QR   BN7164382   1

D1461652

Libraries

Reference and Information Services

THE LONDON BOROUGH

BROMLEY LIBRARIES

3 0128 02141 3409

HAMLYN DICTIONARY OF
DATES AND ANNIVERSARIES

Hamlyn Dictionary of

Dates and Anniversaries

General Editor, J. M. Bailie

Hamlyn

LONDON · NEW YORK · SYDNEY · TORONTO

Published by
The Hamlyn Publishing Group Limited
London · New York · Sydney · Toronto
Astronaut House, Feltham, Middlesex, England

First published 1962
Revised edition 1966
Second revised edition 1978

© Copyright Robert Collison 1962, 1966, 1978

All rights reserved. No part of this publication may be
reproduced, stored in a retrieval system, or transmitted, in
any form or by any means, electronic, mechanical,
photocopying, recording or otherwise, without the
permission of The Hamlyn Publishing Group Limited
and the copyrightholder.

ISBN 0 600 32927 5

Printed in England by
Hazell Watson & Viney Ltd,
Aylesbury, Bucks

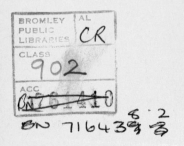

BROMLEY   AL
PUBLIC   CR
LIBRARIES
CLASS
902
ACC

BN 7164 3

INTRODUCTION

It is over 15 years since Robert Collison's *Dictionary of Dates and Anniversaries* first made its appearance. For some time now it has been obvious that a revised edition, which could take in the most significant events of the last decade or so, was becoming a necessity. In offering this new edition the publishers have also taken the opportunity of expanding the *Dictionary* to include much useful material for which space could not previously be found. The biographical entries, in particular, have been enlarged. Nevertheless, despite the substantial work of revision the basic structure of Robert Collison's original book remains and due acknowledgement must be made to his creative spirit.

The first part of the book provides information about more than 12,000 important people and world events – historical, political, economic, scientific and cultural – arranged in alphabetical order. Particular attention has been paid to the achievements of the Space Age, the emergence of newly independent African states and the latest scientific discoveries. The second part, consisting of nearly 6,000 entries, devoted to anniversaries and events for each day, has been likewise updated. Everyone who wants facts at their fingertips – writers, students, teachers, librarians, journalists and the general reader with an enquiring mind – will find that the *Dictionary of Dates and Anniversaries* will amply fulfil all their requirements.

J. M. Bailie
GENERAL EDITOR

DICTIONARY
OF
DATES

A

A1, first British car registration, issued to the 2nd Earl Russell 1903.

Aachen, West Germany, founded A.D. 125; Charlemagne's capital; free city of the Holy Roman Empire; captured by American troops 1944.

Aalto, Hugo Alvar (1899–1976), Finnish architect, designer of modern industrial buildings.

Aaltonen, Waino (1894–1966), Finnish sculptor, noted for his portrait busts.

Aaron (c. 13th cent. B.C.), traditional founder of the Jewish priesthood, led Israelites out of Egypt.

Aasen, Ivar (1813–96), Norwegian philologist, established Norwegian literary language.

Ab, Fast of, Jewish fast, 9th day of Ab.

Abadan, Persian port and refinery, built since 1910; evacuated by British 1951.

Abbas I, the Great (c. 1557–1628), shah of Persia 1586–1628, greatly extended Persian territory.

Abbasid dynasty, founded by Abdul Abbas 750; ended 1258.

Abbe, Ernst (1840–1905), German physicist, noted for his researches into optics.

Abbeville, Treaty of, relinquishing English claims to several French territories, signed 1259.

Abbot, Charles Greeley (1872–1973), American astrophysicist, best known for his work on solar radiation.

Abd-al-Malik (c. 646–705), Omayyad caliph of Damascus 685–705, reunited the Muslim Empire.

Abd-el-Kader (c. 1807–1883), Algerian leader of resistance to French rule.

Abd-el-Krim (c. 1880–1963), Moroccan chieftain in Rif rebellion against Spanish.

Abd-er-Rahman I (731–788), Arab amir of Cordoba 756–788 and founder of Omayyad dynasty in Spain.

Abd-er-Rahman III (891–961), Arab amir 912–929 and caliph 929–961 of Cordoba, whose reign marked the peak of Omayyad power in Spain.

abdominal operation, first successfully performed 1809 by the American surgeon Ephraim McDowell (1771–1830).

Abdul-Hamid II (1842–1918), sultan of Turkey 1876–1909, implicated in the Armenian Massacres; abdicated.

Abdullah ibn Hussein (1882–1951), first king of Jordan, led revolt against Turkish rule during World War I.

Abdul Mejid I (1823–61), sultan of Turkey 1839–61, noted for his reforms.

A' Beckett, Gilbert (1811–56), English humorous writer, author of *Comic History of England* (1848).

Abel, Sir Frederick (1827–1902) English scientist, invented 1879 apparatus for determining flashpoint of petroleum.

Abel, Niels Henrik (1802–29), Norwegian mathematician, studied the theory of elliptic functions.

Abel, Rudolf (1902–72), Soviet spy in the United States.

Abelard, Peter (1079–1142), French scholastic philosopher and lover of Héloïse.

Abercrombie, Lascelles (1881–1938), English poet, author of *Interludes* and *Poems* (1908).

Abercrombie, Sir Leslie Patrick (1879–1957), English architect, noted for his work in town planning.

Aberdeen, incorporated by David I; made a royal burgh by William the Lion 1179; burnt by Edward III 1336.

Aberdeen, George Gordon, Earl of (1784–1860), British statesman, prime minister 1852–55.

Aberfan, mining village, South Wales, where nearly 150 (mainly children) were killed by subsiding coal tip Oct. 1966.

Abershaw, Jerry (c. 1773–1795), English highwayman, hanged for shooting a constable.

Aberystwyth, founded 1109; granted first charter 1277; University College built there 1872.

Abhorrers, political group connected with Tories, first came into prominence 1679.

Abingdon School, Berkshire, English public school, founded 1563.

Abington, Mrs Frances (1737–1815), English actress, created role of Lady Teazel.

Abjuration Oath, rejecting the Stuarts, first required 1701.

Abney, Sir William (1884–1920), English chemist, noted for his work in photographic chemistry.

abortion, made statutory offence in Britain 1803; legalized in certain circumstances 1968.

Aboukir Bay. See **Nile,** Battle of the.

About, Edmond (1828–85), French novelist, author of *Le Roi des Montagnes* (1856).

Abraham (c. 2000 B.C.), traditional first patriarch of the Jews, led his people from Ur to their new settlement in Palestine.

Abraham, Plains of, near Quebec, scene of battle between British and French 13 Sept. 1759.

Abruzzi earthquake, Italy, killing 15,000, occurred 3 Nov. 1706.

absolute zero (−273·16 °C.), idea introduced by Lord Kelvin (*q.v.*).

Abu-Bakr (573–634), first Muslim caliph 632–634, father-in-law and successor to Mohammed.

abu-Nuwas (c. 756–c. 810), Persian poet, noted for his lyric verse.

Abyssinia. See **Ethiopia.**

Académie des Jeux Floraux, Paris, constituted an academy by Louis XIV 1694.

Académie des Sciences, Paris, founded 1666.

Académie Française, Paris, founded 29 Jan. 1635.

Accademia della Crusca, Florence, leading Italian academy, founded 1582.

acceleration due to gravity. See **free fall.**

accelerators, particle, first one developed 1928 by the British scientists Sir John Cockcroft (*q.v.*) and Ernest Walton (b. 1903).

accordion, first patented in Berlin by Friedrich Buschmann 1822.

Accountants, Institute of Chartered, in England and Wales, founded (as the Institute of Accountants) 1870; chartered 1880.

Accra, capital of Ghana since 1876; founded in the 17th century as three fortified trading posts by the British, Dutch and Danes.

accumulator, lead-acid, invented 1859 by the French physicist Gaston Planté (1834–89).

acetylene, discovered 1836 by the English scientist Edmund Davy (1785–1857).

Achaean League, Greece, flourished in the 4th century B.C.; reconstituted *c.* 280 B.C.; dissolved 146 B.C.

Achaemenid dynasty, ruled Persia from *c.* 550 to 300 B.C.

Achard, Franz Karl (1753–1821), German chemist, devised process for extracting sugar from beet.

Acheson, Dean Gooderham (1893–1971), American statesman and lawyer, secretary of state 1949–53.

Acheson, Edward Goodrich (1856–1931), American inventor, discovered silicone carbide.

achromatic lens, developed 1729 by the English inventor Chester Hall (1703–71) and used 1758 in an achromatic telescope by the English optician John Dolland (1706–61).

Ackermann, Rudolph (1764–1834), German-born art publisher in London, best known for his coloured engravings.

Aconcagua, highest mountain in the Andes, first climbed by the Fitzgerald Expedition 1897.

acoustics, first studies reported *c.* 1850; basic theory propounded 1877 by Lord Rayleigh (*q.v.*); architectural acoustics developed and quantified 1900 by the American physicist Wallace Sabine (1868–1919).

Acre, taken by the Crusaders 1104; captured by Saladin 1187; recaptured by Richard Coeur de Lion 1191; finally lost to Christendom 1291.

Act of Settlement. See **Settlement,** Act of.

actinium, radioactive element discovered 1899 by the French chemist André Louis Debierne (1874–1949).

Actium, Battle of, between Octavian and Mark Antony, 2 Sept. 31 B.C.

Acton, John, 1st Baron (1834–1902), English historian, planner of the *Cambridge Modern History.*

actress, first English (name uncertain), played Desdemona 8 Dec. 1660.

Adalbert (*c.* 1000–1072), German archbishop, spread Christianity among the Wends.

Adalbert, Saint (*c.* 955–997), Bohemian bishop, murdered by Prussians.

Adam, Adolphe Charles (1803–56), French composer, wrote the music for the ballet *Giselle* (1841).

Adam, Robert (1728–92), Scottish architect, reintroduced the classical style into domestic British architecture.

Adam de la Halle (*c.* 1235–1285), French trouvère, author of the musical drama *Le Jeu de Robin et de Marion.*

Adamic, Louis (1899–1951), Yugoslav-born American writer, author of *Laughing in the Jungle* (1932).

Adamov, Arthur (b. 1908), Russian-born French dramatist, creator of the Theatre of the Absurd.

Adams, Henry Brooks (1848–1927), American historian, author of *America's Economic Supremacy* (1900).

Adams, John (1735–1826), American statesman, 2nd president of the United States 1797–1801.

Adams, John Couch (1819–92), English astronomer, discovered 1845, independently of Leverrier (*q.v.*), the planet Neptune.

Adams, John Quincy (1767–1848), American statesman, 6th president of the United States 1825–29.

Adams, Samuel (1722–1803), American statesman, played a leading part in the struggle for independence from Britain.

Adams, William (1564–1620), English sailor and navigator, first Englishman to visit Japan.

Addams, Charles (b. 1912), American cartoonist, noted for his macabre humour.

adding machines, first model built *c.* 1642 by Blaise Pascal (*q.v.*); first machine capable of adding, subtracting, multiplying and dividing, commercially available 1820.

Addington, Henry, 1st Viscount Sidmouth (1757–1844), British statesman, prime minister 1801–04.

Addinsell, Richard (b. 1904) English composer of incidental music for films, etc.

Addis Ababa, founded 1887 by Menelek II; became capital of Ethiopia 1889.

Addison, Joseph (1672–1719), English essayist and poet, together with Sir Richard Steele (*q.v.*) founder of the *Spectator*.

Addison's disease, first described 1849 by the English physician Thomas Addison (1793–1860).

Addled Parliament, of James I's reign, sat 5 April to 7 June 1614.

Adelaide (1792–1849), queen of England as wife of William IV.

Adelaide, South Australia, founded 1836 and named after Queen Adelaide.

Aden, annexed by East India Company 1839; became British crown colony 1937; capital of People's Democratic Republic of Yemen since 1968.

Aden Protectorate. See **Yemen,** People's Democratic Republic of.

Adenauer, Konrad (1876–1967), German statesman, chancellor of West Germany 1949–63.

Adler, Alfred (1870–1937), Austrian psychiatrist and psychologist, originated theory of the inferiority complex.

Adler, Larry (b. 1914), American musician, noted as a virtuoso harmonica player.

Adler, Nathan Marcus (1803–90), Jewish rabbi, chief rabbi of the united congregations of the British Empire and founder (1855) of Jews' College, London.

Admiralty Islands, Bismarck Archipelago, discovered by the Dutch 1616.

adoption, made legal in England 1926.

adrenaline, hormone isolated 1901 by the Japanese chemist Jokichi Takamine (1854–1922).

Adrian IV (*c.* 1100–1159), Pope 1154–59, the only English pope, in conflict with the German emperor over papal supremacy.

Adrian VI (1459–1523), Pope 1522–23, noted for his efforts to reform the Church.

Adrian, Edgar Douglas, 1st Baron (b. 1889), English physiologist, made important discoveries about the functioning of the nervous system.

Adrianople, Battle of, 378; city taken by the Ottomans, 1361, and their capital 1366–1453.

Advent, Christian festival comprising the period encompassed by the four Sundays before Christmas.

advertisement duty, newspaper, introduced in England under Cromwell; abolished 1853.

Ady, Endre (1877–1919), Hungarian poet, introduced new literary ideas and forms into Hungarian literature.

A.E. See **Russell,** George William.

Aelfric (*c.* 955–*c.* 1020), English abbot and scholar, author of *Homilies*.

Aemilian Way, Roman road, constructed 187 B.C.

aerial, first built *c.* 1887 by Heinrich Hertz (*q.v.*); first used 1894 for short-distance transmissions by Guglielmo Marconi (*q.v.*), who made first transatlantic transmission 1901.

aerodynamics, study founded by Sir George Cayley (*q.v.*).

aeroplane, first successful flights by Wright brothers 17 Dec. 1903, at Kitty Hawk, North Carolina.

Aescines (389–314 B.C.), Greek orator, opponent of Demosthenes.

Aeschylus (525–456 B.C.), Greek dramatist, author of *The Persians, Seven against Thebes,* etc.

Aesop (620–*c.* 560 B.C.), Greek author of the oldest known collection of animal fables.

Aetius, Flavius (*c.* 396–454), Roman general, defeated Attila at Chalons 451.

Afars and Issas. See **Djibouti.**

Afghanistan, independent kingdom from 1747; independence recognized by Anglo-Russian Convention signed 13 Aug. 1907; republic since 1973.

Afghan Wars, between Britain and Afghanistan, 1838–42, 1878–81, 1919.

Agadir, Morocco, destroyed by earthquake 1960.

Agadir Crisis, between Germany and France and Britain Aug.–Nov. 1911.

Aga Khan I (1800–81), Persian religious leader in India, spiritual head of the Ismaili sect of Islam.

Aga Khan III (1877–1957), Indian statesman, spiritual head of the Ismaili sect of Islam 1885–1957.

Agapemonites, religious sect founded 1840s by the Rev. Henry James Prince (1811–99).

Agasias of Ephesus (2nd cent. B.C.), Greek sculptor, known for his *Borghese Warrior.*

Agassiz, Jean Louis (1807–73), Swiss-born American naturalist, made important contributions to the study of zoology and geology.

Agatha, Saint (d. 251), Christian martyr, patron saint of Malta.

Agesander (1st cent. B.C.), Greek sculptor, whose *Two Sons of Agesander* greatly influenced sculpture in the Renaissance.

Aghrim, Ireland, scene of decisive victory of William III over James II, 12 July 1691.

Agincourt, Battle of, victory of Henry V over the French, 25 Oct. 1415.

Agnes' Eve, Saint, 20–21 Jan.

Agnew, Spiro (b. 1918), American politician, vice-president of the United States 1968–73.

Agnon, Samuel (1888–1970), Israeli novelist, first Israeli to win Nobel Prize for Literature (1966).

agnostic, term first introduced 1869 by the English scientist Thomas Henry Huxley (*q.v.*).

Agostino di Duccio (1418–81), Florentine sculptor, who worked on the Tempio Malatestiano at Rimini.

Agricola, Georg (1494–1555), German

scholar, was the first man to study metals systematically.

Agricola, Gnaeus Julius (37–93 A.D.), Roman general, consolidated Roman power in Britain.

Agricola, Johannes (c. 1494–1566), German Protestant reformer, propounded the doctrine of Antinomianism.

Agriculture, Ministry of, replaced Board of Agriculture (formed 1889) in 1919; merged with Ministry of Food 1955.

Agriculture, Department of, U.S.A., created 1862.

Agrigento, Sicily, founded 582 B.C. by Greek colonists.

Agrippa, Marcus Vipsanius (63–12 B.C.), Roman general, helped Augustus to achieve supreme power.

Agrippa von Nettesheim, Cornelius (c. 1486–1535), German scholar, physician and student of the occult.

Ahmad Shah (1724–73), first amir of Afghanistan 1745–53, invaded India.

Ahmed III (1673–1736), sultan of Turkey 1703–36, lost much territory in Europe in various wars.

Ahmedabad, Indian city, founded by Ahmed Shah 1411.

Ahmediya movement, Muslim sect founded 1889 by Mirza Ghulam Ahmed (1839–1908).

Ahmednagar, Indian city, founded by Ahmed Nizam Shah 1494.

Aidan, Saint (d. 651), Irish monk and missionary, first bishop of Lindisfarne.

Aiken, Conrad Potter (1889–1973), American poet, critic and novelist, whose *Selected Poems* (1930) won a Nobel Prize.

Ainsworth, William Harrison (1805–82), English historical novelist, author of *Tower of London* (1840).

air, first liquefied 1895 by the Bavarian engineer Karl von Linde (1842–1934). See also **atmosphere.**

air brake, first practical type invented 1869 by George Westinghouse (q.v.).

air conditioning, first practical unit designed 1902 by the American inventor Willis Carrier (1876–1950).

air cushion vehicle, designed by Sir Christopher Cockerell (q.v.) in the 1950s; first practical one (hovercraft) launched 1959.

air gun, invented 1656 by Guter of Nuremberg.

airmail service, first (experimental) in Great Britain 1911; first regular in Europe 1919.

Air Ministry, Britain, established 1918; absorbed by Ministry of Defence 1964.

air-pump, invented 1650 by Otto von Guericke (q.v.).

airship, built by Henri Giffard 1852 and by Charles Renard and A. C. Krebs 1884; rigid airship constructed by Zeppelin 1900; first practical one by Lebaudy brothers 1902–03.

Air Training Corps, formed in Britain 1941.

Airy, Sir George Biddell (1801–92), English astronomer, as astronomer royal 1835–91 reorganized Greenwich Observatory.

Aisne, Battles of the, World War I, Sept. 1914, April 1917, May–June 1918, and Sept.–Oct. 1918.

Aix-la-Chapelle, Treaties of, 1668 and 1748; Congress of, Sept.–Nov. 1818.

Ajaccio, Corsica, founded 1492 by Genoese.

Ajanta cave paintings, India, date mostly from the 6th–7th centuries A.D.

Akbar the Great (1542–1605), Mogul emperor of India 1556–1605, patron of the arts, established great empire.

Akhmatova, Anna (1888–1966), Russian poet, wrote love poetry.

Akhnaton (14th cent. B.C.), king of Egypt, introduced the worship of the sun god.

Akimov, Nikolai (b. 1901), Russian theatrical director, notable for his production of classical plays in modern dress.

Akron, Ohio, founded 1825; chartered 1865.

Aksakov, Sergei (1791–1859), Russian novelist, author of *A Family Chronicle* (1846–56).

Alabama, U.S.A., created territory 1817; admitted as state to the Union 1819; seceded 1861; readmitted to Union 1868.

Alabama, Confederate warship, built at Birkenhead 1862; attacked U.S. ships 1862–64; sunk by *Kearsarge* 19 June 1864; Britain paid $15,500,000 in compensation 1873.

Alain. See **Chartier,** Emile.

Alain-Fournier (pseud. of Henri Alain Fournier; 1886–1914), French novelist, author of *Le Grand Meaulnes* (1913).

Alamo, The, San Antonio, Texas, garrison besieged and then massacred by Mexican forces Feb.–March 1836.

Alamein, Battle of, World War II, victory of the British over the Germans, 23 Oct.–4 Nov. 1942.

Alanbrooke, 1st Viscount (1883–1963), British soldier, chief of the Imperial General Staff 1941–46.

Alarcón, Pedro Antonio de (1833–91), Spanish novelist and diplomat, author of *The Three-Cornered Hat* (1874).

Alaric (c. 370–410), Visigothic king 395–410, sacked Rome 410.

Alaska, discovered by Vitus Bering 1741; purchased from Russia by U.S.A. 1867; incorporated as territory 1912; became 49th state 1959.

Alba, Duke of. See **Alva,** Duke of.

Alban, Saint (d. c. 304), first English Christian martyr, executed for sheltering a priest.

Albania, under Turkish suzerainty 1467–1912; principality 1912–24; republic 1925–28; monarchy 1928–46; Communist people's republic from 1946.

Albany, Louisa, Countess of (1752–1824), wife of Charles Edward Stuart (q.v.) and later mistress of Vittorio Alfieri (q.v.).

Albee, Edward (b. 1928), American dramatist, author of *Who's Afraid of Virginia Woolf?* (1962).

Albeniz, Isaac (1860–1909), Spanish composer, wrote the piano suite *Iberia* (1906–09).

Alberoni, Giulio (1664–1752), Italian cardinal, as chief minister of Spain 1715–19 involved that country in a disastrous war.

Albers, Joseph (b. 1888), German abstract painter, member of Bauhaus group.

Albert (1819–61), Prince Consort, husband of Queen Victoria, patron of the arts and sciences.

Albert I (1875–1934), king of the Belgians 1909–34, led resistance to German invasion in World War I.

Albert, Lake, Africa, discovered 1864 by Sir Samuel Baker (q.v.).

Alberta, Canada, organized as a district 1875; created a province 1905.

Albert Bridge, London, built 1873 by the civil engineer R. M. Ordish (1824–86).

Alberti, Domenico (c. 1715–1739), Italian composer, inventor of the Alberti bass.

Alberti, Leone Battista (1404–72), Italian architect and painter, best remembered for his church designs.

Albert Memorial, Kensington Gardens, opened 1872.

Albertus Magnus (c. 1200–1280), German philosopher and writer, teacher of Saint Thomas Aquinas.

Albigenses, heretical sect in southern France; active 12th–13th centuries; destroyed 1209–29.

Albuera, Battle of, Peninsular War, victory of the British over the French, 16 May 1811.

Albuquerque, Affonso d' (1453–1515), Portuguese viceroy of the Indies, founded Portuguese empire in the East.

Albuquerque, New Mexico, founded 1706.

Alcaeus (7th cent. B.C.), Greek lyric poet, originated Alcaic stanza.

Alcibiades (c. 450–404 B.C.), Athenian general and politician, played a leading part in the Peloponnesian War.

Alcock, Sir John William (1892–1919), English pioneer aviator, who, with Sir Arthur Whitten Brown (q.v.), made the first nonstop transatlantic flight.

Alcott, Louisa May (1832–88), American novelist, author of *Little Women* (1868–69).

Alcuin, (735–804), English scholar, helped revival of learning at the court of Charlemagne.

Aldenham, Hertfordshire, English public school, founded by Richard Platt 1597.

Aldershot Camp, English military camp, founded 1854.

Aldhelm, Saint (c. 640–709), English scholar and bishop, author of Latin verse.

Aldington, Richard (1892–1962), English writer, author of *Death of a Hero* (1929).

aldol, chemical compound first synthesized by the French chemist Charles Wurtz (1817–84).

Alecsandri, Vasile (1821–90), Romanian lyric poet and collector of popular songs.

Aleichem, Sholem (1859–1916), Russian-born Jewish writer in America, well known for his humorous stories.

Alekhine, Alexander (1892–1946), Russian chess player, world champion 1927–35 and 1937–46.

Alemán, Mateo (c. 1547–c. 1616), Spanish writer, author of the picaresque novel *Guzman de Alfarache* (1599–1604).

Alembert, Jean le Rond d' (c. 1717–1783), French mathematician and philosopher, helped to edit Diderot's *Encyclopédie*.

Aleppo, Syria, ancient city; sacked by Hittites c. 2000 B.C.; besieged by crusaders 1124; taken by Mongols 1260; captured by Ottoman Turks 1517; destroyed by earthquake 1822.

Aleutian Islands, discovered by Vitus Bering 1741; bought from Russia by U.S.A. 1867.

Alexander (1888–1934), king of Yugoslavia 1921–34, established a dictatorship; assassinated at Marseilles.

Alexander III (d. 1181), Pope 1159–81, engaged in long contest with Emperor Frederick I.

Alexander IV (d. 1261). Pope 1254–61, established Inquisition in France.

Alexander VI (c. 1430–1503), Pope 1492–1503, patron of the arts, endeavoured to increase temporal power of the papacy.

Alexander III, The Great (356–323 B.C.), king of Macedon 336–323 B.C., conquered Greece and Persia and founded an empire stretching as far as India.

Alexander I (1777–1825), tsar of Russia 1801–25, began domestic reforms and founded Holy Alliance.

Alexander II (1818–81), tsar of Russia 1855–81, emancipated the serfs 1861; assassinated by revolutionaries.

Alexander III (1845–94), tsar of Russia 1881–94, repressed liberalism and persecuted the Jews.

Alexander II (1198–1249), king of Scotland 1214–49, joined English barons opposing King John.

Alexander III (1241–85), king of Scotland 1249–85, wrested control of the Western Isles from Norway.

Alexander Nevski (c. 1220–1263), Russian ruler, won great military victories against the Swedes and the Teutonic Knights.

Alexander Obrenovich (1876–1903), king of Serbia 1899–1903, whose repressive measures ended in his assassination.

Alexander of Tunis, 1st Earl (1891–1969), British soldier, led invasion of Italy in World War II.

Alexander Severus (*c.* 208–235), Roman emperor 222–235, defeated Persians; assassinated by his soldiers.

Alexander, Cecil Francis (1818–95), Irish poet and hymn writer, author of 'There is a green hill far away'.

Alexander, Sir George (1858–1918), English actor-manager, produced plays by Pinero and Wilde.

Alexandra (1844–1925), queen of England as wife of Edward VII.

Alexandra Fedorovna (1872–1918), last empress of Russia as wife of Nicholas II.

Alexandria, Egypt, founded 332 B.C.; library built up during 3rd century B.C.; taken by Romans 47 B.C.; captured by Arabs A.D. 646 and by Turks 1517; Battle of, between British and French 1801.

Alexandrian Era, began 5503 B.C.

Alexius I Comnenus (1048–1118), Byzantine emperor 1081–1118, defended the empire against its many enemies.

al-Farabi (*c.* 870–950), Arab philosopher, spread knowledge of Greek philosophy among the Arabs.

Alfieri, Vittorio (1749–1803), Italian dramatist, author of *Cleopatra* (1775) and *Saul* (1782).

Alfonso I (1112–85), king of Portugal 1139–85, freed country from control of Leon.

Alfonso V (1432–81), king of Portugal 1438–81, noted for his victories over the Moors.

Alfonso I (d. 1134), king of Aragon 1104–1134, conquered Saragossa from the Moors.

Alfonso V (1385–1458), king of Aragon 1416–58, also ruled Naples and Sicily; was a patron of the arts.

Alfonso III (*c.* 838–910), king of Leon and Asturias 866–910, extended his territories in wars with the Moors.

Alfonso VI (*c.* 1042–1109), king of Leon from 1065 and of Castile from 1072, established Christian predominance in Spain.

Alfonso VIII (1155–1214), king of Castile 1158–1214, broke Moorish power in Spain by his victory at Las Navas de Tolosa 1212.

Alfonso X (1221–84), king of Castile and Leon 1252–84, encouraged learning and founded a code of laws.

Alfonso XI (1311–50). king of Castile and Leon 1312–50, with Portuguese defeated Moors near Tarifa 1340.

Alfonso XII (1857–85), king of Spain 1874–85, suppressed Carlist opposition and introduced a new constitution.

Alfonso XIII (1886–1941), king of Spain 1886–1931, forced into exile on the establishment of a republic.

Alford, Henry (1810–71), English clergyman and scholar, first editor of the *Contemporary Review.*

Alfred jewel, Ashmolean Museum, Oxford, found at Athelney 1693.

Alfred the Great (*c.* 848–899), king of Wessex 871–99, repelled Danish invasions, strengthened monarchy, instituted legal reforms and encouraged learning.

algebra, earliest extant work by the Greek philosopher Diophantus of Alexandria *c.* A.D. 250; developed from 6th century onwards by Hindu and Arab mathematicians; modern development from 16th century.

Algardi, Alessandro (1602–54), Italian sculptor, well known for his portraiture.

Algeciras, Conference of, concerning Morocco, held 1906.

Algeria, conquered by Vandals A.D. 431; under Arab control 7th century; ruled by Ottoman Turks 16th–18th centuries; annexed to France 1848; conquered by Allies from Axis 1942; nationalist revolt began 1954; independent 1962.

Alhambra, The, Moorish palace near Granada, originally built between *c.* 1250 and *c.* 1360.

Ali (*c.* 600–661), Muslim leader, son-in-law of Mohammed and fourth caliph 656–661.

Aliens Acts, Great Britain, first passed 1793; others 1905, 1918, and 1948. See also **Commonwealth Immigrants Acts.**

Ali, Mohammed (b. 1942), American boxer and world heavyweight champion.

Aliwal, Battle of, First Sikh War, fought between the British and the Sikhs 28 Jan. 1846.

alizarin, red dye, isolated from madder 1827; first synthesized 1868 by the German chemists Karl Graebe (1841–1927) and Karl Liebermann (1842–1914).

Allan, David (1744–96), Scottish painter, noted for his portraits.

All-Blacks, New Zealand Rugby team, made unbeaten tour of British Isles 1924–25.

Allen, Ethan (1738–89), American soldier, active against the British during the Revolutionary War.

Allen, Grant (1848–99), English novelist, author of *The Woman Who Did* (1895).

Allenby, Edmund, 1st Viscount (1861–1936), British soldier, defeated the Turks in Palestine in World War I.

Allende, Salvador (1908–73), Chilean statesman, as president 1970–73 began extensive reforms; killed during coup d'etat.

Alleyn, Edward (1566–1626), English actor-manager, noted for his appearances in *Tamburlaine, Jew of Malta,* etc.

Alleyn's School, Dulwich, English public

school, founded by Edward Alleyn 1619.

All Hallows' Eve, 31 Oct.

Allhallows School, Dorset, English public school founded early 16th century.

All Souls' College, Oxford University, founded 1438 by Henry Chichele.

All Souls' Day, celebrated by Roman Catholic Church 2 Nov., or 3 Nov. if 2 Nov. is a Sunday.

Allston, Washington (1779–1843), American painter, best remembered for his Biblical themes.

All the Talents, Ministry of, formed under Lord Grenville (*q.v.*) 1806–07.

Alma, Battle of the, Crimean War, in which the British and French defeated the Russians, 20 Sept. 1854.

Almack's, London club, founded 1763 by William Almack (d. 1781); established as Brooks's 1778.

Almagro, Diego de (*c.* 1475–1538), Spanish conquistador, took part in conquest of Peru and led expedition to Chile.

almanac duty, abolished in Britain 1834.

Almansa, Battle of, War of the Spanish Succession, in which the French defeated the British, Portuguese and Spanish, 25 April 1707.

Alma-Tadema, Sir Lawrence (1836–1912), Dutch-born painter in England, best known for his studies of classical subjects.

Almeida, Portugal, captured by the Spaniards 1762; by the French 1810; recaptured by Wellington 1811.

Almeida, Francisco de (*c.* 1450–1510), Portuguese soldier, first viceroy of Portuguese India 1505–09.

Almeida-Garrett, João Baptista de (1779–1854), Portuguese statesman and writer, led Romantic movement in Portuguese literature.

Almohades, Berber Muslim sect, ruled North Africa and Spain during 12th and 13th centuries.

Almoravides, Berber Muslim sect, ruled North Africa and Spain during 11th and 12th centuries.

Almqvist, Karl (1793–1866), Swedish novelist, dramatist and poet, author of *The Book of the Briar Rose* (1832–51).

alpaca, first manufactured 1836 by the English wool stapler Sir Titus Salt (1803–76).

Alp Arslan (1029–72), Seljuk Turkish sultan, established Seljuk Empire in Asia Minor after defeating Byzantines.

alpha particle, discovered 1899 by Lord Rutherford (*q.v.*)

Alphege, Saint (954–1012), archbishop of Canterbury 1006–12, murdered by Danes.

Alsace, under French control 1697; ruled by Germany 1871–1918; by France 1918–40; annexed to Germany 1940; part of France since 1945.

Altamira cave paintings, Santander, Spain, discovered 1879.

Altdorfer, Albrecht (*c.* 1480–1538), German painter and engraver, noted for his landscapes.

aluminium, impure form prepared 1825 by Hans Oersted (*q.v.*); pure form isolated 1827 by Friedrich Wöhler (*q.v.*); electrolytic refining method discovered 1866, independently, by the American chemist Charles M. Hall (1863–1914) and the French chemist Paul Héroult (1863–1914).

Alva, Duke of (1508–82), Spanish soldier and statesman, noted for his tyranny as governor of the Netherlands.

Amateur Athletic Association, United Kingdom, founded 1880.

Amateur Athletic Union, U.S.A., founded under the name of National Association of Amateur Athletes of America 1880; assumed present name 1888.

Amati, Nicolò (1596–1684), the most famous member of an Italian family of violin makers.

Amazon river, discovered 1500 by the Spanish navigator Vicente Yañez Pinzón (*q.v.*).

ambassadors, first legally protected in England 1708.

Ambon, Moluccas, Indonesia, discovered by the Portuguese *c.* 1510; seized by the Dutch 1605; English settlers massacred by Dutch 1623.

Ambrose, Saint (*c.* 340–397), German-born bishop of Milan, a father of the Church and opponent of Arianism.

ambulances, introduced 1792 by Baron Dominique Jean Larrey (1796–1842).

Amenhotep IV. See **Akhnaton.**

America, NE coast of North America discovered by Vikings *c.* 1000; Columbus landed in the Bahamas 12 Oct. 1492; in voyages of 1495, 1498 and 1502 touched coasts of Central and South America.

American Academy in Rome, founded 1894.

American Academy of Arts and Sciences, incorporated at Boston 1780.

American Antiquarian Society, founded 1812.

American Bar Association, organized 1878.

American Bible Society, founded 1816.

American Civil War, lasted from April 1861 to April 1865.

American constitution, came into force 21 June 1788.

American Declaration of Independence, made 4 July 1776.

American dialect, of English, first mentioned 1740.

American Duties Act, passed 1764; on tea 1767.

American Federation of Labor, founded 1886.

American football, adopted present form 1880.

American Legion, founded 1919.

American Nautical Almanac, founded 1855.

American Philosophical Society, founded by Benjamin Franklin at Philadelphia 1743.

American Samoa, American trading interests in Samoa (*q.v.*) developed in 19th century; American Samoa effectively ceded to U.S.A. 1899.

American Society for the Prevention of Cruelty to Animals, founded 1866.

American States, Organization of, formed 1948.

American Revolutionary War, lasted from April 1775 to Sept. 1783.

americium, radioactive element first produced 1944 by the American nuclear chemist Glenn T. Seaborg (b. 1912).

Ames, Joseph (1689–1759), English bibliographer and antiquarian, author of *Typographical Antiquities* (1749).

Amherst, Jeffrey, 1st Baron (1717–97), English army officer, led successful expedition against the French in Canada.

Amherst College, Hampshire County, Mass., U.S.A., opened 1821; chartered 1825.

Amici, Giovanni Battista (1786–1863), Italian astronomer, developed achromatic microscope.

Amiel, Henri Frédéric (1821–81), Swiss philosopher and poet, author of *Journal Intime* (1883).

Amiens, cathedral built 1220–70; Burgundian possession 1435–77; captured by Spanish March 1597 and recovered by French Sept. 1597; peace treaty between Britain, France, Spain and Netherlands signed here 25 March 1802.

Amin Dada, Idi (b. 1925), Ugandan army officer and political leader, head of state of Uganda since 1971.

amines, ammonia derivatives, discovered 1849 by the French chemist Charles Wurtz (1817–84).

Amis, Kingsley (b. 1922), English novelist, author of *Lucky Jim* (1954).

Amman, Jost (1539–91). Swiss painter and engraver, best known for his book illustrations.

Ammianus Marcellinus (*c.* 330–*c.* 400), Roman historian, author of a history of the Roman Empire.

ammonia, first isolated 1774 by Joseph Priestley (*q.v.*); first commercially produced, in Germany, by Haber-Bosch process during World War I.

Amos (8th cent. B.C.), minor Hebrew prophet whose predictions are recorded in the Old Testament.

Amoy, former Chinese treaty port; captured by British 1841; opened for trade 1842; occupied by Japanese 1938; returned to China 1945.

Ampère, André Marie (1775–1836), French physicist, noted for his work in electrodynamics.

amphetamine, first clinical use 1935 by Prinzmetal and W. Bloomberg.

amphibian aircraft, first one, designed by Henri Fabre, flew March 1910.

Ampleforth College, York, English public school; exiled at the Reformation; revived 1802.

amplification, electrical. See **triode valve; transistor.**

Amritsar, India, founded 1577 as holy city of Sikhs; Amritsar incident 13 April 1919.

Amsterdam, developed from a fishing village early 12th century; granted charter 1300.

Amundsen, Roald (1872–1928), Norwegian arctic explorer, first man to reach the South Pole, 14 Dec. 1911.

Amyot, Jacques (1513–93), French scholar, translator of Plutarch.

Anabaptists, religious movement, began in Zwickau, Germany, *c.* 1520; first reached England in the mid-16th century.

Anabasis, the account of the Greek mercenaries who, after the defeat of Cyrus by Artaxerxes 401 B.C. marched to the Black Sea; written *c.* 386–*c.* 377 B.C.

Anachreon (*c.* 572–*c.* 485 B.C.), Greek lyric poet, wrote about wine and love.

anaesthesia, general, nitrous oxide used *c.* 1800 by Sir Humphry Davy, 1844 by Horace Wells; ether used 1846 by William Morton; chloroform demonstrated 1847 by Robert Simpson; administered to Queen Victoria 1853 by John Snow; cocaine used 1884 by Carl Koller; procaine used 1905 by Einhorn.

Anastasia (1901–18?), youngest daughter of Tsar Nicholas II of Russia, supposedly murdered by Bolsheviks.

Anaxagoras (*c.* 500–428 B.C.), Greek philosopher, exponent of theory that universe is composed of tiny particles.

Anaximander (611–547 B.C.), Greek astronomer and philosopher, first man to draw a world map.

Anaximenes (6th cent. B.C.), Greek philosopher, claimed that air was primary form of matter.

anchor escapement, clock-making, invented *c.* 1660 by Robert Hooke (*q.v.*)

Ancon, Treaty of, ending War of the Pacific (1879–83) between Chile and Peru, signed 20 Oct. 1883.

Andaman Islands, used as penal settlement by Britain at intervals from 1858 to 1942; occupied by Japanese 1942–45; together with the Nicobar Islands they constitute a centrally administered territory of India.

Andersen, Hans Christian (1805–75), Danish writer, famous for his fairy stories.

Anderson, Carl David (b. 1905), American physicist, awarded Nobel prize for discovery of positron.

Anderson, Elizabeth Garrett (1836–1917), English physician, first woman in Britain to qualify as a doctor, 1865.

Anderson, Maxwell (1888–1959), American dramatist, noted for his verse plays on modern subjects.

Anderson, Sherwood (1876–1941), American short-story writer, poet and novelist, who pictured the frustrations of man in modern society.

Andhra Pradesh, constituted separate Indian state 1953; on enlarging boundaries assumed present name 1956.

Andorra, traditionally granted independence by Charlemagne; created a principality 1278.

Andrada, Antonio de (c. 1580–1634), Portuguese Jesuit missionary and explorer in India.

Andrássy, Gyula, Count (1823–90), Hungarian statesman, first prime minister of Hungary in the Austro-Hungarian monarchy.

André, John (1751–80), British soldier, executed as a spy by the Americans.

Andrea del Sarto (1486–1531), Florentine painter, famous for his frescoes.

Andrée, Salomón August (1854–97), Swedish polar explorer, died in an attempt to cross the North Pole by balloon.

Andrew, Saint (d. c. A.D. 80), one of the 12 apostles, patron saint of Scotland; crucified.

Andrew II (1175–1235), king of Hungary 1205–35, compelled by nobles to limit royal power.

Andrewes, Lancelot (1555–1626), English prelate and scholar, helped preparation of Authorized Version of the Bible.

Andreyev, Leonid (1871–1919), Russian dramatist, author of *He Who Gets Slapped* (1916).

Andrić, Ivo (b. 1892), Yugoslav novelist, author of *The Bridge on the Drina* (1945).

Andronicus I (c. 1110–85), Byzantine emperor 1183–85, whose short reign was marked by administrative reforms.

Andronicus II (1260–1332), Byzantine emperor 1282–1328, abdicated in favour of his grandson.

Andronicus III (c. 1296–1341), Byzantine emperor 1328–41, constantly at war with Turks and Serbs.

Andros, Sir Edmund (1637–1714), English colonial governor of New England 1686–89, deposed by colonists.

Angas, George Fife (1789–1879), English shipowner, founder of South Australia.

angel, gold coin first used in France c. 1340; in England 1465.

Angelico, Fra (1387–1455), Italian Dominican friar, best known as a painter of religious subjects.

Angell, Sir Norman (1874–1967), English economist, noted for his efforts to promote international peace.

Angerstein, John Julius (1735–1823), British merchant and patron of the arts, noted as a collector of paintings.

Angkor Vat, Cambodia, temples built early 11th century.

Anglesey, conquered by the Romans A.D. 61; by the English c. 1295.

Anglican Church, separated from Roman Catholic Church 1534.

Anglo-Afghan Treaty, concluded by the Dobbs Mission in Kabul, 22 Nov. 1921.

Anglo-Irish Treaty, setting up the Irish Free State, signed 6 Dec. 1921.

Anglo-Persian Oil Company, now British Petroleum Company, formed 1909.

Anglo-Saxons, first landed in Britain c. 449.

Angola, discovered by the Portuguese c. 1483; colonized by them from 1575; created an overseas territory 1951; nationalist revolt 1961; achieved independence 1975.

Ångström, Anders Jöns (1814–74), Swedish physicist and astronomer, noted for his work in solar physics; angstrom unit is named after him.

Anguilla, West Indies, discovered by Columbus 1493; colonized by British 1650; part of Associated State of Saint Christopher-Nevis-Anguilla from 1969; reverted to direct British rule 1971.

aniline, first obtained 1826 by O. Unverdorben; used 1856 to prepare mauveine (q.v.) by William Perkin (q.v.).

animism, philosophical doctrine propounded in the 18th century by Georg Ernst Stahl (1660–1734).

Ankara, capital of Turkey since 1923.

Ann Arbor, Michigan, first settled 1824; incorporated 1833.

Anna Comnena (c. 1083–1148), Byzantine historian, author of the *Alexiad*.

Anna Ivanovna (1693–1740), empress of Russia 1730–40, much influenced by her lover Biron (q.v.).

Annam, conquered by Chinese c. 214 B.C.; independent 1428; treaty with France 1787; French protectorate 1884; after World War II part of Vietnam.

Annapolis, Maryland, first settled (under the name of Providence) 1649; assumed present name 1694; incorporated 1708.

Anne (1665–1714), queen of England 1702–14, was the last Stuart sovereign.

Anne Boleyn (1507–36), queen of England, 2nd wife of Henry VIII, beheaded for alleged adultery.

Anne of Austria (1601–66), queen of

France as wife of Louis XIII, regent 1643–61 during minority of Louis XIV.

Anne of Bohemia (1336–94), queen of England as wife of Richard II.

Anne of Brittany (1477–1514), queen of France, wife successively of Charles VIII and Louis XII.

Anne of Cleves (1515–57), queen of England, 4th wife of Henry VIII; marriage annulled.

Anne of Denmark (1574–1619), queen of England as wife of James I.

Annigoni, Pietro (b. 1910). Italian painter, noted for his portraits of Queen Elizabeth II.

Anning, Mary (1799–1847), English palaeontologist, discovered fossils of dinosaurs.

Annual Register, first issued 1759.

Annunciation, Feast of the, celebrated in the Christian Church 25 March each year.

Anouilh, Jean (b. 1910), French dramatist, used Greek classical themes in *Euridice* (1942) and *Médée* (1946).

Anselm, Saint (1033–1109), Italian-born archbishop of Canterbury 1093–1109, was a noted scholastic philosopher.

Ansermet, Ernest (1883–1969), Swiss conductor, founder of the Orchestre de la Suisse Romande (1918).

Anson, George (1697–1762), English admiral, circumnavigated the world 1740–44; introduced important reforms into the Royal Navy.

Anstey, Christopher (1724–1805), English humorous writer, author of *The New Bath Guide* (1706).

Anstey, F. (pseud. of Thomas Anstey Guthrie; 1856–1934), English novelist, author of *Vice Versa* (1882).

antenna. See aerial.

Antheil, George (1900–59), American composer, wrote the opera *Transatlantic* (1929).

Anthesteria, Athenian festival in honour of Dionysus, 11–13 month of Anthesterion (Feb./March).

Anthony, Saint (c. 250–c. 350), Egyptian hermit, considered the founder of Christian monasticism.

Anthony, Susan Brownell (1820–1900), American social reformer, was an active abolitionist and supporter of women's rights.

Anthony of Padua, Saint (1195–1231), Portuguese-born Franciscan friar, noted for his preaching in France and Italy.

anthrax, causative micro-organism isolated 1876 by Robert Koch (q.v.); effective bacterial vaccine used 1881 by Louis Pasteur (q.v.).

anthropology, developed mid-19th century by the American Lewis H. Morgan (1818–81) and the Englishman Edward B. Tylor (1832–1917).

anthropometry, term coined by the French naturalist Georges Cuvier in the 18th century.

anthroposophy, form of theosophy founded by Rudolf Steiner (q.v.).

antibiotics, first one, pencillin, discovered 1928 by Sir Alexander Fleming (q.v.); first successfully produced commercially 1943.

Anticosti, Canadian island, first sighted 1534 by the French explorer Jacques Cartier.

Anti-Corn Law League, founded 1838 by Richard Cobden.

Antietam, Battle of, American Civil War, fought 16–17 Sept. 1862.

Antigonus I (382–301 B.C.), Macedonian soldier, attempted to re-establish Alexander's Asian empire.

Antigua, discovered by Columbus 1493; ceded to Britain 1667; crown colony 1898; Associated State with Britain 1967.

antimony, known by the ancients in compound form and in metal form at beginning of 17th century or possibly earlier.

Antimonian controversy, between Johannes Agricola and the Lutherans, 1527–1540.

Antioch, founded by Seleucus 300 B.C.

Antiochus III (242–187 B.C.), king of Syria 233–187 B.C., expanded Seleucid Empire but defeated by Romans 190 B.C.

antiparticles, elementary particles postulated about 1931 by P. A. M. Dirac (q.v.); first one, the antielectron or positron, discovered 1932 by the American physicist Carl D. Anderson (b. 1905); the antiproton (1955) and antineutron (1956) were discovered by Emilio Segre (q.v.) and the American physicist Owen Chamberlain (b. 1920).

antisepsis, founded 1847 by the Austrian physician Ignaz Semmelweis (1818–65); first applied successfully in England 1865 by Joseph Lister (q.v.).

Antislavery Society, U.S.A., founded 1833 by William Lloyd Garrison (q.v.).

Antisthenes (c. 444–c. 365 B.C.). Greek philosopher, founder of the Cynic school.

Antofagasta, Chile, founded 1870.

Antoine, André (c. 1857–1943), French actor and theatrical manager, introduced modern drama to the French stage.

Antonello da Messina (c. 1430–1479), Sicilian painter, reputedly introduced oil painting into Italy.

Antonescu, Ion (1882–1946), dictator of Romania 1940–44, executed for war crimes.

Antoninus Pius (86–161 A.D.), Roman emperor 138–161 A.D., whose reign marked a period of great prosperity for Rome.

Antonioni, Michelangelo (b. 1912), Italian film director, producer of *L'Avventura* (1961).

Antony, Mark (Marcus Antonius; c. 83–30 B.C.), Roman soldier and politician, rival of Octavian and lover of Cleopatra.

Antraigues, Emanuel, Comte d' (1755–1812), French diplomat in London, murdered by a servant.

Anzac Day, first celebrated in London 25 April 1916.

Anzio landings, Italy, World War II, 22–25 Jan. 1944.

Apache tribe, North American Indians, finally surrendered 1886.

apartheid, official policy of the Republic of South Africa since 1948.

Apollinaire, Guillaume (1880–1918), French poet and art critic, author of *Alcools* (1913), exponent of Cubism.

Apollinaris the Younger (d. *c.* 390 A.D.), bishop of Laodicea, opponent of Arianism.

Apollo 11, spacecraft in which first manned Moon landing was made July 1969 by the American astronauts Neil Armstrong (*q.v.*) and Edwin Aldrin (b. 1930).

Apollonius of Perga (3rd cent. B.C.), Greek mathematician, author of a treatise on conic sections.

Apollonius of Rhodes (3rd cent. B.C.), Greek scholar and epic poet, author of the *Argonautica*.

Apollo-Soyuz linkup, American-Soviet rendezvous in space, July 1975.

Apothecaries' Company. London, incorporated 1606 and 1617.

Apperley, Charles James (*c.* 1777–1843), Welsh sporting writer, author of *The Chase, the Turf and the Road* (1837).

Appian Way, Italy, Roman road, built 312 B.C.

Appleseed, Johnny. See **Chapman,** John.

Appleton layer, of the ionosphere, discovered in the 1920s by the English physicist Sir Edward Appleton (1892–1965).

approved schools, first set up in Britain 1933, superseding reformatory system started 1850s; discontinued on the establishment of community homes 1969.

Apraksin, Feodor (1671–1728), Russian admiral, founder of the Russian navy.

apricots, first planted in England *c.* 1540.

April Fools' Day, celebrated 1st April.

Apuleius, Lucius (2nd cent. A.D.), Roman writer, author of *The Golden Ass.*

aquatint, invented 1768 by the French printmaker J. Le Prince (1733–81).

Aquinas, Saint Thomas (*c.* 1225–1274), Italian scholastic philosopher, founder of Thomism and systematizer of Roman Catholic theology.

Arab League, founded Cairo 1945, consisted of seven Arab states; Libya joined 1953, Sudan 1956, Tunisia and Morocco 1958, Kuwait 1961, Algeria 1962, and People's Democratic Republic of Yemen 1968.

arachnida, invertebrate class to which spiders belong, first distinguished 1815 by Jean Lamarck (*q.v.*).

Arago, François (1786–1853), French scientist, noted for his work in optics and magnetism.

Aragon, conquered by Visigoths 5th century A.D. and by the Moors 8th century A.D.; independent kingdom 1035; united with Castile 1479.

Aragon, Louis (b. 1897), French novelist and poet, influential in the Dadaist and Surrealist movements.

Aram, Eugene (1704–59), English scholar, who recognized similarity of Celtic to Indo-European languages; executed for murder.

Arany, Janos (1817–82), Hungarian poet, author of an epic trilogy *Toldi* (1847–54).

Ararat, Mount, Turkey, reputed resting-place of Noah's Ark, first climbed 1829.

Arber, Edward (1836–1912), English scholar and bibliographer, published many rare texts.

Arblay, Madame d'. See **Burney,** Fanny.

Arbuthnot, Alexander (d. 1585), Scottish printer, brought out the first Scottish Bible 1579.

Arbuthnot, John (1667–1735), Scottish physician and satirical writer, creator of John Bull.

Arcadius (*c.* 377–408), first emperor of the Eastern Roman Empire 395–408.

Arc de Triomphe, Paris, begun 1806; completed 1836.

Arcesilaus (316–241 B.C.), Greek philosopher, exponent of the teachings of Plato and Socrates.

Archangel, Russia, founded 1584; scene of Allied landings 1918 to oppose Bolsheviks.

Archangel Passage, discovered 1553 by the English navigator Richard Chancellor (*q.v.*).

Archbishop Holgate's Grammar School, York, English public school, founded 1546.

Archer, Frederick (1857–86), English jockey, five times Derby winner; committed suicide.

Archer, Frederick Scott (1813–57), English photographer, inventor of the collodion process.

Archer, William (1856–1924), Scottish dramatic critic and playwright, introduced Ibsen to the English stage.

Archimedes (*c.* 287–212 B.C.), Greek mathematician and inventor, best known for his work in mechanics and hydrostatics.

Archipenko, Alexander (1887–1964), Russian sculptor, influenced by Cubism, exponent of abstract sculpture.

Ardashir I (3rd cent. A.D.), king of Persia *c.* 226–241, founder of Sassanid dynasty.

Arden, John (b. 1930), English dramatist, author of *Sergeant Musgrave's Dance* (1959).

Ardingly College, Sussex, English public school, founded 1858.

Arditi, Luigi (1822–1903), Italian composer, wrote operas including *Il Corsaro* (1846).

Ardrey, Robert (b. 1908), American anthropologist, author of studies on human aggression.

Arendt, Hannah (b. 1906), German-born American philosopher, author of *The Origins of Totalitarianism* (1951).

Arensky, Anton (1861–1906), Russian composer, wrote the opera *A Dream on the Volga* (1892).

Arequipa, Peru, founded 1540 by Pizarro on site of Inca town.

Aretaeus (1st–2nd cent. A.D.), Greek physician and writer on the causes and treatment of diseases.

Aretino, Pietro (1492–1556), Italian satirical writer, author of the comedy *La Cortigiana* (1534).

Argand, Jean Robert (1768–1822), Swiss mathematician, a pioneer in the use of complex numbers.

Argentina, discovered 1516; permanent colonization begun by Spain 1536; declared independent 1816; adopted federal constitution 1853.

argon, gaseous element, discovered 1894 by Lord Rayleigh (*q.v.*) and Sir William Ramsay (*q.v.*).

Arianism, heretical Christian doctrine propounded by Arius (*q.v.*); condemned by Council of Nicaea 325.

Ariosto, Lodovico (1474–1533), Italian poet, author of the epic *Orlando Furioso* (1516).

Ariovistus (1st cent. B.C.), German chieftain, invaded Gaul; defeated by Julius Caesar 58 B.C.

Aristarchus of Samos (3rd cent. B.C.), Greek astronomer, reputedly first man to maintain that the Earth revolves around the Sun.

Aristarchus of Samothrace (*c.* 220–*c.* 150 B.C.), Greek scholar, edited Homer and other Greek authors.

Aristides (*c.* 530–*c.* 468 B.C.), Athenian statesman and general, fought at Marathon and Salamis.

Aristippus (*c.* 435–*c.* 356 B.C.), Greek philosopher, founder of hedonistic school of philosophy.

Aristophanes (*c.* 448–*c.* 380 B.C.), Greek dramatist, best known for his comedies including *The Wasps* (422 B.C.).

Aristotle (384–322 B.C.), Greek philosopher, whose work includes natural philosophy, ethics, logic, politics and poetry; profoundly influenced all subsequent thought.

Arius (*c.* 250–335 A.D.), Greek priest at Alexandria, exponent of the doctrine of Arianism, later condemned as heretical.

Arizona, discovered by Spanish expedition 1539; part of New Spain 1598–1845; acquired by U.S.A. 1853; created a territory 1863; admitted to the Union 1912.

Arkansas, settled by French 1686; part of Louisiana Purchase 1803; created a territory 1819; admitted to the Union 1836; seceded 1861; readmitted 1868.

Arkwright, Sir Richard (1732–92), English inventor and manufacturer, introduced mechanical spinning process into the cotton industry.

Arlen, Michael (pseud. of Dikran Kouyoumdjian; 1895–1956), Bulgarian-born novelist in Britain, author of *The Green Hat* (1924).

Arles, Synod of, convened by the Emperor Constantine 314.

Arliss, George (1868–1946), English film actor, noted for his portrayal of famous historical characters.

Armada, Spanish, assembled 1587; defeated by the English July 1588.

Armaments, Limitation of, conference held Washington, D.C., 1921–22.

Armenia, under Turkish rule from 1514; part ceded to Russia 1878; scene of massacres 1895–96; Soviet Republic created 1921; constituent republic of U.S.S.R. 1936.

Armenian Church, separate since 451.

Arminianism, religious movement, founded by the Dutch theologian Jacobus Arminius (1560–1609).

Arminius (*c.* 17 B.C.–A.D. 21), German chieftain, annihilated a Roman army under Varrus A.D. 9.

Armistice Day, World War I, 11 Nov. 1918.

Armour, Philip Danforth (1832–1901), American industrialist, pioneer in food freezing and canning.

armour plate, first proposed for ships of war 1805 by the English scientist and politician Sir William Congreve (1772–1828).

Armstrong, Louis (1900–71), American Negro trumpet player, bandleader, and jazz virtuoso.

Armstrong, Neil (b. 1930), American astronaut, first man to walk on the Moon.

Armstrong, William George (1810–1900), English engineer and inventor, designed a hydraulic crane and breech-loading guns.

Arnauld, Antoine (1612–94), French theologian and advocate of Jansenism.

Arne, Thomas (1710–78), English composer, wrote operas, oratorios and songs, including 'Rule Britannia'.

Arnhem, Battle of, World War II, 17–25 Sept. 1944.

Arnim, Achim von (1781–1831), German writer of romantic stories, author of a collection of folksongs.

Arnold, Benedict (1741–1801), American

army officer, spied for the British during the Revolutionary War.

Arnold, Bion Joseph (1861–1942), American electrical engineer, inventor of the magnetic clutch, 1900.

Arnold, Sir Edwin (1832–1904), English poet, author of the Buddhist-inspired *The Light of Asia* (1879).

Arnold, Matthew (1822–88), English poet, critic and educationalist, author of *The Scholar Gipsy* (1853).

Arnold, Thomas (1795–1842), English educationalist, as headmaster of Rugby School 1828–42 strongly influenced the development of the public school system.

Arnold of Brescia (1100–55), Italian priest and political reformer, executed for revolt against the temporal power of the papacy.

Arnold School, Blackpool, English public school, founded by the first headmaster F. T. Pennington 1896.

Arnolfo di Cambio (*c.* 1232–*c.* 1300), Italian architect, designed the Church of Santa Croce at Florence.

Arnulf (*c.* 850–899), king of Germany and Holy Roman emperor 887–899.

Aroostook War, dispute between U.S.A. and Canada over boundary between Maine and New Brunswick, 1839; settled 1842.

Arp, Jean or Hans (1887–1966), French sculptor and painter, associated with the Blaue Reiter group and an exponent of Dadaism.

Arpád (d. 907), Magyar leader, founded the dynasty that ruled Hungary *c.* 875–1301.

Arrabal, Fernando (b. 1932), Spanish novelist and dramatist, exponent of abstract theatre.

Arras, Peace of, between Charles VII and Philip the Good 1835; Treaty of, between Louis IX and Maximilian I 1482.

Arrhenius, Svante August (1859–1927), Swedish chemist, established theory of electrolytic dissociation.

Arrian (2nd cent. A.D.), Greek historian, author of a life of Alexander the Great.

Arrol, Sir William (1839–1913), Scottish engineer, noted as a bridge builder.

Arrowsmith, Aaron (1750–1823), English geographer and map-maker.

Arsacid dynasty, ruled Persia from *c.* 250 B.C. to A.D. 224.

arsenic, first identified 1649 by Schroeder.

Artaxerxes II (d. 359 B.C.), emperor of Persia 404–359 B.C., crushed revolt by brother Cyrus but failed to recover a rebellious Egypt.

Artevelde, Jacob van (*c.* 1290–1345), Flemish statesman, governor of Flanders 1336–45, supported England in war against France.

Arthur (*c.* 6th cent. A.D.), possibly legendary British king, supposed to have defeated the invading Saxons at Camlan, 537.

Arthur (1187–1203), duke of Brittany, claimant to the English throne, reputedly murdered by King John.

Arthur, Chester Alan (1830–86), American statesman, 21st president of the United States 1881–85.

artichokes, first grown in England in the 17th century.

Articles of Religion, Church of England, 10 drawn up 1536; 13 issued 1538; 42 authorized 1553; reduced to 39 in 1563.

artificial radioactivity, first produced 1934 by the Joliot-Curies (*q.v.*).

artificial satellite, world's first, the Soviet Sputnik I, launched 1957.

Artigas, José Gervasio (1774–1850), Uruguayan soldier, played a prominent part in his country's struggle for independence.

Arts Council of Great Britain, London, founded as the Council for the Encouragement of Music and the Arts (C.E.M.A.) 1940; incorporated under present name 1946.

Artsybashev, Mikhail Petrovich (1878–1927), Russian novelist, author of *Sanin* (1907).

Arundel, Thomas (1353–1414), archbishop of Canterbury 1396–1414 and later chancellor, strongly opposed the Lollards.

asbestos, use recorded in 1st century A.D. by Pliny the Elder although used before that time; assumed commercial importance in 19th-century steam engines.

Asbury, Francis (1745–1816), English-born Methodist leader in America, helped found Methodist Episcopal Church.

Ascalon, Battle of, fought between the Crusaders and the Muslims Aug. 1099.

Ascension, Feast of the, held on a Thursday each year 40 days after Easter Sunday.

Ascension Island, South Atlantic, discovered by the Portuguese navigator João da Nova on Ascension Day 1501; part of colony of Saint Helena (*q.v.*) since 1922.

Asch, Sholem (1880–1957), Polish-born Jewish writer in America, author of *The Nazarene* (1939).

Ascham, Roger (1515–68), English writer and scholar, tutor to Queen Elizabeth and author of *The Scholemaster* (1570).

Asclepiades (2nd cent. B.C.), Greek physician, opposed Hippocrates' theories about disease.

Ascot Gold Cup, instituted 1807.

Ascot race meeting, first held 11 Aug. 1711.

Asen dynasty, ruled Bulgaria *c.* 1185–1280.

Ashanti, Ghana, wars with Britain 1824–27, 1873–74, 1895–1900; formally annexed by Britain 1901; part of Ghana 1957.

Ashbee, Charles Robert (1863–1942),

English architect and interior designer.

Ashcroft, Dame Peggy (b. 1907), English actress, noted for her Shakespearian roles.

Ashdown, Battle of, between the Saxons and the Danes, Jan. 871.

'Ashes, The', instituted 1882.

Ashford, Daisy (b. c. 1890), English writer, author of *The Young Visiters* (1919).

Ashikaga Takauji (1305–58), Japanese ruler, established the power of the shogunate.

Ashmolean Museum, Oxford, founded c. 1677 by the English antiquary Elias Ashmole (1617–92); opened 1683.

Ashmun, Jehudi (1794–1828), American philanthropist, founded Liberia as a home for freed Negro slaves.

Ashton, Sir Frederick (b. 1906), English dancer and choreographer, director of the Royal Ballet.

Aske, Robert (d. 1537), English rebel, executed for his part in the Pilgrimage of Grace (*q.v.*).

Aslib, London, founded as the Association of Special Libraries and Information Bureaux 1924.

Asoka (d. 232 B.C.), Indian emperor, conquered most of India; converted to Buddhism.

Aspasia (c. 470–410), Greek courtesan, mistress of Pericles, celebrated for her beauty and learning.

Aspdin, Joseph (1779–1855), English stonemason, inventor of Portland cement.

asphalt, in use since c. 3000 B.C.; first large commercial source on Trinidad visited by Sir Walter Raleigh 1595.

aspirin, first produced in 1899 by H. Dreser.

Asplund, Gunnar (1885–1940), Swedish architect, made an important contribution to modern design.

Asquith, Herbert Henry (1858–1928), British statesman, as prime minister 1908–16 introduced many important social reforms.

Assam, India, British protectorate 1826; separate province 1919; Indian state 1950; scene of border clash between China and India 1962.

Asser (d. c. 910), Welsh monk, bishop of Sherborne, wrote life of Alfred the Great.

Assignats, French Revolutionary paper money, issued 1789–97.

Assumption of the Blessed Virgin Mary, Feast of the, celebrated each year 15 Aug.

Assur-bani-pal (7th cent. B.C.), king of Assyria 669–626 B.C., whose reign marked the peak of Assyria's achievement.

Astaire, Fred (b. 1899), American dancer and actor, noted for his film musicals.

asteroid, first one, Ceres, discovered 1801 by the Italian astronomer Giuseppe Piazzi (1746–1826).

Astley's circus, founded 1770 by the English equestrian Philip Astley (1742–1814).

Aston, Francis William (1877–1945), English physicist, inventor of the mass spectrograph.

Aston University, Birmingham, founded 1966.

Astor, John Jacob (1763–1848), German-born American millionaire, who made his fortune in the fur trade and real estate.

Astor, Nancy, Viscountess (1879–1964), American-born British M.P., was the first woman to sit in the House of Commons, 1919.

astrolabe, mariner's, adapted from the astronomer's astrolabe c. 1480 by Martin Behaim (*q.v.*).

Aswan dam, Upper Egypt, completed 1902; high dam, begun 1960; became operational 1970.

Atahualpa (c. 1500–1533), last Inca king of Peru, murdered by Spanish conquistadors.

Atatürk, Kemal. See **Kemal Atatürk.**

Athanasius, Saint (c. 293–373), Greek Church father, patriarch of Alexandria 328–373, opponent of Arianism.

Athelstan (895–940), king of Wessex and Mercia from c. 924, conquered much of England.

Athenaeum, British periodical, began publication 1828; absorbed into *The Nation* 1921.

Athenaeum Club, London, founded 1824.

Athens, predominant in Greek civilization 5th century B.C.; declined after war with Sparta 431–404 B.C.; defeated by Macedon 338 B.C.; subjugated by Rome 146 B.C.; conquered by Goths A.D. 267; under Turkish rule 1456–1833.

Atkinson, Sir Harry (1831–92), New Zealand statesman, as prime minister introduced many important social and economic reforms.

Atlantic Charter, signed Aug. 1941.

Atlantic flight, first direct non-stop by J. W. Alcock and A. W. Brown (*qq.v.*) from Newfoundland to Ireland June 1919; first direct non-stop solo by Charles Lindbergh (*q.v.*) from New York to Paris May 1927.

Atlantic telegraph cable, first successfully laid by the S.S. *Great Eastern* 1866.

Atlantic telephone cable, first operational, Sept. 1956.

atmosphere, first analysed in the 1770s by Antoine Lavoisier (*q.v.*) and independently by the Swedish chemist Karl Scheele (1742–86); composition determined 1785 by Henry Cavendish (*q.v.*).

atom, idea postulated by Leucippus of Miletus c. 475 B.C. and developed by Democritus (*q.v.*); modern idea first described 1808 by John Dalton (*q.v.*); structure revealed 1911 by Lord Rutherford (*q.v.*); atomic model proposed 1913 by Niels Bohr (*q.v.*), subsequently modified by Sommefeld and others.

atomic bomb, first successfully exploded at New Mexico 16 July 1945; first used in warfare at Hiroshima 6 Aug. and Nagasaki 9 Aug. 1945.

atomic clock. See **clocks.**

Atomic Energy Research Establishment, British, set up at Harwell 1945.

atomic nucleus, existence established 1911 by Lord Rutherford (*q.v.*); first nuclear reaction (transmutation) observed 1919 by Rutherford; disintegration using a particle accelerator carried out 1932 by the British scientists Sir John Cockcroft (*q.v.*) and Ernest Walton (b. 1903).

atomic pile. See **nuclear reactor.**

atomic-powered ship, world's first, Russian icebreaker *Lenin*, launched 1957.

atomic shell, first, fired in Nevada, U.S.A., 1953.

atomic-powered submarine, world's first, U.S. *Nautilus*, launched Jan. 1954.

atomic weights, pioneer experimental work published 1818, by Jons Jacob Berzelius (*q.v.*); developed 1858 by the Italian chemist Stanislav Cannizzaro (1826–1910).

ATP (adenosine triphosphate), first isolated 1929; proposed 1940 as major energy carrier in living cells by the American biochemist Fritz Lipmann.

atropine, drug extracted from belladonna, discovered by the German scientist Philipp Lorenz Geiger 1833.

Attar (1119–*c.* 1229), Persian mystic poet, best known for his *Language of Birds*.

Atterbom, Per (1790–1855), Swedish Romantic poet, author of *The Isle of the Blessed* (1824–27).

Atticus, Titus Pomponius (109–32 B.C.), Roman scholar and patron of literature, edited Cicero's letters.

Attila (*c.* 406–453), king of the Huns *c.* 433–453, overran much of Europe, creating terror and devastation.

Attlee, Clement Richard, 1st Earl (1883–1967), British statesman, whose period as prime minister 1945–51 saw the introduction of the welfare state.

attorney-general, first English, William Bonneville 1277.

Attwood, Thomas (1783–1856), English political reformer, prominent in the Chartist Movement.

Auber, Daniel François (1782–1871), French composer, wrote operas including *Fra Diavolo* (1829).

Aubigné, Théodore Agrippa d' (1552–1630), French Huguenot soldier and writer, fought in the Wars of Religion.

Aubrey, John (1626–97), English antiquary, author of the biographical *Brief Lives* (published 1813).

Auchinleck, Sir Claude (b. 1884), British soldier, commanded British forces in the Middle East 1941–42.

Auden, Wystan Hugh (1907–73), English poet, a leading figure in the left-wing literary movement of the 1930s; author of *The Orators* (1932).

Audubon, John James (1785–1851), American naturalist, painter and pioneer in ornithology, wrote *The Birds of America* (1827–38).

Auenbrugger, Leopold (1722–1809), Austrian physician, discovered use of percussion in diagnosis of disease.

Augsburg, The Confession of, Lutheran creed, prepared 1530.

Augustine, Saint (d. 604), first archbishop of Canterbury, began conversion of Anglo-Saxons to Christianity.

Augustine of Hippo, Saint (354–430), the greatest of early Church fathers, defended Christianity against heretical beliefs and wrote *The City of God*.

Augustus (63 B.C.–14 A.D.), first Roman emperor 27 B.C.–14 A.D., whose reign was marked by peace, reform and efficient administration.

Augustus II (1670–1733), king of Poland 1697–1733, whose attempts to enlarge his kingdom led to Poland's decline.

Aurangzeb (1618–1707), Mogul emperor of India 1658–1707, whose reign marked the peak of Muslim power in India.

Aurelian (*c.* 212–275), Roman emperor 270–275, reconquered Gaul and Egypt; assassinated.

Aurelius, Marcus (121–180), Roman emperor 161–180, noted as a Stoic philosopher and author of *Meditations*.

Auric, Georges (b. 1899), French composer, writer of ballet music and incidental music for films.

Auschwitz. See **Oswiecim.**

Austen, Jane (1775–1817), English novelist, author of *Pride and Prejudice* (1813), *Emma* (1814), etc.

Austerlitz, Battle of, French victory over the Austrians and Russians, 2 Dec. 1805.

Austin, Alfred (1835–1913), English poet, author of *Sacred and Profane Love* (1908), created poet laureate 1896.

Austin, John (1790–1859), English jurist, made a major contribution to the study of jurisprudence.

Austin, John Langshaw (1911–60), English philosopher notable for his work in linguistic philosophy.

Australia, circumnavigated by Tasman 1642–43; explored by Dampier 1688; eastern part claimed for Britain by Cook 1770; first settlement 1788; self-government given to colonies 1850; Commonwealth of Australia created 1900.

Australian Antarctic Territory, established by Order in Council Feb. 1933.

Australian Capital Territory, formed 1911.

Austria, territory conquered by Rome 15 B.C.; invaded by Huns 5th century A.D.; border state of the Holy Roman Empire 8th century; ruled by Hapsburgs 1278–1918; dual monarchy (Austria-Hungary) 1867–1918; republic 1918–38; annexed by Germany 1938; invaded by Russians 1945; republic re-established 1945; regained sovereignty and independence 1955.

Austrian Succession, War of the, 1740–1748.

Authorized Version of the Bible, made at order of James I, first published 1611.

autogyro, invented by Juan de la Cierva (*q.v.*) 1923.

Avars, entered Europe 6th century A.D.; settled in Hungarian Plain *c.* 550; finally defeated by Charlemagne 805.

Averroës (1126–98), Arab philosopher, whose writings influenced Christian scholasticism.

Avicenna (980–1037), Arab physician and philosopher, regarded as leading medical authority in the Middle Ages.

Avignon, seat of papacy 1309–77; purchased by Pope Clement VI 1348; seat of antipopes 1378–1417; annexed to France 1791.

Avogadro's Law, of gases, formulated 1811 by Italian physicist Amedeo Avogadro (1776–1856).

avoirdupois, generally replaced the merchants' pound in England 1303; gradually superseded in Britain by metric weights in 1960s and 1970s.

Axminster, carpet factory, founded 1755.

Ayer, Alfred Jules (b. 1910), English philosopher, noted for his work on logical positivism.

Azaña, Manuel (1880–1940), Spanish statesman, last president of the Spanish Republic 1936–39.

Azerbaijan, created a Soviet Socialist Republic 1920; made a constituent republic of the U.S.S.R. 1936.

azo dyes, discovered in England *c.* 1860 by the German chemist Johann Peter Griess; commercially exploited in 1870s; first direct azo dye, Congo red, prepared 1884.

Azorín (pseud. of José Martinez Ruiz; 1873–1967), Spanish novelist and critic, a leading figure of the 'generation of 1898'.

Aztec Empire, Mexico, established in the 14th century; destroyed by Spaniards 1519–21.

B

Baader, Franz Xaver von (1765–1841), German Roman Catholic theologian, exponent of a mystical philosophy.

Baalbek, Lebanese town with Roman ruins (1st to 3rd centuries A.D.); damaged by earthquake 1759.

Baal Shem Tov (*c.* 1700–1760), Jewish mystic, founder of the Hasidic sect in Poland.

Babbage, Charles (1792–1871), English mathematician, invented a calculating machine regarded as forerunner of the computer.

Babbitt metal, antifriction alloy invented 1839 by the American Isaac Babbitt (1799–1862).

Babcock test, for butterfat content in milk, invented 1890 by the American agricultural chemist Stephen M. Babcock (1843–1931).

Babel, Isaac (1894–1941), Russian short story writer, author of *Red Cavalry* (1926).

Baber (1483–1530), Persian conqueror of northern India, founded the Mogul dynasty.

Babeuf, François (1760–97), French revolutionary of communist convictions, executed after failure of 1796 conspiracy.

Babi, Persian religious sect, founded 1844 by Mirza Ali Mohammed (*c.* 1821–1850).

Babington plot, to murder Queen Elizabeth and release Mary Queen of Scots, 1586; Anthony Babington and other conspirators executed Sept. 1586.

Bablake School, Coventry, English public school, founded by Queen Isabella 1344; refounded 1560.

Babylon, capital of Babylonia *c.* 2100 B.C.; destroyed 689 B.C.; capital of Neo-Babylonian Empire 625–538 B.C.; later declined in importance.

Babylonian captivity, of the Jews, 586–*c.* 530 B.C.

Babylonish captivity, of the Popes, 1309–77.

Baccarat case, in which the future Edward VII gave evidence concerning gambling at Tranby Croft, tried June 1891.

Bach, Carl Philipp Emmanuel (1714–88), German composer, son of J. S. Bach, worked in Berlin and Hamburg.

Bach, Johann Christian (1725–82), German composer, son of J. S. Bach, was long resident in London.

Bach, Johann Sebastian (1685–1750), outstanding German composer, famous for oratorios, the Brandenburg concertos, fugues, etc.

Bache, Alexander Dallas (1806–67), American physicist, first president of National Academy of Sciences 1863.

Bacon, Francis (1561–1626), English statesman and writer, famous for his *Essays* and as a pioneer of scientific thought.

Bacon, Francis (b. 1909), Irish painter, noted for his powerful portraits of anguished figures.

Bacon, Roger (*c.* 1214–*c.* 1292), English Franciscan friar and philosopher, of legendary scientific or magical powers.

Bacon's Rebellion, American revolt in Virginia 1676, led by Nathaniel Bacon (1647–76).

bacteria, discovered *c.* 1674 by Antonie van Leeuwenhoek (*q.v.*); first cultivated 1776 by the Italian Lazzaro Spallanzani; classified 1872 by the German botanist Ferdinand Cohn (1828–98).

Badajoz, Battle of, Peninsular War, British victory over the French April 1812.

Baden-Powell, Robert, 1st Baron (1857–1941), British soldier, Boer War hero and founder of Boy Scout movement 1908.

badminton, game first played in England in the early 1870s.

Badoglio, Pietro (1871–1956), Italian soldier, formed pro-Allied government after fall of Mussolini.

Badon, Mount, scene of a battle between Britons and Saxons *c.* 500.

Baedeker, Karl (1801–51), German compiler and publisher of world-famous guidebooks.

Baer, Karl Ernst von (1792–1876), Estonian naturalist, notable for pioneer work in embryology.

Baer, Max (1910–59), American heavyweight boxer, world champion 1934–35.

Baeyer, Adolf von (1835–1917), German chemist, noted for his researches into organic chemistry.

Baffin Bay, discovered 1616 by William Baffin (1584–1622).

Bagehot, Walter (1826–77), English writer on economics and politics, author of *The English Constitution* (1867).

Baghdad Pact, mutual defence treaty between Turkey, Iraq, Pakistan and Great Britain, signed 1955; Baghdad Pact Organization set up on permanent footing April 1956; since 1958 known as Central Treaty Organization (*q.v.*) (CENTO).

Baghdad Railway, started 1889; completed 1940.

Bagration, Piotr (1765–1812), Russian general in Napoleonic Wars, killed at Battle of Borodino.

Baha'i, religious sect evolved from Babi by Mirza Husain Ali, known as Bahaullah (1817–92).

Bahamas, islands in west Atlantic, discovered by Columbus 1492; finally ceded to Britain 1783; achieved full internal self-government 1964; independent member of the Commonwealth since 1973.

Bahia Blanca, Argentine port, founded 1828.

Bahrain Islands, Persian Gulf, sheikhdom under British protection since 1861; oil discovered 1932.

Baïf, Jean Antoine de (1532–89), French poet, one of the Pléiade group.

Baikie, William Balfour (1825–64), Scottish naturalist and explorer in West Africa.

Bailey Bridge, invented 1941 by Donald Bailey.

Baillie, Joanna (1762–1851), Scottish poet and dramatist, author of *The Family Legend* (1810).

Bain, Alexander (1818–1903), Scottish psychologist and philosopher, founded the journal *Mind* 1876.

Baird, John Logie (1888–1946), Scottish inventor and pioneer in the development of television.

Bairnsfather, Bruce (1888–1959), English cartoonist, famous for the World War I 'Old Bill' series.

Bajazet I (1347–1403), Ottoman sultan of Turkey overran south-east Europe, but was defeated by Tamerlane.

Bajazet II (1447–1513), Ottoman sultan of Turkey, waged war in Europe and against Persia.

bakelite, invented 1907 by the American chemist Leo Hendrik Baekeland (1863–1944).

Baker, Sir Benjamin (1840–1907), English engineer, designed Forth and Tower bridges.

Baker, Sir Samuel (1821–93), English explorer in Africa, discovered Lake Albert 1864.

Bakerloo Tube, London, opened 1906.

Bakewell, Robert (1725–95), English agricultural pioneer of breeding methods.

Bakst, Leon (*c.* 1866–1924), Russian-born artist, famous for exotic designs for the Russian ballet in France.

Bakunin, Mikhail (1814–76), Russian revolutionary, rival of Karl Marx and founder of modern anarchism.

Balakirev, Mili (1836–1910), Russian composer, noted for his orchestral and piano music and songs.

Balaklava, Battle of, Crimean War, British, French, and Turkish forces fought Russians in indecisive action 25 Oct. 1854.

Balanchine, George (b. 1904), Russian-born American choreographer, notably for the Russian ballet in France.

Balboa, Vasco Nuñez de (1475–1517), Spanish explorer, discovered the Pacific Ocean 1513.

Balbus, Lucius Cornelius (1st cent. B.C.), Spanish-born Roman politician, involved in struggle between Pompey and Caesar.

Balchin, Nigel (1908–70), English novelist, best known for *The Small Back Room* (1943).

Baldovinetti, Alessio (*c.* 1425–1499), Italian painter of the Florentine school.

Baldwin I (1058–1118), king of Jerusalem 1100–18, captured Acre 1104.

Baldwin II (d. 1131), known as Baldwin de Burgh, king of Jerusalem 1118–31.

Baldwin I (1171–1205), leader of the

Fourth Crusade and first Latin emperor at Constantinople 1204–05.

Baldwin II (1217–73), last Latin emperor at Constantinople 1228–61, nephew of Baldwin I.

Baldwin, James (b. 1924), American Negro novelist, author of *Go Tell it on the Mountain* (1953).

Baldwin, Robert (1804–58), Canadian politician, led first responsible government in Canada.

Baldwin, Stanley (1867–1947), British statesman, prime minister,1923–24, 1924–29 and 1935–37.

Bale, John (1495–1563), English bishop and author, wrote the earliest known historical play *King John*.

Balearic Islands, Mediterranean, under Carthaginian occupation 5th century B.C.; taken by Rome 123 B.C.; invaded by Vandals 5th century A.D.; conquered by Arabs 903; Christian kingdom 13th century; occupied by British 18th century; finally ceded to Spain 1802.

Balfe, Michael William (1808–70), Irish singer and composer of operas including *The Bohemian Girl* (1843).

Balfour, Arthur James (1848–1930), British statesman and philosopher, prime minister 1902–05.

Balfour Declaration, favouring the creation of a Jewish national home in Palestine, made by the British government 2 Nov. 1917.

Bali, Indonesian island, first reached by Dutch 1597; Dutch rule firmly established 1908; part of Indonesia from 1950.

Balkan Wars, fought by the Balkan powers over the division of the Turkish empire in Europe 1912–13.

Ball, John (d. 1381), English priest, one of the leaders of the 1381 Peasants' Revolt.

Ballantyne, Robert Michael (1824–94), Scottish writer of boys' stories, often with Canadian backgrounds.

Ballarat, Victoria, founded through discovery of gold nearby, 1851.

Balliol, John de (1249–1315), king of Scotland 1292–96, deposed by Edward I of England.

Balliol College, Oxford University, founded *c.* 1263 by John de Balliol (d. 1269).

ballistic missiles, first operational missile was the German V-2 fired against London 1944; first intercontinental ballistic missile, the American Atlas, was developed 1954 and first fired full-range 1958.

balloons, hot-air, invented by the brothers Joseph and Etienne Montgolfier 1783; first ascent by Montgolfier and Pilatre de Rozier 21 Nov. 1783; first ascent in hydrogen balloon made by the physicist J. A. C. Charles 1 Dec. 1783; first ascents in Britain made 1784.

ballot, voting by, made compulsory in Britain 1872.

ball-point pens, first practical model patented by the Hungarian Lazlo Biro 1938; produced commercially from 1945.

Balmoral Castle, Aberdeenshire, British royal residence, completed 1855.

Balsamo, Giuseppe. See **Cagliostro,** Count.

Baltic Exchange (The Baltic Mercantile and Shipping Exchange), London, developed from informal 17th-century coffeehouse transactions to the formal establishment of the Baltic Club 1823.

Baltimore, Maryland formally founded 1729; settled about 50 years earlier.

Baluchistan, incorporated in India 1887; part of Pakistan 1947; merged with province of West Pakistan 1955; made a separate province 1970.

Balzac, Honoré de (1799–1850), French novelist, wrote large number of works comprising the *Comédie Humaine*.

Bampton Lectures, delivered annually at Oxford University since 1780; founded by John Bampton (*c.* 1690–1751).

Banat, under Turkish rule 1552–1718; under Austrian control 1718–79; inporated in Hungary 1779; ceded by Hungary to Romania and Yugoslavia 1919.

Bancroft, George (1800–91), American historian, wrote a ten-volume *History of the United States* (1834–74).

Bancroft, Sir Squire (1841–1926), English actor, manager of London theatres.

Bancroft's School, Essex, English public school founded by will of Francis Bancroft 1737.

Banda, Hastings Kamuzu (b. 1905), Malawi statesman, president of Malawi since 1966.

Bandaranaike, Sirimavo (b. 1916), prime minister of Sri Lanka 1960–65 and 1970–77; world's first woman prime minister.

Bandaranaike, Solomon (1899–1959), prime minister of Sri Lanka from 1956 to 1959 when he was assassinated.

Bandung Conference, of Asian-African countries, held 18–24 April 1955.

Bangalore, largest town of Karnataka, India, founded 1537.

Bangkok, made capital of Thailand 1782.

Bangladesh, part of Pakistan as province of East Pakistan from 1947; independent republic within the Commonwealth since 1972.

Bangorian Controversy, begun 1717 by Benjamin Hoadly, bishop of Bangor.

Bank for International Settlements, founded 13 Nov. 1929.

Bank for Reconstruction and Development, International, proposed at Bretton Woods Conference 1944; constituted Dec. 1945; started operations 27 June 1946.

Bankhead, Tallulah (1903–68), American

film and stage actress, achieved fame in both comic and dramatic roles.

Bank Holidays Act, passed 1871 establishing present English holidays – Good Friday, Easter Monday, Whit Monday, last Monday in August, Christmas and Boxing Days; New Year's holiday included from 1975; also May Day from 1978.

Bank of England, founded 1694 by William Patterson (1658–1719); nationalized 1946.

Bank of France, founded by Napoleon Bonaparte 1800.

Bank of Scotland, founded by the Scottish Parliament 1695.

Bank of the United States, 1st founded by the Federalists 1791, ended 1811; 2nd founded 1816, ended 1836.

bank robbery, first American, carried out by rebel soldiers at St Albans, Vermont, 1864; first by the James-Younger gang 1866.

Bankruptcy Act, abolished imprisonment for debt in Britain 1870.

Banks, Sir Joseph (1743–1820), English naturalist, accompanied Cook's Pacific expedition 1768–71.

Bannister, Roger (b. 1929), English athlete, first person to run a mile in under four minutes, 1954.

Bannockburn, Battle of, fought between Scots and English, 24 June 1314.

Banting, Sir Frederick Grant (1891–1941), Canadian medical scientist, co-discoverer of insulin.

Banting, William (1797–1878), English undertaker, pioneer of slimming by diet control.

Bantock, Sir Granville (1868–1946), English composer, influenced development of musical life in Midlands.

Bantry Bay, Ireland, scene of unsuccessful French invasion attempts 1689 and 1796.

Bao Dai (b. 1911), last emperor of Annam 1925–55 and president of Vietnam 1949–55.

Baptist Church, first English, formed 1609 at Amsterdam, and c. 1611 in London; the Baptist Union of Great Britain and Ireland formed 1891; in U.S.A. first Baptist Church formed at the Providence settlement of Narragansett Bay 1639.

Bara, Theda (1890–1955), American star of silent films, a famous 'vamp'.

Barbados, West Indies, visited by the English 1605; formally occupied 1625; independent member of the Commonwealth since 1966.

Barbarossa. See **Frederick I.**

Barbarossa Brothers, famous pirates, controlled much of Mediterranean in early 16th century.

barbed wire, invented 1873 by the Ameri-

can Joseph Farwell Glidden (1813–1906).

Barbellion, W. N. P. (pseud. of Bruce Cummings; 1889–1919), English diarist, wrote *Journal of a Disappointed Man* (1919).

Barber, Samuel (b. 1910), American composer, best known for *Adagio for Strings* (1938).

Barbey d'Aurevilly, Jules (1808–89), French writer, author of essays, literary criticism and novels.

Barbirolli, Sir John (1899–1970), English conductor, notably of the New York Philharmonic and Hallé orchestras.

barbiturates, first one, barbitone, introduced in the early 1900s following the discovery, 1864, of barbituric acid by the German chemist Adolf von Baeyer (*q.v.*); phenobarbitone introduced 1912.

Barbizon school, French art movement 1830–70.

Barbon, Nicholas (*c.* 1640–1698), English pioneer of fire insurance.

Barbusse, Henri (1873–1935), French novelist, wrote the World War I classic *Le Feu* (1916).

Barcelona, founded 3rd century B.C.; captured by Moors A.D. 713; incorporated with Aragon 1137; cathedral built 1298–1448; university founded 1430; capital of Republican Spain 1937–39.

Barb College, Annandale-on-Hudson, New York, founded 1860; chartered in its present form and name 1935.

Barebone's Parliament, called by Cromwell during the Commonwealth, sat 4 July to 12 Dec. 1653; named from one of its members, Praise-God Barebone (*c.* 1596–1679).

Barents Sea, named after William Barents (d. 1597), Dutch explorer.

Barham, Richard Harris (1788–1845), English writer of humorous verse, notably *The Ingoldsby Legends.*

Barhebraeus (1226–86), Syrian Christian religious leader and historical writer.

Baring, Maurice (1874–1945), English writer, noted for parody and other humorous work.

Baring Brothers, English merchant banking company, founded by John Baring (1730–1816) and Francis Baring (1740–1810).

Baring-Gould, Sabine (1834–1924), English cleric and writer, composed the hymn 'Onward Christian Soldiers'.

barium, first investigated in mineral form *c.* 1600 by the Italian alchemist Vincenzo Cascariolo; isolated 1808 by Sir Humphry Davy (*q.v.*).

Barker, Harley Granville. See **Granville-Barker,** Harley.

Barker, Sir Herbert (1869–1950), English specialist in manipulative surgery, i.e., done without performing an operation.

Bar-Kochba (d. A.D. 135), leader of Jewish revolt against Roman rule in Palestine A.D. 132–135.

Barlach, Ernst (1870–1938), German sculptor in expressionist style, later successful as a novelist.

Barnabites, Roman Catholic religious order founded 1530 by Saint Antonio Mario Zaccaria (1500–39).

Barnard, Lady Anne (1750–1825), Scottish author of the ballad *Auld Robin Gray*.

Barnard, Christiaan (b. 1922), South African surgeon, first man to perform heart transplant (1967).

Barnard, Edward Emerson (1857–1923), American astronomer, best known for his work in celestial photography.

Barnard Castle School, Co. Durham, English public school, founded 1883.

Barnado's Homes, Dr, founded 1867 by Dr Thomas Barnardo (1845–1905).

Barnato, Barney (1852–97), English financier, made fortune in diamond mining in South Africa.

Barnes, Barnabe (*c.* 1569–1609), English poet, wrote sonnets, madrigals, odes, etc.

Barnes, Thomas (1785–1841), English journalist, edited *The Times* from 1817.

Barnes, William (1801–86), English poet, wrote in Dorset dialect.

Barnet, Battle of, Wars of the Roses, 14 April 1471.

Barnet fair, Hertfordshire, held during first week in Sept.

Barnfield, Richard (1574–1627), English poet, wrote on pastoral themes.

Barnum's show, founded 1871 by the American Phineas T. Barnum (1810–91).

Baroja, Pio (1872–1956), Spanish novelist, noted for his stories of Basque life.

barometer, invented 1643 by Evangelista Torricelli (*q.v.*).

baronet, title created by King James I 1611.

Barr, Robert (1850–1912), Scottish novelist and editor, author of *In the Midst of Alarms* (1894).

Barras, Paul, Vicomte de (1755–1829), French Revolutionary politician, leading member of the Directory 1795–99.

Barrault, Jean Louis (b. 1910), French actor and director, made notable appearance in film *Les Enfants du Paradis* (1944).

Barren Grounds, Canada, first crossed 1770–72 by the English explorer Samuel Hearne (1745–92).

Barrès, Maurice (1862–1923), French writer, of extreme nationalist views.

Barrie, Sir James Matthew (1860–1937), Scottish writer, best known for the play *Peter Pan* (1904).

Barrington, George (1755–1840), Irish pickpocket, transported to Australia, became police official and historian.

barrister, first English woman, qualified 25 May 1921.

Barrow, Sir John (1764–1848), English explorer, founded Royal Geographical Society 1830.

Barry, Sir Charles (1795–1860), English architect of the House of Commons 1840–60.

Barrymore, Ethel (1879–1959), American actress, sister of John and Lionel, played many notable roles on both stage and in films.

Barrymore, John (1882–1942), American actor, famous in both theatre (*Richard III*) and cinema (*Grand Hotel*).

Barrymore, Lionel (1878–1954), American actor, appeared in many films, particularly as Dr Gillespie in the 'Dr Kildare' films.

Bart, Jean (1650–1702), French privateer and naval commander, successful against both Dutch and English fleets.

Barth, Heinrich (1821–65), German explorer, travelled widely in Asia and North Africa.

Barth, Karl (1886–1968), Swiss Protestant theologian, whose works stress the importance of divine grace in Christian belief.

Bartholdi, Frédéric Auguste (1834–1904), French sculptor of the Statue of Liberty, 1885.

Bartholomew, John George (1860–1920), Scottish cartographer, Cartographer Royal from 1913.

Bartholomew fair, held at West Smithfield, London, on Saint Bartholomew's Day from 1133 to 1855.

Bartholomew, Massacre of Saint, of Protestants by Catholics in Paris, 24 Aug. 1572.

Barthou, Jean (1862–1934), French politician, assassinated together with King Alexander of Yugoslavia.

Bartlett, Sir Frederick (1886–1968), English psychologist, professor of experimental psychology at Cambridge 1931–52.

Bartlett, John (1820–1905), American publisher, compiled the standard *Familiar Quotations* (1855).

Bartók, Bela (1881–1945). Hungarian composer, pianist, and folk-music collector, one of the most original figures in 20th-century music.

Bartolommeo, Fra (1475–1517), Italian painter of the Florentine school, whose works include *The Marriage of Saint Catherine*.

Bartolozzi, Francesco (1727–1815), Italian engraver, worked in England for King George III.

Bartram, John (1699–1777), the first American botanist, travelled widely for his naturalistic researches.

Baruch, Bernard Mannes (1870–1965), American financier, active as government economic adviser in World Wars I and II.

Barye, Antoine Louis (1795–1875), French sculptor, chiefly of wild animal subjects.

baseball, supposedly invented 1839 at Cooperstown, New York, by Abner Doubleday (1819–93).

Basel University, founded 1460 by Pope Pius II.

Basevi, George (1794–1845), English architect of the Fitzwilliam Museum, Cambridge.

Bashkirtsev, Marie (1860–84), Russian painter and diarist, left a famous *Journal* (1887).

Basic English, produced 1930 by C. K. Ogden (*q.v.*).

Basil, Saint (*c.* 330–379), Greek prelate, known as Basil the Great, organized Greek monasticism.

Basil I (*c.* 813–886), Byzantine emperor 867–886, a great reformer and warrior.

Basil II (*c.* 958–1025), Byzantine emperor 976–1025, a notable military leader, conquered the Bulgarians.

Basilides (d. *c.* A.D. 140), Syrian-born exponent of Gnosticism at Alexandria.

Baskerville, John (1706–75), English printer and typefounder, noted for his invention of new typefaces.

basketball, invented by James Naismith (1861–1939) at Springfield, Mass., 1891.

Bassano, Jacopo (1510–92), Italian painter of the Venetian Renaissance school.

Bassompierre, François de (1579–1646), French military leader and diplomat, wrote his *Memoirs* during captivity.

Bass Strait, between Australia and Tasmania, discovered 1798 by George Bass, English naval surgeon (d. *c.* 1812).

Bastien-Lepage, Jules (1848–84), French painter of realistic peasant scenes.

Bastille, The, Paris, built by Hugues Aubriot 1370–83; destroyed 14 July 1789.

Basutoland. See **Lesotho.**

Bataan, Philippines, scene of World War II American resistance to Japanese Jan.–April 1942; recaptured by Americans Feb. 1945.

Bataille, Henry (1872–1922), French dramatist, author of *La Femme Nue* (1908).

Batavia, Java, founded by the Dutch colonial administrator Jan Coen 1619.

Bateman, Henry Mayo (1887–1970), Australian-born cartoonist in England, contributed to *Punch.*

Bates, Henry Walter (1825–92), English naturalist, explored the Amazon 1848–59.

Bates, Herbert Ernest (1905–74), English writer, whose many novels include *The Darling Buds of May* (1958).

Bateson, William (1861–1926), English biologist, pioneer in study of genetics.

Bath, Roman watering place 1st century A.D.; destroyed 6th century; received charter 1189; fashionable resort 18th century; university established 1966.

Bath, Order of the, custom in existence by 1127; renewed by George I 1725.

Bathurst, New South Wales, founded by Governor Macquarie 1815.

Batista y Zalvidar, Fulgencio (1901–73), Cuban soldier and politician, dictator of Cuba 1954–59.

Batoni, Pompeo (1708–87), Italian painter, chiefly remembered for his portraits.

Battenberg, title conferred on Julia von Hauke 1851 when she married Prince Alexander of Hesse; their son Louis changed the name to Mountbatten in 1917.

Battersea Bridge, London, built 1887–90 by the English civil engineer Sir Joseph Bazalgette (1819–91); replaced older structure of 1771.

battery, electric, invented 1800 by Alessandro Volta (*q.v.*); dry cell (as used in torches, etc.) invented 1866 by the French engineer Georges Leclanché (1839–82).

battle, ordeal by, valid in English law until 1819.

Battle Hymn of the Republic, The, written 1862 by Julia Ward Howe (*q.v.*).

Battle of Britain, World War II, fought Aug.–Sept. 1940.

Batu Khan (d. 1255), Mongol ruler, conquered Russia and Eastern Europe 1237–41.

Baudelaire, Charles (1821–67), French poet, author of *Les Fleurs du Mal* (1857).

Bauhaus, architectural movement founded 1919 by Walter Gropius (*q.v.*).

bauxite, discovered 1821 by the Belgian P. Berthier; first mined 1882 in France.

Bavaria, ruled by Wittelsbachs 1180–1918; joined German Empire 1871; republic proclaimed 1918; constitution abolished 1933.

Bavarian Succession, War of the, fought 1778–79.

Bax, Sir Arnold (1883–1953), English composer, noted for his use of Celtic themes.

Baxter, George (1804–67), English artist, especially admired for his colour prints.

Baxter, Richard (1615–91), English Nonconformist divine, prolific writer and composer of hymns.

Bayard, Chevalier de (*c.* 1474–1524), French soldier, renowned for his chivalrous behaviour.

Baybars I (1223–77), Turkish-born sultan of Egypt 1260–77 and founder of Mameluke dynasty.

Bay Bridge, San Francisco, built 1936.

Bayeux tapestry, probably embroidered in England in the 11th century; first recorded mention 1476.

Bayle, Pierre (1647–1706), French philosopher and writer, best known for his encyclopedic dictionary.

Baylis, Lilian (1874–1937), English theatre

manager, founded the Old Vic and Sadler's Wells.

Bay Psalm Book, earliest American printed book, published at Cambridge, Mass., 1640.

Bayreuth, Bavaria, founded 1194; Festival Theatre, home of Wagnerian opera, built 1872; opened 1876.

Bazin, René (1853–1932), French novelist, author of *Les Oberlé* (1901).

Beale, Dorothea (1831–1906), English educationalist, founder of colleges for girls and women teachers.

bear-baiting, prohibited in Britain by Act of Parliament 1835.

Beardsley, Aubrey (1872–98), English artist, illustrated *The Yellow Book*.

Beattie, James (1735–1803), Scottish poet, and writer on philosophy, author of *The Minstrel* (1771–74).

Beatty, David, 1st Earl (1871–1936), British admiral, commanded the British battle cruisers at the Battle of Jutland.

Beaufort, Margaret, Countess of Richmond and Derby (1443–1509), English philanthropist, mother of Henry VII and patron of education.

Beaufort scale, of wind speeds, devised 1805 by the British admiral Sir Francis Beaufort (1774–1857).

Beauharnais, Eugène de (1781–1824), French administrator, son of Napoleon's empress Josephine by her first marriage.

Beaumarchais, Pierre Caron de (1732–99), French dramatist, author of *The Barber of Seville* (1775) and *The Marriage of Figaro* (1784).

Beaumont, Francis (1584–1616), English dramatist, with John Fletcher author of *The Knight of the Burning Pestle* (1609).

Beaumont, William (1796–1853), American surgeon, made notable contribution to study of gastric digestion.

Beaumont College, Old Windsor, English public school, founded by the Society of Jesus 1861.

Beauvoir, Simone de (b. 1908), French existentialist writer, noted for her novels and autobiographical works.

Beaverbrook, William Maxwell Aitken, 1st Baron (1879–1964), Canadian-born newspaper magnate and politician, publisher of the *Daily Express*.

bebop, a style of jazz with complex chord patterns; developed in the early 1940s.

Beccaria, Cesare (1738–94), Italian jurist, advocate of criminal law reform.

Bechuanaland. See **Botswana.**

Becket, Thomas (c. 1118–1170), archbishop of Canterbury, quarrelled with Henry II, murdered in Canterbury Cathedral.

Beckett, Samuel (b. 1906), Irish dramatist writing mainly in French, author of *Waiting for Godot* (1953).

Beckford, William (1760–1844), English writer of the oriental fantasy *Vathek* (1787).

Beckmann, Max (1884–1950), German expressionist painter and engraver, exiled by the Nazis.

Becquer, Gustavo Adolfo (1836–70), Spanish Romantic poet, characterized by his melancholy and lyrical verse.

Becquerel, Antoine Henri (1852–1908), French scientist, awarded the Nobel Prize 1903 for research into radioactivity.

Bedales, Hampshire, English coeducational school, founded 1893.

Beddoes, Thomas Lovell (1803–49), English writer, author of *The Bride's Tragedy* (1822).

Bede, Saint (the Venerable Bede; c. 673–735), English theologian and chronicler, author of *Ecclesiastical History of the English Nation*.

Bedford Modern School, English public school, founded through funds left 1566 by Sir William Harper (c. 1496–1573).

Bedford School, English public school, received letters patent from Edward VI 1552, but is much older, possibly founded before the Norman Conquest.

Bedlam (Bethlehem Hospital), London, founded by Simon FitzMary 1247.

Beecham, Sir Thomas (1879–1961), English conductor, played a leading part in the revival of opera in England.

Beecher, Henry Ward (1813–87), American clergyman and social reformer, a strong opponent of slavery.

Beerbohm, Sir Max (1872–1956). English writer and caricaturist, author of *Zuleika Dobson* (1911).

Beethoven, Ludwig van (1770–1827), German composer of outstanding genius, famous for his development of the symphony, also wrote sonatas, concertos, chamber works, etc.

Beeton, Mrs (1836–65), English writer on cooking, of almost legendary authority.

beet sugar, developed 1747 by the German chemist Andreas Sigismund Maggraf (1709–82).

Beguines, lay sisterhoods founded c. 1180 at Liège by Lambert de Bègue (d. c. 1187).

Behaim, Martin (c. 1459–1507), German navigator and geographer, made the first known terrestrial globe, 1492.

Behan, Brendan (1923–64), Irish dramatist, author of *The Quare Fellow* (1956) and *The Hostage* (1959).

Behn, Aphra (1640–89), English woman writer, author of *Oroonoko* (1688).

Behrens, Peter (1868–1938), German architect, notable for his modern industrial design.

Behring, Emil von (1854–1917), German bacteriologist, discovered the antitoxins of diphtheria and tetanus.

Beiderbecke, Bix (1903–31), American

jazz pianist, cornet player and composer.

Beilby enamel glass, introduced 1760.

Beira, Mozambique port, founded 1891 on site of Arab settlement.

Beit, Alfred (1853–1906), British financier, associated with Cecil Rhodes, made fortune in South Africa.

Békésy, Georg von (1899–1972), Hungarian physiologist, awarded Nobel prize 1961 for his study of the inner ear.

Belasco, David (1889–1931), American actor-manager and playwright, renowned as a showman.

Belgian Congo. See **Zaïre.**

Belgium, part of Burgundian and Spanish Netherlands until 1572; Spanish rule until 1700; Austrian rule 1713–94; annexed by France 1797; part of Netherlands 1815–30; became independent kingdom 1830; partly occupied by Germany 1914–18; overrun by Germany 1940; liberated 1944–45.

Belinsky, Vissarion (1811–48), Russian critic, founder of literary criticism in Russia.

Belisarius (505–565), Byzantine general, reconquered North Africa and southern Italy for Byzantium.

Belisha beacons, introduced in Britain 1934 by the minister of transport Sir Leslie Hore-Belisha (1893–1957).

Belize, Central America, settled by British 1638; proclaimed a colony 1862; achieved degree of self-government 1964.

Bell, Alexander Graham (1847–1922), Scottish-born American physicist, inventor of the telephone 1876.

Bell, Andrew (1753–1832), Scottish clergyman and educationalist, founder of the monitorial system of education.

Bell, Sir Charles (1774–1842), Scottish anatomist, discovered the different functions of motor and sensory nerves.

Bell, Gertrude (1868–1926), English traveller, explored interior of Arabia.

Bellarmine, Robert (1542–1621), Italian Jesuit, famous theological controversialist.

Belleau, Remy (1528–77), French poet, was a member of the Pléiade Group.

Belleau Wood, Battle of, World War I, fought between U.S. marines and Germans, June 1918.

Belle Sauvage, London, one of England's oldest coaching inns, first mentioned 1453.

Bellinghausen, Fabian Gottlieb von (1778–1852), Russian naval officer and explorer, leader of an Antarctic expedition.

Bellini, Gentile (c. 1429–1507), Italian painter, was official Venetian state artist.

Bellini, Giovanni (c. 1430–1516), Italian painter, first major Venetian Renaissance artist.

Bellini, Jacopo (c. 1400–1470), Italian painter, father of Gentile and Giovanni, founder of the Venetian School.

Bellman, Karl Michael (1740–95), Swedish poet, writer of popular comic verse and drinking songs.

Belloc, Hilaire (1870–1953), French-born English writer of history, travel, light verse, and Roman Catholic apologetics.

Bellow, Saul (b. 1915), American novelist and Nobel prizewinner, author of *The Adventures of Augie March* (1953).

Bell Rock lighthouse, North Sea, completed 1811.

Belo Horizonte, capital of Minas Gerais, Brazil, since 1897.

Belvoir hunt, Leicestershire and Lincolnshire, dates from 1750; became a fox pack 1762.

Bely, Andrei (1880–1934), Russian symbolist poet and novelist.

Belzoni, Giovanni Battista (1778–1823), Italian explorer and archaeologist, made many discoveries in Egypt.

Bembo, Pietro, Cardinal (1470–1547), Italian scholar and poet, whose writings reflect the ideas of the Renaissance.

Benavente, Jacinto (1866–1954), Spanish dramatist, won Nobel Prize for Literature 1922.

Ben Bella, Ahmed (b. 1916), Algerian politician, first president of independent Algeria 1963–65.

Benbow, John (1653–1702), English naval commander, active in wars against France.

Benchley, Robert (1889–1945), American humorous writer and film actor.

Benda, Julien (1867–1956), French philosopher, author of *La Trahison des Clercs* (1927).

Benday process, illustrative method in printing invented 1879 by the American engraver Benjamin Day (1838–1916).

Benedict VIII (d. 1024), Pope 1012–24, was a notable reformer.

Benedict IX (c. 1012–1056), 'boy' Pope from 1032, twice deposed, finally (according to Roman Catholic view) in 1045.

Benedict XIV (1675–1758), Pope 1740–58, notable as an administrator and scholar.

Benedict XV (1854–1922), Pope 1914–22, made many peace proposals during World War I.

Benedict Biscop (c. 628–690), English churchman, founded monasteries at Wearmouth and Jarrow.

Benedict of Nursia, Saint (c. 480–c. 550), Italian monk, founder of the Benedictine Order, 529.

Benelux, customs union between Belgium, the Netherlands and Luxembourg, came into force Jan. 1948.

Beneš, Eduard (1884–1948), Czech statesman, president of Czechoslovakia 1935–38 and 1945–48.

Benét, Stephen Vincent (1898–1943), American poet, author of *John Brown's Body* (1928).

Bengal, became part of Mogul Empire 1576; under effective British control 1757; made presidency 1773; became autonomous province 1937; divided between India and East Pakistan (now Bangladesh) 1947.

Benghazi, Libya, in World War II captured by British Feb. 1941; by Germans April 1941; retaken by British Dec. 1941; surrendered Jan. 1942; finally retaken by British Nov. 1942.

Ben Gurion, David (1886–1973), Israeli statesman, first prime minister of Israel.

Benin, West Africa, powerful kingdom in 17th century; commercial treaty with France 1851; completely annexed 1894; French overseas territory 1946; independent republic since 1960; people's republic since 1972.

Bennett, Arnold (1867–1931), English novelist, wrote of the Potteries in *Old Wives' Tale* (1908), *Clayhanger* (1910).

Benno, Saint (1010–1106), German bishop, whose canonization (1523) was violently attacked by Martin Luther.

Benois, Alexander (1870–1960), Russian painter and theatrical designer, well known for his work on ballet decor.

Bentham, Jeremy (1748–1832), English legal and political reformer, devised theory of Utilitarianism.

Bentley, Richard (1662–1742), English literary critic, controversialist and classical scholar.

Benz, Karl Friedrich (1884–1929), German engineer, pioneered the construction of internal-combustion engines.

benzene, discovered 1825 by Michael Faraday (*q.v.*); benzene ring structure postulated 1865 by the German chemist August Kekulé (1829–96).

Beowulf, Anglo-Saxon epic poem, written *c.* 1000.

Béranger, Pierre Jean de (1780–1857), French poet, wrote widely popular song lyrics.

Berceo, Gonzalo de (*c.* 1195–*c.* 1268), the earliest known Castilian poet, wrote mainly on devotional subjects.

Berchtold's Day, Swiss annual festival, held 2 Jan.

Berdyaev, Nicolas (1874–1948), Russian philosopher, in exile from 1922, tried to adapt Christianity to modern society.

Berenson, Bernhard (1865–1959), Lithuanian-born American art critic and art historian, particularly of the Italian Renaissance.

Berg, Alban (1885–1935), Austrian composer, whose *Wozzeck* (1922) was a landmark in modern music.

Bergerac, Cyrano de (1619–55), French writer, soldier and duellist.

Bergh, Henry (1811–88), American philanthropist, founder of societies for the prevention of cruelty to animals and children.

Bergius, Friedrich (1884–1949), German industrial chemist, developed process for extracting petrol from coal.

Bergman. Hjalmar Fredrik (1883–1930), Swedish novelist and dramatist, author of *Thy Rod and Thy Staff* (1921).

Bergman, Ingmar (b. 1918), Swedish film director, achieved an international reputation with such films as *The Seventh Seal* (1956).

Bergson, Henri (1859–1941), French philosopher, believed in a 'life force' (*élan vital*) behind evolution.

Beria, Lavrenti (1899–1953), Soviet secret police chief, notorious for his persecution of opponents of the Stalin regime.

Bering Strait, Arctic Ocean, discovered 1728 by Vitus Bering.

Bering, Vitus (1681–1741), Danish-born Russian explorer in waters between Russia and Alaska.

Berio, Luciano (b. 1925), Italian composer, pioneer in modern musical form.

Berkeley, George (1685–1753), Irish philosopher, important for his *New Theory of Vision* (1709).

Berkeley, Sir William (1606–77), English colonial governor of Virginia 1642–76, whose policies led to Bacon's Rebellion (*q.v.*).

berkelium, radioactive element isolated 1949 by S. G. Thompson, A. Ghiorso, and G. T. Seaborg at Berkeley, California.

Berkhampsted School, Hertfordshire, English public school, founded 1541.

Berkman, Alexander (1870–1936), Polish-born American anarchist, associated with Emma Goldman; deported from U.S.A. 1919.

Berlin, founded early 13th century; member of Hanseatic League 14th century; capital of Prussia 1701; captured by French 1806; capital of the German Empire 1871; scene of Congress of Berlin 1878; divided into occupation zones 1945; Berlin Blockade June 1948–May 1949; West Berlin part of West Germany and East Berlin capital of East Germany 1949; wall between East and West built 1961.

Berlin, Irving (b. 1888), Russian-born American composer of popular songs.

Berlioz, Hector (1803–69), leading French 19th-century composer, whose works include *Symphonie Fantastique* (1830).

Bermuda, visited by the Spaniard Juan Bermúdez 1515; settled by the English 1609, and formally taken over 1684; achieved internal self-government 1968.

Bernadette, Saint (1844–79), French peasant girl, whose childhood visions led to the foundation of the shrine at Lourdes.

Bernadotte, Count Folke (1895–1948), Swedish humanitarian, headed wartime

Swedish Red Cross; assassinated working for U.N. in Palestine.

Bernadotte, Jean Baptiste (1763?–1844), French general under Napoleon; from 1814 king of Sweden as Charles XIV John.

Bernanos, Georges (1888–1948), French novelist, author of *Diary of a Country Priest* (1936).

Bernard, Claude (1813–78), French physiologist, conducted important researches into the secretions of the alimentary canal.

Bernardin de Saint Pierre (1737–1814), French writer, whose *Paul et Virginie* (1788) influenced the Romantic movement.

Bernard of Clairvaux, Saint (1090–1153), Cistercian monk, theologian and Church reformer.

Bernhardt, Sarah (1845–1923), French actress of legendary tragic power.

Bernini, Giovanni Lorenzo (1598–1680), Italian Baroque sculptor (*Saint Teresa*) and architect (colonnade, Saint Peter's, Rome).

Bernoulli, the name of a distinguished Swiss family of mathematicians and scientists, including Jacob Bernoulli (1654–1705), Johann Bernoulli (1667–1748), a pioneer in exponential calculus, and Daniel Bernoulli (1700–82).

Bernoulli's principle, of the flow of liquids, formulated 1738 by Daniel Bernoulli.

Bernstein, Leonard (b. 1918), American composer and conductor, wrote the music for *West Side Story* (1957).

Berruguete, Alonso (c. 1486–1561), Spanish sculptor, court sculptor and painter to Charles V.

Berthelot, Marcelin (1827–1907), French chemist, made an important contribution to the study of organic chemistry.

Berthollet, Claude Louis (1748–1822), French chemist, helped to formulate new chemical nomenclature.

Bertillon, Alphonse (1853–1914), French criminologist, devised system of criminal investigation by anthropometry.

Berwick, Peace of, between England and Scotland, signed 1639.

beryllium, discovered as the oxide 1798 by Louis-Nicolas Vauquelin; isolated 1828 by the German scientist Friedrich Wöhler (1800–82).

Berzelius, Jöns Jacob (1779–1848), Swedish chemist, prepared accurate list of atomic weights.

Besant, Annie (1847–1933), English theosophist and social reformer, participated in Home Rule movement in India.

Bessel functions, invented 1817; fully developed 1824 by the German astronomer Friedrich Wilhelm Bessel (1784–1846).

Bessemer process, for steel, originated 1846 by the American William Kelly; developed and patented 1856 by the English engineer Sir Henry Bessemer (1813–98).

Best, Charles Herbert (b. 1899), Canadian physiologist, with Sir Frederick Banting (q.v.) discovered insulin treatment for diabetes.

beta particle, discovered 1896 by Lord Rutherford (q.v.).

betatron, device for producing high-energy electrons, developed 1940 by the American physicist D. W. Kerst.

Bethlen, Gábor (1580–1629), king of Hungary 1620–29, aided Protestant forces in the Thirty Years' War.

Bethmann-Hollweg, Theobald von (1856–1921), German chancellor 1909–17, forced out of office by army chiefs.

Betjeman, Sir John (b. 1900), English poet, appointed poet laureate 1972.

Betterton, Thomas (c. 1635–1710), English actor-manager, a notable interpreter of Shakespeare.

Betti, Ugo (1892–1953), Italian dramatist, author of *Corruption in the Palace of Justice* (1949).

betting houses and lists, abolished by act of parliament 1853; licensed betting shops provided for by 1960 act.

Bevan, Aneurin (1897–1960), British statesman, established National Health Service 1947; controversial figure in British politics.

Beveridge plan, national insurance scheme for Britain, conceived by Lord Beveridge (1879–1963); published 20 Nov. 1942.

Bevin, Ernest (1881–1951), English trade union leader and statesman, foreign secretary 1945–51.

Bewick, Thomas (1753–1828), English wood engraver, notably of birds.

Beza, Theodore (1519–1605), French religious reformer, Calvin's most important follower and successor at Geneva.

Bhave, Vinobha (b. 1895), Indian ascetic, influential disciple of Gandhi.

Bhopal, India, founded 1723; amalgamated with the state of Madhya Pradesh 1956.

Bhutan, Himalayan state, concluded treaty with East India Company 1774; parts annexed to India 1865; Britain assumed responsibility for foreign relations 1910; India assumed similar responsibility 1949.

Biafra, name given to former Eastern Region of Nigeria during its secession 1967–70.

Bialik, Chaim Nachman (1873–1934), Russian-born Jewish poet, author of *In the City of Slaughter* (1903).

Bible, translations of, first complete by Coverdale 1535; authorized version (King James) 1611; revised versions of New

Testament 1881 and Old Testament 1885.

Bibliographical Society, London, founded 1892.

Bibliothèque Nationale, Paris, founded 1721.

bicycle, pedal-operated model invented 1839 by a Scottish blacksmith Kirkpatrick Macmillan; the velocipede produced 1861 by the French Michaux family; the penny farthing built 1870 by the Englishman James Starley; pneumatic tyre introduced 1888 by John Boyd Dunlop (*q.v.*).

Biddle, John (*c.* 1615–1662), English schoolmaster, founder of Unitarianism.

Bierce, Ambrose (1842–*c.* 1914), American humorist and short story writer, author of *Tales of Soldiers and Civilians* (1891).

Biffen, Sir Rowland (1874–1949), English botanist, developed rust-resistant strains of wheat.

bifocal lens, invented 1780 by Benjamin Franklin.

big-bang theory, of the universe, originated about 1927 by the Belgian astronomer Georges Lemaître (1894–1966); elaborated in the 1930s by the Russian-born American physicist George Gamow (1904–68).

Big Ben, London, hour bell cast 1858; clock went into service 1859; chimes first broadcast 1923.

Big Bertha, German long-range gun that shelled Paris 1918.

Bihar, Indian state, treaty made with East India Company 1765; detached from Bengal Province 1912 and united with Orissa; made separate province 1936.

Bikaner, capital of Bikaner state (now part of Rajasthan), India, founded 1488.

Bikini Atoll, Marshall Islands, scene of U.S. atomic bomb tests 1946 and hydrogen bomb tests 1954 and 1956.

billiards, believed to have been invented by Henrique Devigne, French artist, *c.* 1571.

bimetallism, use of gold and silver for currency, first so termed *c.* 1870 by Henri Cernuschi, Italian economist (1821–96).

Binet-Simon intelligence test. See **intelligence quotient.**

Bingham, Hiram (1875–1956), American explorer and archaeologist in Peru.

binomial nomenclature, biology, established *c.* 1753 by Linnaeus (*q.v.*), although introduced much earlier.

binomial theorem, invented before 1676 by Sir Isaac Newton.

Binyon, Laurence (1869–1943), English poet, wrote the famous war poem *For the Fallen*.

biochemistry, established as a separate science *c.* 1897 by the experiments of Eduard Buchner (*q.v.*) following the earlier fermentation experiments of Louis Pasteur (*q.v.*).

Birkbeck College, London University, founded (as the London Mechanics' Institution) 1823 by Dr George Birkbeck (1776–1841).

Birdseye, Clarence (1886–1956), American industrialist, invented method for deep-freezing food.

Birkenhead, Frederick Edwin Smith, 1st Earl of (1872–1930), British statesman and lawyer, was a notably successful lord chancellor 1919–22.

Birkenhead School, Cheshire, English public school, founded 1860.

Birmingham Repertory Theatre, founded 1913 by Sir Barry Jackson (1879–1961).

Birmingham University, founded 1880 as Mason College by Sir Josiah Mason (1795–1881); charter granted 1900.

Biron, Ernst Johann (1690–1772), German-born statesman, favourite of the empress Anna Ivanovna and ruler of Russia.

Birrell, Augustine (1850–1933), English politician, and writer of essays, biography and memoirs.

birth control, 1st clinic opened at Amsterdam 1881; 1st American opened in New York 1916; 1st English opened in London 1921.

Bischof, Werner (1916–56), Swiss photographer, pioneer of modern reportage.

Bishop's Stortford College, Hertfordshire, public school, founded 1868.

Bishop Wordsworth's School, Salisbury, English public school, founded 1890 by John Wordsworth, bishop of Salisbury (1843–1911).

Bisley, National Rifle Association first met at Bisley 1890.

Bismarck, Otto von (1815–98), Prussian statesman and diplomat, architect of German unification.

Bismarck Sea, Battle of the, World War II, naval battle between Allies and Japanese March 1943.

bismuth, identified 1530 by Georg Agricola (*q.v.*).

Bizet, Georges (1838–75), French composer, wrote the opera *Carmen* (1875).

Bjerknes, Vilhelm (1862–1951), Norwegian meteorologist, with his son Jakob (b. 1897) developed accurate method of weather forecasting.

Bjørnson, Bjørnstjerne (1832–1910), Norwegian playwright and novelist, winner of 1903 Nobel Prize for Literature.

Black, Joseph (1728–99), Scottish chemist, developed theory of latent heat.

Black and Tans, nickname of auxiliary police used by the British in Ireland 1920–21.

Black Death, the plague (probably bubonic plague) which affected Asia and North Africa and ravaged Western Europe

Blackett

blood groups

1347–51, finally reaching England 1348.

Blackett, Patrick Maynard Stuart, Baron (1897–1974), English physicist, awarded 1948 Nobel Prize for Physics for his work in cosmic radiation.

Blackfriars, Dominican convent, established London 1276.

Blackfriars Bridge, London, opened 1869.

Black Friday, American financial disaster, 24 Sept. 1869.

Black Hawk (1767–1838), North American Indian chief, fought unsuccessfully against the American army, 1832.

Black Hole of Calcutta, scene of imprisonment of English by Nawab of Bengal, June 1756.

black letter, for English newspaper titles, first used 1679.

Blackmore, Richard (1825–1900), English novelist, wrote the Exmoor romance *Lorna Doone* (1869).

Black Prince, The (1330–76), eldest son of Edward III, renowned for his military exploits in France and Spain.

Black Rod, House of Lords, first appointed 1350.

Blackstone, Sir William (1723–80), English jurist, author of the famous and influential *Commentaries on the Laws of England* (1765–69).

Black Watch, Highland regiment, formed 1725; increased in size 1739; made a royal regiment 1758.

Blackwell, Elizabeth (1821–1910), English-born American physician, the first woman to qualify as a doctor of medicine, 1849.

Blackwood, Algernon Henry (1869–1951), English novelist, noted for his tales of the supernatural.

Blackwood's Magazine, founded 1817 by William Blackwood (1776–1834).

Blaeu, Willem (1571–1638), Dutch publisher, founded well-known firm of map makers.

Blair, Robert (1699–1746), Scottish poet, wrote *The Grave* (1743).

Blake, Robert (1599–1657), English admiral, won great victories over Dutch navy and Mediterranean pirates.

Blake, William (1757–1827), English poet and artist, was gifted with a powerful mystical vision.

Blanc, Jean Joseph (1811–82), French socialist politician and writer, member of government after 1848 Revolution.

Blanc, Mont, highest mountain in the Alps, first climbed by Jacques Balmat and Michel Paccard 1786.

Blanchard, Jean Pierre (1753–1809), French pioneer balloonist and inventor of the parachute.

Blanche of Castile (c. 1187–1252), daughter of Alfonso IX of Castile, wife of Louis VIII of France, was twice regent.

Blanqui, Louis (1805–81), French revolutionary leader, prominent in the Revolution of 1848 and the Commune of 1871.

Blasco-Ibañez, Vicente (1867–1928), Spanish novelist and politician, author of *The Four Horsemen of the Apocalypse* (1916).

Blatchford, Robert (1851–1943), English writer, journalist, and socialist pioneer.

Blavatsky, Madame Helena (1831–91), Russian spiritualist, founder of the Theosophical Society, 1875.

bleaching powder, first successfully manufactured 1799 by the Scottish chemist Charles Tennant (1768–1838).

Blenheim, Battle of, British and Austrian forces defeated French and Bavarians 13 Aug. 1704.

Blenheim Palace, Oxfordshire, built 1705–22 for the Duke of Marlborough by Sir John Vanbrugh.

Blériot, Louis (1872–1936), French aviator, first man to fly across the English Channel, 25 July 1909.

Bligh, William (1754–1817), English admiral, commander of *The Bounty* when the famous mutiny occurred, 1789.

blind, books for the, letters first printed in relief 1771 by the French philanthropist Valentin Haüy (1745–1822).

Bliss, Sir Arthur (1891–1975), English composer of instrumental, ballet and film music, Master of the Queen's Music 1953–75.

Blitz, The (from Blitzkrieg), the bombing by Germany of cities, industrial centres, etc. in Britain during 1940–41.

Blitzkrieg ('lightning war'), name given to the swift campaign, using armoured columns, by which Germany overran Poland (1939) and France (1940).

Bloch, Ernst (1880–1959), Swiss-born American composer, wrote the symphony *America* (1926).

Bloch, Jean Richard (1884–1947), French novelist, described the world of finance.

Blok, Alexander (1880–1921), Russian poet, outstanding figure of the Symbolist movement.

Blomfield, Sir Arthur (1829–99), English architect, notably of the Law Courts, London, 1881.

Blondin, Charles (1824–97), French acrobat, crossed Niagara Falls on a tightrope 1859.

blood, circulation of the, first described 1616 by William Harvey (*q.v.*) but not announced until 1628.

Blood, Colonel Thomas (c. 1618–1680), Irish adventurer, almost succeeded in stealing Crown Jewels 1671.

blood cells, red, first observed 1658 by Jan Swammerdam (*q.v.*).

blood groups, first ones (ABO) discovered

1900 by the American pathologist Karl Landsteiner (1863–1943), enabling first safe blood transfusions to be given.

Bloody Assizes, after the Monmouth Rebellion, held 1685 by Judge Jeffreys.

Bloody Sunday, massacre of St Petersburg workers, Jan. 1905.

Bloomer, Amelia (1818–94), American reformer and advocate of trousers derisively called 'bloomers'.

Bloomfield, Robert (1766–1823), English poet, wrote 'naive' verse, e.g. *The Farmer's Boy* (1800).

Blow, John (1648–1708), English composer, organist at Westminster Abbey.

Bloxham School, English public school, founded by the Rev. P. R. Egerton 1860.

Blücher, Gebhard von (1742–1819), Prussian general, played a decisive part in the Battle of Waterloo.

blueprint process, first used 1842 by Sir John Herschel (*q.v.*).

Blum, Léon (1872–1950), French statesman, was three times prime minister of France.

Blundell's School, Tiverton, English public school, built and endowed by the clothier Peter Blundell 1604.

Blunden, Edmund (1896–1974), English poet, also wrote World War I classic *Undertones of War* (1928).

Blunt, Wilfrid Scawen (1840–1922), English writer, travelled widely in Middle East and India.

Boadicea (d. A.D. 62), British Queen of the Iceni, led anti-Roman revolt A.D. 60.

Board of Trade, London, founded 1661; became Department of Trade and Industry 1970; partially absorbed by other government departments 1974 and renamed Department of Trade.

Boccaccio, Giovanni (1313–75), Italian writer and poet, author of *The Decameron* (1353).

Boccherini, Luigi (1743–1805), Italian composer, was also a cello virtuoso.

Boccioni, Umberto (1882–1916), Italian sculptor, member of the Futurist school.

Böcklin, Arnold (1827–1901), Swiss painter of mysterious, evocative landscapes, often with mythological subjects.

Bodichon, Barbara (1827–91), English feminist, founded Girton College, Cambridge, 1869.

Bodin, Jean (1530–96), French political thinker, expounded theory of sovereignty.

Bodleian Library, Oxford, founded 1598; opened 1602 by Sir Thomas Bodley; new library opened 1946.

Bodoni, Giambattista (1740–1813), Italian printer and typographer, devised first modern 'roman' type.

Boece, Hector (*c.* 1465–1536), Scottish historian, wrote a *Historia Scotorum* (1527).

Boehm, Theobald (1794–1881), German inventor, devised system of finger control for the flute.

Boehme, Jakob (1575–1624), German mystic and writer of theosophical tendencies.

Boer Wars, South Africa, 1st 1880–81; 2nd 1899–1902.

Boethius (*c.* 480–*c.* 524), Roman statesman and philosopher, remembered for his *De Consolatione Philosophiae*, written before execution.

Bogart, Humphrey (1899–1957), American film actor, noted for his gangster roles.

Bogotá, Colombian capital, founded 1538 by Gonzalo Jiménez de Quesada (*q.v.*).

Bohemia, settled by Slavs 5th century A.D.; converted to Christianity 9th century; kingdom within Holy Roman Empire from 12th century; ruled by house of Luxemburg from 1306; ruled by Hapsburgs 1526–1918; part of Czechoslovakia since 1918; incorporated in German Protectorate of Bohemia and Moravia 1939–45.

Bohn, Henry George (1796–1884), English publisher of cheap editions of classics.

Bohr, Niels (1885–1962), Danish physicist, pioneer of atomic structure and quantum theory.

Boiardo, Matteo Maria (1434–94), Italian lyric poet, author of *Orlando Innamorato* (1482).

Boileau-Déspreaux, Nicolas (1636–1711), French critic and poet, defined classical standards for poetry.

Boito, Arrigo (1842–1918), Italian composer of opera *Mefistofile* and distinguished librettist.

Bojer, Johan (1872–1959), Norwegian novelist, wrote of life in fishing communities.

Boldrewood, Rolf (1826–1915), English-born Australian novelist, author of *Robbery Under Arms* (1888).

Boleslav I (d. 1025), king of Poland 992–1025, increased Polish power.

Boleslav II (1039–81), king of Poland 1058–79, asserted national independence but deposed.

Boleslav III (1086–1138), king of Poland 1102–38, won many victories and enlarged his kingdom.

Boleyn, Anne. See **Anne Boleyn.**

Bolingbroke, Henry St John, Viscount (1678–1751), English politician, in exile for some years as Jacobite supporter.

Bolívar, Simón (1783–1830), South American soldier and statesman, led successful revolt against Spain.

Bolivia, part of Inca kingdom from 14th century; conquered by Spanish 1538; proclaimed a republic 1825; boundary with Chile fixed after war 1879–84, with Paraguay after war 1932–35.

Böll, Heinrich (b. 1917), German novelist,

awarded Nobel Prize for Literature 1972.

Bologna, Giovanni da (1524–1608), Flemish sculptor, studied and worked in Italy.

bolometer, invented 1880 by the American scientist Samuel Pierpont Langley (1834–1906).

Bolsheviks, majority faction of Russian Social-Democrat Party at 2nd Congress in London 1903; became Communist Party 1918.

Bolton School, English public school, founded 1524 by William Haighe; rebuilt and endowed by Robert Lever 1641.

Boltzmann, Ludwig (1844–1906), Austrian physicist, known for work on gases and radiation.

Bolyai, Janos (1802–60), Hungarian mathematician, a founder of non-Euclidian geometry.

Bombay, city, acquired by Portuguese 1534; given to England 1661 as part of dowry of Catherine of Braganza; granted to East India Company 1668; university founded 1857; capital of Maharashtra since 1960.

Bombay, state, Portuguese trading stations established in early 16th century; first English settlement 1613; territory of Bombay presidency much enlarged 1818; autonomous province 1936; divided into states of Gujarat and Maharashtra 1960.

Bonaparte, Jérome (1784–1860), brother of Napoleon, king of Westphalia 1807–13.

Bonaparte, Joseph (1768–1844), brother of Napoleon, king of Naples 1806–8, king of Spain 1808–13.

Bonaparte, Louis (1778–1846), brother of Napoleon, king of Holland 1806–10.

Bonaparte, Louis Napoléon. See **Napoleon III.**

Bonaparte, Napoléon. See **Napoleon Bonaparte.**

Bonar Law, Andrew. See **Law,** Andrew Bonar.

Bonaventura, Saint (1221–74), Italian Franciscan friar, theologian and doctor of the Church.

Bond, Sir Edward Augustus (1815–98), English librarian, chief librarian of the British Museum 1878–88.

Bondfield, Margaret (1873–1953), English Labour politician, first woman minister in a British government.

Bone, Henry (1755–1834), English enamel painter, much patronized by royalty.

Bone, Sir Muirhead (1876–1953), Scottish artist, did notable graphic works of scenes in World War I and II.

Bonheur, Rosa (1822–99), French painter, mainly of animal studies.

Bonhoeffer, Dietrich (1906–45), German theologian and prominent member of anti-Nazi resistance movement.

Boniface, Saint (c. 680–754), English

missionary working in Germany; martyred.

Boniface I, Saint (d. 422), Pope 418–422, was an energetic administrator.

Boniface VIII (1235–1303), Pope 1294–1303, asserted papal claims against Philip IV of France.

Boniface IX (d. 1404), Pope 1389–1404, was deeply involved in secular politics and diplomacy.

Bonington, Richard (1802–28), English landscape painter, worked mainly in France.

Bonn, capital of German Federal Republic since 1949.

Bonnard, Pierre (1867–1947), French painter, noted for his interiors and landscapes.

Bonney, William H. (1859–81), American outlaw, known as Billy the Kid, achieved notoriety as a gunman.

Bononcini, Giovanni Battista (1670–1747), Italian opera composer, rival of Handel in London.

book auction, first, the sale of George Dousa's library, held in Leyden 1604.

book jackets, first used in England 1833; came into general use c. 1890.

bookplates, to mark ownership, first introduced in Germany c. 1450.

Booksellers Association, of Great Britain and Ireland, founded as the Associated Booksellers 1895; assumed present name 1948.

Boole, George (1815–64), English mathematician, originated Boolean algebra.

Boone, Daniel (1734–1820), American pioneer and hunter, famous in folklore.

Booth, Charles (1840–1916), English social reformer, author of *Life and Labour of the People in London* (1891–1903).

Booth, Edwin (1833–93), American actor, best known for his Shakespearian roles.

Booth, John Wilkes (1831–65), American actor, brother of Edwin Booth, assassin of Abraham Lincoln.

Booth, William (1829–1912), English evangelist, founder of the Salvation Army.

Booth, William Bramwell (1856–1929), English evangelist, succeeded his father William Booth as general of the Salvation Army.

Bootham School, York, English public school, founded 1823.

Bordeaux, Henri (1870–1963), French novelist, wrote about provincial life.

Bordet, Jules (1870–1961), Belgian bacteriologist, noted for his work in immunology.

Borges, Jorge Luis (b. 1899), Argentinian poet and novelist, author of *Labyrinths* (translated 1962).

Borgia, Cesare (1475–1507), Italian prince, son of Pope Alexander VI, notorious for ruthlessness.

Borgia, Lucrezia (1480–1519), daughter of Pope Alexander VI, duchess of Ferrara, patron of artists including Titian and Ariosto.

Borgia, Rodrigo. See **Alexander VI.**

boric acid, first prepared 1702 by the Dutch chemist Wilhelm Homberg (1652–1715).

boring machine, first practical one invented 1769 by John Smeaton (*q.v.*).

Boris I (d. 907), king of Bulgaria 852–889, established Christianity in his country.

Boris III (1894–1943), king of Bulgaria 1918–43, ally of Germany in World War II.

Boris Godunov. See **Godunov,** Boris.

Borneo, discovered by Portuguese *c.* 1521; Dutch and British trading posts established in early 17th century; Sabah (North Borneo), Sarawak and Brunei (*qq.v.*) declared British protectorates 1888; Borneo occupied by Japanese in World War II; Dutch Borneo became part of Indonesia 1950.

Borodin, Alexander (1833–87), Russian composer of the popular opera *Prince Igor*.

Borodino, Battle of, fought between Napoleon and the Russians 7 Sept. 1812.

boron, isolated 1808 by Sir Humphry Davy (*q.v.*) and independently by Joseph Gay-Lussac (*q.v.*) and Louis-Jacques Thénard.

Borromeo, Saint Charles. See **Charles Borromeo.**

Borromini, Francesco (1599–1667), Italian architect, leading exponent of the Baroque style.

Borrow, George (1803–81), English writer of travel books and about gypsies, author of *Lavengro* (1851).

borstal, system of imprisonment for young criminals, began in England 1902.

Bosanquet, Bernard (1848–1923), English philosopher in the German Idealist tradition.

Bosch, Hieronymus (*c.* 1450–1516), Dutch painter of fantastic, often macabre, scenes.

Bosch, Karl (1874–1940), German chemist, adapted Haber process for commercial production of ammonia.

Boscobel, Shropshire, scene of the hiding-place (in an oak) of Charles II 1651.

Bose, Sir Jagadis Chandra (1858–1937), Indian plant expert, wrote *The Physiology of Photosynthesis*, etc.

Bose, Sabhas Chandra (1895–1945), Indian nationalist politician, led Japanese-supported Indian National Army.

Bosnia, conquered by Turkey 1463; under Austrian rule 1878–1918 as part of province of Bosnia-Hercegovina; part of Yugoslavia since 1918.

Bossuet, Jacques Bénigne (1627–1704), French theologian, bishop of Meaux and a celebrated orator.

Boston, Mass., settled by John Winthrop 1630; Boston Massacre 5 March 1770; Boston Tea Party 16 Dec. 1773.

Boston Symphony Orchestra, founded 1881 by the American philanthropist Henry Lee Higginson (1834–1919).

Boswell, James (1740–95), Scottish diarist and biographer of Dr Johnson.

Bosworth Field, Battle of, fought between Henry VII and Richard III, 22 Aug. 1485.

Botany Bay, New South Wales, discovered 29 April 1770 by Captain James Cook; became British penal settlement 1788; transportation ceased 1840.

Botha, Louis (1862–1919), South African general and statesman, first prime minister of the Union of South Africa 1910–19.

Bothwell, James Hepburn, Earl of (*c.* 1536–1578), Scottish noble, 3rd husband of Mary Queen of Scots.

Bothwell Bridge, Battle of, fought between the English and the Scottish Covenanters 1679.

Botta, Paul Emile (1802–70), French archaeologist, conducted important excavations in Mesopotamia.

Böttger, Johann Friedrich (1682–1719), German manufacturer of porcelain, creator of Dresden china.

Botswana, South Africa, British missionaries arrived early 19th century; conflict between native tribes and Transvaal Boers led to British protectorate 1885; southern part incorporated in Cape Colony 1895; independent republic within the Commonwealth since 1966.

Botticelli, Sandro (1444–1510), Florentine painter, one of the greatest artists of the Italian Renaissance, whose works include *The Birth of Venus* and *Primavera*.

bottles, automatic continuous manufacture introduced commercially 1903 in U.S.A.

Bottomley, Horatio (1860–1933), English politician, financier and founder of magazine *John Bull*; imprisoned for fraud.

Boudicca. See **Boadicea.**

Boucher, François (1703–70), French painter of amorous subjects in rococo style, including *The Toilet of Venus* (1751).

Boucicault, Dion (1822–90), Irish-born dramatist in America, author of many popular plays.

Bougainville, Louis Antoine de (1729–1811), French explorer of Pacific islands.

Boughton, Rutland (1878–1960), English composer, mainly of music for the stage.

Boulanger, Georges (1837–91), French general and politician, whose activities threatened the Third Republic.

Boulanger, Nadia (b. 1887), French musician, composer and influential teacher of music.

Boulder Dam, harnessing the Colorado River, completed 1936.

Boulez, Pierre (b. 1925), French composer

and conductor, best known for his *Le Marteau sans Maître* (1951).

Boulton, Matthew (1728–1809), English manufacturer and inventor, partner of James Watt.

Boumedienne, Houari (b. 1927), Algerian statesman, prime minister of Algeria since 1965.

Bounty, mutiny of the, Indian Ocean 28 April 1789; William Bligh (*q.v.*) and other castaways reached Timor 9 June.

Bourbaki, Charles Denis (1816–97), French general, was an unsuccessful army commander in the Franco-Prussian War 1870–71.

Bourbon dynasty, ruled France 1589–1792 and 1814–1848; Spain 1700–1808, 1814–1868 and 1874–1931; Naples 1759–1799, 1799–1806 and 1815–1860; Parma 1748–1815 and 1847–1860.

Bourbon, Charles, Duc de (1490–1527), constable of France, served both Francis I and the emperor Maximilian.

Bourges cathedral, France, built between *c.* 1200 and *c.* 1250; consecrated 1324.

Bourguiba, Habib (b. 1903), Tunisian statesman, president of Tunisia since 1957.

Bourne, Francis (1861–1935), English cardinal, archbishop of Westminster 1903–35.

Bourse, The, Paris, French Stock Exchange, founded 1724.

Bouts, Dirk (*c.* 1410–1475), Dutch painter, rather austere in manner, noted for his portraits, religious pictures and landscapes.

Bouvet Island, South Atlantic, discovered 1739 by the French navigator Pierre Bouvet; annexed by Norway 1927–30.

Bow porcelain, manufactured 1745–76.

Bowdler, Thomas (1754–1825), English editor of an expurgated *Family Shakespeare* (1818).

Bowdoin College, Maine, founded 1794.

Bowen, Elizabeth (1899–1972), Irish novelist, author of *The Death of the Heart* (1938).

Bowen, York (1884–1961), English composer, wrote *The Lament of Tasso* (1903).

Bow Street Runners, London, organized *c.* 1750; superseded by the police 1829.

Boxer Rebellion, China, 1900, against foreigners, led to siege of European legations in Peking.

boxing, legalized in England 1901.

Boyce, William (1710–79), English composer and organist, worked at Chapel Royal.

Boycott, Captain Charles (1832–97), English land agent in Ireland, object of a 'boycott' by tenants.

Boyd Orr, John, 1st Baron (1880–1971), Scottish nutritionist, awarded Nobel Peace Prize 1949.

Boyle, Richard (1566–1643), the 'Great Earl of Cork', dominant figure in Ireland, lord high treasurer 1631.

Boyle, Robert (1627–91), Irish-born English scientist, son of Richard Boyle, formulated Boyle's Law 1662: that the volume of a gas varies inversely with its pressure.

Boyne, Battle of the, Ireland, victory of William III over James II, 1 July 1690.

Boys' Brigade, The, founded 1883 by Sir William Alexander Smith (1854–1914).

Boys' Brigade of America, United, founded 1887.

Boy Scout movement, organization founded in Britain 1908; in the U.S.A. and several other countries 1910.

Brabançonne, La, Belgian national anthem, composed 1830 by François van Campenhout (1779–1848).

Bracegirdle, Mrs Anne (*c.* 1663–1748), English actress, distinguished notably in comedy.

Bracton, Henri de (d. 1268), English jurist, wrote first systematic treatise on English laws.

Bradfield College (St Andrew's College, Bradfield), English public school, founded 1850 by the Rev. Thomas Stevens.

Bradford Grammar School, English public school, founded 1548.

Bradford University, founded 1966.

Bradlaugh, Charles (1833–91), English reformer, established political rights of atheists and agnostics.

Bradley, Andrew Cecil (1851–1935), English critic, notably of Shakespearian tragedy.

Bradley, Francis Herbert (1846–1924), English philosopher, brother of Andrew Bradley, wrote *Appearance and Reality* (1893).

Bradley, Henry (1845–1923), English lexicographer, senior editor of the *Oxford English Dictionary* 1915–23.

Bradley, James (1693–1762), English astronomer, discovered aberration of light.

Bradman, Sir Donald (b. 1908), Australian cricketer, achieved many batting records.

Bradshaw, John (1602–59), English judge and regicide, presided at trial of Charles I.

Bradshaw's Railway Guide, first published 1839 by George Bradshaw (1801–53); discontinued 1961.

Brady, Matthew (*c.* 1823–1896), American pioneer photographer, took many Civil War pictures.

Bragg, Sir William Henry (1862–1942), English physicist, specialist in X-ray studies of crystal structure.

Bragg, Sir William Lawrence (1890–1971). English physicist, worked with his father, Sir William Bragg, in the study of crystals.

Brahe, Tycho (1546–1601), Danish astronomer, noted for his many accurate observations.

Brahms, Johannes (1833–97), German composer of symphonies, concertos, sonatas, etc., acknowledged master of symphonic style.

Braid, James (c. 1795–1860), Scottish physician, pioneer in study of hypnotism.

Braille alphabet, invented 1834 by the blind Frenchman Louis Braille (1809–52).

Brain, Dennis (1921–57), English musician, noted as a virtuoso French horn player.

Braine, John (b. 1922), English novelist, wrote the best-selling *Room at the Top* (1957).

brakes. See **air brake; hydraulic brake.**

Bramah, Joseph (1748–1814), English engineer, invented safety lock and lavatory flushing system.

Bramalea, near Toronto, Canada's first satellite city, founded 1959.

Bramante, Donato (1444–1514), Italian Renaissance architect, planned rebuilding of St Peter's, Rome.

Brancuşi, Constantine (1876–1957), Romanian-born sculptor in France, created elegant, semi-abstract works.

Brandeis, Louis Dembitz (1856–1941), American legal counsel in progressive causes, associate justice, U.S. Supreme Court 1916–39.

Brandenburg, Slav inhabitants conquered by Germans 12th century; Frederick of Hohenzollen became margrave 1415; acquired Prussia 1618; elector of Brandenburg became king of Prussia 1701; province of German Empire 1871; divided between Poland and East Germany after World War II.

Brandt, Willy (b. 1913), German statesman, chancellor of West Germany 1969–74.

Brandywine, Battle of, Delaware, victory of the British over the Americans 11 Sept. 1777.

Brangwyn, Sir Frank (1867–1956), English artist, gifted as a painter, muralist and etcher.

Brant, Sebastian (1458–1521), German writer, author of the savage satire *Narrenschiff* (1494).

Braque, Georges (1882–1963), French painter, associated with Picasso in creation of Cubism.

Brasília, capital of Brazil, founded 1956; inaugurated 1961.

Brassey's Naval Annual, founded 1886 by Lord Brassey (1836–1918).

Bratby, John (b. 1928), English painter of the 'kitchen sink' school.

Braun, Wernher von (1912–77), German-born rocket designer in U.S.A., worked on missiles and space flight projects.

Bray, Thomas (1656–1730), English clergyman, founded Society for the Propagation of Christian Knowledge 1698.

Brazil, discovered 1500 by Vicente Pinzón and Pedro Cabral; Portuguese coastal settlements 1532; attempts by Dutch at colonization 1630–54; Portuguese rule re-established 1640; independent empire 1822–89; republic since 1889.

Breakspear, Nicholas. See **Adrian IV.**

Breasted, James Henry (1865–1935), American archaeologist, wrote studies on ancient Egypt.

Brecht, Bertolt (1898–1956), German playwright and theatrical producer, was a major innovator with such works as *The Threepenny Opera* (1928).

Breda, Peace of, between England and the Netherlands, 1667.

breech-loading rifle, first adopted in Europe by Prussian army 1848.

'Breeches' Bible, published by the Calvinists at Geneva 1560.

Bremen, joined Hanseatic League 1358; free city 1646; joined North German Confederation 1867.

Brendan, Saint (484–577), Irish abbot, subject of many legends.

Brenner Pass, Swiss Alps, road built 1772; railway 1864–67.

Brentwood School, Essex, English public school, founded by Sir Antony Browne 1557.

Breslau. See **Wroclaw.**

Brest, Blockade of, by the English 1794.

Brest-Litovsk, Treaty of, World War I, confirming Russian armistice with the Central Powers, signed 3 March 1918.

Breton, André (1896–1966), French poet, essayist and critic, a founder of the Surrealist movement.

Breton, Nicholas (c. 1555–c. 1625), English poet, prolific satirist and pastoralist.

Bretton Woods Conference, on international monetary policy, held July 1944.

Breughel, Pieter. See **Bruegel,** Pieter.

Breuil, Henri (1877–1961), French priest and archaeologist, leading authority on prehistoric cave paintings.

Brewster, Sir David (1781–1868), Scottish scientist, made important discoveries about polarized light.

Brezhnev, Leonid (b. 1906), Soviet statesman, secretary-general of the Soviet Communist Party since 1966.

Brian, Havergall (1876–1972), English composer, best known for his symphonies.

Brian Boru (926–1014), king of Ireland from 1002, slain during victory over Danes at Clontarf.

Briand, Aristide (1862–1932), French statesman, several times prime minister, worked for international peace in the 1920s.

Bride, Saint (d. c. 523), Irish abbess of Kildare, second patron saint of Ireland.

bridge, first iron, built 1779 by Wilkinson and Darby at Ironbridge, Shropshire.

bridge, card game, first recorded mention in England 1886.

Bridge of Sighs, Venice, built *c.* 1600.

Bridges, Robert (1844–1930), English poet laureate, remembered for *The Testament of Beauty* (1929).

Bridget (*c.* 1303–1373), Swedish visionary, founded Brigittine order of nuns.

Bridgewater Canal, Worsley to Manchester, completed 1761; extended to Liverpool 1776; engineer James Brindley (*q.v.*) in the service of the Duke of Bridgewater (1736–1803).

Bridie, James (1888–1951), Scottish dramatist, wrote *The Anatomist* (1930) and many other plays.

Brieux, Eugène (1858–1932), French dramatist, whose work was mainly concerned with social problems.

Briggs, Henry (1561–1630), English mathematician, pioneered study of logarithms.

Bright, John (1811–89), English radical politician, worked for repeal of Corn Laws (*q.v.*).

Brighton College, English public school, founded by prominent Brighton residents 1845.

Bright's Disease, first described 1827 by Dr Richard Bright (1789–1858).

Brillat-Savarin, Anthelme (1755–1826), French politician and lawyer, best remembered for gastronomical writings.

Brindley, James (1716–72), English engineer, constructed Manchester Ship Canal.

Brisbane, founded 1824; named after General Sir Thomas Brisbane, governor of New South Wales 1821–25; made capital of Queensland 1859.

Bristol, early settlement *c.* 10th century; received 1st charter 1171; made a county 1373; foremost port outside London and important commercial centre 15th to 18th centuries; university college founded 1876, granted royal charter as university 1909.

Bristol Grammar School, English public school, founded earlier, but chartered 1532.

Bristol porcelain, manufactured 1750–80.

British Academy, London, granted charter 1902.

British and Foreign Bible Society, London, founded 1804.

British Antarctic Territory, part of Falkland Islands (*q.v.*) 1908; became separate colony 1962.

British Association for the Advancement of Science, founded 1831.

British Broadcasting Corporation (preceded by British Broadcasting Company, formed 1922), constituted under royal charter 1 Jan. 1927.

British Columbia, Canada, constituted British colony Aug. 1858; a province of the Dominion of Canada 1871.

British Council, London, established 1934; chartered 1940.

British Drama League, London, founded by Geoffrey Whitworth 1919.

British Empire, Order of the, founded by George V 1917.

British Film Institute, London, founded 1933.

British Guiana. See **Guyana.**

British Honduras. See **Belize.**

British Indian Ocean Territory, created Nov. 1965.

British Interplanetary Society, founded at Liverpool 1933.

British Legion, founded in London by Earl Haig 1921.

British Museum, London, founded 1753; opened 16 Jan. 1759.

British Museum (Natural History), collection moved to South Kensington 1881; extension opened 1914; separated from British Museum 1963.

British North America Act, by which the Dominion of Canada was created, proclaimed 1 July 1867.

British Pharmacopoeia, first published 1864.

British Rail, amalgamating existing regional railway companies under national ownership, inaugurated 1 Jan. 1948.

British Red Cross Society, founded 1870; received royal charter 1908.

British Somaliland, British protectorate established 1884; occupied by Italian forces 1940–41; united with former Italian Somaliland to become independent republic of Somalia 1960.

British Standards Institution, founded 1901 as the Engineering Standards Committee; incorporated by royal charter 1929.

Brittany, conquered by Romans 56 B.C.; invaded by British Celts in 5th and 6th centuries; became an independent duchy 10th century; incorporated in France 1532.

Britten, Benjamin, Baron (1913–76), English composer, best known for his operas including *Peter Grimes* (1945).

Britton, John (1771–1857), English writer on topography, author of *The Beauties of England and Wales* (1801–14).

broadcasting, first regular programmes, by KDKA, Pittsburgh, began 2 Nov. 1920; first British daily broadcasting by British Broadcasting Company, 14 Nov. 1922.

broadcasts, from Britain to the Continent, first began on a weekly basis, 16 Oct. 1925.

Broadmoor, Berkshire, institution for the criminally insane, opened 1863.

Brockhaus, Friedrich Arnold (1772–1823), German publisher and editor of the encyclopedia *Konversations-Lexikon* (1810–11), later called *Der Grosse Brockhaus.*

Brod, Max (1884–1968), Austrian writer born in Prague, literary executor of Kafka.

Broglie, Louis de (1892–1976), French physicist, was awarded 1929 Nobel Prize for Physics for his work on the quantum theory.

bromine, discovered 1826 by the French chemist, Antoine Jérôme Balard (1802–76).

Bromsgrove School, Worcestershire, English public school, founded 1553.

Brontë, Anne (1820–49), English novelist, sister of Charlotte and Emily Brontë, wrote *Agnes Grey* (1848).

Brontë, Charlotte (1816–55), English novelist, author of *Jane Eyre* (1847).

Brontë, Emily (1818–48), English novelist, became famous with her one work, *Wuthering Heights* (1847).

Bronze Age, 4th to 2nd millennium B.C.

Bronzino, Agnolo (1503–72), Florentine painter, noted for his portraits of the Medici family.

Brook, Peter (b. 1925), English theatrical producer, directed many plays for the Royal Shakespeare Company.

Brooke, Henry (c. 1703–1783), Irish writer of dramas, poems and novels.

Brooke, Sir James (1803–68), British soldier, became rajah of Sarawak 1841.

Brooke, Rupert (1887–1915), English poet, author of *1914 and other Poems* (1915).

Brooklands, first purpose-built motor-racing track, opened 6 July 1907.

Brooklyn Bridge, New York, designed by John Augustus Roebling (*q.v.*) and constructed 1869–83 by his son Washington Roebling (1837–1926).

Brooks's Club, London, established 1778.

Brougham, Henry, Lord Brougham and Vaux (1778–1868), Scottish lawyer and politician, lord chancellor 1830–34.

Brouwer, Adriaen (c. 1605–1638), Flemish painter of peasant and low-life scenes.

Brown, Sir Arthur Whitten (1886–1948), British aviator, took part in first non-stop transatlantic aircraft flight.

Brown, Ford Maddox (1821–93), French-born English painter, mainly of historical subjects.

Brown, George Douglas. See **Douglas**, George.

Brown, John (1735–88), Scottish physician and medical pioneer, wrote *Elementa Medicinae* (1780).

Brown, John (1800–59), American anti-slavery crusader, hanged after attempt to seize Harpers Ferry, Virginia.

Brown, Lancelot (1715–83), known as 'Capability Brown', English landscape gardener and architect.

Brown, Tom (1663–1704), English humorous versifier, wrote 'I do not love thee, Dr Fell'.

Browne, Hablot Knight. See **'Phiz'.**

Browne, Robert (c. 1550–1633), English Nonconformist leader, founder of Brownist sect which later developed into the Congregationalists.

Browne, Sir Thomas (1605–82), English writer and physician, author of the ornate *Religio Medici* (1642).

Brownian motion, discovered 1828 by the Scottish botanist Robert Brown (1773–1858).

Browning, Elizabeth Barrett (1806–61), English poet, wife of Robert Browning, wrote *Sonnets from the Portuguese* (1850).

Browning, Robert (1812–89), English poet, noted for his historical imagination and use of the dramatic monologue, as in *Andrea del Sarto* (1855).

Bruce, Robert (1274–1329), king of Scotland 1306–29, victor at Bannockburn 1314.

Bruce, Sir David (1855–1931), Australian-born British physician, expert on tropical diseases.

Bruce, James (1730–94), Scottish explorer in Africa, reached source of Blue Nile.

Bruce, William Speirs (1867–1921), Scottish explorer, made several polar expeditions.

Bruch, Max (1838–1920), German composer, best known for his violin concerto.

Bruckner, Anton (1824–96), Austrian composer of symphonies and religious music.

Bruegel, Pieter, the Elder (c. 1525–1569), Flemish painter, famous for his crowd scenes of extraordinary vitality.

Bruegel, Pieter, the Younger (1564–1638), Flemish painter, son of the above, worked in a similar style.

Brulé, Étienne (c. 1592–1633), French explorer in America, supposedly first white man to visit the Great Lakes.

Brumaire, 2nd month (mid-Oct. to mid-Nov.) in the French Revolutionary calendar, established 1793; Coup d'Etat of, 9 Nov. 1799.

Brummell, 'Beau' (George) (1778–1840), English dandy, friend of the Prince Regent and arbiter of male fashion.

Brunei, North Borneo, sultanate under British protection since 1888.

Brunel, Isambard Kingdom (1806–59), English engineer, son of Sir Marc Brunel, built the Great Western Railway.

Brunel, Sir Marc Isambard (1769–1849), French-born English engineer, built world's first underwater tunnel across the Thames.

Brunel University, Uxbridge, founded 1966.

Brunelleschi, Filippo (1377–1446), Italian Renaissance architect, built dome of Florence Cathedral.

Brunet, Jacques Charles (1780–1867), French bibliographer, author of *Manuel du Libraire* (1860).

Brüning, Heinrich (1885–1970), German statesman, chancellor during economic crisis 1930–32.

Brunner, Heinrich (1840–1915), German legal historian, began systematic study of early Germanic law.

Bruno, Saint (*c.* 1030–1101), German monk, founded the Carthusian Order 1084.

Bruno, Giordano (1548–1600), Italian philosopher, burnt at the stake for his unorthodox beliefs.

Brussels, 1st settlement 6th century A.D.; town granted charter 1312; capital of Spanish Netherlands 1530; capital of Belgium since 1830; occupied by Germans in World Wars I and II; site of World's Fair 1958; headquarters of NATO and EEC since 1967.

Brussels Treaty, concerning Western Union, signed 17 March 1948.

Brutus, Marcus (85–42 B.C.), Roman politician, chief assassin of Julius Caesar, committed suicide after defeat at Philippi.

Bryan, William Jennings (1860–1925), American political leader, Democratic presidential candidate and a notable orator.

Bryanston School, Dorset, English public school, founded 1928.

Bryce, James, Viscount (1838–1922), British diplomat and scholar, author of *The Holy Roman Empire* (1864).

Bryn Mawr College, Philadelphia, American women's college, founded 1880.

bubble chamber, in nuclear physics, developed 1952 by the American physicist Donald Arthur Glaser (b. 1926).

Buber, Martin (1878–1965), Austrian philosopher, exponent of Jewish mysticism.

bubonic plague, bacillus discovered 1894 by the French scientist Alexandre Yersin (1863–1943). See also **Black Death; Great Plague.**

buccaneers, French, English and Dutch pirates active in Caribbean between *c.* 1625 and 1700.

Bucer, Martin (1491–1551), German Protestant religious reformer, active in Switzerland, Germany, and England (where he died).

Buchan, John, 1st Baron Tweedsmuir (1875–1940), Scottish popular novelist, author of *Greenmantle* (1916), governor-general of Canada 1935–40.

Buchan's Days, weather predictions made 1869 by Alexander Buchan (1829–1907).

Buchanan, George (1506–82), Scottish humanist, wrote satires and controversial political works in Latin.

Buchanan, James (1791–1868), American statesman, 15th president of the United States 1857–61, during a period of increasing North-South tension.

Buchanites, Scottish religious sect, founded 1783 by Elspeth Buchan (1738–91).

Buchman, Frank (1878–1961), American evangelist, founder (1921) of Moral Rearmament.

Buchner, Eduard (1860–1917), German chemist, awarded Nobel prize 1907 for work on enzymes.

Büchner, Georg (1813–37), German dramatist, author of *Dantons Tod* (1835).

Buck, Pearl (1892–1973), American novelist, author of *The Good Earth* (1931).

Buckingham, George Villiers, 1st Duke of (1592–1628), English statesman, favourite of James I; assassinated.

Buckingham, George Villiers, 2nd Duke of (1628–87), English statesman, member of Cabal government under Charles II.

Buckingham Palace, built by the Duke of Buckingham 1703; rebuilt 1825–37; official London residence of sovereign since Queen Victoria's reign.

Buckle, Henry Thomas (1821–62), English historian, wrote *History of Civilization in England* (1857–61).

Buddha, The (*c.* 560–*c.* 480 B.C.), Indian prince (proper name Gautama Siddharta), founded Buddhism.

Budé, Guillaume (1467–1540), French humanist scholar, influenced the revival of Greek studies in France.

Budge, Sir Ernest Alfred (1857–1934), English archaeologist, excavated in Near East and Egypt.

Buenos Aires, founded 1536; seat of La Plata viceroyalty 1776; capital of Argentina 1880.

Buenos Aires Standard, first English-language South American daily newspaper, founded 1861.

Buffalo Bill. See **Cody,** William Frederick.

Buffet, Bernard (b. 1928), French painter, exponent of Cubism.

Buffon, Georges, Comte de (1707–88), French naturalist, wrote multi-volume *Histoire Naturelle*, first comprehensive work on natural history.

Bukharin, Nikolai (1888–1938), Russian Communist leader, outstanding Marxist theorist, executed during the Great Purge.

Bulawayo, Southern Rhodesian mining city, founded 1893.

Bulgakov, Mikhail (1891–1940), Russian novelist, author of *The White Guard* (1924).

Bulganin, Nikolai (1895–1975), Soviet statesman, prime minister 1955–58.

Bulgaria, established 7th century; conquered by Byzantines 10th century; revived 12th century; conquered by Turks 14th century; constituted principality under Turkish suzerainty 1878; independent kingdom 1908; became a People's Republic 1946.

Bulge, Battle of the, last major German offensive of World War II, Ardennes region, Dec. 1944–Jan. 1945.

bull-baiting, prohibited in England by act of Parliament 1835.

Bull Run, Battles of, American Civil War, 1st, 21 July 1861; 2nd 30 Aug. 1862.

Buller, Sir Redvers (1839–1908), British soldier, proved an unsuccessful commander-in-chief in the Boer War.

Bullinger, Heinrich (1504–75), Swiss religious reformer, succeeded Zwingli, reconciled with Calvinists 1549.

Bülow, Prince Bernhard von (1849–1929), German diplomat and politician, chancellor 1900–09.

Bülow, Hans Guido von (1830–94), German pianist and conductor, advocate of music of Wagner and Liszt.

Bunche, Ralph Johnson (1904–71), American Negro diplomat, held important U.N. administrative posts.

Bunin, Ivan (1870–1954), Russian poet and novelist, was the first Russian to receive the Nobel Prize for Literature, 1933.

Bunker Hill, Battle of, American Revolution, victory of the British over the Americans 17 June 1775.

Bunsen burner, invented 1855 for laboratory use by the German chemist Robert Bunsen (1811–99).

Buñuel, Luis (b. 1900), Spanish film director, whose works include *Un Chien Andalou* (1929) and *Viridiana* (1961).

Bunyan, John (1628–88), English Nonconformist writer, author of *Pilgrim's Progress* (1678–84).

Buonarroti, Philippe (Filippo) (1761–1837), Italian-born revolutionary, active in France.

Buononcini, Giovanni Battista. See **Bononcini.**

Burbage, Richard (c. 1567–1619), outstanding English actor of Shakespeare's day, first to play Hamlet, Lear, etc.

Burbank, Luther (1849–1926), American horticulturist, improved strains of many plants.

Burchell, William John (c. 1782–1863), English naturalist, travelled widely in Africa and South America.

Burckhardt, Jacob (1818–97), Swiss historian, wrote classic *Civilization of the Renaissance in Italy* (1860).

Burdett, Sir Francis (1770–1844), English radical M.P., supported many reforms.

Burghley, Lord. See **Cecil,** William.

Burgkmair, Hans (1473–1531), German artist, noted for his engravings.

Burgoyne, John (1722–92), British general (known as 'Gentleman Johnny') in the American Revolution, surrendered at Saratoga 1777.

Burgundy, settled by Germanic peoples in early 5th century A.D.; annexed by Franks 534; part of Lotharingia 843; became a duchy in the 9th century; annexed to crown of France 1482.

Burke, Edmund (1729–97), Irish-born British politician, great orator, wrote *Reflections on the French Revolution* (1790).

Burke, Robert O'Hara (1820–61), Irish-born Australian explorer, crossed continent with Wills.

Burke, William (1792–1829), Irish murderer, partner of William Hare, sold victims' bodies for dissection; executed.

Burke's Peerage, founded 1826 by Sir John Burke (1814–92).

Burlington Arcade, Piccadilly, London, opened 20 March 1819.

Burlington House, Piccadilly, built c. 1665; rebuilt 1731.

Burma, partially annexed by Britain 1853; whole country became province of Indian Empire 1886; separated from India 1937; occupied by Japanese in World War II; became independent 4 Jan. 1948.

Burne-Jones, Sir Edward (1833–98), English painter of medieval-mythological subjects, blending eroticism and dreamy spirituality.

Burnet, Sir Frank Macfarlane (b. 1899), Australian virologist, noted for his work in immunology.

Burnet, Gilbert (1643–1715), Scottish divine, bishop of Salisbury from 1689, theologian and historian.

Burnett, Frances Hodgson (1849–86), English-born American writer for children, author of *Little Lord Fauntleroy* (1886).

Burney, Charles (1726–1814), English music historian, father of Fanny Burney.

Burney, Fanny (1752–1840), English novelist, wrote *Evelina* (1778).

burning to death, punishment in England for women convicted of certain crimes, last inflicted 1789; legally abolished 1790.

Burns, John (1858–1943), English Labour leader and politician, served in governments 1905–14.

Burns, Robert (1759–96), regarded as Scotland's national poet, author of lyrics on love and nature, and of satirical verses.

Burr, Aaron (1756–1836), American politician, fought in the Revolutionary War, vice-president 1801–05.

Burt, Sir Cyril (1883–1971), English psychologist, noted for his study of juvenile delinquency.

Burton, Decimus (1800–81), English architect, worked best in Neoclassical style.

Burton, Sir Richard (1821–90), English explorer, visited Mecca and was translator of the *Arabian Nights.*

Burton, Robert (1577–1640), English writer, compiler of the *Anatomy of Melancholy* (1621).

Burundi, Africa, formerly part of Ruanda-Urundi (q.v.); became an independent kingdom 1962; declared a republic 1966.

bus, first London, ran from Marylebone Road to the Bank, 4 July 1829.

Busch, Wilhelm (1832–1908), German poet and humorous illustrator, especially of his own work.

Busoni, Ferruccio (1866–1924), Italian composer, who was also a notable piano virtuoso.

Buss, Frances Mary (1827–94), English educationalist, pioneered secondary education for girls.

Butcher, Samuel Henry (1850–1910), Irish-born British scholar, specialized in ancient Greek literature.

Bute, John Stuart, Earl of (1713–92), Scottish politician, favourite of George III, chief minister 1762–63.

Butler, Joseph (1692–1752), bishop of Durham, whose *Analogy of Religion* was an eloquent defence of Christianity.

Butler, Josephine (1828–1906), English social reformer, a crusader against prostitution.

Butler, Samuel (1612–80), English poet, wrote anti-Puritan satire *Hudibras* (1663–78).

Butler, Samuel (1835–1902), English writer, author of *Erewhon* (1872) and *The Way of All Flesh* (1903).

Butlin, Sir William (1899–1977), South African-born holiday camp pioneer in Britain.

Butt, Dame Clara (1873–1936), English contralto, combined power and delicacy.

Butt, Isaac (1813–79), Irish politician, first leader of Home Rule parliamentary group.

Buxtehude, Dietrich (1637–1707), Danish-born composer in Germany, best known for his church music.

Byng, John (1704–57), British admiral, shot by firing-squad for his failure to relieve the island of Minorca.

Byrd, Richard Evelyn (1888–1957), American aviator and antarctic explorer, made many polar flights.

Byrd, William (c. 1543–1623), English composer of sacred music, madrigals, etc., was organist at the Chapel Royal.

Byrom, John (1692–1763), English poet and diarist, invented an early shorthand system.

Byron, George Gordon, 6th Baron (1788–1824), English poet and satirist, author of *Childe Harold's Pilgrimage* and *Don Juan*, became a symbol for romanticism and political liberalism.

Byzantine Empire, began with building of Constantinople A.D. 330; Rome permanently divided into Eastern and Western Roman Empire 395; Byzantine Empire continued after collapse of Western Roman Empire 476; reached greatest extent under Justinian 527–565; attacked by Arabs, Persians and Bulgars 7th–10th

centuries; finally conquered by Ottoman Turks 1453.

Byzantium, founded c. 658 B.C.; rebuilt as Constantinople (*q.v.*) A.D. 330.

C

Cabal, the secret cabinet of ministers which ruled England under Charles II 1667–73 (from the names of the members: Clifford, Ashley, Buckingham, Arlington and Lauderdale).

Cabell, James Branch (1879–1958), American writer of humorous fantasy, e.g. *Jurgen* (1919).

Cabeza de Vaca, Alvar (1490–c. 1577), Spanish colonist and explorer, led expeditions in Mexico and Brazil.

cabinet, form of British government introduced by Charles II; formally instituted by William III 1693; modern system and name instituted by Sir Robert Walpole (*q.v.*) c. 1720.

Cabinet Noir, French postal censorship, instituted in reign of Louis XI; formally constituted in reign of Louis XV; abolished 1868.

cable, first Atlantic, completed 5 Aug. 1858; first successful cable laid, completed 27 July 1866.

Cabochiens, Parisian rioters led by Simon Caboche, active 1413–14.

Cabot, John (1450–98), Italian navigator, sailed under English patronage, explored Canadian coast.

Cabot, Sebastian (c. 1476–1557), English explorer, son of John Cabot, explored River Plate, founded Merchant Adventurers.

Cabral, Pedro (c. 1467–c. 1520), Portuguese navigator, reached Brazil 1500 and claimed it for Portugal.

Cabrillo, Juan Rodríguez (d. 1543), Portuguese explorer of Mexico and California, in Spanish services.

Cadamosto, Alvise de (c. 1432–c. 1511), Venetian navigator, explored west coast of Africa.

Cadbury, George (1839–1922), English cocoa manufacturer, was a notable social reformer.

Cade, Jack (d. 1450), English rebel, led Kentishmen and briefly controlled London.

Cadets, Russian political party, formed 1905 by Paul Milyukov (1859–1943).

Cadillac, Sieur Antoine de la Mothe (1658–1730), French soldier and official in America, governor of Louisiana 1713–16.

Cadiz, naval raid on, by Sir Francis Drake 1587.

cadmium, first isolated 1817 by the German scientist Friedrich Strohmeyer.

Cadogan, William, Earl (1675–1726), Irish soldier and diplomat, served under Marlborough.

Cadwaladr (d. 1172), Welsh prince, involved in struggles to control North Welsh kingdom.

Caedmon (d. c. 680), Anglo-Saxon poet, wrote on Old Testament subjects.

Caen, Normandy, captured by the English 1346 and 1417; finally retaken by the French 1450.

Caesar, Gaius Julius (100–44 B.C.), Roman general, dictator, statesman and conqueror of Gaul, whose career changed the course of Roman history.

Caesarian section, successfully performed on a living woman as early as 1500.

Caesarion. See Ptolemy XIV.

caesium, first isolated 1860 by the German scientists Robert Bunsen (1811–99), and Gustav Kirchhoff (q.v.).

Café Royal, London, founded 1865; bombed 1940.

Cagliostro, Count (1743–95), title assumed by Giuseppe Balsamo, an Italian adventurer who claimed magical powers.

Cahiers, statements of local grievances submitted to the French States-General 1789.

Caicos Islands, West Indies, discovered c. 1512.

Caillié, René Auguste (1799–1838), French explorer, first white man to travel safely to Timbuktu.

Caine, Sir Hall (1853–1931), English novelist, wrote *The Deemster* (1887).

Ça Ira, French revolutionary song, reputedly written by Ladré 1789.

Caius College, Gonville and, Cambridge University, founded 1348 as Gonville Hall by Edmund Gonville (d. 1351); refounded under present name 1557 by the royal physician John Caius (1510–73).

Cajetan, Cardinal (1469–1534), Italian theologian, attempted to persuade Luther to recant.

Calais, taken by English after siege 1347; only English possession in France after 1450; finally recovered by French 1558.

Calamity Jane (properly Martha Jane Burke; c. 1852–1903), American frontierswoman, reputedly a crack shot.

Calamy, Edmund (1671–1732), English Presbyterian minister, historian of Nonconformity.

Calas, Jean (1698–1762), French Calvinist, victim of judicial murder; Voltaire largely responsible for his rehabilitation.

calcium, first isolated 1808 by Sir Humphry Davy (q.v.).

calculating machine, first model completed 1694 by Gottfried Leibniz (q.v.).

calculus, invented independently c. 1675 by Sir Isaac Newton and Gottfried Leibniz.

Calcutta, capital of West Bengal, founded c. 1690 by Job Charnock; Fort William built 1696; sacked by Nawab of Bengal 1757; capital of British India 1773–1912.

Calder Hall, Cumberland, world's first large-scale atomic energy station, opened Oct. 1956.

Calderón de la Barca, Pedro (1600–81), Spanish dramatist, whose many works include *La Vida es Sueño*.

Caledonian Canal, Scotland, constructed 1803–22 by Thomas Telford (q.v.).

calendar, French Revolutionary, instituted 1793; abolished 1806.

calendar, Gregorian, reformed version of Julian Calendar, introduced by Pope Gregory XIII 1582; not adopted in Britain until 1752.

calendar, Hebrew, calculated from 3761 B.C.; system adopted A.D. 358.

calendar, Julian, reformed version of Roman Calendar, introduced by Julius Caesar 46 B.C.

calendar, Muslim, calculated from the Hegira, A.D. 622.

calendar, Roman, calculated from the supposed date of the foundation of Rome 754 B.C.

Calhoun, John C. (1782–1850), American politician, vice-president 1825–32, defended states' rights.

California, reached by Spaniards 1542; visited by Drake 1579; Jesuit missionaries in lower California 1697; settled by Spain 1769; under Mexican control 1822; gold discovered 1847; ceded by Mexico to U.S.A. 1848; admitted to the Union 1850; University of California founded 1868.

californium, radioactive element discovered 1950 by S. G. Thompson, K. Street, A. Ghiorso, and G. T. Seaborg.

Caligula (A.D. 12–41), Roman emperor 37–41, insane and tyrannical; assassinated.

Caliphate. See Abbasid dynasty; Omayyad dynasty.

Caliphate, Egyptian, ended by Ottoman conquest 1517.

Caliphate, Ottoman, abolished 1924.

Callaghan, James (b. 1912), British statesman, prime minister since 1976.

Callaghan, Morley Edward (b. 1903), Canadian novelist, author of *That Summer in Paris* (1963).

Callas, Maria Meneghini (b. 1923), American-Greek operatic soprano, noted for her roles in Italian opera.

Callimachus (3rd cent. B.C.), Greek poet and scholar, worked in Alexandria.

Callisthenes (c. 360–328 B.C.), Greek historian, accompanied Alexander the Great's expedition.

Callistus II (d. 1124), Pope 1119–24, reconciled German emperor.

Callistus III (1378–1458), Pope 1455–58,

advanced interests of his family, the Borgias.

Callot, Jacques (1592–1635), French engraver, often of grotesque and macabre subjects.

calorimeters, first used 1865 by Marcelin Berthelot (*q.v.*).

calotype, first negative-positive photographic process, patented by W. Fox Talbot (*q.v.*) 1841.

Calpurnia (1st cent. B.C.), wife of Julius Caesar 59–44 B.C.

Calvert, George, 1st Baron Baltimore (*c.* 1580–1632), English colonist, created territory which became Maryland.

Calvin, John (1509–64), French Protestant theologian, leader of the Reformation at Geneva, author of *Institutes* (1536).

Camargo, Marie (1710–70), French ballerina, first to wear skirt showing feet and ankles.

Cambodia, Khmer kingdom founded *c.* A.D. 430; French protectorate 1863; associated state of French Union 1949; granted complete independence 1955 as a constitutional monarchy (later abolished); under Communist control 1975; renamed Khmer Republic.

Cambrai, Treaty of (The Ladies' Peace), renewing Treaty of Madrid, signed 1529.

Cambrian period, Earth history, from *c.* 500 to *c.* 570 million years ago.

Cambridge University, founded in 13th century; first charter granted 1231.

Cambridge University Observatory, opened 1820.

Cambridge University Press, first printer, Thomas Thomas (1553–88) appointed 1582.

Cambridgeshire Stakes, Newmarket, first run 1839.

Cambyses (d. 522 B.C.), king of the Medes and Persians 529–522 B.C.; committed suicide.

Camden, Battles of, South Carolina, American Revolutionary War, victories of the British over the Americans, 16 Aug. 1780, and 25 April 1781.

Camden, Charles Pratt, 1st Earl (1714–94), English judge, lord chancellor 1766–70, defended English and American liberties.

Camden, William (1551–1623), English antiquary, wrote Latin history *Britannia* (1586).

camera, first roll film, marketed 1889 by the American inventor George Eastman (*q.v.*).

camera lucida, invented 1807 by the English scientist William Hyde Wollaston (1766–1828).

Cameron, Sir David Young (1865–1945), Scottish artist, best known for his etchings.

Cameroon, West Africa, German protectorate 1884; occupied by Anglo-French

forces in World War I; put under British and French mandates 1922; U.N. trust territories 1946; French trust territory declared independent republic 1960; southern part of British trust territory joined Cameroon and northern part Nigeria 1961.

Camisards, French Protestant rebels in the Cevennes area, active from 1702 to 1705.

Cammaerts, Émile (1878–1953), Belgian writer, settled in England, notable for World War I poems.

Camões, Luis de (*c.* 1524–1580), Portuguese poet, wrote *The Lusiads*, epic of Portuguese history.

Camorra, Neapolitan secret society, in existence in early 19th century; finally suppressed 1911.

Campagnola, Domenico (*c.* 1484–*c.* 1562), Italian painter, worked mainly in Padua.

Campanella, Tommaso (1568–1639), Italian writer, created an early utopia in *City of the Sun*.

Campbell, Sir Colin (1792–1863), Scottish soldier, suppressed the Indian Mutiny 1857–58.

Campbell, Donald (1921–66), English racing driver, son of Sir Malcolm Campbell, set up world's water speed record 1964.

Campbell, Sir Malcolm (1885–1948), English racing driver, broke both land and water speed records many times.

Campbell, Mrs Patrick (1865–1940), English actress of great beauty, original Eliza Doolittle in Shaw's *Pygmalion* (1914).

Campbell, Robert (1808–94), Scottish explorer of Yukon, Canada.

Campbell, Roy (1901–57) South African poet, author of *The Flaming Terrapin* (1924).

Campbell, Thomas (1777–1844), Scottish narrative poet, author of *Hohenlinden*.

Campbell-Bannerman, Sir Henry (1836–1908), British statesman, prime minister 1905–08.

Campbell College, Belfast, public school, founded 1894.

Campeggio, Cardinal Lorenzo (1474–1539), Italian bishop of Salisbury 1524–34, as papal legate opposed Henry VIII's divorce.

Camperdown, Battle of, naval engagement, victory of the British over the Dutch fleet 11 Oct. 1797.

Campion, Edmund (1540–81), English Jesuit, sent as missionary to Elizabethan England; executed.

Campion, Thomas (1567–1620), English poet, doctor and musician, who set his own lyrics to music.

Campo Formio, Treaty of, between Napoleon Bonaparte and Austria, signed 17 Oct. 1797.

Camus, Albert (1913–60), Algerian-born French writer, author of *The Plague* (1947).

Canada, discovered by Norsemen *c.* 1000; visited by John Cabot 1497; St Lawrence explored by Jacques Cartier 1534; Quebec founded 1608; Canada was a French colony from 1627 to 1763 when whole country was ceded to Britain; divided into two provinces 1791; constituted a dominion 1867; became an independent sovereign state 1931.

Canadian-Pacific Railway, completed 1885.

Canadian-U.S. border, largely defined 1842.

canals, chief period of construction in England, 1755–1827.

Canaletto, Antonio (1697–1768), Italian painter, famous for views of Venice.

Canary Islands, Spanish territory in the Atlantic; occupation completed by Spain 1496.

Canberra, Australian federal capital, founded 1913.

Cancer Research Institute, London, founded 1911.

Candlemas, Festival of Purification of the Virgin, 2 Feb.

Canford School, Wimborne. English public school, founded 1923.

Canning, George (1770–1827), British statesman, prime minister 1827.

canning, to preserve food, using bottles, pioneered 1809 by the Frenchman Nicolas Appert; tin cans for preservation patented 1810 by the Englishman Peter Durand.

Cano, Sebastian del (d. 1526), Spanish navigator, first man to circumnavigate the world 1521–22.

canon law, study developed by the 12th-century Italian monk Gratian in his *Decretum* (1140).

Canossa, Italy, scene of penance of the Emperor Henry IV 1077.

Canova, Antonio (1757–1822), Italian sculptor in Neoclassical style, renowned throughout Europe during his lifetime.

Canterbury, Roman settlement 2nd century A.D.; capital of king of Kent late 6th century; see founded by St Augustine 597; present cathedral built *c.* 1070–*c.* 1090.

Cantor, Georg (1845–1918), Russian-born German mathematician, developed several new theories.

Canute (*c.* 995–1035), king of England 1016–35, of Denmark 1018–35, and of Norway 1028–35.

Cão, Diogo (15th cent.), Portuguese explorer, discovered mouth of Congo River.

Capablanca, José Raoul (1888–1942), Cuban chess player, world champion 1921–27.

Cape Horn, South America, first doubled 1616 by the Dutch navigator Willem Cornelis Schouten (*c.* 1567–1625).

Čapek, Karel (1890–1938), Czech dramatist, author of *R.U.R.* (1920) and *The Insect Play* (1920).

Cape of Good Hope, South Africa, first doubled 1488 by Bartolomeu Diaz (*q.v.*).

Cape Province, South Africa, settled by Dutch 1652; finally ceded to Britain 1814.

Cape St Vincent, Naval Battle of, victory of the British over the Spanish fleet 14 Feb. 1797.

Capet, Hugh (*c.* 940–996), king of France 987–996, founder of Capet dynasty.

Capet dynasty, ruled France 987–1328, Naples 1265–1435, and Hungary 1308–1382.

Cape Verde Islands, Atlantic, discovered by the Portuguese navigator Diogo Gomes 1460; Portuguese overseas province until 1975 when the islands became an independent republic.

Capgrave, John (1393–1464), English friar, wrote Latin hagiology and English historical chronicle.

capillary network, of blood vessels, identified 1661 by Marcello Malpighi (*q.v.*)

capital punishment, in Britain, number of offences punishable by death drastically reduced 1826; death penalty in abeyance 1955–57; Homicide Act 1957 distinguished between two categories of murder; permanently abolished 1969.

Capone, Al (1895–1947), American gangster, built powerful criminal organization in Chicago.

Caporetto, Battle of, World War I, victory of the Austro-German forces over the Italians Oct.–Dec. 1917.

Capote, Truman (b. 1924) American writer, author of *In Cold Blood* (1966).

Capuchin order, founded 1528 by Matteo di Bassi.

Caracalla (186–217), Roman emperor 211–217, notorious for his cruelty; assassinated.

Caractacus (d. *c.* A.D. 54), British king, vainly resisted Romans; captive in Rome from 50 A.D.

Caran d'Ache (pseud. of Emmanuel Poiré; 1858–1909), Russian-born French illustrator and comic cartoonist.

Carausius, Marcus Aurelius (d. A.D. 293), Roman commander, rebelled and maintained independent rule in Britain.

Caravaggio, Michelangelo da (*c.* 1565–1610), Italian painter, introduced new realism and drama into art.

carbolic, first used 1865 as a disinfectant by Joseph Lister (*q.v.*).

carbon, prehistoric discovery; adopted 1961 as the basis for atomic weights.

carbon dioxide, first identified in early 17th century by the Belgian chemist Jan Baptist van Helmont (1580–1644).

Carbonari, members of a secret Italian revolutionary society, formed *c.* 1810.

Carboniferous period, Earth history, from *c.* 280 to *c.* 345 million years ago.

Cardano, Geronimo (1501–76), Italian mathematician and physician, made a notable contribution to the treatment of disease.

Carducci, Giosuè (1835–1907), Italian poet, awarded Nobel Prize for Literature 1906.

Carew, Thomas (*c.* 1595–1640), English poet, one of the Cavalier lyricists.

Carey, Henry (*c.* 1687–1743), English poet, wrote 'Sally in our Alley'.

Carinus (d. 285), Roman emperor 283–285, overthrown by Diocletian.

Carl Rosa Opera Company, founded 1875 by Carl Rosa (1843–89).

Carleton, William (1794–1869), Irish novelist, wrote about country people.

Carlile, Richard (1790–1843), English radical publisher, frequently imprisoned for sedition.

Carlile, Wilson (1847–1942), English clergyman, founded Church Army 1882.

Carlisle, Cumberland, Roman settlement 1st century A.D.; granted charter by Henry II 1158.

Carlisle Grammar School, English public school, probably founded by Henry I 1122; refounded by Henry VIII 1541.

Carlist movement, formed 1820s by supporters of the claims of Don Carlos (1788–1855) and his heirs to the Spanish throne; Carlist revolts finally suppressed 1875; active in support of Nationalists during Civil War 1936–39.

Carlos, Don (1545–68), Spanish prince, son of Philip II, imprisoned by his father and possibly murdered.

Carlota (1840–1927), Belgian princess, empress of Mexico 1864–67 as wife of the archduke Maximilian.

Carlowitz, Treaty of, between Turkey and Austria, Poland and Venice, Jan. 1699.

Carlsbad Decrees, designed to suppress growth of liberalism, signed by the German states 1819.

Carlyle, Jane Welsh (1801–66), Scottish wife of Thomas Carlyle, gifted letter-writer.

Carlyle, Thomas (1795–1881), Scottish historian (*French Revolution,* 1837) and popular prophet.

Carmagnole, French revolutionary song (possibly of Italian origin), composed 1792; suppressed 1799.

Carmelite order, founded about 1155 by the Crusader Berthold; monastic order recognized 1226.

Carmen Sylva (pseud. of Queen Elizabeth of Romania; 1843–1916), wrote many books.

Carnarvon, 4th Earl of (1831–90), English statesman, was a notably progressive colonial secretary.

Carnegie, Andrew (1835–1919), Scottish-born American industrialist and philanthropist, endowed libraries, institutes, etc.

Carnegie Endowment for International Peace, Washington, founded 1910.

Carnot, Lazare (1753–1823), French revolutionary, military organizer of genius.

Carol I (1839–1914), first king of Romania 1881–1914.

Carol II (1893–1953), king of Romania 1930–40, replacing his own son Michael.

Caroline of Anspach (1683–1737), queen of England as wife of George II, gave Sir Robert Walpole powerful support.

Caroline of Brunswick (1768–1821), queen of England as wife of George IV, who failed in his attempt to divorce her.

Carolingian dynasty, ruled France 751–987.

Carpaccio, Vittore (*c.* 1455–*c.* 1525), Italian painter of Venetian school, e.g. *St Ursula's Dream.*

Carpenter, Edward (1844–1929), English writer and social reformer, author of *Towards Democracy* (1905).

Carpentier, Georges (1894–1975), French boxer, world light-heavyweight champion 1920–22.

carpetbaggers, name given in the U.S.A. to Northerners who moved into the South after the Civil War (1861–65) and were prominent in the period of Reconstruction.

carpet sweeper, first practical one designed 1876 by the American businessman Melville R. Bissell.

Carpini, Giovanni de Piano (*c.* 1180–*c.* 1252), Italian Franciscan monk, one of the first Europeans to explore the Mongol Empire.

Carracci, Lodovico (1555–1619) and Annibale (1560–1609), Italian painters, most important members of a gifted family.

Carroll, Lewis (pseud. of Charles Lutwidge Dodgson; 1832–98), English mathematician and writer, author of *Alice's Adventures in Wonderland* (1865).

Carson, Edward (1854–1935), Irish-born British lawyer and politician, organized Ulster Protestant resistance to Home Rule.

Carson, Kit (1809–78), American frontiersman, legendary guide and Indian-fighter.

Carter, Howard (1873–1939), English archaeologist, discovered tomb of Tutankhamun 1922.

Carter, James Earl (b. 1924), American statesman, 39th president of the United States from 1977.

Carteret, Sir George (1610–80), Jersey-born naval officer, proprietor of New Jersey in America 1664–80.

Carteret, John, Baron (1690–1763), English statesman, mainly concerned with foreign affairs.

Cartesian coordinates, theory first propounded 1637 by René Descartes (q.v.).

Carthage, Phoenician city on North African coast, founded 8th century B.C.; destroyed by Romans 146 B.C.; refounded 29 B.C.; occupied by Arabs A.D. 698.

Carthusian order, founded 1086 by Saint Bruno (c. 1030–1101).

Cartier, Jacques (1491–1557), French explorer, discovered St Lawrence River 1534.

Cartwright, Edmund (1743–1823), English inventor of the power loom 1787.

Cartwright, Thomas (1535–1600), English Nonconformist clergyman, opposed Elizabethan settlement.

Carus (d. 283), Roman emperor 282–283, killed in Persian war.

Caruso, Enrico (1873–1921), Italian singer, most famous of all operatic tenors.

Carver, John (c. 1576–1621), English leader of the Pilgrim Fathers.

Cary, Joyce (1888–1957), Anglo-Irish novelist, author of *The Horse's Mouth* (1944).

Casablanca, Morocco, founded in the 18th century; occupied by the French 1907; scene of wartime conference between Roosevelt and Churchill, Jan. 1943, where formula for 'conditional surrender' of Axis powers was agreed.

Casals, Pablo (1876–1973), Spanish cellist of world renown, noted for his interpretation of J. S. Bach.

Casanova, Giovanni (1725–98), Italian adventurer, ardent amorist, wrote fascinating *Memoirs*.

Casaubon, Isaac (1559–1614), Swiss-born classical scholar, in England 1610–14; buried in Westminster Abbey.

Casca, Publius Servilius (d. c. 42 B.C.), Roman conspirator, one of Caesar's assassins.

Casement, Sir Roger (1864–1916), Irish nationalist, sought German help in World War I; executed for treason.

Casey, Richard Gardiner (1890–1976), Australian statesman, governor-general of Australia 1965–69.

cash registers, invented by the American John Ritty of Ohio 1879; first used 1884; introduced into Britain 1885.

Casimir I (1015–58), king of Poland 1040–58, took Silesia from the Czechs.

Casimir III (1310–70), king of Poland 1333–70, strengthened and reformed the state.

Casimir IV (1427–92), king of Poland 1447–92, subjugated the Teutonic Knights.

Casimir V. See **John II Casimir.**

Caslon, William (1692–1766), English type-founder, designed the typeface later named after him.

Cassatt, Mary (c. 1845–1926), American painter, worked in Paris in Impressionist style.

Cassell, John (1817–65), English publisher, founder of the famous firm.

Cassianus, Saint John (360–435), French-born monk, who lived in Egypt as a hermit, was an exponent of Semi-Pelagianism.

Cassini, Giovanni Domenico (1625–1712), Italian-born French astronomer, made many valuable observations.

Cassino, Monte, Italy, monastery founded by Saint Benedict of Nursia 529; destroyed by Allies May 1944; restored early 1950s and reopened 1956.

Cassiodorus (c. 478–570), Roman official in Ostrogothic Italy, founded monastery; was a prolific writer.

Cassius, Gaius (d. 42 B.C.), Roman politician, assassin of Caesar; committed suicide after defeat at Philippi.

Castagno, Andrea del (1423–57), Italian painter, was a notable portraitist of the Florentine School.

Castello Branco, Camilo (1825–95), Portuguese novelist, author of *Disastrous Love* (1862).

Castelnau, Michel de (c. 1520–1592), French diplomat, ambassador to England 1575–85.

Castiglione, Baldassarre (1478–1529), Italian diplomat, author of *The Courtier* (1528), an idealized view of courtly life.

Castiglione, Giovanni Benedetto (1616–70), Italian painter, especially of animal studies.

Castile, Spain, originally a dependency of Leon; became a countship in the 10th century; made a kingdom 1035; united with Leon 1037; expanded 11th–15th centuries; union with Aragon 1479.

Castillon, Battle of, victory of the French over the English 17 July 1453; final battle of The Hundred Years' War.

Castlereagh, Robert, Viscount (1769–1822), British statesman, architect of the 'Grand Alliance' against Napoleon.

Castro, Fidel (b. 1927), Cuban revolutionary leader, prime minister of Cuba since 1959.

catalysis, chemical, first described 1835 by Jons Jakob Berzelius (q.v.).

Caterham School, Surrey, English public school, founded 1811.

Catesby, Robert (1573–1605), English conspirator, led Gunpowder Plot.

Cather, Willa (1873–1947), American novelist, author of *My Antonio* (1918).

Catherine I (1684–1727), empress of Russia, wife of Peter the Great, sole ruler 1725–27.

Catherine II, the Great (1729–96), German-born empress of Russia 1762–96, whose reign was marked by great territorial expansion.

Catherine de Médicis (1519–89), Italian-born queen of France, as regent exerted strong influence over French policy.

Catherine Howard. See **Howard,** Catherine.

Catherine of Aragon (1485–1536), Spanish-born queen of Henry VIII, whose divorce in 1533 led to the English Reformation.

Catherine of Braganza (1638–1705), Portuguese-born queen of England 1662–85 as wife of Charles II.

Catherine of Siena, Saint (1347–80), Italian nun, famous for her visions.

Catherine Parr. See **Parr,** Catherine.

cathode rays, investigated 1869 by the German physicist Johann Hittorf (1824–1914); identified as electrons 1897 by J. J. Thomson (*q.v.*).

Catholic Emancipation Act, 1829, removed most legal disabilities from Roman Catholics in Great Britain and Ireland.

Catholic Hierarchy, restored in Britain 1850.

Catholic Apostolic Church (Irvingites), founded 1829 by the Scottish preacher Edward Irving (1792–1834).

Catiline (Lucius Sergius Catalina; *c.* 108–62 B.C.), Roman conspirator, exposed by Cicero; killed in battle.

Catlin, George (1796–1872), American artist, recorder of American Indian life.

Cato the Elder (Marcus Portius Cato; 234–149 B.C.), Roman political leader, advocated return to austere, simple society.

Cato the Younger (Marcus Portius Cato; 95–46 B.C.), Roman politician, opponent of Caesar; committed suicide.

Cato Street Conspiracy, unsuccessful plot to assassinate members of the British cabinet 1820, planned by Arthur Thistlewood; executed with other accomplices May 1820.

Catt, Carrie Chapman (1859–1947), American campaigner for female suffrage.

Cattermole, George (1800–68), English artist, illustrator of Sir Walter Scott's novels.

Catullus, Gaius Valerius (*c.* 84–*c.* 54 B.C.), Roman lyric poet, master of amorous and satirical verse.

Caudine Forks, Battle of the, fought between the Samnites and the Romans, 321 B.C.

Caughley porcelain, manufactured 1772–99.

Caulaincourt, Marquis de (1773–1827), French soldier and diplomat, foreign minister under Napoleon.

Cavafy, Constantinos (1863–1933), Greek poet, noted for his lyric verse.

Cavalcanti, Guido (*c.* 1255–1300), Italian poet, pioneered the 'sweet new style' (*dolce stil nuovo*).

Cavell, Edith (1865–1915), English nurse in Belgium, executed by Germans for helping Allied prisoners to escape.

Cavendish, Henry (1731–1810), English chemist, determined specific gravity of hydrogen and carbon dioxide.

Cavour, Count Camillo (1810–61), Italian statesman, architect of Italian unification.

Cawnpore, Uttar Pradesh, scene of massacre of English women and children in July 1857 during the Indian Mutiny.

Caxton, William (*c.* 1422–1491), first English printer, began work 1476.

Cayenne, French Guiana, founded 1643.

Cayley, Sir George (1773–1857), English engineer, pioneer in aerial navigation.

Cayman Islands, Caribbean, discovered by Columbus 1503; colonized by Britain in late 17th century; dependency of Jamaica until 1962; now a British dependent territory.

Cecchetti, Enrico (1850–1928), Italian dancer and ballet master, taught many famous ballet dancers.

Cecil, Robert, 1st Earl of Salisbury (*c.* 1563–1612), English statesman, secretary of state under Elizabeth I and James I.

Cecil, William, Baron Burghley (1520–98), English statesman, chief minister of Queen Elizabeth I.

Cecilia, Saint (d. 230), Roman martyr, patron saint of music.

Cedar Creek, Battle of, Union victory over the Confederates in the American Civil War, 19 Oct. 1864.

Celebes, Indonesia, discovered by the Portuguese 1512; first Dutch settlement 1607; part of Indonesia since 1949.

Celestine I, Saint (d. 432), Pope 422–432, said to have sent Saint Patrick to Ireland.

Celestine III (*c.* 1106–1198), Pope 1191–98, crowned Emperor Henry VI.

Celestine V, Saint (1215–96), Pope 1244–46, elected after living many years as a hermit.

Céline, Louis (1894–1961), French writer, made a dramatic impact with his first novel *Voyage au bout de la nuit* (1932).

cell division, studied in the 1840s by the German botanist Hugo von Mohl (1805–72); accurately described and interpreted 1882 by the German anatomist Walther Flemming (1843–1905).

Cellini, Benvenuto (1500–71), Italian gold- and silversmith, wrote famous *Autobiography*.

cellophane, developed commercially 1911 by the Swiss scientist J. E. Brandenberger.

cells, plant cells first observed 1665 by Robert Hooke (*q.v.*), animal cells *c.* 1673 by Antonie van Leeuwenhoek (*q.v.*); recognized as basic to all living matter 1839 by Theodore Schwann (*q.v.*) and Matthias Schleiden.

celluloid, pioneering work on this first

synthetic plastic carried out by the English chemist Alexander Parkes (1813–90); synthesized 1870 by the American chemist John Wesley Hyatt (1837–1920).

cellulose nitrate, violently inflammable compound prepared by method introduced 1845 by the German chemist Christian Schönbein (1799–1868).

Celsius, Anders (1701–44), Swedish astronomer and inventor of centigrade thermometer 1742.

Celsus (1st cent. A.D.), Roman writer on medicine, considered an authority throughout the Middle Ages.

cement. See **portland cement.**

Cenci, Beatrice (1577–99), Italian murderess of a cruel father, whose story inspired a poem by Shelley.

Cennini, Cennino (c. 1370–1440), Italian painter, wrote a notable book on art.

Cenotaph, Whitehall, London, memorial to the dead of both World Wars, unveiled 11 Nov. 1920.

Cenozoic Era, Earth history, from c. 65 million years ago to the present day.

censorship, of printed books, begun in Mainz 1486.

census, first in U.S.A. 1790; first in Britain 1801.

centigrade temperature scale, devised 1742 by Anders Celsius (q.v.).

Centlivre, Mrs Susannah (c. 1667–1723), English dramatist, acted in her own works.

Central African Republic, settled by French c. 1840; part of French Equatorial Africa 1910; French overseas territory 1946; independent republic since 1960.

Central London Electric Railway, opened 27 June 1900.

Central Treaty Organization (CENTO), established 1958 as successor to Baghdad Pact (q.v.).

Ceres, first observed asteroid, sighted 1801 by Giuseppe Piazzi (q.v.).

cerium, chemical element isolated 1803 by Jöns Berzelius (q.v.) and Wilhelm Hisinger, and independently by Martin Klaproth.

CERN, European Council for Nuclear Research, established 1952 at Geneva.

Cerularius, Michael (11th cent.), Byzantine patriarch of Constantinople 1043–59; broke with papacy.

Cervantes, Miguel de (1547–1616), Spanish writer, author of *Don Quixote* (1605).

Cesarewitch Stakes, Newmarket, first run 1839.

Cetewayo (c. 1836–1884), Zulu king, defeated British at Isandhlwana 1879; deposed 1879.

Ceylon. See **Sri Lanka.**

Cézanne, Paul (1839–1906), French painter, pioneer of modern art forms.

Chabrier, Emmanuel (1841–94), French composer, wrote the symphonic work *España* (1883).

Chad, central Africa, settled by French 1890s; part of French Equatorial Africa 1910; French overseas territory 1946; independent republic since 1960.

Chadwick, Sir Edwin (1800–90), English reformer of poor laws and sanitation.

Chadwick, Sir James (1891–1974), English physicist, awarded Nobel prize for discovery of the neutron (1932).

Chaeronea, Battles of, Macedonians defeated Greek states 338 B.C.; Sulla defeated Mithridates 86 B.C.

Chagall, Marc (b. 1887), Russian-born French painter, inspired by Russian folktales and fantasy.

Chain, Ernst Boris (b. 1906), German-born British biochemist, awarded Nobel Prize (1945) for his work on penicillin.

Chaka (1773–1828), Zulu chief, founded vast empire in southwestern Africa.

Chalcedon, Council of, 4th Ecumenical Council, held 451.

Chalgrove Field, Battle of, Oxfordshire, fought between Royalists and Parliamentarians 1643.

Chaliapin, Fyodor (1873–1938), Russian operatic singer, world-famous bass.

Châlons, Battle of, victory of the Romans over the Huns under Attila 451.

Chamber of Commerce, first British, founded at Glasgow 1783.

Chamberlain, Austen (1863–1937), British statesman, foreign secretary 1924–29.

Chamberlain, Houston Stewart (1855–1927), English-born racist writer, settled in Germany.

Chamberlain, Joseph (1836–1914), British statesman, was a noted champion of imperial unity.

Chamberlain, Neville (1869–1940), British statesman, prime minister 1937–40, signed Munich Agreement 1938.

Chamberlain porcelain, manufactured 1786–1840.

Chambers's Encyclopaedia, founded 1859–1868 by the Scottish publishers Robert and William Chambers.

Chambers, Sir William (1723–96), English architect, designed Somerset House.

Chambre Ardente, French special court for trial of heretics, etc., instituted 1535; abolished 1682.

Chamisso, Adalbert von (1781–1838), German writer, author of *Peter Schlemihls Wunderbare Geschichte* (1814).

Champion Hurdle Challenge Cup, Cheltenham, first run 1927.

Champlain, Samuel de (1567–1635), French explorer in Canada, founded Quebec.

Champlain, Battle of, victory of the Americans over the British 1814.

Champollion, Jean François (1790–1832), French Egyptologist, deciphered the Rosetta Stone.

Chancellor, Richard (d. 1556), English navigator, reached Archangel and visited Moscow.

Chancellorsville, Battle of, Confederate victory over the Unionists in American Civil War, May 1863.

Chandernagor, India, town settled by the French 1688; incorporated in India 1952.

Chandler, Raymond (1888–1959), English-born American writer of thrillers, including *The Big Sleep* (1939).

Chandragupta I (4th cent. A.D.), Indian king, founded Gupta dynasty 320.

Channel Tunnel, between England and France, proposed 1802; trial shafts dug 1880–83 near Folkestone and Sangrette; Anglo-French committee recommended rail tunnel 1964; project cancelled 1975.

Channel Islands, part of duchy of Normandy from early 9th century; united to English crown at Norman Conquest 1066; under German occupation July 1940–May 1945.

Channing, William Ellery (1780–1842), American clergyman, founder of Unitarianism as an organized sect in U.S.A.

Chantrey Bequest, to Royal Academy, made by Sir Francis Legatt Chantrey (1781–1841).

Chao K'uang-yin (d. 976), Chinese emperor, founder of the Sung dynasty.

Chaplin, Sir Charles Spencer (b. 1889), English comedian, won international fame with his portrayal of 'The Tramp' in American silent films.

Chapman, George (*c.* 1559–1634), English poet and playwright, translator of Homer.

Chapman, John (1774–1847), American pioneer in the Ohio River valley, celebrated as a folk hero.

Chapman, John Jay (1862–1933), American writer, mainly on literary and cultural topics.

Charcot, Jean Martin (1825–93) French neurologist, best known for his work on hysteria and hypnotism.

Chardin, Jean Baptiste (1699–1779), French painter of interiors and still life.

Charlemagne (742–814), Frankish king, united west-central Europe; first Holy Roman emperor 800–814.

Charles II, the Bald (823–877) king of France 843–877, Holy Roman emperor 875–877; reign marked by conflict.

Charles III, the Fat (839–888), Holy Roman emperor 882–888, was under constant pressure from the Vikings.

Charles IV (1316–78), Holy Roman emperor 1355–78, regulated imperial elections with the 'Golden Bull'.

Charles V (1500–58), Holy Roman emperor 1519–56 and king of Spain 1516–56, held together great empire until voluntary abdication.

Charles VI (1685–1740), Holy Roman emperor 1711–40, tried to ensure succession of his daughter, Maria Theresa.

Charles VII (1697–1745), elector of Bavaria, Holy Roman emperor 1742–45.

Charles I (1887-1922), last emperor of Austria-Hungary 1916–18.

Charles I (1600–49) king of England 1625–49, defeated in Civil War; beheaded.

Charles II (1630–85), king of England 1660–85, restored to throne after the Protectorate.

Charles III, the Simple (879–929), king of France 893–922, dethroned by Robert, count of Paris.

Charles IV, the Fair (1294–1328), king of France 1322–28, last of the Capetian line.

Charles V, the Wise (1337–80), king of France 1364–80, expelled English from much of France.

Charles VI (1368–1422), king of France 1380–1422; reign troubled by civil war and English invasion.

Charles VII (1403–61), king of France 1422–61; period of Joan of Arc and English expulsion from France.

Charles VIII (1470–98), king of France 1483–98, invaded Italy.

Charles IX (1550–74), king of France 1560–74, a period of civil and religious strife.

Charles X (1757–1836), king of France 1824–30, failed in policy of reaction; overthrown.

Charles II (1661–1700), king of Spain 1665–1700; his posthumous disposition of the throne caused War of the Spanish Succession.

Charles III (1716–88), king of Spain 1759–88, conquered Naples and Sicily.

Charles IV (1748–1819), king of Spain 1788–1808, forced to abdicate by Napoleon.

Charles VIII (d. 1470), king of Sweden 1448–57, 1464–65, and 1467–70, involved in struggles with other Scandinavian countries.

Charles IX (1550–1611), king of Sweden 1600–11, usurped effective power 1599.

Charles X (1622–60), king of Sweden 1654–60, incorporated southern provinces into Sweden.

Charles XI (1655–97), king of Sweden 1660–97, strengthened power of the crown.

Charles XII (1686–1718), king of Sweden 1697–1718, suffered disastrous defeat in Russia.

Charles XIII (1748–1818), king of Sweden 1809–18, lost Finland but gained Norway.

Charles XIV, king of Sweden. See **Bernadotte,** Jean Baptiste.

Charles XV (1826–72), king of Sweden 1859–72, was a noted constitutional and legal reformer.

Charles Borromeo, Saint (1538–84),

Italian archbishop of Milan, founded Oblates of Saint Ambrose.

Charles, Prince of Wales (b. 1948), heir apparent to English throne, son of Queen Elizabeth II.

Charles Edward, the Young Pretender. See **Stuart,** Charles Edward.

Charles Martel (*c.* 688–741), ruler of the Franks, defeated Saracens at battle of Tours 732.

Charles the Bold (1433–77), duke of Burgundy 1467–77, famous warrior.

Charlotte Sophia (1744–1818), queen of England 1761–1818 as wife of George III.

Charter, Great. See **Magna Carta.**

Charterhouse School, English public school, founded 1611 by Thomas Sutton (*c.* 1532–1611).

Chartier, Emile (1868–1951), French philosopher and essayist, author of *Les Propos d'Alain* (1920).

Chartist movement, for English social reform, began 1836, ended *c.* 1858; petitions rejected by Parliament 1839, 1842 and 1848.

Chartres cathedral, France, constructed 1194 to 1260.

Chartreuse liqueur, manufactured at La Grande Chartreuse Monastery near Grenoble from 1607 to 1903, when the monks left France for Tarragona in Spain. They returned to France in 1940 and resumed production.

Chastelard, Pierre de (1540–64), French poet, whose passion for Mary Queen of Scots led to his execution.

Chateaubriand, François René de (1768–1848), French Romantic writer, politician and diplomat, author of *Atala* and *René*.

Chatham, Earl of. See **Pitt,** William, the Elder.

Chattanooga, Battle of, Union victory in the American Civil War, Nov. 1863.

Chatterton, Thomas (1752–70), English poet, 'the Marvellous Boy', wrote many fake 15th-century poems.

Chaucer, Geoffrey (*c.* 1340–1400), outstanding English poet of the Middle Ages, wrote *The Canterbury Tales.*

Chausson, Ernest (1855–99), French composer, noted for his songs.

Cheka, Soviet secret police, established 1917; superseded 1922 by O.G.P.U.

Chekhov, Anton (1860–1904), Russian short story writer and playwright, author of *Three Sisters* (1901) and *The Cherry Orchard* (1904).

Chelčický, Peter (*c.* 1390–*c.* 1460), Czech writer, one of the leaders of the Hussite movement.

Chelsea Bridge, London, completed 1937 by G. Topham Forrest and E. P. Wheeler; replaced an older bridge opened 1858.

Chelsea-Derby porcelain, manufactured 1745–84.

Cheltenham College, English public school, founded 1841.

Cheltenham Gold Cup, first run 1924.

Cheltenham Ladies' College, English public school for girls, founded 1853.

Chen Dynasty, China, 557–589.

Chenier, André (1762–94), French poet, precursor of Romanticism, guillotined in Reign of Terror.

Cheops (fl. *c.* 2900 B.C.), Egyptian king, built Great Pyramid.

cheques, first printed by the English banker Lawrence Childs *c.* 1762.

Cherepnin, Nikolai (1873–1945), Russian-born composer, worked in France from 1920s.

Cherokee tribe, North American Indians, disbanded 1906.

Cherubini, Luigi (1760–1842), Italian composer in Paris, made an important contribution to French opera.

Chesapeake Bay, Battle of, between French and British fleets, 5 Sept. 1781.

chess, played in India by 7th century A.D.; brought to Spain between 8th and 10th centuries; to England in late 13th century.

Chester cathedral, England, founded 11th century; created cathedral by Henry VIII 1541.

Chesterfield, Earl of (1694–1773), English politician and diplomat, remembered chiefly for the letters he wrote to his son.

Chesterton, Gilbert Keith (1874–1936), English writer and Catholic apologist, author of the 'Father Brown' detective stories.

Chetham's Library, Manchester, founded by the merchant Humfrey Chetham (1580–1653).

Chevalier, Albert (1861–1923), English music hall performer of songs like 'My Old Dutch'.

Chevalier, Maurice (1888–1972), French music-hall singer and actor, appeared in many films.

Chiang Kai-shek (1887–1975), Chinese soldier and statesman, ruler of China 1928–49; led exiled government in Taiwan from 1949.

Chicago, Illinois, founded early 19th century; largely destroyed by fire 1871; anarchist riots 1886; university founded 1891.

Chichester, Sir Francis (1901–72), English sailor and airman, won first solo transatlantic yacht race (1960).

Chickamauga, Battle of, Confederate victory in the American Civil War, fought Sept. 1863.

Ch'ien Lung (1711–99) emperor of China 1736–96, whose reign marked the zenith of the Manchu dynasty.

Chigwell School, Essex, English public school, founded 1629 by Samuel Harsnett, Archbishop of York (1561–1631).

Childe, Vere Gordon (1892–1957), Australian archaeologist and prehistorian, author of *What Happened in History* (1942).

Childermas. See **Innocents' Day.**

Childers, Erskine (1870–1922), Irish author, wrote *Riddle of the Sands* (1903); executed in Irish Civil War.

Children's Crusade, set out from France and Germany to the Holy Land 1212.

Chile, conquest by Spanish begun 1536; national government set up 1810; complete independence from Spanish rule 1818.

Chiltern Hundreds, first granted to an M.P. as grounds for resignation 1750.

Chimborazo, volcanic mountain in Ecuador; first climbed 1880.

China, earliest dynasty began *c.* 2200 B.C.; under Mongol rule 1279–1368; first Europeans arrived in 16th century; republic since 1912; Communist People's Republic since 1949.

Ch'in Dynasty, China, 255–206 B.C.

Chippendale, Thomas (1718–79), English furniture maker, wrote *The English Cabinet Maker's Director* (1754).

Chirico, Giorgio de (b. 1888), Italian painter, pioneer of Surrealism.

Chiswick Press, London, founded 1811 by the English printer Charles Whittingham (1767–1840).

chlorine, first isolated 1774 by Karl Wilhelm Scheele (*q.v.*).

chloroform, first produced 1831 by Justus von Liebig (*q.v.*) and independently by Samuel Guthrie and by E. Soubeiran; first used as an anaesthetic 1847 by the Scottish physician Sir James Simpson.

chlorophyll, structure determined in the 1930s by the German chemist Hans Fischer (1881–1945).

Chmielnicki, Bogdan (*c.* 1593–1657), Cossack leader, won brief independence from Ukraine.

chocolate, brought to Spain from Mexico as a drink in early 16th century; eating chocolate first produced 1847 by the English firm of Fry and Sons; milk chocolate produced 1876 in Switzerland. See also **cocoa.**

Chodowiecki, Daniel (1726–1801), German artist, was a noted genre painter and engraver.

Choiseul, Duc de (1719–85), French statesman and diplomat, chief minister during Seven Years' War.

cholera, bacillus discovered 1883 by Robert Koch (*q.v.*); last major epidemic in England 1866.

Chomsky, Noam (b. 1928), American linguist, author of *Syntactic Structures* (1957).

Chopin, Frédéric (1810–49), Polish-French composer and pianist, noted for the lyrical quality of his piano music.

Chosroes I (d. 579), king of Persia 531–579, was a constant threat to Byzantium.

Chosroes II (d. 628), king of Persia 590–628, ultimately unsuccessful in war with Byzantium.

Chou Dynasty, China, 1122 to 255 B.C.

Chouans, Breton royalists, rose in revolt 1793; finally subdued 1800.

Chou En-lai (1898–1976), Chinese Communist statesman, prime minister 1949–75.

Chrétien de Troyes (12th cent.), French poet, wrote Arthurian romances.

Christ. See **Jesus of Nazareth.**

Christ Church College, Oxford University, founded 1546.

Christ College, Brecon, Welsh public school, founded 1541.

Christadelphians, religious movement, founded *c.* 1850 in U.S.A. by the English physician John Thomas (1805–71).

Christian I (1426–81), king of Denmark 1448–81, founded Oldenburg dynasty.

Christian II (1481–1559), king of Denmark 1513–23, briefly conquered Sweden; deposed.

Christian III (1503–59), king of Denmark 1534–59, introduced Lutheranism.

Christian IV (1577–1648), king of Denmark 1588–1648, intervened unsuccessfully in Thirty Years' War.

Christian VII (1749–1808), king of Denmark 1766–1808, unstable and finally insane.

Christian VIII (1786–1848), king of Denmark 1839–48, briefly (1814) king of Norway.

Christian IX (1818–1906), king of Denmark 1863–1906, lost Schleswig-Holstein to Germany.

Christian X (1870–1947) king of Denmark 1912–47, and also of Iceland 1918–44.

Christian, Fletcher, English sailor, led mutiny on the *Bounty* 1789 and settled Pitcairn Island.

Christian Science, religious movement, founded 1879 by Mary Baker Eddy.

Christian Socialism, founded *c.* 1850 by John Lulow (1821–1911).

Christie, Agatha (1891–1976), English detective story writer, creator of Hercule Poirot.

Christie's, London auctioneers, founded 1766 by James Christie (1730–1803).

Christina, (1626–89), queen of Sweden 1632–54, abdicated, became a Catholic and died in Rome.

Christine de Pisan (*c.* 1364–*c.* 1431), French poet, wrote courtly love lyrics.

Christmas cards, first examples designed in Britain 1842 for Sir Henry Cole by J. C. Horsley (1817–1903).

Christmas Island, Western Pacific, discovered 1777 by Captain Cook; annexed

1888 by Britain; included in the Gilbert and Ellice Islands Colony since 1919; hydrogen bomb tests 1957.

Christophe, Henri (1767–1820), Negro slave, became king of Haiti; deposed for cruelty, he committed suicide.

Christ's College, Cambridge University, founded 1505.

Christ's Hospital, Sussex, English public school, founded in London 1552 by Edward VI; moved to present site 1902.

chromatography, chemical separation technique first understood and described 1910 by the Russian botanist Mikhail S. Tsvet.

chrome tanning, process invented by Augustus Schultz 1884.

chromium, first isolated 1797 by the French chemist Louis Nicolas Vauquelin (1763–1829).

chromosomes, major studies begun *c.* 1885 by the German biologists Theodor Boveri (1862–1915) and August Weismann (1834–1914).

chromosphere, of the sun, so named 1868 by Sir Joseph Norman Lockyer (*q.v.*).

chronometer, invented 1735 by the English horologist John Harrison (1693–1776); his most accurate design appeared 1762, for which he was awarded by the British government a prize of £20,000.

Church Army, founded in London 1882 by the Rev. Wilson Carlile (1874–1942).

Churchill, Charles (1731–64), English satirical poet (*The Rosciad*, 1761) and journalist associated with John Wilkes.

Churchill, Lord Randolph (1849–95), British statesman, chancellor of the exchequer 1886, father of Sir Winston Churchill.

Churchill, Sarah (1660–1744), English royal favourite, wife of the Duke of Marlborough.

Churchill, Sir Winston (1874–1965), British statesman, national leader during World War II, prime minister 1940–45 and 1951–55.

Churchill College, Cambridge University, opened 1960.

Church of England, established by Saint Augustine 597; separated from the Roman Catholic Church by the Act of Supremacy 1534.

Church of Ireland, (Anglican), disestablished 1869.

Church of Scotland, (Presbyterian), established 1560.

Church in Wales, (Anglican), disestablished 1919.

Churriguera, José de (1665–1725), Spanish architect, worked in an elaborate, colourful Baroque style.

Chu Yüan-chang (1328–98), emperor of China 1368–98, founder of the Ming Dynasty.

Ciano, Galeazzo, Count (1903–44), Italian statesman, foreign minister 1936–43, executed for treason against his father-in-law Mussolini.

Cibber, Colley (1671–1757), English dramatist, whose comedies were popular at Drury Lane; was also Poet Laureate.

Cicero, Marcus Tullius (106–43 B.C.), Roman statesman, lawyer, writer and famous orator; defender of the Roman Republic.

cigarettes, introduced into Britain *c.* 1856.

Cid, The (*c.* 1043–1099), Spanish hero, famous for his legendary exploits against the Moors.

Cierva, Juan de la (1896–1936), Spanish aeronaut, inventor of the autogyro.

Cimabue, Giovanni (*c.* 1240–1302), Italian artist, one of the first Florentine fresco painters.

Cimarosa, Domenico (1749–1801), Italian opera composer, wrote *Il Matrimonio Segreto* (1792).

Cincinnatus, Lucius Quinctius (b. *c.* 519 B.C.), Roman patriot, famous as dictator who renounced power voluntarily.

cinematograph, first model constructed 1895 by the Lumière brothers (*q.v.*), based on a device of Thomas Edison.

cinerama, (and other three-dimensional film processes) came into general use 1952, mainly for travelogues; process abandoned 1960s because of high costs.

Cinna, Lucius Cornelius (d. 84 B.C.), Roman politician, associated with Marius and Popular Party.

Cinq-Mars, Marquis de (1620–42), French noble, executed for conspiracy against Richelieu.

Cintra, Treaty of, concerning the French evacuation of Portugal, signed Aug. 1808.

Circumcision, Christian Feast of the, celebrated 1 Jan.

circulation of the blood. See **blood,** circulation of the.

Cisalpine Republic, Italy, formed 1797; became Italian Republic 1802 and kingdom of Italy 1805–14.

Cistercian Order, founded at Cîteaux, France, 1098 by Saint Stephen Harding (*c.* 1048–1134).

City and South London Railway, first electrified underground line, opened 1890 between King William St and Stockwell.

City of London School, English public school, founded 1442.

City University, London, founded 1966.

Civil Engineers, Institution of, London, founded 1818.

Civil List, instituted by Parliament 1697.

Civil War, English, between Charles I and Parliament, and Charles II and Parliament, 1642–51.

Clair, René, (b. 1898), French film director, e.g. *The Italian Straw Hat* (1927).

Clairvaux, French abbey, founded 1115 by Saint Bernard.

Clare, John (1793–1864), English poet, author of *Shepherd's Calendar* (1827).

Clare College, Cambridge University, founded 1326.

Clarendon, Edward Hyde, Earl of (1608–74), English statesman and historian, chief minister 1660–67; exiled.

Clarendon, Constitutions of, royal proclamation, issued 1164.

Clark, John Grahame (b. 1907), British archaeologist, noted for his work on prehistoric Europe.

Clark, William (1770–1838), American explorer, led first expedition across North America.

Clark, William George (1821–78), English scholar, co-editor of *Cambridge* and *Globe* Shakespeares.

Clarke, John (1609–76), English pioneer settler of Rhode Island 1638.

Clarkson, Thomas (1760–1846), English crusader against the slave trade.

Claudel, Paul (1868–1955), French writer of plays and grandiloquent poetry on religious themes.

Claudius I (10 B.C.–A.D. 54), Roman emperor A.D. 41–54, during whose reign conquest of Britain began; poisoned by his wife.

Claudius II (214–270), Roman emperor 268–270, repelled Barbarian attacks.

Clausewitz, Karl von (1780–1831), Prussian strategist, wrote classic *On War* (1833).

Claverhouse, John Graham of (c. 1649–1689), Scottish soldier, known as 'Bonny Dundee', killed at victory of Killiecrankie.

Clay, Henry (1777–1852), American statesman, architect of Compromises of 1820 and 1850 to avoid civil war.

Clayesmore School, Dorset, English public school, founded 1896.

Clemenceau, Georges (1841–1929), French statesman, was prime minister 1906–09 and 1917–20.

Clement I, Saint (c. A.D. 30–A.D. 100), Pope c. 90–99, wrote an *Epistle to the Corinthians*.

Clement III (d. 1191), Pope 1187–91, preached the Third Crusade.

Clement IV (d. 1268), Pope 1265–68, previously papal legate to England.

Clement V (1264–1314), Pope 1305–14, moved papacy to Avignon 1309.

Clement VI (1291–1352), Pope 1342–52, continued papal residence at Avignon.

Clement VII (1342–94), anti-pope 1378–94, began Great Schism.

Clement VII (1478–1534), Pope 1523–34, became prisoner of emperor Charles V after sack of Rome 1527.

Clement VIII (1536–1605), Pope 1592–1605, ordered revision of Vulgate.

Clement XI (1649–1721), Pope 1700–21, attacked Jansenism as a heresy.

Clement XIV (1705–74), Pope 1769–74, suppressed Jesuits 1773.

Clementi, Muzio (1752–1832), Italian composer, wrote *Gradus ad Parnassum* (1817).

Clement of Alexandria (2nd cent. A.D.), Greek theologian and scholar, one of the fathers of the Church.

Cleopatra (69–30 B.C.), queen of Egypt, mistress of Caesar and Antony; committed suicide after defeat by Octavian (later Augustus).

Cleopatra's Needle, transferred from Egypt to London 1878 by the English surgeon Sir Erasmus Wilson (1809–84).

Clerk-Maxwell, James. See **Maxwell, James Clerk.**

Cleve, Joos van (c. 1480–1540), Flemish painter of religious subjects, active in Antwerp.

Cleveland, Grover (1837–1908), American statesman, 22nd president 1885–89 and 24th president 1893–97.

Clifton College, Bristol, English public school, founded 1862.

Clifton Suspension Bridge, Bristol, opened 1864.

Clive, Kitty (1711–85), English actress, best known for her comedy roles.

Clive, Robert, Baron (1725–74), English soldier and statesman, effectively founded British Empire in India.

clocks, oldest surviving clock in England (Salisbury Cathedral) dates from 1386; small spring-driven clocks made in Germany from 1500; pendulum first used in clocks 1656 by Christiaan Huygens (*q.v.*); anchor escapement invented c. 1660 by Robert Hooke (*q.v.*); minute hand appeared about 1670; battery electric clock invented 1840, developed 1906; mains electric clock 1918; quartz-crystal clock 1929; atomic clock (caesium) 1952.

Clodion, Michel (1738–1814), French sculptor of mythological subjects.

Clontarf, Battle of, victory of the Irish over the Danes, 1014.

Clotaire I (d. 561), Frankish king 558–561, greatly expanded his possessions.

Clotaire II (d. 629), Frankish king 584–629, whose reign was disrupted by civil wars.

Cloth of Gold, Field of the, near Calais, site of conference between Henry VIII and Francis I, 6 June 1520.

Clothworkers, Livery Company, London, founded before 1480; incorporated 1528.

cloud chamber, radiation detector, developed 1896–1912 by the Scottish physicist Charles Wilson (1869–1959).

Clouet, François (c. 1510–c. 1572), French painter, son of Jean Clouet, best known for his court portraits.

Clouet, Jean (*c.* 1485–*c.* 1540), French painter at the court of Francis I, famous for his portraits and religious subjects.

Clough, Arthur Hugh (1819–61), English poet, author of *Tober-na-Vuolich* (1848).

Clovis (*c.* 466–511), Frankish king 481–511, extended rule over much of France.

Cluny Abbey, France, founded 910.

Clynes, John Robert (1869–1949), English Labour politician, home secretary 1929–31.

Cnossos. See **Knossos.**

coal gas, illumination by, developed 1792–96 by the Scottish engineer William Murdock (1754–1839); used in London (Soho) 1803.

coal industry, in Britain, public ownership began 1938; nationalized Jan. 1947.

coalition governments, in Britain, 1757, 1782, 1852, 1915, 1931, 1940.

Coalport porcelain, manufactured from 1790 to present day.

Coates, Eric (1886–1957), English composer of light orchestral works.

cobalt, first isolated *c.* 1735 by the Swedish chemist Georg Brandt (1694–1768).

Cobbett, William (1763–1835), English political journalist, author of *Rural Rides* (1830).

Cobden, Richard (1804–65), English politician, worked for repeal of Corn Laws (*q.v.*).

cocaine, first local anaesthetic, used as such by the Austrian surgeon Carl Kolher, 1884.

cock-fighting, made illegal in England 1849.

Cochran, Sir Charles Blake (1873–1951), English theatrical impresario, producer of many famous reviews.

Cockerell, Sir Christopher Sydney (b. 1910), English engineer, inventor of the hovercraft.

Cockcroft, Sir John Douglas (1897–1967), English physicist, awarded Nobel Prize 1951 for his research into atomic nuclei.

cocoa powder, first produced 1828 by the Dutchman Conrad van Houten. See also **chocolate.**

Cocos Islands, Indian Ocean, discovered by William Keeling 1609; annexed by Britain 1857; Australian external territory 1955.

Cocteau, Jean (1889–1963), French dramatist, poet, novelist and film director of great originality and versatility.

Code Napoléon, promulgated as the French civil law code 1804; assumed its present name 1807.

Codex Sinaiticus, purchased from the Soviet Government by Britain 1933.

Cody, William Frederick (1846–1917), known as 'Buffalo Bill', American frontiersman and Wild West show impresario.

coelacanth, prehistoric fish thought extinct until a living one netted 1938 near the southern coast of Africa.

coffee, first brought to England *c.* 1650.

coherer, radio wave detector, first developed 1890 by the French scientist Edouard Branly (1846–1940).

Coimbra, University of, founded 1290 in Lisbon and transferred to Coimbra 1537.

coke, manufacturing process patented 1621 by Dud Dudley (1599–1684).

Coke, Sir Edward (1552–1634), English jurist, defended common law against royal prerogative.

Colbert, Jean Baptiste (1619–83), French statesman, as minister of finance under Louis XIV made sweeping economic reforms.

Colburn, Zerah (1804–40), American calculating prodigy as a child; widely exhibited.

Colchester, first Roman colony in Britain, founded A.D. 43; destroyed by Boadicea A.D. 60; received first charter 1189; University of Essex founded there 1964.

Coldstream Guards, first raised 1659.

Cole, George Douglas Henry (1889–1959), English political and economic theorist, influential socialist thinker.

Coleridge, Samuel Taylor (1772–1834), English Romantic poet and critic, wrote *Kubla Khan* (1797) and *The Ancient Mariner* (1798).

Coleridge-Taylor, Samuel (1875–1912), English composer of *The Song of Hiawatha* (1898–1900).

Colet, John (*c.* 1467–1519), English theologian and scholar, founded St Paul's School.

Colette (1873–1954), French novelist, author of *Chéri* (1920) and *Gigi* (1944).

Coligny, Gaspard de (1519–72), French Huguenot leader, killed at Massacre of Saint Bartholomew.

college postal stamps, first used by Keble College, Oxford University, 1871; suppressed by the postmaster-general 1885.

Collingwood, Cuthbert, Baron (1750–1810), English admiral, Nelson's second-in-command at Trafalgar.

Collingwood, Robin George (1889–1943), English historian and philosopher, author of *The Idea of History* (1946).

Collins, Michael (1890–1922), Irish nationalist leader in struggle with Britain, negotiated 1921 treaty; assassinated by republican irreconcilables.

Collins, Wilkie (1824–89), English novelist, pioneered detective fiction with *The Woman in White* (1860).

Collins, William (1721–59), English poet, wrote 'How sleep the brave'.

collodion process, invented 1850 by the English photographer Frederick Scott Archer (*q.v.*).

colloidal chemistry, study initiated 1861 by the Scottish chemist Thomas Graham (1805–69).

Collot d'Herbois, Jean Marie (1749–96), French revolutionary, notorious for his cruelty during the Reign of Terror.

collotype, illustration printing process, patented 1855 by the Frenchmen Tessie du Motay and C. R. Maréchal.

Colman, George, the Elder (1732–94), English dramatist, author of *The Jealous Wife* (1761).

Colman, George, the Younger (1762–1836), English dramatist, wrote *The Heir at Law* (1797).

Cologne, made a Roman colony A.D. 50; conquered by Franks *c.* 400; created an archbishopric 785; city secured self-government 1288; university founded 1388 (refounded 1919); incorporated in France during Napoleonic period; annexed to Prussia 1815; cathedral (begun 13th century) completed 1880; occupied by British army 1918–25; heavily bombed in World War II.

Colombia, first settled by Spanish 1525; capital, Bogotá, founded 1538; achieved independence from Spanish rule 1819; part of Greater Colombia 1819–30; became republic of New Granada 1830; transformed into Confederación Granadina 1858; adopted name of United States of Colombia 1863; became Republic of Colombia 1886.

Colonial Office, London, founded as the Council of Foreign Plantations 1660; merged with Commonwealth Office 1966.

Colorado, U.S.A., first settled 1858; made a territory 1861; admitted to the Union 1876.

Colosseum, Roman amphitheatre, built A.D. 72–80.

Colossus, first electronic digital computer; first of the series operational 1943; built in Britain by M.H.A. Newman and Alan Turing and used in Allied war effort.

Colossus of Rhodes, statue built *c.* 285 B.C.; destroyed by earthquake 224 B.C.

colour photography, using subtractive process, suggested 1868 by the Frenchmen Ducos du Hauron and C. Clos and used as a basis for colour-print processes from the 1890s; first commercial colour film based on this (Kodachrome) appeared 1935.

Colt revolver, first patented 1835 by the American Samuel Colt (1814–62).

Colum, Padraic (1881–1972), Irish writer, influential in the Irish literary revival.

Columba, Saint (521–597), Irish missionary, preached gospel in Scotland.

Columban, Saint (*c.* 540–615), Irish missionary, founded monasteries in France.

Columbia River, discovered 1792 by the American explorer Robert Gray (1755–1806).

Columbia University, New York, founded 1754 as King's College; reopened as Columbia College 1784.

columbium. See niobium.

Columbus, Christopher (1451–1506), Italian navigator in service of Spain, discovered America 1492.

Columbus Day, U.S.A., commemorating the discovery of America, 12 Oct.

Combe, William (1741–1823), English writer, author of *The Three Tours of Dr Syntax* (1812–21).

combine harvester-thresher, invented in California 1875.

combustion, first correctly interpreted 1772 by Antoine Lavoisier (*q.v.*).

Comédie Française, Paris, instituted 1658; assumed present name 1680.

Comenius (1592–1670), Czech educationalist, exiled in Poland, Sweden and Holland; devised first pictorial textbook.

comets, first studied in detail by Edmund Halley (*q.v.*) and also by Tycho Brahe and Sir Isaac Newton.

comic strips, originated by the German artist Wilhelm Busch (1832–1908).

Cominform, international Communist body, founded 1947.

Comintern, international Communist body, founded 1919; dissolved 1943.

Commedia dell'Arte, came into being in Italy in the mid-16th century.

Commodus (161–192), Roman emperor 180–192, son of Marcus Aurelius; became insane and was murdered.

Commons, House of, originated in the 13th century. See **Parliament.**

Commonwealth, republican regime in England, 1649–53.

Commonwealth Day, founded as Empire Day 24 May 1902; name changed 1958.

Commonwealth Immigrants Acts, 1962 and 1968, imposed restrictions on numbers of Commonwealth citizens entering Britain.

Commonwealth Relations Office, founded 1925 as the Dominions Office; assumed present name 1947; merged with Foreign Office 1968.

Commune, revolutionary regime established in Paris March-May 1871.

Communism, name first used in modern sense in Karl Marx's *Communist Manifesto* (1848); Bolsheviks renamed Communists in Russia 1918; Communist parties formed in Germany 1918, Britain and France 1920, and China and U.S.A. 1921.

community homes. See approved schools.

Commynes, Philippe de (1447–1511), French chronicler, also wrote memoirs.

Comoro Islands, French protectorate 1886; attached to Madagascar 1914; French overseas territory 1947; independent republic since 1975.

compass, magnetic, first described 1269 by Peregrinus of Maricourt.

compensated pendulum, invented 1722 by the Englishman George Graham (1673–1751).

Complutensian Bible, first polyglot Bible, published 1522.

Compton, Arthur (1892–1962), American physicist, discovered, 1923, the change in wavelength of X-rays when scattered by matter, known as the Compton effect.

Compton-Burnett, Ivy (1892–1969), English novelist, author of *Mother and Son* (1955).

computer, first electronic digital computer, Colossus (*q.v.*) operational 1943.

computer, first mechanical model, the analytical engine, of Charles Babbage (*q.v.*), designed 1834–42 but never completed.

Comstock, Anthony (1844–1915), American crusader against 'immoral' literature.

Comstock silver lode, Nevada, discovered 1859 on land partially owned by Henry Comstock (1820–70).

Comte, Auguste (1798–1857), French positivist philosopher and father of sociology.

Concepción, Chilean city, founded 1550 by the Spanish conquistador Pedro de Valdivia (*q.v.*).

concert hall, London's first public, Hickford's Room, The Haymarket, opened 1697.

concertina, patented 1829 by Sir Charles Wheatstone.

conclave of cardinals, to elect a pope (Gregory X), first held at Viterbo 1268–71.

concrete, reinforced, invention patented 1867 by a Parisian gardener Joseph Monier. See also **portland cement.**

Condé, Prince de (1621–86), French general, 'the Great Condé', served with distinction in the Thirty Years' War and the Third Dutch War.

Condell, Henry (d. 1627), English actor, co-editor with John Heminge of first edition of Shakespeare's plays.

condensed milk, process invented 1856 by the American Gail Borden (1801–74).

Conder, Charles (1868–1909), English painter, who often worked on white silk.

Condillac, Etienne de (1715–80), French philosopher, developed an all-embracing theory of sensationalism.

Condorcet, Marquis de (1743–94), French philosopher, mathematician, and politician, died in prison during the Revolution.

Confederate States of America, formed 4 Feb. 1861; collapsed April-May 1965.

Confederation of the Rhine, Napoleonic organization of German states, formed 1806; ended 1813.

Confucianism, religious movement, founded by the Chinese sage Confucius (*c.* 551–479 B.C.).

Congo. See **Zaïre.**

Congo Republic, region explored by Pierre de Brazza 1870–80; created a French colony 1891; part of French Equatorial Africa 1910; French overseas territory 1946; achieved independence 1960; declared a People's Republic 1969.

Congo River, discovered by the Portuguese navigator Diogo Cão 1482.

Congregational Movement originated *c.* 1580 by Robert Browne (*q.v.*).

Congress of Industrial Organizations, U.S.A., founded 1936.

Congress of the United States, instituted 1789.

Congreve, William (1670–1729), English dramatist, author of sprightly comedies, including *The Way of the World* (1700).

Connecticut, U.S.A., first settled 1634; received constitution 1639; one of the original states of the Union.

Connelly, Marc (b. 1890), American dramatist, wrote *Green Pastures* (1930).

Connolly, James (1870–1916), Irish nationalist politician, played prominent part in Easter Rising 1916; executed.

Conrad I (d. 918), German king 911–918, involved in several wars.

Conrad II (*c.* 990–1039), Holy Roman emperor 1024–39, extended boundaries of empire.

Conrad III (1093–1152), German king 1138–52, founded Hohenstaufen dynasty and led Second Crusade.

Conrad IV (1228–54), German king 1250–54, invaded southern Italy.

Conrad, Joseph (1857–1924), Polish-born English novelist, author of *Lord Jim* (1900).

Conscience, Hendrik (1812–83), Belgian novelist, helped to create modern Flemish literature.

conscription, in England, 1916–18 and, 1939–60 (women 1941–47).

conservation of energy, principle defined 1847 by Hermann von Helmholtz (*q.v.*).

conservation of matter, or mass, principle defined 1789 by Antoine Lavoisier (*q.v.*).

conservation of mass and energy, principle defined 1905 by Albert Einstein (*q.v.*).

conservation of momentum, principle defined 1668 by the English mathematician John Wallis (1616–1703).

Conservative Party, British, origins *c.* 1680 in the Tories; present name began to be adopted 1824–32.

consols, British consolidated annuities, first issued 1751.

Constable, John (1776–1837), English landscape painter, e.g. *The Hay Wain* (1821).

Constance, Council of, Catholic General Council, 1414–18.

Constans I (*c.* 323–350), Roman emperor 337–350, overthrown by Magnus Magnentius.

Constans II (630–668), Byzantine emperor 641–668, was constantly harassed by the Arabs.

Constant, Benjamin (1845–1902), French historical painter and portraitist.

Constant de Rebecque, Benjamin (1767–1830), French writer and political theorist, author of *Adolphe* (1816).

Constantine I, the Great (*c.* 280–337), Roman emperor 306–337, made Christianity the state religion and Constantinople his capital.

Constantine II (*c.* 317–340), Roman emperor 337–340, quarrelled with co-emperor, his brother Constans; killed in battle.

Constantine IV (d. 685), Byzantine emperor 668–685, held off Arab and Bulgar attacks with difficulty.

Constantine V (719–775), Byzantine emperor 741–775, vigorously restored the state.

Constantine VI (771–*c.* 797), Byzantine emperor 780–797, dominated by his mother, Irene, who deposed him.

Constantine VII, 'Porphyrogenitus' (905–959), Byzantine emperor 912–959, also wrote treatises and histories.

Constantine IX (*c.* 1000–1055), Byzantine emperor 1042–55, a period of grave weakness for Byzantium.

Constantine X (*c.* 1007–1067), Byzantine emperor 1059–67, failed to resist Turkish and Magyar incursions.

Constantine XI, Palaeologus (d. 1453), last Byzantine emperor 1448–53, died fighting during fall of Constantinople.

Constantine I (1868–1923), king of Greece 1913–17 and 1920–22; abdicated after disastrous Greco-Turkish war.

Constantine II (b. 1940), ex-king of the Hellenes; left Greece 1967 following coup; deposed 1973; monarchy abolished after referendum 1974.

Constantinople, formerly Byzantium (*q.v.*), rebuilt as Constantinople A.D. 330; captured by Turks 1453 and renamed Istanbul (*q.v.*).

Constantinople, Councils of, 2nd Ecumenical Council 381; 5th Ecumenical Council 533; 6th Ecumenical Council 680.

Constantius I (*c.* 250–306), Roman emperor 305–306, father of Constantine I; died at York.

Constantius II (317–361), Roman emperor 337–361, son of Constantine I, engaged in Persian wars.

Constantius III (d. 421), Roman emperor, successful general, reigned only a few months in 421.

Consulate, The, French government, established 1799; abolished 1804.

contact lenses, first suggested 1827 by Sir John Herschel; first designed 1887 by the German lens maker F. E. Müller.

Contemporary Art Society, London, founded 1910.

Continental Congress, American federal legislative body, established 1774; ended 1789.

continental drift, theory proposed 1912 by the German geologist Alfred Wegener (1880–1931).

Continental System, blockade carried out by Napoleon to prevent British trade with Europe 1806–12.

Conventicle Acts, to suppress Nonconformist worship in Britain, enacted 1593 and 1664; repealed 1689.

Convulsionaries, Jansenist group in Paris who venerated François de Paris (1690–1727).

Conway of Allington, 1st Baron (1856–1937), English mountaineer and art historian, led important expedition to the Karakoram Mountains.

Cook, James (1728–79), English mariner and explorer of Pacific and Antarctic; circumnavigated Australia.

Cook, Thomas (1808–92), English pioneer travel agent, founded Thomas Cook and Son.

Cook Islands, South Pacific, discovered by Captain Cook 1773; British protectorate 1888; part of New Zealand from 1901; internally self-governing in association with New Zealand since 1965.

Cooke, Jay (1821–1905), American financier, had career of spectacular triumphs and disasters.

Cooley, Charles (1864–1929), American sociologist, pioneered studies in primary social groups.

Coolidge, Calvin (1872–1933), American statesman, 30th president of the United States 1925–29.

Coolidge, Susan (1835–1905), American author of *What Katy Did* children's books.

Cooper, James Fenimore (1789–1851), American writer, especially of frontier tales, e.g. *Last of the Mohicans* (1826).

Cooper, Samuel (1609–72), English portrait miniaturist, notable for his picture of Oliver Cromwell.

Co-operative Movement, originated in the Rochdale Society founded 1844; first Co-operative Congress held London 1869; Co-operative Party formed 1917; first M.P. elected 1919.

Copeland, William Taylor (1797–1868), English porcelain manufacturer, started famous firm.

Copenhagen, Battle of, between the British and Danish fleets, 2 April 1801.

Copenhagen University, founded 1479.

Copernicus, Nicolaus (1473–1543), Polish astronomer, whose claim that the planets circle the sun revolutionized modern astronomy.

Copland, Aaron (b. 1900), American composer, mainly on indigenous themes, e.g. *Appalachian Spring*.

Copley, John Singleton (1728–1815), American historical and portrait painter, worked in England 1774–1815.

Coppard, Alfred Edgar (1878–1957), English short story writer, author of *Adam and Eve and Pinch Me* (1921).

Coppée, François (1842–1908), French poet, wrote *Les Humbles* (1872).

copper, discovered in prehistoric times; first used in alloy form (bronze) *c.* 3500 B.C.

Coptic Church, separated from Orthodox Church 451.

Coptic Era, began 29 Aug. 284.

copyright, first act passed in England 1709; law consolidated by act of 1911; further act 1956; first act passed in U.S.A. 1790; comprehensive act 1909; first multilateral copyright convention 1886.

Coquelin, Benoît Constant (1841–1909), French actor, whose classic role was Cyrano de Bergerac.

Coral Sea, Battle of the, World War II, victory of the Americans over the Japanese, May 1942.

Coram, Thomas (1668–1751), English philanthropist, instituted Foundling Hospital, London.

Corday, Charlotte (1768–93), French assassin of Marat (*q.v.*); guillotined.

cordite, invented 1889 by Sir Frederick Abel (*q.v.*) and Sir James Dewar (1842–1923); adopted 1891 as British army's standard explosive.

Corelli, Arcangelo (1653–1713), Italian composer and violinist, established concerto grosso form.

Corelli, Marie (1855–1924), English author of popular sensational novels, including *The Sorrows of Satan* (1895).

Cori, Carl Ferdinand (b. 1896), Czechborn American biochemist, noted for his researches into carbohydrate metabolism.

Corinth, Lovis (1858–1925), German landscape painter, pioneered German Impressionism.

Corinth Canal, Greece, originally begun A.D. 67 by the Roman emperor Nero; ship canal opened 1893.

Corneille, Pierre (1606–84), French playwright, founder of French classical drama, notably with *Le Cid* (1637).

Cornelius, Saint (d. 253), Pope 251–253, died in exile.

Cornelius, Peter von (1783–1867), German painter, chiefly noted for his frescoes.

Cornell, Katherine (b. 1898), American actress, achieved success in plays by Shakespeare, Chekhov and Shaw.

Cornell University, Ithaca, New York State, founded 1865 by the American financier Ezra Cornell (1807–74).

cornet, British cavalry rank, abolished 1871.

Cornford, Frances (1886–1960), English poet, wrote 'O fat white woman whom nobody loves'.

'Corn Law Rhymer'. See **Elliott,** Ebeneezer.

Corn Laws, enacted in Britain 1815, 1828 and 1842; repealed 1846 and 1869.

Cornwallis, Charles, Marquis (1738–1805), English soldier in America, surrendered at Yorktown; governor-general of India 1786–93.

Coronado, Franciso Vasquez de (*c.* 1510–1554), Spanish explorer of south-western U.S.A.

Coronation Cup, Epsom, first run 1902.

Coronation Stone, placed in Westminster Abbey 1296 by King Edward I; stolen by Scottish Nationalists 1950; returned to Westminster 1951.

Corot, Jean Baptiste (1796–1875), French painter, notably of landscapes.

Corpus Christi, feast day, founded 1264 by Pope Urban IV; celebrated on the Thursday after Trinity Sunday.

Corpus Christi College, Cambridge University, founded by the united Guilds of Corpus Christi and of the Blessed Virgin Mary 1352.

Corpus Christi College, Oxford University, founded 1516 by the statesman Richard Foxe (1448–1528).

corpuscles, red. See **blood cells.**

Corpus Juris Civilis, Roman legal code, compiled at the Emperor Justinian I's orders 528–565.

Correggio, Antonio Allegri da (1494–1534), Italian artist, one of the leading painters of the Italian High Renaissance.

Corsica, ruled by Genoa 14th to 18th centuries; sold to France 1768; occupied by British 1794–96 and 1814–15; finally restored to France 1815.

Cort, Cornelis (*c.* 1536–1578), Dutch engraver, copied many old masters.

Cortés, Hernan (1485–1547), Spanish conqueror of Mexico 1519–21.

cortisone, isolated 1935 by the American chemist Edward C. Kendall (1886–1972); first medical usage 1948 by Kendall and Philip S. Hench (1896–1965).

Cortona, Pietro da (1596–1669), Italian artist, noted both as an architect and a painter in the Baroque manner.

Cortot, Alfred (1877–1962), French pianist and conductor, was also a notable teacher of music.

Corvo, Baron. See **Rolfe,** Frederick.

Coryate, Thomas (*c.* 1577–1617), English traveller in northern Europe, described in *Coryate's Crudities* (1611).

Cosa, Juan de la (*c.* 1460–1510), Spanish

navigator and geographer, made first large map of New World.

Cosgrave, William (1880–1965), Irish statesman, first president of the Irish Free State 1922–32.

cosmic rays, first detected about 1900; shown to originate beyond the Earth in the 1920s.

Costa, Lorenzo (c. 1460–1535), Italian painter of the school of Ferrara.

Costa Rica, discovered by Columbus 1502; region conquered by Spain 1530; achieved independence from Spanish rule 1821; joined Mexican Empire 1821 and Central American Federation 1824; completely independent 1848.

Cosway, Richard (c. 1742–1821), English miniaturist, painted many portraits of the nobility.

Cotman, John Sell (1782–1842), English painter and engraver, of the Norwich school.

Cotton, Charles (1630–87), English poet, wrote second part of Walton's *Compleat Angler* (1676).

Cotton, John (1584–1652), English puritan clergyman, influential spiritual leader in Massachusetts colony.

Cotton, Sir Robert Bruce (1571–1631), English collector of coins and medals, Cottonian Collection, now in British Museum.

cotton gin, for cleaning cotton invented 1793 by the American Eli Whitney (1765–1825).

Coué, Emile (1857–1926), French expert in hypnotism, favoured self-help method.

Coulomb, Charles Augustin de (1736–1806), French physicist, pioneered study of electrical attraction and repulsion.

Councils of Constantinople, 2nd Ecumenical Council, 381; 5th Ecumenical Council, 533; 6th Ecumenical Council, 680.

Council of Elders, French Revolutionary government, 1795–99.

Council of Europe, established 1949 at London Conference.

Council of Five Hundred, French Revolutionary government, 1795–99.

Council of Ten, Venetian cabal, set up 1310; abolished c. 1797.

Councils of Nicaea, 1st Ecumenical Council, 325; 7th Ecumenical Council, 787.

Counter-Reformation, within the Roman Catholic Church, began c. 1520; completed at the end of the 16th century.

Countess of Huntingdon's Connexion, Calvinist Methodist sect, founded in the 1740s.

County Hall, Westminster, main building constructed 1912–33; other buildings finally completed 1963, although occupied since 1939.

Couperin, François 'le Grand' (1668–1733), French composer, greatest of a distinguished family.

Couperus, Louis (1863–1923), Dutch writer, author of *The Small Souls*.

Coupon Election, British general election, held Dec. 1918, returned coalition government to power.

Courbet, Gustave (1819–77), French painter, led 19th-century realist movement in France.

Cournand, André Frédéric (b. 1895), French-born American physician, developed new techniques for the treatment of heart disease.

Courtauld, Samuel (1793–1881), English silk manufacturer, was a noted patron of the arts and music.

Courtauld Institute of Art, London, established 1932.

Courtrai, Battle of, victory of the Flemish over the French, July 1302.

Cousin, Jean (c. 1500–c. 1560) and his son, Jean Cousin the Younger (1522–94), French painters and designers, notably of stained glass windows.

Cousins, Samuel (1801–87), English engraver, especially of paintings by Sir Thomas Lawrence.

Cousteau, Jacques-Ives (b. 1910), French underwater explorer, invented aqualung.

Couthon, Georges (1755–94), French revolutionary, close associate of Robespierre; guillotined.

Coutts & Co., London banking house, founded by Thomas Coutts (1735–1822).

Covent Garden Theatre. See **Royal Opera House.**

Coventry Cathedral, built in the 15th century; destroyed by bombing 1940; new cathedral consecrated 1962.

Coverdale's Bible, translated into English by the English divine Miles Coverdale (1488–1569) and published 1535.

Coward, Sir Noël (1899–1973), English dramatist, actor and songwriter; *Private Lives* (1930) is the best known of his light, witty plays.

Cowell, Henry Dixon (1897–1966), American composer, noted for his avant-garde music.

Cowley, Abraham (1618–67), English poet, wrote *The Mistress* (1647).

Cowper, William (1731–1800), English poet, wrote *The Task* (1785).

Cox, David (1783–1859), English painter, chiefly of watercolour country scenes.

Coxwell, Henry Tracey (1819–1900), English balloonist, advised Prussians in War of 1870–71.

Coypel, Noël (1628–1707), French court painter of large-scale historical and religious works.

Cozens, John Robert (1752–97), English watercolourist, painted romantic Italian and Alpine scenes.

Crabbe, George (1754–1832), English poet, wrote realistic narratives, e.g. *The Village* (1770).

Crab Nebula, observed as an exploding star (supernova) 1054 by Chinese astronomers.

Craig, Edward Gordon (1872–1966), English theatre director and designer, son of Ellen Terry (*q.v.*).

Craigavon, James Craig, 1st Viscount (1871–1940), Ulster statesman, first prime minister of Northern Ireland 1921–40.

Craik, Dinah Maria (1826–87), English novelist, author of *John Halifax, Gentleman* (1857).

Cramer, Johann Baptist (1771–1858), German-born composer, pianist and music publisher, spent life in England.

Cranach, Lucas (1472–1553), German painter of erotic, elongated nudes; also a portraitist.

Cranbrook School, Kent, English public school, founded *c.* 1520.

Crane, Hart (1899–1932), American poet, wrote *The Bridge* (1930).

Crane, Stephen (1871–1900), American novelist and poet, author of *The Red Badge Of Courage* (1895).

Crane, Walter (1845–1915), English artist and illustrator, prominent in the aesthetic and socialist movements.

crane, hydraulic, invented *c.* 1845 by William George Armstrong (*q.v.*).

Cranleigh School, Surrey, English public school, founded 1863.

Cranmer, Thomas (1489–1556), archbishop of Canterbury during English Reformation; burnt at the stake.

Crashaw, Richard (*c.* 1613–1649), English religious poet, brilliant and ornate in style.

Crassus, Marcus Licinius (*c.* 115–52 B.C.), Roman political leader, triumvir with Pompey and Caesar; killed fighting Parthians.

Crawford, Francis Marion (1854–1909), American novelist, author of *Via Crucis* (1898).

Crébillon, Claude Prosper de (1707–77), French novelist, son of Prosper Crébillon, author of *Le Sopha* (1740).

Crébillon, Prosper de (1674–1762), French tragic dramatist, wrote *Catilina* (1748).

Crécy, Battle of, victory of the English over the French, 26 Aug. 1346.

Creevey, Thomas (1768–1838), English diarist, whose papers are important historical sources.

Cremona Cathedral, Italy, built 1107–1606.

creosote, discovered 1832 by the German manufacturer Baron von Reichenbach (1788–1869).

Crespi, Giuseppe Maria (1665–1747), Italian artist, called 'Lo Spagnuolo', noted for his genre paintings.

Cretaceous Period, Earth history, from *c.* 65 million to *c* 136 million years ago.

Crete, site of Minoan civilization *c.* 3000–*c.* 1400 B.C.; annexed by Rome 67 B.C.; part of Byzantine Empire; pirate centre in 9th century; ruled by Venetians 1204–1645 and by Turks 1645–1898; part of Greece since 1913; captured by German airborne troops 1941.

Crewe, Marquess of (1858–1945), English politician and diplomat, held many public offices.

Crichton, James (1560–82), Scottish polymath, known as 'the Admirable Crichton', remembered for the variety and brilliance of his attainments.

Crick, Francis Harry (b. 1916), English biologist, shared 1962 Nobel Prize for Physiology for his work on the function of deoxyribonucleic acid (DNA).

cricket, played in England since 13th century; M.C.C. founded 1787.

Crimean War, between Russia and the allied forces of Britain, France, Turkey and Sardinia, 1854–56.

Crippen, Dr Hawley Harvey (1861–1910), American-born wife-poisoner in England, arrested on transatlantic voyage; hanged.

Cripps, Sir Stafford (1889–1952), British statesman, chancellor of the exchequer 1947–50, the period of postwar austerity.

Crivelli, Carlo (*c.* 1434–*c.* 1493), Italian painter with unusual decorative style, e.g. *Annunciation* (1486).

Croatia, independent 924–1102; part of Hungary 1102–1918 and of Yugoslavia since 1918.

Croce, Benedetto (1866–1952), Italian philosopher in Idealist tradition; opposed Mussolini.

Crockett, Davy (1786–1836), American frontiersman of legendary skills, killed at the Alamo (*q.v.*).

Crockett, Samuel Rutherford (1860–1914), Scottish novelist, wrote *The Stickit Minister* (1893).

Croesus (d. *c.* 546 B.C.), king of Lydia *c.* 560–546 B.C., of proverbial wealth; defeated by Cyrus of Persia.

Croker, John Wilson (1780–1857), Irish writer and politician, noted for his rigidly conservative principles.

Crome, John (1768–1821), English landscape painter, most important of the Norwich school.

Cromer, Evelyn Baring, 1st Earl (1841–1917), British administrator, as consul general in Egypt 1883–1907 profoundly influenced that country's development.

Crompton, Richmal (1890–1969), English writer of 'Just William' boys' books.

Crompton's Mule, spinning machine, invented 1799 by the English spinner Samuel Crompton (1753–1827).

Cromwell, Oliver (1599–1658), English

statesman, Puritan leader and general, Lord Protector of England 1653–58.

Cromwell, Richard (1626–1712), Lord Protector of England 1658–59, son of Oliver Cromwell.

Cromwell, Thomas (c. 1485–1540), English statesman, chief minister of Henry VIII 1534–40 and architect of the Reformation in England; beheaded.

Cronin, Archibald Joseph (b. 1896), Scottish novelist, author of *Hatter's Castle* (1931).

Crookes, Sir William (1832–1919), English chemist and physicist, noted for his cathode-ray studies.

crossbow, first used in Europe in the late 11th century.

crossword puzzles, first introduced in England at the beginning of 19th century; first modern crossword appeared in an American newspaper Dec. 1913.

Crowley, Aleister (1875–1947), English self-styled magician, gained notoriety through his supposedly occult practices.

Cruden's Concordance, of the Bible, published 1737, compiled by Alexander Cruden (1701–70).

Cruikshank, George (1792–1878), English caricaturist and illustrator, drew pictures to illustrate *Oliver Twist* and *Grimm's Fairy Tales.*

Crusades, to recover Holy Sepulchre at Jerusalem: 1st 1096–99; 2nd 1147–48; 3rd 1189–92; 4th 1199–1204; 5th 1218–21; 6th 1227–29; 7th 1248–50; 8th 1270; last Crusader strongholds recaptured 1303.

Crystal Palace, designed by Sir Joseph Paxton (*q.v.*); erected in Hyde Park 1851; re-erected at Sydenham 1853–54; destroyed by fire 1936.

Cuba, discovered by Columbus 1492; conquest by Spanish begun 1511; achieved independence from Spain 1898; dictatorship overthrown by revolutionary movement 1959.

cube sugar, manufacturing process invented 1872 by the Englishman Sir Henry Tate (1819–99).

Cubism, art movement, founded in France c. 1907.

Cui, César (1835–1918), Russian composer, one of 'the Five', wrote ten operas.

Culford School, Suffolk, English public school founded as the East Anglian School 1881.

Cullinan diamond, found at Pretoria 1905; presented to Edward VII 1907.

Culloden, Battle of, near Inverness, in which the Jacobites under Prince Charles Edward Stuart were defeated by a British army, 16 April 1746 (last battle fought in Britain).

Culpeper's Herbal, published 1653, compiled by the English physician Nicholas Culpeper (1616–54).

Cumberland, Richard (1631–1718), English philosopher, wrote *De Legibus Naturae* (1672).

Cumberland, William Augustus, Duke of (1721–65), English soldier, son of George II, crushed Jacobites at Culloden; also a prominent military leader in the Seven Years' War.

Cummings, Edward Estlin (1894–1962), American poet, noted for his typographic and other idiosyncrasies.

Cunard, Sir Samuel (1787–1865), British manufacturer, established first regular transatlantic steamship service.

cuneiform, writing first deciphered c. 1835 by Sir Henry Rawlinson.

Cunha, Tristão da (c. 1460–c. 1540), Portuguese explorer in Africa and Asia; discovered Tristan da Cunha.

Cunningham, Alexander (d. 1574), Scottish noble, enthusiastic Protestant and opponent of Mary Queen of Scots.

Cunninghame Graham, Robert Bontine (1852–1936), Scottish traveller and travel writer, e.g. *Mogreb-el-Acksa* (1898).

Cunobelinus (d. c. A.D. 43), British king, was an ally of the Roman emperor Augustus.

Curaçao, island in Netherlands Antilles, discovered 1499; settled by Spanish 1527; became Dutch colony 1634.

Curé d'Ars. See **Vianney,** Jean-Marie.

Curie, Frédéric Joliot. See **Joliot-Curie,** Frédéric.

Curie, Marie (1867–1934), Polish-born French physicist, famous for her work on radioactivity and twice Nobel prizewinner.

Curie, Pierre (1859–1906), French physicist, husband of Marie, with whom he discovered radium.

curium, radioactive element discovered 1944 by Glenn T. Seaborg, Ralph A. James, and Albert Ghiorso.

Curll, Edmund (1675–1747), English bookseller and pamphleteer, involved in many dubious activities.

Curragh Incident, Ireland, March 1914.

Curran, John Philpott (1750–1817), Irish lawyer and politician, defended national and Catholic rights.

Currier, Nathaniel (1813–88), American lithographer, produced work of great documentary value in partnership with J. M. Ives.

Curtiss, Glenn Hammond (1878–1930), American aviator and aeroplane designer, pioneered amphibious aircraft.

Curzon, George Nathaniel, 1st Marquess (1859–1925), British statesman, viceroy of India 1898–1905 and foreign secretary 1919–24.

Cushing, Harvey (1869–1939), American surgeon, made a notable contribution to brain surgery.

Cust, Sir Lionel Henry (1859–1929), English art critic, director of National Portrait Gallery 1895–1909.

Custer, George Armstrong (1839–76), American cavalry officer, killed with all his men in battle with Indians at Little Big Horn, Montana.

Cuthbert, Saint (c. 635–687), English monk of holy life, bishop of Lindisfarne 685–687.

Cuvier, Baron Georges (1769–1832), French naturalist, founder of comparative anatomy.

Cuyp, Albert (1620–91), Dutch painter, famous for his landscapes.

cybernetics, theory of control and communication in man and machines, proposed 1948 by the American mathematician Norbert Weiner.

cyclotron, first successful machine built 1932 by the American physicists E. O. Lawrence (q.v.) and M. Stanley Livingston.

Cymbeline. See Cunobelinus.

Cynewulf (8th or 9th cent.), Anglo-Saxon religious poet, wrote *Juliana* and *Elene.*

Cyprian, Saint (c. 200–258) bishop of Carthage 248–258; Christian martyr.

Cyprus, colonized by Greeks c. 1000 B.C. and by Phoenicians from c. 800 B.C.; ruled successively by Assyrians, Persians and Romans; part of Byzantine Empire; captured during Third Crusade and ruled by Lusignan family 1192–1474; acquired by Venetians 1489; taken by Turks 1571; ceded to Britain 1878; made crown colony 1925; became an independent republic within the Commonwealth 1960.

Cyrano de Bergerac. See Bergerac Cyrano de.

Cyril, Saint (c. 827–869), and his brother Saint Methodius (826–885), Greeks from Thessalonica who Christianized the Slavs and reputedly invented the Cyrillic alphabet.

Cyril of Alexandria, Saint (d. 444), doctor of the Church, bishop and theologian, persecuted Novatians and Nestorians.

Cyril of Jerusalem, Saint (c. 315–386), bishop of Jerusalem, doctor of the Church.

Cyrus the Great (d. 529 B.C.), emperor of Persia 558–528, conquered Medes, Babylonians and Lydians.

Cyrus the Younger (c. 424–401 B.C.), Persian prince, led great revolt against Artaxerxes II; killed in battle.

Cyzicus, Naval Battle of, victory of Greeks under Alcibiades over the Spartans, 410 B.C.

Czechoslovakia, republic founded Oct. 1918; Sudetenland region annexed to Germany 1938; remainder became German Protectorate of Bohemia and Moravia 1939–45; coup established Communist People's Republic 1948; liberalized regime ended by Soviet invasion Aug. 1968.

Czermak, Jaroslav (1831–78), Bohemian painter of historical and rural scenes.

Czerny, Carl (1791–1857), Austrian composer, notably of piano studies.

D

Dabrowski, Jan Henryk (1755–1818), Polish soldier and national hero, fought against Russians and later for Napoleon.

Dachau, Bavaria, site of a Nazi concentration camp erected 1933.

Dadaism, art movement began 1915 in Zurich: ended c. 1922.

Dagobert I (d. 639), Frankish king 629–639, last Merovingian to hold effective power.

Daguerrotype process, developed 1826–39 by the French artist Louis Daguerre (1789–1851) and Nicéphore Niepce (q.v.).

Dahl, Michael (1656–1743), Swedish portrait painter, worked in London from 1688.

Dahlgren, John Adolphus (1809–70), American naval officer and ordnance expert, invented Dahlgren gun.

Dahomey. See Benin.

Daigo II (1287–1339), emperor of Japan 1318–39, ended domination of Kamakura shoguns.

Dáil Eireann, the Chamber of Deputies of the parliament of the Republic of Ireland, instituted 1922.

Daily Courant, first English daily newspaper, founded 1702; ran until 1735.

Daily Express, British newspaper, founded 1900 by C. Arthur Pearson.

Daily Graphic, British newspaper, founded 1890 by W. L. Thomas; absorbed by *Daily Sketch* 1925.

Daily Herald, British newspaper, began publication Jan. 1911; placed under joint control of Odhams and the T.U.C. 1930; ceased publication 1964.

Daily Mail, British newspaper, founded 1896 by Lord Northcliffe.

Daily Mirror, British newspaper, founded 1903 by Lord Northcliffe.

Daily News, British newspaper, founded 1846; merged with *News Chronicle* 1930.

Daily Sketch, British newspaper, founded 1909 by Edward Hulton; merged with *Daily Mail* 1971.

Daily Telegraph, British newspaper, founded June 1855.

Daily Worker. See *Morning Star.*

Daimler, Gottlieb (1834–1900), German automobile pioneer, whose firm produced Mercedes and Daimler engines.

Daladier, Édouard (1884–1970), French politician, prime minister 1933, 1934 and 1938–40; signed Munich Agreement 1938.

Dalai Lama, title of religious and secular leader of Tibet; present incumbent (b. c. 1935) fled to India 1959.

Dale, Sir Thomas (d. 1619), English administrator, ruled Virginia colony harshly 1611–16.

Dalhousie, Marquis of (1812–60), British statesman, governor-general of India 1848–56.

Dali, Salvador (b. 1904), Spanish painter, whose works are influenced by dream symbolism and the unconscious.

Dallapiccola, Luigi (b. 1904), Italian composer, whose work includes *Songs of Liberation* (1955).

Dalmatia, under effective Roman control 155 B.C.; invaded by Slavs 7th century A.D.; ruled by Venice 1480–1797; ruled by Austria intermittently 1797–1918; part of Yugoslavia since 1920; annexed to Italy 1941–45.

Dalton, John (1766–1844), English chemist and physicist, developed the modern atomic theory.

Damascus, captured by Assyrians 732 B.C.; part of empire of Alexander the Great 332 B.C.; occupied by Romans 63 B.C.; captured by Arabs A.D. 635; conquered by Ottoman Turks 1516; taken by T. E. Lawrence and Arabs 1918; capital of Syria since 1946.

Damasus I, Saint (*c.* 304–384), Pope 366–384, ordered Saint Jerome to compose the Vulgate.

Dame Allan's School, Newcastle-upon-Tyne, English public school, founded 1705.

Damão (Daman), India, discovered by Vasco da Gama 1498; under Portuguese rule from 1559; reintegrated with India 1962.

Damiani, Saint Pietro (*c.* 1007–1072), Italian ecclesiastical reformer, presided at Council of Milan 1059.

Damien, Father Joseph (1840–89), Belgian missionary, worked among lepers in Hawaii.

Damocles (4th cent. B.C.), sycophantic Greek courtier, forced to eat a banquet with a sword suspended by a single hair over his head.

Dampier, William (1652–1715), English buccaneer, explorer of northern coast of Australia.

Damrosch, Walter Johannes (1862–1950), German-born American conductor, founded Damrosch Opera Company.

Dana, Charles Anderson (1819–97), American journalist, edited New York *Sun* 1868–97.

Dana, Richard Henry (1815–82), American author of *Two Years Before the Mast* (1840).

Dance, George (d. 1768), English architect, built Mansion House, London.

Dance, George (1741–1825), English architect, son of George Dance, designed Newgate Prison.

Danegeld, tax first levied in England 991; finally abolished 1163.

Danelaw, Anglo-Saxon name applied to those parts of England settled by Danes in the 9th and 10th centuries.

Daniel, Samuel (1562–1619), English poet, author of *A defence of Rhyme* (1603).

Daniel Stewart's College, Edinburgh, Scottish public day school, founded 1855.

Daniell cell, invented 1836 by the English scientist John Frederic Daniell (1790–1845).

D'Annunzio, Gabriele (1863–1938), Italian poet, novelist and dramatist, author of *Il Fuoco* (1900).

Dantan, Joseph Édouard (1848–97), French painter of historical and religious scenes.

Dante Alighieri (1265–1321), Italian poet, the greatest of the Middle Ages, author of *The Divine Comedy*.

Danton, Georges Jacques (1759–94), French revolutionary leader, overthrown by Robespierre; guillotined.

Danube navigation, European Commission appointed under the Treaty of Paris 1856; International Commission appointed 1919; Danube Statute signed 23 Aug. 1921.

Danzig. See **Gdansk.**

Darby, Abraham (1678–1717), English ironmaster, was the first man to use coke to smelt iron.

Dardanelles Campaign, World War I, Feb. 1915 to Jan. 1916.

Darien, Panama, discovered by Spanish explorer Rodrigo de Bastidas 1501; object of 'Darien Scheme', unsuccessful Scottish overseas trading venture 1698–99.

Darío, Rubén (1867–1910), Nicaraguan poet, author of *Songs of Life and Hope* (1905).

Darius I (*c.* 548–486 B.C.), king of Persia 521–486 B.C., reorganized state and built Persepolis; defeated by Greeks at Marathon 490 B.C.

Darius II (d. 404 B.C.), king of Persia 423–405 B.C.; reign was troubled by revolts.

Darius III (d. 330 B.C.), king of Persia 336–330 B.C., conquered by Alexander the Great.

Darling, Grace (1815–42), English heroine of a sea rescue, 1838.

Darling river, Australia, discovered 1828 by the English explorer Charles Sturt (*q.v.*).

Darnley, Henry (1545–67), Scottish noble, husband of Mary Queen of Scots; murdered, probably with her connivance.

Dartmoor Prison, founded 1806; opened 1809 to house prisoners of war; used as a convict prison from *c.* 1850.

Dartmouth College, New Hampshire, founded 1769.

Dartmouth College. See **Royal Naval College.**

Darwin, Charles (1809–82), English biologist, developed theory of evolution in *Origin of Species* (1859).

Darwin, Erasmus (1731–1802), English physician and poet, author of *The Botanic Garden* (1792).

Dasent. Sir George Webbe (1817–96), English scholar, made translations from Norse.

Date Line. See **International Date Line.**

Daubigny, Charles François, (1817–74), French landscape painter, was a member of the Barbizon School.

Daudet, Alphonse (1840–97), French writer, author of *Tartarin de Tarascon* (1872).

Daughters of the American Revolution, founded as a national society 1890.

Daumier, Honoré (1808–79), French painter, graphic artist and sculptor.

Dauntsey's School, Wiltshire, English public school, founded by Alderman William Dauntsey 1543.

D'Avenant, Sir William (1606–68), English playwright and theatre manager, reputedly illegitimate son of Shakespeare.

Davenant porcelain, manufactured 1793–1882.

David (d. *c.* 970 B.C.), Hebrew king, united Judah and Israel and made Jerusalem his capital.

David, Saint (6th cent.), bishop of Menevia (now St David's), patron saint of Wales.

David I (1084–1153), king of Scotland 1124–53, twice unsuccessfully invaded England.

David II (1324–71), king of Scotland 1329–71, defeated and imprisoned by Edward III of England.

David, Gerard (*c.* 1450/60–1523), Flemish painter, worked much in Bruges.

David, Jacques Louis (1748–1825), French mythical, political and portrait painter, e.g. *Death of Marat*.

David, Pierre (David d'Angers; 1788–1856), French sculptor in Neoclassical style.

Davidson, Jo (1883–1952), American sculptor of famous people, e.g. *Marshal Foch*.

Davidson, Randall (1848–1930), archbishop of Canterbury 1903–28, previously Queen Victoria's chaplain.

Davies, (Sarah) Emily (1830–1921), English pioneer in higher education for women, founder of Girton College, Cambridge.

Davies, Sir John (1569–1626), English poet, wrote *Nosce Teipsum* (1599).

Davies, Sir Walford (1869–1941), English composer, influential in musical education.

Davies, William Henry (1871–1940), English poet, also wrote *Autobiography of a Super-tramp* (1908).

Davis, Dwight Filley (1879–1945), American politician and lawn tennis player, established the Davis Cup Competition.

Davis, Jefferson (1808–89), American statesman, president of the Confederate States of America 1861–65.

Davis, John (*c.* 1550–1605), English Arctic explorer, invented Davis's quadrant and discovered Davis Strait, Greenland, 1587.

Davis, Richard Harding (1864–1916), American war correspondent and novelist, author of *Soldiers of Fortune* (1897).

Davitt, Michael (1846–1906), Irish nationalist leader, organized Land League 1879, and United Irish League 1898.

Davy, Sir Humphry (1778–1829), English chemist, made an outstanding contribution to the advancement of science; invented miners' safety lamp 1815.

Dawes Plan, concerning German reparation payments after World War I, devised by the American statesman Charles Gates Dawes (1865–1951).

Dawson, Henry (1811–78), English painter, chiefly of landscapes.

day, mean solar 24 hr, 3 min, 56·6 sec; mean sidereal 23 hr, 56 min, 4 sec.

Day, John (1522–84), English printer, one of the earliest in England to print music.

Day, Thomas (1748–89), English writer, author of *Sandford and Merton* (1783–89).

Daye, Stephen (*c.* 1595–1668), English-born printer, first New England printer.

Day Lewis, Cecil (1904–72), English poet, created Poet Laureate 1968; author of *Collected Poems* (1954).

daylight saving, pioneered in Britain by William Willett (1856–1915); officially adopted 1916.

Day of Atonement. See **Yom Kippur.**

D-Day, World War II, 6 June 1944, when Allied forces landed in Normandy.

DDT (dichlorodiphenyl-trichloroethane), first synthesized 1874; discovered as an insecticide 1939 by the Swiss chemist Paul Hermann Uller (1899–1965).

Deadwood Dick (Richard W. Clarke; 1845–1930), English-born American frontiersman and stagecoach guard.

Dead Sea Scrolls, discovered at Khirbat Qumram, Jordan 1947.

Deaf and Dumb School, first British set up *c.* 1760 at Edinburgh by the Scottish teacher Thomas Braidwood (1715–1806).

Dean Close School, Cheltenham, English public school, founded 1884 in memory of Dean Francis Close (1797–1882).

death duties, revived in England 1894.

Debrett's Peerage, first published 1802 by the English publisher John Debrett (*c.* 1752–1822).

Debs, Eugene (1855–1926), American socialist leader, was five times candidate for the presidency.

Debussy, Claude Achille (1862–1918),

French composer, founded Impressionist school in music: *L'Après-midi d'un faune* (1894), *La Mer* (1905).

Decatur, Stephen (1779–1820), American naval commander, saw distinguished service in the War of 1812.

Decembrists, Russian conspirators involved in the revolt in Dec. 1825 over the accession of Tsar Nicolas I.

decimal coinage, first used in modern form in America 1792; first adopted in Europe (France) 1799; adopted in Britain 1971.

decimal numbers, first used by ancient Hindu and Islamic mathematicians; use in Europe first established by Simon Stevinus (1548–1620).

Decius (A.D. 201–251), Roman emperor 249–251, persecuted Christians.

Declaration of Independence, American Revolution, adopted 4 July 1776.

Declaration of Rights, issued by Parliament Feb. 1689.

Decree of Union (Laetentur caeli), uniting the Latin and Greek Churches, issued 6 July 1439.

Dee, John (1527–1608), English mathematician and philosopher, enjoyed a reputation as an alchemist and astrologer.

Defender of the Faith, English royal title first bestowed by Pope Leo X on Henry VIII 1521; confirmed by Parliament 1544.

Defenestration of Prague, 23 May 1618.

Deffand, Marquise du (1697–1780), leading figure in French society, remembered for her friendships and correspondence with famous men.

Defoe, Daniel (*c.* 1660–1731), English writer, often called first true novelist, author of *Robinson Crusoe* (1719).

Degas, Edgar (1834–1917), French painter, especially of nudes, and ballet and horse-racing scenes.

De Gasperi, Alcide (1881–1954), Italian statesman, as prime minister 1945–53 played a major part in creating western European unity.

De Gaulle, Charles (1890–1970), French soldier and statesman, led Free French in World War II; president of France 1945–46 and 1958–69.

De Havilland, Sir Geoffrey (1882–1965), English aircraft designer, produced the first commercial jet airliner.

dehydration of food, first extensively employed during the American Civil War.

Dekker, Thomas (*c.* 1572–*c.* 1632), English playwright, wrote comedy *The Shoemaker's Holiday* (1599).

De Kooning, Willem (b. 1904), American painter, leading figure in Abstract Expressionist movement in U.S.A.

Delacroix, Eugène (1798–1863), French Romantic painter, e.g., *The Death of Sardanapalus* (1827).

De la Mare, Walter (1873–1956), English poet, author of *The Listeners* (1912).

Delane, John Thaddeus (1817–79), English journalist, edited *The Times* 1841–77.

de la Roche, Mazo (1879–1961), Canadian novelist, author of the 'Whiteoak family' series.

Delaroche, Paul (1797–1856), French painter of historical and anecdotal subjects.

de la Rue, Thomas (1793–1866), English manufacturer, founded well-known playing card and paper firm.

de la Rue, Warren (1815–89), English astronomer, photographed sun and moon.

Delaware, U.S.A., first settled by Dutch 1631; captured by English 1664; part of Pennsylvania until 1776; entered the Union as one of the 13 original states 1787.

De La Warr, Thomas, Lord (1577–1618), English governor of Virginia 1610–18.

Delcassé, Théophile (1852–1923), French statesman, largely responsible for the 'Entente Cordiale' with Britain.

Deledda, Grazia (1875–1936), Italian novelist, awarded Nobel Prize for Literature.

Delibes, Léo (1836–91), French composer, notably of ballet music.

Delius, Frederick (1862–1934), English composer, was a leading figure in the English musical revival.

della Robbia, Luca. See **Robbia,** Luca della.

Delorme, Philibert (*c.* 1512–1570), French architect, built château of Anet.

Delphin Classics, published by the French printer François Didot (1730–1804).

Demetrius I (337–283 B.C.), king of Macedon 294–288 B.C., fought numerous wars against Ptolemies and Seleucids.

Demetrius II (d. 229 B.C.), king of Macedon 239–229 B.C., fought against leagues of Greek states.

Demetrius I (*c.* 187–150 B.C.), king of Syria 162–150 B.C., conquered Babylonia.

Demetrius II (d. 125 B.C.), king of Syria 145–139 B.C. and 129–125 B.C.; continuously involved in civil war.

Demetrius III (d. *c.* 88 B.C.), king of Syria 95–88 B.C., died while a Parthian prisoner.

De Mille, Cecil Blount (1881–1959), American film director, chiefly concerned with epic historical or religious themes, such as in *The Ten Commandments* (1956).

Democratic Party, U.S.A., founded by Thomas Jefferson (*q.v.*) 1792.

Democritus (*c.* 470/60–*c.* 370 B.C.), Greek philosopher, put forward a form of atomic theory.

Demoivre, Abraham (1667–1754), French-born mathematician, in England as refugee 1688–1754.

De Morgan, Augustus (1806–71), English logician, wrote *Budget of Paradoxes* (1872).

De Morgan, William Frend (1839–1917), English ceramic artist, who was also a successful novelist; the son of Augustus de Morgan.

Demosthenes (c. 384–322 B.C.), Athenian orator whose *Philippics* attacked Philip of Macedon; committed suicide when his enemies triumphed.

Denikin, Anton (1872–1947), Russian soldier, led anti-Bolshevik forces after Russian Revolution.

Denmark, settled by Danes 5th–6th centuries A.D.; became a kingdom 10th century; united with Norway and Sweden 1397; ceded Norway to Sweden 1814; adopted new constitution 1953; joined E.E.C. 1972.

Dennis, John (1657–1734), English playwright, wrote *Appius and Virginia* (1709).

Denstone College, Staffordshire, English public school, founded 1868.

deoxyribonucleic acid. See **DNA.**

De Paul University, Chicago, founded 1898.

De Pauw University, Indiana, founded 1837 as the Indiana Asbury College; assumed present name 1884.

Deposition, Bull of, 1st issued by Pope Paul III excommunicating King Henry VIII, 1535; 2nd issued by Pope Pius V excommunicating Queen Elizabeth I, 1570.

Deprès, Josquin (c. 1440–1521), Flemish composer, noted for his church music, including motets, masses and psalms.

Depression, The, began in U.S.A. at the end of 1929.

De Quincey, Thomas (1785–1859), English essayist, wrote *Confessions of an English Opium-Eater* (1822).

Derain, André (1880–1954), French painter, best known for 'Fauve' works in bold colours.

Derby, Epsom Downs, first run 4 May 1780.

Derby, Earl of (1799–1869), English statesman, was three times prime minister: 1852, 1858–59, and 1866–68.

Derby-Chelsea porcelain, manufactured 1770–84.

Derby porcelain, first manufactured 1750.

Desai, Morarji (b. 1896), Indian statesman, prime minister of India since 1977.

Descartes, René (1596–1650), French philosopher, and mathematician, made an outstanding contribution to philosophical method and invented co-ordinate geometry.

De Saussure, Ferdinand (1857–1913), Swiss scholar, pioneer of modern linguistics.

Desmoulins, Camille (1760–94), French revolutionary leader, associate of Danton; guillotined during Terror.

de Soto, Hernan (c. 1496–1542), Spanish explorer of Florida, reached Mississippi.

Despard's Plot, to assassinate King George III, devised by the English officer Edward Marcus Despard, executed with other conspirators 1803.

Despenser, Hugh le (d. 1326), English favourite of Edward II; hanged by rebels.

determinants, mathematical theory originated 1693 by G. W. Leibniz (*q.v.*); developed in the 1770s by the French mathematicians Alexandre Vaudermonde and Pierre-Simon Laplace (*q.v.*).

Detroit University, Michigan, founded 1877.

deuterium. See **heavy hydrogen.**

De Valera, Eamon (1882–1975), Irish statesman, a leading figure in his country's fight for independence, three times prime minister of the Republic of Ireland and president 1959–72.

de Valois, Dame Ninette (b. 1898), Irish dancer and choreographer, director of the Vic-Wells (later Royal) Ballet.

de Vere, Aubrey (1814–1902), Irish poet, precursor of Irish literary revival.

Devil's Island, French Guiana, used as a penal settlement 1854–1938.

De Vinne, Theodore Low (1828–1914), American printer, pioneer of improved design.

Devolution, War of, enforcing the Queen of France's claim to parts of the Spanish Netherlands, 1667–68.

Devonian Period, Earth history, from c. 345 million to c. 359 million years ago.

De Vries, David Pietersen (17th cent.), Dutch pioneer in America, established Staten Island colony.

dew, scientifically investigated 1814 by the American-born doctor Charles Wells (1757–1817).

Dewar, Sir James (1842–1923), Scottish chemist and physicist, inventor of the vacuum flask and (with Sir Frederick Abel) cordite.

De Wet, Christiaan Rudolf (1854–1922), Boer general in South African War and anti-British leader in World War I.

Dewey, John (1859–1952), American philosopher, psychologist, and educationalist, noted for his pragmatic philosophy.

Dewy, Melvil (1851–1931), American inventor of the Dewey Decimal system of library classification.

de Wint, Peter (1784–1849), English landscape painter, often in watercolours.

De Witt, Jan (1625–72), Dutch statesman, leader of anti-Orange party; killed by mob.

Diabelli, Anton (1781–1858), Austrian music publisher and composer, created waltz theme for Beethoven's *Diabelli Variations*.

diabetes. See **insulin.**

Diaghilev, Sergei (1872–1929), Russian impresario, introduced Russian ballet to Western Europe.

diagnosis, medical, established by Thomas Sydenham (*q.v.*) in the 1650s.

Diamond Necklace Affair, involving Queen Marie Antoinette, took place 1785–86.

diamonds, carbon composition demonstrated 1796; first synthesized 1880 by the Scottish chemist James Hannay; commercially produced since 1960.

Diaz, Bartholomew (d. 1500), Portuguese explorer, discovered Cape of Good Hope 1488.

Diaz, Porfirio (1830–1915), Mexican statesman, president 1877–80 and 1888–1911, brought his country peace and stability.

Dibdin, Charles (1745–1814), English songwriter, wrote many sea shanties, including *Tom Bowling*.

Dicey, Albert Venn (1835–1922) English jurist, noted for his work on constitutional law.

Dickens, Charles (1812–70), major English novelist, author of many famous works including *David Copperfield* (1849–50) and *Great Expectations* (1861).

Dickinson, Emily (1830–86), American poet, wrote short lyrics of great intensity.

dictaphone, invented by the American electrician Charles Tainter (1854–1940).

Dictionary of American Biography, published 1872; compiled by Francis Samuel Drake (1828–75).

Dictionary of National Biography, British, published 1885–1900 by George Smith (1824–1901), with later supplements.

Diderot, Denis (1713–84), French philosopher and writer, chief editor of the famous *Encyclopaedia*.

Didius Julianus, Marcus (A.D. 133–193), Roman emperor A.D. 193, bought empire from Praetorian Guard; overthrown almost immediately.

Diemen, Antony van (1593–1645), Dutch colonial administrator, governor-general of Dutch East Indies 1636–45, originated expedition which discovered Van Diemen's Land (Tasmania).

Diesel, Rudolf (1858–1913), German engineer, patented in 1892 the internal-combustion engine which bears his name.

diesel-engined ship, first vessel, the *Selandia*, launched 1912 at Copenhagen.

Dieskau, Dietrich Fischer. See **Fischer-Dieskau,** Dietrich.

Diet of Worms, concerning Martin Luther's actions and writings, held 1521.

Dietrich, Marlene (b. *c.* 1901), German actress and singer in America, first achieved fame with *The Blue Angel* (1930).

differential equations, first studied in the 1690s by Jakob and Johann Bernoulli (*q.v.*), and by Gottfrid Leibniz (*q.v.*).

differential motor gear, invented 1827 by the Frenchman Onésiphore Pecqueur.

Digby, Sir Kenelm (1603–65), English diplomat, writer and courtier, had an eccentric political career; author of *Memoirs* (1827).

Diggers, group of English communists led by Gerrard Winstanley, active 1648–52.

digital computer. See **computer.**

Dilke, Sir Charles (1843–1911), English politician of radical and republican views; ruined by involvement in a divorce case.

Dillinger, John (1902–34), American gangster, specialized in bank robberies.

Dilthey, Wilhelm (1833–1911), German philosopher, noted for his works on literary criticism and the history of ideas.

Dimitrov, Georgi (1882–1949), Bulgarian Communist, one of the accused in Reichstag Fire Trial; prime minister of Bulgaria 1946–49.

Dingaan's Day, South African anniversary commemorating the rout of the Zulu chief Dingaan 16 Dec. 1838.

Diniz (1261–1325), king of Portugal 1271–1325, improved agriculture and was a patron of the arts.

Dio Cassius (*c.* 155–*c.* 230), Roman historian, wrote a vast history of Rome.

Diocletian (245–313), Roman emperor 284–305, introduced far-reaching administrative and financial reforms.

diode valve, invented 1904 by Sir John Ambrose Fleming (*q.v.*).

Diodorus Siculus (1st cent. B.C.), Greek historian, wrote universal history of which 15 books have survived.

Diogenes (*c.* 412–323 B.C.), Greek Cynic philosopher, who, according to legend, lived in a tub.

Dionysius, Saint, Pope 259–268, reorganized Church.

Dionysius Exiguus (d. 560), Scythian monk, made birth of Christ starting point of modern chronology.

Dionysius the Elder (*c.* 430–367 B.C.), Greek tyrant, ruler of Syracuse 405–367 B.C.

Dionysius Thrax (2nd–1st cent. B.C.), Greek grammarian, author of the first Greek grammar.

Dioscorides, Pedanios (1st cent. A.D.), Greek physician, author of a work on remedial substances used in medicine.

diphtheria, antitoxin, discovered 1890 by the German bacteriologist Emil von Behring (1854–1917); made effective by a technique of Paul Ehrlich (*q.v.*).

Dirac, Paul Adrien Maurice (b. 1902), English physicist, best known for his work in quantum mechanics.

Disney, Walt (1901–66), American pioneer of animated cartoon films, e.g. *Snow White* (1938).

Disraeli, Benjamin (1804–81), British statesman, prime minister 1868 and 1874–80; as a novelist author of *Coningsby* (1844).

D'Israeli, Isaac (1766–1848), English writer, author of *Curiosities of Literature*; father of Benjamin Disraeli.

Dissolution of the Monasteries. See **Monasteries,** Dissolution of.

District Line, London. See **Metropolitan District Railway.**

District Nursing Movement, introduced in Britain 1859 by the English philanthropist William Rathbone (1819–1902).

Dittersdorf, Karl Ditters von (1739–99), Austrian violinist and composer of popular operattas.

divorce, for grounds other than adultery, made legal in England 1937.

Djibouti, East Africa, acquired by France 1862–85; made a French overseas territory 1946; voted against independence 1967 when name changed from French Somaliland to Afars and Issas; became independent 1977.

Djilas, Milovan (b. 1911), Yugoslav political theorist, imprisoned 1956–66 for his criticism of Yugoslav Communism.

DNA, first isolated 1869; shown to be genetic material 1944; double helix structure proposed 1953 by the American biochemist James Watson (b. 1928) and the English physicist Francis Crick (b. 1916).

Dobson, Austin (1840–1921), English poet, wrote *Vignettes in Rhyme* (1873).

docking of horses' tails, prohibited by law in Britain since 1948.

Doctor Wall (Worcester) porcelain, manufactured 1751–83.

Doctor's Commons, founded 1568; incorporated 1768; dissolved 1857.

dodo, became extinct *c.* 1680.

Dod's Parliamentary Companion, founded 1832 by the Irish journalist Charles Dod (1793–1855).

Dodsley, Robert (1703–64), English publisher, important as an anthologist.

Doggett's Coat and Badge Prize, Thames rowing competition, founded 1715 by the English actor Thomas Doggett (d. 1721).

Dohnányi, Ernst von (1877–1960), Hungarian composer and folklorist, in U.S.A. 1949–60.

Dolabella (*c.* 70–43 B.C.), Roman general, changed sides several times in civil wars.

Dolci, Danilo (b. 1924), Italian social worker among poor in Sicily, wrote *Waste* (1963).

dole, unemployment payments in Britain, first so named by the *Daily Mail* 1919.

dollar, first issued in U.S.A. *c.* 1794.

Dollfuss, Englebert (1892–1934), chancellor of Austria 1932–34, assassinated by Austrian Nazis.

Döllinger, Johann (1799–1890), German church historian and Catholic theologian, refused to accept doctrine of papal infallibility.

Dolmetsch, Eugene Arnold (1858–1940), Swiss-born musician living in England, noted for his revival of early musical instruments.

Domagk, Gerhard (1895–1964), German chemist, Nobel prizewinner 1939 (refused on government orders).

Domenichino, Il (1581–1664), Italian painter, studied under Carracci, remembered for his landscape paintings.

Domenico, Veneziano (*c.* 1400–1461), Florentine painter, best known for an altarpiece.

Domesday Book, record of William the Conqueror's survey of England during 1085–86.

Dominica, West Indies, discovered by Columbus 1493; settled by French in 18th century; ceded to Britain 1783; administratively part of Windward Islands since 1940; internally self-governing since 1967.

Dominican Order, founded 1216 by Saint Dominic (*c.* 1170–1221).

Dominican Republic, West Indies, discovered by Columbus 1492; achieved independence from Spanish rule 1821; republic founded 1844.

Dominion Day, Canada, celebrated 1 July.

Domitian (A.D. 51–96), Roman emperor A.D. 81–96, persecuted Jews and Christians; assassinated.

Donatello (*c.* 1386–1466), Italian Renaissance sculptor, e.g. bronze *David*.

Donatus, Aelius (4th cent. A.D.), Roman grammarian, whose treatises became standard textbooks in the Middle Ages.

Dongan, Thomas, Earl of Limerick (1634–1715), Irish-born governor of New York 1682–88.

Dönitz, Karl (b. 1891), German naval officer, Nazi supreme commander for a few days in May 1945 after Hitler's death.

Donizetti, Gaetano (1797–1848), Italian opera composer, e.g. *Lucia di Lammermoor* (1835).

Donne, John (1572–1631), English metaphysical poet, also dean of St Paul's.

Donnybrook Fair, Ireland, licensed by King John 1204; discontinued 1855.

Doolittle, Hilda (1886–1961), American imagist poet, author of *Red Roses for Bronze* (1931).

Doppler effect, predicted 1842 by the Austrian physicist Christian Doppler (1803–53).

Doré, Gustave (1833–83), French artist and illustrator of London life.

Doria, Andrea (*c.* 1468–1560), Genoese admiral and statesman, fought against the Turks and Barbary pirates.

Dorr's Rebellion, to extend suffrage to Rhode Island, led 1841 by the American politician Thomas Dorr (1805–54).

Dort, Synod of, held to discuss the Arminian heresy, 1618–19.

Dortmund-Ems canal, Germany, constructed 1892–99.

Dos Passos, John Roderigo (1896–1970), American novelist, wrote the trilogy *U.S.A.* (1930–36).

Dost Mohammed Khan (1793–1863), ruler of Afghanistan, founded dynasty which lasted until 1929.

Dostoyevsky, Feodor (1821–81), Russian novelist of unsurpassed spiritual intensity, authors of *Brothers Karamazov* (1880).

Douai Bible, first English Catholic translation, published 1582 (New Testament) and 1609 (Old Testament).

Douai School, Woolhampton, English public school, founded 1615; at Douai 1818–1903; transferred to Woolhampton 1903.

double refraction, theory developed 1810 by the French physicist Étienne-Louis Malus (1775–1812).

Doughty, Charles Montagu (1843–1926), English explorer in Arabia, wrote *Arabia Deserta* (1888).

Douglas, David (1798–1834), Scottish botanist, introduced many plant species into Britain from North America.

Douglas, Gavin (c. 1475–1522), Scottish poet and bishop, best known for his translation of the *Aeneid.*

Douglas, Sir James (c. 1286–1330), Scottish warrior, 'Black Douglas', a scourge of the English.

Douglas, Norman (1868–1952), Scottish writer, chiefly about Italy, e.g. in *South Wind* (1917).

Douglas-Home, Sir Alec (b. 1903), British statesman, prime minister 1963–64 after renouncing peerage.

Douglass, Frederick (1817–95), American Negro journalist, was a notable orator and campaigner against slavery.

Dounreay, Scotland, site of a fast-breeder nuclear reactor opened 1959.

Dover, Treaty of, to re-establish Catholicism in England, signed between Charles II and Louis XIV 1670.

Dover College, English public school, opened 1871.

Dowland, John (1663–1626), English composer, especially of lute songs; worked in several European countries.

Downing College, Cambridge University, founded by will of Sir George Downing (1684–1749); chartered 1800.

Downside School, Bath, English public school, founded at Douai c. 1606; transferred to Britain 1790, and to Downside 1814.

Doyle, Sir Arthur Conan (1859–1930), English novelist, created the character of Sherlock Holmes.

Doyle, Richard (1824–83), English caricaturist, illustrated Dickens and Thackeray; designed *Punch* cover.

D'Oyly Carte, Richard (1844–1901), English impresario who staged the Gilbert and Sullivan operettas.

Draco (7th cent. B.C.), Athenian statesman, noted for the severity of his code of laws.

dragonnades, persecution of French Protestants by forcibly quartering soldiers upon them; begun 1681; extended to whole of France 1685.

drainage system, London, designed and constructed 1859–65 and completed 1875 by the civil engineer Sir Joseph Bazalgette (1819–91).

Drake, Sir Francis (c. 1540–1596), English admiral, the most famous of the Elizabethan seamen.

Draper, John William (1811–82), English-born American scientist, noted for his work on photochemistry.

Draper, Ruth (1884–1956), American actress, famous for her monologues.

Dreadnoughts, heavily armed warships, launched by Royal Navy 1906.

Dreiser, Theodore (1871–1945), American novelist, author of *An American Tragedy* (1925).

Dresden china, originated c. 1710 by Johann Friedrich Böttger (*q.v.*).

Dreyfus, Alfred (1859–1935), French artillery officer, sent to Devil's Island after wrongful conviction of treason; anti-semitism delayed complete rehabilitation until 1906.

Drinkwater, John (1882–1937), English dramatist, poet and critic, author of *Abraham Lincoln* (1918).

drive-in bank, first American, 1946; first British, 1959.

Drogheda, Ireland, sacked by Cromwell Sept. 1649.

Drummond, Thomas (1797–1840), Scottish engineer, improved surveying equipment.

Drummond, William Henry (1854–1907), Canadian poet, author of *The Habitant* (1897).

Drummond of Hawthornden, William (1585–1649), Scottish poet, also wrote prose *Cypresse Grove* (1623).

Drury Lane theatres, London, opened 1663, 1674, 1794, 1812.

Druses, heretical Muslim sect originating in the 11th century; followers of the Egyptian caliph al-Hakim (996–1044).

Dryden, John (1631–1700), English poet, dramatist and critic, a dominant literary figure of the late 17th century.

dry ice, solid carbon dioxide, first produced commercially c. 1927.

Du Barry, Marie, Comtesse (1743–93), mistress of King Louis XV of France; guillotined during Revolution.

du Bartas, Guillaume (1544–90), French poet, wrote the encyclopedic *La Semaine* (1578).

Dubček, Alexander (b. 1921), Czechoslovak politician, whose attempts to liberalize the country's Communist regime led to Soviet intervention.

du Bellay, Joachim (1522–60), French poet, one of the 'Pléiade' group, and a leading figure in French Renaissance poetry.

Dubois, Guillaume (1656–1723), French statesman and cardinal, virtual ruler of France during the Regency, 1715–23.

Duccio di Buoninsegna (c. 1255–c. 1319), Italian painter, founded the Sienese school.

Duchamp, Marcel (1887–1968), French painter, played an important part in the development of modern art.

Dudintsev, Vladimir (b. 1918), Russian novelist, author of *Not by Bread Alone* (1956).

duel, last fought in England at Priest Hill, Egham, Surrey, 1852.

Dufy, Raoul (1877–1953), French painter, often of brightly coloured outdoor scenes.

Dugdale, Sir William (1605–86), English antiquarian writer and Garter King of Arms, wrote *Baronage of England* (1675).

Du Guesclin, Bertrand (c. 1320–1380), French soldier, was an outstanding military leader in the Hundred Years' War.

Duhamel, Georges (1884–1966), French novelist, wrote the 10-volume *Pasquier Chronicle* (1933–45).

Dukas, Paul, French composer, wrote *The Sorcerer's Apprentice* (1897).

Duke University, North Carolina, founded as Union Institute 1838; assumed present name 1924.

Dulles, John Foster (1888–1959), American statesman, secretary of state 1953–59.

Dulwich College, English public school, founded 1619 as 'The College of God's Gift' by Edward Alleyn (*q.v.*).

Dumas, Alexandre, *père* (1802–70), French writer, notably of historical romances such as *The Three Musketeers* and *The Count of Monte-Cristo*.

Dumas, Alexandre, *fils* (1824–95), French writer, son of Alexandre Dumas, author of *La Dame aux Camélias* (1848).

Du Maurier, George (1834–96), English artist and novelist, drew for *Punch* and wrote *Trilby* (1894).

Dumbarton Oaks Conference, at which the foundations of the United Nations were laid, held Washington, D.C., 1944.

dumdum bullets, use banned by the Hague Conference July 1899.

Dumont, d'Urville, Jules (1790–1842), French navigator, explored Antarctica and discovered Adélie Land.

Dumouriez, Charles François (1739–1823), French revolutionary general, deserted after winning notable victories.

Dunant, Henri (1828–1910), Swiss founder of the International Red Cross 1864.

Dunbar, Battle of, victory of the English over the Scots, 3 Sept. 1650.

Dunbar, William (c. 1460–c. 1522), Scottish poet, best known for *Lament for the Makaris*.

Duncan, Isadora (1878–1927), American dancer whose free improvisatory style influenced modern development.

Duncan-Rubbra, Edmund. See **Rubbra,** Edmund Duncan.

Dunes, Battle of, Dunkirk, victory of the French over the Spanish, 14 June 1658.

Dunham, Katherine (b. 1914), American Negro dancer and choreographer, made extensive use of Caribbean dance rhythms.

Dunkirk, evacuation of, World War II, May–June 1940.

Dunlop, John Boyd (1814–1921), Scottish inventor, patented pneumatic bicycle tyre 1888.

Dunmow Flitch Trial, held at Great Dunmow, Essex, every second August Bank Holiday Monday; ceremony originated in 12th century; revived 1835.

Dunsany, Lord (1878–1957), Irish dramatist, and story writer, author of *Travel Tales of Mr Joseph Jorkens* (1931).

Duns Scotus (c. 1266–1308), Scottish philosopher, founded Scotist school in opposition to Thomists.

Dunstan, Saint (c. 910–988), archbishop of Canterbury 961–988; earlier made Glastonbury great monastic centre.

Dupes, Day of, when Cardinal Richelieu of France foiled attempts to dismiss him, 11 Nov. 1630.

Dupleix, Joseph (1697–1763), French governor-general in India, resisted British but recalled to France 1754.

Durand Line, defining the frontier between India and Afghanistan, determined 1893.

Dürer, Albrecht (1471–1528), German painter and engraver, leading Renaissance artist in Germany.

Durham, Lord (1792–1840), British statesman, governor-general of Canada 1838–39, wrote constitutionally important *Report* (1839).

Durham School, English public school, founded 1414 by Cardinal Thomas Langley (d. 1437).

Durham University, founded by William van Mildert, Bishop of Durham, 1832.

Durkheim, Emile (1858–1917), French sociologist, pioneered methodology in *Rules of Sociological Method* (1895).

Durrell, Lawrence (b. 1912), English poet and novelist, wrote the 'Alexandria Quartet' of novels (1957–60).

Dürrenmatt, Friedrich (b. 1921), Swiss dramatist, author of *The Physicists* (1962).

Duse, Eleanora (1859–1924), Italian actress, notable for her performances in Ibsen's plays.

Dussek, Johann Ladislaus (1761–1812), Czech pianist and composer, especially of piano music.

dust wrappers, for books, first used in Britain 1832; came into general use in the 1890s.

Dutch Guiana. See Surinam.

Duvalier, François (1907–71), Haitian politician, dictator of Haiti 1957–71.

Duveen, Sir Joseph Joel (1843–1908), Dutch-born art dealer in England, contributed to National and Tate Gallery collections.

Dvořak, Antonin (1841–1904), Czech composer, achieved international fame with his symphonic works.

dyes, used by man for probably over 15,000 years. See also **mauveine**.

dynamite, patented in Britain 1867 by Alfred Nobel (*q.v.*).

dynamo, invented 1823 by the English electrician William Sturgeon (1783–1850).

dysentery, bacillus first isolated by the Danish scientist, C. Sonne 1915.

dysprosium, chemical element, first isolated 1886 by the French scientist Paul-Emile Lecoq de Boisbaudran (1838–1912).

E

Eagles, Solomon (1618–83), English Quaker, active in West Indies and New England.

Earhart, Amelia (1898–1937), American aviator, first woman to fly the Atlantic (1928).

Earle, John (*c.* 1601–1665), English writer of *Microcosmographie* (1628).

Early Bird. See satellite communications.

Earth, age of, estimated 1795 as many millions of years by the Scottish naturalist James Hulton (1726–97); reaffirmed in 1830s by the English geologist Sir Charles Lyell (1797–1875); accurately determined following discovery of radioactivity (1896); now taken as *c.* 4,600 million years.

Earth, circumference of, first estimated *c.* 230 B.C. by Eratosthenes (*q.v.*).

Earth, circumnavigation of, 1518–22, by a Spanish expedition led by Magellan (*q.v.*).

Earth, creation of, date calculated by the Irish archbishop James Ussher (1581–1656) as 22 Oct. 4004 B.C.

Earth, density of (and hence mass of) accurately measured 1798 by Henry Cavendish (*q.v.*).

Earth, magnetism of, first described 1600 by William Gilbert (*q.v.*).

Earth, shape of (oblate spheroid), measured by two expeditions led in 1735 by the Frenchman Charles Marie de la Condamine (1701–74) and in 1736 by Pierre Maupertuis (*q.v.*).

earthquakes, major, Lisbon 1755, San Francisco 1906, Tokyo 1923, Agadir and Chile 1960, Yugoslavia 1963, Turkey 1966, Peru 1970, China 1976, Guatemala 1976, Romania 1977.

East, Sir Alfred (1849–1913), English painter of landscapes and graphic artist.

East African Community, providing for cooperation between Kenya, Uganda and Tanzania, formed 1967; it replaced the East African Common Services Organization, founded 1961, which succeeded the East Africa High Commission, established 1948.

Eastbourne College, English public school, founded 1867 by the 7th Duke of Devonshire.

Easter, Christian Feast of the Resurrection, celebrated on the first Sunday after the first full moon after the Vernal Equinox.

East India Company, first chartered 1600; dissolved 1858.

Easter Island, Pacific, discovered by the Dutch admiral Jakob Roggeveen 1722.

Eastlake, Sir Charles Lock (1793–1865), English painter, first director of National Gallery, London, 1855–65.

Eastman, George (1854–1932), American pioneer of improved photographic equipment.

East Prussia, former German province, partitioned between Poland and the U.S.S.R. 1945.

Eberlein, Gustav (1847–1926), German sculptor of monumental works.

Ebers, Georg (1837–98), German novelist, author of *Kleopatra* (1894).

Ebert, Friedrich (1871–1925), German statesman, first president of the Weimar Republic 1919–25.

ebonite, discovered 1839 and first patented 1844 by the American Charles Goodyear (1800–60).

Echegaray, José (1832–1916), Spanish dramatist, won Nobel Prize for Literature 1904.

Echeverría, Esteban (1809–51), Argentine poet, initiated Romantic movement in Argentine literature.

Echo, British newspaper, founded 1876 by John Passmore Edwards (1823–1911); ceased publication 1905.

Eckermann, Johann Peter (1792–1854), German writer, whose *Conversations with Goethe* (1836–48) are a valuable record.

Eckener, Hugo (1868–1954), German aeronautical engineer, was a noted airship designer.

Eckert, John Prosper (b. 1919), American electrical engineer, with J. W. Maunchly designed the first electronic computer.

Eckhart, Johannes (*c.* 1260–*c.* 1327) German mystic and theologian, whose pantheistic philosophy influenced the development of mysticism.

Eclipse Stakes, Sandown Park, first run 1886.

École des Beaux Arts, Paris, founded 1648; adopted present name 1793.

Economist, British periodical founded 1843 by James Wilson (1805–60).

Ecuador, invaded by Spanish 1532; achieved independence from Spain 1822; part of Greater Colombia until 1830.

Eddington, Sir Arthur (1882–1944), English astronomer, wrote *The Expanding Universe* (1933).

Eddy, Mary Baker (1821–1910), American founder of Christian Science.

Eddystone lighthouse, first structure built 1698 and swept away 1703; second completed 1708 and destroyed by fire 1755; third built 1759; present lighthouse built 1879–81.

Edelinck, Gérard (1640–1707), Flemish engraver, worked in France.

Eden, Anthony, Earl of Avon (1897–1977), British statesman, foreign secretary 1935–38, 1940–45, 1951–55, prime minister 1955–57.

Edgar (944–975), king of the English 959–975, had a notably peaceful reign.

Edgar Atheling (c. 1050–c. 1125), English prince, led revolts against William the Conqueror.

Edgehill, Battle of, between King Charles I and the Parliamentary forces, 23 Oct.

Edgeworth, Maria (1767–1849), Irish novelist, wrote *Castle Rackrent* (1800).

Edict of Diocletian, Roman measure to check speculation, issued 301.

Edict of Nantes, granting religious freedom to the Huguenots, signed by Henry IV 1598; revoked by Louis XIV 1685.

Edinburgh, founded c. 617 by Edwin, King of Northumbria.

Edinburgh, Duke of. See **Philip,** Prince.

Edinburgh, Treaty of, between England and Scotland, signed 1560.

Edinburgh Academy, Scottish public school, opened by Sir Walter Scott 1824.

Edinburgh Festival, founded 1947.

Edinburgh Review, British periodical, began publication Oct. 1802; ceased 1929.

Edinburgh University, founded 1582.

Edison, Thomas Alva (1847–1932), prolific American inventor, notably of the phonograph and the incandescent electric lamp.

Edmund, Saint (c. 1175–1240), archbishop of Canterbury, was a notable scholar.

Edmund, Saint (841–870), king of East Anglia 855–870; killed by Danes.

Edmund (c. 922–946), king of the English 940–946, conquered Northumbria; assassinated.

Edmund Crouchback (1245–96), earl of Lancaster, named king of Sicily 1255–63 but never reigned.

Edmund Ironside (c. 981–1016), king of the English 1016; fought and then divided his kingdom with Canute.

Edred (d. 955), king of the English 946–955, incorporated Northumbria into his kingdom.

Education, Ministry of, founded as the Board of Education 1899; received present name 1944.

Edward the Confessor (d. 1066), last Anglo-Saxon king of the English 1043–66, pious (canonized 1161).

Edward the Elder (d. 924), king of the West Saxons 899–924, son of Alfred the Great; united most of England.

Edward, the Black Prince. See **Black Prince,** The.

Edward I (1239–1307), king of England 1272–1307, 'hammer of the Scots', conqueror of Wales, and a great law-giver.

Edward II (1284–1327), king of England 1307–27, weak, involved in factional struggles; defeated and murdered.

Edward III (1312–77), king of England 1327–77, began Hundred Years' War against French; victor at Crécy 1346.

Edward IV (1442–83), king of England 1461–70, and 1470–83; briefly exiled 1470–71 when deserted by Earl Warwick.

Edward V (1470–83), king of England 1483; minority with Richard of Gloucester as protector; murdered in Tower of London.

Edward VI (1537–53), king of England and Ireland 1547–53, when Protestantism became established.

Edward VII (1841–1910), king of Great Britain and Ireland 1901–10, made a notable contribution towards the *Entente Cordiale* with France, 1904.

Edward VIII (1894–1976), king of Great Britain and Northern Ireland Jan.–Dec. 1936; abdicated when marriage opposed; became Duke of Windsor.

Edward, Lake, Uganda, discovered 1889 by Sir Henry Stanley.

Edwards, Edward (1812–86), English librarian, associated with work of William Ewart (*q.v.*).

Edwards, Jonathan (1703–58), American Congregationalist minister, powerful revivalist preacher and writer.

Edwin (c. 585–633), king of Northumbria 617–633, converted to Christianity; defeated and killed by Mercians.

Edwy (c. 940–959), king of the English 955–957, forced to yield northern England to Edgar (*q.v.*) 957.

Egan, Pierce (1772–1849), English journalist, wrote *Life in London* (1821).

Egbert (d. 839), king of the West Saxons 802–839, became overlord of all Anglo-Saxons.

Egerton, Francis, Duke of Bridgewater (1736–1803), pioneer in canal building.

Egerton, Francis, Earl of Ellesmere (1800–57), English politician, secretary for war 1830, and patron of the arts.

Egmont, Lamoral, Count of (1522–68), Flemish soldier, protested against Spanish repression; his execution sparked Netherlands revolt.

Egypt, approximate extent of ancient history (1st to 31st dynasties), c. 3100–332 B.C.; under Ptolemies from 323 B.C.; Roman rule established 30 B.C.; Arab conquest A.D. 640; Turkish conquest 1517; declared British protectorate 1914; proclaimed an independent kingdom 1922; became a republic 1953.

Ehrenburg, Ilya (1891–1967), Russian writer and journalist, author of *Factory of Dreams* (1931).

Ehrlich, Paul (1854–1915), German bacteriologist, discovered salvarsan; Nobel prizewinner 1908.

Eichendorff, Joseph von (1788–1857), German poet and novelist, was a leading figure in the Romantic movement.

Eichmann, Karl Adolf (1906–62), Austrian Nazi, executed in Israel for his part in the wartime mass execution of Jews.

Eiffel Tower, Paris, constructed 1887–89, by the French engineer Alexandre-Gustave Eiffel (1831–1923).

Eijkman, Christiaan (1858–1930), Dutch physician, proved that disease can result from vitamin deficiency.

Eimmart, G. C. (1638–1705), German mathematician, designer and engraver of terrestrial and celestial globes.

Einstein, Albert (1879–1955), German physicist, propounded theory of relativity.

einsteinium, radioactive element first identified 1952 by Albert Ghiorso and co-workers.

Einthoven, Willem (1860–1927), Dutch physiologist, whose work led to great advances in electrocardiography.

Eire, official name of the Republic of Ireland during 1937–48.

Eisenhower, Dwight David (1890–1969), American soldier and statesman, leader of the Allied forces in Europe in World War II and 34th president of the United States 1953–61.

Eisenstein, Sergei (1898–1948), Russian film director, great artistic and technical pioneer, notably in *Battleship Potemkin* (1925).

Eisner, Kurt (1867–1919), German socialist, president of the Bavarian republic 1918–19; assassinated.

Eisteddfod, Welsh national festival reputedly dating from pre-Christian times; first recorded one 1171; held annually since mid-19th century.

El Alamein, Battle of, World War II, between British and Germans, Oct.–Nov. 1942.

elastic, first British patent issued 1832 to J. V. Desgrand.

Eldon, Lord (1751–1838), English jurist, lord chancellor 1804–27, noted for his opposition to reform.

Eleanor of Aquitaine (c. 1122–1204), wife of Louis VII of France 1137–52; divorced; wife of Henry II of England 1152–1204.

Eleanor of Castile (d. 1290), queen of England as wife of Edward I.

Eleanor of Provence (d. 1291), queen of England as wife of Henry III.

Electors (*Kurfürsten*, 'electoral princes'), of Holy Roman Empire, system established in 13th century, revised 1356; ended with abolition of Holy Roman Empire 1806.

electric batteries. See **battery.**

electric clocks. See **clocks.**

electricity, and its connection with magnetism, demonstrated 1820 by Hans Christian Oersted (*q.v.*).

electric lamps, first practical design produced 1880 by Sir Joseph Swan (*q.v.*) and also by Thomas Edison (*q.v.*); in public use (House of Commons) 1881.

electric power station, first English, opened at Godalming, Surrey, 1881.

Electrical Engineers, Institution of, founded as The Society of Telegraph Engineers 1871.

electrified underground railway, first commercial line (City & South London Railway) opened 1890.

electrocardiography, study of heart action, first developed 1903 by the Dutch physiologist Willem Einthoven (*q.v.*).

electrodynamics, theory developed from 1822 by André Marie Ampère (*q.v.*).

electroencephalography, pioneered 1929 by the German neurologist H. Berger.

electrolysis, laws formulated 1833 by Michael Faraday.

electromagnet, invented 1825 by the English scientist William Sturgeon (1783–1850).

electromagnetic induction, discovered 1831 by Michael Faraday.

electromagnetic waves, existence postulated 1864 by James Clerk Maxwell (*q.v.*); demonstrated 1888 by Heinrich Hertz (*q.v.*).

electromagnetism, discovered 1819 by the Danish physicist Hans Christian Oersted (*q.v.*).

electronic music. See **Moog Synthesizer.**

electron microscope, first design built 1933; modified to a practical instrument 1939 by the Russian-born American physicist Vladimir Zworykin (b. 1889).

electrons, discovered 1897 by Sir Joseph Thomson (*q.v.*); charge measured 1906–16 by Robert Millikan (*q.v.*).

electroplating, made possible 1800 by Volta's discovery of the battery; begun on a commercial scale *c.* 1840.

elementary particles See **electrons; neutrinos; neutrons; pions; proton.**

elements, chemical. See **periodic table.**

elevated railway, world's first, opened at Liverpool 1893.

Elgar, Sir Edward (1857–1934), the first of the great modern English composers, wrote *The Dream of Gerontius* (1900), symphonies, concertos, sonatas, etc.

Elgin Marbles, brought from the Parthenon to London 1801–03 by Lord Elgin (1766–1842).

Elijah (9th cent. B.C.), Hebrew prophet, strongly resisted the worship of the Phoenician god Baal.

Eliot, George (pseud. of Mary Ann Evans; 1819–80), English novelist, author of *Middlemarch* (1872).

Eliot, John (1604–90), English missionary to North American Indians.

Eliot, Sir John (1592–1632), English Parliamentarian, imprisoned for his opposition to Charles I.

Eliot, Thomas Stearns (1888–1965), American-born English poet, whose *The Waste Land* (1922) was a major landmark in modern poetry.

Elizabeth, Saint (1207–31), Hungarian princess, daughter of Andrew II of Hungary, noted for her charitable work.

Elizabeth I (1533–1603), queen of England 1558–1603, whose reign was one of the greatest in English history.

Elizabeth II (b. 1926), queen of Great Britain and Northern Ireland since 1952 and head of the Commonwealth of Nations.

Elizabeth (b. 1900), queen consort of George VI 1936–1952; now queen mother.

Elizabeth (1837–98), empress of Austria as wife of Franz Joseph; assassinated by an Italian anarchist.

Elizabeth (1709–62), empress of Russia 1741–62, daughter of Peter the Great.

Elizabeth (1596–1662), daughter of James I, queen of Bohemia 1619–20.

Elizabeth (1437–92), queen of England as wife of Edward IV.

Elizabeth College, Guernsey, public school, founded by Queen Elizabeth I 1563.

Ellenborough, Lord (1750–1818), English jurist, lord chief justice 1802–18; defended Warren Hastings (*q.v.*).

Ellesmere College, Shropshire, English public school founded 1879.

Ellington, ('Duke') Edward Kennedy (1899–1974), American Negro composer and bandleader, established a world-wide reputation as a jazz musician.

Elliott, Ebeneezer (1781–1849), English poet, known as the 'Corn-Law Rhymer', was an active Chartist.

Elliott, George Augustus, Baron Heathfield (1717–90), Scottish soldier, defended besieged Gibraltar 1779–83.

Ellis, Havelock (1859–1939), English writer, pioneered open, rational approach to human sexual behaviour, author of *Studies in the Psychology of Sex* (1897–1928).

Ellsworth, Lincoln (1880–1951), American polar explorer, was the first man to cross the Arctic and Antarctic regions by air.

Elphinstone, William (1431–1514), Scottish bishop of Aberdeen 1483–1514; effective diplomat and royal adviser.

El Salvador, conquered by Spanish 1527; achieved independence from Spain 1821; became an independent republic 1841.

Elssler, Fanny (1810–84), Austrian dancer, rival of Taglioni (*q.v.*), toured widely.

Elssler, Thérèse (1808–78), Austrian dancer, sister and often partner of Fanny Elssler.

Éluard, Paul (1895–1952), French poet, was a leading member of the Surrealist movement.

Eltham College, English public school, founded as 'The School for the Sons of Missionaries' 1842.

Ely Cathedral, built 11th to 14th centuries.

Elyot, Sir Thomas (*c.* 1490–1546), English diplomat, wrote on the education of princes in *Boke named the Governour* (1531).

Elzevir, Louis (*c.* 1540-1617), Dutch bookseller and publisher, founded great family of printers and publishers.

Emancipation Proclamation, concerning the freeing of slaves in the U.S.A., issued by President Lincoln 1 Jan. 1863.

Ember Days, in the Roman Catholic and Anglican Churches, the Wednesday, Friday and Saturday after the first Sunday in Lent, after Pentecost, after 14 Sept. and after 13 Dec.

Emerson, Ralph Waldo (1803–83), American essayist, poet and philosopher, author of *Nature* (1836).

Emin Pasha (Eduard Schnitzer; 1840–92), German explorer in the Sudan and central Africa.

Emmet, Robert (1778–1803), Irish nationalist, led 1803 revolt; hanged.

Emmett, Daniel Decatur (1815–1904), American composer, notably of *Dixie*.

Empedocles (*c.* 490–*c.* 430 B.C.), Greek philosopher, held that affinities and antipathies regulated the universe.

Empire State Building, New York, built 1930–31.

Employment Exchanges, first recorded local office opened in Britain 1885; national system established 1909.

Empson, William (b. 1906), English poet

and critic, author of *Seven Types of Ambiguity* (1930).

Encyclopedia Americana, first published 1829–33.

Encyclopaedia Britannica, first produced and published by Andrew Bell, Colin Macfarquhar and William Smellie in Edinburgh 1768–71.

Enderby Land, Antarctic, discovered 1831 by the English navigator John Biscoe (d. 1848).

Enders, John Franklin (b. 1897), American bacteriologist, joint winner of the Nobel Prize for Medicine 1954 for researches into polio.

energy, concept studied by Galileo and later by James Joule (*q.v.*). See also **conservation of energy.**

Enesco, Georges (1881–1955), Romanian violinist, interpreter of Bach, taught Yehudi Menuhin.

Engels, Friedrich (1820–95), German socialist, close associate of Karl Marx.

Enghien, Louis, Duc d' (1772–1804), French royalist émigré, kidnapped from Baden and shot.

England, inhabited by Celts in pre-Roman times; invaded by Julius Caesar 55 and 54 B.C.; under Roman occupation 1st–5th centuries A.D.; invaded by Angles, Saxons and Jutes in later 5th century and by Danes in the 9th century; Norman conquest 1066; Norman dynasty 1066–1154; House of Plantagenet 1154–1399; House of Lancaster 1399–1461; House of York 1461–1485; Tudors 1485–1603. See also **Great Britain.**

English Folk Dance Society, founded 1911 by Cecil Sharp (*q.v.*).

ENIAC. See **computer.**

Eniwetok Atoll, Marshall Islands, scene of atom bomb tests started by the U.S. Navy 1946.

Ennius, Quintus (239–169 B.C.), Latin poet, wrote epic *Annals.*

Enosis, movement for the union of Cyprus with Greece, had its origins in the Greek government's demand of 1912.

Ensenada, Żenón, Marqués de la (1702–81), Spanish statesman, was a reforming chief minister, 1743–54.

ensign, British infantry rank, abolished 1871.

Entente Cordiale, between France and Britain, signed April 1904.

entropy, concept proposed 1850 by the German physicist Rudolf Clausius (1822–88).

Enver Pasha (c. 1881–1922), Turkish soldier, led Young Turks' revolt 1908; effective ruler of Turkey during World War I.

enzyme reactions, first one (yeast fermentation) discovered 1897 by Eduard Buchner (*q.v.*).

Eocene Epoch, Earth history, from c. 38 million to c. 54 million years ago.

E.O.K.A., nationalist guerrilla force formed in Cyprus 1954 to fight for union with Greece.

Eon, Chevalier d' (1728–1810), French secret agent and transvestite.

Epaminondas (c. 418–326 B.C.), Theban general, defeated Spartans.

Epée, Abbe de l' (1712–89), French priest, devised alphabet for the deaf and dumb.

Épernon, Jean Louis de Nogaret, Duc d' (1554–1632), French administrator, unsuccessfully opposed Richelieu.

Ephesus, Council of, 3rd Ecumenical Council, convened 431.

Epictetus (fl. A.D. 90), Greek philosopher, a freed slave, taught Stoic doctrine at Rome.

Epicurus (c. 342–270 B.C.), Greek philosopher, advocated avoidance of pain and search for pleasure.

Épinay, Louise, Marquise d' (1726–83), French intellectual, intimately associated with Rousseau, Grimm, and others.

epinephrine. See **adrenaline.**

Epiphany, Christian Feast of the Manifestation of Christ to the Gentiles, celebrated 6 Jan.

Epsom, races first run c. 1620.

Epsom College, English public school, founded 1853.

Epsom salts, discovered 1618.

Epstein, Sir Jacob (1880–1959), American-born sculptor in England, whose works include *Adam* (1939).

equations, cubic, general solution obtained by the Italian mathematician Niccolò Tartaglia (c. 1500–1557) and published 1545 by the Italian mathematician Geronimo Cardano (*q.v.*).

equations, of 4th degree, general solution obtained 1540 by the Italian mathematician Lodovico Ferrari (1522–65); published 1545 by Geronimo Cardano.

equations, of 5th degree, shown 1824 by the Norwegian mathematician Niels Henrik Abel (*q.v.*) to have no general solution.

Equatorial Guinea, West Africa, independent republic since 1968. See also **Fernando Po; Rio Muni.**

equinox, time at which day and night are of equal length: vernal equinox, c. 21 March, autumnal equinox, c. 23 Sept.

Erasmus, Desiderius (c. 1466–1536), Dutch humanist writer, brilliantly witty, as in *Praise of Folly.*

Erastus, Thomas (1524–83), Swiss Protestant theologian, from whose name the word 'Erastian' is derived.

Eratosthenes, (c. 276–c. 194 B.C.), Greek philosopher, historian and astronomer; measured the earth's circumference.

erbium, chemical element, first isolated by

the Swedish chemist Karl Gustav Mosander (1797–1858).

Erckmann-Chatrian, pseud. of the French writers Emile Erckmann (1822–99) and Alexandre Chatrian (1826–90), who wrote a series of historical novels in collaboration.

Erebus, Mount, volcanic mountain in the Antarctic, discovered 1841 by Sir James Ross.

Eric I, Evergood (1056–1103), king of Denmark 1095–1103, made pilgrimage to Holy Land.

Eric II, the Memorable (d. 1137), king of Denmark 1131–37, a period of civil wars.

Eric III, the Lamb (d. 1147), king of Denmark 1137–47; abdicated and retired to monastery.

Eric IV, Ploughpenny (1216–50), king of Denmark 1241–50, killed by brother Abel.

Eric V, Klipping (c. 1249–1286), king of Denmark 1259–86, murdered by nobles.

Eric VI, Menved (1274–1319), king of Denmark 1286–1319, involved in struggle with Church.

Eric VII (1382–1459), king of Denmark 1397–1439, and king of Sweden as Eric XIII 1412–39.

Eric IX, Saint (d. 1160), king of Sweden 1150–60 and patron saint; conquered and converted Finns.

Eric XI (1216–50), king of Sweden 1222–50, dominated by a powerful noble.

Eric XII (1339–59), king of Sweden 1356–59, briefly replacing his father Magnus II.

Eric XIII, of Sweden. See **Eric VII,** of Denmark.

Eric XIV (1533–77), king of Sweden 1560–69, a period of expansion; became insane and was deposed.

Eric Bloodaxe (d. c. 954), king of Norway 930–934; notorious for his cruelty; deposed by half-brother.

Eric Magnusson (1268–99), king of Norway 1280–99, at war with Denmark.

Eric the Red (10th cent.), Norwegian discoverer of Greenland c. 981.

Ericsson, John (1803–89), Swedish-born American engineer, greatly improved steamship equipment and armaments.

Ericsson, Leif (b. c. 971), Norwegian navigator, son of Eric the Red, discovered 'Vinland' (North American coast) c. 1000.

Erie Canal, New York State, proposed by Governor De Witt Clinton and constructed 1817–25.

Erigena, Johannes Scotus (9th cent.), Irish scholastic philosopher in France, many of whose ideas were pronounced heretical.

Eritrea, part of ancient Ethiopia, became an Italian colony 1890; invaded by British forces 1941; restored to Ethiopia 1952; independence movement active since mid-1960s.

Erivan, Count. See **Paskevich,** Ivan.

Erkel, Franz (1810–93), Hungarian composer of operas in nationalist spirit.

Erlanger, Joseph (1874–1965), American physiologist, best known for his work on nerve fibres.

Ernle, Rowland, Lord (1851–1937), English politician, journalist and biographical writer.

Ernst, Max (1891–1976), German Surrealist painter, whose works include *The Elephant Celebes* (1921).

Erskine, Ebenezer (1680–1754), Scottish Presbyterian clergyman, founded Secession Church 1733.

Erskine, John (1509–91), Scottish reformer, active in support of John Knox.

Erskine, John. See **Mar,** Earl of.

Erskine, Thomas, 1st Baron (1750–1823), Scottish lawyer, noted defender of personal liberties.

Ervine, St John (1883–1971), Irish dramatist, associated with the Abbey Theatre, Dublin.

escalator, first, installed in New York and Paris 1900; first in England, at Earls Court Station, London, built 1911.

Escorial, Spain, palace built by King Philip II, 1563–84.

Esenin, Sergei (1895–1925), Russian poet, leader of the Imagist group.

Esher, Reginald, 2nd Viscount (1852–1930), English writer and official, governor of Windsor Castle, author of *The Girlhood of Queen Victoria* (1912).

Esperanto, universal language, invented 1887 by the Polish scholar Ludovic Zamenhof (*q.v.*).

Espronceda, José de (1808–42), Spanish poet and revolutionary, leading figure in the Romantic movement in Spain.

Essad Pasha (c. 1863–1920), Albanian politician, claimed throne but assassinated.

Essex, 2nd Earl of (1566–1601), English favourite of Queen Elizabeth I, executed after leading abortive revolt.

Essex, 3rd Earl of (1591–1646), English soldier, led Parliamentary army at beginning of Civil War.

Este, Beatrice d' (1475–97), duchess of Milan, famed for beauty, taste and political ability.

Esterházy, Prince Pal Antal (1786–1866), Hungarian diplomat in Austrian service.

Estienne, Henri (1528–98), French printer, assisted his father, Robert Estienne.

Estienne, Robert (1503–59), French printer, chief of a distinguished family of printers that produced many fine editions.

Estonia, conquered by Danes 1219; passed to Teutonic Knights 1346; under Swedish rule from 1561; ceded to Russian 1721; independent republic 1918; incorporated in U.S.S.R. 1940.

Estrées, Gabrielle d' (1573–99), French noblewoman, mistress of Henry IV.

Ethelbert (c. 522–616), king of Kent, promulgated first English code of laws.

Etheldreda, Saint (1630–79), queen of Northumbria; retired and became abbess of Ely 673.

Ethelred the Unready (c. 968–1016), king of the English 978–1016, notorious for buying off Norse and Danish invaders.

ether, luminiferous, medium for wave transmission, postulated by Sir George Stokes (q.v.); idea discredited 1887 by the Michelson–Morley experiment (q.v.).

ether, soporific qualities discovered 1818 by Michael Faraday (q.v.); first used as anaesthetic 1842 by the American physician Crawford Williamson Long (1815–78).

Etherege, Sir George (c. 1634–1691), English Restoration dramatist, wrote *The Man of Mode* (1676).

Ethiopia, part of ancient kingdom of Aksum; Christianity introduced c. A.D. 330; British expedition 1868; territorial integrity guaranteed by Britain, France and Italy 1906; conquered by Italy 1935–36; regained independence 1941; monarchy overthrown 1974.

Etna, Mount, Sicilian volcano – main eruptions 475, 396, 125, 121 and 43 B.C.; A.D. 1169, 1381, 1444, 1537, 1553, 1639 (major), 1830, 1852, 1865, 1879, 1886, 1892, 1899, 1910, 1923, 1928, 1942, 1947, 1949, 1950, 1955 and 1971.

Eton College, founded 1440 by King Henry VI.

Ettrick Shepherd. See **Hogg,** James.

Etty, William (1787–1849), English painter, notably of nudes.

Euclid (fl. 300 B.C.), Greek mathematician, whose *Elements* were basis of later geometry.

Eudocia (c. 400–460), empress of Byzantium as wife of Theodosius II, exiled c. 441 after court intrigues.

Eudoxia (d. 404), empress of Byzantium as wife of Arcadius, exiled Saint John Chrysostom.

Eudoxus (4th cent. B.C.), Greek scholar, noted for his work in astronomy and mathematics.

Eugene of Savoy, Prince (1663–1736), French-born Austrian general, prominent in War of Spanish Succession; defeated the Turks.

eugenics, movement instigated 1869 by the English scientist Sir Francis Galton (1822–1911).

Eugénie (1826–1920), Spanish princess, empress of France as wife of Napoleon III.

Eugenius II (d. 827), Pope 824–827, was a notable reformer.

Eugenius III (d. 1153), Pope 1145–53, expelled from city by Romans.

Eugenius IV (1383–1447), Pope 1431–47, was in conflict with Council of Basel.

Euler, Leonhard (1707–83), Swiss mathematician, worked in Prussia and Russia: pioneered calculus of variation, etc.

Eumenes (c. 360–316 B.C.), Macedonian general, ruled part of Asia Minor.

Euratom, established by treaty 1957; came into force 1 Jan. 1958; formed single commission and council July 1967 with the European Economic Community and the European Coal and Steel Community.

Euripides (484–406 B.C.), Greek dramatist, introduced realistic and problem-play elements into tragic tradition.

European Coal and Steel Community, established by treaty 1951; came into force July 1952; formed single commission and council with the European Coal and Steel Community and Euratom July 1967.

European Economic Community (Common Market), established by treaty 1957; came into force 1 Jan. 1958; formed single commission and council with Euratom and the European Coal and Steel Community July 1967; U.K. and Ireland joined 1 Jan. 1973.

European Monetary Agreement, signed 5 Aug. 1955.

European Space Research Organization, founded 1962; formally established 1964.

europium, chemical element, discovered 1896 by the French chemist Eugène Demarçay (1852–1904).

Eurovision, television link-up between European countries, first carried out on large scale by the B.B.C. 1954.

Eusebius, Saint, Pope c. 309; exiled by Emperor Maxentius.

Eusebius of Caesarea (c. 260–c. 340), Palestinian theologian, took part in Arian controversy and wrote *Ecclesiastical History*.

Eustachian tube, rediscovered by the Italian anatomist Bartolommeo Eustachio (1520–74); information not published until 1714.

Eustathius (d. c. 1193), Byzantine archbishop of Thessalonica and Greek literary critic.

Euston Station, London's first main line railway terminus, opened 1838.

Eutyches (d. c. 453), Byzantine theologian, whose heretical views were condemned by the Council of Chalcedon.

evacuation, wartime, of mothers and children from British towns began 1 Sept. 1939.

Evans, Sir Arthur (1851–1941), English archaeologist, uncovered Knossos and ancient Cretan civilisation.

Evans, Dame Edith (1888–1976), English actress, played leading roles in plays by Shakespeare and Shaw.

Evans, Sir John (1823–1908), English archaeologist and geologist, expert on ancient implements and coins.

Evans, Oliver (1755–1819), American inventor, constructed first American steam engine.

evaporated milk, first produced 1856 by the American surveyor Gail Borden (1801–74).

Evelyn, John (1620–1706), English diarist and man of letters, contemporary of Pepys.

Evening News, British newspaper, founded 1881; absorbed the *Star* 1960.

Evening Standard, British newspaper, founded 1827 as the *Standard*; absorbed the St James's Gazette 1905.

Everest, Mount, summit first reached 29 May 1953 by Sir Edmund Hillary and the Sherpa Tensing.

Everlasting League, The, Swiss patriotic pact made 1291 between Schwyz, Uri and Nidwalden.

evolution, by natural selection, Darwinian theory first communicated to the Linnean Society of London 1 July 1858.

Ewald, Johannes (1743–81), Danish poet and dramatist, author of *Rolf Krage* (1770).

Ewart, William (1798–1869), English politician, introduced legislation providing for free libraries.

Ewing, Sir Alfred (1855–1935), Scottish physicist, studied magnetization.

Ewing, Juliana Horatia (1841–85), English writer of children's stories, e.g. *The Brownies* (1870).

Exclusion Bill, to prevent the succession of James, Duke of York, introduced 1678.

excursion train, world's first (Leicester–Loughborough return), 5 July 1841, organized by Thomas Cook (*q.v.*).

Exeter Cathedral, built between *c.* 1275 and *c.* 1365.

Exeter College, Oxford University, founded 1314 by Walter de Stapledon, bishop of Exeter (1261–1326).

Exeter School, English public school, founded 1332; refounded 1633.

Exeter University, formerly Exeter University College, created 1955.

Exmouth, Edward Pellew, Viscount (1757–1833), English admiral, defeated dey of Algiers.

expanding universe, theory developed by the Dutch astronomer Wilhem de Sitter (1872–1934).

Eyck, Hubert van (*c.* 1366–1426), Flemish painter, with his brother Jan van Eyck founded Flemish school.

Eyck, Jan van (*c.* 1385–1441), Flemish painter of meticulous realism, e.g. *Arnolfini Marriage.*

Eyre, Edward John (1815–1901), English explorer of central Australia; also a colonial governor.

Eyre, Sir James (1734–99), English lawyer,

involved in controversy with John Wilkes (*q.v.*).

Eyre, Lake, South Australia, discovered 1840 by Edward John Eyre.

Eysenck, Hans Jurgen (b. 1916), German-born British psychologist, noted for his study of human personality.

Ezekiel (6th cent. B.C.), Hebrew prophet, prophesied the overthrow of Judah.

F

Faber, Frederick William (1814–63), English hymn-writer, Anglican clergyman converted to Roman Catholicism.

Fabergé, Peter Carl (1846–1920), Russian goldsmith, whose work includes flowers, animals and Easter eggs.

Fabian Society, London, founded 1884 by the English writers Frank Podmore and Edward R. Pease.

Fabius Maximus, Quintus (d. 203 B.C.), Roman dictator and consul, fought Hannibal by delaying tactics.

Fabre, Jean Henri (1823–1915), French entomologist, produced a major study of insect life.

Fabriano, Gentile da (*c.* 1370–1427), Italian painter of exquisite decorative works, e.g. *Adoration of the Magi.*

Fabricius, Hieronymus (1537–1619), Italian anatomist and surgeon, made advances in both fields.

Fabricius, Johann Christian (1745–1808), Danish entomologist, developed classification of insects.

Fabritius, Carel (*c.* 1624–1654), Dutch painter, pupil of Rembrandt and teacher of Vermeer.

Fabyan, Robert (d. 1513), English writer of *The New Chronicles of England and France* (1516).

Factory Act, first in England passed 1802.

Faeroe Islands, North Atlantic, annexed by Norway 1035; under Danish rule since 1380; became self-governing 1947.

Fahrenheit scale, of temperature, invented *c.* 1714 by the German physicist Gabriel Daniel Fahrenheit (1686–1736).

Fairbairn, Sir William (1789–1874), Scottish engineer, improved building methods.

Fairbanks, Douglas (1883–1939), American film actor, famous for his swash-buckling roles, as in *Black Pirate* (1926).

Fairbanks, Thaddeus (1796–1886), American inventor of the platform scale.

Fairey, Sir Charles Richard (1887–1956), English manufacturer, founded great aircraft company.

Fairfax, Thomas (1612–71), English leader of Parliamentary army in Civil War.

Faisal (1905–75), king of Saudi Arabia 1964–75; assassinated.

Faisal I (1883–1933), Arab (Hashemite

dynasty) leader in World War I; king of Iraq 1921–33.

Faisal II (1935–58), last king of Iraq 1939–58, killed in military coup.

Faithfull, Emily (1835–95), English philanthropist, promoted employment opportunities for women.

Falange, Spanish Fascist Party, founded 1933 by José Antonio Primo de Rivera (*q.v.*); only legal political party in Spain after 1939; dissolved 1966.

Faliero, Marino (*c.* 1278–1355), Venetian doge 1354–55, executed for attempting to seize supreme power.

Falkirk, Battles of, (1) victory of the English over the Scots, 22 July 1298; (2) victory of the Jacobites led by Prince Charles Edward Stuart over the government forces under General Henry Hawley, 17 Jan. 1746.

Falkland Islands, discovered 1592; French, Spanish and British settlements in 18th century; occupied by Britain 1833; made a colony 1892; territory claimed by Argentina.

Falla, Manuel de (1876–1946), Spanish composer, notably of the ballet *The Three-Cornered Hat* (1919).

Fallopian Tubes, first described 1561 by the Italian anatomist Gabriel Fallopius (1523–62).

family allowances, introduced into Britain 1945; already general in France (paid by employers) by 1932.

Fangio, Juan Manuel (b. 1911), Argentinian racing driver, world champion 1951 and 1954–57.

Fanshawe, Sir Richard (1608–66), English Royalist, fought in Civil War; ambassador to Portugal 1662–63 and Spain 1664–66.

Fantin-Latour, Ignace (1836–1904), French painter of flowers and group portraits, including *Homage to Manet* (1869).

Faraday, Michael (1791–1867), English scientist, made many important discoveries, especially in electromagnetism.

Farel, Guillaume (1489–1565), French religious reformer, who brought the Reformation to Switzerland.

Fargo, William George (1818–81), American partner in Wells Fargo company.

Farinelli, Carlo (1705–82), Italian castrato singer of European renown, long resident in Spain.

Farington, Joseph (1747–1821), English landscape artist, kept a notable *Diary* (published 1922–28).

Farman, Henri (1874–1958), French pioneer in aviation and aircraft manufacture.

Farnese, Alessandro (1545–92), Italian soldier in service of Spain at Battle of Lepanto 1571 and in the Netherlands.

Farnese Palace, Rome, built 1517–89.

Farouk (1920–65), king of Egypt 1936–52, overthrown by military coup.

Farquhar, George (1678–1707), Irish-born dramatist, author of *The Beaux' Stratagem* (1707).

Farr, William (1807–83), English pioneer in study of social statistics.

Farragut, David Glasgow (1801–70), American admiral, captured New Orleans 1862 and defeated Confederate navy.

Farrar, Dean Frederick William (1831–1903), English writer of school stories, particularly *Eric, or Little by Little* (1858).

Fascist Party, Italian, founded 1919 by Mussolini; seized power 1922; dissolved 1943.

Fashoda Incident, Sudan, between British and French, 1898.

fast breeder reactor. See **Dounreay.**

Fastolf, Sir John (*c.* 1378–1459), English soldier in French wars, governor of Anjou and Maine 1423–26.

Father's Day, U.S.A., 3rd Sunday in June.

Fatima (*c.* 606–632), daughter of Mohammed, given particularly high place by Shia sect.

Fatima, vision of, Portugal, 13 Oct. 1917.

Fatimids, Arab dynasty in North Africa 909–1171.

fatty acids, first ones, stearic, palmitic, and oleic acids, isolated 1809 by the French chemist Michel-Eugène Chevreul (1786–1889); their use in candles patented 1825 by Chevreul and Gay-Lussac (*q.v.*).

Faulkner, William (1897–1962), American novelist, author of *Sanctuary* (1931), Nobel prizewinner 1949.

Fauré, Gabriel (1845–1924), French composer, notably of songs and piano music.

Faust, Johann (*c.* 1480–*c.* 1540), German magician whose legendary career inspired Marlowe and Goethe.

Faustin I (*c.* 1785–1867), emperor of Haiti 1849–58; deposed.

Fauvism, French modern art movement, began 1905; ended 1908.

Fawcett, Henry (1833–84), English politician and economist, held ministerial office despite blindness.

Fawcett, Dame Millicent Garrett (1847–1929), English champion of women's rights, wife of Henry Fawcett.

Fawcett, Percy Harrison (1867–1925), English explorer in South America, disappeared in the Brazilian jungle.

Fawcett, Sir William (1728–1804), English soldier, translated *Memoirs* of Marshal Saxe.

Fawkes, Guy (1570–1606), English conspirator in Gunpowder Plot, arrested entering House of Commons cellar.

Federal Bureau Of Investigation, U.S.A., established 1908.

Federal Reserve System, American central banking system, founded 1913.

Federation of British Industries, founded 1916.

Fedin, Konstantin (b. 1892), Russian novelist, author of *Cities and Years* (1924).

Fejervary, Geza, Baron (1833–1914), Hungarian politician, prominent in Austro-Hungarian internal affairs.

Felibien, André (1619–95), French architect, wrote several books on the arts.

Felix II (d. 365), Arian anti-pope 356–358, deposed when Liberius (*q.v.*) reinstated.

Felix III, Saint (d. 492), Pope 483–492, began schism between Latin and Greek Churches.

Felix IV, Saint (d. 530), Pope 526–530, chosen by Theodoric, king of the East Goths.

Felix V (1383–1451), anti-pope 1439–49, previously duke of Savoy; submitted to Nicholas V.

Fell, Dr John (1625–86), Anglican scholar, vice-chancellor of Oxford University 1666–69 and bishop of Oxford 1675–86.

Fellini, Federico (b. 1920), Italian film director, whose work includes *La Strada* (1954) and *La Dolce Vita* (1959).

Fellowes, Edmund (1870–1951), English musicologist and madrigal expert.

Felsted School, English public school, founded 1564.

Felton, John (*c.* 1595–1628), English soldier, assassinated duke of Buckingham; executed.

Fénelon, François (1651–1715), French theologian and writer, author of *Dialogues of the Dead* (1700–18).

Fenians, Irish-American revolutionary movement founded 1858 in the U.S.A. by John O'Mahony (*q.v.*).

Feodor I (1557–98), tsar of Russia 1584–98, largely controlled by Boris Godunov.

Feodor II (1589–1605), tsar of Russia 1605, son of Boris Godunov; murdered.

Feodor III (1656–82), tsar of Russia 1676–82, carried out modernizing reforms.

Ferber, Edna (1887–1968), American novelist, wrote *Show Boat* (1926).

Ferdinand I (1503–64), king of Bohemia and Hungary 1526–64, Holy Roman emperor 1556–64.

Ferdinand II (1578–1637), Holy Roman emperor 1619–37, during first part of Thirty Years' War; fiercely anti-Protestant.

Ferdinand III (1608–57), Holy Roman emperor 1637–57, fought Protestants and their allies to end of Thirty Years' War, 1648.

Ferdinand I (1345–83), king of Portugal 1367–83, failed in attempts to expand his possessions.

Ferdinand II (1816–85), Portuguese king-consort of Maria II 1836–53.

Ferdinand I (d. 1065), king of Castile and Leon, began reconquest of peninsula from Moors.

Ferdinand II (d. 1188), king of Leon 1157–88, warred against Castile and Portugal.

Ferdinand III (1199–1252), king of Castile 1217–52 and Leon 1230–52, took Córdoba and Seville from Moors.

Ferdinand IV (d. 1312), king of Castile and Leon 1295–1312, in conflict with the Moors.

Ferdinand V (1452–1516), king of Castile and Leon 1474–1516; by marriage to Queen Isabella, king of Aragon 1479–1516, uniting all Spain.

Ferdinand VI (1713–59), king of Spain 1746–59, followed peaceful policy.

Ferdinand VII (1784–1833), king of Spain 1808 and 1814–33, persecuted liberals.

Ferdinand I (1423–94), king of Naples 1458–94, in conflict with the nobility, the papacy, and the Turks.

Ferdinand II (1469–96), king of Naples 1495–96, repelled French invasion.

Ferguson, James (1710–76), Scottish astronomer, observed transit of Venus.

Ferguson, Patrick (1744–80), Scottish soldier, invented a breech-loading rifle.

Ferguson, Sir James (1832–1907), Scottish administrator, held governorships in Australia, New Zealand and India.

Fermat, Pierre de (1601–65), French mathematician, pioneer of calculus.

Fermi, Enrico (1901–54), Italian physicist, made an important contribution to nuclear physics.

Fernández, Juan (*c.* 1537–*c.* 1603), Spanish navigator along American Pacific coast; island group named after him.

Fernando Po, island off West Africa, discovered by Portuguese navigator Fernão de Po 1472; ceded to Spain 1778; abandoned but repossessed 1844; part of Spanish Guinea – now Equatorial Guinea (*q.v.*).

Fernel, Jean (1497–1558), French polymath, important as writer on medicine.

Ferrar, Nicholas (1592–1637), English leader of religious community at Little Gidding, Huntingdonshire.

Ferrara, Andrea (late 16th cent.), Italian sword-maker, worked as armourer at Belluno 1585.

Ferraris, Galileo (1847–97), Italian physicist, discovered rotary magnetic field 1885.

Ferrer, Francisco (1859–1909), Spanish revolutionary, whose execution caused an international scandal.

Ferrers, Laurence, Earl (1720–60), English nobleman, last to be executed in Britain as a felon.

Ferrier, Kathleen (1912–53), English contralto singer, who won international fame.

Ferrier, Susan (1782–1854), Scottish novelist, wrote *Marriage* (1818).

Ferris wheel, invented 1892 by the American engineer G. W. G. Ferris (1859–96).

Fersen, Hans Axel (1755–1810), Swedish soldier and diplomat, closely associated with French royal family during the Revolution.

fertilizers, chemical, use first promoted in the 1840s by Justus von Liebig (q.v.) and the English agriculturalist Sir John Bennett Lawes (1814–1900).

Festival of Britain, opened 3 May, closed 30 Sept. 1951.

Fettes College, Edinburgh, Scottish public school, founded 1830 by Sir William Fettes (1750–1836).

Feuchtwanger, Lion (1884–1958), German novelist, wrote *Jew Suss* (1925).

Feuerbach, Ludwig Andreas (1804–72), German philosopher, a Hegelian who developed materialist-atheist views.

Feuillet, Octave (1821–90), French novelist, author of *Julia de Trécoeur* (1872).

Féval, Paul (1817–87), French novelist, wrote *Les Mystères de Londres* (1844).

Feydeau, Georges (1862–1921), French writer of farces, including *Occupe-toi d' Amélie* (1908).

Feynman, Richard Phillips (b. 1918), American physicist, best known for his work on quantum electro-dynamics.

Fez, Treaty of, March 1912, established French protectorate in Morocco; terminated March 1956.

Fianna Fail ('Soldiers of destiny'), Irish political party, founded 1926 by Eamon de Valera.

Fibonacci, Leonardo (c. 1180–c. 1250), Italian mathematician, introduced Arabic numerals into Western Europe.

fibre. See **man-made fibres.**

Fichte, Johann Gottlieb (1762–1814), German philosopher, developed Idealist views of Kant.

Fido, airfield fog clearance method developed 1942 by the British engineer A. C. Hartley (1889–1960).

Field, John (1782–1837), Irish pianist and composer, settled in Russia, famous for his nocturnes.

Field, Marshall (1834–1906), American department store (dry goods) pioneer.

Fielding, Henry (1707–54), English comic novelist, wrote *Tom Jones* (1749).

field-marshal, military rank, introduced into Britain in 1736.

Field of Cloth of Gold. See **Cloth of Gold,** Field of.

Fields, Gracie (b. 1898), English comedienne and singer of popular songs.

Fields, W. C. (1879–1946), American film actor, best known for his portrayal of comic characters.

Fifth Monarchy Men, English extremist Puritan movement, active 1642 to 1661.

Fifth Republic, France, constitution came into force Oct. 1958.

Figg, James (d. c. 1735), English pugilist and fencer, won boxing championship 1719.

Figueroa, Francisco de (c. 1536–c. 1617), Spanish poet, wrote in both Spanish and Italian.

Fiji, South Pacific, discovered by Abel Tasman 1643; visited by Cook 1773; made British crown colony 1874; independent member of the Commonwealth since 1970.

Fillmore, Millard (1800–74), American statesman, 13th president of the United States 1850–53, supported compromise on the slavery question.

film, colour, first system (for motion pictures) produced 1906 by the Americans Charles Urban and G. Albert Smith.

film, photographic roll-film, patented 1884 by George Eastman (q.v.). See also **motion films.**

Filmer, Sir Robert (1588–1653), English political writer, defended divine right of kings in *Patriarcha* (1680).

fingerprints, for classification, first employed 1901 at Scotland Yard, using the Galton–Henry system developed by the English anthropologist Sir Francis Galton (1822–1911).

Finland, settled by Finns in 8th century A.D.; conquered by Sweden 13th century; ruled by Russian 1808–1917; independent republic since 1917.

Finsen, Niels (1860–1904), Danish physicist, awarded Nobel Prize in 1903 for his work on skin diseases.

Firbank, Ronald (1886–1926), English novelist, author of *The Flower beneath the Foot* (1923).

Firdausi (c. 940–1020), Persian poet, wrote epic *Book of Kings.*

firearms, first used in Europe in late 13th century; wheel-lock introduced 1510–20; flintlock introduced c. 1610; first percussion detonator patented 1807.

fire engines, first acquired by a London insurance company 1722.

fire extinguisher, first portable, invented 1816 by the English barrackmaster George Manby (1765–1854).

fire insurance, pioneered in England by Nicolas Barbon after Great Fire of London 1666; opened first insurance office 1680.

fireplaces, in Britain, removed from the centre of the hall to the side wall in the late 14th century.

First of June. See **Glorious First of June.**

First Republic, France, proclaimed 21 Sept. 1792; ended 28 May 1804.

Fischer, Bobby (b. 1943), American chess player, won the world chess championship 1972.

Fischer, Emil Hermann (1852–1919), German organic chemist, best known for his work on sugar and the purine derivatives.

Fischer von Erlach, Johann (1656–1723), Austrian architect, built palaces and churches around Vienna and Salzburg.

Fischer-Dieskau, Dietrich (b. 1925), German baritone, known for fine performances of *Lieder* and in opera.

Fisher, John (1459–1535), English Roman Catholic bishop, executed for opposing Henry VIII's Act of Supremacy.

Fisher, John, 1st Baron (1841–1920), British admiral, as first sea lord 1904–10 and 1914–15 carried out naval reforms.

Fish Harvest Festival, held at St Dunstan's-in-the-East, London, on Sunday nearest All Souls' Day.

Fishmongers' Company, London, origins uncertain, · first extant charter granted by King Edward III, 1364.

Fisk University, Nashville, Tennessee, American Negro university, founded 1865.

Fiske, John (1842–1901), American philosopher and historian, wrote *Excursions of an Evolutionist* (1884).

Fitzgerald, Edward (1809–83), English writer, translator of the *Rubáiyát of Omar Khayyám* (1859).

Fitzgerald, Lord Edward (1763–98), Irish revolutionary, plotted French invasion, killed during arrest.

Fitzgerald, (Francis) Scott (1896–1940), American writer, famous for his novels of 'The Jazz Age', including *Tender is the Night* (1934).

Fitzherbert, Mrs Maria (1756–1837), wife of Prince of Wales (later George IV); marriage invalidated.

Fitzwilliam Collection, bequeathed to the University of Cambridge by Viscount Fitzwilliam (1745–1806).

Fiume. See Rijeka.

Five Dynasties, China, 907–960.

Fizeau, Armand (1819–96), French physicist, devised method of measuring the velocity of light.

Flag Day (U.S.A.), celebrated 14 June.

Flagstad, Kirsten (1895–1962), Norwegian opera singer, one of the greatest Wagnerian sopranos.

Flaherty, Robert (1884–1951), American film director, noted for his documentaries including *Nanook of the North* (1920).

Flambard, Ranulf (d. 1128), Norman bishop of Durham, chief adviser of William II.

Flaminian Way, running north from Rome to Ariminum (Rimini) on Adriatic coast, built 220 B.C.

Flaminius, Gaius (d. 217 B.C.), Roman general, defeated and killed by Hannibal.

Flaminius, Titus Quinctius (d. 174 B.C.), Roman consul 198 B.C., defeated Macedonians.

Flammarion, Camille (1842–1925), French astronomer and popular writer on the subject.

Flamsteed, John (1646–1719), English astronomer, first astronomer royal 1675.

Flatman, Thomas (1635–88), English poet, also painter of miniatures.

Flaubert, Gustave (1821–80), major French novelist, author of *Madame Bovary* (1857).

Flavian I (*c.* 320–404), patriarch of Antioch 381–404, in schism with Rome.

Flavian II (d. 518), patriarch of Antioch *c.* 498–512, deposed by Emperor Anastasius.

Flaxman, John (1755–1826), English Neoclassical sculptor and graphic artist, made memorial to Lord Mansfield.

Flecker, James Elroy (1884–1915), English poet and playwright, wrote the exotic *Hassan*.

Fleet Prison, London, dates from late 12th century; burnt down 1666; rebuilt, but against destroyed 1780; rebuilt 1782; pulled down 1844.

Flémalle, Maître de (*c.* 1375–1444), Flemish painter, best known for his altarpiece.

Fleming, Sir Alexander (1881–1955), Scottish biologist, discovered penicillin 1928.

Fleming, Sir John Ambrose (1849–1945), English electrical engineer, responsible for several new applications of electricity.

Fleming, Margaret (1803–11), Scottish child prodigy, wrote poems and a diary.

Fleming, Sir Sandford (1827–1915), Scottish-born Canadian railway engineer, chief engineer to Canadian Pacific 1872–80.

Fletcher, John (1579–1625), English playwright, collaborated with Francis Beaumont (*q.v.*), and possibly with Shakespeare.

Fleury, Cardinal (1653–1743), French ecclesiastic, tutor of Louis XV and effectively first minister 1726–43.

Flight and Barr (Worcester) porcelain, manufactured 1792–1807; Flight period 1783–92.

flintlocks. See firearms.

Flodden, Battle of, victory of the English over the Scots, 9 Sept. 1513.

Floral Games, French poetry competition, first held at Toulouse 1323.

Floréal, French Revolutionary calendar month, 20 April to 19 May.

Florence of Worcester (d. 1118), English monk and chronicler, wrote *Chronicon*.

Florida, discovered by Ponce de León 1513; settled by Spanish 1565; ceded to Britain 1763; returned to Spain 1783; purchased from Spain by U.S.A. 1819; admitted to the Union as a state 1845; seceded 1861; readmitted to Union 1868.

Florio, John (*c.* 1553–1625), English translator of Montaigne's *Essays* 1603.

Flotow, Friedrich (1812–83), German composer, wrote the opera *Martha* (1847).

flour-mill, first steam, erected by the

Scottish engineer John Rennie at Black-friars, London, 1784–88.

fluorescence, nature of studied by Sir George Stokes (*q.v.*).

fluorescent lighting, first marketed 1938.

fluorine, first isolated 1886 by the French chemist Henri Moissan (1852–1907).

flying boat, first flown 1912 by the American aviator Glenn Curtiss (*q.v.*).

flying bombs. See **V-1.**

Flying Doctor Service, Australia, conceived 1912; first base began operating 1928 at Cloncurry, Queensland.

flying saucers. See **unidentified flying objects.**

flying shuttle, weaving, invented *c.* 1733 by the Englishman John Kay (1704–*c.* 1764).

foam rubber, first made 1929 at the Dunlop Latex Development Laboratories, Birmingham.

Foch, Ferdinand (1851–1929), French soldier, commander-in-chief of the Allied armies in France in World War I.

Fogazzaro, Antonio (1842–1911), Italian novelist and poet, wrote *Il Santo* (1905).

Fokine, Michael (1880–1942), Russian dancer and choreographer of *Schéhérazade, Firebird* and *Petrushka.*

Fokker, Antony Hermann (1890–1939), Dutch aviation pioneer, manufactured planes in Germany and (1922–39) U.S.A.

Folger, Henry Clay (1857–1930), American industrialist, founded Folger Shakespeare Library, Washington.

Fontainebleau, Palace of, France, first mentioned 12th century; additions made up to the 19th century, but mostly dating from the 16th century.

Fontane, Theodor (1819–98), German novelist, author of *Effi Briest* (1894).

Fontenelle, Bernard le Bovier de (1657–1757), French scientist and writer, author of *La Pluralité des Mondes* (1686).

Fontenoy, Battle of, victory of the French over the British and their allies, 11 May 1745.

Fonteyn, Dame Margot (b. 1919), English ballerina, outstanding interpreter of classical ballet.

food preservation. See **canning.**

food sales, in Britain, first controlled by legislation 1860.

Football Association, formed 1863.

Foote, Samuel (1720–77), English playwright, was also a gifted mimic and wit.

footlights, in British theatres, first used 1672. See also **limelight.**

Foppa, Vincenzo (*c.* 1427–*c.* 1515), Italian painter of the Milanese school.

Forbes-Robertson, Sir Johnstone (1853–1937), English actor, greatest of a distinguished theatrical family.

Ford, Ford Madox (1873–1939), English novelist, wrote *Parade's End* (1924–28).

Ford, Henry (1863–1947), American industrialist, founded the Ford Motor Company 1903; was the first man to mass-produce motor cars.

Ford, John (1586–*c.* 1639), English Jacobean playwright, wrote *'Tis Pity She's a Whore* (1633).

Ford, John (1895–1973), American film director, best known for his Westerns, including *Stagecoach* (1939).

Forefathers' Day, U.S.A., 21 Dec., celebrating landing of Pilgrim Fathers at Plymouth Rock 1620.

Foreign and Commonwealth Office, created 1968 from merger of Foreign Office (formed 1782) and Commonwealth Relations Office (*q.v.*).

Foreign Legion, French, founded 1831 by King Louis Philippe, with headquarters in Algeria; moved to metropolitan France 1962.

Forest School, London, English public school, founded 1834.

Forli, Melozzo da (1438–94), Italian painter, worked at Rome for the Papacy.

Formosa. See **Taiwan.**

Formosus (d. 896), Pope 891–896; legitimacy of his succession was contested.

Forster, Edward Morgan (1879–1970), English novelist, wrote *A Passage to India* (1924).

Forsyth, Alexander John (1769–1843), Scottish clergyman, invented percussion lock for firearms.

Fort Duquesne, French fort on site of modern Pittsburgh; captured by British 1758.

Forte, Charles (b. 1908), Italian-born British caterer, built restaurant and hotel chain.

Fort Sumter, South Carolina, attack on by Confederate forces 12–13 April 1861 began American Civil War.

Fortescue, Sir John (*c.* 1394–*c.* 1476), English lord chief justice, early writer on constitutional issues.

Forth and Clyde Canal, Scotland, begun 1768; completed 1790.

Forth Bridge, Scotland, designed and constructed 1882–90 by the English engineers Sir Benjamin Baker (1840–1907) and Sir John Fowler (1817–98).

Forth Road Bridge, Scotland, constructed 1958–64.

Forties Field, oil field in North Sea off Aberdeen, discovered late 1970; first production platform established July 1974; pipeline to shore completed Oct. 1974; first oil pumped ashore Nov. 1975.

Foscolo, Ugo (1778–1827), Italian poet, wrote *I Sepolcri* (1807).

Fosse Way, Lincoln to Exeter, Roman road begun as frontier line against raiding forces A.D. 47.

Foster, Myles Birket (1825–99), English

illustrator, made popular drawings and watercolours of rural scenery.

Foster, Stephen Collins (1826–64), American composer of sentimental ballads including *Old Folks at Home* (1851).

Foucault pendulum, to demonstrate Earth's rotation, used 1851 by the French physicist Jean Foucault (1819–68).

Fouché, Joseph (1763–1820), French politician, as minister of police under Napoleon created an elaborate espionage system.

Foulis, Andrew (1712–75), Scottish printer, produced typographical classics.

Foulis, Robert (1707–76), Scottish printer, partnered his brother Andrew Foulis at Glasgow.

fountain pen, first practical design patented 1884 by the American Lewis E. Waterman (1837–1901).

Fountains Abbey, Cistercian house in Yorkshire, founded 1132; building completed 1526.

Fouquet, Jean (c. 1420–c. 1480), French painter, notably of miniatures.

Fouquier-Tinville, Antoine (1746–95), French revolutionary, chief prosecutor during Reign of Terror; guillotined.

Fourier, François (1772–1837), French socialist thinker, advocated organization of society into co-operative units.

Fourier, Jean Baptiste, Baron (1768–1830), French mathematician and physicist, noted for his mathematical theory of heat conduction, described 1822.

Fourneyron, Benoît (1802–67), French engineer, invented the first hydraulic turbine.

Fournier, Alain. See **Alain-Fournier.**

Fournier, Pierre (1712–68), French typefounder, was the first man to devise a points system for measuring type.

Fourth Republic, France, constitution came into force 1946; ended 1958.

Fowler, Henry (1858–1933), English authority on language, wrote *Modern English Usage* (1926).

Fowler, Sir John (1817–98), English engineer, designed Forth Bridge and first London underground railway.

Fowler, John (1826–64), English engineer, inventor of the steam-plough.

Fox, Charles James (1749–1806), British statesman, prime minister 1806, champion of individual liberty.

Fox, George (1624–91), English founder of the Society of Friends ('Quakers').

Foxe, John (1516–87), English martyrologist, author of *The Book of Martyrs* (1563).

Fra Angelico. See **Angelico,** Fra.

Fracastoro, Girolamo (1483–1553), Italian physician, pioneered study of infectious diseases and wrote a poem about syphilis.

Fragonard, Jean Honoré (1732–1806),

French Rococo painter, amorous and light-hearted, e.g. *The Swing* (1765).

Framlingham College, English public school, founded 1864.

Frampton, Sir George (1860–1928), English sculptor of *Peter Pan* in Hyde Park.

France, Anatole (1844–1924), French novelist, master of irony and satire, author of *Penguin Island* (1908).

France, monarchy, Merovingian (481–751), Carolingian (751–987), Capetian (987–1328), Valois (1328–1589), (Bourbon (1589–1792); 1st republic, 1793–1804; 1st empire, 1804–14; restored monarchy, 1814–48; 2nd republic 1848–52; 2nd empire 1852–70; 3rd republic, 1871–1940; German occupation and Vichy regime, 1940–44; 4th republic, 1946–1958; 5th republic since 1958.

Francesca, Piero della (c. 1420–1492), Italian painter, leading figure of the Umbrian school.

Francesca da Rimini (d. c. 1285), Italian heroine, killed with her lover by husband Giovanni Malatesta.

Franceschini, Baldassare (1611–89), Italian painter of Florentine school.

Francis I (1708–65), Holy Roman emperor 1745–65, husband of Maria Theresa of Austria.

Francis II (1768–1835), last Holy Roman emperor 1792–1806, emperor of Austria 1804–35.

Francis I (1494–1547), king of France 1515–47, fought long wars against the Emperor Charles V.

Francis II (1544–60), king of France 1559–60, first husband of Mary Queen of Scots.

Francis Borgia, Saint (1510–72), Italian Jesuit, founded colleges and schools.

Francis of Assisi, Saint (c. 1182–1226), Italian friar and preacher, founded the Franciscan order 1209.

Francis of Sales, Saint (1567–1622), Savoyard ecclesiastic, bishop of Geneva 1602–22, opponent of Calvinism.

Francis Xavier, Saint (1506), Spanish Jesuit, missionary in India and the Far East.

francium, naturally occurring radioactive element, discovered 1939 by the French chemist Marguérite Percy (b. 1909).

Franck, César (1822–90), Belgian-born organist and composer in France, wrote oratorios, symphonic poems, organ music, etc.

Franco, Francisco (1892–1975), Spanish soldier and statesman, led Nationalists in Civil War, head of state 1939–75.

Franco-Prussian War, began July 1870; ended May 1871.

Frank, Anne (1929–44), Dutch Jewish girl, kept *Diary* (pub. 1947) while hiding from Nazis; died in concentration camp.

Frank, Bruno (1887–1945), German novelist, wrote *Trench* (1926).

Frank, Leonhard (1882–1961), German novelist, wrote *Karl and Anna* (1926).

Frankfurter, Felix (1882–1965), American lawyer, Supreme Court judge 1939–62.

Franklin, Benjamin (1706–90), American printer, founding father, diplomat, scientist, moralist, and autobiographer.

Franklin, Sir John (1786–1847), English Arctic explorer, lost on fourth expedition 1845–47.

Franz, Robert (1815–92), German composer of more than 300 songs.

Franz Ferdinand (1863–1914), Austrian archduke, whose assassination at Sarajevo precipitated World War I.

Franz Joseph (1830–1916), emperor of Austria 1848–1916 and king of Hungary from 1867.

Franz Joseph Land, Arctic archipelago, discovered 1873; sovereignty proclaimed by U.S.S.R. 1926.

Frasch, Hermann (1851–1914), German-born American chemist, developed process for extracting sulphur from underground deposits.

Fraser, Claud Lovat (1890–1921), English artist and influential stage designer.

Fraser River, British Columbia, discovered 1793 by the explorer Sir Alexander Mackenzie.

Fraunhofer Lines, in solar spectrum, discovered 1802 by the English physicist William Hyde Wollaston (1766–1828); studied from 1814 by the German physicist Joseph von Fraunhofer (1787–1826).

Frazer, Sir James (1854–1941), Scottish anthropologist, wrote the classic study *The Golden Bough* (1890).

Fréchette, Louis Honoré (1839–1908), French-Canadian poet and politician, wrote patriotic verse.

Fredegunde (d. 597), Frankish queen, involved in bloody dynastic intrigues.

Frederick I, 'Barbarossa' (*c.* 1123–1190), Holy Roman emperor 1155–90, drowned on crusade.

Frederick II (1194–1250), Holy Roman emperor 1212–50, also Frederick I of Sicily 1198–1250; failed to unite Germany and Italy.

Frederick III (1415–93), Holy Roman emperor 1440–93, a period of great disorder.

Frederick I (d. 1533), king of Denmark 1523–33, replaced Christian II.

Frederick II (1534–88), king of Denmark 1559–88, warred against Sweden 1563–70.

Frederick III (1609–70), king of Denmark 1648–70, lost war against Sweden but strengthened monarchy.

Frederick IV (1671–1730), king of Denmark 1699–1730, defeated by Sweden.

Frederick V (1723–66), king of Denmark 1746–66, was a patron of the arts and education.

Frederick VI (1768–1839), king of Denmark 1808–39, ally of Napoleon; lost Norway 1814.

Frederick VII (1808–63), king of Denmark 1848–63, first modern constitutional ruler.

Frederick VIII (1843–1912), king of Denmark 1906–12, father of Haakon VII of Norway.

Frederick IX (1899–1972), king of Denmark 1947–72, succeeded by his daughter Margrethe.

Frederick I (1657–1713), elector of Brandenburg 1688–1701, granted title king in Prussia 1701–13.

Frederick II, 'the Great' (1712–86), king of Prussia 1740–86, outstanding military commander; made Prussia a great power.

Frederick III (1831–88), emperor of Germany 1888, as prince served as an army commander in various wars.

Frederick I (1676–1751), king of Sweden 1720–51, was unable to exert much personal power.

Frederick V (1596–1632), elector palatine of the Rhine 1610–23, and king of Bohemia 1619, ancestor of Hanoverian dynasty in Britain.

Frederick William I (1688–1740), king of Prussia 1713–40, conquered much of Pomerania.

Frederick William II (1744–97), king of Prussia 1786–97, joined in the partitions of Poland.

Frederick William III (1770–1840), king of Prussia 1797–1840; his reign saw a general decline in Prussian power.

Frederick William IV (1795–1861), king of Prussia 1840–61, of reactionary views; insane 1858–61.

Frederick William, 'the Great Elector' (1620–88), elector of Brandenburg 1640–88, increased territory and strengthened state power.

Fredericksburg, Battle of, Confederate victory in the American Civil War, 13 Dec. 1862.

Free Church of Scotland, formed 1843.

free fall, studied and described 1604 by Galileo (*q.v.*).

Freeman, Edward Augustus (1823–92), English historian, wrote *The Norman Conquest* (1867 ff.).

freemasonry, derived from lodges of English and Scottish masons in the 16th century; first Grand Lodge inaugurated in London 1717; introduced in America *c.* 1730 and in Europe during the 18th century.

Freetown, capital of Sierra Leone; first settled (mainly by freed Negro slaves) 1787.

Frege, Gottlob (1848–1925), German mathematician, noted for his work in mathematical logic.

Freiligrath, Ferdinand (1810–76), German poet of radical political views; spent some time in exile in London.

Fremont, John Charles (1813–90), American explorer of Oregon and California.

French, Sir John (1852–1925), British soldier, commander of the British Expeditionary Force in France 1914–15.

French Community, association of states comprising France, its overseas departments and territories and former African territories, formed Oct. 1958.

French Equatorial Africa, former federation of French possessions in West Africa; region first settled 1839; federal constitution adopted 1910; constituent territories independent 1960. See **Chad; Central African Republic; Congo Republic; Gabon.**

French Guiana, South America, first French settlement 1604; further attempts at settlement in 18th century; penal colony established 1854 and finally closed 1947; overseas department of France 1946.

French language, earliest known document, the *Oaths of Strasbourg*, dated 842.

French Polynesia, Pacific, islands under French administration 1903; made a French overseas territory 1946. See also **Tahiti.**

French Revolution, began June 1789; ended with establishment of Consulate Nov. 1799.

French Revolutionary Calendar, began 21–22 Sept. 1792; ended 31 Dec. 1805.

French Revolutionary Wars, 1792–99.

French Somaliland. See **Djibouti.**

French Southern and Antarctic Territories, established 1955.

French Sudan. See **Mali.**

French Union, formed Oct. 1946; superseded by French Community 1958.

French West Africa, mainly acquired in the second half of the 19th century; federal constitution adopted 1895; constituent territories independent 1960. See **Benin; Guinea; Ivory Coast; Mali; Mauretania; Niger; Senegal.**

Freneau, Philip (1752–1832), American poet, wrote political and satirical verse; took part in American Revolution.

Frenssen, Gustav (1863–1945), German novelist, wrote *Jörn Uhl* (1901).

frequency modulation, of radio waves, developed 1933 by the American engineer Edwin H. Armstrong (1890–1954).

Frere, Sir Bartle (1815–84), English colonial administrator in India and South Africa.

Frescobaldi, Girolamo (1583–1643), Italian organist and composer, best known for organ music.

Fresnel, Augustin Jean (1788–1827), French physicist, contributed to the establishment of the wave theory of light.

Freud, Sigmund (1856–1939), Austrian pioneer of psychoanalysis, author of *The Interpretation of Dreams* (1900).

Freytag, Gustav (1816–95), German writer, author of the novel *Debit and Credit* (1855).

Frick, Henry Clay (1849–1919), American industrialist, steel magnate, and patron of the arts.

Fricker, Peter Racine (b. 1920), English composer, wrote the choral *Vision of Judgement* (1956).

Friedrich, Caspar David (1774–1840), German painter, best remembered for his romantic landscapes.

Friends, Society of (Quakers), founded 1650.

Frimaire, French revolutionary calendar month, 21 Nov. to 20 Dec.

Friml, Rudolf (1879–1972), Czech-born American composer of musical comedies, e.g. *Rose Marie.*

Frisch, Max (b. 1911), Swiss dramatist and novelist, author of *Stiller* (1952) and *Andorra* (1962).

Frith, William (1819–1909), English painter, remembered for *Derby Day* (1858).

Froben, Johannes (1460–1527), German pioneer printer, e.g. Erasmus's Greek *New Testament* (1516).

Frobisher, Sir Martin (*c.* 1535–1594), English navigator, sought North–West Passage; fought against Armada.

Fröding, Gustav (1860–1911), Swedish poet, whose best known collection is *Guitar and Concertina* (1891).

Froebel, Friedrich (1782–1852), German educational reformer, founder of the kindergarten 1816.

Froissart, Jean (*c.* 1333–*c.* 1405), French historian, author of chronicles of 14th-century European states.

Fromentin, Eugène (1820–76), French artist, also author of the novel *Dominique* (1862).

Fromm, Erich (b. 1900), German-born American psychoanalyst, concerned with the problems of man in western society.

Fronde, The, period of unrest in France, began 1648; ended 1653.

Frontenac, Comte de (1620–98), French soldier, governor of New France (Canada) 1672–82 and 1689–98.

Fronto, Marcus Cornelius (*c.* A.D. 100–*c.* 170), Roman orator and grammarian, tutor of Marcus Aurelius.

Frost, Robert (1874–1963), American poet, wrote about the New England countryside.

Froude, James Anthony (1818–94), English historian and literary executor of Thomas Carlyle.

Fructidor, French revolutionary calendar month, 18 Aug. to 16 Sept.

Frumentius, Saint (4th cent. A.D.), founder and first bishop of the Ethiopian Christian Church.

Fry, Christopher (b. 1907), English author of verse plays, including *The Lady's Not for Burning* (1948).

Fry, Elizabeth (1780–1845), English Quaker and social reformer, especially of prisons.

Fry, Joseph (1728–87), English Quaker businessman, founded chocolate-manufacturing firm.

Fry, Roger (1866–1934), English painter and art critic, championed Post-Impressionists in Britain.

Fuad I (1868–1936), sultan of Egypt 1917–22, when British protectorate ended; king 1922–36.

Fuchs, Klaus (b. 1912), German-born British spy, imprisoned for passing atom secrets to the Soviet Union.

Fuchs, Leonard (1501–66), German botanist, author of the comprehensive *Concerning the Description of Plants* (1542).

Fuchs, Sir Vivian (b. 1908), English geologist and explorer, led the Commonwealth Antarctic Expedition 1957–58.

fuel cell, first one (using hydrogen and oxygen) invented 1839 by Sir William Grove (1811–96); first successful device patented 1952 by the English engineer F. T. Bacon.

Fugger, Jakob (1459–1525), German financier, turned family business into a powerful international organization; financed the Hapsburgs.

Fujiwara, Michinaga (966–1027), Japanese statesman, brought the Fujiwara clan to the peak of its power.

Fulk (1092–1143), count of Anjou 1109–29 and king of Jerusalem 1131–43.

Fuller, Thomas (1608–61), English clergyman, wrote *The Worthies of England* (pub. 1662).

Fuller, William (1670–c. 1717), English imposter, associated with Titus Oates (*q.v.*).

Fulton, Robert (1765–1815), American engineer, designed a submarine and made great improvements in steamships.

Furness, Christopher, Baron (1852–1912), English shipowner, founded Furness Steamship Line and great shipbuilding concern.

Furniss, Harry (1854–1925), Irish-born illustrator of classics, *Punch* and *Illustrated London News*.

Furry Day, festival held at Helston, Cornwall, on St Michael's Day, 8 May (except when this is a Sunday or Monday).

Furtwängler, Wilhelm (1886–1954), German conductor, active in Berlin and U.S.A.

Fuseli, Henry (1741–1825), Swiss-born English painter, often in a surrealistic, nightmarish vein.

Fustel de Coulanges, Numa Denis (1830–89), French historian, wrote *The Ancient City* (1864).

Futurism, art movement began 1909; ended *c.* 1915.

G

Gabin, Jean (1904–77), French film actor, made a notable appearance in *Le Jour Se Lève* (1939).

Gabinius, Aulus (d. *c.* 47 B.C.), Roman politician and soldier, supported first Pompey, then Caesar.

Gabo, Naum (b. 1900), Russian-born American sculptor, a leader of the Constructivist movement.

Gabon, West Africa, discovered by Portuguese *c.* 1472; first settled by French *c.* 1840; part of French Equatorial Africa 1910; French overseas territory 1946; independent republic since 1960.

Gaborian, Émile (1835–73), French detective story writer, author of *Monsieur Lecoq* (1869).

Gabriel, Jacques Ange (*c.* 1698–1782), French architect, built Petit Trianon at Versailles.

Gabrieli, Giovanni (1557–1612), Italian composer and organist, best known for his choral and instrumental works.

Gaddi, Taddeo (*c.* 1300–1366), Italian painter, notably of a fresco cycle *Life of the Virgin*.

gadolinium, oxide separated 1880 by the Swiss chemist Jean de Marignac (1817–94); element isolated 1886 by the French chemist Paul Lecoq de Boisbaudran (1838–1912).

Gaelic League, founded in Dublin 1893.

Gagarin, Yuri (1934–68), Russian cosmonaut, was the first man to circle the earth in a spaceship, 1961.

Gage, Thomas (1721–87), English soldier, served in American wars; last governor of Massachusetts 1774–75.

Gainsborough, Thomas (1727–88), English painter of landscapes and idealized gentlefolk.

Gaitskell, Hugh (1906–63), British statesman, chancellor of the exchequer 1950–51, Labour Party leader 1955–63.

Gaius (2nd cent. A.D.), Roman jurist, whose *Institutes* provide a useful guide to the elements of Roman law.

Galapagos Islands, archipelago in the Pacific, discovered 1535; annexed by Ecuador 1832.

galaxies, first classified 1926 by the American astronomer Edwin P. Hubble (1889–1953).

Galba (5 B.C.–A.D. 69), Roman emperor A.D. 68–69, appointed and then assassinated by the Praetorian Guard.

Galbraith, John Kenneth (b. 1908), American economist and diplomat, author of *The Affluent Society* (1958).

Galen (*c.* A.D. 130–*c.* A.D. 201), Greek physician, whose writings formed the chief medical authority throughout the Middle Ages.

Galerius (d. A.D. 311), Roman emperor 305–311, persecuted Christians.

Galliani, Ferdinando (1728–87), Italian economist, wrote *Della Moneta* (1751).

Galicia, inhabited by Slavs 6th century A.D.; annexed by Poland 1349; ruled by Austria 1772–1919; part of Poland 1919–39; ruled by U.S.S.R. since 1945.

Galicia, Spain, conquered by Rome *c.* A.D. 137; kingdom founded by Suevi *c.* 410; absorbed by Leon and Castile 11th century.

Galileo Galilei (1564–1642), Italian mathematician and astronomer, made an outstanding contribution to modern scientific thought.

Galla Placidia (d. 450), consort of Roman emperor Constantinius III, regent for son Valentinian III.

Galle, Johann (1812–1910), German astronomer, observed planet Neptune 1846.

Gallegos, Rómulo (1884–1969), Venezuelan novelist, briefly president 1948.

Galli-Curci, Amelita (1862–1963), Italian soprano operatic singer, distinguished in Verdi and Puccini operas.

Gallieni, Joseph Simon (1849–1916), French soldier, governor of Paris 1914; his prompt reinforcement of the army saved the city.

Gallienus (d. A.D. 268), Roman emperor with his father Valerian 253–260, sole emperor 260–268.

Gallipoli, World War I, first Allied landings 25 April 1915; final withdrawal 8 Jan. 1916.

Gallitzin, Demetrius (1770–1840), Russian-born Roman Catholic priest in America, established mission in Pennsylvania.

gallium, chemical element, discovered 1875 by the French chemist Paul Lecoq de Boisbaudran (1838–1912).

gallon, imperial standard, measure legalized in Britain 1824; redefined under the 1963 Weights and Measures Act.

Gallup, George Horace (b. 1901), American statistician, was the first to use scientific methods for sampling public opinion.

Gallus (d. A.D. 253), Roman emperor 251–253, made disgraceful peace with Goths; killed by his own soldiers.

Galois, Evariste (1811–32), French mathematician, contributed important work to the theory of equations.

Galsworthy, John (1867–1933), English novelist, wrote *The Forsyte Saga* (1906–21).

Galt, Sir Alexander (1817–93), British-born Canadian statesman; first high commissioner in Britain 1880–83.

Galt, John (1779–1839), Scottish novelist, father of Alexander Galt, wrote *Annals of the Parish* (1821).

Galton, Sir Francis (1822–1911), English writer on heredity and eugenics, notably *Hereditary Genius* (1869).

Galvani, Luigi (1737–98), Italian anatomist, discovered galvanism.

galvanometer, invented 1820 by the German physicist Johann Schweigger (1779–1857); improved design produced 1836 by the English scientist William Sturgeon (1783–1850).

Gama, Vasco da (*c.* 1460–1524), Portuguese explorer and navigator, discovered sea-route to India.

Gambetta, Léon (1838–82), French statesman, prime minister 1880–82, strong supporter of the 3rd republic.

Gambia, West Africa, discovered by Portuguese 1455; British claim to region recognized 1783; part of Sierra Leone 1807–43 and 1866–88; separate colony 1889; protectorate established in part of Gambia 1894; achieved independence 1965; became a republic 1970.

gamma rays, discovered 1900 by the French physicist Paul-Ulrich Villard (1860–1934).

Gandhi, Indira (b. 1917), Indian stateswoman, first woman prime minister of India 1966–77.

Gandhi, Mohandas (1869–1948), Indian spiritual and political leader, sought independence for his country by nonviolent means (civil disobedience); assassinated.

Gannt, Henry Lawrence (1861–1919), American engineer, devised the Gannt Chart of industrial management.

Gaon, The. See **Wilna,** Elijah.

Gapon, Georgi (1870–1906), Russian priest, led crowd which was fired on by troops on Bloody Sunday 1905.

Garamond, Claude (d. 1561), French type designer, replaced Gothic with roman.

Garbo, Greta (b. 1905), Swedish-born film actress in Hollywood of legendary glamour, starred in *Ninotchka* (1939), etc.

garden city, idea first adopted for England 1898 by Sir Ebenezer Howard (1850–1928); first garden city was Letchworth begun 1903.

Gardiner, Alfred George (1865–1946), English journalist, edited *Daily News* 1902–19.

Gardiner, Samuel Rawson (1829–1902), English historian, wrote on the English Civil War and the Commonwealth.

Gardiner, Stephen (c. 1483–1555), English prelate, bishop of Winchester, took part in Reformation but essentially anti-Protestant.

Gardner, Erle Stanley (1889–1970), American writer, created Perry Mason and other detective characters.

Garfield, James Abram (1831–81), American statesman, 20th president of the U.S.A. 1881; assassinated.

Garibaldi, Giuseppe (1807–82), Italian hero of unification struggle; conquered Sicily and Naples 1860.

Garnett, Constance (1862–1946), English translator of Russian novels, wife of Edward Garnett.

Garnett, David (b. 1892), English novelist, son of Edward Garnett, wrote *Lady into Fox* (1922).

Garnett, Edward (1868–1937), English writer and critic, son of Richard Garnett, author of *The Breaking Point*.

Garnett, Richard (1835–1906), English librarian and scholar, was keeper of printed books in the British Museum library.

Garnier, Francis (1839–73), French explorer, made trip from Cambodia to Shanghai.

Garofalo, Benvenuto da (1481–1559), Italian painter, worked much in his native Ferrara.

Garrick, David (1717–79), English actor and producer, was a leading figure in the English theatre.

Garrison, William Lloyd (1805–79), American abolitionist, founded journal *The Liberator*.

Garter, Order of the, founded by Edward III c. 1348.

Garth, Sir Samuel (1661–1719), English poet, wrote *The Dispensary* (1699).

Garvin, James Louis (1868–1947), Irish-born English journalist, edited the *Observer* 1908–42.

Gary, Indiana, founded 1905 by the U.S. Steel Corporation, and named after the American businessman Elbert Henry Gary (1846–1927).

gas, coal, first produced in quantity 1795 by William Murdock (q.v.).

gas, North Sea, discovered 1959 off Dutch coast, and 1966 off southeast coast of England; commercially produced in Britain from 1967. See also **coal gas.**

gas, poison, first used World War I by the German army against the Russians Jan. 1915 and against the Allies April 1915, and by the British army Sept. 1915; use banned by Geneva Protocol 1925.

Gascoigne, George (c. 1525–1577), English poet, wrote satires and pamphlets.

Gaskell, Elizabeth (1810–65), English novelist, wrote *Cranford* (1853) and *North and South* (1855).

Gas Light and Coke Company, first gas company, granted charter c. 1812.

gas mantle, incandescent, patented 1885 by the Austrian chemist Carl Auer von Welsbach (1858–1929).

Gasparri, Cardinal Pietro (1852–1934), Italian codifier of canon law.

Gassendi, Pierre (1592–1655), French philosopher and scholar, popularized the new astronomy, and attacked Aristotle and Descartes.

gas turbine, first used in Germany 1939 to power aircraft.

Gatling gun, invented 1861–62 by the American engineer Richard Gatling (1818–1903).

G.A.T.T., General Agreement on Tariffs and Trade, came into force Jan. 1948.

Gauden, John (1605–62), English prelate, probably wrote famous defence of Charles I, *Eikon Basilike* (1649).

Gaudí, Antonio (1852–1926), Spanish architect of eccentric Art Nouveau style; worked in his native Barcelona.

Gaudier-Brzeska, Henri (1891–1915), French sculptor, identified with the Vorticist movement; killed in action.

Gaugamela, Battle of, victory of Alexander the Great over Darius III of Persia, 1 Oct. 331 B.C.

Gauguin, Paul (1848–1903), French painter, a leading Postimpressionist, spent later life in Tahiti and the Marquesas Islands.

Gaul, occupied by Celtic tribes from c. 7th cent. B.C.; Roman conquest completed 51 B.C.; invaded by Franks c. A.D. 270; Frankish kingdom established 481. See **France.**

Gaulle, Charles de. See **de Gaulle, Charles.**

Gaunt, John of. See **John of Gaunt.**

Gauss, Karl Friedrich (1777–1855), German mathematician, made major contributions to theory of numbers, electricity, and astronomy.

Gautier, Théophile (1811–72), French poet and story writer, author of *Mademoiselle de Maupin* (1835).

Gavarni, Paul (pseud. of Guillaume Chevalier; 1804–66), French graphic artist, best known for his magazine illustrations.

Gaveston, Piers (d. 1312), French-born favourite of Edward II, executed by opposition party.

Gay, John (1685–1732), English poet and dramatist, author of *The Beggar's Opera* (1728).

Gay-Lussac, Joseph Louis (1778–1850), French scientist, discovered law of volumes.

Gdansk, Poland, capital of the dukes of Pomerania in 13th century; ruled by Teutonic knights 1309–1454; free city

1466–1793; ceded to Prussia 1793; free city 1807–14 and 1919–39; ceded to Poland 1945.

Ged, William (1690–1749), Scottish printer, invented stereotyping.

Geddes, Andrew (1783–1844), Scottish painter and etcher, best known as a portraitist.

Geddes, Sir Eric (1875–1937), English industrialist and politician; 'Geddes Axe' applied to public expenditure 1922.

Geertgen, tot Sint Jans (c. 1465–c. 1493), Dutch painter, e.g. *Lamentation over the Dead Christ.*

Geiger counter, invented 1908 by the German physicist Hans Geiger (1882–1945) and Lord Rutherford; sensitivity increased 1928 by Geiger and W. Müller.

Geikie, Sir Archibald (1835–1924), Scottish geologist, director of the Geological Museum, London 1882–1901.

Gelasius I, Saint (d. 496), Pope 492–496, left letters and other writings.

Gelasius II (d. 1119), Pope 1118–19, driven from Rome; died in France.

Geminiani, Francesco (c. 1679–1762), Italian violinist, spent much of his life in England; wrote on technique.

General Medical Council, London, established 1858.

General Strike, in Britain, 3–13 May 1926.

generator, electric principle demonstrated 1831 by Michael Faraday; first efficient designs produced in the 1870s in France and Germany.

Genet, Jean (b. 1910), French writer, a former criminal, wrote plays *The Maids* (1947) and *The Blacks* (1958).

genetic code, first suggested 1954 by George Gamow; slowly elucidated in the 1960s by many workers.

genetics, experimental study 1857–65 by Gregor Mendel (*q.v.*); results were rediscovered 1900 by the Dutch botanist Hugo de Vries (1848–1935).

Geneva Convention, establishing the International Red Cross, held 1864; revised 1906; further conventions dealing with war victims 1929 and 1949.

Geneviève, Saint (c. 422–512), patron saint of Paris.

Genghis Khan (1162–1227), Mongol warrior, whose empire stretched from China to Poland.

Genlis, Comtesse de (1746–1830), French writer of *Mémoires* (1825).

Genseric (d. A.D. 477), king of the Vandals 428–477 seized North Africa and sacked Rome, 455.

Gentile da Fabriano (c. 1370–1427), Italian painter, leading member of the Umbrian school.

Gentleman's Magazine, founded 1731 by Edward Cave (1691–1754).

gentlemen-at-arms, the English sovereign's personal bodyguard, established by Henry VIII 1509.

Geoffrey of Monmouth (c. 1100–1154), Welsh chronicler, bishop of St Asaph 1152–54, wrote *Historia Britonum.*

Geological Society, London, founded 1807; received royal charter 1925.

geometry, studied by the ancient Egyptians, Babylonians and Greeks; knowledge compiled c. 300 B.C. by Euclid (*Elements*); analytical geometry created 1637 by René Descartes (*q.v.*). See also **non-Euclidean geometry.**

George, Saint (4th cent. A.D.), Christian martyr, made patron saint of England 1349.

George I (1660–1727), elector of Hanover 1698–1727, and king of Great Britain 1714–27.

George II (1683–1760), king of Great Britain and elector of Hanover 1727–60.

George III (1738–1820), king of Great Britain 1760–1820, was also elector (1760–1815) and later king (1815–20) of Hanover.

George IV (1762–1830), king of Great Britain and Ireland 1820–30 and king of Hanover; prince regent 1811–20.

George V (1865–1936), king of Great Britain and Northern Ireland 1910–36 and emperor of India.

George VI (1895–1952), king of Great Britain and Northern Ireland 1936–52; succeeded after abdication of Edward VIII; emperor of India 1936–48.

George I (1845–1913), king of Greece 1863–1913; assassinated.

George II (1890–1947), king of Greece 1922–23; deposed, recalled after plebiscite; reigned 1935–47.

George, Henry (1839–97), American reformer, advocated 'single tax' system in *Progress and Poverty* (1879).

George, Stefan (1868–1933), German poet, led poetical revival in Germany.

George Cross, British order for valour instituted 1940.

George Heriot's School, Edinburgh, Scottish public school, founded 1628.

George Washington Bridge, New York–New Jersey, opened 1931.

George Watson's College, Edinburgh, Scottish public day school, founded 1723.

Georgia, U.S.A., founded as a colony 1733, one of the 13 original states; entered the Union 1788; seceded 1861; readmitted to Union 1870.

Georgia, U.S.S.R., converted to Christianity 4th century A.D.; invaded by Tatars 13th century and by Persians 17th century; annexed to Russia 1801; proclaimed independent 1918; incorporated into U.S.S.R. 1921; became a constituent republic 1936.

Gerard (d. 1108), archbishop of York

1100–1108, involved in investiture conflict; opponent of Anselm (*q.v.*).

Gerard, John (1545–1612), English botanist, wrote famous *Herbal* (1597).

Gerard, John (1564–1637), English Jesuit, involved in Gunpowder Plot.

Gerhardi, William (b. 1895), English novelist, author of *Futility* (1922).

Gerhardt, Charles (1816–56), French chemist, developed a method of classifying organic compounds.

Géricault, Théodore (1791–1824), French painter, e.g. *The Raft of the 'Medusa'* (1819).

German, Sir Edward (1862–1936), English composer, remembered for operetta *Merrie England* (1902).

German Democratic Republic, established Oct. 1949, formerly Russian occupation zone in Germany.

German Federal Republic, established May 1949, formed from the combined British, French and American occupation zones in Germany.

Germanicus Caesar (15 B.C.–A.D. 19), Roman soldier, nephew of Emperor Tiberius, won great victories in Germany; died, probably poisoned, near Antioch.

germanium, chemical element, discovered 1886 by the German chemist Clemens Winkler (1838–1904).

Germany, inhabited by Teutonic peoples from early times; separated from France by Treaty of Verdun 843; ruled by emperors, Saxon 918–1024, Salian 1024–1138, Hohenstaufen 1138–1254, Hapsburg and Luxemburg 1273–1437, Hapsburg 1457–1806; Confederation of the Rhine 1806–13; German Confederation 1815–66; North German Confederation 1866–71; German Empire (Hohenzollern) 1871–1918; Weimar Republic 1919–33; Third Reich 1933–45; divided into 4 zones under Allied occupation 1945. See **German Democratic Republic; German Federal Republic.**

Geronimo (1829–1909), Apache chief, led the last great American Indian rebellion in North America.

Gerry, Elbridge Thomas (1837–1927), American lawyer, noted crusader against cruelty to children and animals.

Gershwin, George (1898–1937), American composer of *Porgy and Bess* and *Rhapsody in Blue*.

Gerson, Jean de (1363–1429), French theologian and mystic, influential in movement for Church reform.

Gerstäcker, Friedrich (1816–72), German traveller, author of many adventure stories.

Gertrude, Saint (1256–c. 1302), German nun, wrote accounts of her visions.

Gervase of Canterbury (d. c. 1210), English chronicler, compiled a history of archbishops of Canterbury.

Gesell, Arnold Lucius (1880–1961), American pioneer in child psychology, wrote *The First Five Years* (1940).

Gesenius, Wilhelm (1786–1842), German theologian and scholar, chiefly of Hebrew.

Gesner, Konrad von (1516–65), Swiss bibliographer and naturalist, was a voluminous writer and collector of plants.

Getty, Jean Paul (1892–1976), American businessman, whose oil interests made him one of the world's richest men.

Gettysburg, Battle of, Union victory in the American Civil War, 1–3 July 1863; address, delivered by Abraham Lincoln 19 Nov. 1863.

Ghana, West Africa, Portuguese settlements by 1482; coastal forts built by British, Danes and Dutch in 17th and 18th centuries; became a British colony 1874; achieved independence 1957; declared a republic 1960.

Ghazali, Abu Hamid Mohammed al (1058–1111), Arab theologian and philosopher, opposed Muslim scholasticism.

Ghent, Treaty of, between the U.S.A. and Great Britain ending the War of 1812, signed 24 Dec. 1814.

Ghent, University of, founded by King William of Württemberg 1816.

Ghent Cathedral, begun 12th century; completed c. 1530.

Ghiberti, Lorenzo (c. 1378–1455), Italian sculptor, made bronze 'Doors of Paradise' for the Baptistery, Florence.

Ghirlandaio (1449–94), Italian painter of Florentine school, particularly noted for his frescoes.

Giacometti, Alberto (1901–66), Swiss sculptor and painter, whose elongated figures have an abstract, surrealist quality.

Gibbon, Edward (1737–94), English historian, wrote *Decline and Fall of the Roman Empire* (1766–88).

Gibbons, Grinling (1648–1721), Dutch-born English sculptor and, especially, woodcarver of impressive naturalism.

Gibbons, Orlando (1583–1625), English composer, organist at Chapel Royal, wrote sacred music, madrigals and keyboard music.

Gibbs, James (1682–1754), Scottish architect in Baroque style, designed Radcliffe Camera, Oxford.

Gibbs, Josiah Willard (1839–1903), American physicist, whose work laid the foundations of modern physical chemistry.

Gibbs, Sir Vicary (1751–1820), English lawyer, attorney-general 1807–12.

Gibraltar, captured by Moors 711; conquered by Spain 1462; captured by British 1704; possession ratified by Treaty of Utrecht 1713; besieged by French and Spanish 1779–83; Spanish claim renewed in the mid-1960s.

Gibson, John (1790–1866), Welsh sculptor

of myths and portraits in neoclassical style.

Giddings, Franklin Henry (1855–1931), American sociologist, author of *Scientific Study of Human Society* (1924).

Gide, André (1869–1951), French writer, author of *Les Faux-Monnayeurs* (1926), won Nobel Prize for Literature 1947.

Gielgud, Sir John (b. 1904), English actor, perhaps most famous in *Richard II* and other Shakespearian parts.

Gieseking, Walter (1895–1956), French-born German pianist, notable interpreter of French music.

Gifford, William (1756–1826), English critic of conservative opinions, edited *Quarterly Review* 1809–24.

Giggleswick School, Yorkshire, English public school, founded 1512.

Gigli, Beniamino (1890–1957), Italian operatic tenor, dominated the generation after Caruso.

Gilbert, Sir Alfred (1854–1934), English sculptor of *Eros* in Piccadilly Circus, London.

Gilbert, Sir Humphrey (c. 1539–1583), English navigator, established Newfoundland colony; drowned.

Gilbert, William (1544–1603), English pioneer in magnetism, wrote *De Magnete* (1600).

Gilbert, Sir William Schwenk (1836–1911), English writer of comic operas with Sir Arthur Sullivan (*q.v.*).

Gilbert and Ellice Islands, Western Pacific, discovered 1765; proclaimed a British protectorate 1892; made a colony 1915; Gilbert Islands seized by Japanese in World War II; Ellice Islands became constitutionally separate 1975, taking new name Tuvalu.

Gildas, Saint (c. 516–570), British monk, wrote history of Britain, valuable for account of near-contemporary events.

Gill, Eric (1882–1940), English sculptor, typographer, engraver and propagandist for revival of craft ideal.

Gillette, King (1855–1932), American inventor, who in 1895 devised the modern safety razor.

Gillray, James (1757–1815), English political caricaturist, satirized Napoleon, the Prince Regent, etc.

Gilmore, Patrick Sarsfield (1829–92), Irish-born American composer of *When Johnny Comes Marching Home* (1863).

Gilpin, Bernard (1517–83), English clergyman, notable for charity and integrity, made preaching tours in north of England.

Ginkgo tree, found in Japan 1690 by the German physician Engelbert Kaempfer; introduced into Europe in the 18th century.

Ginsberg, Allen (b. 1926), American poet, whose *Howl and Other Poems* (1956) made

him a leading figure in the 'beat' movement.

Giono, Jean (1895–1970), French novelist, best known for his books on French peasant life.

Giordano, Luca (1632–1705), Italian painter of Neapolitan school, prolific fresco artist.

Giordano, Umberto (1867–1948), Italian composer of the opera *Andrea Chénier* (1896).

Giorgione (c. 1478–1510), Italian painter, a founder of the Venetian school, whose works include *The Tempest*.

Giotto (Giotto di Bondoni; c. 1266–1337), Florentine artist, the first of the great Italian painters.

Giraldus Cambrensis (c. 1146–c. 1220), Welsh monk, geographer and historian, wrote books about Wales and Ireland.

Giraudoux, Jean (1882–1944), French novelist and playwright, author of *Amphytrion 38* (1929).

Girl Guides Association, movement formed in Britain 1910 by Lord Baden-Powell.

Girl Scouts, U.S.A. founded 1912 by Juliette Gordon Low.

Giro, Post Office banking service, came into operation 1968.

Girondins, group of moderate republicans in French Revolution, formed 1791; dissolved 1794.

Girtin, Thomas (1775–1802), English painter, pioneered freer watercolour style.

Girton College, Cambridge University, opened at Hitchin 1869; acquired present name and site 1872; admitted as college of the University 1947.

Gissing, George (1857–1903), English novelist, wrote *New Grub Street* (1891).

Giulio Romano (c. 1496–1546), Italian painter, engraver and architect in extreme Mannerist style.

Gjellerup, Karl Adolf (1857–1919), Danish novelist, awarded Nobel Prize 1917; worked in Germany.

Gladstone, Herbert John, Viscount (1854–1930), British statesman, son of W. E. Gladstone, first governor-general of South Africa 1910–14.

Gladstone, William Ewart (1809–98), British statesman, Liberal prime minister 1868–74, 1880–85, 1886, and 1892–4, introduced many important reforms.

gland secretion, first studied 1889 by the physiologist Charles Brown-Séquard (1817–94). See also **hormones.**

Glanvill, Joseph (1636–80), English theologian, wrote *The Vanity of Dogmatising* (1661).

Glanvill, Ranulf (d. 1190), English adviser to Henry II, chief justiciar 1180–89.

Glasgow Academy, Scottish public day school, founded 1846.

Glasgow Chamber of Commerce, oldest British chamber of commerce, founded 1783.

Glasgow University, founded 1451.

glass, earliest wholly glass objects date back to *c.* 2500 B.C.; glass blowing discovered 1st century B.C.; English glass industry established *c.* 1230; plate-glass first made commercially in France 1668; float-glass developed in Britain in 1950s.

Glauber's Salts, sodium sulphate, discovered by the German chemist Johann Glauber (1604–68).

Glazunov, Alexander (1865–1936), Russian composer and professor of music, noted chiefly for his symphonies.

Glendower, Owen (*c.* 1350–*c.* 1416), Welsh prince, led rebellion against Henry IV of England.

Glenn, John Herschel (b. 1921), American astronaut, was the first American to orbit the earth, 1962.

Glidden, Joseph (1813–1906), American inventor of barbed wire, 1873.

Glinka, Mikhail (1803–57), Russian composer, introduced national element into operas, e.g. *A Life for the Tsar* (1836).

Glorious First of June, naval battle off Ushant, British victory over the French 1794.

Gloucester, Humphrey, Duke of (1391–1447), the youngest son of Henry IV, protector during Henry VI's minority 1422–29.

Gloucester, Statute of, decreeing necessity of trial before the granting of the royal pardon, 1278.

Gloucester Cathedral, built at end of 11th century.

Glover, Sarah Ann (1785–1867), English inventor of tonic sol-fa system.

Gluck, Christoph Willibald (1714–87), German composer, made opera more dramatic, e.g. *Orpheus and Eurydice* (1762).

glucose, first studied 1799 by the French scientist Joseph Proust (1754–1826).

glycerine, discovered 1779 by Carl Scheele (*q.v.*).

glycogen, isolated 1857 by the French physiologist Claude Bernard (1813–78).

Glyndebourne Festival Opera, founded 1934 by John Christie (1882–1962).

Gmelin, Leopold (1788–1853), German chemist, discovered Gmelin's salt (potassium ferricyanide).

Gneisenau, August von (1760–1831), Prussian field marshal, prominent in war against Napoleon.

Gnosticism, religious movement originating in the 1st century A.D.; reached climax in 2nd-century Alexandrian school under the philosophers Valentinus and Basilides (*qq.v.*).

Goa, India, annexed by Portugal 1510; reintegrated with India 1961.

Gobelins, tapestry works near Paris, founded 1601 (originated as a dye works in 15th century); purchased for Louis XIV 1662, who appointed Charles Le Brun (*q.v.*) director.

Gobineau, Joseph Arthur, Comte de (1816–82), French diplomat and writer, proposed superiority of Teutonic peoples.

Godard, Jean Luc (b. 1930), French film director, a leading figure in the 'New Wave' movement.

Godefroy, Jacques (1587–1622), French jurist, member of a distinguished legal family.

Gödel's Proof, mathematical philosophy, propounded 1931 by the Austrian-born mathematician Kurt Gödel (b. 1906).

Godfrey, Sir Edmund Berry (1621–78), English justice of the peace, whose murder occasioned the anti-Catholic 'Popish Plot'.

Godfrey, Thomas (1736–63), first American playwright, wrote *The Prince of Parthia*.

Godfrey of Bouillon *c.* 1060–1100), French crusader and conqueror of Jerusalem.

Godiva, Lady (11th cent.), wife of Leofric, Earl of Mercia, in legend rode naked through Coventry.

Godolphin, Sidney, Earl of (1645–1712), English politician, as lord high treasurer 1702–10 worked closely with Marlborough (*q.v.*).

Godoy, Manuel de (1767–1851), Spanish statesman, was a notably unsuccessful chief minister.

Godunov, Boris (1552–1605), tsar of Russia 1598–1605, previously a successful general and effective ruler from 1584.

Godwin (d. 1053), earl of Wessex, opposed Edward the Confessor's pro-Norman policy; father of King Harold (*q.v.*).

Godwin, William (1756–1836), English radical reformer, wrote *Political Justice* (1793); married Mary Wollstonecraft (*q.v.*).

Godwin-Austen, Henry Haversham (1834–1923), English geologist, surveyed part of northern India.

Godwin-Austen, Mount (K2), Himalayas, climbed by an Italian expedition 31 July 1954.

Goebbels, Joseph (1897–1945), German Nazi leader, propaganda minister 1933–45; committed suicide.

Goerdeler, Karl Friedrich (1884–1945), German leader in resistance movement to Hitler; executed after failure of July 1944 plot.

Goes, Hugo van der (*c.* 1440–82), Flemish painter of the Portinari altarpiece.

Goethals, George Washington (1858–1928), American builder of Panama Canal 1907–14; first governor of Canal Zone 1914–16.

Goethe, Johann Wolfgang von (1749–1832), German poet, dramatist, scientist, and novelist, author of *Faust* (1808 and 1832), was of supreme importance in the development of German and European literature.

Gogarty, Oliver St John (1878–1957), Irish writer, author of *As I was going down Sackville Street* (1937).

Gogh, Vincent van (1853–90), Dutch painter, one of the greatest Post-impressionists, noted for his vigorous use of brilliant colour.

Gogol, Nikolai (1809–52), Russian playwright (*Inspector General*, 1836) and novelist (*Dead Souls*, 1842).

gold, probably known in Bronze Age; mined in Egypt 2900 B.C.; found in Colombia 1537; near Sacramento (California) Jan. 1848; Ballarat and Bendigo (Australia) 1851; in Otago (New Zealand) June 1861; at Barketon 1882 and Witwatersrand 1886 (South Africa); at Bonanza Creek (Klondike) Aug. 1896.

Gold Coast. See **Ghana.**

Golden Bull, on constitution of Holy Roman Empire promulgated by the Emperor Charles IV 1356.

Golden Gate Bridge, San Francisco, opened 1937.

Golden Spurs, Battle of the. See **Courtrai,** Battle of.

Golding, Louis (1895–1958), English writer, author of *Magnolia Street* (1932).

Golding, William Gerald (b. 1911), English novelist, author of *Lord of the Flies* (1954).

Goldman, Emma (1869–1940), Russian-born American anarchist, wrote *Living My Life* (1931).

Goldoni, Carlo (1707–93), Italian playwright, wrote sophisticated comedies, e.g. *La Locandiera* (1753).

gold rush, California 1849; Australia 1851; South Africa 1886; Klondike 1897–99.

Goldsmith, Oliver (1728–74), Irish-born writer of poetry, novel (*Vicar of Wakefield*, 1766) and comedies.

gold standard, introduced in Britain 1821; finally abandoned Sept. 1931.

Goldwyn, Samuel (1882–1974), American film producer, one of the legendary Hollywood moguls.

golf, origins uncertain, earliest recorded allusion Scotland 1457; first club, Honourable Company of Edinburgh Golfers, 1754; first course in the U.S.A. *c.* 1886.

Golitsyn, Prince Vasily (1643–1714), Russian soldier and statesman, helped reorganize Russian army.

Gollancz, Victor (1893–1967), British publisher, founded Left Book Club.

Goltzius, Hendrik (1558–1617), Dutch painter and pioneer of engraving technique.

Gompers, Samuel (1850–1924), English-born American labour leader; president of American Federation of Labour 1886–94 and 1896–1924.

Gomulka, Wladyslaw (b. 1905), Polish Communist leader 1956–70, represented more independent Polish position in Soviet bloc.

Goncharov, Ivan (1812–91), Russian novelist, created classic slothful Russian type in *Oblomov* (1859).

Goncourt, Edmond de (1822–96), French novelist, author of *La Fille Elisa* (1877); with brother Jules wrote famous *Journals.*

Goncourt, Jules de (1830–70), French novelist collaborated with his brother Edmond on the novel *Germinie Lacerteaux* (1864) and the *Journals.*

Gondomar, Count of (1567–1626), Spanish ambassador in England 1613–18 and 1619–22, strongly influenced James I.

Gongora, Luis de (1561–1627), Spanish poet, wrote in highly elaborate artificial style.

Gonville and Caius College. See **Caius College.**

Gonzaga, Federigo (1500–40), ruler of Mantua 1519–40, duke 1530–40; patron of the arts.

Gooch, Sir Daniel (1816–89), English railway engineer, improved locomotive construction.

Gooch, George Peabody (1873–1968), English historian, specialist in diplomatic history.

Goodyear, Charles (1800–60), American inventor, successfully developed vulcanized rubber.

Good Friday, Christian commemoration of the Crucifixion, the Friday before Easter.

Goodwin Sands, off SE coast of England, first mapped by the Dutch cartographer Lucas Waghenaer 1585.

Goodwood Cup, Goodwood, first run 1812.

Googe, Barnabe (1540–94), English poet, wrote eclogues, epitaphs and sonnets.

Goossens, Sir Eugène (1893–1962), English-born composer and conductor, worked in U.S.A. and Australia.

Goossens, Leon (b. 1897), English oboist of outstanding virtuosity; also an important teacher.

Gorchakov, Prince Alexander (1798–1883), Russian statesman and diplomat, imperial chancellor 1863–83.

Gordian I (A.D. 158–238), Roman emperor 238, killed himself after death of son Gordian II.

Gordian II (A.D. 192–238), Roman emperor 238 with his father; killed in battle.

Gordian III (*c.* A.D. 224–244), Roman emperor 238–244, son of Gordian II, won victories against Persians; assassinated.

Gordon, Adam Lindsay (1833–70), Australian poet, wrote *Bush Ballads and Galloping Rhymes* (1870).

Gordon, Charles (1833–85), English soldier, distinguished in China and Sudan; killed by Mahdists at Khartoum.

Gordon, Lord George (1751–93), Anglo-Scottish noble of eccentric character, led anti-Catholic 'Gordon Riots' 1780.

Gordon Highlanders, raised by the Marquis of Huntly (later Duke of Gordon) 1796.

Gordonstoun School, Elgin, Scottish public school, founded 1934 by Kurt Hahn (*q.v.*).

Gorges, Sir Ferdinando (*c.* 1566–1647), English adventurer, became proprietor of American colony of Maine.

Gorgias (*c.* 485–380 B.C.), Greek philosopher, features in Plato's dialogue, the *Gorgias*.

Göring, Hermann (1893–1946), German Nazi leader, World War I fighter ace, built up Luftwaffe and wielded vast economic power; committed suicide to avoid execution.

Gorki, Maxim (1868–1936), Russian writer of short stories, novels and autobiography; formulated Socialist Realism doctrine.

Gort, John, 6th Viscount (1886–1946), British soldier, commanded army in France 1939–40.

Goschen, George Joachim, 1st Viscount (1831–1907), British statesman, chancellor of the exchequer 1886–92.

Gosse, Sir Edmund (1849–1928), English writer, remembered for his autobiographical *Father and Son* (1907).

Gothic language, earliest recorded Germanic language, first written by Bishop Ulfilas (*q.v.*) 4th century A.D.; a form of it spoken in Crimea up to *c.* 1560.

Goths, Germanic peoples, settled on shores of Black Sea 2nd century A.D.; first attacked Romans 214; attacked by Huns *c.* 370. See also **Ostrogoths; Visigoths.**

Gottfried von Strassburg (late 12th–early 13th cent.), German poet, wrote *Tristan and Isolde*.

Gottschalk (*c.* 804–868), German monk and theologian, involved in controversies over predestination.

Gottsched, Johann Christoph (1700–66), German critic and literary dictator, insisted on classical 'correctness'.

Götz von Berlichingen (1480–1562), German adventurer and outlaw, leader of peasants' revolt; wrote autobiography.

Goucher College, Baltimore, Maryland, American women's college, founded 1885; assumed present name 1910.

Goudy, Frederick William (1865–1947), American type designer, prolific in invention.

Gough Island, South Atlantic, probably discovered by the Portuguese navigator Pero d'Anhaya 1505.

Goujon, Jean (mid-16th cent.), French sculptor in classical style.

Gould, Sir Francis Carruthers (1844–1925), English cartoonist, journalist and book illustrator.

Gould, Jay (1836–92), American financier and speculator in railway stock, attempted to corner gold on 'Black Friday' 1869.

Gounod, Charles (1818–93), French composer of the opera *Faust* (1859).

Gourmont, Remy de (1858–1915), French novelist, dramatist and critic, connected with the Symbolist movement.

Gower, John (*c.* 1325–1408), English poet, wrote in English, French and Latin; was a contemporary of Chaucer.

Goya y Lucientes, Francisco de (1746–1828), major Spanish painter and etcher, depicted Spanish life, horrors of war, terrifying fantasies.

Gozzi, Count Carlo (1720–1806), Italian playwright, wrote *Love of Three Oranges* (1761).

Gozzoli, Benozzo (*c.* 1420–97), Italian painter of frescoes *Procession of the Magi*; belonged to Florentine school.

Gracchus, Caius Sempronius (153–121 B.C.), Roman tribune 122–121 B.C., renewed land reform policy of brother Tiberius; killed in riot.

Gracchus, Tiberius Sempronius (163–133 B.C.), Roman tribune 133 B.C. and land reformer; killed in riot.

Grace, Dr William Gilbert (1848–1915), English cricketer, broke many records both as batsman and bowler in his long career.

Graetz, Heinrich (1817–91), German historian, wrote *History of the Jews* (1853–76).

Graf, Urs (*c.* 1485–1527), Swiss artist, famous for drawings of war scenes.

Graf Spee, German warship, trapped by the British in a naval action 13 Dec. 1939; scuttled 17 Dec.

Graf Zeppelin, German airship, completed first transatlantic flight 15 Oct. 1928; circumnavigated the world 15–29 Aug. 1929.

Grafton, Augustus, Duke of (1735–1811), English statesman, effectively prime minister 1768–70.

Graham, Billy (b. 1918), American evangelist, leader of highly organized revivalist campaigns.

Graham, John, of Claverhouse. See **Claverhouse.**

Graham, Martha (b. 1895), American dancer and choreographer, a leading figure in the evolution of modern dance.

Graham, Thomas, Lord Lynedoch (1748–1843), Scottish soldier, distinguished himself in Peninsular War.

Graham, Thomas (1805–69), Scottish chemist, noted for his work in colloidal chemistry; formulated Graham's Law 1831.

Grahame, Kenneth (1859–1932), Scottish writer of the children's classic *The Wind in the Willows* (1908).

Grahame-White, Claude (1879–1959), pioneer English aviator, established aircraft company.

Grainger, Percy (1882–1961), Australian-born composer and pianist in Britain and U.S.A., noted for his work in folk music.

Gramont, Philibert, Comte de (1621–1707), French noble at courts of Louis XIV and Charles II; his *Memoirs* were written by his brother-in-law.

gramophone. See **phonograph; sound recording.**

Granada, Spain, founded by Moors in 8th century; independent Moorish kingdom from 1238 until captured by Christians 1492.

Granados, Enrique (1867–1916), Spanish composer of nationally inspired music, e.g. *Goyescas.*

Grand Alliance, War of the, between France and Britain, Holland, the Holy Roman Empire and others 1689–97.

Grand Canyon National Park, Arizona, established 1919.

Grand Coulee Dam, Columbia River, Washington, completed 1942; enlarged 1974.

Grand Junction Canal, England, built 1793–1805.

Grand National, Liverpool, first run 1837.

Grand Prix, motor race, first held at Le Mans 1906 (and won by M. Szisz in a Renault); first held in Britain at Brooklands Aug. 1926.

Grand Trunk Canal, England, built 1766 onwards by the English engineer James Brindley (1716–72).

Grand Trunk Herald, first newspaper to be printed in a train, published by the American inventor Thomas Alva Edison.

Granjon, Robert (mid-16th cent.), French type designer, notably of 'civilité' italic.

Grant, Duncan (b. 1885), Scottish painter, pioneer of modern art in Britain.

Grant, Ulysses Simpson (1822–85), American soldier and statesman, commanded Union forces in Civil War, 18th president of the United States 1869–77.

Granville, George, Baron Lansdowne (1666–1735), English politician in reign of Queen Anne; also poet and playwright.

Granville, George, 2nd Earl (1815–91), British statesman, foreign secretary 1870–74 and 1880–85.

Granville-Barker, Harley (1877–1946), English actor, director, and critic (*Prefaces to Shakespeare*), and playwright (*Waste*, 1907).

Grass, Günter (b. 1927), German novelist, poet and dramatist, author of *The Tin Drum* (1959).

Grasse, François, Comte de (1722–88), French admiral, commanded fleet in American Revolutionary War.

Gratian, (A.D. 359–383), Roman emperor 375–383, fought barbarian invaders.

Gratian (12th cent.), Italian monk, whose *Decretum Gratiani* provided the foundation of canon law.

Grattan, Henry (1746–1820), Irish parliamentarian, opposed union with England 1800.

Graves, Robert (b. 1895), English poet and historical novelist, author of *I, Claudius* (1934).

gravitation, law of, established 1684 (published 1687) by Newton; gravitational constant measured 1798 by Henry Cavendish (*q.v.*).

gravity. See **free fall.**

Gray, Elisha (1835–1901), American inventor, claimed to have invented the telephone.

Gray, Thomas (1716–71), English poet, wrote *Elegy in a Country Churchyard* (1751).

Great Australian Basin, largest artesian basin in the world, resources discovered in NW New South Wales 1878.

Great Britain, formed by union of English and Scottish crowns 1603, but name not officially adopted until 1707; Stuarts 1603–49; Commonwealth 1649–53; Protectorate 1653–59; Stuarts 1660–1714; House of Hanover 1714–1837; House of Saxe-Coburg Gotha from 1837 (name changed to Windsor 1917). See also **England; United Kingdom.**

Great Britain, first Atlantic liner built of iron and with screw propulsion, designed by Isambard Kingdom Brunel and launched 1843; scuttled 1937 in the Falkland Islands; raised 1970 and brought back to Bristol.

Great Eastern, steamship designed by Isambard Kingdom Brunel and J. Scott Russell and launched 1858; broken up 1889.

Greater London Council, superseding the London County Council, established 1963.

Great Exhibition, Crystal Palace, London, held 1 May to 15 Oct. 1851.

Great Fire of London, 2–6 Sept. 1666.

Great Plague, of London, bubonic plague epidemic 1664–65, killing over 70,000 out of a population of *c.* 460,000.

Great Schism, within Roman Catholic Church, 1378–1417.

Great Trek, of Boers from Cape Colony to Natal, began 1835; ended 1843. Many moved on from Natal to found the Orange Free State.

Greco, El (1541–1614), Cretan-born Spanish painter, one of the great masters, achieved visionary intensity in such works as *Storm over Toledo*.

Grechaninov, Alexander (1864–1956), Russian composer in the U.S.A., wrote sacred music, symphonies and operas.

Greece, invaded by Greek-speaking peoples c. 1900 B.C.; network of city states formed 8th–6th centuries B.C.; Persian threat finally ended 479 B.C.; rise of Athens and Peloponnesian wars 460–404 B.C.; Macedonia dominant 338 B.C.; Roman conquest completed 133 B.C.; under Roman (and later Byzantine) control until Turkish conquest 1453; achieved independence from Turkey 1821–29; monarchy 1832–1924; republic 1924–35; monarchy 1935–73; republic since 1973.

Greek Orthodox Church, finally separated from Roman Church by Great Schism of 1054.

Greeley, Horace (1811–72), American editor and politician, nominated for the presidency 1872.

Green, Charles (1785–1870), English balloonist, made over 500 ascents.

Green, John Richard (1837–83), English pioneer of social history, wrote *Short History of the English People* (1874).

Green, Thomas (1836–82), English philosopher, wrote *Prolegomena to Ethics* (1883).

green belt, town and country planning scheme, approved by London County Council Jan. 1935; came into operation April 1936.

Greenaway, Kate (1846–1901), English illustrator, chiefly of children's books.

greenbacks, American paper money, first issued 25 Feb. 1862.

Greene, Graham (b. 1904), outstanding English novelist, short story writer and dramatist, whose work is strongly influenced by religious themes.

Greene, Sir Hugh Carleton (b. 1910), English administrator, brother of Graham Greene, director-general of the B.B.C. 1960–69.

Greene, Maurice (c. 1695–1755), English organist and composer, wrote *Jephthah* (1737).

Greene, Nathaniel (1742–86), American soldier, was a successful commander in the Revolutionary War.

Greene, Robert (1558–92), English playwright and pamphleteer, described low life in London.

Greenland, discovered c. 982 by the Norwegian explorer Eric the Red; resettled 1721; first crossed 1888 by the Norwegian explorer Fridtjof Nansen; integral part of Denmark since 1953.

Greenwich meridian, made prime meridian (0° longitude) of world 1884; made basis for standard time (Greenwich mean

time) for Britain 1880 and subsequently for the world.

Greenwich Observatory, Royal, established 1675 by Charles II; completely moved to Herstmonceux, Sussex, by 1958.

Greenwood, Thomas (1851–1908), English advocate of rate-supported free libraries.

Greg, Sir Walter Wilson (1875–1959), English bibliographer, especially of Elizabethan plays.

Gregg, Sir Cornelius (1888–1959), English government official, chairman of Board of Inland Revenue 1942–48, devised P.A.Y.E. system 1944.

Gregg, John Robert (1867–1948), Irish-born inventor of Gregg's shorthand.

Gregorian Calendar. See **Calendar, Gregorian.**

Gregory I, the Great, Saint (c. 540–604), Pope 590–604, church father, enforced strict clerical and monastic discipline; sent Augustine to convert England.

Gregory II, Saint (d. 731), Pope 715–731, asserted authority against Byzantines; sent Boniface to convert Germany.

Gregory III, Saint (d. 741), Pope 731–741, held council at Rome 731 to condemn iconoclasm.

Gregory V (d. 999), Pope 996–999, opposed by anti-pope John XVI.

Gregory VI (d. c. 1047), Pope 1045–46, deposed.

Gregory VII, Saint (c. 1020–85), Pope 1073–85, tried to secure Church supremacy over the state; was a noted reformer.

Gregory IX (c. 1147–1241), Pope 1227–41, involved in constant struggle with Emperor Frederick II.

Gregory X (1208–76), Pope 1271–76, called Council of Lyon 1274, briefly uniting Eastern and Western churches.

Gregory XI (1329–78), Pope 1370–78, brought papacy back to Rome from Avignon.

Gregory XII (c. 1326–1417), Pope 1406–15, resigned to end schism.

Gregory XIII (1502–85), Pope 1572–85, issued reformed (Gregorian) calendar.

Gregory XV (1554–1623), Pope 1621–23, founded Congregation of Propaganda.

Gregory XVI (1765–1846), Pope 1831–46, opposed nationalist and revolutionary movements.

Gregory, Lady Augusta (1852–1932), Irish playwright and writer on folk themes; prominent in Irish literary revival.

Gregory, Sir Augustus Charles (1819–1905), English-born Australian explorer, wrote, with brother, *Journals of Australian Exploration* (1884).

Gregory of Nazianzus, Saint (c. 329–c. 390), bishop of Constantinople 380–381, one of the fathers of the Eastern Church.

Gregory of Nyssa, Saint (c. 331–390),

BATLEY LIBRARY

bishop of Nyssa 371–396, one of the Cappadocian fathers of the Eastern Church.

Gregory of Tours, Saint (538–594), Frankish bishop of Tours 573–594, wrote valuable history of the Franks.

Grenada, West Indies, discovered by Columbus 1498; possession of the French crown 1674; ceded to Britain 1763; held by French 1779–83; headquarters of government of Windward Islands from 1885; member of West Indies Federation 1958–62; associated state with Britain from 1967.

Grenadier Guards, organized on a permanent basis 1740; named 'Grenadier' 1815, after Battle of Waterloo.

Grenfell, Sir Wilfred (1865–1940), English medical missionary active among fishermen and seamen in Newfoundland and Labrador.

Grenville, George (1712–70), British statesman, prime minister 1763–65, offended Americans with Stamp Act 1765.

Grenville, Sir Richard (c. 1541–91), English naval commander, captain of *The Revenge,* which fought alone against Spanish fleet.

Gresham's Law, on the question of coinage, propounded by Sir Thomas Gresham (1519–79).

Gresham's School, Holt, English public school, founded 1555.

Gretna Green, Scotland, scene of runaway marriages by English couples, particularly from 1754 to 1856 when Scottish law became more stringent; from 1940 such irregular marriages were made illegal.

Grétry, André Ernest (1741–1813), Belgian composer of light opera, e.g. *Zémire and Azor* (1771).

Greuze, Jean Baptiste (1725–1805), French painter, became immensely popular with his moralizing pictures.

Greville, Charles Cavendish (1794–1865), English political diarist, wrote *Memoirs* (publ. 1875–87).

Greville, Sir Fulke (1554–1628), English poet, royal servant, and close friend of Sir Philip Sidney (q.v.).

Grey, Charles, 2nd Earl (1764–1845), British statesman, prime minister 1830–34, associated with Reform Bill 1832.

Grey, Edward, Viscount Grey of Fallodon (1862–1933), British statesman, foreign secretary 1905–16.

Grey, Sir George (1812–98), English colonial administrator, governor of South Australia 1841–45, and of Cape Colony 1854–60.

Grey, Lady Jane (c. 1537–54), great-granddaughter of Henry VII, queen of England for nine days; beheaded.

Grey, Zane (1875–1939), American western novels.

greyhound racing, in Britain, began near Welsh Harp, Hendon, 1876; track opened at Belle Vue, Manchester, 1926; at White City, London, 1927.

Grieg, Edvard (1843–1907), Norwegian composer, best known for his *Peer Gynt Suite* (1876).

Grierson, John (1898–1972), Scottish film producer, noted for his documentary films.

Griffith, Arthur (1872–1922), Irish nationalist leader, negotiated Anglo-Irish Treaty 1921; president of Irish Free State 1922.

Griffith, David Wark (1875–1948), American silent film pioneer, directed *Birth of a Nation* (1915).

Griffiths, Ernest Howard (1851–1932), Welsh physicist, investigated measurement of heat.

Grignard reagents, organo-magnesium compounds, discovered 1900 by the French chemist François Victor Grignard (1871–1935).

Grillparzer, Franz (1791–1872), Austrian dramatist, wrote *Sappho* (1819).

Grimald, Nicholas (1519–62), English priest, poet and translator, was chaplain to Nicholas Ridley (q.v.).

Grimaldi, Joseph (1779–1837), English clown of Italian parentage, wrote *Memoirs.*

Grimbald, Saint (c. 820–903), Flemish-born abbot brought to England by Alfred the Great.

Grimm, Jakob (1785–1863), German scholar, collaborated with his brother Wilhelm; formulated Grimm's Law of consonantal shift.

Grimm, Wilhelm Karl (1786–1859), German folklorist, with his brother Jakob made a great collection of fairy tales.

Grimmelshausen, Hans Jakob von (c. 1622–76), German writer, remembered for *Simplicissimus* (1699).

Grimond, Joseph (b. 1913), British politician, leader of the Liberal Party 1955–67.

Grimthorpe, Edmund Beckett, 1st Baron (1816–1905), English lawyer, writer on religion, architecture, etc.

Grindal, Edmund (c. 1519–83), archbishop of Canterbury 1576, suspended 1577 for flouting Queen Elizabeth's policy.

Gringore, Pierre (c. 1475–1538), French poet and satirist, wrote *Jeu du Prince des Sots* (1512).

Gris, Juan (1887–1927), Spanish painter, became leading Cubist in Paris.

Grisi, Carlotta (1819–99), Italian ballerina, noted for her role in *Giselle,* 1841.

Grisi, Giulia (c. 1811–69), Italian operatic soprano, performed in France, England and U.S.A.

Grivas, George (1898–1974), Greek guerrilla leader, led campaign against British rule in Cyprus.

Grocers' Company, London, origins uncertain but at least as early as 1231; Hall built 1427; first charter granted by Edward III 1345.

Grock, (pseud. of Adrien Wettach; 1880–1959), famous Swiss clown, worked mainly in Britain.

Grocyn, William (c. 1446–1519), English humanist scholar at Oxford, pioneered Greek studies.

Grolier, Jean (1479–1565), French collector and connoisseur of books, designed decoration and bindings.

Gromyko, Andrei (b. 1909), Soviet diplomat, foreign minister of the U.S.S.R. from 1957.

Gropius, Walter (1883–1969), German-American architect, founded Bauhaus design school; in England 1934–37, and U.S.A. 1937–69.

Gros, Antoine (1771–1835), French painter, particularly of Napoleonic subjects.

Grosseteste, Robert (d. 1253), English theologian, bishop of Lincoln 1235–53, had wide scientific interests.

Grossmith, George (1847–1912), English actor, with brother Weedon (1854–1919), wrote *Diary of a Nobody* (1892).

Grosz, Georg (1893–1959), German satirical artist, expressed hatred of war and militarism; in U.S.A. 1933–59.

Grote, George (1794–1871), English historian, wrote *History of Greece* (1846–56).

Grotefend, George Friedrich (1775–1853), German scholar, successfully deciphered cuneiform script.

Grotius, Hugo (1583–1645), Dutch jurist, pioneered concepts of international law.

Groton, American boys' preparatory school, originally founded 1793.

Grouchy, Emmanuel, Marquis de (1766–1847), French soldier, failed to prevent Blücher from joining Wellington at Waterloo 1815.

groundnut scheme, in Tanganyika, began 1947; wound up 1955.

Grove, Sir George (1820–1900), English musicologist, compiled standard *Dictionary* (1878–89).

Grove cell. See fuel cell.

Gruber, Franz Xaver (1787–1863), Austrian composer of *Silent Night*.

Grünewald, Matthias (c. 1475–1528), German painter of intense religious feeling, e.g. Isenheim Altar c. 1515.

Guadalcanal, Western Pacific, part of British Solomon Islands protectorate 1893; occupied by Japanese 1942; finally evacuated by them after fierce figiting Feb. 1943.

Guadeloupe, West Indies, discovered by Columbus 1493; occupied by French 1635; held by Britain 1759–63; finally restored to France 1816; French overseas department from 1946.

Guam, Western Pacific, discovered by Magellan c. 1521; ceded by Spain to the U.S.A. 1898; occupied by Japanese Dec. 1941; retaken by Americans Aug. 1944.

Guardi, Francesco (1712–93), Italian painter, famous for scenes of his native Venice.

Guardian, British newspaper, founded 1821 as the *Manchester Guardian*; changed its name 1959.

Guarini, Giovanni (1558–1612), Italian poet, author of *Il Pastor fido*, which enjoyed great contemporary popularity.

Guarnieri, Giuseppe Antonio (1687–1745), Italian violin-maker, greatest of a family of makers.

Guatemala, Central America, conquered by Spanish 1524; proclaimed independence from Spain 1821; established as a separate independent republic 1847.

Guelphs and Ghibellines, rival factions in medieval Italian politics, mainly during 12th–14th centuries. See also **Welf.**

Guericke, Otto von (1602–86), German scientist, invented air pump and demonstrated air pressure.

Guérin, Maurice de (1810–39), French poet, author of *Le Centaure* (1840).

Guernica, Spanish town, largely destroyed by German planes April 1937 during the Spanish Civil War.

Guernsey, Channel Islands, probably acquired by duke of Normandy 933; annexed to English crown 1254; under German occupation 1940–45.

Guesclin, Bertrand du. See **Du Guesclin,** Bertrand.

Guest, Lady Charlotte (1812–95), Welsh writer, translated ancient *Mabinogion* (1838–49).

Guevara, Ernesto ('Che') (1928–67), Argentinian-born Communist guerrilla leader, shot while leading a revolt in Bolivia.

Guggenheim, Meyer (1828–1905), Swiss-born American financier; his son Daniel (1856–1930) set up Guggenheim Foundation 1924.

Guiana, British. See **Guyana.**

Guiana, French. See **French Guiana.**

Guiana, Netherlands. See **Surinam.**

Guicciardini, Francesco (1483–1540), Italian diplomat, wrote histories of Florence and Italy.

Guido d'Arezzo (c. 990–c. 1050), Italian monk, devised system of musical notation.

Guido Reni. See Reni, Guido.

Guilbert, Yvette (1869–1944), French *chanteuse*, sang music hall and other popular Parisian songs.

Guild Socialism, in Britain, National Guilds League formed 1915; movement collapsed by 1922.

Guillaume de Lorris (13th cent.), French poet, wrote *Roman de la Rose*.

guillotine, introduced in France by Dr

Joseph Guillotin (1738–1814) and first used 25 April 1792; similar machines existed in other European countries as early as the 13th century.

Guinea, West Africa, coastal region annexed by France 1849; part of French West Africa 1895; French overseas territory from 1946; became an independent republic 1958.

Guinea, Spanish. See **Equatorial Guinea.**

Guinea-Bissau, West Africa, discovered by Portuguese 1446; made separate Portuguese colony 1879; became an independent republic 1974.

Guinness, Sir Alec (b. 1914), English actor, distinguished on stage and in films.

Guinness, Sir Benjamin Lee (1798–1868), Irish brewer, founded a famous firm.

Guiscard, Robert (c. 1015–1085), Norman soldier, established Norman power in Sicily and southern Italy.

Guise, François, 2nd Duke of (1519–63), French soldier in wars against Charles V; assassinated by Protestant.

Guise, Henri, 3rd Duke of (1550–88), French soldier and political leader, founded anti-Protestant Holy League 1576; assassinated by royal bodyguard.

Guitry, Sacha (1885–1957), French actor, director and writer of plays and films.

Guizot, François (1787–1874), French statesman and historian, prime minister 1840–48.

Gujarat, Indian state, created from part of the former state of Bombay (q.v.) 1960.

Gulbenkian, Calouste (1869–1955), Turkish-born financier and industrialist, founded Iraq Petroleum Company.

Guldberg, Cato Maximilian (1836–1902), Norwegian chemist, established the law of mass action.

gun, first authentic record of use in Europe 1326.

gunpowder, introduced into Europe by end of 13th century.

Gunpowder Plot, attempt to blow up the Houses of Parliament, 5 Nov. 1605.

Gunter, Edmund (1581–1626), English mathematician, invented surveying devices.

Gurney, Sir Goldsworthy (1793–1875), English inventor of London–Bath steam carriage 1829.

Gustavus I Vasa (1496–1560), king of Sweden 1523–60, secured independence from Denmark; introduced Lutheranism.

Gustavus II Adolphus (1594–1632), king of Sweden 1611–32, won many victories in Thirty Years War; killed in battle.

Gustavus III (1746–92), king of Sweden 1771–92, assumed near-absolute power; assassinated.

Gustavus IV (1778–1837), king of Sweden 1792–1809, dethroned after defeat by Napoleon.

Gustavus V (1858–1950), king of Sweden 1907–50, a period of internal prosperity and neutrality.

Gustavus VI (1882–1973), king of Sweden 1950–73, was a noted archaeologist.

Gutenberg, Johann (c. 1398–1468), German inventor of printing in Europe c. 1439.

Guthrie, Thomas (1803–73), Scottish clergyman, worked for 'ragged schools' for the destitute.

Guyana, South America, first settled by Dutch c. 1620; captured by Britain 1781; ceded to Britain 1814; achieved independence 1966; became a republic 1970.

Guy de Lusignan (d. 1194), French noble, king of Jerusalem 1186–87, and of Cyprus 1192–94.

Guy Fawkes Day, 5 Nov., commemorating Gunpowder Plot (q.v.) instigated by Guy Fawkes (q.v.) and others, first celebrated 1607.

Guyon, Madame (1648–1717), French mystic, preached influential quietist doctrine.

Guyot, Arnold (1807–84), Swiss geographer, worked in U.S.A.

Guys, Constantin (1805–92), Dutch-born French illustrator of contemporary manners and fashions.

Guy's Hospital, London, founded 1722 by the English printer and bookseller Thomas Guy (c. 1644–1724).

Gwinnett, Button (1735–77), English-born American patriot, active in Revolutionary politics; president of Georgia 1777.

Gwyn, Nell (1651–87), English actress, mistress of Charles II.

gypsies, reached southeastern Europe in 14th century; spread to Germany, Italy, France and Spain in 15th century; reached England c. 1500.

gyrocompass, invented 1911 by the American Elmer Ambrose Sperry (1860–1930).

gyroscope, invented 1852 by the French scientist Jean Foucault (1819–68).

H

H-bomb. See **hydrogen bomb.**

Haakon I (d. 961), king of Norway 935–961, introduced Christianity; killed in battle.

Haakon II (1147–62), king of Norway 1161–62, failed to establish control over his country.

Haakon IV (1204–63), king of Norway 1217–63, annexed Iceland and Greenland.

Haakon V (1270–1319), king of Norway 1299–1319, at war with Denmark.

Haakon VI (1340–80), king of Norway 1343–80, briefly ruled Sweden 1362–63.

Haakon VII (1872–1957), king of Norway 1905–57, spent World War II in England.

Habberton, John (1842–1921), American novelist, wrote *Helen's Babies* (1876).

Habeas Corpus Act, principle stated in Magna Carta 1215; confirmed by Petition of Right 1627; became law in England 1679.

Haber-Bosch process, for production of ammonia, established 1909 by the German chemist Fritz Haber (1868–1934); developed for industry by the German chemist Carl Bosch (1874–1940).

Haberdashers' Aske's, Elstree, English public school, founded 1690 by bequest of Robert Aske.

Haberdashers' Company, London, origins uncertain; bye-laws drawn up 1371; granted first charter by Henry VI 1448.

Hachette, Louis (1800–64), French publisher and bookseller, founded in 1826 the firm that bears his name.

hackney carriages, used at least as early as 1605 in London; regularized by the Carriage Act 1831.

Haden, Sir Francis Seymour (1818–1910), English surgeon, was also a talented etcher.

Hadfield, Sir Robert Abbott (1858–1940), English metallurgist, invented manganese steel, silicon steel and other steel alloys.

Hadley, John (1682–1744), English astronomer, invented reflecting telescope and reflecting quadrant.

Hadow, Sir William Henry (1859–1937), English musicologist, wrote the *Oxford History of Music* (1901–05).

Hadrian (A.D. 76–138), Roman emperor A.D. 117–138, travelled widely, adopted a generally defensive policy.

Hadrian's Wall, Roman wall across northern England, built under the governorship of Aulus Platorius Nepos, A.D. 122–126.

Haeckel, Ernst Heinrich (1834–1919), German naturalist, developed evolutionary theory.

haematin, colouring matter of blood, chemical structure analysed 1921–29 by the German chemist Hans Fischer (1881–1945).

haemoglobin, prepared in crystalline form 1862 by the German biochemist Ernst Hoppe-Seyler (1825–95); structure determined 1960 by the Austrian-born biochemist Max Perutz (b. 1914).

Hafiz (d. c. 1388), Persian poet, wrote collection of lyrics, the *Divan*.

hafnium, a metal, first isolated 1923 by the Hungarian chemist Georg von Hevesy (1885–1966) and the Dutch physicist Dirk Coster (b. 1889).

Hagedorn, Friedrich von (1708–54), German poet, wrote fables and love songs.

Haggard, Rider (1856–1925), English novelist, best known for his adventure stories, including *King Solomon's Mines* (1885).

Hahn, Kurt (b. 1886), German educationalist, founder of Salem School, Germany, and Gordonstoun, Scotland.

Hahn, Otto (1879–1968), German chemist, Nobel prizewinner 1944, made crucial nuclear fission discoveries.

Hahn, Reynaldo (1875–1947), Venezuelan-born French composer of light operas.

Hahnemann, Samuel (1755–1843), German physician, founder of homeopathy.

Haidar Ali. See Hyder Ali.

Haig, Douglas, 1st Earl (1861–1928), British soldier, commander-in-chief on Western Front 1915–19.

Haile Selassie (1891–1975), king (1928–30) and emperor (1930–74) of Ethiopia; in exile 1936–41; overthrown 1974.

Haileybury, Herts, English public school, founded 1862; absorbed Imperial Service College (founded 1912) 1942.

Haiti, discovered by Christopher Columbus 1492; ruled by French 1697–1792; independent republic 1820; protectorate of U.S.A. 1915–34.

Hakluyt, Richard (c. 1552–1616), English writer of *Principal Navigations of the English Nation* (1589).

Haldane, John Burdon (1892–1964), English biologist, wrote on genetics and Marxism.

Haldane, John Scott (1860–1936), Scottish scientist, made studies of respiration.

Haldane, Richard Burdon, 1st Viscount (1856–1928), British statesman, lawyer, and philosopher, reorganized British army 1905–12.

Hale, Edward Everett (1822–1909), American writer of *The Man Without a Country* (1863).

Hale, George Ellery (1868–1938), American astronomer, best known for his invention of the spectro-heliograph and his researches into sunspots.

Hale, Sir Matthew (1609–76), English lawyer, lord chief justice 1671–76.

Hale, Nathan (1755–76), American patriot, hanged for spying behind British lines during American Revolutionary War.

Halévy, Jacques François (1799–1862), French opera composer, wrote *La Juive* (1835).

halfpenny postage, for postcards, introduced in Britain 1870.

halftone engraving, first practical process invented 1878 by the American Frederic Ives (1856–1937); first commercial production of halftone plates 1881.

Halifax, Earl of (1661–1715), British statesman, man of letters and patron of literature.

Halifax, 1st Earl of (1881–1959), British statesman, governor-general of India 1926–31, foreign secretary 1938–40.

Hall, Charles Francis (1821–71), American explorer, led three arctic expeditions.

Hall, Charles Martin (1863–1914), American chemist, devised an electrolytic process for producing aluminium from bauxite.

Hall, Sir Edward Marshall (1858–1927), English lawyer, outstanding barrister in criminal, libel and divorce cases.

Hall, Joseph (1574–1656), English poet and religious writer, bishop of Norwich 1641–47.

Hall, Marshall (1790–1857), English physiologist, specialized in nervous diseases.

Hall, Peter (b. 1930), English theatrical producer, director of Royal Shakespeare theatre.

Hallam, Henry (1777–1859), English historian, wrote *Constitutional History of England* (1827).

Halle, Adam de la. See **Adam de la Halle.**

Hallé Orchestra, Manchester, established 1857 by Sir Charles Hallé (1819–95); first regular public concert 30 Jan. 1858.

Haller, Albrecht von (1708–77), Swiss anatomist, physiologist, botanist and poet, author of important scientific works.

Halley, Edmund (1656–1742), English astronomer, observed in 1682 the comet now named after him.

Halley's Comet, period (about 76 years) determined 1704; next appearance 1986.

hallmarking, in Great Britain, dates from a statute of 1300 in the reign of Edward I.

Hall of Fame, New York, American national shrine, established 1900.

Hallowe'en (All-Hallows Eve), celebrated 31 Oct.

Hals, Frans (c. 1580–1666), Dutch portrait painter, notably of *The Laughing Cavalier*.

Hamburg, founded by Charlemagne c. 810; became independent 1292; made a free imperial city 1510; ruled by France 1806–14; lost special privileges 1933; heavily bombed in World War II.

Hamburg-America shipping line, founded 1847.

Hamilcar Barca (c. 270–228 B.C.), Carthaginian soldier, father of Hannibal; fought Romans in Sicily.

Hamilton, Alexander (1757–1804), American statesman and founding father, killed in duel by Aaron Burr (q.v.).

Hamilton, Emma, Lady (c. 1765–1815), wife of Sir William Hamilton (q.v.) and mistress of Nelson.

Hamilton, Patrick (c. 1504–28), Scottish Protestant, burnt at the stake.

Hamilton, Sir Robert (1836–95), Scottish administrator, governor of Tasmania 1886–93.

Hamilton, Sir William (1730–1803), Scottish diplomat and archaeologist, envoy at Naples 1764–1800.

Hammarskjöld, Dag (1905–61), Swedish statesman and diplomat, secretary-general of United Nations 1953–61.

Hammerstein, Oscar (c. 1847–1919), American theatre manager and impresario, built many theatres.

Hammerstein, Oscar, II (1895–1960), American librettist and lyricist, in collaboration with Richard Rogers produced many famous musical comedies.

Hammett, Dashiell (1894–1961), American writer, first master of 'hard-boiled' detective fiction, e.g. *Maltese Falcon* (1930).

Hammond, Joan (b. 1912), New Zealand soprano, famous in oratorio and opera.

Hammond, John (1872–1949), English historian, collaborated with wife Barbara (1873–1961) on studies of labouring conditions.

Hammurabi (late 2nd millennium), king of Babylon c. 1792–c. 1750 B.C., great ruler and conqueror, promulgated famous code of laws.

Hampden, John (1594–1643), English parliamentarian, refused to pay ship-money tax; killed in Civil War.

Hampton Court, Treaty of, alliance between Queen Elizabeth I and the Prince de Condé, 1562.

Hampton Court Conference, of English clergy, held 1604.

Hamsun, Knut (1859–1952), Norwegian novelist, author of *Hunger* (1888); Nobel prizewinner 1920.

Han dynasty, China, 206 B.C.–A.D. 220.

Handel, George Frederick (1685–1759), German-born composer in England, best known for his oratorio *Messiah* (1742).

Hannibal (247–c. 182 B.C.), Carthaginian general and opponent of Rome, fought in Italy 218–203 B.C.; defeated at Zama 202 B.C.

Hannington, James (1847–85), English explorer in Africa, bishop of Eastern Equatorial Africa 1884–85.

Hanno, (6th–5th cent. B.C.), Carthaginian navigator, explored West African coast c. 500 B.C.

Hansard, record of British parliamentary debates, begun 1774 by Luke Hansard (1752–1828) who printed House of Commons' *Journals*; debates first printed 1803 by his son Thomas Hansard (1776–1833).

Hanseatic League, North German and Baltic commercial alliance, originating in the 12th century; formal alliance 1241; last meeting 1669.

Hansen, Atmauer Gerhard (1841–1912), Norwegian physician, discovered leprosy bacillus 1879.

Hansom cab, idea patented 1834 by the English architect Joseph Aloysius Hansom (1803–82).

Hapsburg Dynasty, ruled Austria 1278–1918, Netherlands 1477–1579 (and Belgium 1713–92), Spain 1516–1700, Bohemia and (intermittently) Hungary 1526–1918.

hara-kiri, Japanese obligatory suicide, abolished officially 1868.

Harald I (c. 850–933), king of Norway 860–930, forced emigration of many nobles.

Harald III Haadraade (1015–66), king of Norway 1047–66, killed at battle of Stamford Bridge, England.

Harcourt, Sir William (1827–1904), British statesman, chancellor of the exchequer 1886 and 1892–95.

Hardecanute (c. 1019–42), king of Denmark 1035–42 and of England 1040–42; son of Canute.

Hardie, Keir (1856–1915), Scottish Labour leader and miner, M.P. 1892–95 and 1900–15.

Harding, Saint Stephen (d. 1134), English saint, one of the founders of the Cistercian order.

Harding, Warren (1865–1923), American statesman, 29th president of the United States 1921–23, whose period of office was notable for corruption among subordinates.

Hardinge, Henry, Viscount (1785–1856), British soldier, governor-general of India 1844–47.

Hardwicke, Sir Cedric (1893–1964), English actor, notably in plays by Shaw; also had a career in films.

Hardwicke, Philip Yorke, Earl of (1690–1764), English lawyer, lord chancellor, introduced marriage reforms.

Hardy, Thomas (1840–1928), English poet and novelist, author of *Tess of the D'Urbevilles* (1891).

Hare, Augustus (1834–1903), English writer of multi-volume memoirs.

Hare, William (d. c. 1865), Irish murderer, partner of William Burke (q.v.), saved himself by turning king's evidence.

Harewood, Earl of (b. 1923), English artistic director of Edinburgh Festival 1960–65, editor of *Opera* (1950–53), etc.

Hargreaves, James (d. 1778), English inventor of the spinning jenny (q.v.) c. 1764.

Harington, Sir John (1561–1612), English courtier, writer and translator of Ariosto's *Orlando Furioso* (1591).

Harleian Library, started by Robert Harley (q.v.); acquired by British Museum 1753.

Harley, Robert, Earl of Oxford (1661–1724), English statesman, chief minister 1710–14; briefly imprisoned; made notable collection of books and manuscripts.

harmonium, modern design produced 1840 by the French organ manufacturer Alexandre Debain (1809–77).

Harold I Harefoot (d. 1040), king of England 1037–40; illegitimate son of Canute.

Harold II (c. 1022–66), king of England 1066, defeated and killed at battle of Hastings.

Harper's Ferry, Virginia, raided by John Brown, 16–18 Oct. 1859.

Harpignies, Henri (1819–1916), French landscape painter, e.g. *View of Capri.*

Harriman, William Averell (b. 1891), American financier and administrator, ambassador or to the U.S.S.R. 1943–46.

Harris, Frank (1856–1931), Irish-born writer in U.S.A.; later influential British editor, wrote *My Life and Loves* (1922).

Harris, Joel Chandler (1848–1908), American writer of 'Uncle Remus' stories.

Harris, Roy (b. 1898), American composer, whose work includes symphonies and chamber music.

Harris, Thomas Lake (1823–1906), English-born American spiritualist, established several 'brotherhood' communities.

Harrison, Benjamin (1833–1901), American statesman, 23rd president of the United States 1889–93; elected on a protectionist ticket.

Harrison, John (1693–1776), English horologist, invented 1726 a chronometer which could determine longitude accurately.

Harrison, William (1534–93), English topographer, wrote *Description of England* (1577).

Harrison, William Henry (1773–1841), American statesman, 9th president of the United States 1841; grandfather of Benjamin Harrison.

Harrow School, English public school, founded 1571 by John Lyon (1514–92); opened 1611.

Harsha (c. 590–647), king of northern India 606–647, ended the anarchy following the collapse of the Gupta Empire.

Hart, Lorenz (1895–1943), American writer of song lyrics of unusual verbal intricacy, e.g. 'Anything Goes'.

Harte, Bret (1836–1902), American author, best known for his stories of life in the mining camps.

Hartley, Arthur Clifford (1889–1960), English engineer, developed 'Pluto' oil pipeline and 'Fido' airfield fog clearance system.

Hartley, Leslie Poles (1895–1972), English novelist, author of the 'Eustace and Hilda' trilogy and *The Go-Between* (1953).

Hartmann von Aue (c. 1170–c. 1215), German poet, wrote on Arthurian themes.

Harty, Sir Hamilton (1879–1941), Irish conductor of the Hallé Orchestra 1920–33; also a composer.

Harun-al-Rashid (c. 763–809), Abbasid caliph of Baghdad 786–809, ruled vast empire; figured in many legends.

Harunobu, Suzuki (*c.* 1720–*c.* 1770), Japanese colour-print artist, noted for his touching and delicately executed works.

Harvard University, founded 1636; named after the Puritan minister John Harvard (1607–38).

harvester, mechanical, first successful design 1831 by the American manufacturer Cyrus Hall McCormick (1809–84).

harvest moon, the full moon nearest to the autumnal equinox.

Harvey, Gabriel (*c.* 1545–*c.* 1630), English writer, conducted pamphlet war with Thomas Nashe (*q.v.*).

Harvey, Thomas (1812–84), English Quaker philanthropist, removed Mennonites from Russia to Canada.

Harvey, William (1578–1657), English physician, discovered circulation of blood.

Haryana, Indian state, created 1966 from part of former state of Punjab (*q.v.*).

Hasdrubal (d. 207 B.C.), Carthaginian general, brother of Hannibal.

Hašek, Jaroslav (1883–1923), Czech novelist, author of *The Good Soldier Schweik* (1920–23).

Hastings, Battle of, fought at Battle, Sussex, victory of the Normans over the English 14 Oct. 1066.

Hastings, Warren (1732–1818), English administrator, governor-general of Bengal 1773–85; acquitted of corruption after famous trial 1788–95.

Hathaway, Anne (*c.* 1556–1623), wife of William Shakespeare.

Hatton, Sir Christopher (1540–91), English statesman, lord chancellor 1587–91; favourite of Queen Elizabeth.

Hauptmann, Gerhart (1862–1946), German playwright, wrote *The Weavers* (1893)

Haussman, Georges Eugène (1809–91), French administrator, built the great boulevards of Paris.

Haüy, René Just (1743–1822), French mineralogist, helped to found the science of crystallography.

Havas Agency, French press agency, founded 1835 by the French journalist Charles Havas (1785–1858).

Havelock, Sir Henry (1795–1857), English general, during Indian Mutiny relieved Lucknow and withstood siege 1857.

Havelock the Dane, 12th-century Anglo-Danish epic.

Hawaii, Pacific, discovered 1778 by Captain Cook; independence recognized by Britain, France, and U.S.A. 1844; formally annexed by the U.S.A. 1898; admitted to the Union 1959.

Hawes, Stephen (d. *c.* 1523), English poet, wrote *Pastime of Pleasure.*

Hawke, Edward, 1st Baron (1705–81), English admiral, who in 1759 destroyed a French invasion fleet at Quiberon Bay.

Hawker, Robert Stephen (1803–75), Eng-

lish poet, wrote the much anthologized '*And shall Trelawny die?*'.

Hawkins, Sir John (1532–95), English navigator and slave-trader, fought Armada 1588; died on an expedition with Drake.

Hawkins, Sir Richard (*c.* 1562–1622), English navigator, son of Sir John Hawkins.

Hawksmoor, Nicholas (1661–1736), English Baroque architect, built Castle Howard Mausoleum.

Hawthorne, Nathaniel (1804–64), American novelist, wrote *The Scarlet Letter* (1850).

Haydn, Franz Joseph (1732–1809), Austrian composer of symphonies, string quartets, etc., teacher of Mozart and Beethoven.

Haydn, Joseph (d. 1856), English compiler of pioneer *Dictionary of Dates* (1841).

Haydon, Benjamin Robert (1786–1846), English painter, remembered chiefly for his *Autobiography*.

Hayes, Rutherford Birchard (1822–93), American statesman, 19th president of the United States 1877–81, following contested election results.

Hays, William Harrison (1879–1954), American administrator, devised Hays Code defining morally acceptable films.

Hazlitt, William (1778–1830), outstanding English essayist, e.g. collection *The Spirit of the Age* (1825).

Health, Ministry of, Britain, established 1919; merged with Ministry of Social Security 1968.

Healy, Timothy Michael (1855–1931), Irish nationalist and lawyer, first governor-general of the Irish Free State 1922–28.

Heaphy, Charles (*c.* 1821–81), English-born New Zealand administrator, won Victoria Cross in 1867 Maori War.

Hearn, Lafcadio (1850–1904), American writer on oriental subjects, became a naturalized Japanese.

Hearst, William Randolph (1863–1951), American publisher of nationwide chain of newspapers, wielding much influence.

heart, surgery of, pioneered 1896 by the German surgeon Ludwig Rehn (1849–1930).

heart transplant, first operation performed 1967 by the South African surgeon Christiaan Barnard (*q.v.*).

heat, as a form of energy, experiments performed 1798 by Count Rumford (*q.v.*), 1799 by Sir Humphry Davy (*q.v.*), and 1840–49 by James Joule (*q.v.*). See also **thermodynamics.**

heat, latent, concept first developed 1756–61 by Joseph Black (*q.v.*).

Heath, Edward George (b. 1916), British statesman, prime minister 1970–74.

Heathrow. See **London Airport.**

Heaviside, Oliver (1850–1925), English

physicist, made numerous contributions to study of electricity, radio waves, etc.

Heaviside-Kennelly Layer. See **ionosphere.**

heavy hydrogen, discovered 1931 by the American chemist Harold Urey (b. 1893).

heavy water, first prepared 1933 by the American chemist Gilbert Lewis (1875–1946).

Hebbel, Friedrich (1813–63), German poet and playwright, author of *Agnes Bernauer* (1852).

Heber, Reginald (1783–1826), English bishop of Calcutta 1822–26, wrote hymns, e.g. 'Holy, Holy, Holy'.

Hebert, Jacques René (1755–94), French revolutionary of extreme views; guillotined.

Hebra, Ferdinand von (1816–80), Austrian physician, pioneer in the treatment of skin disease.

Hebrides, inhabitants converted to Christianity 6th century; raided by Norsemen from 8th century and later placed under Norse sovereignty; ceded by Norway to Scotland 1266.

hectograph, duplicating process, invented 1780 by James Watt (*q.v.*).

Hedin, Sven (1865–1952), Swedish explorer of central Asia and China.

Hegel, Georg Wilhelm Friedrich (1770–1831), German Idealist philosopher, made philosophy of history central to thought.

Heidegger, Martin (1889–1976), German existentialist philosopher, author of *Being and Time* (1927).

Heidelberg Catechism, instigated by the Elector Frederick III; published 1563 by Zacharias Ursinus (1536–83) and Caspar Olevianus (1536–87).

Heidelberg University, German Federal Republic, founded 1385.

Heidenstam, Verner von (1859–1940), Swedish poet and novelist, began literary renaissance in Sweden.

Heifetz, Jascha (b. 1901), Russian-born American violinist of world fame; originally a child prodigy.

Heine, Heinrich (1797–1856), major German poet, whose works include *Buch der Lieder* (1877); was also a gifted satirist.

Heinsius, Daniel (1580–1655), Dutch scholar and poet, prominent in Renaissance literature in Holland.

Heinz, Henry John (1844–1919), American food manufacturer, pioneer in the use of canned foods.

Heisenberg, Werner Karl (1901–1976), German physicist, formulated theory of indeterminacy in nuclear physics.

Hejaz, Arabia, made Ottoman dependency 1517; proclaimed independent kingdom 1916; annexed to Saudi Arabia 1926.

Hejira, the migration of Mohammed from Mecca to Medina, 622.

Helena, Saint (*c.* 248–*c.* 328), mother of Emperor Constantine the Great; reputedly built churches in Palestine.

helicopter, first machine to make vertical flight, built 1907 by Paul Cornu; first practical machine, the Focke-Achgelis, 1936.

heliocentric theory, first proposed *c.* 270 B.C. by Aristarchus of Samos (*q.v.*); reintroduced 1543 by Copernicus (*q.v.*).

Heliogabalus (A.D. 204–222), Roman emperor 218–222, cruel and degenerate; assassinated.

helium, discovered spectroscopically in the sun 1868 independently by Sir Joseph Lockyer (*q.v.*) and the French astronomer Pierre Janssen (1824–1907); discovered on Earth 1895 by Sir William Ramsay (*q.v.*).

helium, liquid, first obtained 1908 by Heike Kamerlingh Onnes (1853–1926).

Hell Gate Bridge, New York, designed 1902–03 by the Austrian-born engineer Gustav Lindenthal (1850–1935); opened 1917.

Helmholtz, Hermann von (1821–94), German scientist, formulated conservation of energy; made many other discoveries.

Helmont, Jan Baptista van (*c.* 1577–1644), Flemish chemist, was the first man to discover the existence of gases.

Helpmann, Sir Robert (b. 1909), Australian dancer and actor, also a noted choreographer and theatrical producer.

Helsinki, capital of Finland since 1812.

Helvétius, Claude Adrien (1715–71), French philosopher, persecuted for his materialistic *De l'Esprit* (1758).

Hemans, Felicia (1793–1835), English poet, wrote 'The boy stood on the burning deck'.

Heming, John (d. 1630), English actor, edited Shakespeare first folio with Henry Condell (*q.v.*) 1623.

Hemingway, Ernest (1899–1961), American novelist, concerned with the themes of war, love and courage, author of *Farewell to Arms* (1929).

Hémon, Louis (1880–1913), French novelist, wrote of French-Canadian life in *Maria Chapdelaine* (1914).

Henderson, Alexander (*c.* 1583–1646), Scottish Presbyterian leader, drew up the Solemn League and Covenant.

Henderson, Arthur (1863–1935), Scottish Labour Party leader, foreign secretary 1929–31, won Nobel Peace Prize 1934.

Hengist and Horsa (fl. *c.* A.D. 450), two brothers who reputedly led the first Anglo-Saxon settlers in Britain.

Henley, William Ernest (1849–1903), English journalist and poet, collaborated with R. L. Stevenson (*q.v.*) on plays.

Henley Regatta, Henley-on-Thames, founded 1839.

Henrietta (1644–70), duchess of Orleans 1661–70, daughter of Charles I of England.

Henri Christophe. See **Christophe,** Henri.

Henrietta Maria (1609–69), French-born queen of Charles I of England 1625–49, attempted to exert pro-Catholic influence.

Henry I (1068–1135), king of England 1100–35, conquered Normandy and strengthened monarchy.

Henry II (1133–89), king of England 1154–89, conquered Welsh and Irish; ruled much of France.

Henry III (1207-72), king of England 1216–72; reign troubled by civil wars.

Henry IV (1367–1413), king of England 1399–1413, usurped throne from Richard II.

Henry V (1387–1422), king of England 1413–22, defeated French at Agincourt 1415.

Henry VI (1421–71), king of England 1422–61 and 1470–71; reign disrupted by Wars of Roses.

Henry VII (1457–1509), king of England 1485–1509, first Tudor; united country after Wars of the Roses.

Henry VIII (1491–1547), king of England 1509–47, broke with papacy and established himself as head of the English Church.

Henry I (1008–60), king of France 1031–60; warred against nobles and William of Normandy.

Henry II (1519–59), king of France 1547–59, fought long war against Holy Roman Empire; killed in tournament accident.

Henry III (1551–89), king of France 1574–89, a period of unbroken Catholic-Protestant conflict.

Henry IV (1553–1610), king of France 1589–1610, reconciled religious factions and strengthened monarchy; assassinated.

Henry I, the Fowler (c. 875–936), king of Germany 919–36, drove back barbarian invaders of the Empire.

Henry II (973–1024), king of Germany and Holy Roman emperor 1002–24, reformed Church; in conflict with the Poles.

Henry III (1017–56), Holy Roman Emperor 1046–56, conquered Bohemia and Hungary.

Henry IV (1050–1106), king of Germany and Holy Roman emperor 1056–1106, engaged in long struggle with papacy.

Henry V (1081–1125), king of Germany and Holy Roman emperor 1106–25, fought several wars.

Henry VI (1165–97), king of Germany and Holy Roman emperor 1190–97, reconquered Sicily and southern Italy.

Henry VII (c. 1275–1313), king of Germany and Holy Roman emperor 1308–13, failed to subdue southern Italy.

Henry, Joseph (1797–1878), American physicist, discovered method of producing electrical induction.

Henry, O. (pseud. of William Sydney Porter; 1862–1910), American short-story writer of international repute.

Henry, Patrick (1736–99), American patriot, governor of Virginia 1776–79 and 1784–86.

Henry, William (1774–1836), English chemist, formulated Henry's law on weight of gas.

Henryson, Robert (c. 1425–c. 1506), Scottish poet, wrote *Testament of Cresseid.*

Henry the Lion (1129–95), German nobleman, duke of Saxony 1139–80 and of Bavaria 1156–80, quarrelled with Holy Roman emperors.

Henry the Navigator (1394–1460), Portuguese prince, masterminded early Portuguese voyages exploring African coast.

Henschel, Sir George (1850–1934), German-born English singer, conductor and composer; founded Scottish Symphony Orchestra 1893.

Henslowe, Philip (d. 1616), English theatre manager, kept a notable diary of his various theatrical ventures.

Henty, George Alfred (1832–1902), English writer of adventure stories for boys.

Henze, Hans Werner (b. 1926), German composer of symphonies, operas and ballets; notable for use of twelve-note technique.

Hepplewhite, George (d. 1786), English cabinetmaker, wrote *Cabinetmaker and Upholsterer's Guide.*

Hepworth, Dame Barbara (1903–75), English sculptor, created powerful, rounded abstract forms.

Heraclitus (c. 540–475 B.C.), Greek philosopher, believed that 'all is in flux'.

Heraclius (c. 575–641), Byzantine emperor 610–41, victorious until Arab conquest of Syria and Egypt.

Heralds' College, London, founded 1461 by Edward IV; chartered 1484.

Herbart, Johann Friedrich (1776–1841), German philosopher, important for educational theories.

Herbert, George (1593–1633), Welsh-born poet, wrote on religious subjects.

Herbert, Victor (1859–1924), American composer of light opera, e.g. *Naughty Marietta* (1910).

Herbert of Cherbury, Edward, Baron (1583–1648), English philosopher and historian, held the view that all religions agreed in essentials.

Herder, Johann Gottfried (1744–1803), German writer and folksong collector, whose ideas influenced Romanticism.

Heredia, José Maria de (1842–1905), Cuban-born French poet, wrote sonnet collection *Les Trophées* (1893).

heredity, principles established 1865 by Gregor Mendel (*q.v.*). See also **genetics.**

Hereford Cathedral, England, constructed 1079–1148 (crypt Anglo-Saxon, from earlier building burnt 1055).

Hereford Cathedral School, English public school, founded before 1381; reconstituted 1894.

Hereward the Wake (fl. 1070), English rebel against William the Conqueror.

Hereford, William Henry (1820–1908), English educational reformer and teacher, wrote *The Student's Froebel* (1893).

Hergesheimer, Joseph (1880–1954), American novelist, wrote *Java Head* (1919).

Heriot, George (1563–1624), Scottish goldsmith, founded Heriot's Hospital, Edinburgh, opened 1659.

Herkomer, Sir Hubert von (1849–1914), German-born painter, in England 1857–1914; popular portraitist.

Herod Agrippa (10 B.C.–A.D. 44), Jewish ruler of the four tetrarchies under the Romans.

Herod Antipas (d. *c.* A.D. 40), Jewish tetrarch of Galilee and Peraea 4 B.C.–A.D. 40; said to have killed John the Baptist.

Herod the Great (*c.* 73–4 B.C.), king of Judaea 39–4 B.C., with Roman backing rebuilt Temple of Jerusalem.

Herodotus (*c.* 485–*c.* 425 B.C.), Greek historian, the first to collect and sift evidence, wrote a history of the Persian Wars.

Hérold, Louis Joseph (1791–1833), French composer, wrote opera *Zampa* (1831).

Hero of Alexandria (1st cent. A.D.), Greek mathematician, invented many mechanical devices.

Herrera, Ferdinando (*c.* 1534–97), Spanish poet and humanist scholar, wrote Italianate lyrics.

Herrera, Francisco de, the Elder (*c.* 1576–*c.* 1656), Spanish painter, noted for his naturalism.

Herrera, Francisco de, the Younger (1622–85), Spanish painter, son of Francisco de Herrera, appointed court painter 1672.

Herrick, Robert (1591–1674), English poet and clergyman, wrote collection *Hesperides* (1648).

Herrings, Battle of the, victory of the English over the French, 1429.

Herriot, Édouard (1872–1957), French statesman, prime minister 1924–25 and 1932; president of the National Assembly 1946–57.

Herschel, Sir John Frederick (1792–1871), English astronomer, son of Sir William Herschel, studied nebulae.

Herschel, Sir William (1738–1822), German-born English astronomer, discovered Uranus 1781.

Hertford College, Oxford University, founded as Hertford Hall 1282 by Elias de Hertford; incorporated as Hertford College 1740; reincorporated 1874.

Hertslet, Lewis (1787–1870), English librarian to Foreign Office 1810–57, compiled collections of treaties.

Hertz, Heinrich Rudolph (1857–94), German physicist, first man to demonstrate the existence of radio waves.

Hertzog, James Barry (1866–1942), South African soldier and statesman, founded Nationalist Party; prime minister 1924–39.

Hertzsprung, Ejnar (1873–1967) Danish astronomer, discovered the connection between the colour and luminosity of stars.

Herzen, Alexander (1812–70), Russian revolutionary and political journalist, in England 1863–70; wrote memoirs *My Past and Thoughts* (1855).

Herzl, Theodor (1860–1904), Hungarian-born Jewish writer, founded Zionism and wrote *Der Judenstaat* (1896).

Heseltine, Philip. See **Warlock,** Peter.

Hesiod (8th cent. B.C.), Greek poet, wrote *Works and Days.*

Hess, Dame Myra (1890–1965), English pianist, noted for her interpretation of Bach, Mozart and Beethoven.

Hess, Rudolf (b. 1894), German Nazi leader, flew to Scotland 1941; imprisoned at Spandau since 1946.

Hesse, Hermann (1877–1962), German novelist, author of *Steppenwolf* (1927).

Hesychasm, Eastern Christian mystic movement, began 13th century.

Hetton Line, Co. Durham, oldest mineral railway in Britain and first real railway on a prepared surface, built 1819–22 by George Stephenson; closed 1959.

Hevelius, Johannes (1611–87), German astronomer, made careful observations of the surface of the Moon.

Hewlett, Maurice (1861–1923), English writer, author of the romance *The Forest Lovers* (1898).

Heydrich, Reinhard (1904–42), German Nazi leader, deputy chief of the Gestapo, assassinated by Czech patriots.

Heyerdahl, Thor (b. 1914), Norwegian anthropologist, led Kon Tiki Expedition 1947.

Heyward, Dubose (1885–1940), American novelist, author of *Porgy* (1925).

Heywood, John (*c.* 1497–*c.* 1580), English poet and writer of 'interludes' important in drama history.

Heywood, Thomas (*c.* 1574–1641), English playwright, wrote *A Woman Killed With Kindness* (1603).

Hiawatha (16th cent.), North American Indian chief, organized the Iroquois into the Five-Nation Confederacy.

Hibbert Trust, originally for the elevation of the Unitarian ministry, founded 1847 by the British merchant Robert Hibbert (1770–1849).

Hickok, James Butler (1837–76), known as Wild Bill Hickok, American stage-driver, army scout and U.S. marshal; subject of many legends.

Hidalgo y Costilla, Miguel (1753–1811), Mexican priest, led unsuccessful revolt against Spanish rule.

Hiero I (d. 467 B.C.), king of Syracuse 478–467, tyrant, conqueror and patron of poets.

Hiero II (d. 215 B.C.), king of Syracuse (c. 270–215 B.C., became a dependant of Rome.

Higden, Ranulf (d. 1364), English chronicler, wrote *Polychronicon*.

Highgate School, English public school, founded 1565.

Hilary, Saint (d. c. 368), bishop of Poitiers, one of the Doctors of the Church.

Hilary Term, legal term beginning 11 Jan., ending Wednesday before Easter.

Hilda, Saint (614–680), English abbess, founded and ruled Whitby monastery 657–680.

Hildebert (c. 1055–1133), French prelate, archbishop of Tours 1125–33, asserted rights against the king.

Hildebrand, Adolf von (1847–1921), German sculptor, was an influential theorist.

Hildebrandt, Johann Lucas von (1668–1745), Austrian architect, had a notable influence on the development of the Baroque style.

Hildegard, Saint (c. 1098–1179), German nun, founded Rupertsberg convent.

Hill, Octavia (1838–1912), English social reformer, improved housing for the poor.

Hill, Sir Rowland (1795–1879), English administrator, deviser of the penny post.

Hillary, Sir Edmund (b. 1919), New Zealand mountaineer, was, with the Sherpa Tensing, the first man to climb Mount Everest, 1953.

Hillel (c. 60 B.C.–c. A.D. 10), Jewish theologian, leading authority on the interpretation of Biblical law.

Hilliard, Nicholas (c. 1537–1619), English miniaturist, painted Queen Elizabeth and others.

Himachal Pradesh, Indian state, created a union territory 1948; became a state 1970.

Himmler, Heinrich (1900–45), German Nazi, head of the S.S. and Gestapo, largely responsible for policy of extermination of so-called inferior races.

Hindemith, Paul (1895–1963), German composer, in U.S.A. 1939–53, wrote opera *Mathis der Maler* (1938).

Hindenburg, German airship, destroyed by fire in the U.S.A. May 1937.

Hindenburg, Paul von (1847–1934), German soldier, victor of Tannenberg 1914; president of Germany 1925–34.

Hipparchus (c. 160–c. 125 B.C.), Greek astronomer, discovered precession of equinoxes, developed trigonometry, etc.

Hippocrates (c. 460–c. 370 B.C.), Greek physician of legendary skill, said to have devised medical oath.

Hirohito (b. 1901), emperor of Japan since 1926, renounced divinity 1946 after Japanese defeat.

Hiroshige, Ando (1797–1858), Japanese colour-print artist, best known for his landscapes.

Hiroshima, Japanese city, largely destroyed 6 Aug. 1945 by the first atomic bomb used in warfare.

Hirsch, Samson Raphael (1808–88), German-Jewish theologian, pioneered renewal of Orthodox belief.

Hispanic Society of America, New York, founded 1904.

Hispaniola, West Indies, settled by Spanish from 1493; western part ceded to France 1697; whole island briefly united as Republic of Haiti 1804. See **Dominican Republic; Haiti.**

Hitchcock, Alfred (b. 1899), English-born American film director, e.g. *Blackmail* (1929), *Psycho* (1960).

Hitler, Adolf (1889–1945), Austrian-born Nazi leader, dictator of Germany 1933–45, whose aggressive policy led to World War II.

Hoadly, Benjamin (1676–1761), English Anglican bishop, started Bangorian Controversy (q.v.).

Hoban, James (c. 1762–1831), Irish-born American architect, designed White House.

Hobart, capital of Tasmania, founded 1804 as a penal colony.

Hobbema, Meindert (1638–1709), Dutch painter of quiet landscapes, e.g. *The Water Mill.* .

Hobbes, Thomas (1588–1679), English political philosopher whose *Leviathan* (1651) justified state absolutism.

Hobbs, Sir Jack (1882–1963), English cricketer, an outstanding batsman, played for England 1907–30.

Hobhouse, Leonard Trelawney (1864–1929), English writer on sociology, philosophy and morals.

Hoccleve, Thomas. See **Occleve,** Thomas.

Hoche, Lazare (1768–97), French Revolutionary general, put down La Vendée revolt and repulsed Austrian attacks.

Ho-Chi-Minh (1892–1969), Vietnamese Communist leader, first president of the Democratic Republic of Vietnam.

Hockey Association, present body formed 1886.

Hockney, David (b. 1937), English painter, whose work shows the influence of pop art.

Hodgkin, Dorothy (b. 1910), English biochemist, won 1954 Nobel Prize for

Chemistry for her work in determining the structure of biochemical compounds.

Hodgkin, Thomas (1798–1866), English pathologist, first described the glandular disease, lymphadenoma, named after him.

Hodgson, Ralph (1871–1962), English poet, wrote chiefly about nature.

Hodler, Ferdinand (1853–1918), Swiss painter of the mysterious and symbolic.

Hoe, Richard March (1812–86), American inventor of the rotary printing press, 1846.

Hoefnagel, Joris (1542–1600), Dutch miniaturist, best known for his *Missale Romanum.*

Hofer, Andreas (1767–1810), Tyrolese patriot, led rebellion against Franco-Bavarian rule; executed.

Hoff, Jacobus van't (1852–1911), Dutch chemist, laid the foundations of stereo-chemistry.

Hoffman, Ernst Theodor (1776–1822), German writer and composer, whose stories are classics of the fantastic and macabre.

Hoffman, Heinrich (1809–94), German writer of the children's classic *Struwwel-peter* (1847).

Hoffnung, Gerard (1925–59), English musician, cartoonist, and humorous illustrator.

Hofmannsthal, Hugo von (1874–1929), Austrian poet, dramatist and librettist for Richard Strauss, whose plays include *Ariadne auf Naxos* (1912).

Hofmeyr, Jan Hendrik (1854–1909), South African politician and journalist, championed Anglo-Boer conciliation.

Hogarth, David George (1862–1927), English archaeologist, worked in Egypt, Crete and Greece.

Hogarth, William (1697–1764), English painter and engraver, often satirical, e.g. *Rake's Progress* series.

Hogg, James (1770–1835), Scottish poet, called 'the Ettrick Shepherd', also novelist, wrote *Confessions of a Justified Sinner* (1824).

Hogg, Quintin (1845–1903), English founder of Regent Street (London) Polytechnic, 1882.

Hohenlinden, Battle of, Napoleonic Wars, victory of the French over the Austrians, 3 Dec. 1800.

Hohenstaufen dynasty, ruled in Germany 1138–1254.

Hohenzollern dynasty, ruled Brandenburg 1415–1701, Prussia 1701–1871, and Germany 1871–1918.

Hokusai, Katsushika (1760–1849), Japanese painter and colour-print maker, one of the masters of the popular school.

Holbach, Baron d' (1723–89), French philosopher, wrote *Système de la Nature* (1770).

Holbein, Hans, the Elder (c. 1465–1524),

German painter working at Augsburg, noted for his altarpieces.

Holbein, Hans, the Younger (c. 1497–1543), German painter, best known for his portraits, e.g. of Henry VIII and Sir Thomas More.

Holbrooke, Josef (1878–1958), English pianist and composer, notably of a setting of E. A. Poe's *The Raven.*

Holcroft, Thomas (1745–1809), English playwright and radical, wrote *The Road to Ruin* (1792).

Hölderlin, Johann Christian (1770–1843), German lyric poet, deeply influenced by ancient Greece.

Holgate, Robert (c. 1481–1555), English prelate, archbishop of York 1545–54.

Holiday, Billie (1915–59), American Negro singer, outstanding interpreter of jazz music.

holidays with pay, enforced by law in Britain since 1938.

Holinshed, Raphael (d. c. 1580), English historian whose *Chronicles* provided a source for Shakespeare's history plays.

Holl, Frank (1845–88), English painter, one of a family of artists.

Holland, Henry (1745–1806), English architect, built Carlton House, London.

Holland, Henry Fox, 1st Baron (1773–1840), English statesman, a notable reformer, chancellor of Duchy of Lancaster 1830–40.

Holland, John (d. 1772), English founder, 1695, and president of Bank of Scotland.

Hollar, Wenceslaus (1607–77), Bohemian engraver in England, designed valuable views of London.

Hollerith machines, precursor of computers, invented 1890 by the American Herman Hollerith (1860–1929).

Holles, Denzil (1599–1680), English Parliamentarian, exiled 1647–60 for advocating conciliation with the king.

Hollywood, California, founded 1887; incorporated 1903.

Holmes, Oliver Wendell (1809–94), American physician and writer, wrote *The Autocrat of the Breakfast Table* (1858).

Holmes, Oliver Wendell (1841–1935), American lawyer, son of Oliver Wendell Holmes, Supreme Court justice 1902–32.

holmium, chemical element, discovered 1878 by the Swiss chemists J. L. Soret and M. Delafontaine and independently 1879 by the Swede Per Teodor Cleve.

Holocene Epoch, Earth history, the time from c. 8000 B.C. to the present.

holography, three-dimensional photography method, invented 1948 by the Hungarian-born electrical engineer Dennis Gabor (b. 1900); made feasible 1960 by the invention of the laser.

Holst, Gustav (1874–1934), English composer of *The Planets* (1917).

Holstein, Friedrich von (1837–1909), German diplomat, advocated aggressive foreign policy.

Holy Alliance, made between the emperors of Russia and Austria and the king of Prussia 26 Sept. 1815.

Holy Island, England, chosen for the site of his church and monastery by Saint Aidan 635.

Holyoake, George Jacob (1817–1906), English agitator for social reform, wrote *History of Co-operation* (1875–77).

Holyrood Abbey, Scotland, founded 1128 by King David I; Palace begun 1498.

Holy Thursday. See **Ascension.**

Holy Week, the week from Palm Sunday to Easter Saturday.

Homberg, Willem (1652–1715), Dutch chemist, discovered boracic acid.

Home, John (1722–1808), Scottish playwright, wrote *Douglas* (1756).

Home Guard, founded May 1940 as Local Defence Volunteers; adopted new name July 1940; disbanded Dec. 1945.

Home Office, Great Britain, assumed present form 1782.

Homer (8th cent. B.C.), Greek epic poet, reputed author of *Iliad* and *Odyssey*.

Homer, Winslow (1836–1910), American painter and illustrator of war, rural and sea scenes.

Home Rule, for Ireland, movement for begun by Isaac Butt (*q.v.*) 1870; 1st Home Rule Bill 1886, 2nd Home Rule Bill 1893; 3rd Home Rule Bill 1912–14; Home Rule Act 1920.

Home Service, B.B.C., began 1 Sept. 1939.

homoeopathy, principles first enunciated 1796 by the German physician Samuel Hahnemann (1755–1843).

Homo Sapiens, name coined by Linnaeus (*q.v.*); earliest remains, found in Hungary, date back *c.* 425,000 years.

Honduras, Central America, discovered by Columbus 1502; settled by Spanish in the 1520s; independent since 1838.

Honduras, British. See **Belize.**

Hong Kong, ceded to Britain by China 1841; confirmed by treaty 1842; Kowloon also ceded 1860; New Territories leased to Britain 1898; colony occupied by Japanese 1941–45.

Honneger, Arthur (1892–1955), Swiss composer of modern school of music, belonged to French group 'The Six'.

Honorius I (d. 638), Pope 625–638, later (680) condemned as heretic.

Honorius II (d. 1072), anti-pope 1061–64, deposed by Council of Milan.

Honorius II (d. 1130), Pope 1124–30; as cardinal bishop made Concordat of Worms 1122.

Honorius III (d. 1227), Pope 1216–27, called for crusade against Albigensians.

Honourable Artillery Company, received charter of incorporation 1537; possibly founded earlier.

Honourable Corps of Gentlemen at Arms, the sovereign's personal bodyguard, founded 1559.

Honthorst, Gerard van (1590–1656), Dutch painter of dramatic night scenes.

Hooch, Pieter de (1629–*c.* 1685), Dutch painter of ordinary life, e.g. *Courtyard in Delft*.

Hood, Samuel, Viscount (1724–1816), English admiral, gave distinguished service in American and French Revolutionary Wars.

Hood, Thomas (1799–1845), English poet, both comic and also grimly realistic as in *The Bridge of Sighs*.

Hooft, Pieter (1581–1647), Dutch historian, poet and dramatist, a leading Renaissance figure in Dutch literature.

Hook, Theodore (1788–1841), English writer of farces and novels, e.g. *Maxwell* (1830).

Hooke, Robert (1635–1703), English scientist, made astronomical, physical and horological discoveries.

Hooker, Sir Joseph (1817–1911), English botanist, son of Sir William Hooker, introduced many oriental plants to Europe.

Hooker, Richard (*c.* 1554–1600), English Anglican priest, wrote classic *Laws of Ecclesiastical Polity* (1594–97).

Hooker, Sir William Jackson (1785–1865), English botanist, was first director of Botanic Gardens, Kew.

Hooper, John (d. 1555), English prelate, bishop of Worcester 1552; burnt at the stake.

Hoover, Herbert (1874–1964), American statesman, 31st president of the United States 1929–33.

Hoover, John Edgar (1895–1972), American lawyer, director of the Federal Bureau of Investigation 1924–72.

Hope, Anthony (1863–1933), English romantic novelist, remembered for *The Prisoner of Zenda* (1894).

Hope, Thomas (*c.* 1770–1831), English antiquarian, wrote influential *Household Furniture and Interior Decoration* (1807).

Hopkins, Gerard Manley (1844–89), English poet, a Jesuit, wrote in inimitable alliterative 'sprung rhythm' style.

Hopkins, Johns (1795–1873), American financier and philanthropist, founded well-known university and hospital.

Hopkins, Stephen (1707–85), American governor of Rhode Island, supported Revolutionary War.

Hopkinson, Joseph (1770–1842), American lawyer and composer of song *Hail, Columbia.*

Hoppner, John (1758–1810), English painter, mainly of fashionable portraits.

Horace (65–8 B.C.), Roman poet, famous for odes, satires and discourses.

hormones, first extensively studied 1902–05 by the physiologists Sir William Bayliss (1866–1924) and Ernest Starling (1866–1927).

Horn, Count of (1518–68), Dutch soldier and statesman, executed for opposition to Spanish policies.

Horn, Arvid, Count (1664–1742), Swedish statesman, was chief minister 1720–38.

Hornung, Ernest William (1866–1921), English author of 'Raffles' stories, about gentleman-burglar.

Horowitz, Vladimir (b. 1904), Russian-born American piano virtuoso.

Horrocks, Jeremiah (1619–41), English astronomer, first to observe transit of Venus, 1639.

Horsley, Samuel (1733–1806), English Anglican bishop, engaged in controversy with Joseph Priestley (q.v.).

Hortensius, Quintus (114–50 B.C.), Roman orator, Cicero's rival on behalf of the aristocratic party.

Horthy, Miklós (1868–1957), Hungarian naval officer, regent and effectively dictator of Hungary 1920–40.

hot-air blast, in iron-smelting, patented 1828 by the Scottish engineer James Beaumont Neilson (1792–1865).

Hotchkiss, Benjamin (1826–85), American inventor of a machine-gun and a magazine rifle.

Hotspur. See **Percy,** Sir Henry.

Houdini, Harry (1874–1926), American magician and escapologist of unsurpassed skill.

Houdon, Jean Antoine (1741–1828), French sculptor, made portraits of Voltaire, Rousseau, etc.

House, Colonel Edward (1858–1938), American diplomat, friend and special representative of President Wilson.

House of Commons, Great Britain, origins in 13th century.

House of Lords, Great Britain, origins in 13th century.

House of Representatives, U.S. Congress, instituted 1789.

Housman, Alfred Edward (1859–1936), English poet, wrote collection *A Shropshire Lad* (1896).

Housman, Lawrence (1865–1959), English writer, author of *Little Plays of St Francis* (1922); brother of A. E. Housman.

Houston, Sam (1793–1863), American soldier, led Texans in war against Mexico; first president of independent Texas, later state governor.

hovercraft. See **air cushion vehicle.**

Howard, Catherine (c. 1520–42), fifth wife of Henry VIII 1540–42, beheaded for adultery.

Howard, Charles, 2nd Baron of Effingham

(1536–1624), English sailor, commanded the fleet which defeated the Spanish Armada.

Howard, Sir Ebenezer (1850–1928), English pioneer of garden cities.

Howard, Henry (c. 1517–1547), English soldier and poet, executed for treason.

Howard, John (1726–90), English prison reformer, wrote *The State of Prisons* (1777).

Howard, Leslie (1893–1943), English actor, best known for his part in the film of Shaw's *Pygmalion*.

Howard, Sidney (1891–1939), American playwright, author of *They Knew What They Wanted* (1924).

Howard League for Penal Reform, founded 1866.

Howe, Elias (1819–67), American inventor of the sewing-machine, 1846.

Howe, Julia Ward (1819–1910), American author, wrote *The Battle Hymn of the Republic*.

Howe, Richard, Earl (1726–99), English admiral defeated French fleet on 'Glorious First of June' 1794.

Howe, Samuel Gridley (1801–76), American philanthropist, husband of Julia Ward Howe, devoted to care of blind and other causes.

Howell, James (c. 1594–1666), English writer (in prison) of *Epistolae Ho-Eliane*, witty imaginary letters.

Howells, Herbert (b. 1892), English composer of choral and instrumental music.

Howells, William Dean (1837–1920), American novelist, e.g. *Rise of Silas Lapham* (1885); also influential journalist-critic.

Howrah Bridge, Calcutta, opened 1943.

Hoxha, Enver (b. 1908), Albanian political leader, secretary-general of the Albanian Communist party since 1943.

Hoyle, Edmond (1672–1769), English writer on games, especially whist.

Hroswitha (c. 935–1000), German Benedictine nun, author of poems and comedies in Latin.

Hsia dynasty, China, 2205–1766 B.C.

Hsüan Tsang (c. 600–664), Chinese Buddhist traveller, wrote a famous account of his travels in India.

Hsüan Tsung (685–762), emperor of China 713–756, whose reign was marked by the greatest cultural achievements of the T'ang dynasty.

Hubble, Edwin Powell (1889–1953), American astronomer, discovered the existence of independent stellar systems outside the earth's galaxy.

Huber, François (1750–1831), Swiss naturalist, was an expert on bees.

Huber, Wolf (c. 1485–1553), German artist, made woodcuts and drawings of views of the Danube.

Hubert, Saint (d. *c.* 727), bishop of Liège, patron saint of hunters.

Hubert de Burgh (d. 1243), chief justiciar of England 1215–32, effectively regent for Henry III.

Huc, Évariste Régis (1813–60), French Catholic missionary in Tibet, Mongolia and China.

Huch, Ricarda (1864–1947), German novelist, author of *Ludolf Ursleu* (1893).

Hudson, Henry (d. 1611), English navigator, discovered Hudson Bay 1610; set adrift by mutineers.

Hudson, William Henry (1841–1922), Argentine-born English naturalist, wrote romance *Green Mansions* (1904).

Hudson's Bay Company, chartered 1670 in England by Charles II; first governor Prince Rupert (*q.v.*).

Huggins, Sir William (1824–1910), English astronomer, led the development of spectroscopic photography.

Hughes, David Edward (1831–1900), Anglo-American inventor of the teleprinter and an early microphone.

Hughes, Howard (1906–76), American multi-millionaire industrialist, was well-known both as an aircraft manufacturer and a film director.

Hughes, James Langston (1902–67), American Negro poet and novelist, author of *The Weary Blues* (1926).

Hughes, Richard Arthur (1900–76), English novelist, author of *A High Wind in Jamaica* (1929).

Hughes, Ted (b. 1930), English poet, author of *The Hawk in the Rain* (1957) and *Lupercal* (1960).

Hughes, Thomas (1822–96), English author of *Tom Brown's Schooldays* (1857).

Hugo, Victor (1802–83), French poet and novelist, author of *Les Misérables* (1862), a major figure in world literature.

Huguenots, French Protestants, so called from the middle of the 16th century.

Hulagu (1217–65), Mongol ruler, founded the Il-khan dynasty of Persia.

Huli, Festival of, Indian custom similar to April Fools' Day, ending 31 March.

Hull, Cordell (1871–1955), American statesman, secretary of state 1933–44, awarded Nobel Peace prize 1945.

Hull, University of, university college opened 1927; reconstituted as a university 1954.

Hulme Grammar School, Oldham, English public school, founded 1611 by James Assheton.

Hulme, Thomas Ernest (1883–1917), English philosophical writer, killed in World War I; his *Speculations* were published 1924.

Human Rights, Declaration of, adopted by the U.N. General Assembly Dec. 1948.

Humboldt, Alexander von (1769–1859), German naturalist and explorer, best known for his work on ocean currents.

Humboldt, Karl Wilhelm von (1767–1835), German philologist, brother of Alexander von Humboldt, contributed to the development of comparative philology.

Hume, David (1711–76), Scottish philosopher and historian, wrote *Treatise of Human Nature* (1739–40).

Humperdinck, Engelbert (1854–1921), German composer of opera *Hansel and Gretl* (1893).

Hundred Days, the period between Napoleon's arrival in Paris and the 2nd restoration of Louis XVIII, 20 March to 28 June 1815.

Hundred Years' War, between England and France 1337–1453.

Hungary, traditionally invaded by Magyars 896; independent kingdom from *c.* 1000; partitioned between Austria and Turkey 1526–1699; ruled by Hapsburgs 1699–1918 (Dual Monarchy 1867–1918); republic and Communist regime 1918–19; regency 1920–45; republic proclaimed 1946; Communist People's Republic since 1949; revolution Oct.–Nov. 1956.

Huns, invaded Europe *c.* A.D. 370; defeated 453.

Hunt, Leigh (1784–1859), English journalist, critic and poet; also editor of various periodicals.

Hunt, William Holman (1827–1910), English painter of Pre-Raphaelite school, e.g. *Light of the World* (1854).

Hunter, John (1728–93), Scottish surgeon, made important discoveries concerned with arteries.

Hunter, William (1718–83), Scottish surgeon, brother of John Hunter.

Hunter, Sir William Wilson (1840–1900), Scottish administrator, made statistical survey of India.

hunters' moon, the first full moon after the harvest moon in October.

Huntingdon, Selina, Countess of (1707–91), English Methodist, founded her own 'Connexion' (sect).

Huntingdon, Henry Edwards (1850–1927), American railway executive, established well-known art collection and library.

Hunyadi, Janós (*c.* 1387–1456), Hungarian hero, fought many battles against Turks.

Hurst, Fanny (1889–1968), American novelist, wrote *Imitation of Life* (1932).

Hurstpierpoint College, Sussex, English public school, founded 1849.

Hus, Jan (*c.* 1369–1415), Bohemian religious reformer, burnt at the stake; his execution led to Hussite Wars.

Huskisson, William (1770–1830), British statesman, colonial secretary 1827–28; killed in railway accident.

Hussein (b. 1935), king of Jordan since 1952.

Hussein ibn Ali (1856–1931), king of the Hejaz 1916–24, began Arab revolt against Turks 1916 and founded Hashemite dynasty.

Husserl, Edmund (1859–1938), Austrian philosopher, pioneer of phenomenological studies.

Hutcheson, Francis (1694–1746), Irish-born Scottish philosopher, wrote *System of Moral Philosophy* (pub. 1755).

Hutchinson, Anne (1590–1643), English-born American religious reformer, rejected church control of the individual; killed by Indians.

Hutchinson, Thomas (1711–80), American governor of Massachusetts 1771–74, upholder of British authority.

Hutten, Ulrich von (1488–1523), German nobleman and humanist, supported Martin Luther; also a noted satirist.

Hutton, James (1726–97), Scottish pioneer geologist, wrote *Theory of the Earth* (1785).

Huxley, Aldous (1894–1963), English novelist, author of *Brave New World* (1932).

Huxley, Sir Julian (1887–1975), English biologist, brother of Aldous Huxley, wrote *Evolution: the Modern Synthesis* (1942).

Huxley, Thomas Henry (1825–95), English biologist, chief defender of Darwinism in public controversy.

Huygens, Christiaan (1629–95), Dutch scientist, developed wave theory of light, used pendulum in clocks, etc.

Huysmans, Cornelis (1648–1727), Dutch painter, chiefly of landscapes.

Huysmans, Joris Karl (1848–1907), French novelist, influential 'decadent', author of *À Rebours* (1884).

Huysum, Jan van (1682–1749), Dutch painter of exquisite flower-pieces.

Hyder Ali (1722–82), Indian prince, ruler of Mysore, fought two wars against British.

Hyderabad, Indian state, became part of Mogul Empire 1687; independent kingdom 1724; princely state in British Indian Empire; forcibly incorporated into India 1948; divided up among states of Andra Pradesh, Maharashtra and Mysore 1956.

hydraulic brakes, first developed in the 1930s.

hydraulic crane, invented c. 1845 by Lord Armstrong (*q.v.*).

hydraulic press, invented 1796 by Joseph Bramah (1748–1814).

hydrochloric acid, preparation first described by the German alchemist Andreas Libavius (c. 1540–1616).

hydroelectric power station, construction of first begun 1883 in Ireland.

hydrofoil, first successful hydrofoil ship designed by the Italian Enrico Forlanini (1848–1930) and tested 1906; in commercial and military use by 1950s.

hydrogen, first prepared probably by Paracelsus; recognized as a distinct substance 1766 by Henry Cavendish; atomic structure explained 1913 by Niels Bohr.

hydrogen bomb, first American exploded 1951; first Russian 1953; first British 1957.

hydrogen peroxide, obtained 1818 by the French chemist Louis-Jacques Thénard (1777–1857).

hydrophobia. See rabies.

hygrometer, probably invented by Leonardo da Vinci, based on the notes made 1450 by Nicolas Cryfts.

Hymers College, Hull, English public school, founded 1889.

Hyndman, Henry Mayers (1842–1921), English Socialist, founded Social Democratic Federation 1881.

Hypatia (d. A.D. 415), Alexandrian Greek philosopher, famous beauty; murdered by Christian mob.

hypnotism, term coined 1841 by the Scottish scholar James Braid (1796–1860).

hysteresis, law of, discovered 1892 by Charles Proteus Steinmetz (*q.v.*).

I

Ibañez, Vicente Blasco. See **Blasco Ibañez,** Vicente.

Ibert, Jacques (1890–1962), French composer, whose work includes operas, ballets, piano pieces and chamber music.

Ibn Batuta (1304–78), Arab traveller in three continents; reached China.

Ibn Khaldun (1332–1400), Arab historian, author of a general history of the Arab people.

Ibn Saud (1880–1953), founded the kingdom of Saudi Arabia after a career of conquest, king 1932–53.

Ibn Tashfin, Yusuf (d. c. 1105), Berber chieftain, helped to create the Almoravid empire in North Africa and Spain.

Ibrahim Pasha (1789–1848), Egyptian soldier, son of Mehemet Ali (*q.v.*), conquered Syria from Turks.

Ibsen, Henrik (1828–1906), Norwegian playwright, wrote powerful, naturalistic social dramas, including *Hedda Gabler* (1890) and *The Master Builder* (1892).

Ice Age, existence first suggested c. 1840 by Jean Louis Agassiz (*q.v.*); last major glaciation occurred in the Pleistocene Epoch.

ice cream, first made in China before 1000 B.C.; probably introduced into Europe by Marco Polo; water ices known in ancient Greece c. 330 B.C.

Iceland, first settled by Norsemen 874; national parliament (Althing) established 930; united with Norway 1262; rule

passed to Denmark 1380; became sovereign state 1918 by Act of Union; proclaimed itself an independent republic
1944.

Icknield Way, from Berkshire Down to
the Fens, England, natural road of Celtic
origin, first recorded mention A.D. 45.

Iconoclast controversy, in Byzantine
Empire, 726–843.

Ictinus (5th cent. B.C.), Greek architect,
whose masterpiece was the Parthenon at
Athens.

Idaho, U.S.A., first permanently settled
1860; organized as a territory 1863;
admitted to the Union 1890.

identity cards, introduced in Britain 1939;
abolished 1952.

Ido, revision of Esperanto, produced 1907
by Marquis de Beaufront.

Idrisi (c. 1099–c. 1165), Arab geographer,
worked in Sicily; made valuable maps.

Ifni, Morocco, first settled by Spanish
1476–1524; ceded by Morocco to Spain
1860; returned to Morocco 1969.

Ignatius Loyola, Saint. See **Loyola,
Ignatius.**

Ignatius of Antioch, Saint (1st cent.
A.D.), Christian martyr, wrote *Epistles.*

Ignatius of Constantinople, Saint (c.
800–c. 878), patriarch of Constantinople
846–858 and 867–878, rival of Photius
(q.v.).

Ikhnaton. See **Akhnaton.**

Illinois, U.S.A., discovered by the French
1673; settled 1720; ceded by France to
Britain 1763; organized as a territory 1809;
admitted to the Union 1818.

Illuminati, German rationalist society
founded 1776 by the German philosopher
Adam Weishaupt (1748–1830); officially
proscribed and dissolved 1785.

Illustrated London News, British periodical, began publication 1842.

Immaculate Conception, of the Virgin
Mary, Catholic dogma defined 1854.

**Imperial College of Science and Tech-
nology,** London University, established
1907 by royal charter through the federation of the Royal College of Science
(founded 1845), the Royal School of
Mines (1851) and the City and Guilds
College (1884).

Impressionism, major art movement
originating in France, embracing works
produced by a group of artists from c. 1867
to c. 1886.

Inauguration Day, U.S.A., on which
American presidents take the oath of
office every four years; 20 Jan.

Incas, Peru, established capital at Cuzco
supposedly in 11th century; gained control over extensive area of Andes from
early 15th century; empire crumbled
following sacking of Cuzco 1533 by the
Spanish under Pizarro (q.v.).

Inchbald, Elizabeth (1753–1821), English
actress and writer, author of *A Simple
Story* (1791).

income tax, first imposed in Britain 1799–
1802, by William Pitt the Younger;
further period 1803–15; reintroduced
1842 by Sir Robert Peel; P.A.Y.E. (pay as
you earn) scheme introduced 1944.

incunabula, earliest books printed, from
the 1450s up to the end of 1500.

Independence Day, commemorating the
Declaration of Independence 4 July 1776;
public holiday in U.S.A.

Independent Labour Party, founded
1893 by Keir Hardie (q.v.); seceded from
Labour Party 1932 under James Maxton
(q.v.); ceased to have parliamentary representation 1948.

Independent Television Authority,
created July 1954; renamed Independent
Broadcasting Authority July 1972.

Index Librorum Prohibitorum, list of
books condemned by the Roman Catholic
Church, first issued 1557; discontinued
1966.

India, Indus Valley civilization c. 2300–
1750 B.C.; invaded by Indo-Europeans
(Aryans) from c. 1700–1200 B.C., by
Alexander the Great 327–325 B.C., and by
Arabs in 8th century A.D.; Muslim period
c. 1200–1526; Mogul empire 1526–1761;
European trading posts established 16th
and 17th centuries; British East India
Company acquired extensive areas from
1765; government transferred from East
India Company to British crown 1858;
Indian Empire proclaimed 1877; achieved
independence 1947; became a republic
1950.

Indiana, U.S.A., first settled about 1732;
organized as a territory 1800; admitted to
the Union 1816.

Indianapolis, Indiana, founded 1821;
made state capital 1825.

Indian Mutiny, against the British began
May 1857; ended July 1858.

Indian National Congress, founded by
the Englishman Allan Hume, first met
1885.

indiarubber, discovered c. 1740 by the
French traveller Charles de la Condamine
(1701–74).

indium, metallic element, discovered 1863
by the German scientists Ferdinand Reich
(1799–1882) and Theodor Richter (1824–
98).

Indochina, established 1862–87 by the
French in territory of former empire of
Annam; Japanese occupation 1940–45;
France regained control 1946; region
subsequently split up into individual
states. See **Cambodia; Laos; Vietnam,**
Socialist Republic of.

Indo-European languages, spoken for at
least the last 3000 years in most of Europe

and SW and S Asia; common origin of Greek and Sanskrit first postulated 1787 by the English orientalist Sir William Jones (1746–94).

Indonesia, up to 16th century seat of several kingdoms trading with India and China; first visited by Dutch 1595; mostly ruled by Dutch East India Company 1602–1798; governed by the Netherlands 1816–1949; Japanese occupation 1942–45; independent republic since 1949.

induction. See **electromagnetic induction.**

Industrial Revolution, in Britain, c. 1760–c. 1840; term first popularized by Arnold Toynbee (q.v.).

Industrial Workers of the World, Labour organization, founded in U.S.A. 1905.

Indy, Vincent d' (1851–1931), French composer, e.g. opera *Fervaal* (1897).

Infallibility, of the Pope, Catholic dogma, defined 1870.

infinity, first mathematical study c. 1874 by Georg Cantor (q.v.).

Information, Central Office of, London, formed 1946, succeeding the Ministry of Information (1939–46).

infrared radiation, first discovered 1800 by Sir William Herschel (q.v.).

Inge, William (1860–1954), English cleric and writer, dean of St Paul's Cathedral 1911–34.

Inglis, James (d. 1531), Scottish cleric, secretary to Queen Margaret and abbot of Culross.

Ingoldsby, Thomas. Pseudonym of R. H. Barham (q.v.).

Ingres, Jean Auguste (1780–1867), French painter of classical technique and romantic feeling, e.g. *La Grande Baigneuse.*

Inkerman, Battle of, Crimean War, victory of the British and French over the Russians, 5 Nov. 1854.

Inman, Henry (1801–46), American painter, especially of portraits.

Inness, George (1825–94), American painter of landscapes, influenced by European contacts.

Innocent I, Saint (d. 417), Pope 402–417, advanced claims of universal supremacy for papacy.

Innocent II (d. 1143), Pope 1130–43, contested papacy with anti-pope Anacletus.

Innocent III (c. 1160–1216), Pope 1198–1216, humbled King John; deposed Emperor Otto IV; called for Fourth Crusade.

Innocent IV (d. 1254), Pope 1243–54, involved in disputes with Holy Roman emperors.

Innocent VI (d. 1362), Pope 1352–62, resided at Avignon.

Innocent VII (d. 1406), Pope 1404–06 in Rome, opposed by anti-pope Benedict XIII at Avignon.

Innocent VIII (1432–92), Pope 1484–92, called unsuccessfully for a crusade.

Innocent X (1574–1655), Pope 1644–55, mainly involved in Italian political struggles.

Innocent XI (1611–89), Pope 1676–89, quarrelled with Louis XIV of France.

Innocent XII (1615–1700), Pope 1691–1700, reformed abuses in the Church.

Innocents' Day, festival celebrated 28 Dec. in the Roman Catholic Church.

inoculation, for smallpox, introduced c. 1718 into England from Turkey; successful method developed 1796 by Edward Jenner (q.v.).

Inönü, Ismet (1884–1973), Turkish statesman, was three times president of Turkey.

Inquisition, Holy Office of the, founded 1231; Spanish Inquisition instituted 1478; finally suppressed 1820.

insecticides. See **DDT.**

Institute of Contemporary Arts, London, founded 1946.

Institute of International Law, Brussels, founded 1873 by the Swiss writer on law Johann Kaspar Bluntschli (1808–81).

Institute of Physics, London, founded 1874.

insulin, isolated 1921 by the Canadian scientists Sir Frederick Banting (q.v.) and Charles Herbert Best (b. 1899); structure determined 1953 by the English biochemist Frederick Sanger (b. 1918).

insurance, earliest recorded policy issued 1523, London; fire insurance pioneered c. 1666 by the English economist Nicolas Barbon (c. 1640–98); earliest recorded life assurance bond 1228.

integrated circuits, electronics, first demonstrated 1958.

intelligence quotient (IQ), concept suggested by the German psychologist William Stern and adopted 1915 as the Stanford revision of the Binet-Simon intelligence test (1905) by the American psychologist Lewis Terman.

Interdict, Papal, against England under King John, 1208–13.

interference, of light, principles established 1801 by Thomas Young (q.v.). See also **wave theory.**

interferometer, optical device first described 1862 by the French physicist Armand Fizeau (1819–96). See also **radio telescopes.**

internal-combustion engine, invented 1859 by the Belgian-born Frenchman Jean Lenoir (1822–1900); improvement patented 1877 by the German Nikolaus Otto (1832–91).

International, *First* (International Workingmen's Association, Marxist and Anarchist), 1864–76; *Second* (Socialist),

1889–1914, revived 1919 and 1947, re-constituted 1951 as Socialist International; *Third* (Communist) see **Comintern, Cominform**; *Fourth* (Trotskyist), formed 1938.

International Air Transport Association, founded 1945.

International Bank for Reconstruction and Development, Washington D.C., established Dec. 1945; officially began operations June 1946.

International Bureau of Weights and Measures, Paris, established 1875.

International Chamber of Commerce, founded 1919.

International Civil Aviation Organization, proposed 1944, founded 1947.

International Court of Justice, the Hague, set up 1945 as the principal judicial organ of the United Nations.

International Date Line, in Pacific Ocean, coinciding approximately with the 180° meridian, established 1883.

International Geophysical Year, 1 July 1957 to 31 Dec. 1958.

International Herald Tribune, now published with the *New York Times* and *Washington Post,* founded 1887 as the *Paris Herald,* becoming the Paris edition of the *Herald Tribune* after 1924.

International Labour Organization, Geneva, founded 1919; became specialized agency associated with the United Nations 1946.

International Monetary Fund, established Dec. 1945.

International Postal Union, founded at Berne Oct. 1875.

International Power Conference, first session held at Wembley 30 June 1924.

International Telecommunication Union, founded 1865; reorganized as a U.N. agency 1947.

Interpol (International Criminal Police Organization), formed in Vienna 1923.

invar, alloy, first produced 1890 by the Swiss physicist Charles Édouard Guillaume (1861–1938).

invertebrates, first seriously studied and classified 1801–22 by Jean Baptiste Lamarck.

iodine, discovered 1811 by the French chemist Barnard Courtois (1777–1838).

Iona, Hebrides, home of Saint Columba from 563; Iona Community founded 1938 by Rev. George MacLeod.

Ionesco, Eugène (b. 1912), Romanian-born French dramatist, author of *Rhinoceros* (1958), an exponent of the theatre of the absurd.

ionization, electrolytic theory first presented 1884 by Svante August Arrhenius (*q.v.*).

ionosphere, existence suggested *c.* 1839 by Karl Friedrich Gauss (*q.v.*) and again in

1902, independently, by the American electrical engineer Arthur Edwin Kennelly 1861–1939) and the English physicist Oliver Heaviside (1850–1925); first discovered 1925.

Iowa, U.S.A., first settled *c.* 1788; included in Louisiana Purchase (*q.v.*) 1803; territory established 1838; admitted to the Union 1846.

Ipatiev, Vladimir (1867–1952), Russian chemist and an authority on catalytic reactions.

Ipswich School, English public school, founded before 1400.

IQ. See **intelligence quotient.**

I.R.A. See **Irish Republican Army.**

Iran, name officially adopted by Persia (*q.v.*) since 1935.

Iraq, centre of ancient civilization of Mesopotamia (*q.v.*); under Ottoman Turks from 17th century; conquered by British from Turkey 1914–18; British mandate 1919–22; monarchy established 1921; independent state 1932; republic since 1958.

Iraq-Mediterranean oil pipeline, inaugurated 14 Jan. 1935.

Ireland, invaded by Celts *c.* 500 B.C.; converted to Christianity in 5th century A.D.; invasions by Norsemen began 795; beginning of English rule from late 12th century; effective English control established by Cromwell 1652; Act of Union with Britain 1801; Easter Rising 1916; Northern Ireland (*q.v.*) formed 1920; Irish Free State established 1921; renamed Eire 1937 and Republic of Ireland 1949.

Ireland, John (1879–1962), English composer, e.g. of *The Forgotten Rite* (1913).

Ireland, William Henry (1777–1835), English forger of Shakespeare manuscripts, accepted by many as genuine.

Irenaeus, Saint (2nd cent. A.D.), apostle to the Gauls, bishop of Lyons A.D. 177.

Irene (752–803), Byzantine empress, wife of Leo IV 769–780, regent 780–790, and sole ruler 797–802; deposed.

Ireton, Henry (1611–51), English Parliamentarian and soldier, son-in-law of Oliver Cromwell, conducted Irish campaign 1650–51.

iridium, chemical element, discovered 1804 by the English chemist Smithson Tennant (1761–1815).

Irish coffee, invented at Shannon Airport 1947.

Irish Free State. See **Ireland.**

Irish Land League, founded 1879 by Michael Davitt (*q.v.*).

Irish Republican Army, created 1919 from the Irish Volunteers; active 1919–21 and 1922–23; declared illegal 1931 and 1936; carried out bombing attacks in Northern Ireland and England 1938–39;

launched terror campaign against Northern Ireland from 1969 and intermittently against England from 1973.

Irish Volunteers, formed 1913; merged with I.R.A. 1919.

iron, discovered in prehistoric times; widely used in Near East and SE Europe from *c.* 1200 B.C. (beginnings of Iron Age).

iron bridge, first example built across River Severn 1779.

Iron Curtain, between Communist Eastern Europe and the noncommunist West, term first used March 1946 by Sir Winston Churchill.

ironclad ships, first battle of, in the American Civil War between *Monitor* and *Merrimac* 9 March 1862.

Ironmongers' Company, London origins uncertain; first recorded mention 1300; grant of arms 1455; royal charter 1463.

irrational numbers, discovered by Pythagoras (*q.v.*); studied and redefined 1872 by the German mathematician Richard Dedekind (1831–1916).

Irving, Sir Henry (1838–1905), English actor, first to be knighted, manager at London Lyceum 1878–1902.

Irving, Washington (1783–1859), American writer, notably of *Rip Van Winkle* (1819).

Irvingites. See **Catholic Apostolic Church.**

Isaac I (d. 1061), Byzantine emperor 1057–59, abdicated because of illness; was also a scholar.

Isaac II (d. 1204), Byzantine emperor 1185–95, deposed and blinded; restored as puppet ruler by crusaders 1203–04.

Isabella (1214–41), wife of the emperor Frederick II, daughter of King John of England.

Isabella I (1451–1504), queen of Castile 1474–79, and of Castile and Aragon with Ferdinand 1479–1504; financed Columbus's voyage.

Isabella II (1830–1904), queen of Spain 1833–68; deposed; abdicated in favour of her son.

Isabella of Angoulême (d. 1246), queen of England 1200–16 as wife of King John.

Isabella of France (1292–1358), queen of England as wife of Edward II 1308–27; ruled with her lover Mortimer 1327–30.

Isabey, Jean Baptiste (1767–1855), French painter of official portraits and romantic land- and seascapes.

Isaiah (8th cent. B.C.), major Hebrew Old Testament prophet, part-author of the book that bears his name.

Isherwood, Christopher (b. 1904), English novelist and dramatist, author of *Goodbye to Berlin* (1939).

Isidore, Saint (*c.* 560–636), Spanish scholar, archbishop of Seville 600–636, wrote the encyclopaedic *Etymologiae.*

Islam, religion founded *c.* A.D. 610 by the prophet Mohammed (*q.v.*); doctrine laid down in the Koran (*q.v.*).

Ismail I (1486–1524), shah of Persia 1500–24, founder of the Safawid dynasty.

Ismailis, Muslim sect, formed in the mid-8th century.

Ismail Pasha (1830–95), khedive of Egypt 1863–79, sold Suez Canal shares to Britain 1875.

Isocrates (436–338 B.C.), Greek writer and educationalist, conducted school of oratory at Athens.

isomorphism, chemical relationship, principle defined 1820 by the German chemist Eilhardt Mitscherlich (1794–1863).

isotopes, theory developed 1912–13 by Frederick Soddy (*q.v.*); first ones (of neon) identified 1913 by Sir J. J. Thomson (*q.v.*).

Israel, Jewish state, established May 1948 following the partition of Palestine (*q.v.*).

Israëls, Josef (1824–1911), Dutch painter of realistic peasant studies.

Istanbul, capital of Ottoman Empire 1453–1923. See also **Byzantium; Constantinople.**

Isthmian Games, held in ancient Greece, began 581 B.C.

Italian language, earliest known document, the *Placito Capuano*, dated March 960; fully developed in 12th and 13th centuries.

Italian Somaliland. See **Somalia.**

Italy. For early history see **Rome.** Invaded by Ostrogoths and Lombards in 5th–6th centuries A.D.; part of Carolingian Empire from 774 and of Holy Roman Empire from 962; N Italy divided into city-states; S Italy ruled by foreign dynasties; kingdom 1861–1946; Fascist regime 1922–43; republic since 1946.

Ito, Prince Hirobumi (1841–1909), Japanese statesman, promoted policy of expansion and westernization.

Iturbide, Agustin de (1783–1824), emperor of Mexico 1822–23, hero of struggle for independence but tyrannical ruler.

Ivan I (d. 1341), grand duke of Moscow 1328–41, grew powerful as tax collector for Tartar overlords.

Ivan III (1440–1505), grand duke of Moscow 1462–1505, conquered Novgorod; won independence from Tartars.

Ivan IV, the Terrible (1530–84), grand duke of Moscow 1533–84, and first tsar, crushed nobles; unstable and cruel.

Ivan V (1666–96), tsar of Russia 1682–89, was under the influence of his half-sister Sophia.

Ivan VI (1740–64), tsar of Russia 1740–41, spent rest of life in prison; murdered.

Ives, Charles Edward (1874–1954), American composer whose works include symphonies and chamber music, noted for his use of polytonal harmonies.

Ives, Frederick Eugene (1856–1937), American inventor of the half-tone printing process for reproducing pictures.

Ivo of Chartres (c. 1040–1116), French prelate, bishop of Chartres 1090–1116; was an active reformer.

Ivory Coast, West Africa, French treaty with native rulers 1842 leading to French occupation; French protectorate 1889, colony 1893; included in reorganized French West Africa 1895; overseas territory 1946; became an independent republic 1960.

Iyeyasu (1542–1616), Japanese statesman, founder of the Tokugawa shogunate.

J

Jackson, Andrew (1767–1845), American statesman, 7th president of the United States 1829–37; defended New Orleans 1814; was also a famous Indian fighter.

Jackson, Sir Barry (1879–1961), English theatrical manager, founded Birmingham Repertory Company and Malvern Festival.

Jackson, Frederick George (1860–1938), Scottish explorer, notably of the Arctic.

Jackson, Thomas ('Stonewall') (1824–63), American Confederate general, brilliant tactician; accidentally killed by his own soldiers.

Jack the Ripper, the name given to the unknown murderer of prostitutes in Whitechapel, London 1888.

Jacob, Old Testament patriarch, traditional ancestor of the people of Israel.

Jacob, Max (1876–1944), French poet and painter, whose prose poems influenced Surrealism.

Jacobins, French Revolutionary club, founded 1789; suppressed 1794; briefly revived during the 1848 Revolution.

Jacobite glass, manufactured mainly 1745–65.

Jacobites, supporters of James II and his descendants, mainly active 1688–1745.

Jacobs, William Wymark (1863–1943), English writer, especially of riverside stories.

Jacobsen, Arne (1902–71), Danish architect, designer of many notable modern buildings.

Jacobsen, Jens Peter (1847–85), Danish novelist and poet, leader of the naturalist movement in Danish literature.

Jacobus de Voragine (c. 1230–c. 1298), Italian archbishop of Genoa 1293–c. 1298, wrote the hagiological *Golden Legend*.

Jacopone da Todi (c. 1230–1306), Italian friar and poet, said to have written *Stabat Mater*.

Jacquard loom, first to weave patterns,

invented 1801 by the Frenchman Joseph-Marie Jacquard (1752–1834).

Jacquerie, insurrection of French peasants May–June 1358.

Jadassohn, Solomon (1831–1902), German composer, pupil of Liszt, also wrote textbooks.

Jadwiga (1370–99), queen of Poland 1384–99; tried to unite Poland and Lithuania by her marriage.

Jaggard, William (c. 1568–1623), English publisher of Shakespeare.

Jagiellon dynasty, Lithuanian dynasty, ruled Poland 1382–1572.

Jahangir (1569–1627), Mogul emperor of India 1605–27, influenced by wife Nur Jahan.

Jainism, Indian religious movement founded c. 6th century B.C. by Vardhamana Mahavira.

Jalal ad-din Rumi (1207–73), Persian mystical poet and founder of the dancing dervishes.

Jamaica, discovered 1494 by Christopher Columbus; Spanish colony 1509–1655; British colony 1655–1957; full internal self-government 1959; independent member of the Commonwealth from 1962.

Jamboree, World, of Boy Scouts, first held London 1920.

James I (1566–1625), king of Great Britain and Ireland 1603–25, and king of Scotland as James VI 1567–1625.

James II (1633–1701), king of Great Britain and Ireland 1685–88, deposed after failed attempt to impose Catholicism.

James, the Old Pretender (1688–1766), son of James II, claimant to British throne, led 1715 rebellion.

James I (1394–1437), king of Scotland 1406–37, also a poet; murdered by nobles.

James II (1430–60), king of Scotland 1437–60, suppressed power of nobles; accidentally killed.

James III (1451–88), king of Scotland 1460–88, whose reign was disrupted by civil war.

James IV (1473–1513), king of Scotland 1488–1513, killed at Battle of Flodden.

James V (1512–42), king of Scotland 1513–42, struggled against feudal powers of nobles.

James I (1208–76), king of Aragon 1213–76, king of Aragon 1213–76, laid the foundations of an Aragonese empire.

James, Henry (1811–82), American theological writer, follower of Swedenborg.

James, Henry (1843–1916), son of Henry James, American-born novelist in England, author of *The Ambassadors* (1903).

James, Jesse (1847–82), American outlaw and notorious train-robber.

James, Montague Rhodes (1862–1936), English scholar and author, best known for his collection of ghost stories.

James, William (1842–1910), American philosopher, exponent of pragmatism, brother of Henry James.

Jameson, Anna (1794–1860), Irish writer, best known for her works on art.

Jameson, Margaret Storm (b. 1897), English novelist, author of *The Lovely Ship* (1927).

Jameson Raid, Transvaal, 29 Dec. 1895–2 Jan. 1896, led by the Scottish pioneer in southern Africa Sir Leander Starr Jameson (1853–1917).

Jammes, Francis (1868–1938), French poet and novelist, author of *Roman du Lièvre* (1903).

Jammu and Kashmir. See **Kashmir.**

Janáček, Leoš (1854–1928), Czech opera composer, e.g. *Jenufa* (1904).

Janet, Pierre (1859–1947), French psychologist, best known for his researches into the causes of hysteria.

Janin, Jules (1804–74), French novelist and critic, notably of drama.

Janissaries, corp of troops, Ottoman Empire, first levied 1430s; abolished 1826.

Jan Mayen Island, Arctic, discovered 1607 by Henry Hudson (*q.v.*); claimed for Holland 1614 by a Dutch sea captain Jan May; annexed by Norway 1929.

Jannings, Emil (1886–1950), German actor, noted for his tragic roles in films, including *The Blue Angel* (1929).

Jansenism, religious movement deriving from the posthumous publication 1640 of *Augustinus* by the Dutch theologian Cornelis Jansen (1585–1638).

Janssens van Nuyssen, Abraham (d. 1632), Flemish painter, strongly influenced by Italian Renaissance work.

Japan, Jomon culture from *c.* 5th or 4th millennium B.C. to *c.* 250 B.C.; Yayoi culture 250 B.C.–A.D. 250; Yamato imperial court established mid-4th century; first shogunate (military government) set up 1192 by Minamoto Yoritomo; Muromachi shogunate 1338–1573; Europeans first arrived 1543; Tokugawa shogunate 1603–1867; foreign pressure for trade relations began 1840s; first treaty signed 1854, with U.S.A., ending Japan's seclusion; Meiji Restoration 1868–89 returned power to the throne and abolished feudal system; constitutional government 1890; period of expansion from 1890s up to World War II; American occupation 1945–52; new constitution 1947; rapid industrial growth from 1960s.

Jaques-Dalcroze, Émil (1865–1950), Swiss composer and teacher of dancing, invented eurhythmics.

Jarrow March, of unemployed to London, 1936.

Jarry, Alfred (1873–1907), French writer, e.g. play *Ubu Roi* (1896); precursor of Surrealists.

Jaspers, Karl (1883–1969), German philosopher and exponent of existentialism.

Jasper National Park, Canada, established 1907.

Jaurès, Jean (1859–1914), French Socialist leader, founder and editor of *L'Humanité* 1904–14; assassinated.

Java, Indonesia, Indian kingdom established by 8th century A.D.; Madjapahit state flourished 14th century; finally destroyed by Muslims 16th century; Dutch rule began 1619; occupied by British 1811; regained by Dutch 1816; conquered by Japanese 1942; part of Republic of Indonesia from 1950.

Java Man, remains first discovered 1891 in Java by the Dutch anatomist Eugène Dubois (1858–1940).

Jay, John (1745–1829), American lawyer and diplomat, secretary for foreign affairs 1784–89, chief justice of the Supreme Court 1789–95.

jazz, began to develop in New Orleans *c.* 1893–95.

Jean de Meung, (13th cent.), French writer of second part of the classic allegory *Roman de la Rose.*

Jeanne d'Albret (1528–72), queen of Navarre 1562–72, mother of Henry IV of France.

Jeanne d'Arc. See **Joan of Arc.**

Jeans, Sir James (1877–1946), English physicist and astronomer, popularized science in *The Universe Around Us* (1929).

Jefferies, Richard (1848–87), English writer about nature and the countryside.

Jeffers, Robinson (1887–1962), American poet, used rhetoric and narrative poems to underline his cosmic religious belief.

Jefferson, Thomas (1743–1826), American founding father, 3rd president of the United States 1801–09, purchased Louisiana from France 1804.

Jeffreys, George, 1st Baron (1644–89), Welsh-born lord chancellor of England, notorious for savage sentencing at the trials ('the Bloody Assizes') following the Monmouth Rebellion, 1685.

Jehovah's Witnesses, originated in the International Bible Students Association, founded 1872 by the American Charles Taze Russell (1852–1916).

Jellicoe, John, 1st Earl (1859–1935), British naval officer, commanded fleet at Battle of Jutland 1916.

Jemappes, Battle of, victory of the French over the Austrians, 6 Nov. 1792.

Jena, Battle of, victory of the French under Napoleon over the Prussians, 14 Oct. 1806.

Jena glass, first produced 1884 at a glassworks in Jena, founded by Friedrich Schott, Ernst Abbe, and Carl Zeiss (*q.v.*).

Jena University, East Germany, founded 1558.

Jenghiz Khan. See **Genghis Khan.**

Jenkins, Charles Francis (1867–1934), American inventor of a ciné projector, an altimeter, and a braking device for aircraft.

Jenkin's Ear, War of, between Britain and Spain, 1739 to 1741.

Jenner, Edward (1749–1823), English physician, discovered vaccination 1796.

Jensen, Johannes (1873–1950), Danish lyric poet and novelist, author of *The Long Journey* (1908–22), winner of Nobel Prize for Literature 1944.

Jenson, Nicholas (15th cent.), French printer, noted for his work on the roman letter.

Jenyns, Soame (1704–87), English writer, author of *Free Enquiry into the Nature . . . of Evil* (1756).

Jeremiah (*c.* 650–*c.* 585 B.C.), major Old Testament prophet, urged the Jewish people to moral reform.

Jericho, Jordan, settlement dates back to *c.* 9000 B.C.

Jerome, Saint (*c.* 340–420), Christian theologian and scholar, translated Bible into Latin (Vulgate).

Jerome of Prague (*c.* 1365–1416), Bohemian religious reformer, associated with Hus; burnt at the stake.

Jerome, Jerome K. (1859–1927), English humorous writer, above all of *Three Men in a Boat* (1889).

Jerrold, Douglas (1803–57), English humorous writer, e.g. *Mrs Caudle's Curtain Lectures* (1846).

Jersey, Channel Islands, settled by Normans early 11th century and subsequently passed to English crown; occupied by Germans 1940–45.

Jerusalem, continuously occupied since 1800 B.C. or earlier; captured by David 1000 B.C. and became Jewish capital; sacked 922 B.C. by Egyptians, 850 B.C. by the Philistines and Arabians; destroyed by Nebuchadnezzar 587–586 B.C.; rebuilt from 536 B.C. when Babylon overcome by the Persians; desecration of Temple by Antiochus Epiphanes led to Jewish rebellion 167 B.C. and to establishment of Jewish state; destroyed A.D. 70 by Romans under Titus; sacked by the Persians 614; captured by Crusaders 1099, recovered 1187 by Saladin; Egyptian regime 1247–1517; Turkish regime 1517–1917; taken by the British 1917; divided between Israel and Jordan 1948; Jordanian section of the Old City occupied since 1967 by Israel.

Jervis, John, Earl of St Vincent (1735–1823), English admiral, won great naval victory at St Vincent 1797.

Jespersen, Jens Otto (1860–1943), Danish philologist, was a leading authority on the structure of the English language.

Jesuits, order founded 1534 by Saint Ignatius Loyola (*q.v.*); dissolved 1773 by Pope Clement XIV; re-established 1814 by Pope Pius VII.

Jesus Christ (*c.* 4 B.C.–*c.* A.D. 30), founder of Christianity and, according to its teachings, the Son of God.

Jesus College, Cambridge University, founded 1496 by John Alcock, bishop of Ely (1430–1500).

Jesus College, Oxford University, founded by Queen Elizabeth I 1571.

jet engine, first design (turbojet) in England patented 1930 by Sir Frank Whittle (*q.v.*); tested 1937; first flight 1942; independently patented in Germany 1935; first flight (Heinkel He 178) Aug. 1939.

Jewel, John (1522–71), English divine, wrote *Apologia* (1562) for Anglican Church; bishop of Salisbury 1560–71.

Jewett, Sarah Orne (1849–1909), American short story writer, author of *Country of the Pointed Firs* (1896).

Jewish Calendar, calculated from 3761 B.C.; fixed A.D. 358.

Jewish Diaspora, dispersion of the Jews, began with the Assyrian Exile 722 B.C. and the Babylonian Exile 586–538 B.C.

Jewish Disabilities Removal Act, Great Britain, passed 1858.

Jewish M.P., first, Lionel Rothschild (1808–79), took his seat in the House of Commons July 1858.

Jews, expelled from England 1290, from Spain 1492, from Portugal 1497; emancipated in France 1790, in Russia 1917.

Jex-Blake, Sophia (1840–1912), English physician, pioneered women's right to practise medicine.

Jiménez, Juan Ramón (1881–1958), Spanish lyric poet, awarded Nobel Prize for Literature 1956.

Jiménez de Cisneros, Francisco (1436–1517), Spanish prelate, archbishop of Toledo 1495–1517, was politically powerful.

Jinnah, Mohammed Ali (1876–1948), Muslim statesman in British India, secured creation of Pakistan 1947, and was its first governor-general.

Joachim, Joseph (1831–1907), Hungarian violin virtuoso, worked in Germany; formed Joachim Quartet.

Joan (1328–85), English beauty, known as the Fair Maid of Kent, married Edward the Black Prince.

Joan, Pope, according to medieval legend, a woman disguised as man who became Pope.

Joanna I (*c.* 1327–82), queen of Naples 1343–82, whose turbulent reign ended with her murder.

Joanna II (1371–1435), queen of Naples 1414–35, was three times married; reigned during a period of wars and civil unrest.

Joan of Arc, Saint (1412–31), French peasant girl, inspired French to resist

English invaders; burnt as supposed heretic; canonized 1920.

Jocelin de Brakelond (c. 1155–1215), English monk, wrote account of his monastery at Bury St Edmunds.

Jockey Club, of Great Britain, formed c. 1750.

Jodelle, Étienne (1532–73), French playwright, member of Pléiade group.

Jodrell Bank Radio Telescope, planned by Sir Bernard Lovell (q.v.); in operation by 1957.

Joffre, Joseph Jacques (1852–1931), French soldier, commander-in-chief of the French armies in World War I 1914–16.

Johannesburg, South Africa, founded 1886.

John, Saint (1st cent. A.D.), one of the twelve apostles and supposed author of the Fourth Gospel.

John I, Saint (d. 526), Pope 523–526, died in prison after unsuccessful mission to Byzantium.

John VIII (d. 882), Pope 872–882, supported Charles the Bald; murdered.

John X (d. 928), Pope 914–928, drove back Saracens.

John XII (d. 964), Pope 955–964, elected when only a youth, quarrelled with Emperor Otto I.

John XIII (d. 972), Pope 965–972, driven out of Rome for a time.

John XXII (1249–1334), Pope 1316–34, resided at Avignon.

John XXIII (d. 1419), anti-pope 1410–15, deposed by Council of Constance.

John XXIII (1881–1963), Pope 1958–63, a noted reformer who impressed the world with his liberal spirit and benevolence.

John I (925–976), Byzantine emperor 969–976, conquered Bulgaria and Syria.

John II (1088–1143), Byzantine emperor 1118–43, drove back Turks.

John III (1193–1254), Byzantine emperor 1222–54, recovered much of Asia from the Latins.

John IV (c. 1250–c. 1300), Byzantine emperor 1258–61, blinded and imprisoned for life.

John V (1332–91), Byzantine emperor 1341–91, interrupted by usurpation of John VI.

John VI (c. 1292–1383), Byzantine emperor 1347–55, usurping throne of John V; expelled.

John VII (1360–1412), Byzantine emperor 1390, later served as regent.

John VIII (1390–1448), Byzantine emperor 1425–48, ruled only Constantinople; appealed to West for aid against Turks.

John (1167–1216), king of England 1199–1216, lost Normandy; compelled to sign Magna Carta 1215.

John I (1459–1501), king of Poland 1492–1501, fought war against Moldavia.

John II Casimir (1609–72), king of Poland 1648–68; abdicated after a disastrous reign.

John III Sobieski (1624–96), king of Poland 1674–96, famous for his victories against the Turks.

John I (1357–1433), king of Portugal 1385–1433, established independence from Spain with English help.

John II (1455–95), king of Portugal 1481–95, established strong monarchy and encouraged overseas exploration.

John III (1502–57), king of Portugal 1521–57, was much influenced by the Church.

John IV (1604–56), king of Portugal 1640–56, ended Spanish occupation.

John V (1689–1750), king of Portugal 1706–50, a period of national stagnation.

John VI (1769–1826), king of Portugal 1816–26, earlier regent in Brazil 1807–21.

John, Augustus (1878–1961), English painter and etcher, best known for his portraits.

John, Gwen (1876–1939), English painter, sister of Augustus John, was also a noted portraitist.

John Chrysostom, Saint (c. 347–407), Syrian Church Father, patriarch of Constantinople 398–404; famous for his eloquence.

John of Austria, Don (1545–78), illegitimate half-brother of Philip II of Spain, won victory of Lepanto 1571.

John of Beverley, Saint (d. 721), Anglo-Saxon bishop of Hexham 687, built and retired to Beverley monastery.

John of Damascus, Saint (d. c. 754), Syrian monk and scholar, doctor of the Orthodox Church.

John of Gaunt (1340–99), duke of Lancaster, brother of Edward III and father of Henry IV.

John of Lancaster (1389–1435), duke of Bedford, conducted French wars during Henry VI's minority.

John of Leiden (1509–36), Dutch Anabaptist, briefly ruled Münster 1534–35; executed.

John of Nepomuk, Saint (c. 1345–93), Bohemian priest, martyred; Czech patron saint.

John of Salisbury (d. 1180), English prelate, bishop of Chartres 1176–80, wrote history and poetry.

John of the Cross, Saint (1542–91), Spanish Carmelite monk, was a mystic and poet.

John of Trevisa (1326–1412), English cleric, noted for his translations from Latin.

John Rylands Library, Manchester, founded 1899 in memory of the English businessman John Rylands (1801–88).

Johns Hopkins University, Baltimore, founded 1867 by bequest of the American banker Johns Hopkins (q.v.); opened 1876.

Johnson, Amy (1903–41), English aviator,

first woman to fly from England to Australia solo, 1930.

Johnson, Andrew (1808–75), American statesman, 17th president of the United States 1865–69; was vice-president until Lincoln's assassination.

Johnson, Cornelius (1593–1661), English portrait painter, in Holland 1643–61.

Johnson, Lyndon Baines (1908–73), American statesman, 36th president of the United States 1963–69; was vice-president until John F. Kennedy's assassination.

Johnson, Dr Samuel (1709–84), English writer and critic, renowned conversationalist, compiled *Dictionary* (1755).

Johnson, Sir William (1715–74), Irish-born official in the American colonies, negotiated successfully with the Iroquois.

Johnston, Joseph (1807–91), American Confederate general in the Civil War; defeated by Sherman.

John the Baptist (d. *c.* A.D. 28), Christian prophet, a forerunner of Jesus Christ, who urged the people to prepare for his coming.

Johore, Malaysia, Muslim state founded early 16th century; treaty with Britain 1885; became British protectorate 1914; part of Federation of Malaya 1948 and of Malaysia since 1963.

Joinville, Jean, Sire de (*c.* 1224–1317), French chronicler, wrote a life of Louis IX.

Joliet, Louis (1645–1700), French-Canadian explorer of Mississippi.

Joliot-Curie, Frédéric (1900–58), French physicist, awarded 1935 Nobel Prize for Chemistry jointly with his wife Irène (1897–1956), the daughter of Marie and Pierre Curie.

Jolson, Al (1886–1950), American singer and entertainer, appeared in *The Jazz Singer* (1927).

Jones, Daniel (1881–1967), English phonetician, author of an *English Pronouncing Dictionary* (1917).

Jones, Ernest (1879–1958), Welsh psychoanalyst and associate of Sigmund Freud, introduced psychoanalysis into Britain.

Jones, Henry Arthur (1851–1929), English playwright, author of *The Silver King* (1882).

Jones, Inigo (1573–1652), English architect, introduced classical architecture into England.

Jones, John Paul (1747–92), Scottish-born American naval hero of the American Revolutionary War.

Jones, Owen (1809–74), Welsh architect, superintendent of the Great Exhibition of 1851.

Jones, Robert (Bobby) (1902–71), American golfer, winner of the U.S. and British Open Championships.

Jones, Sir William (1746–94), English jurist and orientalist, pioneer of oriental studies in Europe.

Jongkind, Johan (1819–91), Dutch painter, exercised a considerable influence on the development of Impressionism.

Jonson, Ben (1572–1637), English playwright, mainly of comedies of 'humours', such as *The Alchemist* (1610).

Jooss, Kurt (b. 1901), German dancer, teacher, choreographer, worked in Germany and England.

Jordaens, Jacob (1593–1678), Flemish painter, strongly influenced by Rubens, as in *The Triumph of Bacchus*.

Jordan, region inhabited from Lower Palaeolithic times; occupied by Nabataeans from *c.* 7th century B.C.; absorbed into Roman Empire A.D. 106; conquered by Muslims 636; part of Latin kingdom of Jerusalem from 1099; under Ottoman Turkish rule 16th century; new country created as Transjordan out of former Turkish territory 1921; recognized as independent under British protection 1923; achieved full independence 1946; its territory west of Jordan river under Israeli occupation since 1967.

Jordan, Dorothy (1762–1816), English actress, had ten children by Duke of Clarence (later William IV).

Joseph I (1678–1711), Holy Roman emperor 1705–11, carried on War of Spanish Succession.

Joseph II (1741–90), Holy Roman emperor 1765–90, made unsuccessful attempts to centralize and reform.

Joseph, Chief (d. 1904), American Indian, Nez Percé chief; defeated 1877.

Josephine (1763–1814), wife 1796–1809 and empress 1804–09 of Napoleon I; divorced because barren.

Josephus, Flavius (*c.* A.D. 37–*c.* A.D. 100), Jewish rebel against Rome, later reconciled; wrote *Jewish War*.

Josquin Deprès. See **Deprès,** Josquin.

Joubert, Barthélemy (1769–99), French soldier, commanded the French army in Italy 1798–99.

Joubert, Joseph (1754–1824), French writer of aphoristic *Pensées*.

Joule, James Prescott (1818–89), English physicist, established the 1st law of thermodynamics.

Joule's Law, electricity, discovered 1840 by James Joule.

Jourdan, Jean Baptiste (1762–1833), French soldier, one of Napoleon's marshals, served in both the Revolutionary and Napoleonic wars.

Jouvenet, Jean (1644–1717), French painter, worked at Versailles.

Jouvet, Louis (1887–1951), French actor and director, noted for his production of plays by Jean Giraudoux.

Jovian (*c.* 331–364), Roman emperor 363–364, restored Christianity after death of Emperor Julian.

Jowett, Benjamin (1817–93), English scholar, master of Balliol College, Oxford, 1870–93; translated Plato.

Joyce, James (1882–1941), Irish writer, pioneer of new literary methods and a major influence on 20th century literature, author of *Ulysses* (1922).

Joyce, William (1906–46), Irish-born propaganda broadcaster from Nazi Germany; known as 'Lord Haw-Haw'; executed for treason.

Juan Fernandez, Chile, group of Pacific islands discovered *c.* 1563 by the Spanish navigator Juan Fernandez (*c.* 1536–*c.* 1604).

Juana (1479–1555), daughter of Ferdinand and Isabella of Spain, and mother of the emperor Charles V; made insane by her husband's death.

Juarez, Benito (1806–72), Mexican statesman, president 1857–72, during many years of civil war and French occupation.

Judaism, religion of the Jews, in existence *c.* 4000 years, since Abraham entered into a covenant relation with the God of Israel.

Jugurtha (d. 104 B.C.), king of Numidia 113–106 B.C., overthrown by Romans.

Juliana (b. 1909), queen of the Netherlands since 1948.

Juliana of Norwich (1343–1415), English mystic, wrote *Revelations of Divine Love.*

Julian Calendar. See **Calendar,** Julian.

Julian period, astronomical chronological system based on the consecutive numbering of days from 1 Jan. 4713 B.C., devised 1582 by the French scholar Joseph Scaliger.

Julian the Apostate (*c.* 331–363), Roman emperor 361–363, renounced Christianity; tried to reinvigorate pagan beliefs.

Jülich-Cleves, dispute over succession to Westphalian duchy 1609–14.

Julius I, Saint (d. 352), Pope 337–352, opposed Arian heresy.

Julius II (1443–1513), Pope 1503–13, a great warrior and patron of Michelangelo.

Julius III (1487–1555), Pope 1550–55, reconvened Council of Trent.

Julius Caesar. See **Caesar,** Gaius Julius.

July Plot, Germany, to assassinate Adolf Hitler, 20 July 1944.

July Revolution, provoked by the reactionary measures of Charles X of France, 27–29 July 1830.

Juneau, Solomon Laurent (1793–1856), French-Canadian pioneer in Milwaukee.

Jung, Carl Gustav (1875–1961), Swiss psychoanalyst, broke with Freud (*q.v.*), proposed existence of collective unconscious, etc.

Jungfrau, Swiss mountain (13,642 ft [4158 m]), first climbed on the east side by two Swiss brothers, the Meyers, 1811; first climbed on the west side by two Englishmen, Sir George Young and the Rev. H. B. George, 1865.

Jungfrau railway, one of the highest in Europe, constructed 1896–1912.

Junius, English writer of incisive, witty political letters 1768–72; identity never discovered, possibly Philip Francis (1740–1818).

Junqueiro, Abilio (1850–1923), Portuguese poet and political leader, best known for his satirical verse.

Jupiter, principal satellites discovered 1610 by Galileo; Great Red Spot first recorded 1831 by Heinrich Schwabe; planet and and satellites studied 1970s by the Pioneer spacecraft (*q.v.*).

Jurassic Period, Earth history, from *c.* 190 to *c.* 136 million years ago.

Jusserand, Jean Jules (1855–1932), French diplomat and historian, wrote *English Wayfaring Life in the Middle Ages* (1884).

justice of the peace, English judicial and administrative post, first recorded reference 1264.

justiciar, official of Anglo-Norman kings until 1234; also 1258–61.

Justin, Saint (2nd cent. A.D.), also called Justin Martyr, one of the Fathers of the Church.

Justin I (*c.* 450–527), Byzantine emperor 518–527, brought to power by the army.

Justin II (d. 578), Byzantine emperor 565–578, lost much of Italy.

Justinian I (483–565), Byzantine emperor 527–565, codified Roman law, recovered much of Roman territory and built Santa Sophia.

Justinian II (669–711), Byzantine emperor 685–695, banished; regained throne 705–711; killed.

Jutland, Battle of, between the British and German fleets, 31 May 1916.

Juvenal (*c.* A.D. 60–*c.* A.D. 130), Roman satirist, painted a graphic if biased picture of society.

juvenile courts, first established 1889 in Chicago; received statutory recognition in Britain by the Children Act 1908.

Juxon, William (1582–1663), English Anglican prelate, archbishop of Canterbury 1660–63.

K

K2. See **Godwin-Austen,** Mount.

Kabalevsky, Dmitri (b. 1904), Russian composer, whose operas include *The Taras Family* (1944).

Kadar, János (b. 1912), Hungarian politician, effective ruler of Hungary since 1956.

Kafka, Franz (1883–1924), German novelist and short-story writer, author of *The Trial* (pub. 1925).

Kagawa, Toyohiko (1888–1960), Japanese social reformer and writer.

Kaiser, Georg (1878–1945), German playwright, exponent of expressionist drama, e.g. *Burghers of Calais* (1914).

Kaiser, Henry (1882–1967), American industrialist, revolutionized ship-building techniques using prefabricated materials.

Kaiser Wilhelm II Land, Antarctica, discovered 1903 by the German explorer Erich von Drygalski (1865–1949).

kaleidoscope, invented *c.* 1816 by Sir David Brewster (*q.v.*).

Kalevala, Finnish folk epic compiled by Elias Lönnrot (1802–84), and first published by him 1835.

Kalidasa (5th cent. A.D.), Hindu dramatist, wrote *Sakuntala*.

Kalinin, Mikhail (1875–1946), Soviet statesman, president of the U.S.S.R. 1922–46.

Kamenev, Lev (1883–1936), Soviet politician, 'old Bolshevik', imprisoned 1934; later retried and executed.

Kammerlingh Onnes, Heike (1853–1926), Dutch physicist, investigated helium; awarded Nobel Prize 1913.

Kamikaze planes, Japanese suicide aircraft in World War II, used against Allied warships from Oct. 1944.

Kanagawa, Treaty of, establishing trade and diplomatic relations between Japan and the U.S.A., signed March 1854; ended Japan's isolation, 1639–1854, from the West.

Kandinsky, Wassily (1866–1944), Russian-born artist, pioneer of abstract painting.

K'ang-hsi (1654–1722), emperor of China 1662–1722, extended his country's frontiers and encouraged the arts.

Kano, Eitoku (1543–90), Japanese artist, painted screens and landscapes remarkable for their brilliant colours.

Kansas, U.S.A., formed into a territory 1854; admitted to the Union 1861.

Kansas University, Lawrence, Kansas, founded 1866.

Kant, Immanuel (1724–1804), German philosopher, chief figure in modern Idealist tradition.

Kapitza, Peter (b. 1894), Russian physicist, investigated low-temperature conditions, important in space research.

Karg-Elert, Siegfried (1877–1933), German composer, chiefly remembered for his organ music.

Kariba Dam, Zambezi River, constructed 1956–59; opened 1960.

Karlfeldt, Erik Axel (1864–1931), Swedish lyric poet, awarded Nobel Prize for Literature 1931.

Karajan, Herbert von (b. 1908), Austrian conductor, director of Vienna State Opera 1957–64.

Karl Marx University, Leipzig, founded 1409 as the University of Leipzig; renamed 1953.

Karolyi, Count Mihály (1875–1955), Hungarian statesman, president 1919; spent most of life in exile.

Karnataka, Indian state, ruled by Hindu dynasties; expanded territory during reign of Haidar Ali and his son, 1766–99; administered by Britain from 1831; returned to native rulers 1881; part of independent India since 1947.

Karsavina, Tamara (b. 1885), Russian-born dancer, joined Russian ballet in France; settled in Britain.

Karsh, Yusuf (b. 1908), Turkish-born Canadian photographer, famous for his portraits of prominent people.

Kashmir, former princely state, became part of Mogul Empire 1587; annexed to Sikh kingdom 1819; part of British India 1846; maharaja acceded to the Indian Union 1947; partitioned between India and Pakistan 1949, the Indian part forming the state of Jammu and Kashmir.

Kassem, Abdul Karim (1914–63), Iraqi military leader, overthrew monarchy 1958, killed in new army revolt.

Kästner, Erich (1899–1974), German novelist and poet, author of *Emil and the Detectives* (1929).

Katanga, Zaïre, declared independent of central government 1960; secession ended following U.N. intervention 1963.

Kate Greenaway Medal, for the most distinguished work in children's book illustration, awarded annually by the British Library Association since 1956.

Katmandu, capital of Nepal, founded 723 by Raja Gunakamadeva.

Katyn Massacre, mass execution of Polish army officers allegedly by Soviet authorities *c.* May 1940; discovery of the graves announced 1943 by the Germans.

Kaufman, George Simon (1889–1961), American playwright, usually wrote in collaboration, author of *The Man who came to Dinner* (1939).

Kauffmann, Angelica (1741–1807), Swiss painter, notably of portraits; in England 1766–1781.

Kaulbach, Wilhelm von (1805–74), German painter of historical subjects.

Kaunda, Kenneth (b. 1924), Zambian statesman, president of Zambia since 1964.

Kautsky, Karl (1854–1938), German Socialist writer, a disciple of Karl Marx, he opposed Lenin and Bolshevism.

Kazantzakis, Nikos (*c.* 1883–1957), Greek poet, author of *The Odyssey* (1938).

Kean, Charles (1811–68), English actor, son of Edmund Kean, made many successful tours.

Kean, Edmund (1787–1833), English actor, was the leading tragedian of his time.

Keaton, Buster (Joseph) (1895–1966), American cinema actor, best known for his comic roles in silent films.

Keats, John (1795–1821), English poet, one of the greatest of the Romantic period, famous for his *Odes*.

Keble, John (1792–1866), English cleric and poet (*The Christian Year*, 1827), started Oxford Movement (*q.v.*).

Keble College, Oxford University, founded 1870 as a memorial to John Keble.

Kedah, Malaysia, under Thai suzerainty 19th century; became British dependency 1909; invaded by Japanese 1941; joined Malayan Federation 1948.

Keele University, constituted 1962 from University College of North Staffordshire (founded 1949).

Keeling Islands. See **Cocos Islands.**

Keene, Charles (1823–91), English painter and graphic artist, was also a humorous illustrator.

Keir Hardie. See **Hardie,** Keir.

Kekulé von Stradonitz, Friedrich (1829–96), German chemist, discovered the ring structure of the benzene molecule.

Kelantan, Malaysia, conquered by Java and Malacca 14th–15th centuries; under Thai suzerainty 19th century; became British dependency 1909; invaded by Japanese 1941; joined Malayan Federation 1948.

Keller, Gottfried (1819–90), Swiss novelist, wrote autobiographical *Green Henry* (1855).

Keller, Helen (1880–1968), American writer, deaf and blind from 19 months of age, author of *Story of My Life* (1902).

Kellogg-Briand Pact, renouncing war, signed 27 Aug. 1928.

Kelly, Ned (Edward) (1855–80), Australian bushranger, gained notoriety for his daring bank robberies.

Kelly College, Devon, English public school, founded by Admiral Benedictus Kelly, 1867.

Kelmscott Press, private press, founded and operated 1891–98 by William Morris (*q.v.*).

Kelvin, William Thomson, Baron (1824–1907), Irish-born physicist in England, discovered 2nd law of thermodynamics.

Kelvin temperature scale, devised 1848 by Lord Kelvin.

Kemal Atatürk, Mustapha (1881–1938), Turkish army officer and statesman, first president of the Turkish republic 1923–38; modernized his country.

Kemble, Fanny (1809–93), English actress, niece of John Philip Kemble, played all the chief women's parts.

Kemble, John Philip (1757–1823), English actor, brother of Sarah Siddons, was also a noted theatrical manager.

Kemény, Zsigismond, Baron (1814–75), Hungarian writer and politician, author of historical novels.

Ken, Thomas (1637–1711), English pre-

late, bishop of Bath and Wells 1684–91, was a noted hymn-writer.

Kennedy, John Fitzgerald (1917–63), American statesman, 35th president of the United States 1961–63; the 4th to be assassinated.

Kennedy, Joseph (1888–1969), American financier and diplomat, ambassador to Britain 1937–40; father of John Fitzgerald Kennedy.

Kennelly, Arthur (1861–1939), American electrical engineer, proved the existence of ionized layer in the upper atmosphere, 1907.

Kenneth I (d. *c.* 860), first king of Scotland, united Picts and Scots.

Kenneth II (d. 995), king of Scotland 971–995, at war with Anglo-Saxons.

Kensington Gardens, London, once the private gardens of Kensington Palace, laid out 1728–31; opened to the public from early 19th century.

Kensington Palace, London, acquired 1661 by the Earl of Nottingham; purchased by William III, 1689.

Kent, University of, Canterbury, opened 1965.

Kent, Rockwell (1882–1971), American painter and engraver, also wrote *Of Men and Mountains* (1959).

Kent, William (1684–1748), English architect in Palladian style; was also a landscape gardener.

Kentucky, U.S.A., first settled 1774; admitted to the Union 1792.

Kentucky Derby, classic American horse race, run on the first Saturday in May since 1875.

Kenya, annexed to the British crown 1895 as the East Africa Protectorate; became British colony 1920; independent member of the Commonwealth 1963; republic established 1964; formed East Africa Community with Tanzania and Uganda, 1967.

Kenyatta, Jomo (b. 1890), Kenyan statesman, president of Kenya since 1964.

Keokuk (1788–1848), American Indian chief, after whom a town in Iowa is named.

Kepler, Johannes (1571–1630), German astronomer, enunciated first three laws of planetary motion.

Kepler's Laws, of planetary motion, derived 1609 (first two) and 1618 (third) by Kepler from the experimental records of Tycho Brahe (*q.v.*).

Ker, William Paton (1855–1923), Scottish scholar, wrote *Epic and Romance* (1897).

Kerala, Indian state, formed 1956 from the former princely states of Travancore and Cochin.

Kerensky, Alexander (1881–1970), Russian political leader, prime minister of provisional government July–November 1917; overthrown by Bolsheviks.

Kerguelen Archipelago, Southern Indian Ocean, discovered 1772 by the French explorer Yves Kerguelen-Trémarec (1745–97); annexed to France 1893.

Kern, Jerome (1885–1945), American musical comedy composer, e.g. *Showboat* (1927).

Kerouac, Jack (1922–69), American novelist of the 'beat generation', author of *On the Road* (1965).

Keswick Convention, annual religious gathering at Keswick, Cumbria, first held 1875.

Ketch, Jack (d. 1686), English official executioner 1663–86, notorious for his brutality.

Ketèlbey, Albert (1875–1959), English light music composer, wrote *In a Monastery Garden*.

Kett's Rebellion, 1549, led by the English landowner Robert Kett (hanged 1549).

Kew Gardens, Surrey, original botanical collection begun late 1600s by Lord Capel; extended 1759 by Princess Augusta, mother of George III; given to the nation 1841.

Kew Palace, the Dutch House, built 1631; purchased 1781 by George III.

Key, Francis Scott (1779–1843), American poet, wrote *The Star-Spangled Banner* (1814).

Keyes, Sir Roger (1872–1945), English naval commander in Zeebrugge and Ostend operation 1918.

Keynes, John Maynard (1883–1946), English economist, whose theories have profoundly influenced economic thought.

K.G.B., Committee of State Security, political police and intelligence and counter-intelligence agency of the Soviet Union, created 1954.

Khachaturian, Aram (b. 1903), Russian composer of symphonies, ballets and instrumental music.

khaki, first worn as camouflage uniform in the British army 1847, introduced by Sir Harry Burnett Lumsden (1821–96); khaki uniform for service worn for Afghan War 1878–80; approved for all regiments 1882.

Khaki Election, Britain, Sept.–Oct. 1900, won by the Unionists (Conservatives).

Khalid (b. 1913), King of Saudi Arabia since 1975.

Khartoum, capital of Sudan, founded *c.* 1823.

Khayyam, Omar. See **Omar Khayyam.**

Khedive of Egypt, the last, Abbas Hilmi II, deposed 1914.

Khmer Republic, official name of Cambodia (*q.v.*) since October 1970.

Khosru I. See **Chosroes I.**

Khosru II. See **Chosroes II.**

Khrushchev, Nikita (1894–1971), Soviet statesman, head of government 1958–64, began policy of de-Stalinization.

Khufu. See **Cheops.**

Kidd, Captain William (*c.* 1645–1701), Scottish pirate, surrendered on promise of pardon; hanged.

Kiel Canal, small one completed 1784; widened, deepened and straightened into the present canal, opened 1895; enlarged 1914 and 1966.

Kiel Mutiny, of the German Navy, World War I, 3 Nov. 1918.

Kierkegaard, Søren (1813–55), Danish philosopher-theologian, regarded as precursor of Existentialism.

Kilimanjaro, Tanzania, highest African mountain (19,340 ft [5895 m]); discovered 1848 by German missionaries; first climbed 1889.

Killiecrankie, Battle of, victory of the Jacobites over a royal force, 27 July 1689.

Killigrew, Thomas (1612–83), English playwright, wrote *The Parson's Wedding*.

'Kilmainham Treaty', between Gladstone and Parnell, April 1882.

kilogram, international standard, kept at Paris and in use since 1889.

kindergarten, system developed by the German educationalist Friedrich Froebel (1782–1852); first one opened 1837 at Blankenburg, Germany; first English one opened *c.* 1850; first American 1860.

kinetic theory of gases, put into its final form *c.* 1860 by James Clerk-Maxwell (*q.v.*) and Ludwig Boltzmann (*q.v.*).

kinetoscope, invented 1891 by the Americans Thomas Edison and William Dickson. See also **cinematograph.**

King, Martin Luther (1929–68), American Negro civil rights leader, won Nobel Peace Prize 1964; assassinated.

King, Sir Frederick (1858–1938), New Zealand pioneer of mothercraft, established centres in Britain, etc.

King, William Mackenzie (1874–1950), Canadian statesman, prime minister 1921–30 and 1935–48.

King Edward VII School, Lytham, English public school, opened 1908.

King Edward's School, Birmingham, English public school, founded 1552.

King George V Dock, Glasgow, opened 1931.

King George V Dock, London, opened 1921.

King George V Dock, Southampton, opened 1933.

King George's War, waged by Britain and France in North America, 1744–48.

Kinglake, Alexander William (1809–91), English historian and traveller in the East, wrote *Eothen* (1844).

King Philip's War, waged 1675–76 by the American Indian chief Philip (killed 1676) against English settlers.

King's College, Cambridge University, founded by Henry VI, 1441.

King's College, London University, founded 1829; reincorporated 1882.

King's College, Taunton, English public school, in existence 13th century; rebuilt 1522.

King's College Hospital, London, founded 1839; made independent of King's College 1913.

King's College School, Wimbledon, English public school, founded 1829.

Kingsley, Charles (1819–75), English clergyman-novelist, wrote *Westward Ho!* (1855) and *The Water Babies* (1863).

Kingsley, Henry (1830–76), English novelist, brother of Charles Kingsley, wrote *Ravenshoe* (1861).

Kingsley, Mary (1862–1900), English traveller in West Africa, died nursing in Boer War.

King's Messengers. See **Queen's Messengers.**

King's Police Medal. See **Queen's Police Medal.**

King's School, Bruton, English public school founded 1519 by Richard Fitzjames, bishop of London; closed 1538; refounded 1550 by Edward VI.

King's School, Canterbury, English public school, foundation attributed to St Augustine 7th century; reconstituted by Henry VIII 1541; royal charter 1946.

King's School, Chester, English public school, founded by Henry VIII 1541.

King's School, Ely, English public school, existed in 10th century; reconstituted 1541 by Henry VIII.

King's School, Macclesfield, English public school, founded by the will of Sir John Percyvale 1502.

King's School, Rochester, English public school, founded early 7th century.

King's School, Worcester, English public school, established and endowed by Henry VIII 1541.

Kingsway, London, opened Oct. 1905.

Kingswood School, Bath, English public school, founded by John Wesley 1748.

Kinsey, Alfred (1894–1956), American pioneer in sociology of sexual behaviour.

Kinshasa, capital of Zaïre, founded 1881 as Léopoldville by Sir Henry Morton Stanley (*q.v.*); renamed 1966.

Kipling, John Lockwood (1837–1911), English artist, father of Rudyard Kipling.

Kipling, Rudyard (1865–1936), English short-story writer, poet, children's writer, author of *Kim* (1901).

Kircher, Athanasius (1601–80), German scholar, said to have invented magic lantern.

Kirchhoff, Gustav (1824–87), German physicist, who with R. W. Bunsen discovered method of spectrum analysis.

'Kirke's Lambs', English soldiers led at the Battle of Sedgemoor (1685) by the notoriously cruel Percy Kirke (*c.* 1646–91).

Kissinger, Henry (b. 1923), German-born American statesman, U.S. secretary of state 1973–76.

Kit-Cat Club, London, anti-Jacobite dining-club of writers, politicians, etc., existed *c.* 1700–1720.

Kitchener, Herbert, 1st Viscount (1850–1916), British soldier, conquered the Sudan; secretary of state for war 1914–16; drowned.

kites, used by Chinese from *c.* 1000 B.C.; introduced in Europe by 13th century.

Kivi, Alexis (1834–72), Finnish dramatist and novelist, author of *The Seven Brothers* (1870).

Kléber, Jean Baptiste (1753–1800), French Revolutionary general, commander in Egypt 1799–1800; assassinated.

Klee, Paul (1879–1940), Swiss painter, influential pioneer of modern art movements.

Klein, Felix (1849–1925), German mathematician, best known for his work on the theory of functions.

Kleist, Heinrich von (1777–1811), German poet and playwright, e.g. *Prince Frederick of Homburg* (1821).

Klemperer, Otto (1885–1973), German conductor, was a notable interpreter of Beethoven.

Klimt, Gustav (1862–1918), Austrian painter, whose work shows the influence of Art Nouveau.

Klondike gold rush. See **gold; gold rush.**

Klopstock, Friedrich (1724–1803), German poet, wrote *Messias* (1748–73).

Kneller, Sir Godfrey (*c.* 1647–1723), German-born painter in England, leading portraitist of his time.

Knight, Dame Laura (1877–1970), English painter of circus and theatre people.

Knight, William Angus (1836–1916), Scottish philosopher, also editor of Wordsworth's poetry.

Knights Hospitallers. See **Saint John of Jerusalem.**

Knights of Columbus, U.S.A., Roman Catholic organization for men, founded 1882.

Knights Templars. See **Templars.**

knitting machine, invented 1589 (bearded needle type); alternative design (latch needle type) invented 1847.

Knossos, Crete, ancient city and centre of Cretan Bronze Age civilization *c.* 2000–*c.* 1400 B.C.; excavations begun 1900 by Sir Arthur Evans (*q.v.*).

Knowles, James Sheridan (1784–1862), Irish playwright, author of *Virginius* (1820).

Knowles, Sir James (1831–1908), English architect, also founder, 1877, of periodical *Nineteenth Century.*

Knox, John (1505–72), Scottish religious reformer, established Presbyterianism in Scotland.

Knox, Ronald (1888–1957), English Catholic priest and writer; witty essayist, translated Bible.

Knut II. See **Canute.**

Knut III. See **Hardecanute.**

Knut IV, Saint (d. 1086), king of Denmark 1080–86, patron saint of Denmark.

Knut V (d. 1157), king of Denmark 1147–57, involved in continuous civil war.

Knut VI (1163–1202), king of Denmark 1182–1202, a period of Baltic expansion.

Koch, Karl (1809–79), German botanist, worked in Russia and Caucasus.

Koch, Robert (1843–1910), German bacteriologist, discovered tuberculosis bacillus 1882.

Kodak camera, first marketed 1888 by George Eastman (*q.v.*).

Kodály, Zoltán (1882–1967), Hungarian composer, wrote *Háry János* (1926).

Kodiak Island, Alaska, discovered 1764 by a Russian fur trader Stephen Glotov; first settled 1784 by Russians; passed to America 1867.

Koestler, Arthur (b. 1905), Hungarian-born novelist in England, author of *Darkness at Noon* (1940).

Koh-i-noor, diamond, early history in dispute; acquired by the British 1849 and became part of the crown jewels: recut 1852 in London; set in the queen's state crown for the 1937 coronation.

Köhler, Wolfgang (1887–1967), American psychologist, exponent of the Gestalt theory.

Kokoschka, Osker (b. 1886), Austrian painter, mostly in expressionistic style; noted as a portraitist.

Koldewey, Robert (1855–1925), German architect and archaeologist, best known for his excavations of Babylon.

Kollwitz, Käthe (1867–1945), German graphic artist and sculptor, often of grim social subjects.

Komisarzhevsky, Teodor (1882–1954), Russian theatrical director, noted for his practice of Stanislavsky's theories.

Konrad von Würzburg (d. 1287), German poet, wrote epic *Trojan War*.

Kon-Tiki, raft sailed 1947 from the west coast of South America to Polynesia by Thor Heyerdahl and five others.

Kooning, Willem de. See **de Kooning, Willem.**

Koran, sacred book of Islam revealed to Mohammed, written fragments being collected after his death, 632; present text established by the caliph 'Uthman, 643–656.

Korda, Sir Alexander (1893–1956), Hungarian-born film producer, gained international status for British films.

Korea, under Chinese influence from earliest times; period of three kingdoms from *c.* 57 B.C.; united as a single kingdom under Silla dynasty A.D. 668; ruled by Yi dynasty 1392–1910; annexed by Japan 1910; occupied by U.S.A. and U.S.S.R. 1945.

Korea, North, under Soviet occupation from 1945; became independent as the People's Democratic Republic of Korea 1948.

Korea, South, under American occupation from 1945; became independent as the Republic of Korea 1948.

Korean War, between U.N. forces (mainly American and South Korean) and North Korean and Chinese forces, June 1950 to July 1953; truce signed 27 July 1953.

Kornilov, Lavr (1870–1918), Russian soldier, leader of Don Cossacks against the Bolshevik regime.

Kościuszko, Tadeusz (1746–1817), Polish leader of 1794 rebellion against Russia.

Kossuth, Lajos (1802–94), Hungarian patriot, led revolt against Austrian Empire 1848–49.

Kotzebue, August von (1761–1819), German playwright, whose work enjoyed great popularity; assassinated as Russian agent.

Koussevitsky, Serge (1874–1951), Russian-born conductor and musical patron in the U.S.A., popularized modern music.

Krafft-Ebing, Richard (1840–1902), German neurologist, wrote *Psychopathia Sexualis* (1886).

Krakatoa, Indonesian volcano, violent eruption 27 Aug. 1883.

Krebs cycle, biochemistry, first described 1937 by the German biochemist Sir Hans Krebs (b. 1900).

Kreisler, Fritz (1875–1962), Austrian-born violinist and composer in the U.S.A.

Kremlin, Moscow, built as a fortress 1156; rebuilt 1367; became centre of Russian government from *c.* 1620 to 1712, and after 1918.

Kreuger, Ivar (1880–1932), Swedish industrialist and financier ('the match king'), engaged in large-scale fraud; committed suicide.

Kreutzer, Rodolphe (1766–1831), German-French composer and violinist; Beethoven's *Kreuzer Sonata* was dedicated to him.

Krishna Menon, Vengalil (1896–1975), Indian statesman, was his country's first high commissioner in London and subsequently Indian ambassador to the U.N.

Krishnamurti (b. 1895), Indian spiritual teacher, rejected his own theosophical upbringing and stressed individual striving.

Krogh, August (1874–1949), Danish physiologist, discovered the regulation of the motor mechanism of capillaries.

Kronstadt, Russian naval base founded 1710; scene of mutiny against Soviet government March 1921.

Kropotkin, Prince Peter (1842–1921), Russian Anarchist leader, wrote *Mutual Aid* (1902).

Kruger, Paul (1825–1904), Boer leader against the British, president of Transvaal 1883–1900.

Kruger National Park, South Africa, established 1898.

Krupp Works, cast-steel factory founded 1810 at Essen, Germany, by Friedrich Krupp (1787–1826) and developed as a munitions factory by his son Alfred (1812–87) and his descendants.

Krusenstern, Adam von (1770–1846), first Russian circumnavigator of world, 1803–06.

Krylov, Ivan (1768–1844), Russian poet, created classic fable collection.

krypton, gaseous element, discovered 1898 by Sir William Ramsay (*q.v.*) and Morris W. Travers.

Kubelik, Jan (1880–1940), Czech violin virtuoso and composer.

Kublai Khan (1216–94), Mongol emperor, grandson of Ghenghis Khan, founded Mongol dynasty in China.

Ku Klux Klan, American terrorist secret society founded 1866 at Pulaski, Tennessee; formally disbanded 1869; revived 1915; at peak strength 1920s; again revived in mid-1960s.

Kulturkampf, Bismarck's struggle with the Roman Catholic Church in Germany *c.* 1872–1887.

Kun, Béla (1886–1939), Hungarian Communist, led 1919 revolution; fled to Russia; shot during purges.

kuomintang, Chinese Nationalist party, evolved 1912; ruled all or part of mainland China 1928–49 under Chiang Kai-shek (*q.v.*); after defeat by Communists moved to Taiwan 1949.

Kuprin, Alexander (1870–1938), Russian writer, notably of short stories about army life.

Kurchatov, Igor (1903–60), Russian physicist, leading figure in the development of Soviet nuclear weapons.

Kurds, name first used in 7th century to describe a race of people living in mountainous region divided since 1920 between Turkey, Iraq and Persia.

Kuropatkin, Alexei (1848–1925), Russian general, war minister 1898–1904; defeated by Japanese 1905.

Kurosawa, Ahira (b. 1910), Japanese film director, whose work includes *Rashomon* (1951) and *Seven Samurai* (1954).

Kut, Mesopotamia, World War I, captured by the British 1915; surrendered to the Turks 1916; retaken by the British 1917.

Kutuzov, Mikhail (1745–1813), Russian military commander, victorious against the French, 1812.

Kuwait, independent amirate on Arabian Gulf, ruling dynasty founded 1756; came under British protection 1899; British protectorate established 1914; became fully independent 1961.

Kyd, Thomas (c. 1558–94), English playwright, whose *Spanish Tragedy* was first of the 'revenge play' type.

Kynaston, Edward (*c.* 1640–1706), English actor, one of the last to take female parts.

Kyoto, capital of Japan from 794 to 1868.

L

Labé, Louise (*c.* 1525–66), French poet, was a member of the Lyons school.

Labiche, Eugène Marin (1815–88), French writer of farce, e.g. *Italian Straw Hat* (1851).

Labienus (d. 45 B.C.), Roman tribune, assisted Caesar in Gallic Wars; later sided with Pompey.

Labor Day, U.S.A. and Canada, first Monday in September; inaugurated 1882; officially adopted 1894.

Labouchère, Henry (1831–1912), English politician and investigative journalist, founded *Truth* 1877.

Labour, Ministry of, created 1916; became Ministry of Labour and National Service 1939; reverted to original name 1959; reorganized 1968 as Ministry of Employment and Productivity.

Labour Day, 1 May, celebrated as a public holiday in Britain from 1978.

Labour Exchanges. See **Employment Exchanges.**

Labour Party, British parliamentary party founded 27 Feb. 1900 as the Labour Representation Committee; present name adopted 1906; constitution adopted 1918; modified 1937; formed first government 1924.

La Bruyère, Jean de (1645–96), French writer of *Characters,* describing contemporary types.

Labuan, island off NW coast of Borneo, ceded to Britain 1846 by the Sultan of Brunei; crown colony 1848; made part of colony of North Borneo (now Sabah) 1946.

La Calprenède, Gauthier de (*c.* 1610–63), French writer of romances (*Cassandre,* 1642–50) and plays.

Laccadive Islands, Arabian Sea, discovered 1498 by the Portuguese; annexed by Britain 1877 and included in Madras province; since 1956 part of the Laccadive, Minicoy, and Amindivi Islands.

lace-making, began in Europe early 16th century, mainly in Italy and Flanders.

La Chaise, François de (1624–1709), French Jesuit, confessor of Louis XIV.

Laclos, Pierre Choderlos de (1741–1803), French novelist, author of *Les Liaisons dangereuses* (1782).

Lactantius Firmianus (2nd–3rd cent. A.D.), Christian writer, tutor of Constantine the Great's son Crispus.

Ladies' Peace. See **Cambrai,** Treaty of.

Ladislas I, Saint (1040–95), king of Hungary 1077–95, enlarged his territorial possessions.

Ladislas IV (1262–90), king of Hungary 1272–90, defeated Ottokar of Bohemia; assassinated.

Ladislas V (1440–57), king of Hungary 1444–57 and of Bohemia 1453–57; fled his kingdom.

Ladislas II Jagiello (1350–1434), king of Poland 1386–1434, joined Lithuania to Poland and founded the Jagiellon dynasty.

Lady Margaret Hall, Oxford University, founded 1878.

Ladysmith, Natal, South Africa, besieged during Boer War from 1 Nov. 1899 to 28 Feb. 1900.

Laetare Sunday, the fourth Sunday in Lent.

La Fayette, Comtesse de (1634–93), French novelist, author of *La Princesse de Clèves*.

Lafayette, Marquis de (1757–1854), French soldier and statesman, fought in American Revolution; prominent in the French Revolution.

Laffite, Jean (*c.* 1780–*c.* 1826), French-born pirate, helped Americans in War of 1812.

Lafitte, Jacques (1767–1844), French banker, governor of Bank of France 1814–19 and prime minister 1830–31.

La Follette, Robert (1855–1925), American politician of radical and isolationist views.

La Fontaine, Jean de (1621–95), French poet, author of classic *Fables* (1668–94).

Laforgue, Jules (1860–87), Uruguayan-born French poet, early exponent of free verse.

Lagerkvist, Pär (b. 1891), Swedish poet and novelist, awarded Nobel Prize for his novel *Barabbas* (1951).

Lagerlöf, Selma (1858–1940), Swedish novelist, wrote *Gösta Berlings Saga* (1891).

Lagrange, Joseph Louis (1736–1813), Italian-born mathematician and astronomer, worked in Germany and France.

La Guardia, Fiorello (1882–1947), American lawyer and politician, as mayor of New York 1934–45 instituted many reforms.

Laing, Alexander Gordon (1793–1826), Scottish explorer, discovered the source of the Niger.

Lake Erie, Naval Battle of, victory of the Americans over the British, Sept. 1813.

Lalande, Le Français de (1732–1807), French astronomer, director of Paris observatory.

Lalo, Édouard (1823–92), French composer, e.g. of *Symphonie Espagnole* (1875).

Lamarck, Jean Baptiste (1744–1829), French naturalist, proposed theory of evolution, Lamarckism, 1809.

Lamartine, Alphonse de (1790–1869), French Romantic poet and statesman, author of *Méditations Poétiques* (1820); effective head of provisional government after 1848 Revolution.

Lamb, Charles (1775–1834), English essayist, wrote *Elia* (1823) and *Last Essays of Elia* (1833).

Lambert, Constant (1905–51), English composer, notably of *Rio Grande* (1929); also wrote perceptive study *Music Ho!* (1934).

Lambert, Daniel (1770–1809), English fat man, weighed 52¾ stone (739 lb.) at death.

Lambert, John (1619–84), English Parliamentary general, briefly controlled country before Restoration of 1660.

Lambeth Articles, concerning predestination and election, drawn up 1595 by the archbishop of Canterbury, John Whitgift (*c.* 1530–1604).

Lambeth Bridge, London, opened 1862; pulled down 1929; new bridge opened 1932.

Lambeth Conference, Anglican bishops' assembly, first convened 1867.

Lambeth Palace, London residence of the archbishops of Canterbury since 1207; building started late 12th century; chapel built 1245–73.

Lamennais, Félicité de (1782–1854), French reformer-priest, left Church when condemned; became radical republican.

La Mettrie, Julien (1709–51), French physician and philosopher, propounded a materialistic view of man.

Lamond, Frederic (1868–1948), Scottish pianist and composer, was a pupil of Liszt.

La Motte Fouqué, Friedrich (1777–1843), German poet and author of novel *Undine* (1811).

lamp, electric. See **electric lamps.**

Lancaster, Duchy of, established 1265; attached to the Crown since 1399.

Lancaster, Joseph (1778–1838), English educationalist, noted for his use of the monitorial system of teaching.

Lancaster Royal Grammar School, founded 1469.

Lancers, form of quadrille, came into fashion in Britain *c.* 1850.

Lancet, The, British medical journal, founded 1823 by the English surgeon Thomas Wakley (1795–1862).

Lancing College, Sussex, English public school, founded by the Rev. Nathaniel Woodward, 1848.

Lancret, Nicolas (1660–1743), French painter, worked in style of Watteau (*q.v.*).

Land, Edwin Herbert (b. 1909), American scientist, inventor of the Polaroid camera.

Landau, Lev (1908–68), Russian physicist, awarded 1962 Nobel Prize for Physics for his work on helium gas.

Land Registry, British, established 1862; operates at present under Land Registration Acts, 1925 to 1971.

Landor, Walter Savage (1775–1864), English poet and writer of *Imaginary Conversations.*

Landowska, Wanda (1877–1959), Polish-born harpsichord virtuoso, worked in France and U.S.A.; began harpsichord revival.

Landru, Henri Désiré (1869–1922), French murderer, guillotined for the murder of 11 people.

Landseer, Sir Edwin (1802–73), English painter of sentimental animal scenes, e.g. *Monarch of the Glen.*

Landsteiner, Kerl (1868–1943), Austrian pathologist, discovered the four main types of human blood.

Lane, Sir Allen (1902–70), English publisher, founder of Penguin Books and pioneer in paperback publishing.

Lane Bequest, Impressionist paintings, bequeathed by the Irish art dealer Sir Hugh Lane (1875–1915); shared between London and Dublin 1959.

Lanfranc (*c.* 1005–1089), Italian-born archbishop of Canterbury 1070–89; advisor to William the Conqueror.

Lang, Andrew (1844–1912), Scottish writer on folklore and mythology, also a poet and children's writer.

Lang, Fritz (1890–1976), Austrian film director, notably of the expressionistic *Metropolis* (1926); also made many films in the U.S.A.

Langevin, Paul (1872–1946), French physicist, known for his work on gases and magnetism.

Langham, Simon (d. 1376), English chancellor 1363, archbishop of Canterbury 1366–68.

Langland, William (*c.* 1332–*c.* 1400), English poet, wrote allegorical *Piers Plowman.*

Langley, Samuel (1834–1906), American astronomer and aeronautical pioneer, invented instrument for measuring radiant heat.

Langmuir, Irving (1881–1957), American chemist, awarded Nobel Prize 1932 for his work on surface chemistry.

Langton, Stephen (*c.* 1150–1228), English cleric and scholar, archbishop of Canterbury 1207–28, helped secure Magna Carta.

Langtry, Lillie (1852–1929), English actress, born in Jersey, noted for her beauty; mistress of Edward VII.

Languedoc Canal, Bay of Biscay to Mediterranean, started 1666; opened 1681 and completed 1692; built by the French engineer Pierre-Paul Riquet (1604–80).

Lanier, Sidney (1842–81), American poet and theorist, wrote *Science of English Verse* (1880).

Lansbury, George (1859–1940), English Labour Party leader 1931–35, was a noted pacifist.

Lanston, Tolbert (1844–1913), American inventor, devised Monotype typesetting machine.

lanthanum, metallic element, discovered 1839 by the Swedish chemist Carl Gustav Mosander (1797–1858).

Laos, Buddhist kingdom, Lanxang, founded 14th century; became French protectorate 1893; independent sovereign state within the French Union 1949; withdrew from French Union 1956; intermittent civil war 1953–73; Communist People's Democratic Republic of Laos proclaimed Nov. 1975.

Lao-tzu (*c.* 604–531 B.C.), Chinese religious philosopher, founded Taoism.

La Paz, founded 1548 by the Spanish explorer Alonso de Mendoza; capital of Bolivia since 1898.

La Pérouse, Jean, Comte de (1741–88), French navigator, explored Pacific Ocean.

Laplace, Pierre, Marquis de (1749–1827), French astronomer, investigated planetary motions.

Laporte, Pierre de (1603–50), French valet to Louis XIV, used position to intrigue.

Larbaud, Valéry (1881–1957), French novelist, wrote *Fermina Marquez* (1911).

Lardner, Ring (1885–1933), American writer of satirical short stories.

Largillière, Nicolas de (1656–1746), French painter of portraits, worked in London and Paris.

La Rochefoucauld, François de (1613–80), French writer of *Maxims*, unequalled in penetration and polish.

Larousse, Pierre (1817–75), French lexicographer, founded *Grand Dictionnaire Universel du XIXᵉ Siècle.*

Larousse Encyclopedia, first published 1866–76 (supplements 1878 and 1890) by Larousse publishing house, Paris, founded 1852.

La Salle, Robert de (1643–87), French explorer navigated Mississippi to Gulf of Mexico, 1682.

Las Casas, Bartolomé de (1474–1566), Spanish missionary, opposed slavery in Spanish America; wrote *History of the Indies.*

Lascaux Cave, Dordogne, SW France,

containing examples of palaeolithic art, discovered 1940 by four boys; closed to the public 1963.

laser, suggested 1958 by Charles H. Townes (*q.v.*); first one (ruby laser) constructed 1960 by the American physicist Theodore H. Maiman (b. 1927).

Lasker, Emmanuel (1868–1941), German world chess champion 1894–1921, retained powers into old age; also a noted philosopher.

Laski, Harold (1893–1950), English political thinker, influential at London School of Economics and in Labour Party.

Lassalle, Ferdinand (1825–64), German Socialist, creator of German social democracy; killed in a duel.

Lasso, Orlando di (*c.* 1531–94), Flemish composer of over 1,000 motets and many other pieces.

László, Philip (1869–1937), Hungarian-born painter in England, noted for portraits.

La Tène, name applied to Iron Age period extending from *c.* 500 to *c.* 15 B.C.

Lateran Councils, ecumenical councils of the Roman Catholic Church held in Rome: 1st, 1123; 2nd, 1139; 3rd, 1179; 4th, 1215; 5th, 1512–17.

Lateran Treaty, between the Holy See and the kingdom of Italy, 1929.

lathe, wood-cutting lathe used 1570s in France; screw-cutting lathe invented 1797 by the English engineer Henry Maudslay (1771–1831).

Latimer, Hugh (*c.* 1485–1555), English Protestant martyr, burnt at the stake.

Latin American Free Trade Association, set up Feb. 1960.

La Tour, Georges de (1593–1652), French painter, whose mainly religious paintings are notable for their effects of light and shade.

La Tour, Maurice Quentin de (1704–88), French pastel portraitist and court painter to Louis XV.

Latvia, in Middle Ages consisted mainly of the Baltic provinces of Kurland and Livonia; subjugated by the Teutonic knights in 12th century; ruled by Poland from 1561 and (in part) by Sweden from 1629; annexed by Russia 1795; independent republic 1918; incorporated into the U.S.S.R. 1940.

Latvian language (Lettish), earliest known text dated 1585.

Latymer Upper School, London, English public day school, founded 1624.

Laud, William (1573–1645), English prelate, as archbishop of Canterbury 1633–45 persecuted dissenters; beheaded.

laudanum, opium-based medicine first prepared by Paracelsus (*q.v.*); modern alcoholic tincture of opium first prepared *c.* 1660 by Thomas Sydenham (*q.v.*).

Lauder, Sir Harry (1870–1950), Scottish music hall comedian and composer of popular songs.

Lauderdale, John Maitland, Duke of (1616–82), Scottish statesman, secretary of state for Scotland 1660–80; ruled country for Charles II.

laughing gas. See **nitrous oxide.**

Laughton, Charles (1899–1962), English actor in plays and films, notably *The Hunchback of Notre-Dame.*

Laurent, Auguste (1807–53), French chemist, classified organic compounds according to their atomic groupings.

Laurier, Sir Wilfred (1841–1919), French-Canadian statesman, prime minister 1896–1911.

Lausanne, Treaty of, between Italy and Turkey Oct. 1912; between World War I Allies and the newly formed Turkish Republic July 1923.

Lautréamont, Comte de (pseud. of Isidore Ducasse; 1846–70), French writer of *Chants de Maldoror.*

Lautrec, Henri de Toulouse-. See **Toulouse-Lautrec,** Henri de.

Laval, Pierre (1883–1945), French politician, prime minister of the Vichy government; executed for treason.

La Vallière, Louise de (1644–1710), French mistress of Louis XIV of France 1661–74; subsequently entered a convent.

Lavater, Johann Kaspar (1741–1801), Swiss writer, founded study of physiognomy.

lavender, introduced to England from Naples; believed first grown at Hitchin 1568.

Lavoisier, Antoine Laurent (1743–94), French chemist, founder of modern chemistry, identified oxygen; guillotined in Revolution.

Law, Andrew Bonar (1858–1923), Canadian-born British statesman, prime minister 1922–23.

Law, John (1671–1729), Scottish financier, became French controller-general; fled when 'Mississippi scheme' collapsed 1720.

Law, William (1686–1761), English theologian, writer of *Serious Call to a Devout and Holy Life* (1728).

Lawes, William (d. 1645), English composer of 'Gather ye rosebuds while ye may'.

Lawrence, Saint (3rd cent.), Christian martyr, said to have been burnt on a grid.

Lawrence, David Herbert (1885–1930), English novelist, author of *Sons and Lovers* (1913).

Lawrence, Ernest (1901–58), American physicist, inventor of the cyclotron, 1931.

Lawrence, Gertrude (1898–1952), English actress, best known for her roles in musical comedy and review.

Lawrence, Sir Henry (1806–57), English

administrator in the Punjab; killed during Indian Mutiny.

Lawrence, John Laird, 1st Baron (1811–79), English administrator, brother of Sir Henry Lawrence, governor-general of India 1863–69.

Lawrence, Sir Thomas (1769–1830), English painter, was a notable portraitist.

Lawrence, Thomas Edward (1888–1935), English soldier and scholar, known as 'Lawrence of Arabia'; led Arab revolt against the Turks 1917–18.

lawrencium, transuranic element, discovered 1961 by Albert Ghiorso, T. Sikkeland, A. E. Larsh, and R. M. Latimer.

Layamon (fl. *c.* 1200), English writer of *Brut* (i.e. Brutus), first important vernacular work.

Layard, Sir Austen Henry (1817–94), English archaeologist, made impressive discoveries at Nineveh.

L.D.V. See **Home Guard.**

Leacock, Stephen (1869–1944), Canadian writer of humorous stories, e.g. *Literary Lapses* (1910).

lead, chemical element, known before recorded history; used for water pipes by Romans.

League of Nations, created 1919 by the Treaty of Versailles; dissolved April 1946 and superseded by the United Nations.

Leakey, Louis (1903–72), English archaeologist and anthropologist, discovered important fossil remains in E Africa.

Leaning Tower of Pisa, built 1174–1350.

leap year, system by which an extra day (29 Feb.) is added to every fourth year divisible by 4 but only to those century years divisible by 400.

Lear, Edward (1812–88), English 'nonsense' poet, e.g. *Owl and the Pussycat*; was also a watercolour artist.

leather hose, for fire fighting, first designed 1672.

Léautaud, Paul (1872–1956), French writer, famous in old age for *Journal* (1954–56) and radio interviews.

Lebanon, occupied since Phoenician times or earlier; inhabited from 7th century A.D. by Maronites (*q.v.*); came under French influence 1861–1914; became French mandate 1920; occupied by British and French forces in World War II; achieved full independence 1946; armed insurrection 1958; base for Palestinian guerrillas in the 1960s; state of civil war in the mid-1970s.

Leblanc process, industrial chemical process for manufacturing sodium carbonate, developed 1783 by the French chemist Nicolas Leblanc (1742–1806).

Lebon, Philippe (1769–1804), French chemist, pioneer in the use of gas as a means of illumination.

Le Brun, Charles (1619–90), French royal painter, decorated Versailles and managed Gobelins tapestry works.

Lecky, William (1838–1903), Irish historian, wrote *Rationalism in Europe* (1865).

Leclanché cell, invented *c.* 1866 by the French engineer Georges Leclanché (1839–82).

Lecocq, Charles (1832–1918), French composer, mainly of melodious operettas.

Leconte de Lisle, Charles (1818–94), French poet, founded Parnassian movement.

Le Corbusier (1887–1965), Swiss architect, pioneer in modern design, e.g. Unité d'Habitation, Marseilles.

Lecouvreur, Adrienne (1692–1730), French actress, mistress of Marshal de Saxe; reputedly poisoned by rival.

Lee, Ann (1736–84), English-born religious enthusiast, founded Shaker sect; settled in U.S.A.

Lee, Nathaniel (*c.* 1653–1692), English playwright, wrote *The Rival Queens* (1677).

Lee, Robert E. (Edward) (1807–70), American soldier, leading Confederate general; despite early victories lost Battle of Gettysburg, 1863.

Lee, Sir Sidney (1859–1926), English scholar, editor of *Dictionary of National Biography* 1891–1917.

Lee, Tsung-Dao (b. 1926), Chinese-born American physicist, awarded (with C. N. Yang) Nobel Price for Physics, 1957.

Leech, John (1817–64), English cartoonist for *Punch* and illustrator of Dickens' works.

Leeds Grammar School, English public school, founded by Sir William Sheafield 1552; enlarged by John Harrison 1634.

Leeds University, originated as medical school 1831; granted university status 1904.

Leeuwenhoek, Anton van (1632–1723), Dutch naturalist, devised microscope and observed corpuscles, spermatozoa, etc.

Le Fanu, Sheridan (1814–73), Irish novelist, best known for his ghost stories, including *Uncle Silas* (1864).

Lefèvre d'Etaples, Jacques (*c.* 1455–*c.* 1536), French humanist scholar, often persecuted for suspected Protestant sympathies.

Le Gallienne, Richard (1866–1947), English poet and general writer, e.g. *Prose Fancies* (1894–96).

legal memory, in England, dates back to accession of Richard I, 1 Sept. 1189.

Legendre, Adrien (*c.* 1752–1833), French mathematician, noted for his work on elliptic functions and the theory of numbers.

Léger, Fernand (1881–1955), French painter, associated with the Cubist movement.

Legion of Honour, created by the French consular law of 19 May 1802.

legitimacy, by subsequent marriage of parents, made legal in England and Wales 1926; act amended 1959.

Legros, Alphonse (1837–1911), French painter, e.g. *The Ex-Voto* (1861); settled in England.

Lehár, Franz (1870–1948), Hungarian composer of operettas, including *The Merry Widow* (1905).

Lehmann, Beatrix (b. 1903), English actress, also a writer, sister of John and Rosamond.

Lehmann, John (b. 1907), English poet and editor, founded *New Writing* and *London Magazine*.

Lehmann, Lilli (1848–1929), German operatic singer, distinguished in Wagnerian roles.

Lehmann, Lotte (1888–1976), German opera singer, mainly in U.S.A.

Lehmann, Rosamond (b. 1903), English novelist, wrote *Dusty Answer* (1927).

Leibniz, Gottfried Wilhelm (1646–1716), German philosopher, developed theory of monads; discovered calculus.

Leicester, Robert Dudley, Earl of (*c.* 1531–88), English noble, favourite of Queen Elizabeth.

Leicester University, founded as a university college 1921; gained university status 1957.

Leichhardt, Friedrich (1813–48), German explorer, made the first crossing of Australia, 1844–45.

Leiden University, Netherlands, founded 1575 by William of Orange.

Leif Ericsson. See **Ericsson,** Leif.

Leighton, Frederick, Lord (1830–96), English painter, extremely popular in Victorian times.

Leighton Park School, Reading, English public school, founded 1890 under the direction of the Quakers.

Leipzig, University of. See **Karl Marx University.**

Lekeu, Guillaume (1870–94), Belgian composer, left much unfinished at premature death.

Leland, John (*c.* 1506–52), English antiquary, published his account of collecting in *Itinerary*.

Lely, Sir Peter (1618–80), Dutch-born English portrait painter, fashionable in the period 1650–80.

Le Mans Grand Prix, 24-hour motor race, run annually, with few exceptions, since 1923.

Lemon, Mark (1809–70), English editor of *Punch* 1841–70, and prolific general writer.

Lemonnier, Pierre Charles (1715–99), French astronomer, observed Uranus before it was known to be a planet.

Le Moyne, Charles (1626–85), French pioneer in Canada, founded dynasty of French colonial administrators.

Le Moyne, François (1688–1737), French decorative painter, worked at Versailles.

Le Nain, brothers Antoine (1588–1648), Louis (1593–1648), and Mathieu (1607–77), French painters, noted for their portrayal of peasant life.

Lenbach, Franz von (1836–1904), German painter, especially of portraits of Bismarck and other notabilities.

Lenclos, Ninon de (1620–1705), French society woman, kept brilliantly intellectual salon.

Lend-Lease, programme of U.S. aid, mainly to Britain, during World War II, authorized 1941; made reciprocal 1942; ended 1945.

L'Enfant, Pierre Charles (1754–1825), French soldier in American Revolution, planned design of Washington, D.C.

Lenin (pseud. of Vladimir Ilyich Ulyanov; 1870–1924), Russian Bolshevik, leader of October Revolution 1917; prolific writer on Marxism.

Leningrad, founded 1703 by Peter the Great as St Petersburg; capital of Russia 1712–1918; name changed 1914 to Petrograd; renamed Leningrad 1924; besieged by Germans Sept. 1941–Jan. 1943.

Lennox, Charlotte (1720–1804), American-born English novelist, author of *The Female Quixote* (1752).

Leno, Dan (1860–1904), English comedian, was a music-hall and pantomime star.

Lenormand, Henri René (1882–1951), French playwright, author of *Le Lâche* (1925).

Le Nôtré, André (1613–1700), French designer of formal gardens for palaces and châteaux.

lenses, magnified properties studied by the Arab physicist Alhazan (*c.* 965–1038).

Lent, period of 40 days of fasting (excluding Sundays) preceding Easter, starting Ash Wednesday.

Lenz, Heinrich (1804–65), Russian physicist, formulated the law governing the direction of an induced current.

Leo I, Saint (d. 461), Pope 440–461, one of the greatest of the early period; negotiated successfully with the Huns.

Leo III, Saint (*c.* 750–816), Pope 795–816, crowned Charlemagne 800, thus establishing Holy Roman Empire.

Leo IV (d. 855), Pope 847–855, held off Saracen attacks on Rome.

Leo VIII (d. 965), Pope 963–965, deposed and then reinstated 964.

Leo IX, Saint (1002–54), Pope 1049–54, warred with Normans in southern Italy.

Leo X (1475–1521), Pope 1513–21, son of Lorenzo de' Medici (*q.v.*); a great patron of the arts.

Leo XII (1760–1829), Pope 1823–29, attempted financial reforms.

Leo XIII (1810–1903), Pope 1878–1903,

condemned Socialism and other modern ideas; refused recognition to Italian authority in Rome.

Leo I (*c.* 400–474), Eastern Roman emperor 457–474, warred unsuccessfully against the Vandals.

Leo III, the Isaurian (*c.* 680–741), Byzantine emperor 717–741, founder of the Isaurian dynasty; was a successful soldier and administrator.

Leo V, the Armenian (d. 820), Byzantine emperor 813–820, campaigned successfully against the Bulgarians.

Leo VI, the Wise (866–912), Byzantine emperor 866–912, was a noted scholar; completed code of laws.

Leo Africanus (*c.* 1485–*c.* 1554), Arab traveller, author of *Description of Africa*.

León, Juan Ponce de. See **Ponce de León,** Juan.

León, Luis Ponce de. See **Ponce de León,** Luis.

Leonardo da Vinci (1452–1519), Italian artist, scientist, and engineer of universal genius, painted *Mona Lisa*.

Leonidas I (d. 480 B.C.), king of Sparta, died attempting to hold the pass at Thermopylae against a Persian army.

Leoncavallo, Ruggiero (1858–1919), Italian composer, wrote opera *I Pagliacci*.

Leopardi, Giacomo (1798–1837), Italian poet, great master of lyric, usually wrote in a pessimistic vein.

Leopold I (1640–1705), Holy Roman emperor 1658–1705; successful in wars against Turkey.

Leopold II (1747–92), Holy Roman emperor 1790–92, previously duke of Tuscany 1765–90; formed alliance with Prussia against France.

Leopold I (1790–1865), king of the Belgians 1831–65, was the first sovereign of an independent Belgium.

Leopold II (1835–1909), king of the Belgians 1865–1909; as personal ruler of the Congo 1885–1908 notorious for his cruel exploitation of the inhabitants.

Leopold III (b. 1901), king of the Belgians 1934–51, unpopular because of his conduct in World War II; abdicated.

Léopoldville. See **Kinshasa.**

Lepanto, Battle of, naval victory of the Holy League under Don John of Austria over the Turks, 7 Oct. 1571.

Lepidus, Marcus Aemilius (d. 13 B.C.), Roman soldier, triumvir with Octavian and Antony; defeated by Octavian 36 B.C.

Le Play, Pierre (1806–82), French engineer, pioneer of economic studies.

leprosy, mentioned 1500 B.C. (Egypt) and 1400 B.C. (India); bacillus discovered 1872 by Gerhard Hansen (*q.v.*).

Lepsius, Karl Richard (1810–84), German archaeologist, led an important expedition to Egypt, 1842–45.

Lermontov, Mikhail (1814–41), leading Russian Romantic poet, also wrote the novel *A Hero of Our Times* (1840).

Le Sage, Alain (1668–1747), French writer of picaresque novels, notably *Gil Blas* (1715–35).

Leschetizky, Theodor (1830–1915), Polish composer and piano teacher, worked in Russia and Austria.

Leskov, Nikolai (1831–95), Russian novelist and short story writer, author of *Lady Macbeth of the Mtsensk District* (1865).

Lesotho, southern Africa, annexed by Britain 1868; became part of Cape Colony 1871; made a British protectorate 1884; achieved independence within the Commonwealth 1966, changing its name from Basutoland to Lesotho.

Lespinasse, Julie de (1732–76), French hostess, a noted letter writer, held an influential literary salon.

Lesseps, Ferdinand de (1805–94), French diplomat, masterminded building of Suez Canal.

Lessing, Gotthold Ephraim (1729–81), German dramatist and critic, introduced realistic ordinary-life subjects into his plays.

L'Estrange, Sir Roger (1616–1704), English pamphleteer and journalist, published the *Public Intelligencer* and the *Observator*.

Le Sueur, Eustache (1616–55), French painter of the *Life of St Bruno* cycle.

Le Sueur, Jean François (1760–1837), French composer, important mainly as a teacher.

Letchworth, England's first garden city, founded 1903.

Letter Office, General, first established in England by Act of Parliament 1660.

Letters of Marque, licences granted to private persons to fit out armed ships in time of war, abolished by the Treaty of Paris, 1856.

Levant Company, English trading venture, founded 1581; chartered 1592.

Le Vau, Louis (1612–70), French architect, designed part of the Louvre and Tuileries.

Levellers, English republican and democratic group formed 1646 around John Lilburne (*q.v.*); suppressed by Cromwell 1649.

Lever, Charles (1806–72), Irish novelist, wrote *Harry Lorrequer* (1837).

Leverhulme, William Lever, 1st Viscount (1851–1925), English soap manufacturer, created Port Sunlight, the model factory town.

Leverrier, Urbain (1811–77), French astronomer, predicted existence of an unknown planet (Neptune).

Lévi-Strauss, Claude (b. 1906), Belgian anthropologist, author of *A World on the Wane* (1955).

Lewes, Battle of, victory of Simon de

Montfort over Henry III of England, 1264.

Lewis, Clive Staples (1898–1963), English critic, children's writer, Christian apologist and science-fiction novelist.

Lewis, John Llewellyn (1880–1969), American mineworkers' leader, helped found the Congress of Industrial Organizations.

Lewis, Meriwether (1774–1809), American explorer, with William Clark, of the Far West.

Lewis, 'Monk' (1775–1818), English author of *The Monk* (1796), a 'Gothic' horror novel, once universally admired.

Lewis, Percy Wyndham (1884–1957), English painter, chief of Vorticist group, and writer, e.g. *The Childermass* (1928).

Lewis, Sinclair (1885–1951), American novelist, author of *Babbitt* (1922); awarded Nobel Prize for Literature 1930.

Lewis machine-gun, invented and patented 1911 by the American army officer Isaac Newton Lewis (1858–1931).

Leyden, Lucas van (1494–1533), Dutch painter and engraver, noted for his woodcuts.

Leyden Jar, electric capacitor, first made 1746 by the Dutch physicist Pieter van Musschenbroek (1692–1761) and independently 1745 by the German G. E. von Kleist.

Leys School, Cambridge, English public school, founded 1875; incorporated 1878.

Leyte Gulf, Battle of. See **Philippine Sea.**

Lhote, Henri (b. 1903), French archaeologist, noted for his work on the prehistory of the Sahara.

Liadov, Anatol (1855–1914), Russian composer, collected and arranged folk-songs.

Liang dynasty, China, 502–557.

Libby, Willard Frank (b. 1908), American scientist, best known for his work in carbon-14 dating.

Liberal Party, British origins in the Whigs (*q.v.*); name adopted officially 1830; first Liberal government 1846 led by Lord John Russell (*q.v.*); supplanted 1918 by Labour Party as a major political party in Britain.

Liberals, Spanish supporters of 1812 constitution; French opponents of 'Ultras' in 1815 and during 1820–30; Italian opponents of Austrian rule after 1815; European supporters of the revolutions of 1848.

Liberia, West Africa, settlement of freed American slaves established 1822; state constituted 1847 as an independent republic.

Liberius, Saint (d. 366), Pope 352–366, struggled against anti-pope Felix II.

Liberty Bell, Independence Hall, Philadelphia, hung 1753; cracked 1835.

library, first public, built in Rome by C. Asinius Pollio 39 B.C.; Vatican, begun by

Pope Nicolas V 1447; Bodleian opened 1602; British Museum, founded 1753; Congress, established 1800; London, opened 1841.

Library Association, American, established 1876.

Library Association, British, established 1877.

library service, public, first proposed in Britain 1831; established by the Public Libraries Act 1850.

Libreville, capital of Gabon, founded 1848.

Libya, North Africa, ancient region colonized by Greeks; annexed to Rome 2nd century B.C.; conquered by Vandals A.D. 476 and by Arabs 647; under Ottoman domination 1551–1911; conquered by Italy 1911; scene of several campaigns 1940–43 in World War II; under British and French administration 1943–51; achieved independence as a monarchy 1951; monarchy overthrown and republic proclaimed 1969.

Lichfield Cathedral, Staffordshire, constructed in 13th and early 14th centuries.

Licinius (d. A.D. 324), Roman emperor 308–324, defeated by Constantine and executed.

Lichtenstein, Roy (b. 1923), American artist, an exponent of pop art.

Lick Observatory, Mount Hamilton, California, constructed 1876–88, endowed by the philanthropist James Lick (1796–1876).

Lie, Jonas (1833–1908), Norwegian novelist, author of *The Commodore's Daughters* (1886).

Lie, Trygve (1896–1968), Norwegian statesman, foreign minister 1941–46, U.N. secretary-general 1946–53.

Lieber, Francis (1800–72), German-born American writer, conceived and edited *Encyclopedia Americana* (1829–33).

Liebermann, Max (1847–1935), German painter, best known for his Impressionist work.

Liebig, Justus von (1803–73), German chemist and biochemist, pioneered agricultural chemistry; made many discoveries.

Liebknecht, Karl (1871–1919), German Marxist, led Spartacist rising 1919; captured and shot.

Liebknecht, Wilhelm (1826–1900), German Socialist, co-founder of Social Democratic Party, father of Karl Liebknecht.

Liechtenstein, formed 1342 as the Principality of Vaduz; enlarged to present size 1434; constituted 1719 as the Principality of Liechtenstein; united with Switzerland in a customs union 1924.

lie-detector, modern version constructed 1921 by an American medical student John A. Larson.

Liège Cathedral, Belgium; first cathedral

destroyed 1794; second, originally built 10th century as a church.

lifeboat, first 'unsinkable' one designed and built in 1790s at Newcastle.

Life Guards, first raised 1660 after the Restoration.

life-line, first practical one invented 1807.

lift, first hydraulic passenger lift invented 1853 by the American Elisha Graves Otis (1811–61); first used 1857 in New York.

light, colour composition of, discovered 1666 by Sir Isaac Newton.

light, theories of. See **particle theory; wave theory.** See also **interference; polarization of light; refraction.**

light, velocity of, first calculated 1675 by the Danish astronomer Olaus Roemer (1644–1710); recalculated by the French physicists Armand-Hippolyte Fizeau (1819–96) in 1849 and Jean Foucault (1819–68) in 1850.

Light Brigade, Charge of the, Balaklava, Crimean War, 25 Oct. 1854.

Lightfoot, Joseph Barber (1828–89), English prelate, bishop of Durham 1879–89, noted for his work on the New Testament.

Light Programme, B.B.C., began 29 July 1945; replaced 30 Sept. 1967 by Radio 1 and Radio 2.

Lights, Festival of, Jewish festival, Kislev 25th.

lighthouses, first man-made design built c. 280 B.C. at Pharos, Alexandria. See also **Eddystone Lighthouse.**

lightning conductor, principle discovered 1747 by Benjamin Franklin (q.v.).

Ligne, Charles, Prince de (1735–1814), Austrian diplomat, remembered for his writings, especially his correspondence with famous people.

Liguori, Saint Alfonso (1696–1787), Italian ecclesiastic, founded Redemptorists.

Lilburne, John (c. 1614–57), English pamphleteer, 'Freeborn John', persecuted under both king and Commonwealth.

Liliencron, Detlev von (1844–1909), German poet, also war novelist, e.g. *Krieg und Frieden* (1891).

Lilienthal, Otto (1848–96), German engineer and gliding pioneer; killed in flying accident.

Liliuokalani (1838–1917), last queen of Hawaii 1891–93, overthrown by American-inspired revolt.

Lillie, Beatrice (b. 1898), Canadian-born actress in Britain and U.S.A., best known as a comedienne.

Lilliput, British periodical, 1937–60, founded by the Hungarian-born American journalist Stefan Lorant (b. 1901).

Lillo, George (1693–1739), English playwright, wrote *The London Merchant* (1731), the first 'ordinary life' tragedy.

Lilly, William (1602–81), English astrologer, issued almanacs.

Lima, capital of Peru, founded c. 1535 by Francisco Pizarro (q.v.).

limejuice, introduced on board ships c. 1779 as a preventative of scurvy by the physician Sir Gilbert Blane (1749–1834); made compulsory in the Royal Navy 1795.

limelight, invented 1816 by Thomas Drummond (1797–1840), following work by the American chemist Robert Hare (1781–1858).

Limousin, Leonard (c. 1505–c. 1577), French enamel painter, head of royal works at Limoges.

Linacre, Thomas (c. 1460–1524), English humanist, scholar and founder of Royal College of Physicians.

Lincoln, Abraham (1809–65), American statesman, 16th president of the United States 1861–65 during Civil War; emancipated slaves 1863; assassinated by J. W. Booth (q.v.).

Lincoln Cathedral, England, construction began 1086; consecrated 1092.

Lincoln Cathedral School, English preparatory school, founded 1090 or before; closed 1919; reopened 1961 as an independent school.

Lincolnshire Insurrection, largely against religious and fiscal oppression, began 1536; suppressed 1536–37.

Lind, Jenny (1820–87), 'Swedish nightingale', world-famous soprano.

Lindbergh, Charles (1902–74), American aviator, made first solo non-stop transatlantic flight 1927.

Lindemann, Ferdinand (1852–1939), German mathematician, proved that π is a transcendental number.

Lindisfarne. See **Holy Island.**

Lindley, John (1799–1865), English botanist, attempted classification of plants.

Lindsay, Nicholas Vachel (1879–1931), American poet, author of *General Booth enters Heaven* (1913).

linear accelerator, for accelerating subatomic particles, first built 1927 by the Swiss physicist Rolf Wideröe (b. 1902).

Linear B, syllabic script used by the ancient Greeks in Crete and Mycenae c. 1500–c. 1150 B.C.; deciphered 1952 by the English architect Michael Ventris.

Ling, Pehr Henrik (1776–1839), Swedish pioneer of gymnastics.

Lingard, John (1771–1851), English historian, wrote 8-volume *History of England*.

Linklater, Eric (1899–1974), Scottish novelist, author of *Poet's Pub* (1929).

Linnaean Society, London, founded 1788 by the English botanist Sir James Edward Smith (1759–1828).

Linnaeus, Carl (1707–78), Swedish botanist, devised modern system of naming and classifying.

linoleum, patented 1860 by the Englishman Frederick Walton.

linotype, typesetting machine, patented 1884 by the German inventor Ottmar Mergenthaler (1854–99).

Lin Piao (1908–71), Chinese Communist political leader and soldier, prominent in struggle against Nationalists and Japanese.

Linus, Saint (d. c. A.D. 79), bishop of Rome, said to have succeeded St Peter.

Liotard, Jean Étienne (1702–89), Swiss painter, best known for his pastel portraits.

Lipchitz, Jacques (1891–1973), Lithuanian sculptor, whose early style was influenced by Cubism.

Li Po (d. 762), Chinese court poet, noted for the vigour and exuberance of his verse on wine and women.

Lippershey, Hans (d. c. 1619), Dutch lens-maker, said to have made a telescope c. 1608.

Lippi, Fra Filippo (c. 1406–69), Italian painter, remarkable for his delicate linear style.

Lippmann, Walter (1889–1974), American journalist, author and political commentator.

Lipton, Sir Thomas (1850–1931), Scottish merchant, built up a famous chain store.

liquefaction of gases, principle discovered 1878 by the French scientist Louis-Paul Cailetet (1832–1913).

Lisbon earthquake (greatest of many suffered by the city), 1 Nov. 1755.

Lissitzky, Eliezer (1890–1941), Russian sculptor and painter, strongly influenced modern art movements.

List, Friedrich (1789–1846), German-born American economist, advocate of protective tariffs.

Listener, The, British periodical, first published 16 Jan. 1929.

Lister, Joseph, 1st Baron (1827–1912), English surgeon, pioneer of antiseptics.

Liszt, Franz (1811–86), Hungarian composer and piano virtuoso, and a leading figure in the Romantic movement.

lithium, discovered 1817 by the Swedish chemist Johann August Arfwedson (1792–1841).

lithography, printing method, invented 1798 by the German engraver Aloys Senefelder (1771–1834).

Lithuania, grand duchy formed early 14th century; merged with Poland 1569; acquired and ruled by Russia 1795–1918; Soviet republic proclaimed 1918; overthrown 1919 and an independent democratic republic set up; incorporated in U.S.S.R. 1940.

Lithuanian language, earliest known text printed 1547.

Litolff, Henry Charles (1818–91), English composer, later head of well-known music publishers.

Littell, Frank Bowers (1869–1951), American astronomer, catalogued over 23,000 stars.

Little Entente, mutual defence arrangement between Czechoslovakia, Yugoslavia, and Romania based on treaties of 1920–21; Permanent Council established 1833; agreement ended 1938.

Littleton, Sir Thomas (1402–81), English lawyer, wrote classic account of land law.

Littré, Maximilian Paul (1801–81), French lexicographer, remembered for his *Dictionary of the French Language* (1863–72).

Litvinov, Maxim (1876–1951), Soviet diplomat foreign minister 1930–39, ambassador to U.S.A. 1941–43.

Lin Sung dynasty, China, 420–479.

Liutprand (c. 922–972), Italian bishop of Cremona 961–972, historian of Italy and Germany.

Livermore, Mary Ashton (c. 1820–1905), American social reformer, leading advocate of women's suffrage.

Liverpool, Robert Jenkinson, 2nd Earl (1770–1828), British statesman, prime minister 1812–27, a period of internal unrest.

Liverpool Cathedral, Anglican, founded 1904, consecrated 1924; Roman Catholic, founded 1967.

Liverpool College, English public school, founded 1840.

Liverpool University, started as a university college 1881; achieved full university status 1903.

Livery Companies, London, see under individual names – Skinners, Vintners, etc.

Livia Drusilla (c. 55 B.C.–A.D. 29), first Roman empress, wife of Augustus and mother of Tiberius.

Livingston, Edward (1764–1836), American statesman and lawyer, secretary of state 1831–33.

Livingston, Robert (1654–1728), Scottish-born administrator in New York, founded distinguished family including Edward Livingston.

Livingstone, David (1813–73), Scottish explorer and medical missionary in Africa, discovered Victoria Falls and Lake Nyasa; exposed slave trade.

Livius Andronicus, Lucius (3rd cent. B.C.), Greek slave in Rome, father of Latin poetry and drama.

Livonia, conquered and made Christian 13th century by Teutonic Knights; taken by Sweden 1629; ceded to Russia 1721; in 1918 north region became part of Estonia and south region part of Latvia.

Livy (Titus Livius; 59 B.C.–A.D. 17), outstanding Roman historian, wrote a history of Rome from its origins.

Li Yüan (565–635), emperor of China 618–627, founder of the T'ang dynasty.

Llandaff Cathedral, East Glamorgan, begun 1120; fell into decay 18th century;

restored 1844–69; bombed 1941; restored 1957.

Llandovery College, Welsh public school, founded by Thomas Phillips, 1848.

Llewelyn I (d. 1240), prince of North Wales 1194–1240, perpetually at war with the English.

Llewelyn II (d. 1282), prince of North Wales 1246–82, struggled against English infiltration; killed in battle.

Lloyd, Marie (pseud. of Matilda Wood; 1870–1922), English music-hall and pantomime singer and comedienne.

Lloyd-George, David (1863–1945), Welsh-born British statesman and radical reformer; prime minister 1916–22.

Lloyd's of London, insurance market, had its origins in a coffee house opened 1686 by Edward Lloyd.

Lloyd's List and Shipping Gazette, London, founded 1734.

Lloyd's Register, of shipping, first printed 1760.

Llull, Ramón (*c.* 1235–1315), Catalan scholastic philosopher, mystic and writer of poetry, novels, etc.

Lobachevsky, Nikolai (1793–1856), Russian mathematician, developed non-Euclidean geometry.

Lobel, Matthias de (1538–1616), Flemish botanist, James I's physician, gave name to lobelia.

Lobengula (1833–94), king of the Matabele tribe, opposed British colonization of Rhodesia.

Locarno Pact, series of treaties, signed 1 Dec. 1925, guaranteeing peace and frontiers in Europe; denounced March 1936 by Germany.

Lochner, Stefan (d. *c.* 1451), German painter, notably of Cologne cathedral altarpiece.

Locke, John (1632–1704), English empirical philosopher, wrote *Two Treatises of Government,* propounding theory of social contract.

Locke, Joseph (1805–60), English railway engineer, assisted Stephenson and built many railway lines.

Lockhart, John Gibson (1794–1854), Scottish writer, biographer of Sir Walter Scott.

Lockwood, James Booth (1852–84), American polar explorer, reached northern Greenland.

Lockyer, Sir Joseph (1836–1920), English astronomer, made discoveries in solar chemistry.

locomotives, early models (steam) built 1803 by Richard Trevithick (*q.v.*) and 1814 by George Stephenson (*q.v.*). See also *Rocket.*

Lodge, Sir Oliver (1851–1940), English physicist, who also did important work in psychic research.

Lodge, Thomas (*c.* 1558–1625), English writer, author of *Rosalynde,* basis of Shakespeare's *As You Like It.*

Loeb, Jacques (1859–1924), German-born American biologist, studied the chemical processes of living organisms.

Loeb, James (1867–1933), American banker and philanthropist, financed Loeb Classical Library, founded 1912.

Loeffler, Charles Martin (1861–1935), American violinist, composer of symphonic poems, including *A Pagan Poem* (1909).

Loewe, Johann Karl (1796–1869), German musician, notable ballad composer, e.g. *The Erl King.*

Loewi, Otto (1873–1961), German-born American pharmacologist, noted for his work on the chemical transmissions of nerve impulses.

Löffler, Friedrich (1852–1915), German bacteriologist, cultured diphtheria (Klebs-Löffler) bacillus; specialized in animal diseases.

Lofting, Hugh (1886–1947), English-born children's writer in U.S.A.; creator of Dr Dolittle.

logarithms, common, first tables published 1617 and 1624 by the English mathematician Henry Briggs (1561–1630).

logarithms, natural, first tables published 1614 after 20 years' work by John Napier (*q.v.*).

logic, study founded 4th century B.C. by Aristotle.

Logical Positivism, philosophical movement originating in Vienna in 1920s.

Logue, Michael (1840–1924), Irish Roman Catholic cardinal and primate of Ireland from 1888.

Loisy, Alfred (1857–1940), French Roman Catholic theologian and biblical scholar, excommunicated for his modernist views.

Lollards, group of Church reformers, formed *c.* 1380 as followers of John Wyclif (*q.v.*); active during early 15th century; revival *c.* 1500; eventually merged with Protestant groups *c.* 1530.

Lombard, Peter (*c.* 1100–*c.* 1160), Italian theologian, bishop of Paris 1159–*c.* 1160, wrote standard text, *Sententiae.*

Lombard League, of cities in Lombardy, originally formed 1167; renewed 1198 and 1208; second league formed 1226; dissolved after 1250.

Lombardo, Pietro (*c.* 1435–1515), Italian sculptor, carved tombs of Dante and other well-known people.

Lombards, invaded Italy 568 and established kingdom; conquered by Franks 774.

Lombroso, Cesare (1836–1909), Italian pioneer of criminology, tried to prove that the criminal is a distinct human type.

Lomonosov, Mikhail (1711–65), Russian scientist and poet, effective creator of literary Russian language.

London, Jack (1876–1916), American novelist, whose experiences as a sailor, tramp and Klondike digger are reflected in *Martin Eden* (1909) and other novels.

London, City of, Roman town founded A.D. 43; sacked by Boadicea 61; fortified in 4th century; fortifications destroyed by Danes in 9th century, but restored by Alfred; Tower of London (*q.v.*) begun 1078; received 1st charter 11th century; effective capital of England by late 12th century.

London, Conference of, on naval disarmament, 1930.

London Airport, Heathrow, opened for civilian use 1946; Terminal 1 opened 1969; Terminal 2 and Queen's Building, 1955; Terminal 3, 1961.

London Bridge, new, designed by the Scottish engineer John Rennie (1761–1821) and constructed 1824–31 by his son John (1794–1874); replaced in 1960s and transported to Arizona, U.S.A.

London Bridge, old, built 1176–1209 by Peter, Chaplain of St Mary's Colechurch; rebuilt in 1750s and replaced in 1830s.

London Company, formed to colonize part of Virginia, chartered 1606.

London County Council, formed 1888; absorbed into the Greater London Council 1965.

London Fire Brigade, set up April 1965 with the establishment of the Greater London Council.

London Gazette, first published as *Oxford Gazette* 1665; renamed 1666.

London Library, subscription library, founded 1840; opened 1841.

London Museum. See **Museum of London.**

London Naval Conference, concerning war at sea, held 1908–09.

London Naval Treaty, ratified 1930.

London Oratory, established 1849 by the English theologian and hymnist Frederick William Faber (1814–63).

London–Paris daily air service, inaugurated 25 Aug. 1919.

London–Paris phone service, opened 1891.

London Passenger Transport Board. See **London Transport Executive.**

London postal districts, established 1858.

London Salvage Corps, founded 1866.

London School of Economics and Political Science, founded 1895 as part of London University.

London Symphony Orchestra, first concert given 9 June 1904.

London Transport Executive, established 1948 to control most of London's transport services, replacing the London Passenger Transport Board formed 1933; London transport services controlled by Greater London Council since 1969.

London University, chartered 1836 following establishment of University College 1828, and Kings College 1829.

London Zoo, opened 1828; country branch (Whipsnade Zoo) opened 1931.

Long, Huey (1893–1935), American politician, populist governor of Louisiana 1928–31 and senator 1931–35; assassinated.

Long, John Luther (1861–1927), American writer, whose short story, *Madame Butterfly*, became basis of Puccini's opera.

Longchamp, William (d. 1197), English prelate, bishop of Ely 1189–97, effectively regent during Richard I's absence.

Longfellow, Henry Wadsworth (1807–82), American poet, author of *Hiawatha*, enjoyed great popularity with his contemporaries.

Longhi, Pietro (1702–85), Italian painter, chiefly of scenes from his native Venice.

Longinus (d. A.D. 273), Greek philosopher, advised Zenobia (*q.v.*); beheaded when captured by Romans.

Long Island, first settled *c.* 1623; annexed to New York 1664.

Longman, Thomas (1699–1755), English publisher, founded well-known firm.

Long March, 6000-mile trek of the Chinese Communists Oct. 1934 to *c.* Oct. 1935 led by Mao Tse-tung and Lin Piao.

Longomontanus (1562–1647), Danish astronomer, initiated building of observatory at Copenhagen.

Long Parliament, called Nov. 1640 by Charles I; most members expelled 1648; remainder, forming the Rump Parliament (*q.v.*), expelled 1653; finally dissolved 1660.

Longus (2nd–3rd cent. A.D.), Greek writer of the pastoral romance *Daphnis and Chloë.*

Longworth, Nicholas (1782–1863), American pioneer of grape production.

Lönnrot, Elias (1802–84), Finnish scholar, collected folk materials which he edited into national epic, *Kalevala.*

Löns, Hermann (1866–1914), German writer, author of *Mein Grünes Buch*; killed in battle.

Lonsdale Belt, boxing award created 1909 by the 5th Earl of Lonsdale (1857–1944).

Loomis, Mahlon (1826–86), American pioneer of wireless telegraphy.

looping the loop, aviation, first performed 20 Aug. 1913 at Kiev by the Russian pilot Peter Nesterov.

Lope de Vega. See **Vega,** Lope de.

Lopez, Carlos Antonio (1790–1862), president and dictator of Paraguay 1844–62, attempted to modernize his country's institutions.

Lopez, Francisco (1827–70), dictator of Paraguay 1862–70, launched disastrous war against Argentina and Brazil.

Lopez de Ayala, Pedro (1332–1407), Spanish statesman, historian and poet, best known for his chronicles of the kings of Castile.

Lorca, Federico García (1899–1936), Spanish poet and playwright, author of *Blood Wedding* (1933); killed by Falangists.

Lord Howe Island, SW Pacific, dependency of New South Wales, discovered 1788.

Lord Mayor of London, office (of mayor) first filled *c.* 1191 to 1212 by Henry Fitz Ailwyn; first chosen annually 1215; term 'lord mayor' generally used from late 15th century.

Lord Mayor's Show, London, takes place second Saturday in Nov.; first held 1215.

Lords, House of, separated from House of Commons (*q.v.*) in reign of Edward III; name in use by 16th century; absolute power of veto abolished 1911 by Act of Parliament; granting of judicial life peerages for men formalized by an Act of 1876; non-judicial life peerages first granted 1958; debarring of women members, as life peers, removed 1958 and as hereditary peers, 1963.

Lords Appellant, group of English nobles, held power 1386–97.

Lord's Cricket Ground, London, headquarters since 1814 of the Marylebone Cricket Club. See **M.C.C.**

Lords Ordainers, group of nobles whose reform ordinances of 1310 were confirmed by Parliament 1311; repealed 1322.

Lorentz, Hendrik Antoon (1853–1928), Dutch physicist, co-discoverer of Zeeman Effect; Nobel prizewinner 1902.

Lorentz-Fitzgerald Contraction, of length with velocity, formulated 1895–96 by Hendrik Antoon Lorentz (*q.v.*) and the Irish physicist George FitzGerald (1851–1901).

Lorenz, Adolf (1854–1946), Austrian orthopaedic surgeon, found cures for several bone ailments.

Lorenz, Konrad (b. 1903). Austrian psychologist, noted for his studies on animal behaviour, including *On Aggression* (1966).

Lorenzetti, Ambrogio (d. *c.* 1348), Italian painter, painted *Good and Bad Government* frescoes in town hall at Siena.

Lorenzetti, Pietro (d. *c.* 1348), Italian painter, brother of Ambrogio Lorenzetti, painted frescoes at Assisi.

Lorenzo de' Medici. See **Medici, Lorenzo de'.**

Loreto, Italy, reputed site of the house of the Virgin Mary, miraculously deposited there 1295.

Loretto School, Scottish public school, founded 1862 by Dr Hely Hutchinson Almond (1832–1903).

Lorimer, George Horace (1868–1937), American writer and journalist, editor of *Saturday Evening Post* 1899–1936.

Lorrain, Claude (1600–82), French painter of large classical landscapes and seascapes.

Lorraine, part of realm of Lothair I 843; German Duchy created 959; came under French domination from mid-16th century; ruled by France 1766–1870; ceded as part of Alsace-Lorraine to Germany 1871; returned to France 1918; under German occupation from 1940; restored to France 1944.

Lorris, Guillaume de. See **Guillaume de Lorris.**

Lortzing, Albert (1801–51), German opera composer, wrote *Tsar and Carpenter* (1837).

Lothair I (795–855), Holy Roman emperor 840–855, accepted division of Carolingian empire at Verdun 843.

Lothair II (*c.* 1070–1137), Holy Roman emperor 1125–1137, fought civil war against Hohenstaufens.

Lotharingia. See **Lorraine.**

Loti, Pierre (1850–1923), French novelist, famous for his exotic settings.

Lotto, Lorenzo (*c.* 1480–1556), Italian painter, most successful as a portraitist.

Lotze, Rudolf (1817–81), German philosopher and physiologist, belonged to Idealist school.

Loudon, John Claudius (1783–1843), Scottish writer on horticulture, compiled reference books.

Loughborough Grammar School, English public school, founded traditionally 1495 by Thomas Burton.

Loughborough University, of Technology, created 1966 from the Loughborough College of Technology.

Louis I (778–840), Holy Roman emperor and king of France 814–840.

Louis II (846–879), king of France 877–879, son of Charles the Bald.

Louis III (921–954), king of France 879–882, jointly with his brother; beat off Viking attacks.

Louis IV (*c.* 921–954), king of France 936–954, dominated by Hugh Capet.

Louis V (*c.* 967–987), king of France 986–987, last Carolingian; succeeded by Hugh Capet.

Louis VI (1081–1137), king of France 1108–37, expanded royal control and encouraged the communes.

Louis VII (*c.* 1121–80), king of France 1137–80, overshadowed by Henry II of England's French possessions.

Louis VIII (1187–1226), king of France 1223–26, as crown prince led expedition to England 1216–17.

Louis IX, Saint (1214–70), king of France 1226–70, pious and conciliatory; crusaded in Egypt.

Louis X (1289–1316), king of France 1314–16, a period of baronial discontent.

Louis XI (1423–83), king of France 1461–83, destroyed power of Burgundy and greatly strengthened crown.

Louis XII (1462–1515), king of France 1499–1515, made internal reforms; waged fruitless Italian wars.

Louis XIII (1601–43), king of France 1610–43; strongly influenced by Cardinal Richelieu (q.v.).

Louis XIV (1638–1715), king of France 1643–1715, the 'Sun King', exercised absolute authority over the most powerful country in Europe in a period of expansion.

Louis XV (1710–74), king of France 1715–75; influenced by his mistresses during a period of lessening royal power.

Louis XVI (1754–93), king of France 1774–92; deposed during Revolution and guillotined.

Louis XVII (1785–95), son of Louis XVI, titular king of France 1793–95; died in prison.

Louis XVIII (1755–1824), king of France 1814–24, after fall of Napoleon.

Louis II (c. 804–876), king of Germany 843–876, usually regarded as the founder of Germany.

Louis III (893–911), king of Germany 899–911, last Carolingian in Germany.

Louis IV (c. 1287–1347), king of Germany and Holy Roman emperor 1314–47; in conflict with papacy.

Louis, Joe (b. 1914), American Negro boxer, world heavyweight champion 1937–49.

Louis Ferdinand (1772–1806), Prussian prince, soldier in French wars; killed in 1806 campaign.

Louisiana, U.S.A., first settled 1699; region E of Mississippi ceded by France to Britain 1763; admitted to Union 1812; seceded 1861; readmitted 1868.

Louisiana Purchase, from France of territory west of the Mississippi, completed 1803 by the American president Thomas Jefferson.

Louis Napoleon. See **Napoleon III.**

Louis Philippe (1773–1850), king of France 1830–48, 'citizen king', abdicated after 1848 revolution.

Lourdes, first visions of Bernadette Soubirous at, 1858. Festival of Our Lady at Lourdes celebrated 11th Feb.

Loutherbourg, Philippe de (1740–1812), French painter in England, known for marine and sea-battle scenes.

Louvois, Marquis de (1641–91), French minister of war, reorganized and modernized the French army.

Louvre, Paris, rebuilding of the original medieval castle started 1546 by the French architect Pierre Lescot (c. 1515–1578).

Louÿs, Pierre (1870–1925), French writer in 'decadent' vein, author of *Aphrodite* (1896).

Lovejoy, Owen (1811–64), American abolitionist, prominent supporter of Abraham Lincoln.

Lovelace, Richard (1618–58), English Cavalier poet, wrote *To Althea from Prison.*

Loveless, George (1792–1874), English labourer, one of the Tolpuddle martyrs (q.v.).

Lovell, Sir Bernard (b. 1913), English astronomer, director of Jodrell Bank Observatories since 1951.

Lover, Samuel (1797–1868), Irish comic novelist, author of *Handy Andy* (1842).

Low, Sir David (1891–1963), New Zealand-born cartoonist in Britain, shrewd and funny political commentator.

Low, Juliette (1860–1927), American founder of Girl Scouts in the U.S.A., 1912.

Low, Sampson (1797–1886), English publisher, founded well-known firm, 1848.

Lowe, Sir Hudson (1769–1844), Irish-born British soldier, captor of Napoleon on St Helena 1815–21.

Lowell, Amy (1874–1925), American poet, belonged to Imagist group.

Lowell, James Russell (1819–91), American poet, wrote the satirical *Biglow Papers* (1848).

Lowell, Robert (b. 1917), American poet, author of *Lord Weary's Castle* (1946).

Lowell Observatory, Arizona, founded 1894 by the American astronomer Percival Lowell (1855–1916).

Lowestoft, Battle of, victory of the English fleet over the Dutch, 3 June 1665.

Lowie, Robert (1883–1957), Austrian-born American anthropologist, studied American Indian life.

Lowndes, William Thomas (c. 1798–1843), English author of *Bibliographer's Manual of English Literature* (1834).

Lowry, Malcolm Boden (1909–57), English novelist, author of *Under the Volcano* (1947).

Lowry, Laurence Stephen (1887–1976), English painter, noted for his pictures of northern industrial towns.

Low Sunday, first Sunday after Easter.

Loyalty Islands, Pacific, discovered early 19th century; annexed by France 1864; became dependency of New Caledonia 1946.

Loyola, Saint Ignatius (1491–1556), Spanish soldier, founded Society of Jesus (Jesuits) 1541.

Loyola University, Chicago, founded 1870 as St Ignatius College; established as Loyola University 1909.

Luanda, capital of Angola, founded 1576.

Lubbock, Sir John (1834–1913), English banker, wrote popular texts on prehistory, natural history, etc.

Lubin, David (1849–1919), Polish-born American merchant, pioneered and organized scientific agriculture.

Lubitsch, Ernst (1892–1947), German film director in U.S.A., made many sophisticated Hollywood comedies including *Ninotchka* (1939).

Lucan (A.D. 39–65), Spanish-born Roman poet, wrote epic *Pharsalia*; forced to commit suicide by Nero.

Lucaris, Cyril (*c.* 1572–1637), Greek prelate, controversial patriarch of Constantinople; strongly influenced by Protestantism.

Lucas, Edward Verrall (1868–1938), English journalist, novelist, anthropologist and critic.

Lucas, Frank Laurence (1894–1967), English writer, poet and critic, author of play *Land's End* (1938).

Lucas van Leyden (*c.* 1494–1533), Dutch painter and engraver, created a notable *Ecce Homo*.

Luce, Clare Boothe (b. 1903), American playwright and diplomat, wife of Henry Robinson Luce; U.S. ambassador to Italy 1953–56.

Luce, Henry Robinson (1898–1967), American founder-publisher of *Time* (1923) and *Life* (1936).

Lucian (*c.* A.D. 120–*c.* A.D. 180), Greek writer, satirist of contemporary manners in *Dialogues of the Dead*.

Luckner, Felix von (1881–1966), German sailor, served in World War I, toured world in yacht *Sea Devil* 1937–39.

Lucknow, India, ancient city probably dating back to 12th century; capital of Oudh 18th century; residency besieged 1 July–25 Sept. 1857 during the Indian Mutiny.

Lucrece (d. *c.* 510 B.C.), Roman matron, said to have been raped by Tarquinius Sextus; committed suicide.

Lucretius (*c.* 94–*c.* 55 B.C.), Roman poet, expounded Epicurus' philosophy in *De Rerum Natura*.

Lucullus, Lucius Licinius (*c.* 110–57 B.C.), Roman general, defeated Mithridates in Asia Minor: notorious for luxurious living.

Lucy, Saint (2nd cent. A.D.), patron saint of the blind, martyred under Diocletian at Syracuse.

Lucy, Sir Thomas (1532–1600), English squire, said to have prosecuted Shakespeare for deer-stealing.

Luddites, English machine wreckers, active 1811–16.

Ludendorff, Erich von (1865–1937), German general, helped to formulate World War I strategy; supported Hitler's Munich putsch, 1923.

Ludlow, Edmund (*c.* 1617–92), English Parliamentary leader and regicide; after Restoration fled to Switzerland.

Ludwig I (1786–1868), king of Bavaria 1825–48, lover of Lola Montez; forced to abdicate.

Ludwig II (1845–86), king of Bavaria 1864–86, patron of Wagner and extravagant builder; committed suicide while insane.

Ludwig III (1845–1921), last king of Bavaria 1913–18.

Ludwig, Emil (1881–1948), German writer of popular biographies.

Lugard, Frederick, 1st Baron (1858–1945), English pioneer colonial administrator, chiefly in Nigeria.

Luini, Bernadino (*c.* 1481–1532), Italian painter of Milanese school, noted for his religious frescoes.

Lukács, György (1885–1971), Hungarian philosopher and critic, an authority on Marxist thought.

Luke, Saint (1st cent. A.D.), traditionally a physician, was the author of the third New Testament gospel.

Lull, Ramón. See **Llull, Ramón.**

Lully, Jean Baptiste (1632–87), Italian-born French composer, established the characteristically French type of opera.

Lumière, Auguste (1862–1954), French pioneer of cinematography with his brother Louis (1864–1948).

luminescence, first investigated 1603 by the Italian alchemist Vincenzo Cascariolo (1571–1624).

Lumumba, Patrice (1925–61), first prime minister of independent Zaïre; dismissed and subsequently murdered.

Luna, Álvaro de (d. 1453), Spanish constable of Castile, acquired almost unlimited power under John II.

Lunacharsky, Anatoli (1875–1933), Soviet Communist leader, commissar for education 1917–29; writer and patron of the arts.

Lundy, Benjamin (1789–1839), American philanthropist, prominent in the antislavery movement.

Lunéville, Treaty of, between France and Austria, signed Feb. 1801.

Luna, or Lunik, series of Soviet spacecraft: Luna 3 circumnavigated the Moon Sept. 1959 sending back first photographs of far side; Luna 9 made first successful lunar soft landing 1966.

Lusaka, became capital of Northern Rhodesia, (now Zambia) 1935.

Lusitania British Atlantic passenger liner, launched 1906; torpedoed by German submarine 7 May 1915.

lutetium, metallic element, discovered 1907 independently by Charles Urbain and the Austrian chemist Baron von Welsbach (1858–1929).

Luther, Martin (1483–1546), German religious reformer, began Protestant Reformation; translated Bible into German.

Lutheran Church, first established 1522.

Luthuli, Albert John (1899–1967), South African nationalist leader, opponent of apartheid, awarded Nobel Peace Prize, 1960.

Lutyens, Sir Edwin Landseer (1869–1944), English architect, designed Cenotaph; planned New Delhi.

Lützen, Battle of, Swedish victory over the Imperialists in the Thirty Years' War, Nov. 1632.

Luxembourg, emerged as a county in Holy Roman Empire 10th century; became duchy 1354; passed to Spanish and then Austrian Hapsburgs as part of Netherlands; Grand Duchy created 1815 by Congress of Vienna; part of Netherlands 1815–30; western half given to Belgium 1839, rest remaining as Grand Duchy in union with Netherlands; neutrality and independence guaranteed 1867; under German occupation 1914–18 and 1940–44; joined Benelux Union (q.v.) 1947.

Luxembourg Palace, Paris, built 1615–c. 1627.

Luxemburg, Rosa (1870–1919), German revolutionary Socialist, with Karl Liebknecht (q.v.) led Spartacist rising; murdered.

Luynes, Charles d'Albert, Duc de (1578–1621), French royal favourite, constable of France 1621.

Lvov, Alexei (1799–1871), Russian composer of operas and national anthem.

Lyall, Edna (1857–1903), English novelist, author of *Donovan* (1882).

Lyautey, Louis (1854–1934), French soldier, progressive colonial administrator in Morocco 1912–25.

Lycurgus (9th cent. B.C.), Spartan reformer, whose laws gave Sparta its unique character.

Lydekker, Richard (1849–1915), English naturalist, worked in India 1874–82.

Lydgate, John (c. 1370–c. 1450), English poet, wrote *The Troy Book* (1412–20).

Lyell, Sir Charles (1797–1875), Scottish geologist, whose *Principles of Geology* (1830–33) founded modern study of the subject.

Lyly, John (c. 1554–1606), English writer whose *Euphues* (1579) set fashion for elaborate 'euphuistic' writing.

lynching, term derived possibly from the American Charles Lynch (1736–96) who headed an irregular organization for punishment of offenders during the American Revolution.

Lyndhurst, John Singleton, Baron (1772–1863), English lawyer and statesman, three times lord chancellor.

Lyndsay, Sir David (1490–1555), Scottish poet, wrote satire *The Three Estates* (1540).

Lyon, Mary (1797–1849), American advocate of advanced education for women.

Lyon, Nathaniel (1818–61), American soldier, served in Mexican War and American Civil War; killed in action.

Lyons, France, founded 43 B.C. by Lucius Plancus as Roman military colony; Ecumenical Councils held here, 1st 1245, 2nd 1274.

Lyons, Joseph Aloysius (1879–1939), Australian statesman, prime minister 1932–39.

Lysander (d. 395 B.C.), Spartan commander, captured Athens 404.

Lysenkoism, doctrines on heredity proposed by the Soviet biologist T. D. Lysenko (1898–1977) and accepted in the Soviet Union from 1940s; discredited in 1960s.

Lysimachus (d. 281 B.C.), Macedonian soldier, ruled Macedon and Asia Minor after Alexander the Great's death.

Lysippus (late 4th cent. B.C.), Greek sculptor, worked for Alexander the Great.

Lysistratus (4th cent. B.C.), Greek sculptor, brother of Lysippus.

Lyte, Henry Francis (1793–1847), Scottish-born Anglican clergyman, wrote *Abide with me* and other hymns.

Lyttleton, George, Baron (1709–73), English politician, poet and literary patron.

Lytton, Bulwer (1803–73), English novelist, wrote *Last Days of Pompeii* (1834).

Lytton, Edward Bulwer. See **Meredith, Owen.**

M

M1, London–Birmingham motorway, main section officially opened 2 Nov. 1959.

Maartens, Maarten (1858–1915), Dutch novelist, author of *God's Fool* (1893).

Mabillon, Jean (1632–1707), French Benedictine monk and scholar, wrote a history of his order.

Mabinogion, Welsh epic collection, compiled 14th–15th centuries.

Mabuse (c. 1470/80–c. 1533), Flemish painter, influenced by visit to Italy, e.g. *Neptune and Amphitrite.*

macadamized roads, introduced c. 1815 by the Scottish surveyor John Loudon McAdam (1756–1836).

McAdoo, William Gibbs (1863–1941), American politician and railway executive; secretary of the treasury 1913–18.

Macao, China, first settled 1557 by Portuguese; Portuguese suzerainty recognized by China 1887; greater autonomy granted by 'organic statute' of 1976.

MacArthur, Douglas (1880–1964), American soldier, commander in the Pacific in World War II and in Korea 1950–51.

McArthur, John (1767–1834), English pioneer in New South Wales, created Australian wine and wool trade.

Macaulay, Dame Rose (1881–1958), English novelist, author of *Towers of Trebizond* (1956).

Macaulay, Thomas Babbington (1800–1859), English historian (*History of England*); also essayist and poet.

Macbeth (d. 1057), king of Scotland 1040–1057; overthrown by Malcolm III.

Maccabees, Jewish leaders against the Syrians from *c.* 168 B.C.; restored Jewish worship in Jerusalem 164 B.C. under Judas Maccabeus (d. 161 B.C.); rulers until 63 B.C. when Judaea annexed to Roman Empire.

MacCarthy, Sir Desmond (1878–1952), English writer, best known as a dramatic critic.

McCarthy, Joseph Raymond (1908–57), American politician, notorious for 'witch-hunt' of Communists 1950–54.

McCarthy, Justin (1830–1912), Irish journalist, novelist and nationalist politician, wrote *History of Our Own Times.*

McCarthy, Mary (b. .1912), American novelist and critic, author of *Memories of a Catholic Girlhood* (1957).

McClellan, George Brinton (1826–85), American Unionist general in Civil War; held Confederates at Antietam 1862.

McClintock, Sir Francis (1819–1907), Irish polar explorer, discovered fate of Franklin (*q.v.*).

McClure, Sir Robert (1807–73), Irish naval officer and explorer, discovered North-West Passage.

McCormack, Count John (1884–1945), Irish-born American tenor, internationally famous for opera roles and Irish songs.

McCormick, Cyrus Hall (1809–84), American inventor of a successful reaping machine, 1831.

McCoy, Sir Frederick (1823–99), Irish naturalist and geologist, active in England and Australia.

McCullers, Carson (1917–67), American novelist, author of *The Heart is a Lonely Hunter* (1940).

MacCunn, Hamish (1868–1916), Scottish composer and conductor, wrote opera *Jeannie Deans* (1894).

MacDiarmid, Hugh (b. 1892), Scottish poet, pioneer in the Scottish literary revival.

Macdonald, Flora (1722–90), Scottish Jacobite heroine, helped the Young Pretender escape, 1746.

Macdonald, George (1824–1905), Scottish children's author, novelist, fantasy-writer (*Phantastes*, 1858), and dialect poet.

MacDonald, James Ramsay (1866–1937), Scottish statesman, first British Labour prime minister 1924.

Macdonell, Alastair (*c.* 1725–61), Scottish Jacobite, became English spy, known as 'Pickle the Spy'.

Macdonough, Thomas (1786–1825), American naval commander, defeated British at Plattsburg 1814.

McDougall, William (1871–1938), English-born American psychologist, wrote *Social Psychology* (1908).

MacDowell, Edward Alexander (1861–1908), American composer, notably of symphonic poems.

Macedonians, ruled Greece 338–307 B.C.

McEntee, Jervis (1828–91), American painter of atmospheric landscapes.

McEvoy, Ambrose (1878–1927), English painter, for a time associated with Augustus John (*q.v.*); noted as a portraitist.

MacEwen, Sir William (1848–1924), Scottish surgeon, distinguished for his work in bone surgery.

McGill University, Montreal, founded 1821 by the legacy of James McGill (1744–1813); opened 1829.

McGillivray, Alexander (d. 1793), American Indian chief, was a skilled diplomat and warrior in his resistance to white advance.

McGonagall, William (b. 1830), Scottish poet, wrote much doggerel verse.

Macgregor, Robert. See **Rob Roy.**

Mach, Ernst (1838–1916), Austrian physicist and philosopher, noted for his work on supersonic projectiles.

Machado, Antonio (1875–1939), Spanish poet, best known for his lyric verse including *Castilian Fields* (1912).

Machado, Bernardino (1851–1944), Portuguese statesman, twice president between periods of exile.

Machaut, Guillaume de (*c.* 1300–77), French composer and poet, was a skilled versifier.

Machen, Arthur (1863–1947), English writer, especially of fantasy, e.g. *Hill of Dreams* (1907).

Machiavelli, Nicolò (1469–1527), Italian diplomat, wrote of politics with brutal realism in *The Prince.*

machine-gun, true repeating gun first patented 1718 by the Englishman James Puckle (d. 1724); modern weapons include the Gatling 1862, Nordenfeldt 1873, Hotchkiss 1878, Maxim 1884, Lewis 1911, and Browning 1917.

Machu Picchu, location of ancient Inca city, discovered 1911 by the American archaeologist Hiram Bingham (1875–1956).

Macintosh, Charles (1766–1843), Scottish chemist, invented waterproofs 1823.

Mackay, Charles (1814–89), Scottish journalist and light-verse writer, e.g. in *Voices from the Crowd* (1846).

McKaye, Steele (1842–94), American actor and dramatist, wrote *Hazel Kirke* (1880).

Macke, August (1887–1914), German painter, prominent in *Blaue Reiter* school; killed in action.

Mackensen, August von (1848–1945), German soldier, was a successful commander in Eastern Europe in World War I.

Mackenzie, Sir Alexander (1755–1820), Scottish explorer in Canada, first white man to make overland journey across North America.

Mackenzie, Sir Compton (1883–1972), Scottish novelist, wrote *Sinister Street* (1913–14) and *Whisky Galore* (1947).

Mackenzie, Henry (1745–1831), Scottish novelist, wrote *The Man of Feeling* (1771).

Mackenzie, William Lyon (1795–1861), Scottish-born Canadian politician, led rebellion, 1837.

Mackinac Bridge, Michigan, U.S.A., completed 1957.

McKinley, Mount, Alaska discovered 1794 by the English navigator George Vancouver; first successfully climbed 1913 by a party led by the American missionary Hudson Stuck.

McKinley, William (1843–1901), American statesman, 25th president of the United States 1897–1901; assassinated by anarchist.

Mackintosh, Charles Rennie (1868–1928), Scottish architect and artist, whose work shows the influence of Art Nouveau.

Mackintosh, Sir James (1765–1832), Scottish lawyer, in India 1804–11; wrote on philosophy and history.

Macklin, Charles (*c.* 1697–1797), Irish actor, notably as Shylock; was also a playwright.

Maclaren, Ian (pseud. of John Watson; 1850–1907), Scottish novelist, wrote *Beside the Bonnie Brier Bush* (1894).

Maclaurin, Colin (1698–1746), Scottish mathematician, author of *Treatise on Fluxions* (1742).

MacLennan, Hugh (b. 1907), Canadian novelist, author of *Two Solitudes* (1945).

McLean, Sir Donald (1820–77), Scottish-born New Zealand statesman, known for conciliatory policies towards Maoris.

MacLeish, Archibald (b. 1892), American poet, e.g. *Conquistador* (1932), and verse playwright.

Macleod, Fiona. See **Sharp,** William.

Maclise, Daniel (1806–70), Irish painter of historical scenes; was also a notable illustrator.

McLuhan, Marshall (b. 1911), Canadian writer on mass communications, author of *The Medium is the Message* (1967).

Maclure, William (1763–1840), Scottish-born American geologist, made geological map of the United States.

MacMahon, Maurice de (1808–93), French soldier, in Crimea and Franco-Prussian War, president of France 1873–1879.

McMahon Line, delineating the northeastern frontier of India, agreed at the 1913–14 Simla Conference; named after the British representative Sir Henry McMahon (1862–1949).

McMaster, John Bach (1852–1932), American historian, wrote *Daniel Webster* (1902).

Macmillan, Daniel (1813–57), Scottish publisher, started famous firm, 1844.

McMillan, Edwin Mattison (b. 1907), American physicist, discovered neptunium and plutonium.

Macmillan, Harold (b. 1894), British statesman, prime minister 1957–63.

McMillan, Margaret (1860–1931), American-born British pioneer of school clinics, with her sister Rachel (1859–1917).

MacNaghten Rules, legal definition of insanity under English law, formulated after the trial for murder of Daniel MacNaghten, 1843.

Macon, Nathaniel (1758–1837), American political leader, was speaker of the House of Representatives 1801–07.

Maconchy, Elizabeth (b. 1907), English composer, best known for her string quartets.

McPherson, Aimée Semple (1890–1944), American evangelist, whose career was disrupted by scandals.

Macpherson, James (1736–96), Scottish poet, made 'translations' (mostly invented) of Gaelic poet Ossian; deeply influenced European literature.

Macpherson, Samuel Charters (1806–60), Scottish administrator in India, suppressed human sacrifice in Orissa 1845.

Macready, William Charles (1793–1873), English actor, outstanding in Shakespearian tragedy.

Macrinus (A.D. 164–218), Roman emperor A.D. 217–18, defeated by Parthians.

MacSwiney, Terence (1879–1920), Irish nationalist leader, imprisoned 1920; starved to death after hunger strike.

McTaggart, John (1866–1925), English philosopher, wrote *Nature of Existence* (1921–27).

MacVeagh, Wayne (1833–1917), American lawyer, attorney-general 1881.

Macy, Anne Sullivan (1866–1936), American teacher of Helen Keller (*q.v.*).

Madagascar. See **Malagasy Republic.**

Madame Tussaud's Waxworks, London, founded 1835 by the Swiss show-woman Marie Tussaud (1760–1850); new building opened 1928.

Madariaga, Salvador de (b. 1886), Spanish writer and diplomat, represented Spain at League of Nations.

Madden, Sir Frederic (1801–73), English paleographer, edited early English texts.

Madeira Islands, North Atlantic, Portuguese possessions, first sighted 1418, and later visited, by a Portuguese navigator Gonçalvez Zarco.

Madeleine, Parisian church, construction began 1746; completed 1842.

Maderna, Carlo (1556–1629), Italian architect, was a noted exponent of baroque Church architecture.

Madero, Francisco (1873–1913), Mexican statesman, as president 1911–13 attempted to introduce social reform.

Madhya Pradesh, Indian state, region conquered by Marathas in 18th century; annexed to Britain 1853; adopted present name 1950.

Madison, James (1751–1836), American statesman, 4th president of the United States 1809–17.

Madog (12th cent.?), Welsh prince, legendary hero long believed to have sailed to America.

Mad Parliament, summoned June 1258 at Oxford.

Madras. See **Tamil Nadu.**

Madrid University, founded 1508 at Alcalá; transferred to Madrid 1836.

Maecenas, Gaius (c. 70–8 B.C.), Roman administrator, generous patron of Virgil and Horace.

Maes, Nicolaes (1632–93), Dutch painter of interiors, e.g. *Card Players.*

Maeterlinck, Maurice (1862–1949), Belgian writer in mystical vein, author of *The Blue Bird* (1909); Nobel prizewinner 1911.

Mafeking, Cape Province, besieged by the Boers 12 Oct. 1899; relieved by the British 17 May 1900; Mafeking Night 18 May 1900.

Magdalen College, Oxford University, founded 1458 by William of Waynflete (c. 1395–1486).

Magdalen College School, Oxford, English public school, founded c. 1478 by William of Waynflete.

Magdalene College, Cambridge University, founded 1542 by Baron Audley of Waldon (1488–1544).

Magdeburg hemisphere, by which air pressure was demonstrated, invented 1654 by Otto von Guericke (q.v.).

Magellan, Ferdinand (c. 1480–1521), Portuguese navigator in Spanish service; killed in Philippines but his ship was the first to circumnavigate the world.

Magellanic Clouds, nearby galactic systems, sighted 1520 by Ferdinand Magellan; identified as star accumulations in 1830s by Sir John Herschel (q.v.).

Magendie, François (1783–1855), French physiologist, introduced new drugs and investigated anatomy.

Magenta, Battle of, victory of the Franco-Piedmontese army over the Austrians, 4 June 1859.

magic lantern. See **slide projector.**

Maginn, William (1793–1842), Irish writer, co-founder of *Fraser's Magazine,* wrote comic stories and verse.

Maginot Line, French defence system, construction began 1928; named after André Maginot (1877–1932), minister of war.

magistrate, first British stipendiary, Henry Fielding, appointed 1748; first British woman, Emily Duncan, appointed 26 May 1913.

Magliabechi, Antonio (1633–1714), Italian bibliophile, accumulated 30,000-volume library still preserved.

Magna Carta, granted by King John at Runnymede, 15 June 1215.

magnesium, first isolated 1808 by Sir Humphry Davy.

magnetic compass. See **compass.**

Magnetic Pole, North, located June 1831 by Sir James Clark Ross (q.v.).

Magnetic Pole, South, located Jan. 1909 by T. W. Edgeworth David of the Shackleton expedition.

magnetic recording, recording device of magnetic steel wire patented 1898 by the Danish inventor Valdemar Poulsen (1869–1942); magnetic paper tape patented 1927 (U.S.A.) and 1928 (Germany).

magnetism, first described 1600 by William Gilbert (q.v.); connection with electricity demonstrated 1820 by Hans Christian Oersted (q.v.) and François Arago (q.v.).

magnets. See **electromagnets.**

Magnus I (d. 1047), king of Norway 1035–1047, and of Denmark 1042–47.

Magnus II (d. 1069), king of Norway 1066–1069, divided kingdom with brother Olaf.

Magnus III (1073–1103), king of Norway 1093–1103, led expeditions against Britain; killed in Ireland.

Magnus IV (d. 1139), king of Norway 1130–35, lost civil war; blinded.

Magnus V (d. 1184), king of Norway 1162–1184, overthrown after long civil war.

Magnus VI (1238–80), king of Norway 1263–80, was a noted legal reformer.

Magnus VII (1316–74), king of Norway 1319–43; resigned crown to his son; king of Sweden as Magnus II 1319–65.

Magnusson, Finnur (1781–1847), Icelandic archaeologist, wrote on Norse literature and mythology.

Magritte, René (1898–1967), Belgian Surrealist painter, cool and enigmatic in feeling.

Magsaysay, Ramón (1907–57), Philippino soldier and statesman, president 1953–57.

Mahabhārata, Indian epic, evolved c. 400 B.C. to c. A.D. 200.

Mahan, Alfred Thayer (1840–1914), American naval historian, wrote *Influence of Sea Power Upon History* (1890).

Maharashtra, Indian state, formed 1960 from Bombay (q.v.).

Mahavira (6th cent. B.C.), Indian sage, founder of Jainism.

Mahdi, The (title assumed by Mohammed Ahmed; *c.* 1843–1885), Sudanese religious leader, led uprising in which Charles Gordon (*q.v.*) was killed.

Mahler, Gustav (1860–1911), major Austrian composer, noted for his symphonic works; also a famous conductor.

Mahmud I (1696–1754), sultan of Turkey 1730–54; recovered Belgrade from Austria 1739.

Mahmud II (1785–1839), sultan of Turkey 1808–39, forced to grant Greek independence, 1829.

Mahomet. See Mohammed.

Mahon, Charles James (1800–91), Irish adventurer, served in several European armies and in the Union army in the U.S.A.

Maiden Castle, Dorset, developed as a cattle corral in early Iron Age; fortified *c.* 250 B.C.; stormed and captured by the Romans A.D. 43; inhabitation ended A.D. 70; excavated 1934–37 by Sir Mortimer Wheeler.

Mailer, Norman (b. 1923), American novelist, author of *The Naked and the Dead* (1948).

Maillol, Aristide (1861–1944), French sculptor, chiefly of nude figures.

Maimonides (1135–1204), Spanish-born Jewish philosopher; his *Guide for the Perplexed* synthesized Judaism and Aristotelianism.

Maine, Sir Henry (1822–88), English legal expert, much involved in Indian affairs, wrote *Early Law and Custom* (1883).

Maine, U.S. battleship, blown up in Havana Harbour 1898.

Maine, U.S.A., first successful settlement 1623; admitted to the Union 1820.

mainspring, invented *c.* 1510 by a German locksmith Peter Henlein.

Maintenon, Françoise, Madame de (1635–1719), queen of France as wife of Louis XIV 1685–1715, influenced him towards piety and intolerance.

Maistre, Joseph de (1753–1821), French writer and diplomat, upholder of conservatism in politics.

Maitland, Frederick William (1850–1906), English legal historian, wrote several standard works.

Maitland, William (*c.* 1528–73), Scottish noble, much involved in intrigues of Mary Queen of Scots' reign.

Majorca, Spanish Mediterranean island, conquered 1229 by James I of Aragon; united to Aragon in mid-14th century.

Majorian (d. A.D. 461), Roman emperor 457–61, attempted reforms but forced to abdicate.

Makarios III (1913–77), Cypriot archbishop and statesman, president of Cyprus 1959–77.

Malacca, Malaysia, founded 14th century;

taken for Portugal by Albuquerque 1511; captured by Dutch 1641; became British colony 1824; under Japanese control 1942–1945; part of independent Federation of Malaya 1957; a state of Malaysia since 1963.

Malachy, Saint (*c.* 1094–1148), Irish monk, archbishop of Armagh, introduced Cistercian order to France.

Malagasy Republic, discovered 1500 by the Portuguese navigator Diego Diaz; became a united Kingdom 1810; made a French protectorate 1895 and a colony 1896; French overseas territory 1946; achieved independence as a republic 1960.

Malamud, Bernard (b. 1914), American novelist, author of *The Fixer* (1966).

Malan, Daniel François (1874–1959), South African statesman, as prime minister 1948–54 introduced apartheid.

malaria parasite, discovered 1897 in the anopheles mosquito by Sir Ronald Ross (*q.v.*).

Malatesta, Enrico (1850–1932), Italian anarchist, edited periodicals in Italy, France and U.S.A.

Malatesta, Sigismonde (*c.* 1417–68), Italian tyrant, ruler of Rimini; patron of the arts.

Malawi, constituted 1891 as the British protectorate of Nyasaland; federated with Rhodesia 1953–63; achieved independence as Malawi 1964; became a republic 1966.

Malaya, occupied over 6000 years, under influence of India and other SE Asian empires and later of European trading nations; united 1826 as the Straits Settlements; placed under direct British rule 1867; Japanese occupation 1941–44; Federation of Malaya (now peninsular Malaysia) formed 1948 out of smaller federation of Malay states 1896; became independent 1957; joined federation of Malaysia 1963.

Malaysia, independent federation, formed Sept. 1963, consisting of the Federation of Malaya, Singapore, Sabah and Sarawak; Singapore seceded 1965.

Malcolm I (d. 954), king of Scotland 943–954, received Cumbria by treaty 945.

Malcolm II (d. 1034), king of Scotland 1005–34, recognized overlordship of Canute.

Malcolm III (d. 1093), king of Scotland 1057–93, overthrew Macbeth.

Malcolm IV (1141–65), king of Scotland 1153–65, lost Northumberland and Cumberland.

Malcontents, Treaty of the, between Catholic nobles in the Netherlands and the Prince of Parma, 19 May 1579.

Maldive Islands, Indian Ocean, under British protection 1887–1965; achieved complete independence 1965; became a republic 1968.

Maldon, Battle of, victory of the Danes over the Anglo-Saxons, 991.

Mâle, Émile (1862–1954), French art historian, wrote *L'An Mil.*

Malebranch, Nicolas (1638–1715), French philosopher, wrote *Recherche de la Vérité* (1674–75).

Malenkov, Georgi (b. 1902), Soviet statesman, prime minister of the U.S.S.R. 1953–1955.

Malesherbes, Chrétien de (1721–94), French statesman, held ministerial office 1775–76 and 1787–88; guillotined during the Terror.

Malherbe, François de (1555–1628), French court poet, influential in advocacy of clarity and exactness.

Mali, became part of French West Africa 1899 as French Sudan; French overseas territory 1946; became a republic within the French Community 1958; formed Federation of Mali with Senegal 1959; achieved complete independence 1960; federation with Senegal dissolved 1960.

Malinowski, Bronislaw (1884–1942), Polish-born pioneer of anthropology in Britain and U.S.A.

Malipiero, Gian Francesco (1882–1973), Italian composer of both traditional and 12-tone music.

Mallarmé, Stéphane (1842–98), French poet, a leading figure in Symbolist movement, wrote *Après-midi d'un faune* (1876).

Mallet, David (c. 1705–65), Scottish poet, wrote *William and Margaret* (1723).

Mallorca. See **Majorca.**

Malmö, Treaty of, signed 1523 between the Danes and the Swedish national leader, later king, Gustavus Vasa.

Malone, Edmund (1741–1812), Irish critic, published an edition of Shakespeare.

Malory, Sir Thomas (d. 1471), English writer of *Le Morte D'Arthur*, a landmark in English prose narrative.

Malpighi, Marcello (1628–94), Italian anatomist, used microscope to make discoveries, including the capillary network.

Malplaquet, Battle of, victory of an Anglo-Dutch-Austrian army under the Duke of Marlborough (*q.v.*), over the French, 11 Sept. 1709.

Malraux, André (1901–76), French novelist and Gaullist minister, author of *La Condition humaine* (1933); active participant in Chinese and Spanish Civil Wars.

Malta, conquered by Arabs 870; joined to Sicily 1090–1530; ruled by Knights of St John of Jerusalem 1530–1798; captured by Napoleon Bonaparte 1798; annexed to Britain by the Treaty of Paris; awarded George Cross by George VI April 1942; became independent 1964 and a republic within the Commonwealth 1974.

Malta, Knights of. See **Saint John of Jerusalem,** Order of the Knights of.

Malthus, Thomas (1766–1834), English clergyman, wrote pioneering *Essay on the Principle of Population* (1798).

Malvern Hill, Battle of, American Civil War, last of a series of actions in which the Confederates defeated the Union army, 1 July 1862.

Malvern College, English public school, founded 1862; opened 1865.

Malvern Festival, of English drama, instituted 1928.

Mamluks, ruled Egypt and Syria 1250–1517; power finally destroyed by a massacre in Cairo 1811.

Mamun, al- (786–833), Arab caliph of Baghdad 813–33, patron of the arts and sciences.

man. See **Homo Sapiens.**

Man, Isle of, Viking invasions 9th and 10th centuries; sold to Scotland by Norway 1266; annexed by Edward I of England 1290; ruled by the Stanley family 1406–1651 and 1660–1736, and by James Murray, Duke of Atholl 1736–64; passed to the British crown 1765; achieved considerable autonomy by 1866.

Manasseh ben Israel (1604–57), Jewish scholar in Holland, petitioned for admission of Jews to England, 1655.

Manchester Grammar School, English public school, founded by Hugh Oldham, bishop of Exeter, 1515.

Manchester Guardian. See *Guardian.*

Manchester–Liverpool railway, opened 1830. See also *Rocket.*

Manchester November Handicap, first run 1876; held at Doncaster since 1964.

Manchester Ship Canal, construction began 1887; opened 1894.

Manchester University, founded 1851 as Owens College by the bequest of John Owens (1790–1846); received charter and opened 1903 as the Victoria University of Manchester.

Manchu dynasty, China, 1644–1912.

Manchuria, region occupied by Mongols from c. 12th century; conquered China 17th century and founded Manchu dynasty; subject of dispute between Russia and Japan at end of 19th century; occupied by Japanese 1929 and established as puppet state of Manchukuo 1932; reverted to China 1945.

Mancini, Pasquale (1817–88), Italian statesman, as foreign minister 1881–85 signed Triple Alliance.

mandate system, introduced 1920 by the League of Nations; replaced 1946 by the U.N. Trusteeship system.

Mandeville, Bernard de (1670–1733), Dutch-born English writer, author of *Fable of the Bees* (1705).

Manes (c. A.D. 216–c. A.D. 276), Persian sage, founder of Manichaeism; crucified.

Manet, Édouard (1832–83), French

painter, was a noted innovator and precursor of Impressionism.

Manetho (3rd cent. B.C.), Egyptian historian, whose work is known through other writers.

Manfred (c. 1232–1266), king of Naples and Sicily 1258–66, illegitimate son of the emperor Frederick II.

manganese, recognized 1774 by Carl Scheele as an element; isolated 1774 by the Swedish scientist Johann Gahn (1745–1818).

manganese steel, developed and patented 1883 by the English metallurgist Sir Robert Hadfield (1859–1940).

Manhattan Island, bought from Indians 1626 by Peter Minuit (c. 1580–1638) for the Dutch West India Company.

Manhattan Project, for U.S. nuclear bomb development, activated June 1942; experimental bomb detonated July 1945 at Alamogordo, New Mexico; bombs dropped on Japan Aug. 1945.

Mani. See **Manes.**

Mangla Reservoir, Indus Basin, Pakistan, comprising three dams, completed 1967.

Manila Bay, Battle of, victory of the U.S. navy over the Spanish Pacific fleet, 1 May 1898.

Manila Conference, held Sept. 1954, led to formation of South East Asia Treaty Organization.

Manin, Daniele (1804–57), Italian revolutionary-nationalist, president of Venetian republic 1848–49; overthrown by Austrians.

Manipur, Indian state, first established treaty relations with Britain 1762; uprising 1890; invaded by Japanese 1944; centrally administered territory of India from 1947; established as a state 1972.

Manitoba, Canada, Hudson's Bay Company post established 1670; Red River Settlement founded 1811; admitted to the Canadian confederation 1870.

Manley, Mary de la Rivière (c. 1663–1724), English author of scandalous *Secret Memoirs* (1709); was also a pamphleteer and playwright.

Manlius, Capitolinus (d. 384 B.C.), Roman consul, repelled invasion of city by Gauls.

Manlius, Titus (4th cent. B.C.), Roman general and political leader, executed own son for disobedience.

man-made fibres, first one produced 1883 by Sir Joseph Swan (q.v.); industry established (for rayon) c. 1885 by the French chemist Hilaire, Comte de Chardonnet (1839–1924).

Mann, Heinrich (1871–1950), German novelist, whose *Professor Unrat* (1904) was made into the film *The Blue Angel.*

Mann, Thomas (1875–1955), a major German novelist, author of *Buddenbrooks* (1901); brother of Heinrich Mann.

Mann Act (White Slave Traffic Act), U.S. congressional act 1910, put through by James Robert Mann (1856–1922).

Mannerheim, Baron Carl von (1867–1951), Finnish soldier and statesman, president of Finland 1944–46.

Mannheim, Karl (1893–1947), Austrian sociologist, author of *Ideology and Utopia* (1940).

Manning, Henry, Cardinal (1808–92), English Anglican clergyman converted to Catholicism; archbishop of Westminster 1865–92.

Mannying, Robert (d. c. 1340), English poet and chronicler, wrote *Handlyng Synne.*

Mansart, François (1598–1666), French architect, designed Val-de-Grâce, Paris, and also châteaux, churches, etc.

Mansart, Jules Hardouin (1645–1708), French architect, great-nephew of François Mansart, designed parts of Hôtel des Invalides and Versailles.

Mansell, Sir Robert (1573–1656), English admiral, active against Spanish, Portuguese and Algerians.

Mansfield, Katherine (1888–1923), New Zealand-born short story writer in England, author of *The Garden Party* (1922).

Mansfield College, Oxford University, founded 1886.

Manship, Paul (1885–1966), American sculptor, e.g. *Abraham Lincoln.*

Mansion House, London, designed 1739 by the English architect George Dance the elder (q.v.); finished 1753; reconstructed 1930–31.

Mansur (d. 775), Abbasid caliph 754–775, established Baghdad as capital 762.

Mantegna, Andrea (1431–1506), Italian painter, strongly influenced by classical antiquity, e.g. *Triumphs of Caesar.*

Mantell, Gideon (1790–1852), English palaeontologist, studied dinosaur remains and wrote popularizing books.

Manu, Laws of, Brahman code, composed before 3rd century B.C.

Manuel I (c. 1120–1180), Byzantine emperor 1143–80, survived many threats from foreign enemies.

Manuel II (1350–1425), Byzantine emperor 1391–1425, tried to secure help from the West against the Turks.

Manuel I (1469–1521), king of Portugal 1495–1521, the great age of Portuguese discoveries.

Manuel II (1889–1932), king of Portugal 1908–10, overthrown by revolution.

Manutius, Aldus (1450–1515), Italian printer and scholar in Venice, produced many superb editions.

Manzoni, Alessandro (1785–1873), Italian novelist, wrote *I Promessi Sposi* (1827).

Maoism, Communist doctrine developed in 1950s by Mao Tse-tung (q.v.).

Maori Wars, New Zealand, began 1860; ended 1872.

Mao Tse-tung (1893–1976), Chinese revolutionary leader, founder of the Chinese Communist state.

Map, Walter (d. *c.* 1208), Welsh writer, in Latin, of witty mélange *De Nugis Curialium.*

Mapungubwe, northern Transvaal, ruins of a late Iron Age trading centre, erected 12th to 16th centuries.

Mar, John, Earl of (1675–1732), Scottish Jacobite leader in 1715 rebellion.

Marat, Jean Paul (1743–93), French Revolutionary leader and influential journalist, assassinated by Charlotte Corday (*q.v.*).

Marathon, Battle of, victory of the Greeks over the Persians Sept. 490 B.C.

Marbeck, John (d. *c.* 1585), English composer, adapted plain chant to Protestant prayerbook; narrowly escaped burning for heresy.

Marble Arch, London, built 1828 at entrance to Buckingham Palace; re-erected at Cumberland Gate, Hyde Park, 1851.

marbling, printing process, came into use in England late in the 17th century.

Marburg Colloquy, Protestant conference, held 1529.

Marc, Franz (1880–1916), German painter, notably of expressively coloured animals.

Marcellinus, Saint (d. 304), Pope 296–304, during persecutions by Diocletian.

Marchand, Jean Baptiste (1863–1934), French soldier and explorer, figured prominently in the 'Fashoda Incident'.

Marchmont, Patrick Hume, Earl of (1641–1724), Scottish statesman, lord chancellor of Scotland 1696–1702.

Marcion of Sinope (2nd cent. A.D.), Christian Gnostic, founded Marcionite sect.

Marco Polo. See **Polo,** Marco.

Marconi, Guglielmo (1874–1937), Italian physicist, pioneer in the use of wireless telegraphy; awarded Nobel Prize for Physics 1909.

Marcus Aurelius (A.D. 121–180), Roman emperor 161–180, a period of stability; wrote stoic *Meditations.*

Marcuse, Herbert (b. 1898), American sociologist, noted for his criticism of the values of Western society.

Mardi Gras, the last day of carnival, celebrated on Shrove Tuesday.

Marées, Hans von (1837–87), German painter, notably of frescoes.

Marengo, Battle of, victory of Napoleon and the French army over the Austrians, 14 June 1800.

Marey, Étienne Jules (1830–1904), French physiologist, inventor of the ciné camera.

Margaret, Saint (d. 1093), Anglo-Saxon princess, married Malcolm III of Scotland; re-founded Iona.

Margaret (1353–1412), queen of Denmark, Norway and Sweden, effectively united Scandinavia under her rule.

Margaret (1283–90), known as the Maid of Norway, titular queen of Scotland 1286–90; died on journey to England.

Margaret of Anjou (1430–82), queen of England as wife of Henry VI, involved in dynastic struggles of York and Lancaster.

Margaret of Navarre (1492–1549), queen of Henry II of Navarre, wrote *L'Heptaméron,* modelled on Boccaccio's tales.

Margaret Tudor (1489–1541), queen of Scotland as wife of James IV; after his death embroiled in internal politics.

margarine, invented in 1860s by the French chemist H. Mège-Mouriès (1817–80).

Margraaf, Andreas (1709–82), German chemist, discovered existence of sugar in sugar-beet.

Margrethe II (b. 1940), queen of Denmark since 1972.

Maria I (1734–1816), queen of Portugal 1777–86, feeble minded and dominated by others.

Maria II (1819–53), queen of Portugal 1826–53; period of conflict between Conservatives and Liberals.

Maria Cristina (1806–78), queen of Spain 1829–33 as wife of Ferdinand VII; regent during Carlist Wars.

Maria Cristina (1858–1929), queen of Spain as wife of Alfonso XII and regent after his death in 1885.

Maria Theresa (1717–80), empress of Austria as wife of Francis I, and queen of Hungary and Bohemia; involved in long struggle to retain Hapsburg possessions.

Marianas, Pacific Islands, discovered 1521 by Ferdinand Magellan; colonized 1668; Japanese mandate from 1919; except for Guam (*q.v.*), became part of the Trust Territory of the Pacific Islands, 1947, administered by the U.S.A.

Marianus Scotus (*c.* 1028–1083), Irish monk, wrote a *Universal Chronicle.*

Marie Amélie (1782–1866), queen of France 1830–48 as wife of Louis Philippe.

Marie Antoinette (1755–93), Austrian-born queen of France as wife of Louis XVI; guillotined during Revolution.

Marie Byrd Land, or Byrd Land, Antarctica, discovered 1929 by the American Richard E. Byrd (*q.v.*).

Marie de France (12th cent.), French poet, author of *Fables* and *Lais.*

Marie de Médicis (1573–1642), Italian-born queen of Henry IV of France, regent 1610–17; vainly opposed Richelieu.

Marie Leszczynska (1703–68), queen of France as wife of Louis XV.

Mariette, Auguste (1821–81), French Egyptologist, relocated many important monuments.

Marie Louise (1791–1847), Austrian archduchess, second wife of the emperor Napoleon I, later duchess of Parma.

Marignano, Battle of, French victory over the Swiss, 13–14 Sept. 1515.

Marin, John (1872–1953), American painter, was a noted water-colour artist.

Mariner, series of unmanned American spacecraft: *Mariners* 4 (1965), 6 and 7 (1969), and 9 (1971–72) photographed Mars; *Mariner* 10 (1974) photographed Venus cloud cover and Mercury.

Marinetti, Filippo (1876–1944), Italian writer, pioneered the Futurist movement in literature.

Marini, Marino (b. 1901), Italian sculptor, chiefly of equestrian figures.

Mario, Giuseppe (1810–83), Italian operatic tenor, gifted interpreter of Verdi.

Marion, Francis (c. 1732–95), American soldier in the Revolutionary War, used swamps as a guerrilla base.

Mariotte, Edme (c. 1620–84), French physicist, whose discoveries included the independent formulation of Boyle's Law.

Maris, Willem (1844–1910), Dutch painter of landscape and animals, worked extensively in Britain.

Marischal College, Aberdeen, founded 1593 by George Keith, Earl Marischal (c. 1553–1623); united 1860 with King's College as the University of Aberdeen.

Marisco, Geoffrey de (d. 1245), English justiciar, ruled Ireland for King John and Henry III.

Marists, Catholic orders: Fathers, founded 1824 by Jean-Claude-Marie Colin (1790–1875), received papal approval 1836; Brothers, founded 1817; Sisters, founded 1816; Third Order, founded 1850.

Maritain, Jacques (1882–1973), French neo-Thomist philosopher, wrote *Art and Scholasticism* (1920).

Marius, Gaius (c. 155–86 B.C.), Roman soldier and consul, defeated Jugurtha, destroyed Cimbri and Teutones; rival of Sulla (q.v.).

Marivaux, Pierre de (1688–1763), French novelist and writer of wittily analytical plays about love.

Mark, Saint (1st cent. A.D.), Christian apostle and evangelist, author of the second New Testament gospel.

Mark Antony. See **Antony,** Mark.

Markham, Sir Clement (1830–1916), English geographer and historian, wrote extensively about his travels in South America, the Arctic, India, etc.

Markham, Gervase (1568–1637), English poet and writer, notably on husbandry, forestry, etc.

Markova, Dame Alicia (b. 1910), English ballerina, performed with Russian Ballet and Vic-Wells; headed Festival Ballet 1949–52.

Marlborough, John Churchill, Duke of (1650–1722), English soldier, won major victories over the French in the War of the Spanish Succession.

Marlborough, Sarah, Duchess of (1660–1744), wife of the Duke of Marlborough, favourite of Queen Anne until 1710.

Marlborough College, English public school, founded 1843; incorporated by royal charter 1958, replacing original charters of 1845 and 1853.

Marlowe, Christopher (1564–93), major English poet and playwright, wrote *Doctor Faustus*; killed in tavern brawl.

Marmont, Auguste (1774–1852), French soldier, one of Napoleon's marshals; went over to Bourbons 1814.

Marmontel, Jean (1723–99), French playwright and critic, disciple of Voltaire.

Marne, Battle of the, World War I, 1st 5–9 Sept. 1914; 2nd 15 July–7 Aug. 1918, leading to German retreat.

Maronites, Christian community, appeared in the Lebanon c. 681; reconciled to Rome 1182; massacred by the Druses 1860.

Marot, Clément (c. 1495–1544), French poet, noted for his graceful satirical verse.

Marprelate, Martin (16th cent.), pseudonym of unidentified author(s) of puritan tracts against English episcopacy 1588–89.

Marquesas Islands, south Pacific, annexed by the French 1842; became an administrative division of the Overseas Territory of French Polynesia 1958.

Marquette, Jacques (1637–75), French Jesuit missionary in America, made extensive explorations.

Marquis, Don (1878–1937), American humorist, wrote *archy and mehitabel* (1927).

marriages, clandestine, abolished in England 1754; civil marriages legalized 1836.

Married Women's Property Act, Britain, became law 1883.

Marryat, Frederick (1792–1848), English naval officer and novelist of the sea, e.g. *Mr Midshipman Easy* (1836).

Mars, orbit studied 1609 by Kepler (q.v.); surface and atmosphere investigated by *Mariner* spacecraft (q.v.); first Mars soft landings 1976 by the American *Viking* spacecraft.

Marseillaise, composed and written 1792 by Rouget de Lisle; finally accepted as French national anthem 1879.

Marsh, James (1794–1846), English chemist, worked on poisons and devised Marsh test for arsenic.

Marshal, William (d. 1219), English nobleman, trusted royal adviser-administrator during three reigns.

Marshall, Alfred (1842–1924), English economist, noted for his development of the concept of marginal utility.

Marshall, John (1755–1835), American

jurist, chief justice of the Supreme Court 1801–35.

Marshall Islands, Pacific, discovered 1529; Japanese mandate from 1919; became part of the Trust Territories of the Pacific Islands, 1947, administered by the U.S.A.

Marshall Plan, concerning European post-war recovery, proposed 1947 by the U.S. secretary of state, George C. Marshall (1880–1959); implemented 1948–52.

Marshalsea Prison, London, established by 1310; demolished 1849.

Marsilius of Padua (*c.* 1275–1342), Italian writer of *Defensor Pacis* (1324), arguing state supremacy over the Church.

Marston, John (*c.* 1575–1634), English playwright, wrote *Antonio and Mellida* (1602).

Marston Moor, Battle of, Parliamentarian victory over the Royalists, 2 July 1644.

Martello Towers, English coastal defences, built at the end of the 18th century.

Marten, Maria (d. 1827), English village girl murdered by William Corder; subject of famous melodrama 1830.

Martha's Vineyard, Mass., discovered 1602 by the English navigator Bartholomew Gosnold (d. 1607).

Marti, José (1853–95), Cuban revolutionary hero, killed leading revolt against Spain.

Martial (*c.* A.D. 40–104), Roman epigrammatic poet born in Spain, was a shrewd, often obscene social commentator.

Martianus Capella (5th cent. A.D.), Latin writer born in North Africa, whose miscellany *Satyricon* is of historical value.

Martin, Saint (*c.* 316–*c.* 399), bishop of Tours, patron saint of France and also of innkeepers.

Martin I, Saint (d. 655), Pope 649–655, deposed by Emperor Constans II.

Martin IV (*c.* 1210–1285), Pope 1281–85, tried to intervene on French side in Sicily.

Martin V (1368–1431), Pope 1417–31; his election ended Great Schism.

Martin, John (1789–1854), English painter, often on large scale depicting heroic or catastrophic events.

Martin du Gard, Roger (1881–1958), French novelist, wrote multi-volume *Les Thibault*; Nobel prizewinner 1937.

Martineau, Harriet (1802–76), English writer of didactic popular stories.

Martini, Giovanni Battista (1706–84), Italian monk, composer, distinguished music scholar and teacher.

Martini, Simone (*c.* 1283–1344), Italian painter, one of the leaders of the Sienese school.

Martinique, Caribbean, sighted 1493; visited 1502 by Christopher Columbus; French possession since 1635 except for British occupation 1762–63, 1794–1802

and 1809–14; became a French overseas department 1946.

Martinmas, Feast of St Martin, celebrated 11th Nov.

Martinson, Harry (b. 1904), Swedish poet and dramatist, author of *The Songs of Aniara* (1956).

Martinů, Bohuslav (1890–1959), Czech composer of operas and symphonic works, lived mainly in Paris and U.S.A.

Martyn, Henry (1781–1812), English missionary in India, made Bible translations.

Marvell, Andrew (1621–78), English poet and satirist, wrote *Cromwell's Return from Ireland* (1650).

Marx, Groucho (1890–1977), American actor, with his brothers made famous comedy films.

Marx, Karl (1818–83), German Socialist, in London 1849–83, developed complete world-view underlying modern Marxism and Communism; author of *Das Kapital*.

Marxism, Communist doctrine first developed *c.* 1848 by Karl Marx and Friedrich Engels (*q.v.*).

Marxism–Leninism, Soviet Marxism developed by Lenin in 1890s; modified by Joseph Stalin in late 1930s.

Mary I (1516–58), queen of England and Ireland 1553–58, known as 'bloody Mary'; restored Catholicism and persecuted Protestants.

Mary II (1662–94), queen of England, Scotland and Ireland 1689–94, jointly with husband William III.

Mary (known as Mary Queen of Scots; 1542–87), queen of Scotland 1542–68; overthrown and imprisoned in England 1568–87; implicated in plots; beheaded.

Mary (1867–1953), queen of Great Britain and Northern Ireland 1910–36 as wife of George V.

Mary Celeste, ship, found abandoned 5 Dec. 1872 in the Atlantic.

Maryland, U.S.A., first settled 1634; one of the 13 original states of the Union.

Maryland University, Baltimore, founded 1807; enlarged 1920.

Marylebone Cricket Club. See **M.C.C.**

Mary of Burgundy (1457–82), duchess of Burgundy, married Maximilian of Austria 1477, making the Low Countries a Hapsburg possession.

Mary of Guise (1515–60), queen of Scotland as wife of James V and later regent 1554–59; mother of Mary Queen of Scots.

Mary of Hungary (1505–58), queen of Hungary 1522–26 and regent of the Netherlands 1531–55.

Mary of Modena (1658–1718), queen of England, Scotland and Ireland as wife of James II.

Masaccio (1401–*c.* 1428), Italian painter, revolutionized art with new realism and emotional force.

Masaniello (c. 1623–1647), Italian fisherman, led anti-Spanish revolt, but later murdered by mob.

Masaryk, Jan (1886–1948), Czech statesman, foreign minister 1940–48, died after Communist coup in mysterious circumstances.

Masaryk, Tomáš (1850–1937), Czech statesman, first president of Czechoslovakia 1918–37.

Mascagni, Pietro (1863–1945), Italian composer of opera *Cavalleria Rusticana* (1890).

Masefield, John (1878–1967), English poet and dramatist, poet laureate 1930–67; wrote much about the sea.

maser, microwave amplifier, first constructed 1953 by Charles H. Townes (q.v.) and colleagues; development work also done 1950 by the German-French physicist Alfred Kastler (b. 1902).

Masham, Abigail, Lady (d. 1734), English favourite of Queen Anne, replacing Duchess of Marlborough, 1710.

Maskelyne, Nevil (1732–1811), English astronomer, whose work led to great advances in navigation.

Masolino (c. 1383–c. 1447), Italian painter, associate and perhaps master of Masaccio.

Mason, Alfred Edward Woodley (1865–1948), English novelist and playwright, author of *Fire over England* (1936).

Mason, John (1586–1635), English founder of New Hampshire 1629–31.

Mason, Lowell (1792–1872), American composer of hymn and psalm tunes.

Mason and Dixon Line, boundary fixed between Maryland and Pennsylvania 1763–67 by the English surveyors Charles Mason and Jeremiah Dixon.

Maspero, Gaston (1846–1916), French Egyptologist, discovered royal mummies at Deir-el-Bahri 1881.

Massachusetts, U.S.A., first settled 1620; one of the 13 original states of the Union.

Massachusetts Bay Company, granted territory 1628 by the Council of New England; grant ratified by royal charter 1629.

Massachusetts Institute of Technology, founded Boston 1861; opened 1865; moved to Cambridge, Mass., 1916.

mass action, law of, formulated 1864 by the Norwegian scientists Cato M. Guldberg (1836–1902), and Peter Waage (1833–1900); translated and published 1879 in Germany.

Masséna, André (1758–1817), French soldier, one of Napoleon's marshals, fought in Italy, Switzerland, Austria and Spain.

mass-energy. See **conservation of mass and energy.**

Massenet, Jules (1842–1912), French composer of opera *Manon* (1884).

Massey, Vincent (1887–1967), Canadian statesman and diplomat, governor-general of Canada 1952–59.

Massine, Léonide (b. 1896), Russian dancer and choreographer, created such ballets as *The Three-Cornered Hat* (1919).

Massinger, Philip (1583–1640), English playwright, wrote *A New Way to Pay Old Debts* (1633).

Massingham, Henry William (1860–1924), English journalist, edited the *Nation* (1907–23).

Masson, David (1822–1907), Scottish editor and critic, wrote *Life of Milton* (1859–80).

mass production, originated in 18th century; modern technique begun 1913 by Henry Ford (q.v.) at the Ford Motor Company.

mass spectrometers, focusing types, first built 1919 by Francis William Aston (q.v.).

Massys, Quentin (c. 1466–1530), Flemish painter, leading figure in the Antwerp school.

Master-gunner of England, office last held from 1709 by Colonel James Pendlebury (d. c. 1758).

Master of the Queen's Music, title originated c. 1625; first master Nicholas Lanier (1588–1666).

Masters, Edgar Lee (1869–1950), American poet, wrote *Spoon River Anthology* (1915).

mastoid, operation first successfully performed 1774 by the French surgeon Jean Louis Petit.

Masurian Lakes, Battles of the, German victory over the Russians 6–15 Sept. 1914; 2nd German offensive Feb. 1915.

Mata Hari (pseud. of Gertrud Zelle; 1876–1917), Dutch dancer, executed by French as a German spy.

Matapan, Battle of, World War II, victory of the British Navy over an Italian fleet 27–28 March 1941.

matches, friction, using phosphorus, invented 1816 by the Frenchman François Derosne; 'promethean' matches invented 1828 by the Englishman Samuel Jones; safety matches patented 1855 by the Swede J. E. Lundström; book matches invented 1892 by the American Joshua Pusey.

Mather, Cotton (1663–1728), American Congregational clergyman, associated with Massachusetts witchcraft trials 1692–93.

Mather, Increase (1639–1723), American Congregationalist clergyman, father of Cotton Mather, helped calm fears of witchcraft.

Mathews, Charles James (1803–78), English comedian and dramatist, played in England, France and the U.S.A.

Matilda (1102–87), wife of the Holy Roman emperor Henry V and claimant to the English throne; mother of Henry II of England.

Matisse, Henri (1869–1954), French painter, at first a Fauve and later a colourist, working with calm, simplified forms.

Matsys, Quentin. See **Massys,** Quentin.

Matteotti, Giacomo (1885–1924), Italian Socialist leader, murdered by Fascists.

Matterhorn, mountain on Swiss–Italian frontier, first climbed 1865 by Edward Whymper (q.v.).

Matthay, Tobias (1858–1945), English piano virtuoso and teacher, wrote books on piano technique.

Matthew, Saint (1st cent. A.D.), Christian apostle and evangelist, author of the first New Testament gospel.

Matthew of Paris. See **Paris,** Matthew of.

Matthew, Tobias (1546–1628), English prelate, archbishop of York 1606–28, enforced conformity.

Matthews, Sir Stanley (b. 1915), English footballer, the first to receive a knighthood.

Matthias (1557–1619), Holy Roman emperor 1612–19; the end of his reign marked the beginning of the Thirty Years' War.

Matthias Corvinus (1440–90), king of Hungary 1458–90, created powerful monarchy.

Maturin, Charles (1782–1824), Irish novelist, wrote Gothic tale *Melmoth the Wanderer* (1820).

Maud (1080–1118), queen of England as wife of Henry I.

Maudslay, Henry (1771–1831), English engineer, made a number of useful inventions including a screwcutting lathe.

Maugham, William Somerset (1874–1965), English novelist and playwright, achieved vast popularity with *Of Human Bondage* (1915), etc.

Mau Mau, terrorist movement in Kenya in early 1950s; state of emergency declared Oct. 1952; ended 1957.

Maundy Thursday, commemoration on the Thursday before Easter of Christ's washing of the Apostles' feet.

Maupassant, Guy de (1850–93), French short-story writer, author of *Boule de Suif* (1880).

Maupeou, René de (1714–92), French statesman, chancellor 1768–74.

Maupertuis, Pierre Louis (1698–1759), French mathematician, worked in Berlin; ardent supporter of Newton.

Maurepas, Jean de (1701–81), French statesman, held ministerial office 1738–49 and 1774–81.

Mauretania, Atlantic passenger liner, launched 20 Sept. 1906.

Mauriac, François (1885–1970), French novelist, author of *Thérèse Desqueyroux* (1927), awarded Nobel Prize 1952.

Maurice (A.D. 540–602), Byzantine emperor 582–602, defeated Persians and Avars.

Maurice of Nassau (1567–1625), Dutch soldier, leader of his country's forces in the struggle with Spain.

Mauritania, West Africa, region opened up by Portuguese 15th century; became French protectorate 1903, and a colony 1921; created a French overseas territory 1946 and an autonomous republic within the French Community 1958; achieved independence 1960 as the Islamic Republic of Mauritania.

Mauritius, Indian Ocean, discovered 1505 by the Portuguese; occupied by the Dutch 1598–1710, by the French 1715–1810; ceded to Britain 1814; became independent 1968.

Maurois, André (1885–1967), French writer, notable as a biographer of Shelley, Hugo, Chateaubriand, Balzac, etc.

Maurras, Charles (1868–1952), French writer, editor of royalist *Action Française,* imprisoned as a collaborator after World War II.

Maury, Jean Siffrein (1746–1817), French prelate, archbishop of Paris 1810–14; supported Napoleon.

Maury, Matthew Fontaine (1806–73), American naval officer, engaged in oceanographic research.

Mauve, Anton (1838–88), Dutch painter of atmospheric landscapes, in both oils and watercolours.

mauveine, first synthetic dye, discovered 1856 by Sir William Perkin (q.v.).

Mavrocordato, Alexander (1791–1865), Greek patriot, one of the leaders in the struggle for independence.

Mawson, Sir Douglas (1882–1958), English explorer and geologist, took part in several Antarctic expeditions.

Maxentius (d. A.D. 312), Roman emperor 306–312, lost Battle of the Milvian Bridge to Constantine.

Maxim, Sir Hiram Stevens (1840–1916), American-born inventor of the machine-gun named after him, 1884.

Maximian (d. 310), Roman emperor 286–305; abdicated, recalled by son 306–308; failed to overthrow Constantine; committed suicide.

Maximilian I (1459–1519), Holy Roman emperor 1493–1519; made advantageous marriage alliances.

Maximilian II (1527–76), Holy Roman emperor 1564–76, tolerated Protestants; made truce with Turks.

Maximilian (1832–67), Austrian archduke, emperor of Mexico 1864–67 with French support; overthrown and executed.

Maximilian I (1756–1825), elector 1799–1805 and king of Bavaria 1806–25, supported Napoleon.

Maximilian II (1811–64), king of Bavaria 1848–64, came to the throne as a result of the 1848 revolution.

Maximinus (d. A.D. 238), Roman emperor 235–238, overthrew Severus; killed by his own soldiers.

Maximinus (d. A.D. 314), Roman emperor 308–314, ruled Asian provinces; defeated by Licinius.

Maximus, Saint (c. 580–662), Byzantine Christian monk, opposed Monothelite heresy.

Maximum (d. A.D. 388), Roman emperor 383–388, controlled Gaul, Spain and Britain; defeated by Theodosius.

Max-Müller, Friedrich (1823–1900), German-born philologist in England, pioneer of oriental studies.

Maxton, James (1885–1946), Scottish Socialist, chairman of the Independent Labour Party 1926–31 and 1934–39.

Maxwell, James Clerk (1831–79), Scottish physicist, developed electromagnetic theory.

Maxwell's Equations, concerning electromagnetic waves, formulated 1864–73 by James Clerk Maxwell.

May, Phil (1864–1903), English cartoonist of 'guttersnipes' and other low-life types.

Mayakovsky, Vladimir (1893–1930), Russian poet, combined futurist–modernist style with Communist dedication.

May, Thomas (1595–1650), English poet and historian of the Long Parliament.

Mayan Civilization, in parts of Mexico and Central America, developed 1st millennium B.C.; flourished from c. A.D. 300 to Spanish conquest in mid-16th century.

Maybach, Wilhelm (1847–1929), German engineer, partnered Gottfried Daimler (q.v.) in the production of internal-combustion engines.

May Day, festival dates back to pre-Christian Europe; public holiday in medieval and Tudor England; designated International Labour Day by the International Socialist Congress 1889; now an important holiday in Communist and some other countries; public holiday in Britain from 1978.

Mayenne, Charles, Duc de (1554–1611), French Catholic leader against Henry IV; reconciled 1596.

Mayer, Joseph (1803–86), English antiquary, pioneered study of Greek coins.

Mayerling Tragedy, suicide of Crown Prince Rudolf of Austria and Marie Vetsera, 30 Jan. 1889.

Mayflower. See **Pilgrim Fathers.**

Mayhew, Henry (1812–87), English writer, e.g. *London Labour and the London Poor* (1851), and founder of *Punch.*

Maynard, François (1582–1646), French poet, wrote *Philandre* (1619).

Maynooth, Irish seminary for Catholic priesthood, founded 1795.

Mayo Clinic and **Mayo Foundation for Medical Education and Research,** founded respectively 1889 and 1915 in Rochester, Minnesota, by the American surgeons and brothers William James Mayo (1861–1939) and Charles Horace Mayo (1865–1939).

mayor, first woman, Elizabeth Garrett Anderson (q.v.), elected mayor of Aldeburgh 1908.

Mayow, John (1640–79), English physician and chemist, investigated combustion and oxygen.

Mazarin, Jules, Cardinal (1602–61), Italian-born French prelate and statesman, guided France through Louis XIV's minority.

Mazarine, public library of Paris founded 1643 by Cardinal Mazarin; absorbed 1930 into the Bibliothèque Nationale.

Mazeppa, Ivan (c. 1644–1709), Ukrainian Cossack leader, failed to win independence from Russia; died in exile.

Mazzini, Giuseppe (1805–72), Italian republican revolutionary, organized Young Italy movement; triumvir of Roman Republic, 1849.

Mboya, Thomas Joseph (1930–69), Kenyan politician, prominent in pan-African politics; assassinated.

M.C.C., Marylebone Cricket Club, founded 1787; first match 1788; present ground (Lords) opened 1814.

Mead, Margaret (b. 1901), American anthropologist, author of *Coming of Age in Samoa* (1928).

Mead, Richard (1673–1754), English physician, investigated poisons and scabies.

Meade, Richard James (1832–1907), British admiral, served in Crimean War.

Meagher, Thomas Francis (1823–67), Irish-born Unionist general in the American Civil War.

Meal Tub Plot, alleged Papist conspiracy conceived and disclosed 1679 by the Englishman Thomas Dangerfield (1650–1685).

Mecca, holiest of Muslim cities, birthplace of Mohammed; captured by him 630 after his flight 622; occupied by Ottoman Turks 1517; taken Oct. 1924 by Ibn Saud, becoming part of Saudi Arabia.

Mechnikov, Ilya. See **Metchnikov,** Elie.

Medawar, Sir Peter Brian (b. 1915), English zoologist, noted for his work on immunology.

Medical Research Council, incorporated by royal charter 1920, succeeding the Medical Research Committee appointed 1913; new charter granted 1966.

Medici, family powerful in Florence from mid-14th century; became extinct 1737.

Medici, Catherine de'. See **Catherine de Médicis.**

Medici, Cosimo de' (1389–1464), Italian banker, effective ruler of Florence and a patron of the arts.

Medici, Cosimo de' (1519–74), duke of Florence 1537–74, granted title duke of Tuscany; an energetic, capable but cruel ruler.

Medici, Ferdinand de' (1549–1609), Italian ruler, duke of Tuscany 1587–1609, was an able administrator.

Medici, Giovanni de' (1498–1526), Italian soldier, killed at Battle of Mantua.

Medici, Giulio de'. See **Clement VII.**

Medici, Lorenzo de' (1449–92), Italian ruler of Florence 1469–92, poet, skilful diplomat and patron of the arts.

Medici, Maria de'. See **Marie de Médicis.**

Medina, ancient city in Saudi Arabia, home of Mohammed after his flight from Mecca 622.

Medina-Sidonia, Duke of (1550–1615), Spanish noble, commanded the Spanish Armada 1588.

Medtner, Nilolai (1879–1951), Russian composer, notably of piano music.

Meer, Jan van der (1628–91), Dutch painter specializing in landscapes.

Meerut, scene of outbreak of Indian Mutiny 10 May 1857.

Meghalaya, Indian state, created a union territory 1970; became a state 1972.

Mehemet Ali (1769–1849), Albanian-born soldier in the service of Turkey, viceroy of Egypt 1805–48.

Méhul, Étienne (1763–1817), French composer of operas, e.g. *Uthal* (1806).

Meigs, Return Jonathan (1740–1823), American soldier in Revolutionary War; later pioneer in Tennessee.

Meiji Period, era of modernization in Japan, 1868–1912, following the restoration of the Meiji emperor to the throne 1867.

Meikle, Andrew (1719–1811), Scottish engineer, invented first successful threshing machine.

Meiklejohn, John Miller (1836–1902), Scottish educationalist, wrote extensively on language.

Meilhac, Henri (1831–97), French playwright, often wrote in collaboration.

Meillet, Antoine (1866–1936), French philologist, author of studies of Indo-European languages.

Meir, Golda (b. 1898), Israeli stateswoman, prime minister 1969–73.

Meissonier, Jean Louis (1815–91), French painter of epic Napoleonic scenes.

Meitner, Lise (1878–1968), Austrian-Swedish physicist, best known for her work on nuclear physics.

Melanchthon, Philip (1497–1560), German Protestant leader and scholar, worked closely with Luther.

Melba, Dame Nellie (1861–1931), Australian soprano of remarkable virtuosity, became world famous.

Melbourne, William Lamb, 2nd Viscount (1779–1848), English statesman, as prime minister 1834–41, guided the young Queen Victoria in her duties as sovereign.

Melbourne University, Victoria, Australia, founded 1854; opened 1855.

Melchers, Gari (1860–1932), American painter, traditional in approach, e.g. *Dutch Skaters.*

Melchett, Alfred Moritz Mond, Baron (1868–1930), English industrialist and politician, son of Ludwig Mond.

Melchiades, Saint (d. 314), bishop of Rome c. 310–314, period of triumph of Constantine.

Melchior, Lauritz (1890–1973), Danish-born American singer, a notable interpreter of Wagner.

Meletius, Saint (c. 310–381), Greek prelate, bishop of Antioch, in conflict with Arians.

Mellon, Andrew William (1855–1937), American financier, ambassador to Britain 1932–33.

Melozzo da Forli. See **Forli,** Melozzo da.

Melrose Abbey, Scotland, founded by King David I 1136.

Melville, Herman (1819–91), American novelist, wrote much about the sea, notably in *Moby Dick* (1851).

Melville,' James (1556–1614), Scottish Protestant, moderator of General Assembly 1589, left a *Diary.*

Member of Parliament, 1st Quaker, 1833; 1st Jewish, Baron Lionel de Rothschild, 1858; 1st atheist Charles Bradlaugh, 1886; 1st woman (to sit in House of Commons), Lady Astor, 1919.

Memling, Hans (c. 1433–c. 1494), German-born painter in Flemish tradition, e.g. Portinari portraits.

Memorial Day, U.S.A., 30 May; first observed 1869.

Memphis Race Riot, attack by whites on black residents of Memphis, Tennessee, May 1866.

Menai Suspension Bridge, designed and built 1818–26 by Thomas Telford (*q.v.*).

Menander (342–c. 291 B.C.), Greek playwright of sophisticated 'new comedy'; only one complete play survives.

Mencius (372–c. 289 B.C.), Chinese philosopher, follower of Confucius; his *Sayings* have survived.

Mencken, Henry Louis (1880–1956), American journalist and pungent essayist, edited *American Mercury* 1924–33, wrote *The American Language* (1919).

Mendel, Gregor (1822–84), Austrian monk, pioneer of genetics, the value of whose work was recognized after his death. See **genetics.**

Mendele Moisher Sforim (1835–1917), Jewish writer, pioneer of realistic everyday literary language in both Yiddish and Hebrew.

Mendeleyev, Dmitri (1834–1907), Russian chemist, classified chemical elements.

mendelevium, transuranic element, discovered 1955 by Albert Ghiorso, Bernard G. Harvey and others.

Mendelsohn, Erich (1887–1953), German architect, e.g. Einstein Observatory, Potsdam; after 1933 worked in England, Palestine and U.S.A.

Mendelssohn-Bartholdy, Felix (1809–1847), German composer, leading figure in the Romantic movement, wrote symphonies, concertos, chamber music, incidental music, etc.

Mendelssohn, Moses (1729–86), German philosopher in Enlightenment tradition; grandfather of Felix Mendelssohn-Bartholdy.

Mendès, Catulle (1841–1909), French poet, member of Parnassian school, also a journalist and novelist.

Mendès-France, Pierre (b. 1907), French statesman, prime minister 1954–55, ended French role in Vietnam.

Menelik II (1844–1913), emperor of Ethiopia 1889–1913, defeated Italians at Adowa 1896 and secured independence.

Menendez Pidal, Ramón (1869–1968), Spanish philologist, founded Madrid Centre of Historical Studies.

Menendez y Pelayo, Marcelino (1856–1912), Spanish historian and critic, was a notable literary scholar.

Mengelberg, Willem (1871–1951), Dutch musician, conductor of the Concertgebouw Orchestra, Amsterdam, 1895–1945.

Mengs, Anton Raphael (1728–79), German painter, worked in Italy in Neo-Classical style.

Menin Gate, Ypres, Belgium, World War I memorial to the armies of the British Empire, unveiled July 1927.

Menken, Adah Isaacs (1835–68), American actress, made a sensationally successful appearance (tied naked to a horse) in *Mazeppa*.

Mennonites, Protestant movement originating along Anabaptists, founded 1537 by the Dutch priest Menno Simons (1496–1561).

Menorca. See **Minorca.**

Menotti, Gian Carlo (b. 1911), Italian-born American opera composer, e.g. *The Telephone* (1947).

Menpes, Mortimer (c. 1859–1938), Australian-born painter in England, produced many illustrations of his war experiences.

Mensheviks, moderate minority faction of the Russian Social Democratic Workers' Party, formed 1903 and led by L. Martov; expelled from party 1912 by Lenin and the Bolsheviks (q.v.).

Menshikov, Alexander (c. 1670–1729), Russian soldier, influential under Peter the Great and his successors.

mental hygiene, modern study founded by the Swiss-born psychiatrist Adolf Meyer (1866–1950).

Menton, elected by plebiscite to be annexed to France 1860.

Menuhin, Yehudi (b. 1916), American-born violin virtuoso, child prodigy, also outstanding musical organizer.

Menzies, Sir Robert (b. 1894), Australian statesman, prime minister 1939–41 and 1949–66.

Merbecke, John. See **Marbeck,** John.

Mercator, Gerardus (1512–94), Flemish cartographer, published world map 1538, and a map with 'Mercator' projection 1569.

Mercer, John (1791–1866), English chemist and calico printer, invented mercerizing process 1850.

Mercers' Company, London livery company, first recorded reference 1172; chartered 1393.

Mercers' School, London, English public school, formerly school of Hospital of St Thomas, Cheapside; refounded 1447; taken over by the Mercers' Company 1542.

Merchant Adventurers, company of English merchants chartered 1407; charter abrogated 1689; dissolved 1806.

Merchant Taylors' Company, London livery company, origins uncertain; 1st charter granted 1327 by Edward III, 6th charter by Henry VII, 1502.

Merchant Taylors' School, Crosby, English public school, founded by the merchant tailor John Harrison of London 1620.

Merchant Taylors' School, Northwood, English public school, founded by the Company of Merchant Taylors 1561.

Merchiston Castle School, Edinburgh, Scottish public school, established 1833.

Mercia, Anglo-Saxon kingdom prominent from mid-7th to early 9th century.

Mercier, Louis Sébastien (1740–1814), French playwright and critic, particularly important for his attack on classical conventions.

Merciless Parliament, condemned five of King Richard II's supporters to death, 1388.

mercury, element, known to the ancient Chinese and Hindus; found in an Egyptian tomb of c. 1500 B.C.

Mercury, planet, transit predicted by Johannes Kepler (q.v.) and first observed 1631 by Pierre Gassendi (q.v.); surface photographed by *Mariner* 10.

mercury-vapour lamp, first marketed 1901; improved 1903, by the American electrical engineer Peter Cooper Hewitt (1861–1921).

Meredith, George (1828–1909), outstanding English novelist and poet, wrote *The Egoist* (1879).

Meredith, Owen (pseud. of Lord Lytton; 1831–91), English poet, son of Bulwer Lytton (*q.v.*), author of *The Wanderer* (1857).

Merezhkovsky, Dmitri (1865–1941), Russian symbolist writer, in France 1919–41; wrote philosophical-historical novels.

Mergenthaler, Ottmar (1854–99), German-born inventor of the linotype printing process.

Mérimée, Prosper (1803–70), French writer, author of *Carmen* (1845).

Merit, Order of, Great Britain, founded 1902.

Mermaid Theatre, first English theatre in the City of London since The Restoration, opened Puddle Dock 1959.

Merovingian dynasty, ruled France 481–751.

Merriman, Henry Seton (1862–1903), English adventure novelist, author of *In Kedar's Tents* (1897).

Merry de Val, Rafael, Cardinal (1865–1930), English priest, papal secretary of state 1904–14, secretary of the Holy Office 1914–30.

Mersen, Treaty of, dividing the kingdom of Lothair II between Charles the Bald and Louis the German, signed 870.

Mersey Tunnel, Road, Liverpool–Birkenhead, construction began 1925; opened 1934; 2nd tunnel opened 1971.

Merton, Walter de (d. 1277), English prelate, justiciar and chancellor of England.

Merton College, Oxford University, founded 1264–74 by Walter de Merton.

Meryon, Charles (1821–68), French engraver, chiefly of Parisian scenes.

mesmerism, founded 1776 by the German physician Franz Mesmer (1734–1815).

mesons, subatomic particles, predicted 1935 by the Japanese physicist Hideki Yukawa (b. 1907); first one (pion) discovered 1947 by the English physicist C. F. Powell (1903–69).

Mesopotamia, centre of ancient civilizations of Sumer, Babylon and Assyria from *c.* 3000 B.C. to 7th century B.C.; subsequently under Persian, Parthian, Roman and Sassanian rule; conquered by Arabs in mid-7th century; annexed by Ottoman Turks in 17th century; became kingdom of Iraq (*q.v.*) after World War I.

Mesozoic Era, Earth history, from *c.* 65 to *c.* 225 million years ago.

Messager, André (1853–1929), French composer of light opera, e.g. *Véronique* (1898).

Messala, Corvinus (64 B.C.–A.D. 8), Roman general, took part in battles of Philippi and Actium; conquered Aquitania.

Messalina (d. A.D. 48), 3rd wife of the Roman emperor Claudius, credited with flamboyant vices; executed.

Messerschmitt, Willy (b. 1898), German aircraft designer, produced planes for the Luftwaffe in World War II.

Messiaen, Olivier (b. 1908), French composer and organist, drew on many sources, e.g. *Turangalîla Symphony* (1948).

Meštrović, Ivan (1883–1962), Yugoslav sculptor of religious and Slav subjects, in U.S.A. 1947–62.

Metaphysical Society, London, founded 1869 by the English architect Sir James Knowles (1831–1908).

Metastasio, Pietro (1698–1782), Italian poet and librettist, poet laureate at Viennese court.

Metaurus, Battle of, Roman victory over the Carthaginians, 207 B.C.

Metcalf, John (1717–1810), English road and bridge builder, despite blindness which earned him the name 'Blind Jack of Knaresborough'.

Metchnikov, Élie (1845–1916), Russian-born French bacteriologist, Nobel prizewinner 1908.

Metellus Macedonicus, Quintus (d. 115 B.C.), Roman general, won victories in Macedon and Greece.

meteor crater, Arizona, discovered 1891; formed by a meteorite 15,000 to 40,000 years ago.

Meteorological Office, Bracknell, Berkshire, founded 1850 by James Glaisher (1809–1903).

meteors, great shower (Leonid meteors) recorded 12 Nov. 1833.

Methodism, founded 1738 by John Wesley (*q.v.*); spread throughout Britain and to America by 1770; in Britain separated from Church of England 1795; World Methodist Council founded 1881; reorganized 1951; Methodist Church in Great Britain united 1932 by merging of the original Wesleyan with the Primitive (formed 1811) and United Methodist (merged 1857) Churches.

Methuen Treaty, concerning trade between England and Portugal, negotiated Dec. 1703 by the English diplomat John Methuen (*c.* 1650–1706).

Meton (5th cent. B.C.), Greek astronomer, worked out 19-year moon cycle (Metonic cycle).

metre, defined 1795 in terms of Earth's circumference; redefined 1889 as length of a standard bar; redefined 1960 in terms of wavelengths of a spectral line of krypton.

metric system, introduced 1791–95 and legally adopted 1801 in France; new standards adopted 1889 and 1960; change to metric system began in U.K. and U.S.A. in 1970s.

metronome, invented 1812 by the Dutchman Dietrich Nikolaus Winkel (*c.* 1776–1826).

Metropolitan Board of Works, London,

established 1855; functions transferred 1888 to the London County Council.

Metropolitan District Railway, London, first section opened Dec. 1868 between Mansion House and South Kensington.

Metropolitan Museum of Art, New York, founded 1870; opened 1872.

Metropolitan Opera House, New York, opened 22 Oct. 1883 under the management of Henry Abbey; 'golden age' 1898–1903; new Metropolitan Opera House, Lincoln Center, opened Sept. 1966.

Metropolitan Police, London, set up 1829 by Sir Robert Peel (q.v.).

Metropolitan Railway, London, first underground passenger service, opened Jan. 1863 between Paddington and Farringdon Street; extended to Moorgate Dec. 1865; electrified between Baker Street and Harrow 1904; Inner Circle service completely electrified Sept. 1905.

Metsu, Gabriel (c. 1629–67), Dutch painter mainly of quiet, genre scenes.

Metternich, Clemens, Prince (1773–1859), Austrian diplomat, foreign minister 1809–1848, dominated post-Napoleonic Europe.

Metz, Siege of, Franco–Prussian War, Aug.–Oct. 1870.

Meulen, Adam van der (1632–90), Flemish-born court painter to Louis XIV of France.

Meung, Jean de. See **Jean de Meung.**

Mexican War, between Mexico and U.S.A., May 1846–Feb. 1848.

Mexico, centre of Inca and Maya empires; Spanish conquest 1519–21; part of viceroyalty of New Spain 1521; revolution against Spanish rule began 1810, leading to independence 1821; became federal republic 1824; new constitution 1857; revised 1917; period of political and social revolution 1910–21.

Meyer, Conrad (1825–98), Swiss novelist, author of The Saint (1880).

Meyer, Julius Lothar (1830–95), German chemist, discovered periodic law.

Meyer-Förster, Wilhelm (1862–1934), German novelist and playwright, wrote Old Heidelberg (1901).

Meyerbeer, Giacomo (1791–1864), German-born composer of Les Huguenots (1836), worked in Venice and Paris.

Meyerhof, Otto (1884–1951), German physiologist, investigated muscle spasm, Nobel prizewinner 1922.

Meyerhold, Vsevolod (1874–1940), Russian actor and theatrical producer, noted for his innovations.

Meynell, Alice (1847–1922), English poet and prose writer, author of Rhythm of Life (1893).

Meyrink, Gustav (1868–1932), Austrian novelist, mystical and eccentric, wrote The Golem (1915).

mezzotint process, invented c. 1642 by the Dutch-born engraver Ludwig von Siegen (c. 1609–1680).

M.G.B., Ministry of State Security, U.S.S.R., in operation as secret police organization 1946–53; combined with the M.V.D. (q.v.) 1953 after Stalin's death.

Miami, University of, Florida, founded 1925; opened 1926.

Michael IV (d. 1041), Byzantine emperor 1034–41; real power in hands of his brother John the Eunuch.

Michael VII (d. 1078), Byzantine emperor 1071–78, lost territory in Italy and Asia.

Michael VIII (1234–82), Byzantine emperor 1260–82, drove Latins from Constantinople.

Michael (1596–1645), tsar of Russia 1613–1645, the first Romanov; reorganized government.

Michael (b. 1921), king of Romania 1927–1930 and 1940–47, abdicated after Communist takeover.

Michaelis, Johann David (1717–91), German theologian, early exponent of 'higher criticism' of the Bible.

Michaelmas (Feast of St Michael the Archangel), celebrated 29 Sept.

Michaud, Joseph François (1767–1839), French historian, compiled Biographie Universelle (1811–28).

Michelangelo (1475–1564), Italian sculptor, painter, architect and poet, one of the outstanding artists of the Renaissance.

Michelet, Jules (1798–1874), French historian, wrote histories of France and the Revolution.

Michelozzo, Michelozzo (1396–1472), Italian Renaissance architect, designed Palazzo Medici-Riccardi, Florence.

Michelson, Albert Abraham (1852–1931), American physicist, awarded Nobel Prize for Physics 1907.

Michelson–Morley Experiment, for testing theory of the ether, first performed 1881, and repeated 1887, by A. A. Michelson and the American chemist Edward W. Morley (1838–1923).

Michigan, U.S.A., settled by French in 17th century; ceded to Britain 1763 and to U.S.A. 1783; independent U.S. territory 1805; admitted to the Union 1837.

Mickiewicz, Adam (1798–1855), Polish poet and nationalist, wrote epic Pan Tadeusz (1834).

microbes, or micro-organisms, postulated 1546 as agents of disease by the Italian scholar Girolamo Fracastoro (1483–1553); first observed 1680s by the microscopist Leeuwenhoek (q.v.).

microphone, invented 1877 by the German-born American Emile Berliner (1851–1929); carbon microphone invented 1878 by the Anglo-American David Edward Hughes (1831–1900).

microscope, compound, invented *c.* 1590, traditionally by the Dutch opticians Hans and Zacharias Janssen or by Hans Lippershey (*q.v.*), or Galileo (*q.v.*).

Middle Ages, in western Europe, roughly from the fall of the Western Roman Empire, 476, to the end of the 15th century; now often taken to extend from *c.* 1100; in eastern Europe, the period of the Eastern Roman Empire 330–1453.

Middle English, in use from the 12th century to *c.* 1500.

Middleton, Conyers (1683–1750), English scholar, involved in theological controversies.

Middleton, Thomas (1580–1627), English playwright, author of *The Changeling* (1622).

Midrash, Rabbinical commentary on the Scriptures compiled 2nd to 13th centuries.

midsummer day (Feast of the Nativity of St John the Baptist), 24 June; summer solstice 21 or 22 June.

Midway, Battle of, World War II, victory of American naval and air units over the Japanese, 4–7 June 1942.

midwinter, winter solstice, 21 or 22 Dec.

Mieris, Frans van (1635–81), Dutch painter, achieved effects of great richness of texture.

Mies van der Rohe, Ludwig (1886–1969), German-born architect, in U.S.A. 1937–1969, a leading exponent of modern architecture.

Mignard, Pierre (1612–95), French painter, rival of Le Brun at French court.

Migne, Jacques Paul (1800–75), French Catholic theologian, important publisher of religious books.

Mignet, François (1796–1884), French historian, wrote a history of the Revolution (1824).

Mihailović, Draža (1893–1946), Serbian nationalist and guerrilla leader, executed for collaboration with the Germans.

Mikoyan, Anastas (b. 1895), Soviet statesman, held numerous important government posts during his long career.

Milan Cathedral, Italy, constructed 1386–1813; consecrated 1577.

Milan Decree, extending ban on British goods, issued by Napoleon 1807.

Mildenhall treasure, Roman silver tableware, discovered near Mildenhall, Suffolk, 1942–43.

mile, British statute, established by law 1593.

Miles, Nelson (1839–1925), American soldier, served in Civil War, Indian wars, Cuba and Puerto Rico.

Milhaud, Darius (1892–1974), French composer, member of the 'Six' group, used technique of polytonality.

Military Cross, British award, instituted 1914.

Mill, James (1773–1836), English utilitarian philosopher and historian (*History of India*, 1818).

Mill, John Stuart (1806–73), English political philosopher, son of James Mill, wrote *On Liberty* (1859).

Millais, Sir John (1829–96), English painter, a founder of the Pre-Raphaelites.

Millay, Edna St Vincent (1892–1950), American poet, used sonnet and other traditional forms.

millennium, period of 1,000 years, particularly that of Christ's return to reign in person on Earth.

Miller, Arthur (b. 1915), American playwright, best known for *Death of a Salesman* (1949).

Miller, Henry (b. 1891), American writer, pioneer of sexual frankness, as in *Tropic of Cancer* (1934).

Miller, Joe (1684–1738), English actor, famous for his comic roles in the Drury Lane company.

Millerand, Alexandre (1859–1943), French statesman, prime minister 1920 and president 1920–24.

Millet, Jean François (1814–75), French painter of realistic peasant scenes, e.g. *The Gleaners* (1857).

Millikan, Robert Andrews (1868–1954), American physicist, was the first to measure the charge on the electron.

Millin, Sarah Gertrude (1889–1968), South African writer of novels and biographies.

Mills, Sir Charles (1825–95), Hungarian-born British soldier in India, the Crimea and South Africa.

Milman, Henry Hart (1791–1868), English historian, dean of St Paul's, wrote *History of the Jews* (1830).

Milne, Alan Alexander (1882–1956), Scottish writer of children's books, notably *Winnie the Pooh* (1926).

Milner, Alfred, 1st Viscount (1854–1925), English administrator in Egypt and South Africa.

Milo, Titus Annius (95–48 B.C.), Roman politician, supported Pompey against Clodius.

Milovanović, Milovan (1863–1912), Serbian statesman, prime minister 1911–12.

Miltiades (d. *c.* 489 B.C.), Athenian soldier, defeated Persians at Marathon 490 B.C.

Milton, John (1608–74), major English poet, wrote *Paradise Lost* (1667) despite blindness; also effective prose pamphleteer.

Milwaukee, Wisconsin, originated as a French–American fur-trading post in the late 18th century.

Milyukov, Pavel (1859–1943), Russian politician, leader of Cadet Party, foreign minister 1917; in France 1919–43.

Minden, Battle of, Seven Years' War, victory of the Prussians, English and Hanoverians over the French, 1 Aug. 1759.

Mindszenty, Jozsef, Cardinal (1892–1975), Hungarian Roman Catholic prelate, imprisoned under Communist regime.

Ming dynasty, China, 1368–1644.

Minnesota, U.S.A., organized as a territory 1849; admitted to the Union 1858.

Minoan Civilization, Crete, dating from *c.* 3000 to *c.* 1200 B.C. or later; destruction at Cnossos and other sites, possibly by earthquake, *c.* 1500 B.C.; palace at Cnossos destroyed about 1400 B.C.; archaeological excavations from 1900 by Sir Arthur Evans (*q.v.*).

Minoan script. See **Linear B.**

Minorca, part of the Balearic Island province of Spain, captured by the British from the Spanish 1709; taken by France 1756; ceded to Britain 1763; finally returned by Britain to Spain 1802.

Minot, Laurence (14th cent.), English poet, wrote patriotic battle songs.

Mint, The Royal, origins uncertain although mentioned in records 1229; Tower Hill building erected 1809–10; moved to Llantrisant, Mid Glamorgan, 1972–74.

Minto, Gilbert, 4th Earl (1845–1914), Scottish administrator, governor-general of Canada 1898–1904 and viceroy of India 1905–10.

Minuit, Peter (*c.* 1580–1638), Dutch purchaser of Manhattan Island from Indians 1626.

Miocene Epoch, Earth history, from *c.* 7 to *c.* 26 million years ago.

Mirabeau, Honoré, Comte de (1749–91), French politician, played a leading role early in the French Revolution.

miracle plays, originated in France, performed in England from early 14th to 16th centuries.

Miranda, Francisco (1750–1816), Venezuelan revolutionary, failed to overthrow Spanish.

Miró, Joan (b. 1893), Spanish painter, developed personal 'calligraphic' Surrealist idiom.

Missionary Ridge, Battle of. See **Chattanooga,** Battle of.

Mississippi River, first seen by a white man, the Spaniard Hernando de Soto 1541; navigated 1682 by Robert Cavelier, Sieur de La Salle (1643–87).

Mississippi Scheme, for colonial development of the lower Mississippi, inaugurated 1717 as the Western Company by John Law (*q.v.*); company bankrupted 1720.

Missouri, U.S.A., first settled 1735; made a territory 1812; admitted to the Union 1821.

Mistral, Frédéric (1830–1914), French poet, wrote in Provençal; Nobel prizewinner 1904.

Mistral, Gabriella (1889–1957), Chilean poet, Nobel prizewinner 1945.

M.I.T. See **Massachusetts Institute of Technology.**

Mitchell, Reginald Joseph (1895–1937), English aircraft designer, creator of the Spitfire.

Mitchell, Sir Thomas (1792–1855), Scottish explorer of Australian interior.

Mitford, Mary Russell (1787–1855), English writer of country life tales, collected in *Our Village* (1824–32).

Mithridates V (d. *c.* 123 B.C.), king of Pontus *c.* 150–*c.* 123 B.C., was an ally of the Romans.

Mithridates VI (*c.* 131–63 B.C.), king of Pontus 120–63 B.C., fought three wars against Romans; defeated by Pompey.

mitosis, cell duplication, first observed in the 1870s and described 1882 by the German anatomist Walther Flemming (1843–1905).

Mitré, Bartolomé (1821–1906), Argentine statesman, president 1862–68, victorious in war against Paraguay 1865–70.

Mitropoulos, Dimitri (1896–1960), Greek-born conductor and composer, headed Minneapolis Symphony Orchestra 1937–60.

Mitscherlich, Eilhard (1794–1863), German chemist, made important discoveries about isomorphism.

Mivart, George Jackson (1827–1900), English biologist, opposed Darwinism.

Moabite Stone, inscribed *c.* 850 B.C.; discovered at Dibon, near the Dead Sea, 1868 by a German missionary F. Klein.

modern face, type design, introduced *c.* 1788 by the English publisher John Bell (1745–1831).

Modigliani, Amadeo (1884–1920), Italian painter and sculptor, developed characteristic linear, quasi-primitive style.

Modjeska, Helena (1844–1909), Polish-born American actress, notable as a tragedienne in Shakespeare and Ibsen.

Moe, Jörgen (1813–82), Norwegian poet, and collector of folk-songs and fairy tales.

Moeran, Ernest John (1894–1950), English composer, often on rural or folksong themes.

Mogul Empire, India, lasted from 1526 to 1761, although began disintegrating after 1707.

Mohammed (A.D. 570–632), Arabian prophet, founder of Islam.

Mohammed I (1387–1421), sultan of Turkey 1413–21, consolidated empire after period of defeats.

Mohammed II (1430–81), sultan of Turkey 1451–81, captured Constantinople; made extensive Balkan conquests.

Mohammed III (1566–1603), sultan of Turkey 1595–1603, at war with Persia.

Mohammed IV (1641–91), sultan of Turkey 1648–87; real power exercised by viziers.

Mohammed V (1844–1918), sultan of Turkey 1909–18, succeeded his brother Abdul Hamid II.

Mohammed VI (1861–1926), last sultan of Turkey 1918–22.

Mohl, Hugo von (1805–72), German botanist, investigated plant cells; coined term 'protoplasm'.

Moir, David Macbeth (1798–1851), Scottish physician and writer, e.g. novel *The Life of Mansie Wauch* (1828).

Moiseiwitsch, Benno (1890–1963), Russian-born British piano virtuoso, interpreter of romantic music.

Moissan, Henri (1852–1907), French chemist, isolated fluorine and developed electric furnace; Nobel prizewinner 1906.

Molay, Jacques de (c. 1243–1314), last grand master of the Templars 1297–1314; burnt at the stake.

Moldavia, founded early 14th century, achieving independence 1349; under Turkish domination from 1513; placed under Russian protection 1774; united with Walachia 1859 to form the state of Romania (q.v.).

Moldavian S.S.R., created a constituent republic of the U.S.S.R. 1940; formed from the Moldavian Autonomous S.S.R. (organized 1924) and Bessarabia.

molecules, first differentiated from atoms 1811 by Amedeo Avogadro whose work was extended 1858 by the Italian chemist Stanislao Cannizzaro (1826–1910).

Molesworth, Sir Guilford (1828–1925), English civil engineer, wrote on various subjects.

Molesworth, Mary Louisa (1839–1921), Dutch-born writer in Scotland, mainly of books for children.

Molière (pseud. of Jean Baptiste Poquelin; 1622–73), French playwright, great master of prose and verse comedy, e.g. *Le Misanthrope* (1666).

Molinism, Jesuit reconciliation of divine grace and free will, proposed by the Spanish theologian Luis de Molina (1535–1600) in his *Concordia* (1588).

Molinos, Miguel de (1640–97), Spanish priest, practised a form of quietism; denounced as heretical and imprisoned.

Mollison, James (1909–59), Scottish aviator, married to Amy Johnson 1932–38, broke many flying records.

Molly Maguires, secret organization of Irish-American coal miners active c. 1862–1877 in Pennsylvania; originally a group of Irish agitators led in the 1840s by Molly Maguire.

Molnár, Ferenc (1878–1952), Hungarian playwright, witty and sophisticated in tone, e.g. *Liliom* (1909).

Molotov, Vyacheslav (b. 1890), Soviet statesman, commissar for foreign affairs and foreign minister 1939–56.

Moltke, Helmuth von (1800–91), German soldier, organized and directed Prussian army in victories of 1866–71.

molybdenum, metallic element isolated 1782 by the Swedish chemist Peter Jacob Hjelm (1746–1813) following a suggestion of Carl Wilhelm Scheele (q.v.).

Mommsen, Theodor (1817–1903), German historian of Roman Empire, Nobel prizewinner 1902.

Mompou, Federico (b. 1893), Spanish composer, wrote almost exclusively for the piano.

Monaco, sovereign principality, ruled by the Grimaldi family from 1297; allied to France from 1512 except 1524–1641 when under Spanish protection; under Sardinian protection 1815–61; constitutional monarchy established 1911; constitution suspended 1959; replaced 1962.

monasteries, English, dissolved 1536–40 at the orders of Henry VIII.

monastery, first Christian, founded in Egypt c. 320 by Saint Pachomius (c. 290–346).

Monck, Charles, Viscount (1819–94), Irish-born administrator, governor-general of Canada 1861–68.

Monck, George, Duke of Albemarle (1608–1670), English soldier, Cromwell's governor of Scotland 1654–60; organized Charles II's restoration.

Monckton, Mary, Countess of Cork and Orrery (1746–1840), English bluestocking, entertained many distinguished writers.

Mond, Ludwig (1839–1909), German-born chemist in Britain, made many scientific discoveries and built up a great business concern.

Mondrian, Piet (1872–1944), Dutch artist, pioneer in abstract painting.

Monet, Claude (1840–1926), French painter, one of the founders of Impressionism.

Monge, Gaspard (1746–1818), French mathematician, invented descriptive geometry.

Mongolia, Mongols secured supremacy over other nomadic tribes 13th century under Ghenghis Khan (q.v.), leading to Mongol expansion; came under Chinese control in 17th century and divided: Inner Mongolia, formed 1644, made autonomous region of China after World War II; Outer Mongolia was Chinese province 1691–1911, 1919–21, and under Russian protection 1912–19; independence declared 1921; became Mongolian People's Republic 1924.

Mongols, invaded China 1207–15, Transoxiana 1219, Caucasia 1221, Persia 1222, Russia 1237–40, central Europe 1241, Mesopotamia 1258. Ruled China (Yuan dynasty) 1297–1368, Persia 1225–1386, and Russia 1242–1380.

Moniz, Antonio (1874–1955), Portuguese physician, noted for his work in brain surgery.

Monk, Maria (c. 1817–50), Canadian writer of *Awful Disclosures* (1836) of nunnery life; exposed as a fraud.

Monkton Combe School, Somerset, English public school, founded by the Rev. F. Pocock 1868.

Monmouth, Battle of (New Jersey), American Revolutionary War 28 June 1778.

Monmouth School, English public school, founded by William Jones 1614.

Monmouth, James, Duke of (1649–85), natural son of Charles II and claimant to the English throne; led rebellion June–July 1685 against James II; executed.

Monocacy, Battle of, American Civil War, victory of Confederates over the Union army 8 July 1864.

Monophysitism, Christian heresy, condemned at Council of Chalcedon, 451.

Monothiletism, Christian heresy similar to Monophysitism, condemned at Council of Constantinople, 680.

monotype, typeface, invented 1887 by the American Tolbert Lanston (1844–1913).

Monroe, James (1758–1831), American statesman, 5th president of the United States 1817–25; promulgated Monroe Doctrine 1823.

Monroe, Marilyn (1926–62), American film actress, appeared in *Some Like it Hot* (1959).

Mons, retreat from, World War I, by the British army, Aug. 1914.

Montagna, Bartolommeo (c. 1450–1523), Italian painter of religious subjects, worked in northern Italy.

Montagu, Lady Mary Wortley (1689–1762), English traveller, at Constantinople 1716–18, much involved with writers; author of witty *Letters*.

Montague, Charles Edward (1867–1928), English journalist and novelist, wrote *Rough Justice* (1926).

Montaigne, Michel Eyquem de (1533–1592), French writer, created the essay as a literary form and made it a vehicle for personal reflection.

Montalembert, Charles, Comte de (1810–1870), French politician and journalist, champion of liberal Catholicism.

Montalembert, Marc René, Marquis de (1714–1800), French military engineer, wrote on fortifications.

Montana, U.S.A., first settled 1809; made a territory 1864; admitted to the Union 1889.

Montanism, Christian heresy, flourished in Asia Minor in 2nd century.

Mont Blanc, highest peak in western Europe, summit first reached 1786 by the Frenchmen Michel-Gabriel Paccard and Jacques Balmat.

Mont Blanc Tunnel, construction started 1959 from both ends; completed Aug. 1962.

Montcalm, Louis Joseph de (1712–59), French soldier, defeated by Wolfe and killed at Battle of Quebec.

Mont Cenis Pass, between France and Italy, completed 1810; tunnel opened 1871.

Montefiore, Sir Moses (1784–1885), Italian-born British financier and philanthropist, did much for Jews in the East.

Montemayor, Jorge de (c. 1520–61), Spanish poet, wrote *La Diana Enamorada* (1559).

Montenegro, independent since 14th century; in alliance with Russia against Turkey in 18th–19th centuries; independent 1878; monarchy proclaimed 1910; voted union with Serbia and other territories 1918 to form kingdom of Yugoslavia; made a constituent republic of Yugoslavia 1946.

Montes, Ismael (1861–1933), Bolivian statesman, president 1904–09 and 1913–1917; also held diplomatic posts in Britain and France.

Montespan, Marquise de (1641–1707), French noblewoman, mistress of Louis XIV 1667–c. 1685.

Montesquieu, Charles de (1689–1755), French writer of *L'Esprit des Lois* (1748), an epoch-making study of institutions.

Montessori, Maria (1870–1952), Italian educationalist, developed c. 1907 the method named after her of educating children.

Monteverdi, Claudio (1567–1643), Italian composer, greatly developed opera and emotional expressiveness of music.

Monteux, Pierre (1875–1964), French conductor, worked much in England and the U.S.A.

Montez, Lola (1818–61), Irish dancer, mistress of Ludwig I of Bavaria (*q.v.*).

Montezuma I (1390–1464), Aztec emperor 1436–64, ruled most of Mexico.

Montezuma II (1466–1520), last Aztec emperor 1502–20, died a prisoner of Cortés (*q.v.*).

Montfort, Simon de (c. 1208–65), English statesman and soldier, led opposition to Henry III; killed at Battle of Evesham.

Montgolfier, Joseph (1740–1810), French hot-air balloon pioneer, together with his brother Jacques Étienne (1745–99).

Montgomerie, Alexander (c. 1566–c. 1610), Scottish poet, wrote *The Cherrie and the Slae* (1597).

Montgomery, Bernard, Viscount (1887–1976), Irish-born British soldier, victor at El Alamein 1942; commanded Allied armies in northern France, 1944.

month, in astronomy, 29–53 days (synodic), 27–32 days (sidereal); in calendar,

28 (or 29), 30, or 31 days; in law, 28 days.

Montherlant, Henri de (1896–1972), French novelist and dramatist, author of *The Dead Queen* (1942).

Montholon, Charles (1783–1853), French general, shared Napoleon's exile at Saint Helena.

Monticelli, Adolphe (1824–86), French painter, fashionable in the Second Empire, especially for his portraits.

Montmorency, Anne, Duc de (1493–1567), French soldier, fought on Catholic side in the Wars of Religion.

Montpensier, Duchesse de (1627–93), French noblewoman, known as 'La Grande Mademoiselle', involved in Fronde revolt.

Montreal, Canada, founded 1642.

Montreal University (Université de Montréal), French-speaking university, Canada, founded 1876.

Montrose, James Graham, Marquis of (1612–50), Scottish soldier, supported Charles I; captured and executed.

Mont Saint Michel, France, oratory founded c. 708 by Saint Aubert, bishop of Avranches; monastery founded 966.

Montserrat, West Indies, British colony from 1632; part of West Indies Federation 1958–62.

Montt, Jorge (1847–1922), Chilean sailor and statesman, led revolution of 1891; president 1891–96.

Montt, Manuel (1809–80), Chilean statesman, as president 1851–61 encouraged economic development.

Monvel (pseud. of Jacques Boutet; 1745–1812), French actor and playwright, wrote *L'Amant Bourru* (1777).

Moody, Dwight Lyman (1837–99), American revivalist, toured Britain and U.S.A. with Ira Sankey (*q.v.*).

Moog Synthesizer, for electronic music, developed in the 1960s by the American physicist Robert Moog.

Moon, first pictures of far side taken 1959 by *Luna* 3 (*q.v.*); first soft landing 1966 by *Luna* 9; first manned landing July 1969 by *Apollo* 11 (*q.v.*); subsequent *Apollo* landings: Nov. 1969 (*Apollo* 12), Jan. and July 1971 (14 and 15), April and Dec. 1972 (16 and 17).

Moon Alphabet, for the blind, invented 1845 by the Englishman William Moon (1818–94).

Moorcroft, William (c. 1765–1825), English veterinary surgeon and explorer in central Asia.

Moore, George (1852–1933), Irish novelist, author of *Esther Waters* (1894).

Moore, George Edward (1873–1958), English philosopher, leader in the revolt against Idealism.

Moore, Grace (1901–47), American soprano, at first in musical comedy, and from 1928 in opera and films.

Moore, Henry (b. 1898), major English sculptor, famous for reclining figures, often with internal spaces.

Moore, Sir John (1761–1809), Scottish soldier, commander in Portugal, killed during retreat from Corunna.

Moore, Marianne (1887–1972), American poet, whose works include *What are Years?* (1941).

Moore, Thomas (1779–1852), Irish poet, author of *Lalla Rookh* (1817).

Mor, Antonio. See **Moro,** Antonio.

Moraes Barros, Prudente de (1841–1902), Brazilian statesman, president 1894–98, the first civilian president.

Morales, Luis de (c. 1509–86), Spanish religious painter, often obtained striking effects by painting on copper.

morality plays, played mainly in the 15th and 16th centuries.

Moral Rearmament, nondenominational religious movement founded 1922 by the American religious leader Frank Buchman (1878–1961).

Moran, Edward (1829–1901), English-born American painter, known for his marine subjects.

Morand, Paul (1888–1976), French novelist, author of *L'Europe Galante* (1925).

Moravia, Alberto (b. 1907), Italian novelist, author of *The Woman of Rome* (1947).

Moravian Brethren, Protestant sect appeared c. 1457, as Unitas Fratrum, among followers of Jan Hus (*q.v.*); independent church formed 1467; revival from 1722 at the Herrnhut colony under Graf von Zinzendorf (1700–60); missionary work began 1732; Moravian Church in America founded 1739 by Bishop Spangenberg (1704–92); Moravian Episcopal Church in England recognized 1749.

More, Hannah (1745–1833), English writer of religious tracts and stories, set up Sunday schools, etc.

More, Paul (1864–1937), American writer, e.g. *Pages from an Oxford Dictionary* (1937).

More, Sir Thomas (1478–1535), English statesman, lord chancellor 1529–32, wrote *Utopia* (1516); executed for refusal to accept Henry VIII's Act of Supremacy.

Moreau, Gustave (1826–98), French painter, moved away from literal realism in *Salomé* and similar works.

Moreau, Jean Victor (1763–1813), French soldier, commanded Revolutionary and Napoleonic armies; conspired against Napoleon.

Morgagni, Giovanni (1682–1771), Italian physician, founder of pathological anatomy.

Morgan, Charles (1894–1958), English novelist, wrote *The Fountain* (1932).

Morgan, Sir Henry (c. 1635–1688), Welsh buccaneer, conducted successful operations against the Spanish; became lieutenant-governor of Jamaica.

Morgan, John Pierpont (1837–1913), American financier, built railroad and industrial empire.

Morgan, Lewis Henry (1818–81), American ethnologist, made a study of the Iroquois Indians.

Morgan, Thomas Hunt (1866–1945), American zoologist, noted for his work in genetics.

Morgan, William de. See **De Morgan,** William.

Morgenstern, Christian (1871–1914), German poet, was most successful in 'nonsense' humorous vein.

Morgenthau, Henry (1856–1946), German-born American diplomat, ambassador to Turkey 1913–16 and Mexico 1920.

Morier, James (c. 1780–1849), English diplomat in the East, wrote the novel *Adventures of Hajji Baba* (1824).

Mörike, Eduard (1804–75), German poet and novelist, one of the greatest German lyricists.

Morison, James (1816–93), Scottish founder of the Evangelical Union 1843, which broke away from the United Secession Church.

Morison, Stanley (1889–1967), English typographer, had a great influence on newspaper and book design.

Morisot, Berthe (1841–95), French painter, one of the leading Impressionists.

Morland, George (1763–1804), English painter of rural life, often sentimentalized village scenes.

Morley, Henry (1822–94), English writer and editor of *Morley's Universal Library* and others.

Morley, John, Viscount (1838–1923), English statesman and writer, notably of *Life of Gladstone* (1903).

Morley, Thomas (c. 1557–c. 1602), English composer, wrote madrigals, church music and canzonets.

Mormon Movement, or Church of Jesus Christ of Latter-Day Saints, founded 1830 in Fayette, New York State, by Joseph Smith (q.v.); headquarters moved to Salt Lake City, Utah, 1847.

Mornay, Philippe de (1549–1623), French Huguenot leader, for some years chief adviser of Henry of Navarre (later Henry IV).

Morning Star, British newspaper, founded 1932 as the *Daily Worker*; suppressed 1941–42; name changed 1966.

Moro, Antonio (c. 1519–c. 1575), Flemish portrait painter, worked for Philip II of Spain.

Morocco, Muslim invasion 7th century; dynastic governments 788–1911, first Berber dynasty being founded 1056; protectorates of French Morocco and Spanish Morocco established 1912; Tangier set up as international zone 1923–56; independence restored 1956; became a constitutional monarchy 1962.

Moroni, Giambattista (c. 1525–78), Italian painter, notably of ordinary life, e.g. *Portrait of a Tailor*.

Moronobu, Hishikawa (1618–1703), Japanese painter, founder of the realistic (Ukiyoye) school.

morphine, isolated 1806 by the German chemist F. W. A. Sertürner and about the same time by the French chemist Bernard Courtois (1777–1838); structure analysed 1925 by the English chemist Sir Robert Robinson (1886–1975).

Morphy, Paul (1837–84), American chess champion, defeated all European opposition 1857–59.

Morris, Gouverneur (1752–1816), American diplomat whose diary is a valuable record of the French Revolution.

Morris, William (1834–96), English artist-craftsman, poet and Socialist; pioneered improved design; wrote *News from Nowhere* (1891).

Morrow, Dwight Whitney (1873–1931), American financier, politician and diplomat; ambassador to Mexico 1927–30.

Morse, Henry (1595–1645), English Jesuit missionary in England; executed.

Morse, Samuel (1791–1872), American inventor of the electrical telegraph and the Morse code.

mortar (hydraulic cement), not known since ancient times, developed 1756 by John Smeaton (q.v.).

Mortimer, Edmund (1391–1425), English noble, imprisoned by Henry IV 1399–1413, but served Henry V loyally.

Mortimer, Roger (c. 1287–1330), English noble, opponent of Edward II, lover of Queen Isabella; effectively ruled England 1327–30; executed.

Morton, John, Cardinal (c. 1420–1500), English prelate, Lancastrian supporter and adviser to Henry VII; archbishop of Canterbury 1486–1500.

Morton, Thomas (1781–1832), Scottish shipwright, invented patent slip for docking.

Morton, William (1819–68), American dentist, first man to employ ether as a general anaesthetic, 1846.

Mosander, Karl Gustav (1797–1858), Swedish chemist, discovered several elements.

Moscheles, Ignaz (1794–1870), Austrian piano virtuoso and composer, in London 1826–46.

Moschus (2nd cent. B.C.), Greek poet of Syracuse, wrote *Lament for Bion*.

Moscow, first recorded mention 1147; threatened by Tatar (Mongol) armies 13th–15th centuries; became capital of principality of Moscow 1341; occupied and burnt by the French under Napoleon Sept. 1812; French retreat from began 19 Oct. 1812; became capital of Russian S.F.S.R. 1918, and of the U.S.S.R. 1922; besieged by the Germans autumn 1941; much reconstruction and expansion since World War II.

Moseley, Henry (1887–1915), English physicist, determined atomic numbers of elements by X-ray spectra.

Moses (c. 13th cent. B.C.), Hebrew prophet and lawgiver, led the escape of the Jewish people from Egypt.

Moses, 'Grandma' (1860–1961), American painter, one of the first primitives to gain recognition.

Mosley, Sir Oswald (b. 1896), English politician, founded British Union of Fascists 1932 and British Union Movement 1948.

Mossadegh, Mohammed (1881–1967), Persian statesman, nationalized oil industry in Persia 1951.

Mössbauer, Rudolf (b. 1929), German physicist, showed that gamma rays can be emitted by atoms without recoiling.

Moszkowski, Moritz (1854–1925), Polish composer and pianist, worked in Paris; wrote opera *Boabdil* (1892).

Mother's Day: 2nd Sunday in May (U.S.A.); 4th Sunday in Lent (Great Britain).

Motherwell, Robert (b. 1915), American painter, known for his abstract expressionist work.

Motherwell, William (1797–1835), Scottish poet, wrote *Jeannie Morrison* (1832).

motion, laws of, published 1687 by Sir Isaac Newton.

motion films, first film taken with a still camera 1882 by the French physiologist Étienne-Jules Marey (1830–1904); first film made with a movie camera (the cinematograph [*q.v.*]) 1895; 'sound' movies (talkies) first demonstrated 1923.

Motley, John Lothrop (1814–77), American diplomat and historian, wrote *Rise of the Dutch Republic* (1856).

motor, electric, principle demonstrated 1821 by Michael Faraday; first one built 1835 by Thomas Davenport; first commercial model demonstrated 1873 by the Belgian engineer Zénobe Gramme (1826–1901); first alternating-current motor invented 1888 by Nikola Tesla (*q.v.*).

motorcars, developed 1885–90 independently by Gottlieb Daimler (*q.v.*) and Carl Benz (*q.v.*).

motorcycles, first (tricycle) built 1884 by the Englishman Edward Butler; first petrol-engine motorcycle (modified bicycle) built 1885 by Gottlieb Daimler.

motor scooter, first one produced in New York 1915; first in Britain 1919; revived in Italy 1946.

motorways, major routes in Britain: M1 started March 1958, southern extension completed May 1975; M6 constructed June 1956–May 1972; M4 constructed 1959–Dec. 1971; M5 under construction since early 1960; M2 constructed Sept. 1960–May 1963; M62 constructed mid-1966–Nov. 1976.

Mott, Lucretia (1793–1880), American Quaker agitator against slavery and for women's rights.

Mountbatten of Burma, 1st Earl (b. 1900), English sailor, supreme Allied commander in South-East Asia 1943–46; last viceroy of India, 1947.

Mounties. See **Royal Canadian Mounted Police.**

Mount Palomar Observatory, California, planned by the American astronomer George E. Hale, opened 1949; 200-inch reflecting telescope completed 1948.

Mount St Mary's College, Derbyshire, English public school, founded by the Society of Jesus 1842.

Mount Wilson Observatory, California, planned by the American astronomer George E. Hale, opened 1904; 100-inch reflecting telescope completed 1918.

Mowbray, Thomas, Duke of Norfolk (c. 1366–1399), English noble, gained dukedom by supporting Richard II; later exiled.

Mozambique, discovered 1498 by Vasco da Gama's fleet; became Portuguese colony 1505; created an overseas territory of Portugal 1951; achieved independence June 1975 as the People's Republic of Mozambique.

Mozart, Wolfgang Amadeus (1756–91), Austrian composer, supreme musical genius of the classical school, wrote operas, symphonies, concertos and chamber music.

Muawiyah I (602–680), Arab caliph 661–680, founder of the Omayyad dynasty.

Mudie, Charles Edward (1818–90), English founder of Mudie's Lending Library 1842–1937.

Muggletonians, religious sect, founded c. 1651 by the Englishmen Lodowick Muggleton (1609–98) and his cousin John Reeve (1608–58).

Mühlenberg, Heinrich Melchior (1711–87), German-born pioneer of American Lutheranism.

Muir, Edwin (1887–1959), Scottish poet, author of *Chorus of the Newly Dead* (1926).

Muir, Sir Robert (1864–1959), Scottish pathologist, expert on diseases of blood cells.

Mukden, Battle of, Japanese victory over the Russians, Feb.–March 1905.

Mulberry, artificial harbour used at Arromanches, Normandy, 1944.

Mulcahy, Richard (1886–1971), Irish political leader, commanded Free State army 1922–23.

Mulhall, Michael (1836–1900), Irish-born editor and statistician, published English-language newspaper in Argentina.

Müller, Friedrich Max-. See **Max-Müller,** Friedrich.

Müller, Fritz (1827–97), German naturalist, early advocate of Darwinism.

Müller, Johannes (1801–58), German physiologist, best known for his work on the nervous system.

Müller, Paul (1899–1965), Swiss chemist, first man to synthesize DDT, 1939.

Müller, Wilhelm (1794–1827), German poet, wrote *Die Schöne Müllerin* cycle, set to music by Schubert.

Mulock, Dinah Maria. See **Craik,** Mrs.

Mulready, William (1786–1863), Irish painter of landscapes and rural scenes.

Mumbles Railway, Swansea, Britain's oldest passenger railway, first recorded journey 1806; closed 1 Jan. 1960.

Mumford, Lewis (b. 1895), American writer on social, and particularly, urban, subjects, e.g. *Culture of Cities* (1938).

Munch, Edvard (1863–1944), Norwegian painter, intense expressionist, as in *The Scream* (1893).

Münchhausen, Baron Karl von (1720–97), German soldier, reputedly told grotesquely boastful tales. See **Raspe,** Rudolf.

Munday, Anthony (1553–1633), English playwright, wrote *Downfall of Robert of Huntingdon*.

Munich Agreement, between Britain, France, Germany and Italy, determining fate of Sudetenland (Czechoslovakia), dated 29 Sept. 1938, signed 30 Sept.

Munich Putsch, unsuccessful coup by Adolf Hitler, 8 Nov. 1923.

Munkácsy, Mihály (1844–1900), Hungarian painter, was a realist in the style of Courbet.

Munnings, Sir Alfred (1878–1959), English painter, notably of horses.

Munro, Hector Hugh. See **Saki.**

Munro, Sir Thomas (1761–1827), Scottish colonial administrator; had a long career in India.

Munroe, Charles Edward (1849–1938), American chemist, developed explosives.

Münzer, Thomas (c. 1489–1525), German Anabaptist preacher, led insurrection during Peasants' War (q.v.).

muon, subatomic particle, discovered 1935 by the American physicists Carl David Anderson and S. H. Neddermeyer.

Murad I (1319–89), sultan of Turkey 1359–89, killed in battle.

Murad II (d. 1451), sultan of Turkey 1421–1451, extended Turkish power in the Balkans.

Murad III (d. 1595), sultan of Turkey 1574–95, defeated Persians.

Murad IV (1609–40), sultan of Turkey 1623–40, a period of stabilization.

Murad V (1840–1904), sultan of Turkey 1876; declared insane and replaced by Abdul Hamid II.

Murasaki, Lady (11th cent.), Japanese courtier, wrote classic novel *Tale of Genji*.

Murat, Achille, Prince (1801–47), French writer, settled in U.S.A. and wrote studies of government.

Murat, Joachim (1767–1815), French soldier, skilled Napoleonic cavalry commander; king of Naples; executed.

Murchison, Sir Roderick (1792–1871), Scottish geologist, made numerous contributions to the subject.

Murdoch, Iris (b. 1919), Irish novelist, author of *The Sand Castle* (1957).

Murdock, William (1754–1839), Scottish engineer, inventor of coal-gas lighting.

Murfreesboro, Battle of, American Civil War, victory of Union army over Confederates, 31 Dec. 1862–2 Jan. 1863.

Murger, Henri (1822–61), French novelist, wrote *La Vie de Bohème* (1848), on which Puccini's opera *La Bohème* is based.

Murillo, Bartolomé (1617–82), Spanish painter of sentimental religious and everyday scenes.

Murphy, Jeremiah (1806–24), Irish child prodigy, learned seven languages and wrote poetry.

Murphy, William (b. 1892), American physician, discovered means of treating pernicious anaemia.

Murray, Gilbert (1866–1957), Australian-born classical scholar in England, was a notable translator from the Greek.

Murray, Sir James (1837–1915), English writer, chief editor of *The Oxford English Dictionary*.

Murray, Sir John (1841–1914), Canadian-born oceanographer in England, was also active as marine zoologist.

Murray, John (1778–1843), Scottish publisher, founded *Quarterly Review* 1809.

Murray, Margaret (1863–1963), English Egyptologist, author of *The Witch Cult in Western Europe* (1921).

Murrow, Edward Roscoe (1908–65), American journalist, noted for his London broadcasts during the Blitz.

Murry, John Middleton (1889–1957), English writer and critic, editor of the *Athenaeum* 1919–21; husband of Katherine Mansfield (q.v.).

Muscovy Company, English trading company, formed 1555 to trade with Russia.

Museum of London, amalgamating former Guildhall and London Museums, opened 1976.

Museum of Modern Art, New York, established 1929.

Museums Association, London, founded 1889.

music printing, earliest records 1457 (printed staves only) by associates of Gutenberg and 1473 (first printed notes); double printing of staves and notes in separate processes perfected by Ottaviano dei Petrucci (1466–1539) of Venice, who began music printing 1501; single printing process first used 1525 by Haultain of Paris.

Musil, Robert (1880–1942), Austrian novelist, wrote long, unfinished philosophical novel *The Man Without Qualities* (publ. 1930–43).

Muslim Era, began 16 July 622.

Muslim League, political group founded in India 1906.

Muslim religion. See **Islam.**

Musschenbroek, Pieter van (1692–1761), Dutch physicist, discovered the principle of the Leyden jar.

Musset, Alfred de (1810–57), French Romantic poet and playwright, lover of George Sand.

Mussolini, Benito (1883–1945), Italian statesman, creator of Fascism, effective dictator of Italy 1922–43; executed.

Mussorgsky, Modest (1839–81), Russian composer, of 'nationalist' school, e.g. *Boris Godunov.*

Mustafa Kemal Atatürk. See **Kemal Atatürk,** Mustafa.

Mustapha I (1591–1639), sultan of Turkey 1617–18 and 1622–23; deposed.

Mustapha II (1664–1704), sultan of Turkey 1695–1703, lost much territory in Europe; deposed.

Mustapha III (1717–74), sultan of Turkey 1757–74, defeated in war against Russia.

Mustapha IV (1779–1808), sultan of Turkey 1807–08, a puppet of the Janissaries.

mutation, biological variation, study first developed 1901 by Hugo de Vries (*q.v.*).

mutinies, *Bounty* 1789; Spithead and Nore, England, 1797; Indian 1857–58; Curragh army camp, Ireland, 1914; Kiel, Germany, 1918; Kronstadt, U.S.S.R., 1921.

Mutsuhito (1852–1912), emperor of Japan 1867–1912, during whose reign the power of the shoguns was crushed.

Muybridge, Eadweard (1830–1904), English-born American photographer, noted for his pictures of animals in motion.

Muzaffar-ed-din (1853–1907), shah of Persia 1896–1907, a period of concessions to colonial powers.

Muziano, Girolamo (*c.* 1528–92), Italian painter of landscapes and a noted mosaic artist.

M.V.D., Ministry of Internal Affairs, U.S.S.R., took over functions of the N.K.V.D. (*q.v.*) 1946; combined 1953 with the M.G.B. (*q.v.*) under Lavrenti Beria (*q.v.*); reorganized 1954; disbanded 1960. See also **K.G.B.**

Myddleton, Sir Hugh (*c.* 1560–1631), English builder of 'New River' (i.e. canal) supplying London with water.

Myers, Frederick William (1843–1901), English writer, a founder of the Society for Psychical Research, 1882.

myoglobin, protein, structure determined 1960 by the English biochemist John Kendrew (b. 1917).

Myron (5th cent. B.C.), Greek sculptor, best known for his *Discus Thrower.*

Mysore. See **Karnataka.**

Mytens, Daniel (*c.* 1590–*c.* 1647), Dutch court painter to James I and Charles I of England.

N

Nabokov, Vladimir (1899–1977), Russian-born American writer, best known for *Lolita* (1955).

Nabonidus (d. *c.* 539 B.C.), last king of Babylonia, defeated by Cyrus the Great.

Nachtigal, Gustav (1834–85), German explorer in Africa, later annexed parts of West Africa for Germany.

Nadir Shah (1688–1747), king of Persia 1736–47, restored Persian rule over northern India.

Nagaland, Indian state, established 1961.

Nagasaki, target of 2nd atomic bomb dropped on Japan, 9 Aug. 1945.

Nagy, Imre (1895–1958), Hungarian Communist leader, prime minister during 1956 revolution; executed.

Naidu, Sarajini (1879–1949), Indian woman politician, president of Congress 1925; was also a noted poet.

Nairne, Caroline (1766–1845), Scottish ballad writer, author of *Charlie is My Darling.*

Namibia, South West Africa, visited by Bartholomew Dias 1486; annexed by Germany 1884; mandated territory administered by Union (now Republic) of South Africa from 1919; mandate terminated by U.N. resolution 1966.

Namier, Sir Lewis (1888–1960), Polish-born British historian, revolutionized ideas on 18th-century politics.

Nanak (1469–1538), Indian religious leader, founder of Sikh faith.

Nana Sahib (*c.* 1820–*c.* 1859), one of the leaders of the Indian Mutiny; took refuge in Nepal.

Nancy, Battle of, victory of the Swiss over Charles the Bold of Burgundy, 5 Jan. 1477.

Nanga Parbat, Himalayas, climbed by a German–Austrian expedition 3 July 1953.

Nansen, Fridtjof (1861–1930), Norwegian polar explorer, who also worked for the League of Nations; winner of Nobel Peace Prize 1922.

Nantes, Edict of, granting tolerance to

French Protestants, signed by Henry IV 1598; revoked by Louis XIV 1685.

Nanteuil, Robert (1623–78), French portrait engraver, from both his own and others' works.

Napier, Sir Charles (1786–1860), English naval commander, in Brazilian–Portuguese service as well as British.

Napier, John (1550–1617), Scottish inventor of logarithms, 1614.

Napier, Sir William (1785–1860), Irish soldier in, and historian of, the Peninsular War.

Naples, city founded c. 600 B.C. by Greek colonists; captured by the Romans 326 B.C.

Naples, kingdom of, ruled by the Normans, with Sicily (q.v.), 1130–94, by Hohenstaufen 1194–1266, by the Angevins 1268–1435, breaking with Sicily 1282; reunited with Sicily under the Aragonese 1442–1501; ruled by Spanish Hapsburgs 1504–1707, by Austrians 1707–35, by Spanish Bourbons 1735–99, 1802–05, and 1815–1860; united with northern Italy 1860.

Napoleon Bonaparte (1769–1821), Corsican-born first consul 1799–1804 and emperor 1804–15 of France; his military genius made France dominant in Europe; his supreme administrative ability created the institutions which have shaped the history of modern France.

Napoleon II (1811–32), son of Napoleon I, never in fact ruled France.

Napoleon III (1808–73), president 1848–1851 and emperor 1852–70 of France, nephew of Napoleon I; deposed.

Napoleonic Wars, waged between the Allies and the French 1800 to 1814.

Narses (c. 478–c. 573), Byzantine soldier and eunuch, reconquered Italy for Justinian.

Narvik, Norway, scene of unsuccessful Allied expedition, World War II, 28 May–9 June 1940.

N.A.S.A., National Aeronautics and Space Administration, American agency, established 1958.

Naseby, Battle of, English Civil War, victory of Parliamentarians over the Royalists, 14 June 1645.

Nash, 'Beau' (Richard) (1674–1762), English gambler, as master of ceremonies at Bath made the city fashionable.

Nash, John (1752–1835), English architect, planned the great Regent's Park development; also designed Royal Pavilion, Brighton.

Nash, Ogden (b. 1902), American poet, noted for his humorous verse.

Nash, Paul (1889–1946), English painter, notable for work as official war artist in both World Wars.

Nashe, Thomas (1567–c. 1602), English writer of an early novel *The Unfortunate Traveller* (1594).

Nashville, Battle of, American Civil War, Unionist victory over the Confederates, 15–16 Dec. 1864.

Nasmyth, James (1808–90), Scottish engineer, invented steam hammer, 1839.

Nasr-ed-Din (1829–96), shah of Persia 1848–96, at war with Britain 1856–57; assassinated.

Nassau-Siegen, Charles, Prince de (1745–1808), French commander of Russian fleets against Turks and Swedes.

Nasser, Gamal Abd-al (1918–70), Egyptian soldier and statesman, president 1956–70, was a dominant figure in the Arab world.

Natal, coastline first sighted 1497 by Vasco da Gama; European trading posts set up 1824; Republic of Natal proclaimed 1838 by the Afrikaners; annexed as a colony 1843 by the British; joined Union (now Republic) of South Africa as a province, 1910.

Nathan, George Jean (1882–1958), American critic, associated as a journalist with H. L. Mencken (q.v.).

Nation, Carry (1846–1911), American temperance crusader, famous for wrecking saloons.

National Assembly, of France, formed 17 June 1789, renamed 9 July 1789 National Constituent Assembly; replaced by Legislative Assembly Sept. 1791; joint name for the two houses of the French parliament 1875–1940; from 1946 name of the lower house only.

National Assistance Board, set up 1948; merged with Ministry of Pensions and National Insurance 1966 to become Ministry of Social Security (Ministry of Health and Social Security from 1968).

National Bureau of Standards, U.S. Department of Commerce, Washington D.C., founded 1901.

National Debt, established in England Jan. 1693.

National Economic Development Council, set up in Britain 1961.

National Enterprise Board, Britain, proposed 1974; established 1975.

National Farmer's Union, London, founded 10 Dec. 1908.

National Gallery, London, founded 1824.

National Gallery, of Scotland, Edinburgh, founded 1850.

National Geographic Magazine, monthly American magazine, first published 1888 by the National Geographic Society, founded 1888.

National Guard, U.S.A., evolved from the militia, organized from 1790s; established as the country's reserve force 1903.

National Health Service, Britain, enacted 1946; came into effect July 1948, reorganized from April 1974 (England, Scotland, and Wales), and Oct. 1973 (Northern Ireland).

National Insurance Act, Britain, passed Dec. 1911; came into effect July 1912; Ministry set up 1944, now part of the Ministry of Health and Social Security. See also **National Assistance Board.**

nationalization, Britain: Bank of England 1946; coal industry 1946; civil aviation 1946; railways 1948; electricity industry 1948; gas industry 1948; road transport 1948 (largely denationalized 1953); steel industry 1949–51 (largely denationalized 1953, renationalized 1967); shipbuilding industry 1977; aircraft industry 1977.

National Liberation Front, Vietnamese political organization, formed 1960.

National Park, Britain's first, started by a gift of 300 acres near Snowdon 1935.

National Physical Laboratory, Britain, founded 1899.

National Playing Fields Association, Britain, granted charter Jan. 1933.

National Portrait Gallery, London, founded 1856; opened 1859.

National Savings Certificates, Britain, first issued 1916 as War Savings Certificates.

National Society for the Prevention of Cruelty to Children, London, founded 1884.

National Theatre, London, money allocated by Parliament for construction 1949; building began 1969; officially opened 1976.

National Trust, for places of historic interest or natural beauty, Britain, founded 1895.

National Trust for Scotland, for places of historic interest or natural beauty, founded 1895.

National University of Ireland, Dublin, came into being 1908; previously Royal University of Ireland, founded 1882, superseding the Queen's University in Ireland, founded 1849.

N.A.T.O., North Atlantic Treaty Organisation, founded on the signing of the treaty 4 April 1949.

Nattier, Jean Marc (1685–1766), French painter, fashionable portraitist, also painted historical and mythological subjects.

Natural Environment Research Council, Britain, established by royal charter 1965.

Natural History Museum, British Museum (Natural History), moved from British Museum to present site 1881; made independent 1963.

natural selection. See **evolution.**

natural gas, first discovered in England 1659. See also **gas,** North Sea.

Nature, British scientific journal, first published 1869; first editor, Sir Joseph Lockyer (q.v.).

nature conservancy, Britain, established 1949; became a committee of the Natural Environmental Research Council, 1965.

Naundorff, Karl Wilhelm (d. 1845), French pretender, claimed to be Louis XVII (q.v.).

Nauru, Pacific, annexed by Germany 1888; under League of Nations mandate 1920; jointly administered by Britain, Australia and New Zealand from 1947 as a U.N. trust territory; became an independent republic 1968.

Nautilus, first nuclear submarine, launched 1954; passed under the Arctic ice cap and beneath the North Pole, 1958.

Naval Architects, Royal Institution of, London, founded 1860.

Naval Limitation Conference, Washington, D.C., held 1921–22.

Navarino, Battle of, Greek War of Independence, victory of a combined British, French and Russian fleet over an Egyptian-Turkish fleet, 20 Oct. 1827.

Navarre, became independent kingdom 10th century; united with Castile and León and formed 1035 into kingdoms of Navarre, Aragon and Castile; reunited with Aragon 1086–1134; under French dynastic rule 1234–1328; southern part conquered by Ferdinand II of Aragon 1512; incorporated with Castile 1515; northern part remained separate kingdom until united with France 1589.

Navarrete, Battle of, Hundred Years War, victory of the English led by the Black Prince over a Spanish and French army, 3 April 1367.

Nayler, James (1618–60), English Quaker, believed himself incarnation of Jesus; branded and imprisoned 1656.

Nazianzen, Saint Gregory. See **Gregory Nazianzen,** Saint.

Nazi Party, National Socialist German Workers' Party, evolved 1920 from German Workers' Party (1919) with Adolf Hitler a founder member; reconstructed 1925; achieved power 1933 under Hitler; dissolved 1945.

Neal, Daniel (1678–1743), English clergyman, wrote a *History of the Puritans* (1732–88).

Neale, John Mason (1818–66), English hymn-writer, e.g. *Jerusalem the Golden* (1865).

Neander, Johann (1789–1850), German Protestant theologian, wrote a history of the Church.

Neanderthal Man, remains discovered 1856 near Dusseldorf; probably lived *c.* 85,000 to *c.* 35,000 years ago.

Nearchus (4th cent. B.C.), Macedonian soldier, commanded Alexander the Great's fleet.

Nebraska, U.S.A., first visited 1541 by Francisco Vasquez de Coronado; acquired from France 1803 as part of the Louisiana Purchase; first settled 1823; became a territory 1854; admitted to the Union 1867.

Nebraska, University of, Lincoln and Omaha, founded 1869; opened 1871.

Nebuchadnezzar (d. 562 B.C.), king of Babylon 604–562, built prosperous empire and destroyed Jerusalem.

Necker, Jacques (1732–1804), Swiss-born French financier and statesman, chief minister 1776–81 and 1789–90.

Nefertiti (14th cent. B.C.), Egyptian queen, wife of Akhnaton, noted for her beauty.

negatives, photographic, first produced 1841 by the English inventor William Fox Talbot (1800–77).

Negri, Pola (b. *c.* 1899), Polish-born actress in Hollywood silent films, e.g. *Forbidden Pleasure.*

Nehru, Pandit Jawaharlal (1889–1964), Indian nationalist leader, first prime minister of independent India 1947–64.

Neill, Alexander Sutherland (1883–1973), Scottish educationalist, noted for his progressive views.

Neilson, Samuel (1761–1803), Irish nationalist and journalist, co-founder of United Irishmen; exiled.

Nekrasov, Nikolai (1821–77), Russian poet, radical opponent of tsarism, wrote *Who is Happy in Russia?*

Nelson, Horatio, Viscount (1758–1805), English naval hero, victor of the Battle of the Nile 1798 and Trafalgar 1805; killed in action.

Nemours, Louis, Duc de (1814–96), French soldier, son of King Louis Philippe (*q.v.*); lived in England 1848–70.

Nenni, Pietro (b. 1891), Italian statesman, foreign minister 1968–69.

Nennius (8th cent.), Welsh writer, whose *Historia Britonum* has the earliest known reference to King Arthur.

neodymium, metallic element, discovered 1885 by the Austrian chemist, Baron von Welsbach (1858–1929).

Neolithic, or New Stone Age, began *c.* 15,000 to 20,000 years ago; ended *c.* 3000 B.C. at start of Bronze Age.

neon, discovered 1898 by the English chemists Sir William Ramsay (*q.v.*) and Morris W. Travers.

neon lights, invented *c.* 1910 and developed for lighting and advertising signs by the French chemist Georges Claude (1870–1960).

neoprene, synthetic rubber, developed *c.* 1930 by the American chemists Julius Arthur Nieuwland (1878–1936) and Wallace H. Carothers (1896–1937).

Nepal, ancient kingdom, conquered by Gurkhas 1769, who established modern state; virtually ruled by Rana family 1846–1951; constitutional monarchy proclaimed 1951; new constitution 1962; amended 1975.

Nepomuk, John of. See **John of Nepomuk.**

Nepos, Cornelius (*c.* 100–*c.* 25 B.C.), Roman historian; only some of his biographies of famous people survive.

Nepos, Julius (d. *c.* A.D. 480), penultimate Roman emperor 474–475; deposed.

Neptune, planet, position predicted 1845 by John Couch Adams and, independently, 1846 by Urbain Leverrier (*q.v.*); observed Sept. 1946 by Johann Galle (*q.v.*) at Leverrier's suggestion.

neptunium, first transuranic element to be synthesized, discovered 1940 by the American physicists Edwin M. McMillan (b. 1907) and Philip H. Abelson (b. 1913).

Neri, Saint Philip (1515–95), Italian priest, founded Fathers of the Oratory 1564.

Nernst, Walther (1864–1941), German scientist, did research in electricity, thermodynamics, etc.; Nobel prizewinner 1920.

Nero (A.D. 37–68), Roman emperor 54–68, became increasingly cruel and unstable; overthrown; committed suicide.

Neruda, Jan (1834–91), Czech writer, author of *Mala Strana* (1878).

Neruda, Pablo (1904–73), Chilean poet and diplomat, author of *Canto General* (1950).

Nerva (*c.* A.D. 30–98), Roman emperor 96–98, succeeded Domitian; restored order.

Nerval, Gérard de (1808–55); French writer of hallucinatory brilliance; achieved belated recognition as a gifted poet.

nerve cells, or neurons, existence suggested by the German anatomist Heinrich von Waldeyer (1836–1921); observed in detail in the 1880s by the Italian scientist Camillo Golgi (1843–1926) and the Spanish scientist Santiago Ramón y Cajal (1852–1934).

nerves, function first studied by the Swiss physiologist Albrecht von Haller (1708–1777).

Nervi, Pier Luigi (b. 1891), Italian architect, noted for his innovations in style and technology.

Nesselrode, Karl, Count (1780–1862), Russian statesman, was foreign minister for over 30 years.

Nestorian Church, Middle Eastern religious movement dating from the deposition 431 of Nestorius, patriarch of Constantinople (d. 451).

Nestorius (d. *c.* 451), patriarch of Constantinople, deposed and banished for preaching heretical doctrine.

Netherlands, came under dukes of Burgundy 14th century, passing to Spanish Hapsburgs 1504; struggle for independence 1568–1609; Spanish authority reestablished in south (now Belgium and Luxembourg) 1579; war of north region with Spain 1621–48 leading to recognition of Dutch independence 1648; republic 1650–72 and 1702–47; under French rule 1795–1813; restored as independent monarchy 1814; reunited with Belgian provinces to form Kingdom of the Netherlands 1815; Belgium seceded 1830; under German occupation 1940–45; became part of Benelux Union 1947.

Netherlands Antilles, West Indies, made an integral part of the Netherlands 1954.

Neuhof, Theodor (1686–1756), German king of Corsica as Theodor I 1736–38; expelled by Genoese.

Neuilly, Treaty of, between the World War I Allies and Bulgaria, signed 1919.

Neumann, Alfred (1895–1952), German historical novelist, author of *The Devil* (1926).

Neumann, Johann Balthazar (1687–1753), German Baroque architect, whose best-known work is the Vierzehnheiligen Church in Bavaria.

Neumann, Theresa (1898–1962), German stigmatic, reputed to have taken no food after 1922.

neutrinos, subatomic particles, existence postulated 1931 by Wolfgang Pauli (*q.v.*); first detected 1956 by the American physicists Frederick Reines (b. 1918) and Clyde L. Cowan.

neutrons, nuclear particles, discovered 1932 by the English physicist Sir James Chadwick (b. 1891).

neutron stars, postulated 1934 by the astronomers Walter Baade (1893–1960), Fritz Zwicky (b. 1898), and others. See **pulsars.**

Nevada, U.S.A., first settled 1849; created a territory 1861; admitted to the Union 1864.

Nevada University, Reno, founded 1873; opened 1874.

Neville, George (*c.* 1433–76), English prelate, archbishop of York and chancellor, involved in civil war as a Lancastrian supporter.

Neville's Cross, Battle of, victory of the northern levies over the invading Scottish army, 17 Oct. 1346.

Nevin, Ethelbert Woodbridge (1862–1901), American composer, e.g. *Narcissus* (1891).

Nevinson, Henry Woodd (1856–1941), English journalist, worked for the *Nation* and *Manchester Guardian*; also an essayist.

New Amsterdam, early name of New York City until 1664.

Newberry Library, Chicago, public reference library, founded 1887 at the bequest of Walter L. Newberry (1804–68).

New Brunswick, Canada, region first settled by French early 17th century; first English settlement 1762; part of French province of Acadia, then of Nova Scotia; became separate province 1784; joined Dominion of Canada 1867.

Newbolt, Sir Henry (1862–1938), English writer, mainly remembered for patriotic verse, e.g. *Drake's Drum* (1914).

New Caledonia, Pacific, discovered 1774 by Captain Cook; annexed by France 1853; penal colony 1864–94; became part of French overseas territory of New Caledonia 1946.

Newcastle, William Cavendish, Duke of (1592–1676), English Royalist, active in Civil War, was also a playwright and patron of writers.

Newcastle upon Tyne, University of, became a division of the University of Durham 1908; assumed independent status 1963.

Newcastle upon Tyne, Royal Grammar School, English public school, founded 1545.

New College, Oxford University, founded 1379 by William of Wykeham (*q.v.*).

New Deal, U.S.A., policy of President Franklin D. Roosevelt from 1932 onwards.

Newcomen, Thomas (1663–1729), English inventor of a steam-engine used for pumping water from mines.

New Delhi, capital of India, built 1911–29; officially inaugurated 10 Feb. 1931.

Newdigate Prize, Oxford University, for English verse, endowed 1805 by Sir Roger Newdigate (1719–1806).

New England Confederation, formed 1643 for defence against the Indians; dissolved 1684.

New Forest, Hampshire, England, proclaimed a royal hunting preserve 1079 by William the Conqueror; under the control of the Forestry Commission since 1924.

Newfoundland, discovered by John Cabot 1497; British sovereignty recognized 1713, the French retaining fishing rights; granted responsible government 1855; suspended 1934; with Labrador became a Canadian province 1949.

Newgate, London prison, originated 13th century or earlier; rebuilt 1770–83 by the English architect George Dance (1741–1825); finally demolished 1904.

New Guinea, Pacific, island first visited by the Dutch in 17th century; frontiers of Dutch and British claims fixed 1884; now divided into Indonesian province of Irian Taya (formerly West Irian) and the independent state of Papua New Guinea (*q.v.*).

New Hampshire, U.S.A., first settled 1623; one of the 13 original states, entering the Union 1788.

New Hebrides, Pacific, discovered 1606 by the Portuguese navigator Pedro Fernandez de Queiras (1560–1614); under joint administration of France and Britain since 1906.

New Jersey, U.S.A., first settled 1623; one of the 13 original states, entering the Union 1787.

Newman, Ernest (1868–1959), English music critic, wrote the exhaustive *Life of Richard Wagner* (1933–46).

Newman, John Henry, Cardinal (1801–90), English leader of Oxford Movement (*q.v.*), became a Catholic 1845; wrote *Apologia* (1864).

Newmarket, English horse-racing centre, first cup race instituted there 1634 by Charles I.

New Mexico, U.S.A., first explored 1540 and settled 1598 by the Spanish; became part of Mexico 1821; taken by and finally ceded to the U.S.A. 1846–48, becoming a territory 1850; admitted to the Union 1912.

New Model Army, brought into existence 1645 by Oliver Cromwell.

Newnes, Sir George (1851–1910), English newspaper and magazine publisher.

New Orleans, Louisiana, founded 1718 by the French-Canadian explorer Jean-Baptiste le Moyne, Sieur de Bienville (1680–1768).

Newport, Rhode Island, U.S.A., first settled 1639.

New River, water supply system, London, built 1609–13 by the Welsh politician Sir Hugh Myddleton (*c.* 1560–1631).

News Chronicle, British daily newspaper, formed by merger of *Daily News* and *Daily Chronicle* 1930; incorporated in the *Daily Mail* 1960.

News of the World, British Sunday newspaper, founded Oct. 1843.

New South Wales, Australia, discovered and claimed, as the entire eastern coast, for the British crown 1770 by Captain Cook; first settled (Botany Bay) by marines and convicts 1788; separate colonies of Victoria, Queensland, South Australia, and Tasmania set up in mid-19th century; became part of the Commonwealth of Australia 1901.

newspapers, first appeared in England 1621 (*Corante*); first daily, the *Daily Courant*, began 11 March 1702, lasting until 1735.

newspaper advertisement duty, abolished in Britain 1853.

newspaper stamp tax, introduced in Britain 1712; abolished 1855.

newsreels, first introduced 1909 by the French photographer Charles Pathé (*q.v.*).

New Statesman, British periodical, founded 1913; absorbed *The Nation* 1931.

New Stone Age. See **Neolithic.**

New Territories, part of Hong Kong (*q.v.*); leased to Great Britain by China 1898 for 99 years.

New Tokaido Line, high-speed railway, Tokyo–Osako, Japan, opened 1964; extended 1972.

Newton, Sir Isaac (1642–1727), English mathematician and physicist, outstanding figure in history of science, discovered laws of gravity.

Newton's laws of motion. See **motion,** laws of.

Newton, John (1725–1807), English clergyman, a leading figure in the Evangelical movement, was also a hymn-writer and a noted abolitionist.

new towns, in Britain, proposed in the New Towns Act 1946; development corporations formed 1947 for Crawley, Sussex, and Hemel Hempstead, Herts, and 1948 for Hatfield and Welwyn, Herts; substantially completed, respectively, 1962 and 1966.

New Year's Day, changed 1660 (Scotland) and 1752 (England) from 25 March to 1 Jan., following introduction of Gregorian Calendar (*q.v.*); public holiday in Britain.

New York, city, founded as New Amsterdam 1626; renamed New York 1664 when seized by the British from the Dutch; national capital of U.S.A. 1789–90; state capital 1784–97.

New York, state, explored by Henry Hudson 1609; first permanent settlement, by Dutch, at Albany 1624; came under British rule 1664; formed one of the 13 original states of the Union 1788.

New York Herald Tribune, American newspaper, formed 1924 by merging the *New York Tribune,* founded 1841 by Horace Greeley (1811–72), and the *New York Herald,* founded 1835 by James Gordon Bennett (1795–1872); ceased publication 1967.

New York Public Library, founded 1695.

New York Times, American newspaper, founded 1851 by the American editor and politician Henry Jarvis Raymond (1820–1869); called the *New York Daily Times* 1851–57.

New York University, founded 1831.

New Zealand, discovered probably between A.D. 400 and A.D. 700 by Polynesians (Maoris); well-established settlements by 950; rediscovered 1642 by Abel Tasman (*q.v.*); visited and charted by Captain Cook, from 1769; northern lands ceded by Maoris to Britain 1840; annexed by Britain as a crown colony 1841, leading to Maori Wars (*q.v.*); became a dominion 1907.

Nexö, Martin (1869–1954), Danish novelist, wrote about the working classes in *Pelle the Conqueror* (1906–10).

Ney, Michel (1769–1815), French soldier, one of Napoleon's marshals, distinguished himself at Borodino; executed for supporting Napoleon during the Hundred Days.

Niagara Falls, first crossed 1859, on a tightrope, by the French acrobat Blondin (1824–97).

Nibelungenlied, German epic poem, compiled *c.* 1190.

Nicaea, scene of two ecumenical councils of the Christian Church, first convened there 325; second one 787.

Nicaragua, Central America, settled and colonized by the Spanish in 1520s; achieved independence from Spain 1821, becoming a fully independent republic 1838; new constitution 1974.

Nice, founded *c.* 350 B.C.; came under protection of House of Savoy 1388; ceded to France 1860.

Nicene Creed, origin now uncertain; believed to have been proposed 381 at Council of Constantinople but not, as once thought, as an enlargement of the statement formulated at the Council of Nicaea of 325.

Nicephorus I (d. 811), Byzantine emperor 802–811, overthrew Irene; killed fighting Bulgarians.

Nicephorus II (*c.* 912–969), Byzantine emperor 963–969, reconquered Syria.

Nicephorus III (d. 1081), Byzantine emperor 1078–81, proclaimed by his troops; later abdicated.

Nicholas, Saint (4th cent.), bishop of Myra, Asia Minor; patron saint of children and sailors and giver of dowries; origin of Santa Claus.

Nicholas I, Saint (d. 867), Pope 858–867, asserted papal claims to supremacy.

Nicholas II (d. 1061), Pope 1059–61, laid down papal election procedure.

Nicholas III (d. 1280), Pope 1277–80, gave Rome a new constitution.

Nicholas V (*c.* 1398–1455), Pope 1447–55, was a notable patron of the arts.

Nicholas I (1796–1855), tsar of Russia 1825–55, a period of severe repression.

Nicholas II (1868–1918), tsar of Russia 1894–1917, abdicated after February 1917 revolution; murdered by Bolsheviks.

Nicholson, Ben (b. 1894), English painter, best known for his abstract work.

Nicholson, Francis (1665–1728), English colonial administrator, governed several American colonies.

Nicholson, John (1821–57), Irish soldier, deputy commissioner in Punjab 1851–56; killed in Indian Mutiny.

Nicholson, Sir William (1872–1949), English painter, pioneer poster designer, with J. Pryde, as one of the 'Beggarstaff Brothers'.

Nicias, Peace of, negotiated between the Athenians and Spartans 421 B.C. by the Athenian statesman and general Nicias (executed 413 B.C.).

nickel, isolated 1751 by the Swedish chemist Baron Axel Fredrik Cronstedt (1722–1765).

Nicobar Islands, Bay of Bengal, annexed by the British 1869; joined to Andaman Islands (*q.v.*) 1872; now together forming a union territory of India.

Nicolai, Otto (1810–49), German composer, chiefly remembered for the opera *Merry Wives of Windsor* (1849).

Nicolls, Richard (1624–72), first English governor of New York 1664–68.

Nicol prism, for polarizing light, invented 1828 by the Scottish physicist William Nicol (*c.* 1768–1851).

Nicot, Jean (*c.* 1530–1600), French diplomat, introduced tobacco into France, whence 'nicotine'.

nicotine, purified form obtained 1828; first synthesized 1904.

Niebuhr, Reinhold (1892–1971), American theologian, author of *Nature and Destiny of Man* (1941–43).

Nielsen, Carl August (1865–1931), Danish composer, best known for his symphonies.

Niemöller, Martin (b. 1892), German Protestant pastor, imprisoned for his opposition to the Nazis.

Niepce, Nicéphore (1765–1833), French pioneer of photography, produced first permanent image 1822.

Nietzsche, Friedrich (1844–1900), German philosopher, of great and continuing influence, author of *Thus Spake Zarathustra* (1883–92).

Niger, West Africa, first European exploration late 18th century; became part of French West Africa 1904; created a French overseas territory 1946 and an autonomous republic within the French Community 1958; achieved independence 1960.

Niger, River, navigated 1795–96, and 1805–06 by Mungo Park (*q.v.*).

Nigeria, West Africa, established 1914 as the colony and protectorate of Nigeria by amalgamation of the British protectorate of Northern Nigeria (formed 1900) with the British colony and protectorate of Southern Nigeria (formed 1906); became a federation 1954; achieved independence within the Commonwealth 1960, becoming a republic 1963; civil war 1967–70.

'Night of the Long Knives', Nazi purge in Germany, 30 June 1934.

Nightingale, Florence (1820–1910), English nurse in the Crimea War, founded the modern nursing profession.

Nightingale School for Nurses, first modern school of nursing, established 1860 at St Thomas's Hospital, London.

Nihilism, Russian revolutionary movement, founded *c.* 1860.

Nijinsky, Vaslav (1890–1950), Russian ballet dancer of legendary fame, outstanding member of the Diaghilev company.

Nikisch, Arthur (1855–1922), Hungarian conductor, worked in Germany and the U.S.A.

Nikon (1605–81), Russian ecclesiastic, patriarch of Moscow 1652–60; his reforms led to secession of 'Old Believers' from the Church.

Nile, source of the Blue Nile located 1613 by Pedro Páez; source of the White Nile discovered 1862 by the English explorers John Hanning Speke (*q.v.*) and James Augustus Grant (1827–92); Lake Albert discovered 1864 by Sir Samuel Baker (*q.v.*).

Nile, Battle of the, Aboukir Bay, victory of a British fleet, under Nelson, over the French, 1 Aug. 1798.

Nimitz, Chester William (1885–1966), American admiral, commanded the U.S. Pacific Fleet 1941–45.

Nine Lessons and Nine Carols, festival held at King's College Chapel, Cambridge, each year on Christmas Eve.

Nineveh, settlement dates from 7th millennium B.C.; capital of the Assyrian Empire *c.* 700 B.C.–612 B.C.; excavated from 19th century onwards, in particular by Sir Henry Layard (*q.v.*), 1845–51.

Ninian, Saint (*c.* 360–*c.* 432), British bishop, studied at Rome; apostle to the Picts.

Ninon de Lenclos. See **Lenclos,** Ninon de.

niobium, discovered 1801 by the English chemist Charles Hatchett (*c.* 1765–1847); name established *c.* 1950.

nitric acid, discovered by 1300 by alchemists; chemical composition established 1816 by Joseph Louis Gay-Lussac (*q.v.*) and Claude Berthollet (*q.v.*). See also **Ostwald Process.**

nitrocellulose. See **cellulose nitrate.**

nitrogen, discovered 1772 by the Scottish doctor Daniel Rutherford (1749–1819) and about the same time by Joseph Priestley, Henry Cavendish, and Carl Scheele.

nitrogen trichloride, discovered 1811 by the French chemist Pierre-Louis Dulong (1785–1838).

nitroglycerine, first prepared 1846 by the Italian chemist Ascanio Sobrero.

nitrous oxide, or laughing gas, discovered 1772 by Joseph Priestley; physiological properties reported 1800 by Sir Humphrey Davy; first used 1844 as an anaesthetic by the American dentist Horace Wells (1815–1848).

Nixon, Richard (b. 1913), American statesman, 37th president of the United States 1969–75; resigned because of Watergate scandal.

Nkrumah, Kwame (1909–72), Ghanaian statesman and advocate of Pan-Africanism, prime minister from 1957 and president from 1960; deposed 1966.

N.K.V.D., Soviet Commissariat of Internal Affairs (including secret police), founded 1934 as successor to O.G.P.U.; functions taken over 1946 by M.V.D. (*q.v.*).

Noailles, Adrien, Duc de (1678–1766), French soldier, one of a distinguished military family.

Nobel, Alfred (1833–96), Swedish chemist and engineer, inventor of dynamite and founder of the Nobel prizes.

nobelium, transuranic element, discovered 1958 by Albert Ghiorso, T. Sikkeland, J. R. Walton, and Glenn T. Seaborg.

Nobel prizes, awarded annually under the terms of the will of Alfred Nobel, in physics, chemistry, physiology or medicine, literature, and peace, since 1901; economics prize first awarded 1969.

Nobile, Umberto (b. 1885), Italian designer of airships, in which he explored the Arctic.

Noble, Sir Andrew (1832–1915), Scottish physicist, noted for his work on ballistics.

Nobunaga (1534–82), Japanese soldier, subjugated feudal lords and began process of unification.

No **Drama,** classical Japanese lyric drama dating from early 14th century or earlier; perfected 17th century.

Noguchi, Hideyo (1876–1928), Japanese bacteriologist, worked in U.S.A., pioneer in treatment of syphilis.

Nolan, Sidney (b. 1917), Australian painter, best known for his landscapes depicting the Australian outback.

Nollekens, Joseph (1737–1823), English Neo-Classical sculptor, popular for his portrait busts.

non-Euclidean geometry, founded 1829 by Nikolai Lobachevski (*q.v.*).

Nonjurors, body of English Anglican and Scottish Episcopalian clergy who refused to take the oath of allegiance to William and Mary after 1688; last Nonjuring bishop died 1805.

Nordenskjöld, Otto (1869–1928), Swedish explorer, especially of the Antarctic; was also a geologist.

Nordic Council, of Scandinavian countries, inaugurated Feb. 1953; Nordic Council of Ministers established 1971.

Nordraak, Rikard (1842–66), Norwegian composer of his country's national anthem.

Nore Mutiny, at the naval anchorage at Nore, Thames Estuary, 1797, led by Richard Parker (hanged 1797).

Norfolk, Hugh Bigod, 1st Earl of (d. *c.* 1177), English noble, actively rebellious against the throne.

Norfolk, Roger Bigod, 4th Earl of (d. 1270), English noble, involved in civil wars of Henry III's reign.

Norfolk, Thomas Howard, 3rd Duke of (1473–1554), English noble, uncle of Anne Boleyn and Catherine Howard, held high office under Henry VIII.

Norfolk Island, Pacific, discovered by Captain Cook 1774; penal colony 1788–1813 and 1825–55; settled 1856 by the population of Pitcairn Island (*q.v.*); became a Territory of the Australian Commonwealth government 1913.

Norham, Peace of, between Scotland and England, made Aug. 1209.

Norman, Montagu, 1st Baron (1871–1950), English financial expert, governor of Bank of England 1920–44.

Norman Conquest, of England, by William the Conqueror 1066.

Normandy, established *c.* 911 after Viking invasions; united with England 1066; conquered by French 1204; under English control from 1417 until French reconquest 1450; French province until divided into *départements* 1790.

Normandy, Alphonse de (1809–64), French-born chemist in England, invented a distiller for seawater 1851.

Normandy Invasion, World War II, Allied invasion of Europe under the command of General Eisenhower (*q.v.*), began on D-Day, 6 June 1944.

Norris, Frank (1870–1902), American novelist, noted for social realism, as in *The Pit* (pub. 1903).

North, Christopher (1785–1854), Scottish writer of criticism and sketches in *Noctes Ambrosianae* (1822–35).

North, Frederick, Lord (1732–92), English statesman, prime minister 1770–82, with support of George III, during American Revolutionary War.

North, Sir Thomas (*c.* 1535–*c.* 1601), English translator of Plutarch, whose version was used by Shakespeare.

Northampton, Treaty of, recognizing independence of Scotland, signed 1328.

North Atlantic Treaty, signed at Washington, D.C., 4 April 1949. See **N.A.T.O.**

North Borneo. See **Sabah.**

North Carolina, U.S.A., first permanently settled 1650s; formed part of the Caroline grant 1663 from Charles II; became royal province 1729; one of the 13 original states of the Union 1789; seceded May 1861; readmitted to the Union 1868.

Northcliffe, Alfred Harmsworth, 1st Viscount (1865–1922), Irish-born British newspaper magnate.

Northcote, Henry, Lord (1846–1911), English governor-general of Australia 1904–08.

North Dakota, U.S.A., first settled 1819; formed part of the Dakota Territory 1861; separated from South Dakota (*q.v.*) and admitted to the Union 1889.

Northeast Passage, first navigated 1878–1879 by the Swedish explorer Baron Adolf Erik Nordenskiöld (1832–1901).

Northern Ireland, part of the United Kingdom, accepting administration by separate Parliament and executive government established by Government of Ireland Act 1920; scene of civil strife since 1969; direct rule by British government imposed 1972. See also **Ireland**; **Ulster.**

Northern Line, underground railway,

London, opened 1904 as the Great Northern and City Railway.

Northern Rhodesia. See **Zambia.**

Northern Territory, Australia, part of New South Wales (*q.v.*) until annexed by South Australia 1863; transferred to the Commonwealth of Australia 1911 under the control of an administrator; divided into North and Central Australia 1927; reunited 1931; Legislative Council of fully elected members took office Oct. 1974.

North Pole, first reached 6 April 1909 by the American explorers Robert Peary (*q.v.*) and Matthew Henson; first reached by plane 1929 by Richard Byrd (*q.v.*) and by airship 1926 by Roald Amundsen (*q.v.*), Lincoln Ellsworth, and Umberto Nobile (*q.v.*).

North Sea Fisheries Convention, held 1882.

North Sea oil, first direct flow from British sector pumped ashore Nov. 1975 from the Forties Field (*q.v.*).

North Staffordshire, University College of, Keele, founded 1949; became Keele University 1962.

Northumberland, Henry Percy, Earl of (1342–1408), English noble, helped Henry IV win throne, later rebelled; killed in battle.

Northumberland, Thomas Percy, Earl of (1528–72), English Catholic noble, led revolt against Elizabeth I; beheaded.

Northwest Frontier Province, region annexed by British from Sikhs 1849; separated from Punjab and created a province 1901; part of Pakistan 1947; integrated with West Pakistan 1955; regained provincial status 1970.

Northwest Mounted Police. See **Royal Canadian Mounted Police.**

Northwest Ordinance, providing for the government of the northwestern territories of the U.S.A., passed 1787.

Northwest Passage, sought since late 15th century; first journey completed 1850–54 by the British navigator Robert McClure (1807–73), partly over ice; first sailed 1906 by Roald Amundsen.

Northwestern University, Illinois, founded 1851.

Northwest Territories, Canada, first recorded exploration 1770–72 by Samuel Hearne; original region, Northwestern Territory, ceded to Canada 1869, greatly enlarged 1869–82; administered by a commissioner since 1952.

Norton, Charles Bowyer (1814–1905), English politician, president of Board of Trade 1874–78.

Norton, Thomas (1832–84), English poet, with Thomas Sackville (*q.v.*) wrote *Gorboduc* (1561), the first English tragedy.

Norway, converted to Christianity 10th century; united with Sweden 1319–71, with Denmark 1380–89, with Sweden and Denmark 1389–1450, with Denmark 1450–1814; ceded to Sweden 1814 and given a separate constitution; dissolved union 1905 becoming an independent kingdom; under German occupation 1940–45.

Norwich, granted first charter by Henry II 1158.

Norwich Cathedral, founded 1096; cloisters built 14th century, spire 15th century and vaulted roofs 15th–16th century.

Norwich School, English public school, origins uncertain; earliest recorded mention 1256; refounded 1547.

Nostradamus (1503–66), French physician-prophet whose obscure verse *Prophecies* (1555) still causes interpretative controversy.

Notre Dame de Paris, construction began 1163; consecrated 1189; largely completed by 1240.

Nottingham, Charles Howard, Earl of (1536–1624), English admiral, commanded the fleet which defeated the Armada 1588.

Nottingham High School, English public school, founded by Agnes Mellers 1513.

Nottingham University, opened as a university college 1881; achieved university status 1948.

Novalis (pseud. of Georg von Harbenberg; 1772–1801), German Romantic poet and novelist, aphorist of profound mystical feeling.

Nova Scotia, Canada, first settled by the French 1604; ceded to Britain 1713; became a province of the Dominion of Canada 1867.

Novatian (3rd cent.), anti-pope 251, founded sect of Novatians.

Novello, Ivor (1893–1951), English composer of musical comedies, e.g. *Perchance to Dream* (1945).

Novello, Vincent (1781–1861), English musician and pioneer music publisher.

Noverre, Jean Georges (1727–1810), French dancer-choreographer, made ballet more fluent and dramatic.

Novi, Battle of, victory of an Austro-Russian army over the French, 15 Aug. 1799.

Noyes, Alfred (1880–1958), English poet, author of *Drake* (1908).

Noyes, John Humphrey (1811–86), American religious leader, founded Oneida Community, 1848.

Noyon, Treaty of, between France and Spain, signed 1516.

nuclear disintegration, or transmutation, first observed 1919 by Lord Rutherford.

nuclear fission, first observed, in uranium atoms, 1938 by the German chemists Otto Hahn (1879–1968) and Fritz Strassman

(b. 1902); results published 1939 by the Austrian physicist Lise Meitner (1878–1968).

nuclear fusion, as the energy source in stars, proposed 1938 by the German-born physicist Hans Albrecht Bethe (b. 1906). See also **hydrogen bomb.**

Nuclear Nonproliferation Treaty, approved by the United Nations 4 June 1968, ratified by 62 nations, including U.S.A., U.S.S.R., and United Kingdom by 1 July 1968.

nuclear reactor, first built at Chicago University 1942 by Enrico Fermi (*q.v.*).

nuclear reactor, British, first, built at Harwell 1947.

Nuclear Test-Ban Treaty, signed in Moscow by the U.S.A., U.S.S.R., and United Kingdom 5 Aug. 1963; went into effect 10 Oct. 1963 with over 100 signatories.

nuclear weapons. See **atom bomb; hydrogen bomb.**

nucleic acid. See **DNA.**

nucleus, of the cell, first observed (in plant cells) *c.* 1830 by Robert Brown (*q.v.*).

nucleus. See **atomic nucleus.**

Nuffield, William Morris, 1st Viscount (1877–1963), English motor-car manufacturer, built up great mass-production industry.

Nuffield College, Oxford University, founded 1937 by Lord Nuffield (*q.v.*); opened 1958; became a full college of the University 1963.

Nuffield Foundation, established 1943 at the bequest of Lord Nuffield.

Nuñez Cabeza de Vaca, Álvaro (d. *c.* 1557), Spanish adventurer in Latin America, participated in Florida expedition 1527–28; governor of Paraguay 1542–1544.

Nuremberg, War Crimes Tribunal, held Nov. 1945–Oct. 1946.

Nureyev, Rudolf (b. 1939), Russian-born ballet dancer, partnered Margot Fonteyn (*q.v.*) in many roles.

Nuri-es-Said (1888–1958), Iraqi statesman, many times prime minister, murdered in 1958 military coup which overthrew the monarchy.

Nyasa, Lake, existence reported 1616 by the Portuguese Caspar Boccaro; reached by David Livingstone (*q.v.*) 1859.

Nyasaland. See **Malawi.**

Nyerere, Julius (b. 1922), Tanzanian statesman, president since 1962.

nylon, developed in 1930s by a research team led by the American chemist Wallace H. Carothers (1896–1937) at the American firm Du Pont de Nemours; first nylon stockings on general sale in U.S.A. 1940.

Nyon Conference, on the suppression of Mediterranean submarine piracy, held Sept. 1937.

O

Oak Apple Day, 29 May, celebrating the Restoration of Charles II, 1660.

Oakham School, Rutland, English public school, founded by Archdeacon Johnson 1584.

Oaks, The, Epsom, first run 1779.

Oates, Titus (1649–1705), English imposter, 'revealed' Popish Plot which caused political crisis and judicial murder of Catholics.

Oath of Strasbourg, sworn between Charles the Bald and Louis the German against Lothair I, 842.

Oberammergau, Germany, scene of the decennial presentation of the Passion Play since 1634 (now occurring in decimal years).

Oberlin, Jean Frédéric (1740–1826), French pastor, renowned for his philanthropic work.

Oberth, Hermann (b. 1894), German scientist, pioneered the development of rockets.

Obregon, Álvaro (1880–1928), Mexican soldier and statesman, as president 1920–1924 instituted social and economic reforms.

O'Brien, Murrough (1614–74), Irish soldier, after defeat by Cromwell took service with the French.

O'Brien, William Smith (1803–64), Irish nationalist, transported to Tasmania for his part in an insurrection in 1848.

Observer, British newspaper, began publication 1791.

O'Casey, Sean (1884–1964), Irish playwright, author of *Juno and the Paycock* (1924).

Occleve, Thomas (c. 1368–c. 1450), English poet, wrote *The Regiment of Princes.*

Ochs, Adolph (1858–1935), American newspaper publisher, made the *New York Times* one of the world's leading newspapers.

Ockham, William of (d. 1349), English scholastic philosopher, formulated 'Ockham's razor' principle.

O'Clery, Michael (1575–1643), Irish historian, compiled king-list and digest of Irish annals.

O'Connell, Daniel (1775–1847), Irish political leader, helped to secure Catholic Emancipation 1829.

O'Connor, Feargus (1794–1855), Irish politician, prominent in the Chartist Movement.

O'Connor, Frank (1903–66), Irish writer, best known for his short stories including *Guests of the Nation* (1931).

O'Connor, Roderic (1116–98), last Irish high king, submitted to Henry II of England 1175.

Octavia (d. 11 B.C.), wife of Mark Antony, and sister of Octavian; divorced by Antony 32 B.C.

Octavia (c. A.D. 42–62), wife of the Roman emperor Nero, who had her executed.

Octavian. See Augustus.

October Revolution, by which Bolsheviks seized power in Russia, 24–25 Oct. (6–7 Nov. New Style) 1917.

October War, between Israel and Egypt, Syria, Jordan and Iraq, 6 Oct.–23 Oct. 1973.

Oddfellows, Independent Order of, secret fraternal benefit society, founded in Manchester 1813, and in U.S.A. 1819.

Oder–Neisse Line, Polish–German border determined by the Allied powers 1945.

Odo de Cluny (d. 942), French monk, pioneer in development of musical theory.

Odoacer (d. 493), barbarian warrior, overthrew last Roman emperor 476; defeated by Theodoric (*q.v.*).

O.E.C.D., Organization for Economic Co-operation and Development, founded Sept. 1961.

O.E.E.C., Organization for European Economic Cooperation, established April 1948; superseded 1961 by O.E.C.D.

Oecolampadius, Johannes (1482–1531), German Protestant, helped introduce Reformation at Basel.

Oersted, Hans Christian (1777–1851), Danish physicist, founded electro-magnetic studies.

Offa's Dyke, Welsh border defence, constructed some time between 784 and 796 by Offa, king of Mercia 757–796.

Offenbach, Jacques (1819–80), German-born French composer of popular operettas, especially *Tales of Hoffmann.*

offset printing, method discovered 1798 by the German Aloys Senefelder (1771–1834).

O'Flaherty, Liam (b. 1896), Irish novelist, famous for *The Informer* (1925).

Ogadai (1185–1241), Mongol khan 1229–1241, extended empire of his father Genghis Khan.

Ogden, Charles Kay (1889–1957), English linguist, founder of Basic English.

ogham, alphabetic script probably dating from 4th century A.D. used on Irish and Pictish monuments.

Oglethorpe, James (1696–1785), English soldier, founded colony of Georgia 1733.

O.G.P.U., United State Political Administration, Soviet secret police agency, established 1922 as the G.P.U.; renamed 1923; replaced by the N.K.V.D. (*q.v.*) 1934.

O'Higgins, Bernardo (1776–1842), Chilean soldier, defeated Spaniards; dictator 1817–1823.

Ohio, U.S.A., first settled 1788; admitted to the Union 1803.

Ohio Company, organization of Englishmen and Virginians chartered 1749 for colonizing the Ohio Valley.

Ohm's Law, electricity, pronounced 1827 by the German physicist Georg Simon Ohm (1787–1854).

Ohthered (9th cent.), Norse explorer, commissioned by King Alfred, reached the White Sea.

oil, first well drilled 1858 in Pennsylvania by the American Edwin Drake (1819–80); oil struck 1859.

oil lighting, first used for London streets 1681.

oil tankers, prototype built 1886 at Tyneside; first 100,000 dead weight tonnage built 1958; supertankers of over 250,000 tons built late 1960s and of 500,000 tons and over in early 1970s.

Oireachtas, National Parliament of the Republic of Ireland, founded 1937.

Oistrakh, David (1908–74), Russian violin virtuoso, for whom many works were specially composed.

Oistrakh, Igor (b. 1931), Soviet violin virtuoso, son of David Oistrakh.

Ojeda, Alonso de (c. 1466–c. 1515), Spanish explorer of South American coastline; later colonial governor.

okapi, African mammal first noted c. 1880 by the Russian-born explorer Wilhelm Junker (1840–92).

O'Keeffe, John (1747–1833), Irish playwright, wrote *Tony Lumpkin in Town* (1778).

Okinawa, Battle of, World War II, between the Japanese and the invading Americans, 1 April–22 June 1945; Okinawa reverted to Japan May 1972.

Oklahoma, U.S.A., acquired 1803 by the Louisiana Purchase (*q.v.*); first settled 1889; western region created a territory 1890; merged with the original Indian Territory, formed 1820s, and admitted to the Union 1907.

Okyo (1733–95), Japanese painter, noted for his realism.

Olaf II (1370–87), king of Denmark 1376–1387, as Olaf V king of Norway 1380–87; his mother Margaret acted as regent.

Olaf I (969–1000), king of Norway 995–1000, introduced Christianity.

Olaf II, Saint (995–1030), king of Norway 1016–28 and patron saint; driven out by under-kings.

Olaf III (d. 1093), king of Norway 1066–93, enjoyed a peaceful reign.

Olaf IV (d. 1115), child king of Norway 1103–15, ruled jointly with his brothers.

Olaf V. See **Olaf II** of Denmark.

Olbers, Heinrich (1758–1840), German astronomer, studied asteroids and comets.

Olcott, Chauncey (1860–1932), American actor and singer in musical comedy.

Old Age Pensions, Britain, first introduced 1909.

Old Believers, section of Russian Orthodox Church that refused to accept liturgical reforms 1652–58 of the Moscow patriarch Nikon; excommunicated 1667 and greatly persecuted to mid-19th century; officially recognized 1881.

Old Catholics, religious movements, separated from Rome, formed 1724 (Netherlands), 1870–71 (Germany, Austria and Switzerland).

Oldcastle, Sir John (d. 1417), English religious reformer and Lollard leader; hanged.

Oldenbarneveldt, Jan van (1547–1619), Dutch republican leader, negotiated peace with Spain 1609; executed.

Old English, or Anglo-Saxon, spoken and written in England before 1100–50.

Oldham Hulme Grammar School, Lancashire, English public school, founded by James Assheton 1611.

Old Pretender. See **Stuart,** James Edward.

Old Stone Age. See **Palaeolithic.**

Old Style, British calendar (Julian), superseded by New Style 1752.

Olduvai Gorge, Tanzania, site of rich hominid fossil beds dating back over two million years; excavated from 1931 by the Leakey family.

Old Vic Theatre, London, opened 1818 as the Royal Coburg; reopened 1833 as the Royal Victoria, soon known as the Old Vic; management taken over 1912 by Lilian Baylis (*q.v.*); first Shakespeare season 1914; closed June 1963, becoming, Oct. 1963, the temporary home of the National Theatre Company.

Oldys, William (1696–1761), English antiquary, cataloguer of Harleian Library (*q.v.*).

oleic acid. See **fatty acids.**

Olga, Saint (d. c. 969), princess of Kiev, wife of Prince Igor, ruled as regent 945–955.

Oligocene Epoch, Earth history, from c. 38 to c. 26 million years ago.

Oliphant, Laurence (1829–88), South African-born British travel writer, later wrote mystical works.

Olivares, Gaspar (1587–1645), Spanish chief minister of Philip IV 1621–43, entered Thirty Years War.

Oliver, Isaac (c. 1566–1617), French-born English miniaturist, pupil and later rival of Hilliard.

Olivier, Laurence, Lord (b. 1907), English actor of great distinction, noted for his Shakespearean roles on the stage and in films; first director of National Theatre Company.

Ollivier, Emile (1825–1913), French statesman, chief minister in Napoleon III's 'liberal empire'.

Olmsted, Denison (1791–1859), American scientist, investigated weather phenomena.

Olympiad, ancient Greek 4-year period, calculated by the Olympic Games.

Olympias (d. 316 B.C.), wife of Philip II of Macedon, inveterate intriguer, influenced her son Alexander the Great.

Olympic Cup, instituted 1906 by the French scholar Baron Pierre de Coubertin (1863–1937).

Olympic Games, ancient, held 776 B.C. to A.D. 393.

Olympic Games, modern idea of revival introduced 1894 by Pierre de Coubertin; first modern games held at Athens 1896. Games were then held as follows: Paris 1900, St Louis 1904, London 1908, Stockholm 1912, Antwerp 1920, Paris 1924, Amsterdam 1928, Los Angeles 1932, Berlin 1936, London 1948, Helsinki 1952, Melbourne 1956, Rome 1960, Tokyo 1964, Mexico City 1968, Munich 1972, Montreal 1976.

Olympic Games, Winter, first held at Chamonix, France, 1924; skating events included in the 1908 (London) and 1920 (Antwerp) Olympic Games.

O'Mahoney, John (1816–77), Irish nationalist, prominent Fenian leader in U.S.A.

Oman, independent sultanate, Arabian Peninsula, close ties with Britain since early 19th century, affirmed by treaty 1939; renewed 1951.

Oman, Sir Charles (1860–1946), English historian, wrote studies of wars and military techniques.

Omar (c. 581–644), second Muslim caliph, great organizer and conqueror, subdued Persia, Syria and Egypt.

Omar Khayyam (d. c. 1123), Persian poet, wrote famous *Rubaiyat*; was also an astronomer.

Omayyad dynasty, of Arabian caliphs, 661 to 750.

Omdurman, Battle of, victory of Anglo-Egyptian forces under Kitchener (q.v.) over the Mahdists, 2 Sept. 1898.

O'Meara, Barry (1786–1836), Irish surgeon, Napoleon's physician at St Helena 1815–18, wrote *Napoleon in Exile* (1822).

Omer Pasha (1806–71), Croatian-born Turkish general, put down many revolts and was successful in war against the Russians.

Onassis, Aristotle (1906–75), Greek multi-millionaire shipping magnate.

Oneida Community, New York State, founded 1848 by the American reformer John Noyes (1811–86).

O'Neill, Eugene (1888–1953), American playwright, author of *The Iceman Cometh* (1946); Nobel prizewinner 1936.

O'Neill, Hugh, Earl of Tyrone (c. 1540–1616), Irish leader in resistance to English rule.

Ontario, Canada, settled by the French; British territory from 1763; organized as Upper Canada 1791; made a province of the Dominion of Canada 1867.

O.P.E.C., Organization of the Petroleum Exporting Countries, established 1960.

Open Door Policy, initiated by the U.S.A. 1899 concerning trade with, and integrity of, China.

open-hearth process, major steel-making process up to 1970s, invented 1864 by the French engineer Pierre-Emile Martin (1824–1915), based on the open-hearth furnace invented 1856 by Sir William Siemens (q.v.) and his brother Friedrich, and patented 1861.

Open University, Milton Keynes, Buckinghamshire, founded 1969, opened May 1970.

opera, first real, *La Dafne* (1597) by Rinuccini and Peri.

ophthalmoscope, invented 1851 by Herman von Helmholtz (q.v.) and independently 1847 by Charles Babbage (q.v.).

Opie, Amelia (1769–1853), English novelist, wrote *Father and Daughter* (1801); wife of John Opie.

Opie, John (1761–1807), English historical painter, e.g. *Assassination of Rizzio* (1787).

Opium War, between Britain and China, waged 1839–42.

Oppenheimer, Sir Ernest (1880–1957), German-born South African mining magnate, was prominent in the diamond industry.

Oppenheimer, John (1904–67), American physicist, played a leading part in the development of the atomic bomb.

optics, geometric, founded by Johann Kepler (q.v.); greatly developed and described 1841 by Karl Friedrich Gauss (q.v.).

oral contraceptives, first effective 'pills' developed in late 1950s following the work in 1955 of the American biologist Gregory Pincus (1903–67).

Orange Free State, South Africa, first settled 1820s; main settlement followed the Great Trek of the Boers 1836; proclaimed British territory 1848; became independent Boer state 1854; annexed by Britain 1900; became a province of the Union (later Republic) of South Africa 1910.

Orangemen, Irish Protestant association, formed by 1795.

Oratorians, religious order, founded 1575 by Saint Philip Neri (1515–95); introduced into England 1847 by Cardinal Newman.

oratorio, earliest surviving, by Emilio del Cavaliere (c. 1550–1602), produced 1600.

Oratory, The, London, established 1849; moved to Brompton site 1854; church completed 1884.

Orcagna, Andrea (c. 1308–68), Italian artist, painted and sculpted in Gothic style.

Orchardson, Sir William (1832–1910), Scottish painter, notably of *Napoleon on board the 'Bellerophon'* (1880).

Ord, Sir Harry (1819–85), English colonial administrator, first governor of the Straits Settlements 1867–73.

Ordericus Vitalis (1075–*c.* 1143), Anglo-Norman monk and chronicler, wrote *Historia Ecclesiastica*.

Order of Merit, created 1902.

Ordnance Survey, of Britain, established 1791.

Order of the Garter, founded by Edward III 1348.

Ordovician Period, Earth history, from *c.* 500 to *c.* 430 million years ago.

Oregon, U.S.A., first settled *c.* 1830; made a territory 1848; admitted to the Union 1859.

Oregon, University of, founded 1872, opened 1876.

Oregon Trail, Missouri to Oregon, first travelled 1805; main migrations early 1840s.

Orellana, Francisco de (*c.* 1500–49), Spanish soldier and explorer, first man to navigate the Amazon to its mouth.

Orff, Carl (b. 1895), German composer, whose best-known work is *Carmina Burana* (1936).

Orford, Earl of. See **Walpole,** Robert.

organic chemistry, developed in early 19th century by the work of the French and German chemists Michel-Eugene Chevreul (1786–1889), Friedrich Wohler (1800–82), Marcelin Berthelot (*q.v.*), and Adolphe Kolbe (1818–84).

Organization of African Unity (O.A.U.), founded at Addis Ababa May 1963.

Organization of American States (O.A.S.), founded at Bogotá, Colombia, April 1948.

Orgetorix (d. *c.* 60 B.C.), leader of the Helvetii tribe against Julius Caesar.

Oriel College, Oxford University, founded by Edward II 1326.

Origen (*c.* 185–*c.* 254), theologian of Alexandria, one of the Greek Fathers of the Church.

Orinoco, South American river, first explored 1531 independently by Spanish expeditions led by Diego de Ordaz and by Antonio de Berrio.

Orissa, India, conquered by the British 1803; constituted a separate province 1936; recognized as a state of the Indian Union 1950.

Orkneys, passed (by default) from Danish to Scottish ownership 1468; formally annexed to the Scottish crown 1472.

Orlando, Vittorio Emanuele (1860–1952), Italian statesman, prime minister 1917–19 and negotiator at the peace conference 1919–20.

Orleanists, French royalist political party, formed *c.* 1790; ceased to exist after 1883.

Orléans, Charles d' (1391–1465), French poet, one of the greatest courtly poets, exiled in England for many years.

Orléans, Gaston de France, Duc d' (1608–1660), French prince, brother of Louis XIII, involved in conspiracies against Richelieu and Mazarin.

Orléans, Henri, Prince d' (1867–1901), French explorer in Asia and Africa.

Orléans, Louis de France, Duc d' (1372–1407), French prince, whose assassination led to the long feud between Burgundians and Armagnacs.

Orléans, Louis-Philippe, Duc d' (1747–1793), French prince, known as 'Philippe Egalité' during the Revolution; guillotined.

Orléans, Philippe, Duc d' (1647–1723), French prince, regent of France 1715–23, during the minority of Louis XV.

Orley, Bernard (*c.* 1491–1542), Flemish Renaissance painter, was also an influential tapestry designer.

Orlov, Prince Alexei (1737–1809), Russian noble, with brother Grigori (1734–83), dethroned and killed Peter III.

Orm (13th cent.), English poet, also known as Ormin, wrote *Ormulum.*

Ormandy, Eugene (b. 1899), Hungarian-born American conductor of the Philadelphia Symphony Orchestra.

Ormonde, James Butler, 1st Duke of (1610–88), Irish soldier and statesman, advanced Protestant cause in Ireland.

Orosius (4th–5th cent.), Spanish historian, wrote a (Latin) *History against the Pagans.*

Orozco, José (1883–1949), Mexican fresco painter, produced more stylized versions of Rivera's social realism.

Orpen, Sir William (1878–1931), Irish painter, best known for his *Homage to Manet* (1909).

Orrery, Roger, Earl of (1621–79), Irish soldier, served Cromwell; transferred allegiance to Charles II; was also a playwright.

Orsini, Felice (1819–58), Italian revolutionary, attempted to assassinate Napoleon III; executed.

Ortega y Gasset, José (1883–1955), Spanish writer, denounced emergence of mass values in *Revolt of the Masses* (1930).

Ortelius (1527–98), Flemish geographer, produced the first modern atlas.

Orthodox Eastern Church, finally separated from the Western Church 1054.

Orton, Arthur (1834–98), English impostor, whose claim to the Tichborne title led to a famous court case.

Orwell, George (pseud. of Eric Blair; 1903–50), English writer on social-political subjects, including the satirical *Animal Farm* (1945) and *Nineteen Eighty-Four* (1949).

Osborne, Dorothy (1627–95), gifted English letter-writer – to Sir William Temple (*q.v.*), whom she eventually married.

Osborne, John (b. 1929), English playwright, made a great impact on the English theatre with *Look Back in Anger* (1956).

Osborne, Ruth (1680–1751), English 'witch', last victim of popular superstition; killed by mob.

Oscar I (1799–1859), king of Sweden and Norway 1844–59, son of Marshal Bernadotte (*q.v.*).

Oscar II (1829–1907), king of Sweden 1872–1907 and Norway 1872–1905; played conciliatory role between the two countries.

oscilloscope, cathode ray, invented 1897 by the German physicist Karl Ferdinand Braun (1850–1918).

O'Shanassy, Sir John (1818–83), Irish-born Australian statesman, three times prime minister of Victoria.

Osiander, Andreas (1498–1552), German theologian, prominent in establishing Reformation at Augsburg.

Osler, Sir William (1849–1919), Canadian physician, wrote widely on medicine and general topics.

Osman I (1259–1326), Turkish ruler, founder of the Ottoman dynasty.

Osman Pasha (*c.* 1835–1900), Turkish soldier, famous for his defence of Plevna against the Russians, 1877.

osmium, metallic element, discovered 1803 by the English chemist Smithson Tennant (1761–1815).

osmosis, first detailed study 1877 by the German botanist Wilhelm Pfeffer (1845–1920).

Ossendowski, Ferdynand (1876–1945), Polish writer, author of *The Devils* (1938).

Ossian. See **Macpherson,** James.

Ossietzky, Carl von (1889–1938), German pacifist, imprisoned for his views by the Nazis.

Ostade, Adriaan van (1610–85), Dutch painter of country and tavern scenes.

Ostenso, Martha (1900–63), Norwegian-born American writer, author of the novel *Wild Geese* (1925).

osteopathy, principles formulated 1874 by the American physician Andrew Taylor Still (1828–1917).

Osterman, Andrei (1686–1747), Russian diplomat, served three rulers but exiled by the Empress Elizabeth.

Ostrog Bible, first Russian Bible, published by order of Konstantin, Prince Ostrogski, 1581.

Ostrogoths, eastern branch of the Goths, divided in late 4th century; settled in Hungary in 5th century; founded kingdom in Italy *c.* 490–552.

Ostrovsky, Alexander (1823–1886), Russian dramatist, author of *The Storm* (1880).

Ostwald process, for nitric acid production, developed 1901 by the German chemist Wilhelm Ostwald (1853–1932).

Osuna, Pedro Giron, Duke of (1575–1624), Spanish viceroy of Sicily 1611 and Naples 1616; suspected of plotting; imprisoned.

Oswald, Saint (*c.* 605–642), king of Northumbria 634–642; killed in battle against pagan Mercians.

Oswald, Saint (d. 992), English monk, archbishop of York 972–992; one of leaders of the 10th-century ecclesiastical revival.

Oswiecim, Poland, site of German concentration camp 1941–45, in which more than one million people died.

Othman (*c.* 574–656), third Muslim caliph 644–656, conquered North Africa and Armenia; assassinated.

Otho (A.D. 32–69), Roman emperor A.D. 69, overthrew Galba; defeated by Vitellius; committed suicide.

Otis, Elisha Graves (1811–61), American inventor, notably of lift machinery.

Ottawa, Canada, settlement developed from 1827, as Bytown, with construction of Rideau Canal by John By; renamed 1855; became capital 1857.

Ottawa Conference, British imperial economic conference held 21 July–20 Aug. 1932.

Otterburn, Battle of, victory of the Scots over the English Aug. 1388.

Otto I (912–973), Holy Roman emperor 936–973, crushed Lombards and Magyars.

Otto II (955–983), Holy Roman emperor 973–983, victorious in France but defeated in Italy.

Otto III (980–1002), Holy Roman emperor 996–1002, made Rome his capital.

Otto IV (*c.* 1174–1218), Holy Roman emperor 1198–1218, crowned 1209 after long civil war.

Otto I (1815–67), king of Greece 1832–62, never popular with his subjects; deposed.

Ottocar I (d. 1230), king of Bohemia 1197–1230, became powerful in Germany but failed to control Church.

Ottocar II (*c.* 1230–78), king of Bohemia 1253–78, defeated by Emperor Rudolf II.

Otto cycle, four-stroke engine cycle, patented 1877 by the German inventor Nikolaus August Otto (1832–91).

Ottoman Empire, established 1288; at peak of its power from late 15th to mid-16th centuries; ended 1922 when Turkey became a republic.

Otway, Thomas (1652–85), English playwright, chiefly remembered for *Venice Preserved* (1682).

Ouchy, Treaty of. See **Lausanne,** Treaty of.

Oudenaarde, Battle of, victory of the British and Imperialists under the Duke of

Marlborough and Prince Eugene over the French, 11 July 1708.

Oughtred, William (1575–1660), English mathematician, inventor of the slide rule.

Ouida (pseud. of Maria Louise Ramée; 1839–1908), English popular novelist, author of *Under Two Flags* (1867).

ounce, troy, for precious metals and stones, legalized in Britain 1853.

Oundle School, Peterborough, founded 1556 from the bequest of Sir William Laxton to the Grocers' Company.

outlawry, civil proceedings in, abolished in Britain 1879; proceedings finally abolished 1938 in England and 1949 in Scotland.

Outram, Benjamin (1764–1805), English engineer, first to use iron rails for colliery railways.

Outward Bound Trust, for schools, established 1946.

ova, or egg cells, first described 1827 by the Russian-born German embryologist Karl Ernst von Baer (1792–1876).

ovaries, human, structure described 1673 by the Dutch anatomist Regnier de Graaf (1641–73).

Overbeck, Johann Friedrich (1789–1869), German painter, leader of Nazarene group of religious artists.

Overbury, Sir Thomas (1581–1613), English writer (*Characters*), adviser to Earl of Somerset; poisoned as a result of court intrigue.

Overland Mail, Southern, U.S.A., from St Louis to San Francisco, via El Paso, Texas, and Tucson, Arizona, began service Sept. 1858.

Ovid (43 B.C.–A.D. 17), Roman poet, wrote *Metamorphoses*; exiled after scandal.

Owen, Sir Richard (1804–92), English zoologist, expert in vertebrate palaeontology.

Owen, Robert (1771–1858), English social reformer, set up model industrial community; was an early trade unionist.

Owen, Wilfred (1893–1918), Welsh poet whose work expresses his feelings at the futility of war.

Owen Falls Dam, Jinja, Uganda, opened 1954.

Owen Glendower. See **Glendower,** Owen.

Owens, Jesse (b. 1913), American Negro athlete, remembered for his achievements at the 1936 Berlin Olympic Games.

Owens College. See **Manchester University.**

Oxenstierna, Count Axel (1583–1654), Swedish statesman, chancellor for many years; directed national policy after death of Gustavus Adolphus (*q.v.*).

OXFAM, founded 1942 as the Oxford Committee for Famine Relief; name changed 1965.

Oxford, Edward, Earl of (1550–1604),

English poet and dramatist, in the opinion of some was the author of Shakespeare's works.

Oxford, Robert, Earl of (1362–92), English courtier, was a leading supporter of Richard II.

Oxford and Cambridge Boat Race, first held 1829.

Oxford English Dictionary, first suggested to the Philological Society of London 1857; editorial work began 1878; published 1884–1928 as *A New English Dictionary on Historical Principles*; reissued as *The Oxford English Dictionary* 1933; reprinted 1961 and 1970; supplements (A–N) published 1972 and 1976.

Oxford Group. See **Moral Rearmament.**

Oxford Movement, centred at Oxford University, led by John Keble, John Henry Newman and E. B. Pusey (*qq.v.*), launched 14 July 1833.

Oxford Tracts (*Tracts for the Times*), issued 1833–41 by the Oxford Movement.

Oxford University, in existence before 1200; first colleges, University, Balliol, and Merton, founded in 1260s and 1270s; incorporated by Elizabeth I 1571; religious tests abolished 1871; Rhodes scholarships founded 1902; women admitted to degrees 1920.

Oxford University Press, founded 1856.

Oxley, John (1781–1828), English-born Australian surveyor, explored New South Wales interior.

oxygen, discovered 1774 by Joseph Priestley (findings published 1774) and independently *c.* 1772 by Carl Wilhelm Scheele (findings published 1777); recognized as element, named and role in combustion explained 1775–79 by Antoine Lavoisier.

oxygen, liquid, first produced 1877 by the French physicist Louis-Paul Cailletet (1832–1913).

oxyhydrogen blowpipe, antecedant of the welding torch, invented 1801 by the American chemist Robert Hare (1781–1858).

ozone, discovered 1840 by the German chemist Christian Friedrich Schönbein (1799–1868).

P

Paasikivi, Juho Kusti (1870–1956), Finnish statesman, president 1946–56.

Pachmann, Vladimir de (1848–1933), Russian pianist, was a notable Chopin interpreter.

Pachomius, Saint (4th cent.), Christian monk in Egypt, founded first true monastery.

Pacific, War of the, between Chile and Bolivia and Peru 1879–84.

Pacific Islands, Trust Territory of the, administered by the U.S.A., created 1947.

Pacific Ocean, first sighted 1513 by the Spanish navigator Vasco Nuñez de Balboa (*q.v.*); first sailed 1520 by Ferdinand Magellan (*q.v.*).

Pacific Security Treaty, between the U.S.A., Australia and New Zealand, signed 1 Sept. 1951.

Packard, Alpheus Spring (1839–1905), American entomologist, founded and edited *American Naturalist* (1867–87).

paddle steamers, introduced in 1780s following the invention of the steam engine (*q.v.*); superseded in 1850s by vessels with screw propellers (*q.v.*).

Paderewski, Ignacy Jan (1860–1941), Polish pianist, composer, and statesman, was prime minister 1919–20.

Padua, University of, founded 1222.

Paganini, Nicolò (1782–1840), Italian violin virtuoso and composer, who led a turbulent, adventurous life.

Page, Thomas (1803–77), English builder of Chelsea and Westminster bridges; constructed Albert Enbankment.

Paget, Sir James (1814–99), English surgeon, was an authority on tumours and bone diseases; described 'Paget's disease'.

Paget, William, Lord (1505–63), English administrator, employed by Henry VIII and Queen Mary.

Pahang, state of Malaysia, entered into treaty relations with Britain 1887; member of Federated Malay States 1895; part of Federation of Malay 1948 and of Malaysia since 1963.

Pain, Barry (1864–1928), English humorous writer for *Cornhill Magazine* and *Punch*.

Paine, Thomas (1737–1809), English radical, wrote *Rights of Man*, 1791–92; active in American and French revolutions.

Painlevé, Paul (1863–1933), French statesman, prime minister 1917, 1925; as minister of war and air encouraged aviation.

Painter, William (*c.* 1540–94), English translator, published *Palace of Pleasure* (1566–67).

Pakistan, created an independent state Aug. 1947 from the predominantly Muslim parts of the former Indian Empire; proclaimed an Islamic republic within the Commonwealth 1956; eastern province seceded Dec. 1971 to become the independent state of Bangladesh (*q.v.*); Pakistan left the Commonwealth 1972; adopted new constitution 1973.

Palaeocene Epoch, Earth history, from *c.* 65 to *c.* 54 million years ago.

Palaeolithic, or Old Stone Age, began with the appearance of the first man-like forms using simple stone tools, dating back 2,500,000 years or earlier.

palaeontology, founded in 1790s by the

French anatomist Georges Cuvier (1769–1832) and developed by the English zoologist Sir Richard Owen (1804–92).

Palaeozoic Era, Earth history, from *c.* 570 to *c.* 395 million years ago (Lower) and from *c.* 395 to *c.* 225 million years ago (Upper).

Palafox y Melzi, José de (1780–1847), Spanish soldier, defended Saragossa against the French during the Peninsular War.

Palamas, Kostes (1859–1943), Greek poet, author of *Life Immovable* (1904).

Paléologue, Maurice (1859–1944), French diplomat in Bulgaria 1907–12; ambassador to Russia 1914–17.

Palestine, conquered by Egypt *c.* 1550 B.C.; Israelite occupation from 12th century B.C.; part of Assyrian, Persian and Roman empires; conquered by Arabs in 7th century A.D.; part of Ottoman Empire 1516–1917; conquered by British 1917–1918; British mandate proclaimed 1923; ended 1948 when Palestine divided between new state of Israel and Jordan (*qq.v.*).

Palestine Liberation Organization, set up May 1964.

Palestrina, Giovanni da (*c.* 1525–94), Italian composer of masses and motets.

Paley, William (1743–1805), English philosopher-theologian, argued for existence of God as 'great clockmaker'.

Palgrave, Francis Turner (1824–97), English compiler of famous verse anthology *Golden Treasury* (1861).

Palissy, Bernard (*c.* 1509–89), French potter, produced characteristic ware decorated with modelled relief snakes, fish, etc.

Palladio, Andrea (1518–80), Italian architect, developed villa style from ancient Roman practice.

palladium, metallic element, isolated 1803 by the English scientist William Hyde Wollaston (1766–1828).

Pallavicino, Pietro Sforza (1607–67), Italian Jesuit, wrote history of Council of Trent.

Palma, Jacopo (*c.* 1480–1528), Italian painter of Venetian school, mainly of historical or allegorical subjects.

Palmer, Arnold (b. 1924), American golfer, several times winner of U.S. Open Tournaments.

Palmer, Edward Henry (1840–82), English professor of Arabic, murdered in Egypt on diplomatic mission.

Palmer, George (1818–97), English biscuit manufacturer, with Thomas Huntley founded well-known firm 1841.

Palmer, Samuel (1805–81), English painter of visionary intensity, was a disciple of William Blake.

Palmerston, Henry, Viscount (1784–1865), British statesman, as foreign secretary and, later, prime minister, was a dominant figure in British politics over many years.

Palmgren, Selim (1878–1951), Finnish composer, wrote mostly for the piano.

palmitic acid. See **fatty acids.**

Palm Sunday, the Sunday before Easter.

Palomar. See **Mount Palomar Observatory.**

Panama, region settled by Spanish early in 16th century; part of viceroyalties of Peru and New Granada; joined Greater Colombia 1821; became independent 1903.

Panama Canal, first attempted construction 1879–89 by the French under Ferdinand de Lesseps (q.v.); construction begun again 1904 by the Americans; completed Aug. 1914; major improvements completed 1970.

Panama Canal and Canal Zone, treaty between Panama and the U.S.A. giving U.S. government use of the canal zone in perpetuity signed 18 Nov. 1903; negotiations for new treaty begun 1964.

Pan-American Highway, connecting North and South America, projected 1923; still under construction in Chile, Argentina and Brazil.

Pan-American Union, established 1890; reconstituted 1948 as the Organization of American States (q.v.).

Panchatantra, Sanskrit collection of fables, assembled c. 5th century or possibly earlier.

Panchen Lama, title of the line of reincarnated lamas at the Tashilhunpo monastery, Tibet; first one 'reappeared' 1663.

Pancras, Saint (c. 290–304), child martyred during Diocletian's persecutions of Christians; patron saint of children.

Pandit, Viljaya Lakshmi (b. 1900), Indian diplomat, first woman president of the U.N. General Assembly, 1953–54.

Pandulf (d. 1226), Italian-born bishop of Norwich and papal legate, enjoyed great influence in England.

Pan-German League (*Alldeutschen Verband*), German nationalist organization evolved 1894 from the earlier General German League, founded 1891.

Panizzi, Sir Anthony (1797–1897), Italian-born librarian 1856–66 of the British Museum.

Pankhurst, Dame Christabel (1880–1958), English suffragette, daughter of Emmeline Pankhurst; later turned to revivalism.

Pankhurst, Emmeline (1858–1928), English suffragette, led violent agitation for votes for women.

Pankhurst, Sylvia (1882–1960), English suffragette, daughter of Emmeline Pankhurst; later became a pacifist and Socialist.

Pannartz, Arnold (15th cent.), German printer, worked in Italy.

Pannini, Giovanni Paolo (c. 1691–1765), Italian painter of ruins and architectural 'caprices'.

Panthéon, Paris, designed by Jacques-Germain Soufflot (q.v.); built c. 1757–c. 1790 as a church; secularized 1789; served as a church 1828–30 and 1851–85.

Pantheon, Rome, built c. 27 B.C.; rebuilt c. A.D. 120 by Hadrian; transformed into a Christian church 609.

pantomimes, introduced into England in early 18th century, in ballet form, by the English dancing-master John Weaver (1673–1760).

Panzini, Alfredo (1863–1939), Italian novelist, wrote *Santippe* (1914).

Paoli, Pasquale (1725–1807), Corsican leader of independence struggle against Genoa and France.

Papagos, Alexandros (1883–1955), Greek soldier and statesman, prime minister 1952–55.

Papal States, papacy's temporal power began with Donation of Pepin 754; greatly extended in 12th–13th centuries; annexed to France 1809–15; finally incorporated in kingdom of Italy 1859–60 and 1870.

Papen, Franz von (1879–1969), German statesman, chancellor 1932, helped Hitler to achieve power 1933.

paper, traditionally invented A.D. 105 by Ts'ai Lun, a Chinese official at the imperial court; manufacture from wood pulp suggested 1800; chemical wood pulp process first used 1852 in England.

Papin, Denis (c. 1647–1712), French physicist, inventor of the steam safety valve.

Papini, Giovanni (1881–1956), Italian writer, author of *Un Uomo Finito* (1912).

Papinian (c. A.D. 140–212), Roman jurist, author of *Quaestiones*; executed.

Pappus (4th cent.), Greek geometer, author of a comprehensive work on mathematics.

Papua, first visited c. 1526 by the Portuguese navigator Jorge de Menezes; annexed by the Queensland government 1883; created a territory of Australia 1906; united with Trust Territory of New Guinea 1947. See **Papua New Guinea.**

Papua New Guinea, created 1947 by uniting the Territory of Papua (q.v.) with the Trust Territory of New Guinea (q.v.); achieved self-government Dec. 1973; became a fully independent state Sept. 1975.

Paracelsus (1493–1541), Swiss physician and occultist, credited with remarkable cures.

parachutes, probably invented 1785 by the French balloonist Jean-Pierre Blanchard (1753–1809); first used successfully 1802 by the Frenchman André-Jacques Garnevin (1769–1823); first descent from an aeroplane, 1912, by the American Captain Albert Berry.

paraffin, or kerosene, first produced in the 1850s from coal tar and shale; obtained from petroleum 1859.

paraffin lamps, widely used from the 1860s up to the development of electric lights in the 1880s.

Paraguay, colonized by Spain 1530s; declared independence 1811; proclaimed a republic 1813; new constitution adopted 1844; at war with Brazil, Argentina and Uruguay 1865–70, and with Bolivia 1932–1935.

paratroops, first paratroop assault division formed 1934 by the Soviet army; first used in war by the Germans 1940.

parcel post, inland, began in Britain 1883.

parchment, traditionally invented by Eumenes II of Pergamon in the 2nd century B.C.

Paré, Ambroise (1510–90), French pioneer of surgery, improved treatment of wounds, obstetrics, etc.

Parents' National Educational Union, London, founded 1888.

Pareto, Vilfredo (1848–1923), Italian economist and sociologist, often regarded as a precursor of Fascism.

Paris, Matthew (d. 1259), English chronicler, wrote account of contemporary events.

Paris, first settlement established by 3rd century B.C.; made a bishopric c. A.D. 250; became capital of France 987; besieged by Germans 1870–71; occupied by Germany 1940–44.

Paris-Match, French weekly magazine, first published 1949.

Paris, Treaty of, adjusting the claims of Henry III of England, 1259; ending the Seven Years' War, 1763; ending American Revolutionary War, 1783; ending the Napoleonic Wars, 1814 and 1815; ending Crimean War, 1856; ending Spanish–American War, 1898.

Paris, University of, founded c. 1170; foundation charter 1200; replaced 1970–1971 by the 13 independent faculties of the Universities of Paris: Paris I to Paris XIII.

Paris Observatory, founded by Louis XIV at the instigation of Jean-Baptiste Colbert (q.v.); construction began 1667; enlarged several times.

Paris Peace Conference, inaugurating international settlement after World War I 1919–20; on ending Vietnam War 1968, 1969–70 and 1973.

parity, conservation of, proposed 1927 by the physicist Eugene Wigner (b. 1902); shown not to apply to certain nuclear reactions 1956 by the Chinese-born physicists Tsung-Dao Lee (b. 1926) and Chen Ning Yang (b. 1922).

Park, Mungo (1771–1806), Scottish explorer of Niger River, drowned on second expedition.

Parker, Dorothy (1893–1967), American humorous writer, best known for her poems and short stories.

Parker, Matthew (1504–75), English prelate, archbishop of Canterbury 1559–75, one of the founders of Anglicanism.

Parker, Richard (c. 1767–97), English sailor, leader of Nore mutineers; hanged.

Parker, Sir Thomas, Earl of Macclesfield (c. 1666–1732), English lord chancellor 1718–25, impeached and found guilty of defalcation.

Parkes, Alexander (1813–90), English inventor of celluloid.

Parkhurst, John (c. 1512–75), English prelate, bishop of Norwich 1560–75.

parking meters, first introduced in the U.S.A. in Oklahoma 1935; in Britain in Westminster 1958.

Parkinson's Disease, first described by the English physician James Parkinson (1755–1824); treatment with the drug L-Dopa began 1967.

Parkman, Francis (1823–93), American historian and traveller, wrote *California and Oregon Trail* (1849).

Parliament, England, originated in meeting of citizens called by Simon de Montfort 1265.

Parliament of Dunces, in reign of Henry IV, met at Coventry 1404.

Parmenides (6th–5th cent. B.C.), Greek philosopher, wrote poem *Nature*, of which only fragments survive.

Parmigianino, Francesco (1503–40), Italian Mannerist painter, of characteristically elongated figures.

Parnell, Charles Stewart (1846–91), Irish nationalist, created powerful Home Rule party; ruined by divorce scandal 1890.

Parr, Catherine (1512–48), last (sixth) wife of Henry VIII 1543–47.

Parr, 'Old' (Thomas) (c. 1483–1635), said to have been the longest-lived Englishman.

Parrish, Maxfield (1870–1966), American illustrator, mainly of children's or humorous books.

Parry, Sir Charles Hubert (1848–1918), English composer, especially of choral works, e.g. *Blest Pair of Sirens.*

Parry, Sir William Edward (1790–1855), English naval officer and arctic explorer, attempted to reach the North Pole.

Parsees, followers of the prophet Zoroaster (q.v.) who originally fled from Persia to India in 7th century A.D.

Parsons, Sir Charles (1854–1931), English engineer, invented a steam-turbine engine.

Parsons, Elizabeth (1749–1807), English child impostor, 'Cock Lane Ghost'; denounced by Samuel Johnson.

Parsons, Robert (1546–1610), English Jesuit, missionary in England; founded several seminaries for English Catholics abroad.

parthenogenesis, biology, first recognized by Aristotle; studied by the Swiss naturalist Charles Bonnet (1720–93).

Parthenon, Athens, begun 447 B.C. under direction of Pericles (*q.v.*); temple and cult statues dedicated 438 B.C.; work completed 432 B.C.; converted into a Christian church 5th century A.D.; became a Turkish mosque 15th century; partly destroyed 1687 when a Turkish powder magazine exploded during Venetian siege. See also **Elgin Marbles.**

Parthian Empire, lasted from 247 B.C. to A.D. 224.

particles, subatomic or elementary. See **elementary particles.**

particle theory, of light, evolved by Sir Isaac Newton; revised early 20th century by the theories of Max Planck, Albert Einstein (*q.v.*) and Arthur Holly Compton (*q.v.*).

Parton, James (1822–91), English-born writer of famous American lives.

Partridge, John (1644–1715), English astrologer, issued almanac; victim of a parody by Jonathan Swift.

Pascal, Blaise (1623–62), French mathematician, and Jansenist writer on religious themes; author of *Pensées* (1670).

Paschal II (d. 1118), Pope 1099–1118, quarrelled with emperors and Henry II of England over investitures.

Paschall III (d. 1168), anti-pope 1164–68, opposed Pope Alexander III.

Pascin, Jules (1885–1930), Bulgarian-born painter, worked in France and U.S.A.

Pascoli, Giovanni (1855–1912), Italian poet, author of *Hymns and Odes* (1906).

Paskevich, Count Ivan (1782–1856), Russian soldier, suppressed Polish and Hungarian rebellions.

Pasquier, Etienne (1529–1615), French writer, author of *Recherches de la France*.

Passchendaele, Belgium, scene of 3rd Battle of Ypres, World War I, 31 July–10 Nov. 1917.

Passion Play. See **Oberammergau.**

Passover (*Pesah, Pesach*), Jewish feast, beginning on the night of 14/15 Nisan, the eve of the Exodus.

Passy, Frédéric (1822–1912), French economist, politician and peace campaigner; first winner of Nobel Peace Prize 1901.

Pasternak, Boris (1890–1960), Russian writer and major poet, wrote novel *Dr. Zhivago* (1957); forced to decline Nobel Prize for Literature.

Pasteur, Louis (1822–95), French chemist, pioneer of bacteriology, made an invaluable contribution to scientific progress.

pasteurization, first demonstrated 1860s by Louis Pasteur.

Paston, John (1421–66), English letter-writer, prominent member of family whose correspondence is of great historical value.

Pastor, Ludwig von (1854–1928), German historian of the popes.

patents, first introduced in 15th century in certain Italian states; earliest English patent granted by Henry VI to the Flemish-born John of Utynam, 1449.

Pater, Walter (1839–94), English essayist and critic, noted for his delicate style, also wrote the novel *Marius the Epicurean* (1885).

Paterson, Emma (1848–86), first woman admitted to the Trade Union Congress, 1875.

Paterson, William (1658–1719), Scottish financier, founder of the Bank of England.

Pathé, Charles (1863–1957), French pioneer film producer, started newsreels.

pathology, anatomical, founded by the Scottish surgeon John Hunter (1728–93) and by the Italian anatomist Giovanni Morgagni (1682–1771).

pathology, scientific, founded by Rudolph Virchow (*q.v.*) and Sir James Paget (*q.v.*).

Patmore, Coventry (1823–96), English poet, wrote on domestic themes, e.g. *Angel in the House* (1854–62).

Paton, Alan Stewart (b. 1903), South African novelist, opponent of apartheid and author of *Cry the Beloved Country* (1948).

Paton, John Brown (1830–1911), Scottish Congregational minister, founded many moral improvement societies.

Patrick, Saint (d. *c.* 462), Romano-British missionary in, and patron saint of, Ireland.

Patterson, Joseph (1879–1944), American journalist, founder of the New York *Daily News* 1919.

Patti, Adelina (1843–1919), Italian coloratura soprano, internationally famous for technique and subtlety.

Pattinson, Hugh Lee (1796–1858), English chemist, devised improved lead desilvering process.

Patton, George Smith (1885–1945), American soldier, commanded U.S. 3rd Army in Allied invasion of Europe.

Paul, Saint (d. *c.* 65), Jewish apostle to the Gentiles, said to have been martyred at Rome.

Paul II (1417–71), Pope 1464–71, credited with the introduction of printing in Rome.

Paul III (1468–1549), Pope 1534–49, initiated Counter-Reformation by establishing Jesuits and Council of Trent.

Paul IV (1476–1559), Pope 1555–59, had earlier founded Theatine Order, 1524.

Paul V (1522–1621), Pope 1605–21, notable as a scholar and patron of the arts.

Paul VI (b. 1897), Pope since 1963, convened Vatican II (Ecumenical Council).

Paul I (1754–1801), tsar of Russia 1799–1801, took part in war against the French; assassinated.

Paul, Jean (1763–1825), German writer, romantic and often whimsical, author of *Titan* (1803).

Paulhan, Louis (1883–1963), French aviator, won *Daily Mail* London–Manchester race 1910.

Pauli, Wolfgang (1900–58), Austrian physicist, discovered the exclusion principle, awarded Nobel Prize for Physics 1945.

Pauling, Linus (b. 1901), American chemist, won Nobel Prize for Chemistry 1954 and Nobel Peace Prize 1962.

Paulinus (d. 644), Christian missionary to Anglo-Saxons, bishop of York.

Paul of the Cross, Saint (1694–1775), Italian founder of the Passionists.

Paulus, Lucius Aemilius (*c*. 229–*c*. 160 B.C.), Roman soldier, defeated Perseus of Macedon 168 B.C.

Pausanias (d. *c*. 470 B.C.), Spartan soldier, defeated Persians at Plateau 479 B.C.; later turned traitor.

Pausanias (2nd cent. A.D.), Greek traveller, wrote guide to Greece of great historical interest.

Pavlov, Ivan (1849–1936), Russian physiologist, discovered conditioned reflex, Nobel prizewinner 1904.

Pavlova, Anna (1885–1931), Russian ballerina, famous above all as *The Dying Swan*.

pawnbroking, public pawnshops appeared briefly in Bavaria in late 12th–early 13th century; funds for granting loans to the poor first established 1462 by the Franciscans in Perugia, Italy.

Paxton, Sir Joseph (1801–65), English designer of the Crystal Palace for the Great Exhibition 1851.

P.A.Y.E. (Pay as You Earn), British income tax system, introduced 1944.

Payne, John Howard (1791–1852), American writer of *Home, Sweet Home* (1823).

Peabody, Elizabeth Palmer (1804–94), American pioneer in kindergarten education.

Peabody, George (1795–1869), American merchant and philanthropist, founded a number of U.S. institutions.

Peace, Charles (*c*. 1832–79), English murderer, and 'gentleman' burglar; hanged.

Peace Corps, U.S.A., government volunteer agency, established March 1961 by John F. Kennedy; merged with other volunteer programmes in a new agency, Action, 1971.

Peace Pledge Union, founded 1936 by the Rev. Dick Sheppard (1880–1937).

Peacock, Thomas Love (1785–1866), English writer of humorous novels, including *Headlong Hall* (1816).

Peale, Charles Willson (1741–1827), American painter, studied in England, was a successful portraitist.

Pearl Harbor, American naval base, Honolulu, attacked by Japanese 7 Dec. 1941.

Pearse, Padraic (1879–1916), Irish nationalist, one of leaders of 1916 Easter Rebellion; tried and shot.

Pearson, Sir Arthur (1866–1921), English newspaper owner, founded *Pearson's Weekly* (1890).

Pearson, John (1613–86), English theologian, ardent Royalist and Anglican, bishop of Chester 1673–86.

Pearson, Lester (1897–1972), Canadian statesman, prime minister 1963–68, won Nobel Peace Prize 1957.

Pearson, William (1767–1847), English astronomer, chief founder of London Astronomical Society, 1820.

Peary, Robert (1856–1920), American explorer, first man to reach North Pole, 1909.

Peasants' Revolt, led by Wat Tyler (*q.v.*) 1381.

Peasants' War, South Germany, 1524–25, led by Thomas Münzer.

Peck, Francis (1692–1743), English antiquary, wrote *Desiderata Curiosa* (1732–1735).

Peckham, John (d. 1292), English prelate, archbishop of Canterbury 1279–92; author of treatises and poems.

Pecock, Reginald (*c*. 1395–*c*. 1460), Welsh theologian, wrote *Repressor of Overmuch Blaming of the Clergy* (1455).

Peculiar People, Protestant sect of faith-healers, founded London 1838.

pedal bicycle. See **bicycle.**

pedestrian crossings, first in Britain established 1926 in Parliament Square, London; standardized crossing with flashing Belisha beacons (*q.v.*) introduced 1934; zebra crossings introduced 1951.

Pedrarias, Davila (*c*. 1440–1531), Spanish soldier and administrator, founder of Panama City.

Pedro I (1798–1834), emperor of Brazil 1822–31, abdicated; also Pedro IV of Portugal.

Pedro II (1825–91), emperor of Brazil 1831–89, forced to abdicate despite progressive views.

Pedro the Cruel (1334–69), king of Castile and Léon 1350–69, on withdrawal of English support overthrown and killed.

Peel, Sir Robert (1788–1850), English statesman, as home secretary established police force and as prime minister founded modern Conservative Party.

Peele, George (*c*. 1558–*c*. 1597), English poet and playwright, author of *David and Bethsabe*.

Peenemünde, East Germany, during World War II German rocket and missile research and testing site; bombed by the Allies Aug. 1943; captured by Soviet troops 1945.

Péguy, Charles (1873–1914), French poet and philosopher, wrote *Les Mystères de Jeanne d'Arc* (1912).

Peine Forte et Dure (strong and hard punishment), for refusing to submit to trial, introduced 1275; used in England up to 1741; officially abolished 1772.

Peirce, Benjamin (1809–80), American astronomer, applied mathematical skills to the subject.

Peirce, Charles Sanders (1839–1914), American mathematician and logician, son of Benjamin Peirce, noted for his work in formal logic.

Peisistratus. See Pisistratus.

Peking, capital of China for most of the period 1267–1928; made capital of People's Republic of China 1949.

Peking Man, first remains discovered 1927 near Peking; thought to have lived *c.* 350,000 years ago.

Pelagius (*c.* 360–*c.* 420), British theologian, disputed with Saint Augustine, founded Pelagian heresy.

Pellegrini, Carlo (1839–89), Italian-born caricaturist in Britain, 'Ape' in *Vanity Fair* magazine.

Pelletier, Pierre Joseph (1788–1842), French chemist, discovered strychnine, quinine, etc.

Pelopidas (d. 364 B.C.), Greek statesman and soldier, with Epaminondas established Theban dominance in Greece.

Peloponnesian League, organized by Sparta in the 6th century B.C., possibly *c.* 550–540 B.C.; dissolved 366 B.C.

Peloponnesian War, between the city states of Sparta and Athens, 431–404 B.C., leading ultimately to a Spartan victory.

Peltier effect, in an electric circuit, discovered 1834 by the French physicist Jean-Charles Peltier (1785–1845).

Pembroke, Mary Herbert, Countess of (1561–1621), English writer, patron of poets and sister of Sir Philip Sidney.

Pembroke, William Herbert, Earl of (*c.* 1501–1570), English noble, loyal to Tudors, crushed Wyatt's Rebellion 1554.

Pembroke College, Cambridge University, founded 1347 as the Hall or House of Valence-Mary by Mary de St Paul, widow of the Earl of Pembroke.

Pembroke College, Oxford University, founded 1624 by James I.

P.E.N. Club, London, world association of writers, founded 1921.

Penang, formerly Prince of Wales Island, founded 1786 as first British settlement in Malay Peninsula; mainland region added 1800; incorporated with Malacca and Singapore 1826 under a single government, known from 1867 as the Straits Settlements; part of Federation of Malaya 1948 and of Malaysia since 1963.

pencils, possibly invented much earlier,

but certainly in use by the mid-16th century.

Pendleton, Edmund (1721–1803), American lawyer and politician, Federalist Party leader in Virginia.

pendulum, constancy of its period first noted about 1582 by Galileo (*q.v.*). See also **compensated pendulum.**

pendulum clock, first accurate model built 1657 by Christiaan Huygens (*q.v.*).

penicillin, discovered 1928 by Sir Alexander Fleming (*q.v.*); isolated and purified *c.* 1939 by the Australian-born English pathologist Sir Howard Florey (1898–1968) and the German-born biochemist Ernst Boris Chain (b. 1906); first manufactured 1943.

Peninsular War, between the allied British, Spanish and Portuguese forces and the French, in Portugal and Spain, 1808–14.

Penn, Sir William (1621–70), English naval commander in both the Commonwealth and Restoration periods.

Penn, William (1644–1718), English Quaker, founded Pennsylvania 1682; son of Sir William Penn.

Pennell, Joseph (1860–1926), American artist, best known as an etcher and lithographer.

Pennsylvania, U.S.A., first settled by Swedes 1643; seized from the Dutch by the British 1664; given by royal charter 1681 to the Quaker William Penn (*q.v.*), who established a colony 1682; one of the 13 original states of the Union 1787.

Pennsylvania, University of, Philadelphia, founded 1740 as a charity school, becoming an academy 1753; made a university 1765.

penny postage, in Britain, proposed 1837 and put into effect 1840 by Sir Rowland Hill (*q.v.*).

Penrose, Francis Cranmer (1817–1903), English architect and archaeologist; was also a noted astronomer.

pens, quill pens used in Europe from 6th century; metallic pens and nibs introduced in early 19th century. See also **ball-point pen; fountain pen.**

Pentecost, Christian feast of the Holy Spirit, celebrated on Whit Sunday (*q.v.*).

Pentecostal Churches, group of Protestant Churches originated in U.S.A. in the late 19th century; meetings first held in London 1907.

P.E.P. (Political and Economic Planning), London, association formed 1931.

Pepin I (d. 640), Frankish mayor of the palace for Merovingian king Dagobert I 628–639 and effective ruler.

Pepin II (d. 714), Frankish mayor of the palace and effective ruler 687–714.

Pepin III, the Short (d. 768), king of the Franks 751–768, founded Carolingian dynasty.

Pepper, John Henry (1821–1900), English chemist, exhibited 'Pepper's Ghost', optical illusion produced by an ingenious apparatus.

pepsin, digestive enzyme, first prepared 1836 by Theodor Schwann (q.v.).

Pepurch, John Christopher (1667–1752), German-born composer of music for John Gay's *The Beggar's Opera*.

Pepys, Samuel (1633–1703), English administrator, secretary to the navy and famous diarist.

Perak, Malaysian state, ceded to Britain 1875; joined Federated Malay States 1895; part of Federation of Malaya 1948 and of Malaysia since 1963.

Perceval, Spencer (1762–1812), English statesman, prime minister 1809–12; assassinated.

Percier, Charles (1764–1838), French architect, undertook many official commissions.

percussion caps, muskets fitted with these first regularly manufactured for the British and U.S. armies 1842.

percussion lock, invented 1805 by the Rev. Alexander John Forsyth (q.v.).

Percy, Sir Henry ('Hotspur') (1364–1403), English soldier, defeated Scots 1402; rebelled against Henry IV; killed in battle.

Percy, John (1817–89), English metallurgist, improved steel manufacturing and silver extraction.

Perdiccas (d. 321 B.C.), regent of the Macedonian empire after Alexander the Great's death.

Perdita (pseud. of Mary Robinson; 1758–1800), English actress, also mistress of the Prince of Wales.

Perelman, Sidney Joseph (b. 1904), American writer, best known for his humorous short stories.

Peretz, Isaac (1852–1915), Polish writer of Yiddish stories, mainly about poor village Jews.

Pérez de Ayala, Ramón (1880–1962), Spanish novelist, author of *Tiger Juan* 1926.

Pérez de Montalván, Juan (1602–1638), Spanish playwright, wrote *The Lovers of Teruel*.

Pérez Galdós, Benito (1843–1920), Spanish novelist, whose prolific and wide-ranging work includes *Fortunata and Jacinta* (1887).

Pergolesi, Giovanni (1710–36), Italian composer of the opera *La Serva Padrona* (1733).

Pericles (d. 429 B.C.), Athenian statesman, encouraged growth of democracy and brought his country to political and cultural supremacy in Greece.

Perim, island off tip of Arabian Peninsula, under British control as part of Aden Protectorate 1857–1967; became part of People's Democratic Republic of Yemen 1967.

Periodic Law, of chemical elements, proposed 1869 by Dmitri Mendeleyev (q.v.) following work announced 1864 by the English chemist John Alexander Newlands (1838–98).

Periodic Table, of chemical elements, first published 1869 by Dmitri Mendeleyev; amended with discovery of new elements; order of elements determined by atomic number confirmed 1913 by H. G. J. Moseley (q.v.).

periscopes, first designed for submarine use 1854; prisms substituted for mirrors 1872.

periwig, use general in western Europe approximately 1660–1800.

Perkin, Sir William (1838–1907), English chemist, produced first artificial dyes.

Perkins, Loftus (1834–91), English engineer and pioneer of refrigeration.

Perkins, William (1558–1602), English theologian of strong Calvinist views, wrote *Armilla Aurea* (1590).

Permanent Court of International Justice, established by the League of Nations 1921; first meeting 1922; succeeded by the International Court of Justice (q.v.) 1945.

Permian Period, Earth history, from c. 280 to c. 225 million years ago.

pernicious anaemia, described by Thomas Addison (q.v.); successful vitamin treatment developed by the American physicians George H. Whipple (b. 1878), George R. Minot (1885–1959) and William P. Murphy (b. 1892).

Perón, Juan (1895–1974), Argentine soldier and statesman, president 1946–55 and 1973–74.

Perrault, Charles (1628–1703), French collector of fairy tales, published 1697.

Perrault, Claude (1613–88), French architect, brother of Charles Perrault; built main front of Louvre, Paris.

Perrers, Alice (d. 1400), English courtier, mistress of Edward III.

Perret, August (1874–1954), French architect, pioneered modern techniques of reinforced concrete construction.

Perronet, Edward (1721–92), English hymn-writer, e.g. 'All Hail the Power of Jesu's Name.'

Perronneau, Jean Baptiste (c. 1715–83), French painter, created charming pastel portraits.

Perrot, Sir John (c. 1527–92), English administrator, lord-deputy of Ireland 1584–88.

Perry, John (1670–1732), English traveller and canal builder in Russia.

Perry, Matthew (1794–1858), American naval officer, concluded treaty which ended Japan's isolation.

Perry, Stephen (1833–89), English astronomer, initiated regular delineation of solar surface by projection, 1880.

Perse School, Cambridge, English public school, founded 1615 by provision of the will of Stephen Perse (1548–1615).

Perseus (c. 212–c. 165 B.C.), last king of Macedon, defeated by Rome.

Pershing, John Joseph (1860–1948), American soldier, commanded U.S. army in France in World War I.

Persia, occupied by Aryan tribes from c. 9th century B.C.; Kingdom of the Medes established c. 730 B.C. and Persian empire 550 B.C.; ruled by Achaemenids 550–330 B.C., Parthians c. 227 B.C.–c. A.D. 224, Sassanids 226–651, Muslims 651–1231, Mongols and Turks 1231–1502, Safavids 1502–1736, Qajars 1796–1925 and by Pahlavis since 1925; known in the West as Persia until 1935.

Persian Gulf States. See **Bahrain**; **Kuwait**; **Qatar**; **United Arab Emirates.**

Persian Wars, with the Greek city-states 499–448 B.C.

Persigny, Jean Fialin, Duc de (1808–72), French politician, supporter of Napoleon III, minister of the interior 1852–54 and 1860–63.

Persius (A.D. 34–62), Latin writer, whose satires were influenced by Stoic philosophy.

Perth, John Drummond, Duke of (d. 1747), Scottish Jacobite, active in the 1745 rebellion.

Perthes, Justus (1749–1816), German publisher, founded family business.

Pertinax (A.D. 126–193), Roman emperor 193, killed by Praetorian Guards.

Peru, seat of the Inca civilization from early 13th century; conquered by the Spanish 1530s; declared its independence from Spain 1821.

Perugino (c. 1445–1523), Italian painter, worked on Sistine Chapel, was the master of Raphael.

Peruzzi, Baldassare (1481–1536), Italian architect, designed Villa Farnesina and Palazzo Massini, Rome.

Pervigilium Veneris, anonymous Latin poem, probably written in the 2nd century A.D.

Pestalozzi, Johann Heinrich (1746–1827), Swiss educationalist, pioneer in progressive elementary school teaching.

Pétain, Henri (1856–1951), French soldier, defended Verdun 1916, reorganized armies 1917; head of state of Vichy France 1940–1944; imprisoned.

Peter, Saint (d. c. 67), disciple of Jesus, said to have been martyred at Rome.

Peter I, the Great (1672–1725), tsar of Russia 1689–1725, was a ruthless modernizer and reformer.

Peter II (1715–30), tsar of Russia 1728–30, died just before his wedding.

Peter III (1728–62), tsar of Russia 1762; partially insane, was murdered and replaced by his wife Catherine II (q.v.).

Peterborough, Charles Mordaunt, Earl of (1658–1735), English politician and successful military commander in Spain 1705–07.

Peterborough Cathedral, England, present building begun 1117; consecrated 1237.

Peter Damian, Saint. See **Damiani, Saint Peter.**

Peter des Roches (d. 1238), French bishop of Winchester; active in English and European politics; joined the Crusades.

Peter I Island, Antarctica, discovered by Bellinghausen (q.v.) 1821; annexed by Norway 1931.

Peterhouse, Cambridge University, founded by Hugh de Balsam, bishop of Ely, 1284.

Peter Lombard. See **Lombard, Peter.**

Peterloo Massacre, at a parliamentary reform meeting, St Peter's Fields, Manchester 16 Aug. 1819.

Petermann, August (1822–78), German cartographer, associated with African exploration.

Peter Martyr, Saint (d. 1252), Italian Dominican inquisitor; killed by Cathars.

Peter Martyr (1457–1526), Italian historian at Spanish court, wrote about the discovery of America.

Peter Martyr (1500–62), Italian Protestant scholar, worked in Germany, England and Switzerland.

Peter's Pence, annual English offering to the pope, first sent 787; abolished 1534.

Peter the Hermit (d. c. 1115), French monk, preached and accompanied First Crusade.

Petipa, Marius (1819–1910), French dancer and choreographer, first dancer and ballet master at St Petersburg.

Petitioners, English political group (connected with Whigs) became prominent 1680.

Petition of Right, submitted by the House of Commons to Charles I and accepted by him 1628.

Petit Trianon, Versailles, constructed 1762–68 by Jacques Gabriel (q.v.).

Petlura, Semyon (1879–1926), Ukrainian political leader, fought Bolsheviks 1918–1920; settled in Paris.

Petöfi, Sandor (1823–49), Hungarian poet, broke new ground with *János Vitéz* (1844); killed in revolution.

Petra, ancient ruined city, Jordan, made the capital of the Nabataeans 312 B.C.; became part of Roman province of Arabia A.D. 106, declining after trade routes changed; rediscovered 1812 by John Lewis Burckhardt.

Petrarch (1304–74), Italian poet and humanist, wrote in Latin and Italian; was the first modern lyric poet.

Petre, Sir Edward (1631–99), English Jesuit, adviser to James II.

Petri, Egon (1881–1962), German-born pianist, played and taught in Europe and U.S.A.

Petrie, Sir William Flinders (1853–1942), English Egyptologist, discovered valuable papyri and sites.

Petrified Forest, Arizona, established as a national monument 1906 and as a national park 1962.

petrol engine, constructed 1883 as a high-speed internal-combustion engine (*q.v.*) by Gottlieb Daimler.

petroleum. See **oil.**

petroleum refining, cracking processes developed from 1913; catalytic cracking introduced 1930s; catalytic reforming and hydrocracking developed 1950s and 1960s.

Petronius, Gaius (d. *c.* 66), Roman writer of *The Satyricon*, traditionally a favourite of Nero; committed suicide.

Petrucci, Ottaviano dei (1466–1539), Italian printer, pioneered use of movable type for printed music.

Pettie, George (1548–89), English writer, author of *A Petite Pallace* (1576).

Petty, Sir William (1623–87), English economist, was an early advocate of greater freedom of trade.

Pevsner, Antoine (1886–1962), Russian sculptor and leading exponent of constructivism.

petunia, double, first grown (in France) *c.* 1855.

Pfister, Albrecht (*c.* 1420–*c.* 1465), German printer, one of the first in Germany.

pH, of acids and alkalis, concept introduced 1909 by the Danish chemist Søren Sørensen (1868–1939).

Phaedo (5th–4th cent. B.C.), Greek philosopher, known only through dialogue by Plato.

Phalaris (d. *c.* 554 B.C.), Greek tyrant of Agrigento, Sicily, 570–544 B.C., reputedly cruel.

Pharmaceutical Society, Britain, founded 1841; incorporated by royal charter 1843.

Pharnaces II (d. 47 B.C.), king of Pontus *c.* 63–47 B.C., ally of Pompey; defeated by Caesar.

Pharos, near Alexandria, site of the lighthouse which was one of the Seven Wonders of the Ancient World; built *c.* 280 B.C.; demolished in 14th century.

Pharsalus, Battle of, Greece, victory of Julius Caesar over Pompey 48 B.C.

Pheidippides (5th cent. B.C.), Athenian long-distance runner, sent to Sparta to seek help before the Battle of Marathon.

Phelps, Samuel (1804–78), English actor-manager of Sadler's Wells Theatre.

Phelps, Thomas (1694–*c.* 1777), English astronomer, first in England to observe the comet of 1743.

Phidias (*c.* 490–*c.* 432 B.C.), Greek sculptor, designed the sculptures for the Parthenon.

Philadelphia, Pennsylvania, founded 1682 under a charter granting land to William Penn from Charles II, 1681.

Philby, Harry St John (1885–1960), English explorer in Arabia, wrote *The Heart of Arabia* (1922).

Philby, Kim (Harold Adrian) (b. 1911), English diplomat, son of Harry Philby, earned notoriety as a Soviet spy.

Philemon (*c.* 360–*c.* 263 B.C.), Greek playwright, known only as rival of Menander.

Philidor, André Danican (1726–95), French composer and leading chess player.

Philip, Prince (b. 1921), Duke of Edinburgh, consort of Queen Elizabeth II since 1947.

Philip II (382–336 B.C.), king of Macedon and father of Alexander the Great, conquered whole of Greece; assassinated.

Philip V (d. 179 B.C.), king of Macedon 220–179 B.C., defeated by Romans.

Philip I (1052–1108), king of France 1060–1108, overshadowed by great nobles.

Philip II, Augustus (1165–1223), king of France 1180–1223, made extensive conquests, especially from the English.

Philip III (1245–85), king of France 1270–1285, influenced by favourites; achieved little.

Philip IV, the Fair (1268–1314), king of France 1285–1314, strengthened monarchy and suppressed Templars.

Philip V (1294–1322), king of France 1316–22, carried out some administrative reforms.

Philip VI (1293–1350), king of France 1328–50; his reign marked the beginning of the Hundred Years' War.

Philip I (1478–1506), king of Spain 1504–1506; his marriage arrangements left a vast empire to his son Charles V (*q.v.*).

Philip II (1527–98), king of Spain 1556–98, added Portugal to his vast empire but failed to subdue England and the Netherlands.

Philip III (1578–1621), king of Spain 1598–1621, took little part in government.

Philip IV (1605–65), king of Spain 1621–1665, relied on his favourite Olivares (*q.v.*).

Philip V (1683–1746), king of Spain 1700–1746, first of the Bourbon dynasty.

Philippe Égalité. See **Orléans,** Louis-Philippe, Duc d'.

Philip Neri, Saint. See **Neri,** Saint Philip.

Philippi, Battle of, victory of Mark Antony and Octavian over Brutus and Cassius, 42 B.C.

Philippines, discovered 1521 by Ferdinand Magellan; first settled by the Spanish 1565; ceded by Spain to the U.S.A. 1898; Commonwealth of the Philippines established 1935; under Japanese rule 1941–44; became an independent republic 1946.

Philippine Sea, Battles of, World War II, victories over the Japanese by the invading American forces 19–20 June and, at Leyte Gulf, 23–25 Oct. 1944.

Philips, John (1676–1709), English poet remembered for didactic poem *Cyder* (1708).

Philip the Bold (1342–1404), duke of Burgundy 1364–1404, made co-regent of France when Charles VI became insane.

Philip the Good (1396–1467), duke of Burgundy 1419–67, was a notable patron of the arts.

Philip the Magnanimous (1504–67), landgrave of Hesse 1509–67, was a leading figure in the Reformation in Germany.

Philistines, originating in the Aegean, settled on coast of Palestine 12th century B.C. shortly before the Israelites; defeated by King David 10th century B.C.

Phillimore, Greville (1821–84), English hymn-writer, joint editor of *Parish Hymn Book* (1863).

Phillipps, Sir Thomas (1792–1872), English book and manuscript collector, published important works using his own printing press.

Phillpotts, Eden (1862–1960), English novelist, author of *Widecombe Fair* (1913).

Philo Judaeus (c. 15 B.C.–c. A.D. 50), Jewish philosopher of Alexandria, tried to reconcile Judaic with Platonic teaching.

Philopoemen (c. 253–183 B.C.), Greek general of the Achaean League, defeated the Spartans.

Phipps, Charles (1835–97), English theatre architect in both London and the provinces.

Phiz (pseud. of Hablot Browne; 1815–82), English artist and illustrator, especially of Charles Dickens' novels.

phlogiston theory, proposed c. 1730 by George Ernst Stahl (q.v.), adapted from the views, propounded 1669, of Johann Becker (1635–82).

Phocion (c. 402–317 B.C.), Athenian general and statesman, ruled the city for a time; executed.

Phoenix Park murders, Dublin, of Lord Frederick Cavendish and Thomas Henry Burke by Irish patriots 6 May 1882.

Phoenicians, arrived in the region corresponding to present-day Lebanon and parts of Syria and Israel c. 3000 B.C.; flourished greatly 1200–1000 B.C.

'Phoney War', at beginning of World War II, from Oct. 1939 until the German offensive 10 May 1940.

phonograph, first sound-recording apparatus, invented 1877 by Thomas Alva Edison.

phosphorus, discovered c. 1669 by the German alchemist Hennig Brand.

Photius (c. 820–891), patriarch of Constantinople, began East–West schism by disputes with papacy.

photoelectric effect, discovered 1887 by Heinrich Hertz (q.v.); explained 1905 by Albert Einstein.

photoengraving, first successfully carried out in France 1827.

photograph, first one produced 1826 by Joseph-Nicéphore Niepce (q.v.); first reproducible one made 1835 by William Fox Talbot (q.v.).

photography, two pioneering processes developed late 1830s by Louis Daguerre and Niepce (see **Daguerrotype process**) and by Fox Talbot.

photography, colour, first successfully practised commercially 1907 by August Lumière (q.v.); first film with three emulsion layers (Kodachrome) appeared 1935.

photogravure, first successful method invented 1878 and used commercially 1895 by the Czech-born graphic artist Karl Klič (1841–1926).

photons, energy packets (quanta) of light, X-rays, etc., conceived 1905 by Albert Einstein; shown to exist 1923 and named 1926 by Arthur H. Compton (q.v.).

photosynthesis, first described 1779 by the Dutch physician Jan Ingenhousz (1730–99); mechanisms deduced 1949–57 by the American biochemist Melvin Calvin (b. 1911).

phototypesetting, proposed 1866; first machine designed 1894; computerized machines developed 1960s.

Phraates II (d. 128 B.C.), king of Parthia c. 138–128 B.C., defeated Medes but killed by nomad invaders.

Phraates III (d. 57 B.C.), king of Parthia 70–57 B.C., forced to make concessions to Romans.

Phraates IV (d. c. 2 B.C.), king of Parthia c. 37–c. 2 B.C., lost Armenia to Mark Antony 34 B.C.

phrenology, conceived c. 1800 by the German physician Franz Joseph Gall (1758–1828).

Phyfe, Duncan (1768–1854), Scottish-born American cabinetmaker, made much-admired furniture.

Physick, Philip Synge (1768–1837), American surgeon, pioneer in ligature technique.

piano, first practical one invented c. 1710 by the Italian harpsichord-maker Bartolommeo Cristofori (1655–1731).

Piaget, Jean (b. 1896), Swiss psychologist, best known for his researches into child behaviour.

Piatigorsky, Gregor (1903–1977), Russian-born American cellist, also a noted teacher.

Piazzi, Giuseppe (1746–1826), Italian monk and astronomer, discovered first asteroid.

Picard, Jean (1620–82), French astronomer, first man to measure accurately the degree of a meridian.

Picasso, Pablo (1881–1973), Spanish painter, generally considered the greatest of the 20th-century masters; creator of Cubism.

Piccard, Auguste (1884–1962), Swiss physicist, explorer of the stratosphere and the ocean depths.

Piccard, Jacques (b. 1922), Swiss oceanographer, son of Auguste, made a record descent in a bathyscaphe 1960.

Piccolomini, Prince Octavio (1599–1656), Italian soldier, distinguished himself in the Spanish and Imperial service in the Thirty Years' War.

Pickens, Andrew (1739–1817), American soldier, served in the Revolutionary War.

Pickering, Edward (1846–1919), American astronomer, inventor of the meridian photometer.

Pickering, John (d. 1537), English Dominican, a leader of the Pilgrimage of Grace rebellion 1536; executed.

Pickering, Timothy (1745–1829), American statesman, secretary of state 1795–1800.

Pickering, William (1796–1854), English publisher, introduced cloth bindings.

Pickford, Mary (b. 1893), American film actress, won worldwide fame with her appealing 'little girl' roles.

Pickle the Spy. See **Macdonell,** Alastair.

Pico della Mirandola, Giovanni (1463–1494), Italian humanist, was an exponent of Renaissance learning.

picric acid (trinitrophenol), known since 1771; effective use as explosive ('lyddite' or 'melinite') dates from the 1880s.

Picton, Sir Thomas (1758–1815), English soldier, served in the Peninsular War; killed at Waterloo.

Picts, early inhabitants of Scotland, menaced Roman Britain in late 4th century; extensive kingdom established by 8th century; united with rest of Scotland c. 840.

Picture Post, British periodical, published 1938–57.

Pierce, Franklin (1804–69), American statesman, 14th president of the United States 1853–57, a period of tension over the Kansas–Nebraska crisis.

Pierné, Gabriel (1863–1937), French composer, wrote *Entry of the Little Fauns.*

Piero della Francesca. See **Francesca,** Piero della.

Piero di Cosimo (c. 1462–c. 1521), Italian painter, whose works include *Death of Procris.*

Pietermaritzburg, capital of Natal, founded 1839.

Pietism, 17th-century movement in the German Lutheran Church started by Philipp Jakob Spener (1635–1705).

piezoelectricity, phenomenon discovered 1880 by Pierre Curie (q.v.) and his brother.

Pigalle, Jean Baptiste (1714–85), French sculptor, worked for the royal court and fashionable circles.

pigeon post, first employed by the Persians in mid-12th century; used for wartime messenger service since then, notably in the Franco–Prussian War 1870–71.

pig-iron, quality improved 1709 by use of coke-fired furnace by the English ironmaster Abraham Darby (c. 1677–1717).

Pike, Zebulon (1779–1813), American soldier-explorer, reached Colorado and 'Pike's Peak'.

Pilate, Pontius (1st cent. A.D.), Roman procurator in Judaea under Tiberius; said to have condemned Jesus to death.

Pilgrim Fathers, set sail from Plymouth, England, for New England 6 Sept. 1620; anchored at Cape Cod 11 Nov. 1620; reached Plymouth, Mass., 16 Dec. 1620.

Pilgrimage of Grace, 1536, Yorkshire insurrection led by Robert Aske (q.v.).

pill, the. See **oral contraceptives.**

Pilon, Germain (1537–90), French sculptor, one of the leading Renaissance artists in France.

Pilsudski, Jozef (1867–1935), Polish revolutionary and statesman, helped gain his country's independence; dictator for most of the period 1920–35.

Piltdown skull, discovered 1912; exposed as a fraud 1953–54.

Pinckney, Charles Cotesworth (1746–1825), American diplomat, involved in controversial negotiations with France 1796–97.

Pindar (c. 522–c. 440 B.C.), Greek poet, famous for his *Odes.*

Pindar, Peter (pseud. of John Wolcot; 1738–1819), English writer, noted for his satirical verse.

Pinero, Sir Arthur (1855–1934), English playwright, wrote *The Second Mrs Tanqueray* (1893).

Pinkerton Detective Agency, U.S.A., founded c. 1852 by the American detective Allan Pinkerton (1819–84).

Pinkie, Battle of, victory of the English over the Scots, 10 Sept. 1547.

Pinter, Harold (b. 1930), English dramatist, author of *The Birthday Party* (1957).

Pinturicchio, Bernardino (c. 1454–1513), Italian Renaissance painter, worked in a brilliantly decorative style.

Pinzón, Martín Alonso (c. 1440–93), Spanish navigator, accompanied Columbus, commanded the *Pinta.*

Pinzón, Vicente Yañez (c. 1460–c. 1524),

Spanish navigator, brother of Martín Pinzón, commanded the *Nina* and later explored the South American coast.

Pioneer spacecraft, American unmanned planetary probes; *Pioneer* 10, launched March 1972, reached Jupiter Dec. 1973; *Pioneer* 11, launched April 1973, reached Jupiter Dec. 1974; estimated flyby of Saturn 1979.

pions, or pi-mesons. See **mesons.**

Piozzi, Hester Lynch. See **Thrale,** Hester Lynch.

Piper, John (b. 1903), English painter, was a distinguished war artist.

Pipe Rolls, or Great Rolls of the Exchequer, annual records introduced by Roger, Bishop of Salisbury (d. 1139); earliest surviving record 1130; discontinued 1834.

Pirandello, Luigi (1867–1936), Italian playwright, often experimental in form, as in *Six Characters in Search of an Author* (1918).

Piranesi, Giambattista (*c.* 1720–1778), Italian engraver of fantastic imagination, e.g. *Imaginary Prisons.*

Pisa, Council of, convoked by the cardinals 1409 to unite Christendom under a new pope.

Pisa, Leaning Tower of, built 1174–1350.

Pisa, University of, founded 1343.

Pisanello, Antonio (*c.* 1395–*c.* 1450), Italian artist, achieved fame both as a painter and as a medallist.

Pisano, Nicola (1220–84), Italian sculptor in the Romanesque style and a forerunner of the Renaissance.

Pisano, Giovanni (1245–1314), Italian architect and sculptor, son of Nicola Pisano, whom he helped to create the pulpit of Siena Cathedral.

Pisistratus (d. 527 B.C.), Greek statesman, tyrant of Athens 560 and 554–527 B.C.

Piso Caesoninus, Lucius Calpurnius (d. *c.* 40 B.C.), Roman politician, much involved in intrigues in the Civil War period.

Pissarro, Camille (1830–1903), French painter, one of the earliest Impressionists.

Pissarro, Lucien (1863–1944), French painter, son of Camille Pissarro, worked in England.

pistols, possibly in use in Germany by 1512; introduced into England in 1540s.

Piston, Walter (1894–1976), American composer of instrumental music and the ballet *The Incredible Flutist.*

Pitcairn Island, Pacific, discovered 1767 by Philip Carteret (d. 1796); settled by mutineers from the *Bounty* (*q.v.*) 1790; became a British settlement 1887; administered by the governor of Fiji 1952–70 and by the British high commissioner in New Zealand from 1970.

Pitman, Sir Isaac (1813–97), English inventor of a system of shorthand, 1837.

Pitt, William, The Elder, Earl of Chatham (1708–78), British statesman, chief minister 1756–61, noted for his skilful conduct of the Seven Years' War.

Pitt, William, the Younger (1759–1806), British statesman, prime minister 1783–1801 and 1804–05, reorganized the country's finances.

Pius II (1405–64), Pope 1458–64, humanist scholar, known to literature as Aeneas Silvius, and a prolific writer.

Pius IV (1499–1565), Pope 1559–65, reconvened Council of Trent; tried to unite Catholics.

Pius V (1504–72), Pope 1566–72, active against both Protestants and Turks.

Pius VI (1717–99), Pope 1775–99, became a prisoner of the French Revolutionary army.

Pius VII (1740–1823), Pope 1800–23, made concordat with France; restored Jesuits, 1814.

Pius IX (1792–1878), Pope 1846–78, proclaimed dogma of papal infallibility; lost temporal power.

Piux X, Saint (1835–1914), Pope 1903–14, was a noted reformer.

Piux XI (1857–1939), Pope 1922–39; his concordat with Mussolini established the Vatican City.

Piux XII (1876–1958), Pope 1939–58; was previously a skilled papal diplomat.

Pizarro, Francisco (*c.* 1478–1541), Spanish conqueror of Peru 1532–33; killed in factional war.

Pizarro, Gonzalo (d. 1548), Spanish conquistador, half-brother of Francisco Pizarro, governor of Quito 1539–46.

P.L.A. See **Port of London Authority.**

Place, Francis (1771–1854), English radical, prominent in repeal of anti-trade-union laws and Reform Bill agitation.

plague. See **bubonic plague.**

Plaid Cymru, Welsh Nationalist Party, founded 1925.

Planck, Max (1858–1947), German physicist, formulated quantum theory, awarded Nobel Prize for Physics 1918.

planetarium, invented and designed 1913 by Walther Bauersfeld of the Zeiss Optical Company; first modern design built 1923 by this firm.

planetary motion. See **Kepler's Laws.**

Planquette, Robert (1848–1903), French composer of popular operettas.

Plantin, Christophe (1514–89), French printer, worked in Antwerp, published many famous books including *Polyglot Bible.*

plants, first systematically classified 1730s by Linnaeus (*q.v.*).

Plassey, Battle of, victory of the British under Robert Clive (*q.v.*) over Indian forces, 23 June 1757.

plastics, first one exhibited 1862 by Alexander Parkes; first manufactured plastic was celluloid (q.v.); first wholly synthetic plastic was bakelite (q.v.); polymer basis demonstrated 1920s by the German chemist Hermann Staudinger (1881–1965), leading to production of many different types.

plastic surgery, nose surgery practised in India since 5th century; first operation in Britain performed 1814 in London; first practised extensively during World War I.

plate tectonics, geological theory explaining continental drift (q.v.), put forward c. 1967 by W. Jason Morgan and others.

platform scales, invented 1831 by the American engineer Thaddeus Fairbanks (1796–1886).

Plath, Sylvia (1932–63), American poet, author of *Ariel* (pub. 1965).

platinum, possibly known in mid-16th century; discovered in South America 1735 by the Spaniard Antonio de Ulloa and 1741 by the British metallurgist Sir Charles Wood, who brought it to England.

Plato (c. 427–c. 347 B.C.), Greek philosopher, famous for style and dialectical brilliance of his dialogues, e.g. *The Republic*.

Platt Amendment, measure concerning Cuba, adopted by U.S. Congress 1901; drawn up by Senator Orville H. Platt (1827–1905); abrogated by Cuban Treaty 1934.

Plautus (c. 250–184 B.C.), Roman comic playwright, whose *Menaechmi* was the basis of Shakespeare's *Comedy of Errors*.

Playboy, American monthly magazine, published since 1953.

Playfair, Sir Nigel (1874–1934), English actor-manager of the Lyric Theatre, Hammersmith, 1918–32.

Playfair, William Henry (1789–1857), Scottish architect, designed National Gallery of Scotland.

Playford, John (1623–86), English music publishing pioneer, wrote *Introduction to the Skill of Music* (1654).

Pléiade, group of seven French writers and poets of the late 16th century including Pierre de Ronsard (q.v.).

Pleistocene Epoch, Earth history, the great ice age extending from c. 2,500,000 to c. 10,000 years ago.

Plekhanov, Georgi (1856–1918), Russian Marxist, influenced Bolsheviks although opposed to October Revolution.

Plesiosaurus, extinct marine reptile, remains first discovered 1821 by the English fossil-collector Mary Anning (q.v.).

Plimsoll Line, brought into force by the 1876 Merchant Shipping Act through the efforts of the English politician Samuel Plimsoll (1824–98).

Pliny, the Elder (A.D. 23–79), Roman writer of an encyclopedic *Natural History*.

Pliny, the Younger (A.D. 62–c. 113), Roman administrator, wrote polished letters including an account of the eruption of Vesuvius.

Pliocene Epoch, Earth history, from c. 7,000,000 to c. 2,500,000 years ago.

Plomer, William (1903–73), South African poet and novelist, author of *Turbott Wolfe* (1926).

Plotinus (A.D. 205–270), Greek philosopher, developed mystical Neoplatonic system.

Plücker, Julius (1801–68), German mathematician, pioneered analytical geometry; also studied magnetism.

Plumptre, Edward Hayes (1821–91), English theologian and classical scholar, worked on Revised Version of Old Testament.

Plunkett, Sir Horace (1854–1932), Irish politician and pioneer of agricultural co-operatives.

plural voting, discontinued in Britain by Act of Parliament 1948.

Plutarch (c. A.D. 46–c. 120), Greek writer of *Lives* of famous Greeks and Romans.

Pluto, planet, predicted and sought 1905–1916 by the American astronomer Percival Lowell (1855–1916); discovered 1930 by the American astronomer Clyde William Tombaugh (b. 1906).

Pluto, 'pipe line under the ocean', supplying petrol across the English channel to Allied forces in France, first used Aug. 1944.

plutonium, first produced 1940 in U.S.A. by Glenn T. Seaborg, Edwin M. McMillan, J. W. Kennedy and A. C. Wahl; traces since found in uranium ores.

Plymouth Breakwater, constructed 1811–41 by John Rennie (q.v.) and his son Sir John Rennie (1794–1874).

Plymouth Brethren, religious movement established at Plymouth, England, 1830 by John Nelson Darby (1800–82).

Plymouth College, English public school, formed 1896 by the amalgamation of Mannamead School (founded 1854) and Plymouth College (founded 1877).

Plymouth Colony, Mass., first settled permanently by the Pilgrim Fathers 1620.

pneumatic tyre, first, patented 1845 by R. W. Thompson (q.v.); first pneumatic bicycle tyre made by J. B. Dunlop (q.v.) 1888.

Pocahontas (c. 1595–1617), American Indian chief's daughter, saved life of John Smith (q.v.); married an Englishman and sailed to England 1616.

Pocklington School, Yorkshire, English public school, founded by Dr John Dolman 1514.

Pococke, Edward (1604–91), English orientalist, expert in Syriac and Arabic literature.

Podebrad, George of (1420–71), king of Bohemia 1458–71, successfully held off Hungarian invasion.

Poe, Edgar Allan (1809–49), American poet and short story writer, master of the macabre and grotesque.

Poel, William (1852–1934), English actor-manager, used original staging methods for Elizabethan plays.

poet laureate, office originated in the granting of a pension to Ben Jonson by James I 1616.

Pogany, Willy (1882–1955), Hungarian-born painter and illustrator, was also a cinema art director.

Poggendorff, Johann Christian (1796–1877), German physicist, wrote a history of science and biographies of scientists.

Poggio, Gian Francesco (1380–1459), Italian humanist scholar, discovered numerous lost Latin texts.

Poincaré, Raymond (1860–1934), French statesman, president 1913–20 and several times prime minister.

Point Pleasant, Battle of, defeat of the Indian nations by the Virginia Militia, 10 Oct. 1774.

points rationing, World War II, first introduced in Britain June 1941.

poison gas, first effectively used in World War I by the Germans 22 April 1915; first used by the British 25 Sept. 1915.

Poissy, Colloquy of, to reconcile French Catholics and Protestants, held 1561.

Poitiers, Battle of, Hundred Years' War, victory of the English over the French, 19 Sept. 1356.

Poland, founded 966, becoming an independent kingdom from 1025; first partition, 1772 between Russia, Prussia and Austria; second, 1793 between Russia and Prussia; third, 1795 between Russia, Prussia and Austria; independent republic proclaimed 1918; German and Russian occupation 1939–45; Communist regime established 1947; became the Polish People's Republic 1952 under a new constitution, amended 1976.

polarization, of light, studied by the French physicists Etienne-Louis Malus (1775–1812) in 1809 and Jean-Baptiste Biot (1774–1862) in 1815; further studied 1848 by Louis Pasteur.

polaroid, polarizing material, invented 1932 by the American Edwin Herbert Land (b. 1909).

Polaroid land camera, invented 1947 by Edwin Herbert Land.

Polder, arable land reclaimed from water, as in the Netherlands with the Zuiderzee project enclosing the Ijsselmeer, completed 1932.

Pole, Margaret, Countess of Salisbury (1473–1541), English noblewoman, mother of Reginald Pole; beheaded.

Pole, Reginald, Cardinal (1500–58), English prelate, archbishop of Canterbury under Queen Mary.

Polignac, Prince Jules de (1780–1847), French statesman, minister under Charles X; his reactionary decrees provoked 1830 revolution.

poliomyelitis, vaccine using dead virus developed 1954 by the American scientist Jonas Edward Salk (b. 1914); oral vaccine (live) developed 1957 by the Polish-born American scientist Albert Bruce Sabin.

Polish Succession, War of the, 1733–35.

Politian (1454–94), Italian scholar and poet, who wrote in both Italian and Latin.

Polk, James Knox (1795–1849), American statesman, 11th president of the United States, annexed Texas and waged successful war with Mexico.

Pollaiuolo, Antonio (c. 1432–1498), Italian Renaissance painter, worked with brother Piero (1443–96) on *Martyrdom of St Sebastian*.

Pollard, Albert Frederick (1869–1948), English historian, notably of Tudor period.

Pollitt, Harry (1890–1960), English politician, secretary of the British Communist Party 1929–39 and 1941–56.

Pollock, Sir Frederick (1845–1937), English lawyer and writer on legal matters, author of *Principles of Contract* (1876).

Pollock, Jackson (1912–56), American painter, exponent of Abstract Expressionism.

poll-tax, first levied in England 1377; increased 1380; abolished 1689.

Polo, Marco (1254–1324), Italian merchant and explorer, visited China, India, central Asia, described in his *Milione*.

polonium, radioactive element, discovered 1898 by Marie and Pierre Curie (qq.v.).

Poltava, Battle of, victory of the Russians over the Swedes, 8 July (N.S.) 1709.

Polybius (c. 205–123 B.C.), Greek historian, lived many years in Rome, of which he wrote a history.

Polycarp, Saint (d. c. 155), bishop of Smyrna; burnt at the stake.

Polyclitus (5th cent. B.C.), Greek sculptor, best known for his bronze *Doryphorus*.

Polycrates (d. 522 B.C.), tyrant of Samos, built a great navy; crucified by his enemies.

polyethylene, first manufactured in Britain 1939; new production method invented 1953 by the German chemist Karl Ziegler (1898–1973).

Polyglot Bibles, first one, the Complutensian, begun 1502 in Spain; first circulated 1522.

polystyrene, large-scale manufacture began in late 1930s.

polythene, first produced 1933 at the laboratories of Imperial Chemical Industries.

polyurethane, first developed 1937.

Pombal, Sebastião, Marquess of (1699–1782), Portuguese statesman, chief minister 1750–77, introduced many reforms.

Pompadour, Madame de (1721–64), French courtier, mistress of Louis XV, strongly influenced policy.

Pompeii, Italy, Roman city devastated by the eruption of Mt Vesuvius A.D. 79; ruins first excavated 1748.

Pompey (106–48 B.C.), Roman general and statesman, member of the First Triumvirate 60 B.C.; defeated by Julius Caesar.

Pompidou, Georges (1911–74), French statesman, prime minister 1962–68 and president 1969–74.

Ponce de León, Juan (1460–1521), Spanish explorer, discoverer of Florida 1513.

Ponce de León, Luis (1527–91), Spanish scholar and Augustinian monk, made important translations.

Pond, John (c. 1767–1836), English astronomer, improved instruments and methods of observation.

Pondicherry, India, settled by the French 1683; administration transferred to the government of India 1954.

Pons, Lily (1904–76), French-born opera singer and film actress, worked in U.S.A.

Ponsonby, George (1755–1817), Irish political leader, opposed union with England; led Whigs in Parliament 1808–17.

Ponsonby, William, Baron (1744–1806), Irish politician, supporter of Charles James Fox.

Ponte Vecchio, Florence, completed 1345; ascribed to the Florentine artist Taddeo Gaddi (1300–c. 1366); only bridge spared from destruction 1944 by retreating German army.

Pontiac's Rebellion, 1763–64, led by the American Indian chief Pontiac, reputedly murdered 1769.

Pontian, Saint (3rd cent.), Pope 230–235; exiled to Sardinia.

Pontius Pilate. See **Pilate,** Pontius.

pontoon bridge, first used 480 B.C. for transporting the Persian army under Xerxes across the Hellespont.

Pontoppidan, Henrik (1857–1943), Danish novelist, author of *The Kingdom of the Dead* (1912–16).

Pontormo, Jacopo da (1494–1556), Italian painter of Florentine school, was a noted Mannerist fresco painter and portraitist.

Pony Express, American mail delivery system run April 1860–Oct. 1861 between St Joseph, Montana, and Sacramento, California.

Poole, William Frederick (1821–94), American bibliographer, compiled valuable index to periodical literature.

Poor Clares, order of Franciscan nuns founded between 1212 and 1214 by St Clare (c. 1193–1253).

Poore, Richard (d. 1237), English prelate, bishop and builder of Salisbury Cathedral.

Poor Law, old system begun in Britain 1601; new system 1834; care of poor transferred to local authorities 1930; superseded 1948 by the National Assistance Act.

Pope, Alexander (1688–1744), English poet, master of urbane wit, author of *Rape of the Lock* (1714).

Pope, Sir Thomas (c. 1507–59), English administrator, founded Trinity College, Oxford.

Popish Plot, fictitious allegation of a Roman Catholic plot to murder Charles II, fabricated 1678 by Titus Oates (*q.v.*); popular agitation 1678–81.

Poppaea Sabina (d. A.D. 65), wife of the Roman emperor Nero, who ultimately killed her.

Popper, Sir Karl (b. 1902), Austrian-born philosopher in England, author of *The Open Society and its Enemies* (1944).

porcelain, primitive form made in China during Tang dynasty (618–907); true (hard) form made during Yuan dynasty (1279–1368); soft-paste form first made in Florence c. 1575; secret of true Chinese-like porcelain discovered c. 1707 at the Meissen factory.

Pordenone, Giovanni Antonio (1483–1539), Italian painter, settled in Venice, for a time rivalled Titian.

Porphyry (A.D. 233–c. 304), Greek philosopher; a Neoplatonist, he was a disciple of Plotinus and an opponent of Christianity.

Porson, Richard (1759–1808), English classical scholar and a notable editor of Euripides.

Port Arthur, China, naval base surrendered to Japan by Russia Jan. 1905; under shared supervision by U.S.S.R. and China 1945; Soviet forces withdrawn 1955.

Port Arthur, Tasmania, penal colony 1830–70.

Port Elizabeth, South Africa, founded 1820.

Porteous Riot, Edinburgh, at a public execution 1736, at which the captain of the City Guard, John Porteous, was lynched.

Porter, Cole (1893–1964), American popular composer and lyric-writer, e.g. *Night and Day*.

Porter, Katherine Anne (b. 1890), American novelist, author of *Pale Horse, Pale Rider* (1939).

Porter, William Sydney. See **O. Henry.**

Portland, Maine, first settled 1632; assumed present name 1786.

Portland, Oregon, founded 1845; chartered 1851.

portland cement, invented 1824 by the English stonemason Joseph Aspdin (1779–1855).

Portland Vase, Roman cameo glass vessel

of 1st century A.D. or late 1st century B.C.; bought 18th century by the Duke of Portland; lent to the British Museum (smashed 1845); bought by the Museum 1945.

Port of London Authority, constituted by Act of Parliament 1908.

Portola, Gaspar de (d. *c.* 1785), Spanish explorer and governor of California.

Port-Royal, French Jansenist convent near Paris, founded 1204; transferred to Paris 1626; finally dispersed 1709.

Port Said, Egypt, founded 1859.

Portora Royal School, Enniskillen, Northern Ireland, public school, founded 1618.

Portsmouth, England, granted a charter by Richard I 1194.

Portsmouth, Treaty of, ending the Russo–Japanese War, signed 5 Sept. 1905.

Portsmouth Grammar School, English public school, founded by Dr William Smith 1732.

Portugal, declared an independent monarchy 1143; ruled by Spain 1580–1640; Braganza monarchy 1640–1910; proclaimed a republic 1910; dictatorship established 1932; overthrown 1974.

Portuguese East Africa. See **Mozambique.**

Portuguese Guinea. See **Guinea-Bissau.**

Portuguese India, west coast of India, under Portuguese rule 1505–1961; invaded by Indian troops 1961, proclaimed the Union Territory of Goa, Daman, and Diu 1962.

Portuguese Timor. See **Timor.**

Portuguese West Africa. See **Angola.**

positivism, philosophical system developed in 1820s and 1830s by Auguste Comte (*q.v.*).

positron, antiparticle (*q.v.*) of the electron, discovered 1932 by Carl Anderson.

Post, Emily (1873–1960), American writer and arbiter of the rules of etiquette.

Post, Wiley (1899–1935), American pioneer aviator, killed in a crash.

Post Office Savings Bank, system introduced in Britain 1861.

postage stamps, first government postage stamp, the British Bishop Mark date stamp, introduced 1661; first adhesive stamp, the penny black, introduced 6 May 1840 by Sir Rowland Hill (*q.v.*).

postal orders, first used in Britain 1881.

postcards, stamped, introduced in Britain Oct. 1870; unstamped blank cards introduced 1894.

postcodes, first introduced in Britain 1968.

Postgate, John (1820–81), English pioneer of legislation against food adulteration.

Post Office, crown services for carriage of government despatches set up *c.* 1516; conveyance of public correspondence began 1635; Post Office established 1657

making mail service a parliamentary responsibility; telegraphs passed under Post Office control 1870; ceased to be a government department Oct. 1969.

Post Office Tower, London, completed 1965.

potassium, discovered 1807 by Sir Humphry Davy.

potatoes, introduced into England 1587 by Sir Walter Raleigh (*q.v.*).

potato famine, in Ireland, 1845–48.

Potemkin, Grigori (1739–91), Russian favourite and chief minister of Catherine the Great.

Potsdam Conference, Germany, World War II, held 17 July–2 Aug. 1945.

Pott, Percivall (1714–88), English surgeon, introduced improvements and identified Pott's disease.

Potter, Beatrix (1866–1943), English writer-illustrator of children's books, including *Tale of Peter Rabbit.*

Potter, Stephen (1900–70), English writer, best known for his humorous books, including *Lifemanship* (1950).

Potter, Sir Thomas (1773–1845), English joint-founder (with his brother) of the *Manchester Guardian.*

potter's wheel, invented in Neolithic times.

Poulenc, Francis (1899–1963), French composer, member of 'Six' group, wrote opera *Dialogues des Carmelites* (1957).

Poulsen, Valdemar (1869–1942), Danish electrical engineer, made an important contribution to wireless telegraphy.

Pound, Ezra (1885–1972), major American poet (*Cantos*) and cultural pundit; pro-Fascist, lived in Italy during World War II.

pound, imperial standard weight established in Britain 1844.

Pourtalès, Louis de (1823–80), Swiss-born naturalist in U.S.A., investigated marine life.

Poussin, Nicolas (1594–1665), French painter, developed characteristic classical style, e.g. *Bacchanal.*

Powell, Anthony (b. 1905), English novelist, author of *The Music of Time* series.

Powell, Humphrey (d. *c.* 1556), English printer, established Ireland's first printing press at Dublin 1551.

Powell, Vavasor (1617–70), Welsh preacher, created band of itinerant preachers.

Power, Tyrone (1869–1931), English-born American actor, grandson of the Irish comedian Tyrone Power (1795–1841), father of the American film actor Tyrone Power (1913–58).

power loom, first crude design patented 1785 by Edmund Cartwright (*q.v.*).

Powys, John Cowper (1872–1963), English writer, author of *A Glastonbury Romance* (1933).

Powys, Llewellyn (1884–1939), English writer, brother of J. C. Powys, author of *Apples Be Ripe* (1930).

Powys, Theodore Francis (1875–1953), English writer, notably of *Mr Weston's Good Wine* (1927), brother of J. C. and L. Powys.

Poynings' Law, regulating Irish government, passed 1495 by the lord-deputy of Ireland Sir Edward Poynings (1459–1521).

Poznán Riots, uprising of Polish workers, June 1956.

Prado, Spain, national museum of paintings and sculpture, opened 1819.

Praed, Winthrop (1802–39), English poet, lightly humorous in manner, wrote *Goodnight to the Season*.

Praetorian Guard, household troops of the Roman emperors, formed by Augustus from praetorian cohorts (general's bodyguard) 2 B.C.; disbanded by Constantine A.D. 312.

Pragmatism, philosophical movement introduced late 1870s by American philosophers including Charles Sanders Peirce (1839–1914).

Prague, Czech capital, site first settled in late 9th century.

Prague, Treaty of, ending the war between Austria and Prussia, signed 23 Aug. 1866.

Prague University, or Charles University, founded 1348 by the emperor Charles IV.

Prasad, Rajendra (1884–1963), Indian statesman, first president of India, 1950–1962.

praseodymium, metallic element, isolated 1885 by the Austrian chemist Baron Carl von Welsbach (1858–1929).

Pratt, Charles. See **Camden,** Charles Pratt, Earl.

Pratt, Silas Gamaliel (1846–1916), American composer, wrote the opera *Zenobia* (1882).

Pratt Institute, New York, founded 1887.

Pratt Institute, Pittsburgh, founded by Silas Gamaliel Pratt 1906.

Pravda, established 1917 as the official newspaper of the Communist Party of the Soviet Union.

Praxiteles (*c.* 390–*c.* 322 B.C.), Greek sculptor, was the first to portray gods in the nude.

Prayer Book, English, or Book of Common Prayer, first published 1549 at the suggestion of Thomas Cranmer (*q.v.*), amended 1552; reissued as the Elizabethan Book of Common Prayer 1559; revised version came out 1662; attempted revision 1928.

Precambrian Time, Earth history, from formation of Earth's crust *c.* 4,600 million years ago to *c.* 570 million years ago.

prefabrication, first house designed in this way built *c.* 1830 at Birmingham; factory designed 1905 in Chicago for manufacturing concrete modules for use some distance away.

Premium Bonds, first issued in Britain 1956.

Premonstratensian Canons, religious order founded 1120 by St Norbert (*c.* 1080–1134).

Pre-Raphaelites, English art movement, flourished in the mid-19th century.

Presbyterianism, developed by John Calvin (*q.v.*) and other reformers in 16th century; introduced to Scotland by John Knox (*q.v.*) 1559–60; finally established 1690.

Prescott, William Hickling (1796–1859), American historian, remembered for his histories of the Mexican and Peruvian conquest.

Press Association, London, founded 1868.

Press Council, London, established July 1953; new constitution 1963; amended 1973.

Pressburg, Treaty of, between France and Austria, signed 26 Dec. 1805.

Prester John, mythical medieval king, believed to rule mighty empire in Asia or Africa (Ethiopia).

Preston, Battles of, first, English Civil War, victory of the Parliamentarians over the Royalists, 17–19 Aug. 1648; second, victory of a royal army over the Jacobites, 13 Nov. 1715.

Preston Bypass, first section of a British motorway (M6) to be completed, opened Dec. 1958.

Prestonpans, Battle of, victory of the Jacobites over a royal army, 21 Sept. 1745.

Pretoria, capital of the Republic of South Africa, founded 1855.

Pretorius, Andries (1799–1853), Dutch South African colonist, one of the Great Trek leaders; founder of the Transvaal.

Prevost, Sir George (1767–1816), English colonial administrator, governor-general of Canada 1811–16.

Prévost, Marcel (1862–1941), French novelist, wrote *Les Demi-Vierges* (1894).

Prévost, The Abbé (1697–1763), French priest, led a scandalous, adventurous life; wrote *Manon Lescaut* (1731).

Price, Hugh (*c.* 1495–1574), Welsh founder of Jesus College, Oxford 1571.

Price Commission, Britain, set up April 1973.

Prices and Consumer Protection, Department of, Britain, set up March 1974.

Prideaux, Humphrey (1648–1724), English orientalist, dean of Norwich, wrote about Jewish history.

Pride's Purge, of the Long Parliament, carried out 1648 by the Parliamentary general Thomas Pride (d. 1658).

Priestley, John Boynton (b. 1894), English novelist, achieved great success with *The Good Companions* (1929); also a noted playwright and broadcaster.

Priestley, Joseph (1773–1804), English scientist and Unitarian minister of radical views; discovered oxygen; settled in U.S.A.

Primaticcio, Francesco (1504–70), Italian painter, worked at Fontainebleau, France, creating dazzling, intricate decorations.

prime minister, first to hold the office, from 1721, was Sir Robert Walpole (*q.v.*); office legally recognized 1905.

Primitive Methodists. See **Methodism.**

Primrose League, British Conservative organization, founded 1883 by Lord Randolph Churchill (*q.v.*).

Prince, Thomas (1600–73), English administrator, three times governor of Massachusetts.

Prince Edward Island, Canada, discovered 1534 by Jacques Cartier; entered the Canadian Confederation as a province 1873.

Princeton, Battle of, American Revolutionary War, victory of the Americans over the British, 3 Jan. 1777.

Princeton, New Jersey, first settled 1696.

Princeton University, chartered 1746 as the College of New Jersey; renamed 1896.

Princip, Gavrilo (*c.* 1893–1918), Serbian nationalist, assassinated Archduke Franz Ferdinand at Sarajevo, 1914.

Principe. See **São Tomé e Principe.**

printed circuits, first produced late 1940s; made obsolescent 1970s by integrated circuits (*q.v.*).

printer's device, first known example printed in Fust and Schoeffer's Mainz Psalter, 1484.

printing, known in China 2nd century A.D.; wood blocks used 8th century in China and Japan; movable type invented *c.* 1041 in China and *c.* 1440 in Europe.

printing offices, English provincial, suppressed (except for one press at Oxford) by a decree of the Star Chamber 1585.

printing press, invention *c.* 1440s attributed to Johannes Gutenberg (*q.v.*); cylinder press invented 1811 by the German Friedrich Koenig (1774–1833).

Prior, Matthew (1664–1721), English poet and diplomat, author of *Alma* (1718).

Priscian (5th–6th cent. A.D.), Latin grammarian, lived at Constantinople; his text book was used throughout the Middle Ages.

Priscillian (d. 385), Spanish heretic, founded Priscillianist sect; executed.

prisons, first used in England as a means of punishment during 16th century.

privy councillor, first woman, Margaret Bondfield, appointed 1929.

Probability, Theory of, founded 1654 by

Blaise Pascal (*q.v.*) and Pierre de Fermat (*q.v.*).

Probus (d. A.D. 282), Roman emperor A.D. 276–282, a successful soldier; killed in mutiny.

Procession of the Holy Spirit, from the Father *and the Son* ('filioque'), added to Roman Catholic doctrine at or shortly after the 3rd Council of Toledo, 589.

Proclus (*c.* A.D. 410–485), Greek philosopher, last significant Neoplatonist; opposed Christianity.

Proclus (*c.* A.D. 410–485), Greek philosopher, last significant Neoplatonist; opposed Christianity.

Procopius (d. *c.* 563), Byzantine historian of Justinian's reign and author of a scandalous *Secret History* about the court.

Proctor, Richard (1837–88), English astronomer, was also a popular writer on the subject.

Proctor, Robert (1868–1903), English bibliographer at Bodleian Library and British Museum, compiled *Index of Early Printed Books* (1898).

Prohibition, came into effect in the U.S.A. 16 Jan. 1920; repealed 5 Dec. 1933.

projector, film, invented 1895 by the Lumière brothers (*q.v.*).

Prokofiev, Sergei (1891–1953), major Russian composer of the 20th century, wrote operas, ballets, film music, etc.

Promenade Concerts, London, founded 1895 by Sir Henry Wood (*q.v.*).

promethium, chemical element, identified 1945 in the U.S.A. by J. A. Marinsky, L. E. Glendenin and C. D. Coryell.

prontosil, first sulphonamide drug, medical powers discovered 1935 by the German bacteriologist Gerhard Domagk (b. 1895).

Propertius, Sextus (*c.* 48–*c.* 14 B.C.), Roman elegiac poet, author of *Cynthia*.

protactinium, isotope first identified 1913 by K. Fajans and O. H. Göhring; metal isolated 1934 by the Russian-born chemist Aristid V. Grosse (b. 1905).

Protagoras (*c.* 490 B.C.–*c.* 420 B.C.), Greek philosopher, was a leading member of the Sophists.

Proterozoic Era, Earth history, from *c.* 1,500 million to *c.* 600 million years ago.

Protestant Episcopal Church, organized in Philadelphia 1789 as the successor to the Church of England in the American colonies.

Protestantism, origins in the early 16th century; name derived from the members of the Diet of Speyer, 1529, who protested against the decision to revoke the toleration granted to followers of Martin Luther (*q.v.*) in 1526.

Prothero, Sir George (1848–1922), English historian, co-editor of *The Cambridge Modern History*.

Protogenes (4th cent. B.C.), Greek painter,

in Rhodes; none of his work survives.

proton, elementary particle, identified with the nucleus of the hydrogen atom 1919 by Lord Rutherford.

proton synchroton, type of particle accelerator, proposed 1943 by the Australian physicist Marcus Oliphant (b. 1901); first constructed in 1950s.

protoplasm, living cellular material, studied and named 1846 by the German botanist Hugo von Mohl (1805–72).

protozoa, unicellular animals, discovered 1674 by Antony van Leeuwenhoek (q.v.).

Proudhon, Pierre Joseph (1809–65), French Socialist and journalist, wrote extensively; disputed with Karl Marx.

Proust, Marcel (1871–1922), major French novelist, author of *À la Recherche du Temps Perdu* (1913–27).

Prout, Ebenezer (1835–1909), English music theorist, wrote standard works on technique.

Prout, William (1785–1850), English chemist, best known for his work on atomic theory.

Proxima Centauri, nearest star to the Earth, discovered 1916 by the Scottish astronomer Robert Innes (1861–1933).

Prudentius, Aurelius Clemens (348–c. 410), Spanish poet, wrote (in Latin) on Christian themes.

Prud'hon, Pierre Paul (1758–1823), French painter, was a portraitist of romantic warmth, e.g. *Empress Josephine*.

Prussia, conquered by the Teutonic Knights 13th century; western part ceded to Poland 1466; eastern part became a duchy 1525 under Polish suzerainty; passed under direct control of Electors of Brandenburg 1618; became a kingdom 1701, greatly expanding in 18th and 19th centuries; united Germany under its leadership 1871; became a state in the German Reich 1918; abolished as an administrative region 1947.

prussian blue, pigment, first made 1704 by the German scientist Johann Dippel (1673–1734).

prussic acid, hydrogen cyanide solution, discovered 1782 by Carl Wilhelm Scheele (q.v.).

Prynne, William (1600–69), English Puritan pamphleteer, whose ears were cut off as punishment; later became a Royalist.

Pryor, Roger (1828–1919), American statesman and lawyer, New York supreme court justice 1894–99.

Psalmanazar, George (c. 1679–1763), French literary impostor in London; later confessed and became a writer.

psychoanalysis, study founded c. 1895 by Sigmund Freud (q.v.).

Ptolemaic system, in which the Earth is the centre of the Universe, formulated c. A.D. 140 by Ptolemy (q.v.).

Ptolemy I, Soter (d. 283 B.C.), Greek king of Egypt 323–285 B.C., his share of Alexander the Great's empire.

Ptolemy II (309–246 B.C.), king of Egypt 285–246 B.C., built Pharos lighthouse and Nile–Red Sea canal.

Ptolemy III (d. c. 222 B.C.), king of Egypt 246–c. 222 B.C., builder and patron of arts.

Ptolemy IV (d. 203 B.C.), king of Egypt 221–203 B.C., a weak ruler but eventually defeated the Syrians.

Ptolemy V (c. 210–181 B.C.), king of Egypt 203–181 B.C., began dependence on Rome.

Ptolemy VI (c. 186–145 B.C.), king of Egypt 181–145 B.C., twice deposed but restored by Romans.

Ptolemy VII (161–144 B.C.), king of Egypt 145–144 B.C., killed by his uncle Ptolemy VIII.

Ptolemy VIII (c. 184–116 B.C.), king of Egypt 144–116 B.C., earlier joint king 170–164 B.C. with his brother Ptolemy VI.

Ptolemy IX (d. 80 B.C.), king of Egypt, jointly with mother 116–108 B.C.; sole ruler 88–80 B.C.

Ptolemy X (d. 88 B.C.), king of Egypt 108–88 B.C., brother of Ptolemy IX.

Ptolemy XI (d. 51 B.C.), king of Egypt 80–58 B.C., exiled; restored by Romans 55 B.C.

Ptolemy XII (61–47 B.C.), king of Egypt 51–47 B.C., expelled sister/wife Cleopatra; defeated and killed by Caesar.

Ptolemy XIII (d. 44 B.C.), king of Egypt 47–44 B.C., jointly with sister Cleopatra; killed, probably by her.

Ptolemy XIV (47–30 B.C.), known as Caesarion, son of Caesar and Cleopatra, ruled jointly with his mother; killed after Octavian's victory.

Ptolemy, Claudius (2nd cent. A.D.), Alexandrian astronomer and geographer; his geocentric description of the planets was accepted until Copernicus's time.

Public Health Act, Britain, first enacted 1875, modification of earlier legislation on English sanitary law; amended 1883.

Public Health Laboratory Service, set up 1939 as an emergency wartime service, retained on a permanent basis 1945; administered by the Medical Research Council until 1969 when it became an agent for the Department of Health and Social Security.

Public Libraries Act, first, permitting the establishment of public libraries in England, passed 1850, second 1855; first library opened 1856 at Westminster.

Public Records Office, London, established 1838.

Public Safety, Committee of, French Revolution established Sept. 1793; diminished in importance after July 1794.

Public Trustee Office, London, opened 1908.

Puccini, Giacomo (1858–1924), Italian

composer, master of melody and drama, e.g. *La Bohème* (1896).

puddling furnace, invented 1784 by the English ironmaster Henry Cort (1740–1800).

Puerto Rico, discovered by Christopher Columbus 1493; first Spanish settlement 1509; ceded by Spain to U.S.A. 1898; became a commonwealth in association with U.S.A. 1952.

'Puffing Billy', pioneer adhesion locomotive, patented 1813 by the Englishman William Hedley (1779–1843).

Pugachev, Emelyan (*c.* 1742–1775), Russian soldier, led rebellion against Catherine the Great.

Puget, Pierre (1620–94), French sculptor, e.g. *Milo of Crotona* (1683).

Pughe, William Owen (1759–1835), Welsh antiquary and lexicographer, compiled Welsh-English dictionary.

Pugin, Augustus Welby (1812–52), English architect, was a pioneer in the revival of Gothic architecture.

Pulaski, Count Casimir (1748–79), Polish soldier, fought in George Washington's army.

Pulcheria (A.D. 399–453), Byzantine empress 450–453, involved in many intrigues.

Pulitzer Prizes, for American writing, awarded since 1917 through the philanthropy of the Hungarian-born newspaper owner Joseph Pulitzer (1847–1911).

Pullman sleeping car, devised by the American financier George Mortimer Pullman (1831–97); first appeared 1865.

pulsars, massive dying stars, first discovered 1967 by the English astronomers Anthony Hewish (b. 1924), and Jocelyn Bell; identified with neutron stars (*q.v.*).

pumps. See **air-pump; steam engine.**

Punch, British periodical founded 1841 by Ebenezer Landells (1808–60), Mark Lemon (1809–70) and Henry Mayhew (1812–87).

Punch and Judy, puppet play, origins (probably Italian) uncertain; introduced into England via France in the 17th century.

Punic Wars, between Rome and Carthage, first, 264–241 B.C.; second, 218–201 B.C.; third, 149–146 B.C.

Punjab, invaded by Alexander the Great 326 B.C.; conquered by Muslims in 10th century; part of Sultanate of Delhi 1206–1526; ruled by Mogul emperors 16th to 18th centuries; under Sikh control 1799–1849; annexed by Britain 1849; constituted an autonomous province of India 1937; partitioned between India and Pakistan 1947.

Punjab, or Punjabi Suba, Indian state, formed 1966.

Purcell, Henry (1659–95), major English composer, wrote *Dido and Aeneas* (1689).

Purchas, Samuel (*c.* 1575–1626), English compiler of travel books, including *Purchas, His Pilgrimage* (1613).

purchase tax, levied on certain goods manufactured and sold in Britain 1940–1973; replaced by V.A.T. (*q.v.*).

Purdue University, Lafayette, Indiana, founded 1869; teaching began 1874.

Purification of the Virgin, Festival of (Candlemas), 2 Feb.

Puritanism, reform movement in the Church of England during late 16th and 17th centuries.

Purkinje, Johannes (1787–1869), Czech physiologist, made important discoveries in both physiology and anatomy.

Pusey, Edward (1800–82), English Anglican writer, one of the founders of the Oxford Movement (*q.v.*) and Anglo-Catholicism.

Pushkin, Alexander (1799–1837), Russian Romantic poet, wrote *Eugene Onegin* (1831); killed in duel.

Putnam, George (1814–72), American publisher, founded well-known firm.

Puvis de Chavannes (1824–98), French painter, chiefly of murals in a cool decorative style.

Pu Yi, Henry (1906–67), last Chinese emperor 1908–12; Japanese puppet emperor of Manchukuo (Manchuria) 1934–1945.

PVC, polyvinyl chloride, first produced 1912.

pygmies, African, first discovered *c.* 1870 by the German ethnologist Georg August Schweinfurth (1836–1925).

Pym, John (1584–1643), English Parliamentary leader in struggle with Charles I.

Pynson, Richard (d. 1530), French-born printer, introduced Roman type into England.

Pyramids, Battle of the, victory of Napoleon over the Mamelukes, 21 July 1798.

Pyrenees, Peace of the, ending war between France and Spain, signed Nov. 1659.

pyridine, organic base, discovered 1851 by the Scottish chemist Thomas Anderson (1819–74).

Pyrrho of Elio (*c.* 360–*c.* 270 B.C.), Greek philosopher, a sceptic, from whose name Pyrrhonism is derived.

Pyrrhus (*c.* 318–272 B.C.), king of Epirus, defeated Romans in Sicily, at great cost: hence 'Pyrrhic victory'.

Pythagoras (6th cent. B.C.), Greek philosopher, and mathematician, developed mystical beliefs and (with his followers) made advances in geometry and astronomy.

Pytheas (4th cent. B.C.), Greek navigator and geographer, explored Atlantic coast of Europe.

Q

'Q'. See **Quiller-Couch,** Sir Arthur.

Qatar, Persian Gulf state, in special treaty relations with Britain since 1868; regulated by treaty 1916; became an independent sovereign state 1971.

Quadragesima, the forty days of Lent; or, sometimes, the first Sunday in Lent.

quadrant, reflecting, invented 1730 by John Hadley (*q.v.*) modified from the octant of Robert Hooke (*q.v.*), and independently by Newton and Thomas Godfrey (1704–49) of Pennsylvania.

quadrille, first introduced into Britain 1815.

Quadruple Alliance, of Britain, Russia, Austria and Prussia against Napoleon, 1814–15; officially renewed Nov. 1815 to prevent further French aggression.

Quadruple Alliance, of Britain, France, Spain and Portugal, guaranteeing the constitutional monarchies of Spain and Portugal, 1834.

Quakers, Society of Friends, religious movement founded *c.* 1650 by George Fox (*q.v.*).

quantitative analysis, first used 1750s by Joseph Black (*q.v.*); developed 1760s by Antoine Lavoisier (*q.v.*).

quantum electrodynamics, theory developed late 1940s independently by the American physicists Richard P. Feynman (b. 1918) and Julian S. Schwinger (b. 1918) and the Japanese physicist Sin-Itiro Tomonaga (b. 1906).

quantum mechanics, developed and published 1926 (as wave mechanics) by Erwin Schrödinger (*q.v.*) and 1925 (as matrix mechanics) by Werner Heisenberg (*q.v.*), based on work in 1923 by Louis de Broglie (*q.v.*) and by Paul Dirac (*q.v.*) and Max Born (1882–1970).

quantum theory, formulated and published 1900 by Max Planck (*q.v.*).

Quare, Daniel (1648–1724), English clockmaker, invented repeating watches 1687.

Quaritch, Bernard (1819–99), German-born bookseller in England, published a valuable catalogue of old books.

quarks, hypothetical particles in the substructure of certain subatomic particles, postulated 1963 independently by the American physicists Murray Gell-Mann (b. 1929) and George Zweig.

Quarles, Francis (1592–1644), English poet, wrote collection *Emblems* (1635).

Quarter Days, in England, Wales and Northern Ireland, 25 March, 24 June, 29 Sept., 25 Dec.; in Scotland, 2 Feb., 15 May, 1 Aug., 11 Nov.

Quarterly Review, founded by the London publisher John Murray (*q.v.*), first appeared 1809; ceased publication 1967.

Quarter Sessions, British court of record, held at least four times a year since 1388; abolished 1972.

quartz-crystal clock. See **clocks.**

quasars, quasi-stellar objects, first discovered 1960 by radioastronomers; immense red shift discovered 1963 by the Dutch-born astronomer Maarten Schmidt (b. 1929).

Quasimodo, Salvatore (1901–68), Italian poet, awarded Nobel Prize for Literature 1959.

Quaternary Period, the last 2,500,000 years of Earth history.

quaternions, in mathematics, discovered 1843 by the Irish mathematician Sir William Rowan Hamilton (1805–65).

Quatre Bras, Battle of, victory of the British over the French, 16 June 1815.

Quebec, Canada, founded 1608 by Samuel de Champlain (*q.v.*).

Quebec Act, concerning the government and territory of the Province of Quebec, 1774.

Quebec Conferences, World War II, held Aug. 1943 and Sept. 1944.

Queen Alexandra's Day, first held 26 June 1912.

Queen Anne's Bounty, ecclesiastical fund, founded in England 1704.

Queen Elizabeth, transatlantic liner, launched Sept. 1938; became a troopship during World War II; caught fire and sank, Hong Kong harbour Jan. 1972.

Queen Elizabeth 2, (QE2), transatlantic liner, launched Sept. 1967; maiden voyage May 1969.

Queen Elizabeth's Grammar School, Blackburn, founded by Thomas, Earl of Derby, 1509; re-established and chartered by Elizabeth I 1567.

Queen Elizabeth Grammar School, Wakefield, founded by royal charter 1591.

Queen Mary, transatlantic liner, launched Sept. 1934; became a troopship during World War II; sold 1967 to an American company and berthed at Long Beach, California.

Queen Maud Land, Antarctica, discovered by a Norwegian expedition 1930; claimed by Norway 1939.

Queensberry Rules, in boxing, drafted *c.* 1866 by the 8th Marquess of Queensberry (1844–1900).

Queen's College, Cambridge University, founded 1448 by Queen Margaret of Anjou; refounded 1465 by Elizabeth Woodville, consort of Edward IV.

Queen's College, Taunton, English public school, founded 1843.

Queen's College, The, Oxford University, founded 1340 by Robert de Eglesfield; new charter conferred 1585 by Elizabeth I.

Queensland, Australia, part of New South

Wales until 1859; became one of the states of the Commonwealth of Australia 1901.

Queen's Messengers, in operation by 1454; first so called 1485; formed into a corps 1772.

Queen's Police Medal, instituted by royal warrant 1909.

Queen's University, The, Belfast, established 1845 as Queen's College, Belfast; assumed full university status 1908.

Quental, Antero de (1842–92), Portuguese poet, best known for his *Sonnets* (1886).

Quérard, Joseph (1791–1865), French bibliographer, compiler of a literary bibliography.

Quercia, Jacopo della (1374–1438), Italian sculptor, noted for his tombs and bronze reliefs.

Quesada. Gonzalo de (*c.* 1500–1579), Spanish conquistador, conqueror of New Granada.

Quételet, Adolphe (1796–1874), Belgian mathematician, noted for his work on statistics.

Quetta, Pakistan, annexed by the British 1876; severely damaged by earthquake May 1935.

Quevedo, Francisco de (1580–1645), Spanish poet, wrote elaborate, often astringent lyrics.

Quiberon Bay, Battle of, British naval victory over the French, 20 Nov. 1759.

Quietism, contemplative mystical movement in the Catholic Church in the 17th century.

Quiller-Couch, Sir Arthur (1863–1944), English writer, especially on Cornwall, e.g. *Troy Town* (1888).

Quilter, Roger (1877–1953), English composer, wrote *A Children's Overture* (1900).

Quin, James (1693–1766), English actor, rival of Garrick; famous as Falstaff.

Quincey, Thomas de. See **De Quincey,** Thomas.

Quinet, Edgar (1803–75), French writer, in exile 1852–71, published a contemporary history and some verse.

quinine, appeared in Europe in early 1630s; synthesized 1944 by the American chemists Robert Burns Woodward (b. 1917) and William von Eggers Doering (b. 1917).

Quinquagesima, the fifty days immediately preceding Easter; or the Sunday before Ash Wednesday.

Quintana, Manuel José (1772–1857), Spanish poet and biographer of famous Spaniards.

Quintero, Serafín (1871–1938) and Joaquín (1873–1944), Spanish playwrights, brothers and collaborators, e.g. *Fortunato.*

Quintillian (*c.* A.D. 35–*c.* 100), Roman orator, wrote on education and the art of rhetoric.

Quirinal Palace, Rome, designed 1574 by The Italian architect Domenico Fontana (1543–1607).

Quisling, Vidkun (1887–1945), Norwegian politician, formed Nazi party in Norway; puppet ruler 1940–45; executed.

Quito, capital of Ecuador, pre-Columbian town captured by the Incas 1487; taken by the Spanish 1534.

quiz programme, first, broadcast in Canada 15 May 1935.

quiz programme, first British, the Inter-Regional Spelling Competition broadcast Nov. 1937 onwards.

R

R 100, British airship, first trials 16 Dec. 1929; transatlantic flight (to Montreal) 29 July 1930; sold for scrap after R 101 crash.

R 101, British airship, first trials 14 Oct. 1929; crashed at Beauvais, France, while en route to India, 5 Oct. 1930.

Rabelais, François (*c.* 1490–1553), French humanist and writer of the satirical masterpieces *Pantagruel* and *Gargantua.*

rabies, vaccine treatment developed and first effectively used 1885 by Louis Pasteur (*q.v.*).

Race Relations Board, Britain, set up 1966 by the terms of the Race Relations Act 1965.

Rachel (1821–58), Swiss-born French actress, supreme in French classical tragedy.

Rachmaninov, Sergei (1873–1943), Russian composer and piano virtuoso, settled in U.S.A.; composed in rich Romantic vein.

Racine, Jean (1639–99), French playwright, leading figure of French classical drama, author of *Phèdre* (1677).

Rackham, Arthur (1867–1939), English illustrator of children's books in brilliant, sometimes grotesque, style.

R.A.D.A. See **Royal Academy of Dramatic Art.**

radar, first practical demonstration made 1935 by a team led by the English scientist Sir Robert Watson-Watt (*q.v.*).

Radcliffe, Ann (1764–1823), English 'Gothick' novelist, wrote the influential *Mysteries of Udolpho* (1794).

Radcliffe Observatory, Oxford University, founded 1771 through the benefaction of John Radcliffe (1650–1714).

Radek, Karl (1885–*c.* 1939), Soviet Communist, prominent until mid-1920s; denounced and later imprisoned as a Trotskyite.

Radetzsky, Josef (1766–1858), Austrian soldier, fought successfully in Napoleonic and Italian Independence Wars; was a military reformer and national hero.

Radhakrishnan, Sarvepalli (1888–1975),

Indian scholar and statesman, president of India 1962–67.

radiation, black-body, theory (quantum theory) proposed 1900 by Max Planck (*q.v.*) explaining work in 1890s of Wilhelm Wien (*q.v.*) and Lord Rayleigh (*q.v.*).

Radiguet, Raymond (1903–23), French novelist, author of *Le Diable au Corps* (1923).

radioactivity, first discovered in uranium, 1896 by Antoine Henri Becquerel (*q.v.*); studied 1898 by Marie and Pierre Curie (*qq.v.*).

radio astronomy, developed following the discovery 1932 by the American radio engineer Karl Jansky (1905–50) of radio signals from beyond the Earth's atmosphere.

radiocarbon dating, developed 1947 by the American chemist Willard Frank Libby (b. 1908) following the isolation 1940 of the long-lived radioisotope carbon-14.

radiology, in medicine, developed soon after discovery, 1896, of X-rays.

radiometer, invented *c.* 1875 by Sir William Crookes (*q.v.*).

radio receivers. See **superheterodyne receiver.**

radio signals, first transmitted over short distances 1895 and across the Atlantic (Cornwall to Newfoundland) 1901 by Guglielmo Marconi (*q.v.*).

radio telegraphy, or wireless telegraphy, developed 1895 by Guglielmo Marconi.

radio telescopes, first one built 1937 by the American radio engineer Grote Reber (b. 1911); radio interferometers developed late 1940s in England and Australia.

Radio Times, British periodical, first published 28 Sept. 1923.

radio tuning, selective, basic principles defined 1898 by Sir Oliver Lodge (*q.v.*).

radio waves, first generated and detected 1888 by Heinrich Hertz (*q.v.*) following their prediction 1864 by James Clerk Maxwell (*q.v.*).

Radisson, Pierre (*c.* 1636–*c.* 1710), French explorer and fur trader, opened up Hudson Bay area.

radium, discovered 1898 by Marie and Pierre Curie (*q.v.*); pure metal isolated 1910 by Marie Curie and the French chemist André-Louis Debierne (1874–1949).

Radley College, Berkshire, English public school, founded by the Rev. William Sewell; opened 1847; incorporated by royal charter 1890.

radon, radioactive gaseous element, discovered 1900 by the German physicist Friedrich Ernst Dorn (1848–1916).

Raeburn, Sir Henry (1756–1823), Scottish painter of Edinburgh and Highland notables.

Raemaekers, Louis (1869–1956), Dutch cartoonist, noted for his anti-German works.

R.A.F. See **Royal Air Force.**

Raff, Joseph Joachim (1822–82), Swiss composer, remembered for his *Cavatina*.

Raffles, Sir Stamford (1781–1826), English colonial administrator, founded Singapore, 1819.

Raglan, Fitzroy, Lord (1788–1855), English soldier, commander-in-chief of the British army during the Crimean War.

Rahere (d. 1144), English founder of St Bartholomew's Hospital, London, 1123.

Rahman, Tunku Abdul (b. 1903), Malaysian statesman, first prime minister of independent Malaya (later Malaysia) 1957–1970.

Raikes, Robert (1735–1811), English founder of Sunday school movement.

railways, mining railways used in Europe from 16th century; first public railway (Wandsworth to Croydon) opened 1803; first to use locomotive traction, Stockton and Darlington railway (*q.v.*), opened 1825; Liverpool and Manchester railway opened 1830; first public electric (City and South London) opened 1890; first diesel locomotive in use 1925.

Raimondi, Marcantonio (*c.* 1480–*c.* 1534), Italian engraver, first artist to specialize in reproductions.

Rainier (b. 1923), prince of Monaco since 1944.

Rais, Gilles de (1404–40), marshal of France, satanist, and mass-murderer of children; executed.

Rajasthan, Indian state, established 1947; reorganized 1956.

Rákóczy, Francis II (1676–1735), prince of Transylvania and Hungary, briefly, 1703–08, independent of the Hapsburgs.

Raleigh, Sir Walter (1552–1618), English courtier, poet and colonizer of Virginia; executed.

Ramadan, Islamic month of fasting during daylight hours, the 9th month of the Muslim year.

Ramakrishna (1834–86), Indian religious leader, preached the underlying unity of all religions.

Raman effect, discovered 1928 by the Indian physicists Sir Chandrasekhara Venkata Raman (1888–1970) and K. S. Krishnan.

Rambert, Dame Marie (b. 1889), Polish-born English dancer and teacher, helped found modern ballet in Britain.

Rambouillet, Catherine, Marquise de (1588–1665), French patron of writers; her salon deeply influenced cultural life.

Rameau, Jean Philippe (1683–1764), French composer, established the French opera in rivalry with Italian.

Rameses I (d. *c.* 1314 B.C.), king of Egypt

c. 1315–*c.* 1314, began building hypostyle hall, Karnak.

Rameses II (d. 1225 B.C.), king of Egypt 1292–1225, builder on a vast scale, including Abu Simbel temple.

Rameses III (d. 1167 B.C.), king of Egypt 1198–1167, made war on Libyans and Syrians.

Ramillies, Battle of, War of the Spanish Succession, victory of the British over the French, 23 May 1706.

Ramon Berenguer IV (12th cent.), count of Barcelona 1131–62, united Aragon with Catalonia.

Ramsay, Allan (1685–1758), Scottish poet and playwright, early collector of folk poetry.

Ramsay, Allan (1713–84), Scottish painter, son of Allan Ramsay, best known for his portraits.

Ramsay, Sir William (1852–1916), Scottish chemist, discovered argon, helium and other gases; Nobel prizewinner 1904.

Ramsden, Jesse (1735–1800), English instrument-maker, improved sextant, barometer, etc.

Ramus, Petrus (1515–72), French humanist, was a notable critic of Aristotle.

Ramuz, Charles Ferdinand (1878–1947), Swiss novelist, wrote about life in his native Vaud.

Ranavalona III (*c.* 1861–1916), last queen of Madagascar 1883–1916.

Randolph, Thomas, Earl of Moray (d. 1332), Scottish nobleman, close adviser of Robert Bruce, later regent of Scotland.

Randolph, Thomas (1605–35), English writer, author of *Amyntas.*

Randolph, William (*c.* 1650–1711), English founder of William and Mary College, Virginia, 1693.

Ranelagh, London pleasure gardens, opened to the public 1742; closed 1803.

Ranjit Singh (1780–1839), Sikh ruler 1799–1839, built powerful Punjab state; ally of the British.

Ranjitsinhji, Prince (1872–1933), outstanding Indian cricketer, played for England.

Ranke, Leopold von (1795–1886), German historian of the papacy and the Reformation.

Rankin, Thomas (1738–1810), Scottish Methodist reformer, close associate of Wesley; worked in America 1773–77.

Rankine, William (1820–72), Scottish civil engineer and molecular physicist.

Rapallo, Treaties of, settling the frontiers between Yugoslavia and Italy, signed 1920; between Germany and U.S.S.R. renouncing claims to war reparations, signed 1922.

Raphael (1483–1520), major Italian Renaissance painter, master of composition, e.g. *School of Athens.*

Rapin du Thoyras, Paul de (1661–1725), French historian, author of a history of England.

Rashi (1040–1105), French Jewish scholar, wrote Biblical and Talmudic commentaries.

Rashid al-Din (*c.* 1250–1318), Arab historian and statesman, author of *History of the Mongols of Persia.*

Rasmussen, Knud (1879–1933), Danish polar explorer and ethnologist born in Greenland, wrote much about Eskimos.

Raspe, Rudolf (1737–94), German writer, worked in England; wrote *Baron Münchhausen* (*q.v.*) stories.

Rasputin (1871–1916), Russian mystic, credited with healing powers; had great influence at court; assassinated.

Ratcliffe College, Leicestershire, English public school, founded with funds provided by Lady Mary Arundel of Wardour 1844; opened 1847.

Ratdolt, Erhard (*c.* 1443–*c.* 1528), German pioneer printer, was the first to publish decorated title pages.

Rathbone, William (1819–1902), English founder of the District Nurse movement, 1859.

Rathenau, Walther (1867–1922), German statesman, foreign minister 1922; assassinated.

rationing, of food in Britain, in World War I, 1917–18; in World War II, began 8 Jan. 1940; finally ended 3 July 1954. See also **points rationing.**

Rattigan, Sir Terence (b. 1911), English dramatist, author of *French Without Tears* (1936), *The Deep Blue Sea* (1946), etc.

Ratzel, Friedrich (1844–1904), German geographer, pioneer in the study of human communities in relationship to their natural environment.

Ravel, Maurice (1875–1937), French composer, best known for his symphonic works, including the ballet *Daphnis and Chloé* (1909–12).

Ravenna, Italy, chief residence of the Roman emperors A.D. 404–476, and of the Byzantine exarchs 540–751; came under the dominion of the archbishops of Ravenna, then under papal rule, almost continuously 1278–1859.

Rawalpindi, Treaty of, by which Britain recognized complete independence of Afghanistan, 8 Aug. 1919.

Rawlins, Thomas (*c.* 1620–1670), English medallist and playwright, wrote *The Rebellion* (1640).

Rawlinson, Sir Henry (1810–95), English Assyrologist, continued work of Layard (*q.v.*).

Rawsthorne, Alan (b. 1905), English composer, wrote *Canticle of Man* (1952).

Ray, John (1627–1705), English naturalist, did much pioneer work in classification.

Rayleigh, John, Baron (1842–1919), English physicist, joint discoverer of argon; Nobel prizewinner 1904.

Raymond IV (d. 1105), count of Toulouse 1088–1105, led army in First Crusade.

Raymond VI (d. 1222), count of Toulouse 1196–1222, ally of Albigenses, defeated but regained possessions.

rayon. See **man-made fibres.**

Ray Society, London, for the publication of works on natural history, founded in honour of John Ray (*q.v.*) 1844.

Razin, Stenka (d. 1671), Cossack peasant, led rebellion against the tsar; executed.

razor, safety, invented 1901, first sold 1903, by the American manufacturer King Camp Gillette (*q.v.*).

Read, Sir Herbert (1893–1968), English poet, novelist and critic of modern art.

Reade, Charles (1814–84), English novelist, wrote *The Cloister and the Hearth* (1861).

Reader's Digest, American monthly magazine, founded 1922.

Reading, Rufus Isaacs, 1st Marquess (1860–1935), English lawyer, was lord chief justice; viceroy of India 1921–26.

Reading University, founded 1892 as the University Extension College; attained university status 1926.

Real Academia Española (Royal Spanish Academy), Madrid, founded 1713; charter granted 1714 by Philip V.

reaper, invented *c.* 1826 by the Scottish clergyman Patrick Bell (1799–1869); first practical machine patented 1834 by the American Cyrus Hall McCormick (1809–1884).

Réaumur scale, of temperature, devised 1730 by the French scientist René-Antoine Réaumur (1683–1757).

Rebecca Riots, Wales, occurred briefly 1839 and more violently during 1842–44; chief disturbances 1843.

Récamier, Madame Jeanne (1777–1849), French society woman, famous for her beauty, whose salon attracted many famous men.

Rechabites, Independent Order of, temperance society, founded at Salford 1835.

Recife, Brazil, settled *c.* 1535.

Reclus, Elisée (1830–1905), French geographer, author of the influential *Nouvelle Géographie Universelle* (1875–94).

Reconstruction Acts, U.S.A., passed 1 March, 23 March and 19 July 1867, and 11 March 1868, during the Reconstruction period following the American Civil War.

Records. See **Public Records Office.**

Red Cross, International, originated 1863; first Geneva Convention signed 1864.

Red Guards, China, formed 1966 from groups of students during the Cultural Revolution; movement gradually died out 1967.

Redmond, John (1856–1918), Irish nationalist leader of moderate views, advocate of Home Rule; outbid by extremists.

Redon, Odilon (1840–1916), French painter and engraver, was a forerunner of Surrealism.

Redouté, Pierre (1759–1840), French artist, best known for his paintings of flowers.

Reed, Talbot Baines (1852–1903), English writer of boys' books.

Reed, Walter (1851–1902), American bacteriologist, proved that mosquitoes carried yellow fever.

Reed's School, Cobham, Surrey, English public school, founded 1813.

Reeves, John Sims (1818–1900), English tenor singer in opera and oratorio.

referendum, first in Britain, on the question of membership of the European Economic Community, held 5 June 1975.

reflecting telescope, first designed, but not built, 1663 by the Scottish astronomer James Gregory (1638–75); first constructed 1668 by Sir Isaac Newton; Gregory's design first built 1674 by Robert Hooke (*q.v.*).

reflex action, first explained scientifically 1837 by the English physiologist Marshall Hall (1790–1857).

Reformation, 16th- and 17th-century religious revolution in the Western Church, started 1517 by the German reformer Martin Luther (*q.v.*).

reformatory. See **approved schools.**

refracting telescope. See **telescopes.**

refraction, double, discovered 1669 by the Danish physician Erasmus Bartholin (1625–98); finally explained by the wave theory (*q.v.*) of Thomas Young and Augustin Fresnel.

refraction, of light, law proposed 1621 by the Dutch mathematician Willebrord Snell (1591–1626) and published 1638.

refrigerators, domestic, widely used after the preparation 1930 of the first safe refrigerant (Freon) by the American chemist Thomas Midgley (1889–1944).

refrigerators, for industry, developed 1840s and 1850s in U.S.A. by John Gorrie and Alexander C. Twinning, in Australia by James Harrison, and in France by Ferdinand Carré.

Regency Period, Britain, approximately 1810 to 1820.

Reger, Max (1873–1916), German composer and organ virtuoso, wrote much organ music.

Regiomontanus (1436–76), German astronomer and mathematician, established observatory at Nuremberg.

registrar-general, first for England and Wales, Thomas Henry Lister (1800–42), appointed 1836.

registration, of births, marriages and deaths, instituted in England and Wales 1538 by Thomas Cromwell; made compulsory 1837.

Regnault, Henri (1843–71), French painter of mythological scenes.

Regnault, Henri Victor (1810–78), French chemist and physicist, conducted researches on the properties of gases.

Regnier, Henri de (1864–1936), French poet, whose work shows both Symbolist and Parnassian influence.

Regnier, Mathurin (1573–1613), French satirical writer, author of *Macette*.

Regulus (3rd cent. B.C.), Roman hero, reputedly returned voluntarily to Carthage after failure of peace mission, where he was tortured to death.

Rehan, Ada (1860–1916), Irish-born American actress, mainly in light comedy roles.

Reichstadt, Duc de. See **Napoleon II.**

Reichstag, parliamentary assembly of the German Empire 1871–1918 and the Weimar Republic 1919–33; building burnt down 27 Feb. 1933.

Reid, Mayne (1818–83), Irish-born writer, drew on experiences in U.S.A. for adventure novels.

Reid, Sir William (1791–1858), English soldier and administrator, governor of the Bermudas 1839–46.

Reign of Terror, during the French Revolution, from 5 Sept. 1793 to 27 July 1794, when Robespierre (*q.v.*) fell from power.

Reims Cathedral, France, construction began 1211; west front erected 14th century; partially destroyed in World War I; restored 1927–38.

Reinach, Salomon (1858–1932), French archaeologist, wrote extensively on the history of art and religion.

reinforced concrete. See **concrete.**

Reinhardt, Max (1873–1943), Austrian theatre director, famous for his spectacular sets.

Reith, John Charles, 1st Baron (1889–1971), Scottish government official, first director-general of the B.B.C. 1927–38.

Réjane, Gabrielle (1857–1920), French actress, founded her own theatre.

Relativity, Special Theory 1905 and General Theory 1916, propounded by Albert Einstein (*q.v.*).

Remarque, Erich Maria (1898–1970), German novelist, wrote *All Quiet on the Western Front* (1929).

Rembrandt (1606–69), outstanding Dutch painter, whose works include *The Night Watch, Bathsheba*, etc.

Remembrance Day, Sunday following 11 Nov. (Armistice Day, World War I), commemorating the dead of both world wars; founded 1927 by the *Daily Express*;

organized by the British Legion since 1929.

Remington, Frederick (1861–1909), American artist, painted scenes of the American West; was also a sculptor.

Remizov, Aleksei (1877–1957), Russian novelist and short story writer, author of *The Fifth Pestilence* (1912).

Remonstrants, group of Dutch Protestants who set forth their doctrines in a Remonstrance, 1610; not fully tolerated until 1795.

Rémusat, Charles, Comte de (1797–1875), French statesman, foreign minister 1871–1873; also historian of 18th-century England.

Renaissance, began in Italy in the 14th century, spreading to other European countries and lasting until the 16th century.

Renan, Ernest (1823–92), French writer, whose *Life of Jesus* (1863) scandalized by treating Jesus as a human being.

Rendcomb College, Cirencester, English public school, founded and endowed 1920 by Noel Wills.

Reni, Guido (1575–1642), Italian painter of Bolognese classical school, e.g. *Aurora* (1610).

Rennie, John (1761–1821), Scottish civil engineer, designed London, Southwark and Waterloo bridges.

Renoir, Auguste (1841–1919), French painter, one of the greatest Impressionists, best known for his female nudes, café scenes, etc.

Renoir, Jean (b. 1894), French film director, son of Auguste Renoir, whose work includes *La Règle du Jeu* (1934).

Renouvier, Charles (1815–1903), French philosopher, exponent of neocriticism.

Renwick, James (1662–88), Scottish Covenanter, outlawed for rejection of royal authority; hanged.

Reparations, German, after World War I, paid 1921–31.

Repington, Philip (d. 1424), English cardinal, follower of Wyclif but recanted; bishop of Lincoln 1405–19.

Repplier, Agnes (1858–1950), American writer, author of *Books and Men* (1888).

Repton School, Derbyshire, English public school, founded under the will of Sir John Port 1557.

Republic, French, First 1792–1804, Second 1848–52, Third 1870–1940, Fourth 1946–58, Fifth since 1958; English, 1649–60; Spanish, 1873–74 and 1931–39; Portuguese, since 1910; Italian since 1946; German, 1918–33 and (East and West Germany) since 1949; Greek, 1924–35 and since 1974; Turkish, since 1923.

Republican Party, U.S.A., present one formed 1854.

Respighi, Ottorino (1879–1936), Italian composer of *La Boutique Fantasque* (1919).

Restif de la Bretonne, Nicolas (1734–1806), French novelist, also autobiographer (*Monsieur Nicolas*, 1797).

Restoration, English, of Charles II, 26 May 1660.

Restoration, French, of Louis XVIII, 1814.

Reszke, Edouard de (1855–1917), Polish opera singer, best known in Wagnerian roles.

Reszke, Jean de (1850–1925), Polish operatic tenor, brother of Edouard de Reszke, outstanding in Romantic opera.

Retz, Paul de, Cardinal (1613–79), French ecclesiastic and political intriguer, remembered for his *Memoirs*.

Reuchlin, Johann (1455–1522), German humanist, pioneer Hebrew scholar.

Réunion, Indian Ocean, discovered *c.* 1507; colonized by the French 1660s; became an overseas department of France 1946.

Reuters, news agency founded in London 1851 by the German-born Paul Julius Reuter (1816–99).

Reuther, Walter Philip (1907–70), American labour leader, organized the Union of Automobile Workers.

Revere, Paul (1735–1818), American patriot, rode from Boston to Lexington to warn of British approach 1775.

Revised Version, of the Bible, completed 1885; Apocrypha 1895.

Reykjavik, capital of Iceland, founded *c.* 870.

Reymont, Wladislaw (1867–1925), Polish novelist, e.g. *The Peasants* (1904); Nobel prizewinner 1924.

Reynolds, George Nugent (*c.* 1770–1802), Irish poet, wrote *Kathleen O'More* (1800).

Reynolds, Sir Joshua (1723–92), English painter, best known as a portraitist; first president of the Royal Academy.

Reza Shah Pahlavi (1877–1944), shah of Persia 1925–41.

Rhangaves, Alexandros (1810–92), Greek archaeologist and writer, excavated around Argos.

Rhee, Syngman (1875–1965), president and effective dictator of South Korea 1948–60.

Rheinberger, Josef (1839–1901), German composer of organ sonatas; child prodigy as an organist.

rhenium, metallic element, predicted 1869 by Dmitri Mendeleyev (*q.v.*); discovered 1925 by the German chemists Ida and Walter Noddack and Otto Berg.

Rhesus (Rh) blood groups, discovered in U.S.A. independently by Philip Levine and R. E. Stetson 1939 and by Karl Landsteiner and Alexander S. Wiener 1940.

Rhine, Joseph (b. 1895), American psychologist, noted for his investigations into parapsychology.

Rhine, Confederation of the, of German states, formed by Napoleon 1806; collapsed 1813.

Rhineland, occupied by the Allies 1918–1930 as part of the terms of the Treaty of Versailles; reoccupied by Germany March 1936.

Rhode Island, U.S.A., first settled 1636; one of the 13 original states of the Union; admitted to the Union 1790.

Rhodes, Cecil (1853–1902), English statesman and financier, made fortune in diamonds, opened up Rhodesia; prime minister of Cape Colony 1890–96.

Rhodes, Greek island, independent kingdom *c.* 1400 B.C.; part of Delian league 5th century B.C. seized by the Knights Hospitallers 1309; evacuated 1522 and ceded to the Turks; taken by the Italians 1912; ceded to Greece 1947.

Rhodes, Colossus of, statue built *c.* 285 B.C.; destroyed by an earthquake *c.* 224 B.C.

Rhodes Scholarships, for the education at Oxford University of overseas students, set up 1902 by the will of Cecil Rhodes.

Rhodesia, southern Africa, region explored by Portuguese in early 16th century; Bantu migrations began 1830s; administered by British South Africa Company from 1889 to 1923 when it became a self-governing colony; federated with Northern Rhodesia and Nyasaland 1953–1963; declared unilateral independence 1965; proclaimed a republic 1970.

Rhodesia, Northern. See **Zambia.**

rhodium, discovered 1803–04 by William Hyde Wollaston (*q.v.*).

Rhondda, Margaret, Viscountess (1883–1958), English feminist, founder and editor 1920–58 of *Time and Tide.*

Rialto Bridge, Venice, designed 1587 and built by the Venetian architect-engineer Antonio da Ponte (1512–*c.* 1595).

Ribault, Jean (*c.* 1520–65), French navigator, tried to establish French colony in South Carolina.

Ribbentrop, Joachim von (1893–1946), German Nazi leader, ambassador to Britain 1936–38, foreign minister 1938–45; executed.

ribbing machine, for stockings, etc., patented 1758–59 by the English inventor Jedediah Strutt (1726–97).

Ribera, Jusepe de (*c.* 1591–1656), Spanish painter in Italy, worked in dramatic Baroque style.

Ricardo, David (1772–1823), English economist, wrote *Principles of Political Economy* (1817).

Ricci, Matteo (1552–1610), Italian Jesuit missionary in China, founded a mission at Peking.

Rice, Elmer (1892–1967), American playwright, remembered for the expressionistic *Adding Machine* (1923).

Rich, Richard (16th–17th cent.), English traveller and writer of *News from Virginia* (1610).

Richard I (1157–99), king of England 1189–99, neglected his country for the Crusades.

Richard II (1367–1400), king of England 1377–99, deposed in favour of Bolingbroke (Henry IV).

Richard III (1452–85), king of England 1483–85; defeated and slain at Bosworth.

Richard de Bury (1287–1345), English divine and book collector, wrote handbook on the subject.

Richard of Cirencester (*c.* 1335–1401), English chronicler, wrote *Speculum Historiale*.

Richard of Devizes (late 12th cent.), English chronicler of Richard I's reign and deeds.

Richards, Alfred Bate (1820–76), English journalist, first editor of *Daily Telegraph* 1855.

Richards, Frank (1875–1961), English writer of 'Billy Bunter' books for boys.

Richards, Sir Gordon (b. 1904), English jockey, was many times champion jockey.

Richards, Theodore (1868–1928), American chemist, best known for his accurate determination of atomic weights.

Richardson, Dorothy (1873–1957), English novelist, pioneered stream-of-consciousness technique in her *Pilgrimage* novels.

Richardson, Jonathan (1665–1745), English painter, was a popular portraitist.

Richardson, Samuel (1689–1761), English novelist, author of *Pamela* (1740), the first English novel of character and psychology.

Richelieu, Armand, Cardinal and Duc de (1585–1642), French statesman, chief minister of Louis XIII 1624–42, greatly strengthened monarchy in France.

Richelieu, Armand, Duc de (1766–1822), French statesman, prime minister 1815–1818 and 1820–21.

Richepin, Jean (1849–1926), French poet, author of *Les Blasphèmes* (1884); was also a playwright.

Richmond Bridge, London, built 1774–1777 by the English architects James Paine (1725–89) and Kenton Couse (1721–90).

Richter, Ernst Friedrich (1808–79), German composer, remembered as a harmonic theorist.

Richter, Hans (1843–1916), German conductor, popularized the operas of Wagner in England.

Richter, Johann Paul (1763–1825), German novelist, author of *The Titan* (1800–1803).

Richter scale, for earthquake measurements, developed by the American geophysicist Charles Francis Richter (b. 1900).

Richthofen, Manfred von (1892–1918), German aviator, outstanding air ace in World War I.

Rickenbacker, Edward Vernon (1890–1973), American aviator in World War I, later chairman of Eastern Air Lines.

Rickover, Hyman George (b. 1900), American admiral, directed the project for the first atomic-powered submarine.

Ricordi, Giovanni (1785–1853), Italian music publisher, founded well-known firm.

Riddell, George Allardyce, Baron (1865–1934), English newspaper owner, notably of the *News of the World*.

Ridley, Nicholas (*c.* 1500–55), English prelate, bishop of London 1550–55; burnt at the stake.

Ridolfi, Roberto di (1531–1612), Italian conspirator, plotted to place Mary Queen of Scots on the English throne 1571.

Ridpath, George (*c.* 1717–72), Scottish historian, wrote *Border History* (1776).

Riebeeck, Jan van (1634–77), Dutch surgeon and colonist in South Africa, founded Cape Town, 1652.

Riefenstahl, Leni (b. 1902), German film director, best known for her film of the 1936 Olympic Games.

Riel, Louis (1844–85), French Canadian political leader, executed after unsuccessful rebellion.

Riemann, Georg Friedrich (1826–66), German mathematician, made notable advances in the theory of geometry.

Riemann, Hugo (1849–1919), German musicologist, compiled well-known *Musiklexikon* (1882).

Riemannian geometry, non-Euclidean geometry (*q.v.*) developed 1854 by Georg Friedrich Riemann.

Riemenschneider, Tilman (*c.* 1460–1531), German sculptor whose work includes *Ascension of the Virgin*.

Rienzi, Cola di (*c.* 1313–54), Italian revolutionary, dictator at Rome 1347–48 and 1354; murdered by mob.

rifle, invented in central Europe in late 15th century; British army first equipped (with Baker rifles) 1805; greatly improved in 19th century by breech-loading designs and the expanding Minié ball (1849); semi-automatic rifles used in World War II; fully automatic assault rifles in use in 1960s.

Riga, capital of Latvia, founded *c.* 1200.

Rigaud, Hyacinthe (1659–1743), French court painter, notably of Louis XIV.

Rigaud, Stephen (1774–1839), English mathematician and astronomer, was a notable scholar.

Rights, Declaration of, accompanying the offer of the British crown to William and Mary jointly, Feb. 1689; parliamentary enactment (Bill of Rights) Dec. 1689.

Rights of Man, Declaration of, adopted Aug. 1789 by French National Assembly; formed preface to the 1791 Constitution.

Rijeka, Yugoslavia, at various times under Austrian, French and Hungarian rule; seized by D'Annunzio (*q.v.*) 1919; ruled by Italy 1924–47 and by Yugoslavia since 1947.

Riley, James Whitcomb (1849–1916), American poet, wrote in Indiana (Hoosier) dialect, e.g. *Little Orphan Annie.*

Riley, John (1646–91), English court painter, also made portraits of servants.

Rilke, Rainer, Maria (1875–1926), outstanding German poet, author of the *Duino Elegies* (1923).

Rimbaud, Arthur (1854–91), major French Symbolist poet, author of *Les Illuminations*; ceased writing at the age of 20.

Rimini, Francesca da. See **Francesca da Rimini.**

Rimmer, William (1816–79), English-born American sculptor, mainly of portraits and mythological subjects.

Rimsky-Korsakov, Nikolai (1844–1908), Russian composer in nationalist Romantic idiom, e.g. *Coq d'Or.*

Rinehart, William Henry (1825–74), American sculptor, worked in Italy.

Rio de Janeiro, Brazil, site traditionally discovered 1502 by the Portuguese; settled 1535 by the French and 1567 by the Portuguese; capital of Brazil until 1960.

Rio Muni, West Africa, first settled by Spanish 1843; with Fernando Po formed Spanish Guinea (now Equatorial Guinea).

Ripley, Thomas (*c.* 1683–1758), English architect, built the Admiralty, London.

Ripon, George Robinson, Marquess of (1827–1909), English Liberal politician, held many ministerial offices.

Risorgimento, 19th-century movement for Italian unity culminating in the annexation of Venetia, 1866, and papal Rome, 1870, to the new kingdom of Italy, formed 1861.

Ritchie, Charles, Baron (1838–1906), English politician, responsible for the Local Government Act 1888.

Ritschl, Albrecht (1822–89), German Protestant theologian, emphasized ethics rather than dogma.

Ritson, Joseph (1752–1803), English antiquary and controversialist, wrote *Bibliographia Poetica* (1802).

Rittenhouse, David (1732–96), American astronomer, built first American telescope; took part in the Revolutionary War.

Ritter, Hermann (1848–1926), German inventor of the viola alta, 1876.

Ritter, Karl (1779–1859), German geographer, founder of modern scientific geography.

Rivera, Diego (1886–1957), Mexican painter of murals in bold 'social realist' style.

River Plate, Battle of the, World War II, fought between British cruisers *Exeter*, *Ajax* and *Achilles*, and the German pocket-battleship *Graf Spee* (*q.v.*), 13 Dec. 1939.

Rivers, William (1864–1922), English anthropologist, author of *History of Melanesian Society* (1914).

Rizzio, David (*c.* 1533–66), Italian secretary to Mary Queen of Scots, murdered by Lord Darnley (*q.v.*).

RNA, or ribonucleic acid, discovered 1869, with DNA (*q.v.*) by the Swiss biochemist Friedrich Miescher (1844–95); function in protein formation studied from late 1950s.

Robbe-Grillet, Alain (b. 1922), French novelist, author of *Dans le Labyrinthe* (1959).

Robbia, Luca della (*c.* 1399–1482), Italian sculptor in classical style, e.g. 'Singing Gallery' bas relief made for Florence cathedral.

Robbins, Jerome (b. 1918), American dancer and choreographer, whose work includes such musicals as *West Side Story.*

Robert I (d. 923), king of France 922–923 in rivalry with Charles III; defeated.

Robert II (*c.* 970–1031), king of France 996–1031, enjoyed a mainly peaceful reign.

Robert I, the Bruce (1274–1329), king of Scotland 1306–29, defeated English at Bannockburn 1314.

Robert II (1316–90), king of Scotland 1371–90, first of the Stuart dynasty.

Robert III (*c.* 1340–1406), king of Scotland 1390–1406, controlled by younger brother, the Duke of Albany.

Robert Gordon's College, Aberdeen, Scottish public school, founded 1729.

Robert of Gloucester (13th cent.), English chronicler, wrote history of England in the vernacular.

Roberts, Frederick, Earl (1832–1914), British soldier, commanded in Afghanistan and in the Boer War.

Roberts, Richard (1789–1864), Welsh inventor of self-acting mule and other cotton manufacturing machinery.

Robertson, Thomas William (1829–71), English playwright, author of *Caste* (1867).

Robertson, William (1721–93), Scottish historian, best remembered for his *History of America* (1777).

Robertson, Sir William (1860–1933), British soldier, was Chief of the Imperial General Staff during World War I.

Robeson, Paul (1898–1976), American Negro singer and actor, and campaigner for civil rights for Negroes.

Robespierre, Maximilien (1758–94), French Revolutionary leader, identified with the Reign of Terror 1793–94; guillotined.

Robin Hood, legendary English hero, probably lived in the 13th or 14th century.

Robinson, Edwin (1869–1931), American poet, author of *Captain Craig* (1902).

Robinson, Henry Crabb (1775–1867), English journalist, friend of writers, kept valuable *Diary*.

Robinson, Mary. See **Perdita.**

Rob Roy (Robert Macgregor; 1671–1734), Scottish outlaw.

Robsart, Amy (*c.* 1532–1560), English noblewoman, wife of Earl of Leicester, died in obscure circumstances.

Rochambeau, Jean, Comte de (1725–1807), French soldier, commanded army which, with Washington's, forced British surrender of Yorktown 1781.

Rochdale Canal, Lancashire, constructed by John Rennie (*q.v.*); opened 1804.

Rochester, John Wilmot, Earl of (1647–1680), English poet and courtier, noted for his satirical and frequently obscene verse.

Rockall, tiny island, Outer Hebrides, formally annexed by Britain 1955.

rock drill, invented 1871 by the American Simon Ingersoll (1818–94).

Rockefeller, John Davison (1839–1937), American industrialist and philanthropist, made a fortune in oil.

Rocket, The, first successful high-speed steam locomotive built 1929 by George and Robert Stephenson (*qq.v.*) and used on the Liverpool and Manchester railway.

Rockingham, Charles Wentworth, Marquess of (1730–82), English statesman, led his own Whig faction, prime minister 1765–66 and 1782.

Rocroi, Battle of, Thirty Years' War, victory of the French over the Spanish, 19 May 1643.

Roderic (d. 1198), king of Connaught and last high king of Ireland; submitted to Henry II.

Rodgers, Richard (b. 1902), American musical comedy composer, collaborated with Lorenz Hart and Oscar Hammerstein.

Rodin, Auguste (1840–1917), French sculptor, e.g. *The Thinker, The Kiss.*

Rodney, George, Baron (1719–92), English admiral, achieved unbroken success in naval battles in the West Indies against French and Spanish.

Rodrigues, Indian Ocean, island dependency of Mauritius (*q.v.*), ceded to Britain by France 1814.

Roebling, John Augustus (1806–69), German-born American engineer, designed several bridges and planned Brooklyn Bridge.

Roedean School, Brighton, English girls' public school, founded 1885; incorporated by royal charter 1938.

Roerich, Nikolai (1874–1947), Russian painter, lived in India, painted the Himalayas.

Rogation Days, the three days before Ascension Day.

Roger I (1031–1101), Norman conqueror and ruler of Sicily, and later of Malta.

Roger II (1097–1154), Norman ruler of Sicily 1112–1154, king 1130–54; in conflict with the Byzantines.

Roger de Wendover (d. 1236), English chronicler, wrote *Flores Historiarum.*

Roger of Salisbury (d. 1139), English administrator, chancellor, bishop of Salisbury 1102–39; created exchequer system.

Rogers, Henry Darwin (1808–66), American geologist, worked in U.S.A. and Scotland.

Rogers, Samuel (1763–1855), English poet, wrote *The Pleasures of Memory* (1792).

Rogers, Will (1879–1935), American humorist, starred on Broadway and in films.

Rogers, William (1819–96), English clergyman and educationalist, founded many schools.

Roget's Thesaurus, compiled 1852 by the English scholar Peter Mark Roget (1779–1869).

Rojas, Fernando de (*c.* 1465–1541), Spanish writer of *La Celestina*, a dialogue-novel of great originality.

Rolfe, Frederick (1860–1913), English writer, also called himself Baron Corvo; best known for *Hadrian the Seventh* (1904).

Rolfe, John (1585–1622), English colonist in Virginia, discovered how to cure tobacco; married Pocahontas (*q.v.*).

Rolland, Romain (1866–1944), French novelist, whose *Jean Christophe* (4 vols., 1904–12) traces the development of a composer.

Rolle, Richard (*c.* 1290–1349), English mystical writer in both English and Latin.

Rollo (*c.* 860–931), Norse chieftain, led Viking settlement in Normandy.

Rolls, Charles Stewart (1877–1910), English motor-car manufacturer and aviator, co-founder of Rolls Royce Ltd.

Rölvaag, Ole Edvart (1876–1931), Norwegian-born American novelist, wrote *Giants of the Earth* (1924–25), in Norwegian, about immigrants.

Romains, Jules (1885–1972), French novelist, wrote the multi-volume *Les Hommes de Bonne Volonté* (1932–47).

Roman Catholic Church, origins traced back to teaching of the Apostles, 1st century A.D.; schism between Eastern and Western Churches 11th century; Protestant Church broke away in the 16th century in the Reformation.

Roman Empire, established 27 B.C. under

Augustus (*q.v.*); divided 395 A.D. into an Eastern Empire (Byzantine Empire), which survived until the fall of Constantinople 1453, and a Western Empire, overrun in 4th–5th centuries by invading tribes of Visigoths, Vandals, Ostrogoths, and others; last emperor deposed 476. See also **Rome.**

Romanes Lectures, Oxford University, founded 1891 by the Canadian-born scientist Georges John Romanes (1848–94).

Romanesque art, European medieval art style, flourished in the period 1075–1125; superseded by Gothic art.

Romania, formed 1861 when principalities of Moldavia and Wallachia formally united; complete independence from Turkey recognized 1878; monarchy 1881–1947; Communist People's Republic proclaimed 1947; new constitution 1965.

roman type, first used in 1460s in Europe; perfected 1470 by the Venetian printer and publisher Nicolas Jenson (*c.* 1420–1480).

Romanus I (d. 948), Byzantine emperor 919–944, deposed after trying to establish a new dynasty.

Romanus II (939–963), Byzantine emperor 959–963, captured Crete from the Saracens.

Romanus III (d. 1034), Byzantine emperor 1028–34, possibly murdered by wife Zoë.

Romanus IV (d. 1071), Byzantine emperor 1067–71, utterly defeated by Suljuks at Manzikert.

Romberg, Sigmund (1887–1951), Hungarian-born composer of musical comedies, e.g. *The Student Prince* (1924).

Rome, traditionally founded 753 B.C. by Romulus and Remus; monarchy until early 6th century B.C. (traditional date 509 B.C.); republic 509–31 B.C.; Roman Empire (*q.v.*) established under Augustus 27 B.C.

Rome, Treaties of, establishing the European Economic Community (E.E.C.) and European Atomic Energy Community (Euratom) (*qq.v.*), signed March 1957.

Rome, University of, founded 1303.

Römer, Olaus (1644–1710), Danish astronomer, calculated velocity of light 1675.

Romilly, Sir Samuel (1757–1818), English reformer, did much to mitigate severity of criminal law.

Rommel, Erwin (1891–1944), German soldier, commanded the Afrika Korps during World War II.

Romney, George (1734–1802), English painter, was a notable portraitist; Lady Hamilton (*q.v.*) was his favourite subject.

Romulus Augustulus (d. A.D. 476), last Roman emperor in the West, 475–476.

Ronald, Sir Landon (1873–1938), English conductor of the Royal Albert Hall Orchestra 1908–38.

Ronsard, Pierre de (1524–85), French poet, chief of the Pléiade group, noted for his sonnets and odes.

Röntgen, Wilhelm von (1845–1923), German physicist, awarded first Nobel Prize for Physics, 1901, for his discovery of X-rays.

Roosevelt, Eleanor (1884–1962), American author and diplomat, wife of Franklin Roosevelt; U.S. delegate to the U.N. General Assembly 1945–52.

Roosevelt, Franklin Delano (1882–1945), American statesman, 32nd president of the United States 1933–45; instituted the New Deal; the only president to be re-elected three times.

Roosevelt, Theodore (1858–1919), American statesman, 26th president of the United States 1901–09; noted for his anti-trust legislation.

Root, Elihu (1845–1937), American statesman and diplomat, worked for disarmament; awarded Nobel Peace Prize 1912.

Roper, Margaret (1505–44), English scholar, daughter of Sir Thomas More.

Rops, Félicien (1833–98), Belgian artist, worked in Paris, produced morbid and 'decadent' drawings.

Rorschach test, devised 1921 by the Swiss psychiatrist Hermann Rorschach (1884–1922).

Rosa, Carl (1843–89), German-born founder of Carl Rosa Opera Company.

Rosa, Salvator (1615–73), Italian painter of wild, dramatic landscape scenes.

Rosamund, Fair (d. *c.* 1176), mistress of Henry II of England, said to have been poisoned by Queen Eleanor.

rosaniline, red dye, synthesized 1858 by the German chemist August Wilhelm von Hofmann (1818–92).

Roscius, Quintus (*c.* 130–*c.* 62 B.C.), famous Roman comic actor, promoted to equestrian rank by Sulla.

Roscoe, William (1753–1831), English writer on Renaissance history.

Roseberry, Archibald Primrose, 5th Earl of (1847–1929), English statesman, prime minister 1894–95.

Rosegger, Peter (1843–1918), Austrian novelist and poet, author of *Man and Wife* (1879).

Rosenberg, Alfred (1893–1946), German Nazi official, proponent of racialist doctrines; executed as a war criminal.

Rosenberg, Isaac (1890–1918), English poet, wrote *Break of Day in the Trenches*; killed in action.

Rosenberg, Julius (1917–53), American spy, with his wife Ethel (1916–53), convicted and executed for passing atomic secrets to the Soviet Union.

Rose of Lima, Saint (1586–1617), Peruvian nun, first person to be canonized in the New World.

Roses, Wars of the, between the houses of Lancaster and York, 1455–85.

Rosetta Stone, ancient Egyptian stone bearing inscriptions in Greek and Egyptian (hieroglyphic and demotic), discovered 1799; deciphered *c*. 1810–*c*. 1822, by the physicist Thomas Young and the orientalist Jean-François Champollion (*qq.v.*).

Rosh ha-Shanah (Feast of the Trumpets), the Jewish New Year, 1st day of Tishri.

Rosicrucians, occult society in 17th century; revived in 18th century and several times since.

Ross, Sir James Clark (1800–62), Scottish explorer, made several expeditions to the Arctic and Antarctic.

Ross, Sir John (1777–1856), Scottish Arctic explorer, twice sought North-West Passage.

Ross, Sir Ronald (1857–1932), British physician born in India, pioneer in cure of malaria; Nobel prizewinner 1902.

Rossall School, Lancashire, English public school, founded 1844; incorporated by royal charter 1890.

Ross Dependency, Antarctica, administered by New Zealand since 1923.

Rosse, William Parsons, 3rd Earl of (1800–1867), English astronomer, pioneered building of larger telescopes.

Rossellino, Antonio (1427–*c*. 1479), Italian sculptor of busts and tombs.

Rossellino, Bernardo (1409–64), Italian sculptor and architect, brother of Antonio Rossellino, whose best known work is the tomb of Leonardo Bruni.

Rossetti, Christina (1830–94), English poet, mainly religious in inspiration, wrote *Goblin Market* (1862).

Rossetti, Dante Gabriel (1828–82), English Pre-Raphaelite painter (*Beata Beatrix*) and poet (*Blessed Damozel*).

Rossi, Charles (1762–1839), English sculptor of monuments in St Paul's Cathedral.

Rossini, Gioacchino (1792–1868), Italian opera composer, notably *The Barber of Seville* (1816).

Rostand, Edmond (1868–1918), French playwright, author of *Cyrano de Bergerac* (1897).

Rostropovich, Mtislav (b. 1927), Russian cellist and composer, professor of music at the Moscow Conservatoire.

Rosyth, Scotland, construction of naval base and dockyard began 1909.

Rotary International, founded U.S.A. 1905; Britain 1914.

rotary printing press, invented 1846 by the American Richard March Hoe (1812–1886).

Rothamsted Experimental Station, world's first agricultural research station, established 1843 by the English agriculturalist Sir John Bennet Lawes (1814–1900).

Rothenstein, Sir John (b. 1901), English art historian, wrote *Modern English Painters* (1952–56).

Rothenstein, Sir William (1872–1945), English painter, principal of Royal College of Art 1920–35, noted for his portraits.

Rotherhithe Tunnel, first under-river tunnel, under the Thames, constructed 1825–43 by Sir Marc Isambard Brunel and his son, Isambard Brunel, using a protective shield; road tunnel built 1904–08.

Rothermere, Harold Harmsworth, Viscount (1868–1940), English newspaper publisher, brother of Lord Northcliffe (*q.v.*).

Rothko, Mark (1903–70), Russian-born American painter, an exponent of Abstract Expressionism.

Rothschild, Meyer Amshel (1743–1812), German Jewish financier, founder of the famous banking family.

Rotrou, Jean de (1609–50), French playwright, pioneered the development of drama in France.

Rouault, Georges (1871–1958), French painter, best known for his religious work.

Roubiliac, Louis François (*c*. 1705–62), French-born sculptor, made career in England with portrait busts of well-known people.

Rouen, invaded by the Normans 876; became subject to the English crown 1066; captured by the French 1204; taken 1419, after a long siege, by Henry V of England; recaptured by the French 1449.

Rouen Cathedral, construction began *c*. 1202.

Rouget de l'Isle, Claude (1760–1836), French composer of the *Marseillaise* (1792).

Roundheads, nickname of Parliamentary supporters during the English Civil War 1642–51.

Rousseau, Henri, 'Le Douanier' (1844–1910), French primitive painter, e.g. *La Chasse au Tigre*.

Rousseau, Jean Jacques (1712–78), French writer, profoundly influential as a novelist, educationalist and political philosopher.

Rouvray, Battle of, Hundred Years' War, victory of the English over the French, 12 Feb. 1429.

Roux, Pierre (1853–1933), French bacteriologist, associated with Pasteur; did pioneer work on diphtheria.

Rover Scouts, movement formed in Britain 1918.

Rowan, Archibald (1751–1834), Irish nationalist, joined United Irishman, exiled in France and U.S.A. 1794–1803.

Rowe, Nicholas (1674–1718), English playwright, edited Shakespeare's plays.

Rowlandson, Thomas (1756–1827), English painter, noted for his watercolour caricatures of English life.

Rowley, William (*c.* 1585–*c.* 1642), English playwright, wrote *A Woman Never Vext* (1632).

Rowley Poems, supposedly written by a 15th-century poet, Thomas Rowley, in fact composed in late 1760s by Thomas Chatterton (*q.v.*).

Rowntree, Joseph (1836–1925), English Quaker manufacturer of cocoa, was a model employer and philanthropist.

Rowton House, poor men's hostels in London, founded 1892 onwards by the philanthropist Baron Rowton (1838–1903).

Roxana (d. 310 B.C.), wife of Alexander the Great; murdered.

Royal Academy of Arts, London, founded 1768.

Royal Academy of Dramatic Art, London, founded 1904 by Sir Herbert Tree (*q.v.*); royal charter granted 1920.

Royal Academy of Music, London, founded 1822; incorporated 1827.

Royal Aeronautical Society, founded 1866 as the Aeronautical Society of Great Britain; acquired present name 1919.

Royal Agricultural Society, of England, founded 1838.

Royal Air Force, formed 1918.

Royal Air Force College, Cranwell, founded 1920.

Royal Albert Hall, London, built in memory of Prince Albert 1867–71; opened by Queen Victoria 29 March 1871.

Royal and Ancient Golf Club of St Andrews, founded 1754.

Royal Astronomical Society, London, founded 1820; chartered 1831.

Royal Automobile Club, London, founded 1897.

Royal Ballet, English ballet company and school, formed 1956 under a royal charter granted to Sadler's Wells Ballet, Theatre Ballet, and School.

Royal Belfast Academical Institution, Northern Ireland public school, founded 1810.

Royal Canadian Mounted Police, founded as the North-West Mounted Police 1873; assumed present title 1920.

Royal College of Physicians, London, founded 1518.

Royal College of Surgeons of Edinburgh, founded 1505.

Royal College of Surgeons of England, before 1843 'of London', founded 1800.

Royal Dutch Petroleum Company, The Hague, established June 1890; interests consolidated with those of the Shell Transport and Trading Company, Ltd., 1907.

Royal Exchange, London, founded 1566 by Sir Thomas Gresham; opened 1571.

Royal Festival Hall, opened 1951; Queen Elizabeth Hall and Purcell Room opened 1967.

Royal Flying Corps, established 1912; superseded by the Royal Air Force 1918.

Royal Geographical Society, London, founded 1830 by Sir John Barrow (*q.v.*).

Royal George, The, sank at Portsmouth 1782.

Royal Grammar School, High Wycombe, English public school, founded 1562; moved to present site 1914.

Royal Grammar School, Newcastle-upon-Tyne, English public school, founded by Thomas Horsley early 16th century; royal charter granted by Elizabeth I 1600.

Royal Grammar School, Worcester, English public school, origins uncertain; earliest recorded mention 1290.

Royal Hospital, Chelsea, founded 1682 by Charles II; built by Sir Christopher Wren; opened 1692.

Royal Hunt Cup, Ascot, first run 1843.

Royal Institute of International Affairs, London, founded 1920.

Royal Institution of Great Britain, London, founded 1799.

Royal Marines, Corps of, constituted 1664 as the Duke of York and Albany's Maritime Regiment of Foot.

Royal Marriages Act, passed 1772.

Royal Masonic School, Bushey, English public school, founded 1798.

Royal Military Academy, Sandhurst, formed 1946 by the amalgamation of the Royal Military Academy, Woolwich (founded 1741) and the Royal Military College, Sandhurst (founded 1799).

Royal Naval College, Dartmouth, opened 1905.

Royal Naval College, Greenwich, opened 1873.

Royal Naval Reserve, formed in Britain under the Royal Naval Reserve (Volunteer) Act of 1859.

Royal Observatory, Greenwich, founded 1675 by Charles II; transferred to Herstmonceux, Sussex, in 1950s.

Royal Opera House, Covent Garden, London, opened 15 May 1858.

Royal Shakespeare Theatre, Stratford-upon-Avon, opened 1879; burnt down 1926; new building opened 1932; received present name 1961.

Royal Society, The, organized 1660; constituted by royal charter 1662.

Royal Society for the Prevention of Cruelty to Animals, London, founded 1824.

Royal Society of Arts, London, founded 1754.

Royal Society of Edinburgh, founded 1783.

Royce, Josiah (1855–1916), American philosopher, author of *The World and the Individual* (1900).

Royden, Maude (1876–1956), English suf-

Ruadri

Russia

fragette and evangelist, first regular woman preacher.

Ruadri. See **Roderic**.

Ruanda-Urundi, part of German East Africa from 1891; Belgian mandate established 1919; became a United Nations trust territory administered Belgium, 1949; split 1962 into the independent republic of Rwanda and the kingdom of Burundi (*qq.v.*).

rubber, first synthesized in 1890s; practical varieties developed in World War II.

rubber, vulcanization of, developed 1839 by Charles Goodyear (*q.v.*).

rubber trees, first cultivated in Kew Gardens from seeds collected 1876 from the Amazon jungle by Sir Henry Wickham (1846–1928); introduced from Kew into the Far East *c.* 1885.

Rubbra, Edmund (b. 1901), English composer and pianist, influenced by earlier English music.

Rubens, Peter Paul (1577–1640), Flemish painter and diplomat, whose work includes *Rape of the Sabine Women*; excelled as a colourist.

rubidium, chemical element, discovered 1861 by Robert Bunsen and Gustav Kirchhoff (*q.v.*).

Rubinstein, Anton (1829–94), Russian piano virtuoso, also composer, e.g. *Dmitri Donskoi*.

Rubinstein, Artur (b. 1889), Polish-born American concert pianist of international fame.

Rubinstein, Nikolai (1835–81), Russian pianist, brother of Anton Rubinstein; founded Moscow Conservatory.

Rudé, François (1784–1855), French sculptor, best in romantically patriotic vein, e.g. *La Marseillaise*.

Rudolf I (1218–91), Holy Roman emperor 1273–91, first of the Habsburg dynasty.

Rudolf II (1552–1612), Holy Roman emperor 1576–1612; forced to yield Hungary and Bohemia to his brother.

Rueda, Lope de (*c.* 1510–*c.* 1565), Spanish playwright, author of *Medora*.

Rufinus, Tyrannius (*c.* 342–410), Italian theologian and controversialist, translated Greek Christian works into Latin.

Rugby football, traditionally started by William Webb Ellis of Rugby School 1823; rules adopted 1846.

Rugby League, seceded from Rugby Union 1895 as Northern Union; adopted present name 1922.

Rugby School, English public school, founded by Lawrence Sheriff 1567.

Rugby Union, British, founded 1871.

Ruhmkorff, Heinrich Daniel (1803–77), German physicist, invented Ruhmkorff induction coil, 1851.

Rule Britannia, first published 1740; words by the Scottish poet James Thomson

(1700–48); music by Thomas Arne (*q.v.*).

Rumania. See **Romania**.

Rumford, Count. See **Thompson,** Benjamin.

Rump Parliament, England, sat 1648–53 and 1659–60.

Rundstedt, Gerd von (1875–1955), German soldier, was a prominent commander in World War II.

Runyon, Damon (1884–1946), American writer and journalist, best known for his short stories.

Rupert (1352–1410), king of Germany 1400–10, led unsuccessful expedition to Italy.

Rupert, Prince (1619–82), German-born soldier, nephew of Charles I of England, Royalist cavalry commander in English Civil War.

Rush, Benjamin (1746–1813), American physician and political leader, active in Revolutionary War period; established first free dispensary in U.S.A.

Rush-Bagot Agreement, between Britain and the U.S.A., limiting naval forces on the Great Lakes between Canada and U.S.A., signed April 1817.

Rushworth, John (1669–1736), English surgeon at Northampton, promoter of local infirmaries and dispensaries.

Rusk, David Dean (b. 1909), American statesman, secretary of state 1961–68.

Ruskin, John (1819–1900), English art and social critic, had a profound influence on accepted ideas of good taste.

Russell, Bertrand, 3rd Earl (1872–1970), English philosopher, writer and mathematician, advocate of nuclear disarmament; awarded Nobel Prize for Literature 1950.

Russell, George (1867–1935), Irish writer, author of *The Candle of Vision* (1919).

Russell, Henry Norris (1877–1957), American astronomer, noted for his work on the relationship between the luminosity and temperature of stars.

Russell, Lord John (1792–1878), English statesman, prime minister 1846–52 and 1865–66.

Russell, John Scott (1808–82), Scottish naval architect, constructed the *Great Eastern*.

Russell, Sir William Howard (1821–1907), English journalist for *The Times*, as war correspondent exposed shortcomings of British army in Crimean War.

Russia, settled by Slavs during 1st millennium A.D.; Scandinavian rulers established in 9th century; under Mongol (Tatar) domination from *c.* 1240 to late 14th century; importance of Muscovy increased from *c.* 1328; Romanov dynasty 1613–1917; tsarist regime overthrown 1917 by the Bolsheviks; civil war 1918–20; Union of Soviet Socialist Republics formed 1922.

Russian Revolutions, 22 Jan. (Bloody Sunday) to Oct. 1905; February Revolution 8–14 March (new style) 1917; Bolshevik Revolution 7 Nov. (Oct. 25 old style) 1917.

Russo–Japanese War, fought 1904–05.

Russo–Turkish Wars, 1676–81, 1687, 1689, 1695–96, 1710–12, 1735–39, 1768–1774, 1787–91, 1806–12, 1828–29, 1853–1856 (Crimean War), 1877–78.

Rutebeuf (d. *c.* 1286), French poet and playwright, author of *Le Miracle de Théophile.*

Rutgers University, New Brunswick, New Jersey, U.S.A., founded as Queen's College 1766; name changed to Rutgers College 1825; became Rutgers University 1924.

Ruth, 'Babe' (1895–1948), American champion baseball player.

ruthenium, metallic element, discovered 1844 by the Russian chemist Karl Klaus (1796–1864), following earlier work, 1828, by Gottfried Osann.

Rutherford, Daniel (1749–1819), Scottish physician, discovered nitrogen 1772.

Rutherford, Ernest, Baron (1871–1937), New Zealand-born British physicist, pioneer investigator of radioactivity and possibility of atomic fission.

Rutherford, Mark (pseud. of William Hale White; 1831–1913), English writer, author of the novel *The Revolution in Tanner's Lane* (1887).

Rutherford, Samuel (1600–61), Scottish Covenanter controversialist; his *Lex Rex* was burnt by hangman 1661.

Ruthven, Raid of, conspiracy against James VI of Scotland 1582, named after one of the conspirators William Ruthven, Earl of Gowrie (*c.* 1541–1584).

Ruysbroek, Jan van (1293–1381), Dutch mystic, wrote *Spiritual Marriage.*

Ruysdael, Jakob (*c.* 1628–82), Dutch painter, especially noted for his sombre landscapes.

Ruyter, Michel de (1607–76), Dutch admiral, distinguished in Anglo–Dutch wars; died in battle against French.

Rwanda, independent African republic, formed 1962 from the U.N. trust territory Ruanda-Urundi (*q.v.*).

Rydal School, Colwyn Bay, Welsh public school, founded by Thomas Osborn 1885.

Rye House Plot, conspiracy of Whigs to assassinate Charles II, April–June 1683.

Rymer, Thomas (1641–1713), English writer, court historiographer and editor of historical documents.

Rysbrack, John Michael (1694–1770), Flemish sculptor, settled in England; rival of Roubiliac (*q.v.*).

Ryswick, Treaty of, ending the war between France and England, Holland and Spain, signed Sept. 1697.

S

Saarinen, Eero (1910–61), Finnish architect, whose work includes the General Motors Technical Center, Michigan; son of Eliel Saarinen.

Saarinen, Eliel (1873–1950), Finnish architect, pioneer of modern style.

Saarland, West German state, administered by League of Nations 1919–35; by France 1945–56.

Sabah, made a British protectorate 1888; became a colony 1946; incorporated in Malaysia 1963.

Sabatier, Auguste (1839–1901), French Protestant theologian, applied historical criteria to the Bible.

Sabatini, Rafael (1875–1950), Italian-born writer of romances in English, e.g. *Captain Blood* (1922).

Sabbath, Jewish day of rest, seventh day of week; Christian day of rest, first day of week since 4th century.

Sabin, Joseph (1821–81), English-born book dealer and writer of the *Bibliotheca Americana* (1868–84).

saccharin, discovered 1879 by the American chemist Ira Remsen (1846–1927) and the Russian-born chemist Constantin Fahlberg.

Sacco, Nicola (1891–1927), American anarchist, convicted, with Bartolomeo Vanzetti of robbery and murder; executed.

Sacheverell, Henry (*c.* 1674–1724), English clergyman, preached intolerantly Tory-Anglican sermons 1709, leading to political crisis.

Sachs, Hans (1494–1576), German poet, mastersinger of Nuremberg; subject of Wagner opera.

Sachs, Julius von (1832–97), German botanist, best known for his researches into the metabolism of plants.

Sackville, Charles, Earl of Dorset (1638–1706), English poet and patron, notably of Dryden.

Sackville, Thomas, Earl of Dorset (1536–1608), English playwright, wrote *Gorboduc* with T. Norton (*q.v.*).

Sackville-West, Victoria (Vita) (1892–1962), English novelist, author of *The Edwardians* (1930).

Sadat, Anwar (b. 1918), Egyptian statesman, president of Egypt since 1970.

Sade, Donatien, Marquis de (1740–1814), French writer, whose sexual perversions, described in his novels, gave rise to the word sadism.

Sadi (*c.* 1184–1291), Persian poet, wrote the *Gulistan* ('Rose Garden'), mixing stories and aphorisms, verse and prose.

Sadleir, Michael (1888–1957), English writer, biographer of Trollope and novelist, e.g. *Fanny by Gaslight* (1940).

Sadler's Wells, London theatre, opened in late 17th century; reconstructed 1879; closed 1906; rebuilt 1931.

Sadowa, Battle of, victory of the Prussians over the Austrians, 3 July 1866.

safety lamp, miner's invented 1815 by Sir Humphry Davy (*q.v.*).

safety razor. See **razor.**

Sagan, Françoise (b. 1935), French novelist, won immediate fame at 19 with *Bonjour Tristesse* (1954).

Sage, Russell (1816–1906), American financier, rose from grocery clerk to a prominent position on the stock exchange.

Sahagun, Bernardino de (c. 1499–1590), Spanish missionary and historian of Mexico.

Sahara, Western, Spanish settlement established late 15th century; Spanish protectorate proclaimed 1884; boundary with French Sahara defined by treaty 1900; made an overseas province of Spain 1968; became independent 1976.

Sailors' Rests, founded by the English philanthropist Agnes Elizabeth Weston (1840–1918).

Saint Albans Abbey, England, built 793 on supposed site of Saint Alban's martyrdom 303; abbey church became cathedral 1877.

Saint Albans School, English public school, founded 1570; original foundation said to have been by Abbot Ulsinus c. 948.

Saint Andrew's University, Scotland, founded by Bishop Wardlaw 1411.

Saint Andrew's Cathedral, Scotland, built 1159–1318.

Saint Andrew's Day, 30 Nov., national day of Scotland.

Saint Anne's College, Oxford University, founded 1879 for women students; incorporated as a college of the university 1952.

Saint Anthony's College, Oxford University, founded 1950.

Saint Bartholomew's Day, Massacre of Protestants in Paris 24–25 Aug. 1572.

Saint Bartholomew's Hospital, London, founded 1137; rebuilt 1730.

Saint Bees School, Cumbria, English public school, founded by Edmund Grindal, archbishop of Canterbury, 1583.

Saint Benedict's School, Ealing, English public school founded by Abbot Hugh Edmund Ford, 1902.

Saint Benet's Hall, Oxford University, founded 1897 by the Benedictine abbey of Ampleforth.

Saint Catharine's College, Cambridge University, founded by Robert Woodlark, provost of King's College, 1473.

Saint Catherine's College, Oxford University, founded 1963, replacing Saint Catherine's Society for non-collegiate students, founded 1868.

Saint Christopher-Nevis. See **Saint Kitts-Nevis.**

Saint Columba's College, Dublin, Irish public school, founded 1843; incorporated 1913.

Saint Cyr, French girls' school, founded 1686; taken over by Napoleon 1806 for establishment of military training college 1808; destroyed 1944.

Saint David's Cathedral, Wales, founded late 12th century.

Saint David's Day, 1 March, Welsh national day.

Saint Dunstan's, London and Brighton, homes for blinded servicemen, founded 1915 by Sir Arthur Pearson (*q.v.*).

Saint Dunstan's College, London, English public school in existence from early 15th century; refounded 1888.

Saint Chapelle, Paris, constructed 1245–1248.

Saint Edmund Hall, Oxford University, founded 13th century; incorporated as full university college 1958.

Saint Edmund's School, Canterbury, founded 1749; transferred to Canterbury 1855.

Saint Edward's School, Oxford, English public school, founded by the Rev. Thomas Chamberlain 1863.

Saint-Évremond, Charles (1613–1703), French essayist, lived at English court.

Saint-Exupéry, Antoine de (1900–44), French writer and aviator, author of *Night Flight* (1931).

Sainte-Beuve, Charles (1804–69), French critic, had a lasting influence on literary taste through his essays, *Causeries du Lundi.*

Saint Gaudens, Augustus (1848–1907), Irish-born American sculptor, carved Farragut Monument in Madison Square, New York.

Saint George's Day, 23 April, English national day; traditionally Shakespeare's birthday.

Saint Germain, Treaty of, made between World War I Allies and Austria 1919.

Saint Gotthard Pass, carriage road constructed 1820–30; replaced by a motorway.

Saint Gotthard Tunnel, constructed 1872–80 by Louis Favre; railway through tunnel opened 1882; new road tunnel under construction in the 1970s.

Saint Helena, South Atlantic island, discovered by Portuguese João de Nova 1502; granted to British East India Company 1661; Napoleon's place of exile 1815–21; British crown colony since 1834.

Saint Hilda's College, Oxford University, founded for women students 1893.

St James's Gazette, British newspaper, founded 1880; absorbed into *Evening Standard* 1905.

Saint James's Palace, London, built by Henry VIII 1532–36; gatehouse is main Tudor survival in present building.

Saint John, Henry. See **Bolingbroke,** Lord.

Saint John, Oliver (c. 1598–1673), English lawyer, prominent supporter of Parliamentarians against Charles I.

Saint John of Jerusalem, Order of the Knights of, founded c. 1070; recognized by papacy 1113; moved to Cyprus 1291 and to Rhodes 1309; settled in Malta 1530–1798; permanently established in Rome since 1834.

Saint John's College, Cambridge University, founded by Lady Margaret Beaufort (q.v.) 1511.

Saint John's College, Oxford University, founded 1555 by a London alderman, Sir Thomas White (1495–1567).

Saint John's School, Leatherhead, English public school, founded 1851.

Saint Just, Louis de (1767–94), French Revolutionary leader, follower of Robespierre; guillotined with him.

Saint Katherine Docks, Port of London, built 1826–29 by Thomas Telford (q.v.).

Saint Kitts-Nevis, West Indian islands (St Kitts, Nevis, Sombrero) discovered by Columbus 1493; ceded to Britain 1713; with Anguilla became a fully independent state (St Kitts-Nevis-Anguilla) in association with Britain 1967; Anguilla (q.v.) reverted to British control 1971.

Saint Laurent, Louis (1882–1973), Canadian statesman, prime minister 1948–1957.

Saint Lawrence College, Ramsgate, English public school, founded 1879; incorporated 1892.

Saint Lawrence River, North America, explored 1535–36 by the French navigator Jacques Cartier (q.v.).

Saint Lawrence Seaway, Canadian–American navigational project, officially launched 1954; opened to deep-draught merchant shipping April 1959.

Saint Leger, Doncaster, one of the classic horseraces, first run 1776.

Saint Lucia, West Indian island, probably discovered by Columbus 1502; finally ceded to Britain 1814; independent in association with Britain 1967.

Saint Mark's, Venice, built 1042–85; gilded domes in 13th century; further additions in 15th century.

Saint Martin-in-the-Fields, London church, built 1722–26 by the Scottish architect James Gibbs (q.v.).

Saint Mary Redcliffe, Bristol church, built 1325–1475.

Saint Olave's and Saint Saviour's Grammar School, London, founded by bequest of the merchant Henry Leeke, 1561.

Saint Patrick's Cathedral, New York, built 1858–79.

Saint Patrick's Day, 17 March, Irish national day.

Saint Paul's Cathedral, London, medieval Old Saint Paul's destroyed in Great Fire 1666; present building, by Sir Christopher Wren (q.v.), constructed 1675–1710.

Saint Paul's School, London, English public school founded by John Colet (q.v.), dean of St Paul's, 1509.

Saint Peter's, Rome, Old St Peter's, built by Constantine the Great; demolished 1506 for present building, constructed over following 100 years.

Saint Peter's College, Radley. See **Radley College.**

Saint Peter's Hall, Oxford University, private hall for students, founded 1929; made a university college 1961.

Saint Peter's School, York, English public school, founded 627.

Saint-Pierre, Charles, Abbé de (1658–1743), French writer, author of *Project for Perpetual Peace* (1713).

Saint Pierre and Miquelon, North Atlantic, islands settled by French in early 17th century; several times occupied by British in 18th century; restored to France 1816; made an overseas territory of France 1946.

Saint-Saëns, Camille (1835–1921), French composer, whose most popular work was the opera *Samson and Delilah* (1877).

Saints, Battle of the, West Indies, English naval victory over the French, 12 April 1782.

Saintsbury, George (1845–1933), English literary historian, enjoyed considerable influence as a critic of both English and French literature.

Saint-Simon, Claude, Comte de (1760–1825), French reformer, advocated a form of socialist industrial organization.

Saint-Simon, Louis, Duc de (1675–1755), French noble, wrote classic account of court life in *Memoirs.*

Saint Swithin's Day, 15th July.

Saint Valentine's Day (Old Candlemas), 14 Feb.

Saint Vincent, Earl. See **Jervis,** John.

Saint Vincent, West Indian island, discovered by Columbus 1498; ceded to Britain by France 1783; self-governing in association with Britain since 1969.

Saki (pseud. of Hector Hugh Munro; 1870–1916), English writer of humorous short stories, including *Beasts and Superbeasts* (1914); killed in action.

Saklatvala, Shapurji (1874–1936), Indian politician, first Communist M.P. in Britain 1922–29.

Saladin (1138–93), sultan of Egypt and

Syria, led Muslim armies against the crusaders.

Salazar, Antonio de Oliveira (1889–1970), Portuguese statesman, prime minister and effectively dictator of Portugal 1932–70.

Sale, George (c. 1697–1736), English scholar, translated *Koran* 1734.

salicylic acid, first prepared 1838 by the Italian chemist Rafaelle Piria (1815–65).

Salinas, Pedro (1892–1951), Spanish poet and critic, wrote mainly love-lyrics.

Salinger, Jerome David (b. 1919), American novelist, author of *Catcher in the Rye* (1951).

Salisbury, John de Montacute, Earl of (c. 1350–1400), English soldier-diplomat and Lollard, served Richard II; murdered by anti-Lollard mob.

Salisbury, Robert, 3rd Marquess (1830–1903), English statesman, prime minister 1885–92 and 1895–1902.

Salisbury Cathedral, England, construction began 1220; consecrated 1258.

saliva, digestive action discovered by the Italian scientist Lazaro Spallanzani (1729–1799).

Salk, vaccine. See **poliomyelitis.**

Sallust (86–c. 34 B.C.), Roman historian, wrote *Catiline* and *War against Jugurtha*.

Salmasius, Claudius (1588–1653), French scholar, engaged in political controversy with Milton.

Salomon, Erich (1886–1944), German photographer, famous for revealing shots of public personalities; died in a concentration camp.

Salten, Felix (1869–1945), Austrian writer, noted for his animal stories, including *Bambi* (1929).

Salter, Arthur, Baron (1881–1975), English economist, worked for the League of Nations.

Salters' Company, London livery company, originated under Edward III; incorporated 1559.

Salt Lake City, Utah, U.S.A., founded by Mormons 1847.

Saltykov, Mikhail (1826–89), Russian writer of novel *Golovlyov Family* (1876–1880) and of political satire.

Salvador, El. See **El Salvador.**

salvarsan, first effective drug for treating syphilis, discovered 1909 by Paul Ehrlich (q.v.).

Salvation Army, evangelical Christian movement, founded in London 1865 by William Booth (q.v.).

Salzburg Festival, major European music festival in honour of Mozart, founded 1877.

samarium, metallic element discovered 1879 by the French scientist Paul-Émile de Boisbaudran (1838–1912).

Samoa, Pacific, first visited by Dutch 1722; in 19th century conflicting U.S.,

British and German interests in the islands; under joint administration of all three countries 1889–99; divided between U.S.A. and Germany 1899. See **American Samoa; Western Samoa.**

Samuel, Herbert, Viscount (1870–1963), English statesman, notable for his social legislation, was leader of the Liberal Party 1931–35.

Sancho I (d. 1211), king of Portugal 1185–1211, notable as a builder of cities.

Sancho II (1208–48), king of Portugal 1223–48, fought his brother Alfonso III.

Sancho III (970–1035), king of Navarre 1000–35, conquered Castile and Léon.

sanctuary, right of, in churches, abolished in England 1623.

Sand, George (pseud. of Armandine Dupin; 1804–76), French woman novelist, author of *Lélia* (1833); mistress of Musset and Chopin.

Sandburg, Carl (1878–1967), American poet and biographer of Lincoln.

Sandby, Paul (1725–1809), English landscape artist, eminent as a painter and aquatint engraver.

Sandhurst. See **Royal Military Academy.**

Sandow, Eugene (1867–1925), famous German strong man and wrestler.

Sandringham House, Norfolk, British royal residence, purchased by Edward VII (then Prince of Wales) 1862; house rebuilt 1871.

Sand River Convention, recognizing the independent South African Republic (Transvaal), signed by Britain 1852.

Sandwich, Edward Montagu, Earl of (1625–72), English admiral in Dutch Wars, killed in battle.

Sandwich Islands, older name for Hawaii (q.v.).

Sandys, Sir Edwin (1561–1629), English organizer of the colonization of Virginia.

Sandys, George (1578–1644), English poet and translator, spent ten years in Virginia, which he helped found with his brother Sir Edwin Sandys.

San Francisco Conference, held 25 April–26 June 1945 to establish United Nations organization.

San Francisco earthquake, took place 18–19 April 1906.

Sangallo, Antonio da (1485–1546), Italian architect, designed the Farnese Palace, Rome.

Sanger, 'Lord' George (1825–1911), English circus manager, put on shows at Astley's Amphitheatre, London.

Sanger, John (1816–89), English circus manager, brother and partner of 'Lord' George Sanger.

Sankey, Ira David (1840–1908), American evangelist and hymn-writer, toured as a revivalist with Dwight Moody (q.v.).

San Marino, world's smallest republic, enclave in northern Italy, founded 9th–10th century; independence recognized by papacy 1631; customs union with Italy 1862.

San Martín, José de (1778–1850), South American soldier and statesman, liberator of Chile and Peru from Spanish rule.

Sannazaro, Jacopo (1458–1530), Italian poet, author of the pastoral romance *Arcadia* (1504).

San Nicandro, Italy, place where Judaic sect developed in 1930s led by Donato Manduzio (1885–1948); sect emigrated to Israel 1949.

San Quentin, California, state prison opened 1852.

Sansovino, Jacopo (1486–1570), Italian architect, designed Renaissance churches and palaces in Venice.

Santa Anna, Antonio de (c. 1796–1876), Mexican soldier and statesman, several times president; twice defeated in war by U.S.A.

Santa Claus. See **Nicholas,** Saint.

Santa Cruz Islands, Pacific, discovered 1595 by Spanish navigator Alvaro Mendaña (1541–95); administratively attached to Solomon Islands (*q.v.*).

Santa Fe Trail, U.S.A., wagon route from Missouri to New Mexico, much used 1822–80.

Santa Sophia, Istanbul, famous Byzantine church built for Justinian 532–537; converted into a mosque 1453.

Santayana, George (1863–1952), Spanish-born philosopher, spent youth in U.S.A.; wrote *Life of Reason* (1905–06).

Santillana, Iñigo, Marquis of (1398–1458), Spanish poet, introduced sonnet form to Spain.

Santos-Dumont, Alberto (1873–1932), Brazilian-born aviator in France, built and flew airships.

São Paulo, Brazilian city, founded by the Portuguese 1554.

São Tomé e Príncipe, islands off west coast of Africa, discovered in 1470s; settled in 16th century; formed a Portuguese overseas territory until they achieved independence as a republic 1975.

Sappho (7th–6th cent. B.C.), Greek woman poet, known only through fragmentary lyrics.

Sarajevo, capital of Bosnia and Herzogovina, Yugoslavia; under Austrian rule 1878–1918; scene of Archduke Franz Ferdinand's assassination 28 June 1914.

Sarasate, Pablo (1844–1908), Spanish violinist, also a composer in nationalist idiom.

Saratoga, Battle of, victory of American colonists over the British 17 Oct. 1777.

Sarawak, governed by Brooke family 1841–1946; under British protection 1888–1946; crown colony 1946–63; incorporated in Malaysia 1963.

Sardinia, annexed by Carthage 6th century B.C.; came under Roman rule 238 B.C.; conquered by Byzantium c. A.D. 533; ruled by Spanish 1297–1713; ruled by Savoy-Piedmont 1720–1860; incorporated in Italy 1861.

Sardou, Victorien (1831–1908), French playwright, notable for his stagecraft, author of *Madame Sans Gêne* (1893).

Sargent, John Singer (1856–1925), American painter in England, was an admired portraitist.

Sargent, Sir Malcolm (1895–1967), English conductor, best remembered for his work at the Promenade Concerts.

Sargon I (3rd millennium B.C.), king of Babylonia, created a substantial empire.

Sargon II (d. 705 B.C.), king of Assyria 722–705; his conquests included Babylonia and Israel.

Saroyan, William (b. 1908), American writer of sentimental-surrealistic fantasy, e.g. *Daring Young Man on the Flying Trapeze* (1934).

Sarsfield, Patrick (d. 1693), Irish soldier, with James II in Ireland 1689–90; joined French army.

Sarto, Andrea del (1486–1531), Italian painter, one of the leading 16th-century Florentines.

Sartre, Jean Paul (b. 1905), French existentialist philosopher, playwright and novelist (*Roads to Freedom*, 1946–49); refused Nobel Prize 1964.

Saskatchewan, Canadian province, created 1905.

Sassanids, Persian dynasty, ruled A.D. 226–651; overthrown by Muslim Arabs.

Sassoon, Siegfried (1886–1967), English writer, best known for *Memoirs of a Fox-Hunting Man* (1928).

satellite, first one, Sputnik I, launched Oct. 1957 by the Soviet Union.

satellite, communications, first passive one, Echo 1, launched Aug. 1960 by U.S.A.; first active one, Telstar 1, launched July 1962 by U.S.A.; first commercially used one, Early Bird, launched April 1965 by U.S.A.

satellite, weather, first one, Tiros 1, launched April 1960 by U.S.A.

Satie, Erik (1866–1925), French composer, in individual modernist idiom, e.g. ballet *Parade* (1917).

Saturday closing, in Britain, started in Liverpool c. 1843; Manchester 1844.

Saturn, first observed telescopically 1610 by Galileo; largest satellite, Titan, discovered 1655 by Christiaan Huygens (*q.v.*); flyby by Pioneer II (*q.v.*) due 1979.

Saturninus, Lucius Appuleius (d. 100 B.C.), Roman tribune, follower of Marius (*q.v.*); murdered.

Saturn's rings, observed as a single ring 1655–59 by Christiaan Huygens; two rings divided by a dark gap discovered 1675 by Giovanni Cassini (*q.v.*).

Saturn rocket, developed from 1958 by a NASA team led by Wernher von Braun (*q.v.*) as the launch vehicle for the American Apollo spacecraft, first fired 1961; Saturn V first launched 1967.

Saud, Ibn. See **Ibn Saud.**

Saudi Arabia, kingdom created by Ibn Saud (*q.v.*) through conquest of Hejaz 1926; kingdom formally proclaimed 1932.

Saul (11th–10th cent. B.C.), first king of Israel, killed in battle with Philistines.

Saumarez, James (1757–1836), English admiral, distinguished in battle at Cape St Vincent and under Nelson.

Saunders, Sir Edwin (1814–1901), English pioneer in training for dentistry.

Saussure, Horace Benedict de (1740–99), Swiss physicist, was a wide-ranging investigator; member of a distinguished scientific family.

Savage, Edward (1761–1817), American painter, notably of George and Martha Washington.

Savage, Richard (*c.* 1697–1743), English poet, subject of a famous *Life* by Dr Johnson.

Savannah, first steam-propelled ship to cross the Atlantic, 1819.

Savary, Anne Jean Marie René (1774–1833), French soldier and administrator under Napoleon.

Savery, Thomas (*c.* 1650–1715), English engineer, invented first practical steam engine, for pumping water.

Savigny, Friedrich Karl von (1779–1861), German writer, pioneered history of jurisprudence.

Savile, Sir Henry (1549–1622), English classical scholar, one of the translators of the Authorized Version of the Bible.

savings banks, in Britain, first established by Priscilla Wakefield at Tottenham 1804 and Henry Duncan at Ruthwell, Scotland, 1810; National Savings Bank established 1861.

Savonarola, Girolamo (1452–98), Italian Dominican monk and puritanical reformer, virtually ruled Florence 1494–97; burnt as heretic.

Savoy, became a duchy in 14th century; ruled Sardinia from 1720; joined France after plebiscite 1860.

Saxe, Maurice, Comte de (1696–1750), French soldier, won several victories in the War of Austrian Succession; created a marshal of France.

saxhorn, invented *c.* 1844 by the Belgian instrument-maker Adolphe Saxe (1814–1894).

Saxo-Grammaticus (*c.* 1150–*c.* 1205), Danish chronicler, wrote *Gesta Danorum.*

saxophone, invented *c.* 1844 by Adolphe Saxe.

Saxton, Christopher (16th cent.), English draughtsman, mapped every English and Welsh county.

Say, Jean Baptiste (1767–1832), French economist, advocate of free trade.

Say, Léon (1826–96), French economist, three times minister of finance; fierce opponent of socialism.

Saye and Sele, William Fiennes, Viscount (1582–1662), English politician, prominent in parliamentary opposition to Charles I.

Sayers, Dorothy Leigh (1893–1957), English writer of detective stories, creator of Lord Peter Wimsey.

Sayers, Tom (1826–65), English pugilist, active 1849–60, was middleweight boxing champion.

Scaevola, Quintus Mucius (d. 82 B.C.), Roman politician of conservative views; murdered by partisans of Marius.

Scaliger, Joseph (1540–1609), Italian pioneer of precise classical scholarship, son of Julius Caesar Scaliger.

Scaliger, Julius Caesar (1484–1558), Italian humanist scholar, influenced literary standards.

scandium, metallic element, predicted 1871 by Dmitri Mendeleyev (*q.v.*); discovered 1879 by the Swedish chemist Lars Fredrik Nilson (1840–99).

Scapa Flow, Scotland, scene of scuttling of German battle fleet, 21 June 1919.

Scarlatti, Alessandro (1660–1725), Italian opera composer, e.g. *Griselda* (1721).

Scarlatti, Domenico (1685–1757), Italian keyboard virtuoso and composer of harpsichord music; son of Alessandro Scarlatti.

Scarron, Paul (1610–60), French writer, noted for his burlesque poems, comedies and a novel *Le Romant comique* (1651–57).

Scève, Maurice (*c.* 1500–*c.* 1564), French poet, author of *Délie.*

Schacht, Hjalmar (1877–1970), German financier, effectively in charge of German economy 1934–37.

Schadow, Johann Gottfried (1764–1850), German Neo-Classical sculptor, e.g. *Frederick the Great.*

Scharnhorst, Gerhard von (1755–1813), Prussian soldier, helped reorganize the Prussian army after its defeat by Napoleon.

Scharnhorst, German battleship, sunk by British navy off North Cape, 26 Dec. 1943.

Scharwenka, Xaver (1850–1924), German composer, piano virtuoso, and director of music schools in Berlin and New York.

Schaudinn, Fritz Richard (1871–1906), German zoologist, discovered the organism which causes syphilis.

Scheele, Carl Wilhelm (1742–86), Swedish chemist, made numerous discoveries, including oxygen, independently of Joseph Priestley (*q.v.*).

Scheer, Reinhard (1863–1928), German admiral, commanded fleet at Battle of Jutland 1916.

Scheffer, Ary (1795–1858), Dutch-born painter in France, was mainly a portraitist.

Schelling, Friedrich von (1775–1854), German philosopher, made artistic experience central to his thought.

Scherer, Wilhelm (1841–86), Austrian-born German historian of language and literature.

Schiaparelli, Giovanni (1835–1910), Italian astronomer, discovered asteroid Hesperia and observed 'canal' markings on Mars.

Schick test, for immunity to diphtheria, introduced 1913 by the Hungarian-born scientist Bela Schick (1877–1967).

Schiller, Friedrich von (1759–1805), major German playwright and poet, author of *The Robbers* (1782); closely associated with Goethe.

Schinkel, Karl Friedrich (1781–1841), German architect, adopted classical style to the design of modern buildings.

Schirmer, Gustave (1829–93), German-born American music publisher, founded well-known firm.

Schism, Great, period of rival popes 1378–1417; also applied to schism between Papacy and Eastern Orthodox Church, begun 9th century, complete 1054.

Schism of Photius, 9th-century schism in which patriarch Photius (*q.v.*) was involved; began Great Schism.

Schlegel, August von (1767–1845), German Romantic critic, made important translation of Shakespeare.

Schlegel, Friedrich von (1772–1829), German poet and critic, who influenced the Romantic movement in Germany; brother of August Schlegel.

Schleiermacher, Friedrich (1768–1834), German theologian and philosopher, helped union of Lutheran and Reform Churches.

Schleswig-Holstein, under Danish crown 1460–1864; jointly administered by Austria and Prussia 1864–66; annexed to Prussia 1866; North Schleswig passed to Denmark 1920; remainder a West German state since 1946.

Schlick, Moritz (1882–1936), German philosopher, leading exponent of logical positivism.

Schlieffen, Alfred, Graf von (1833–1913), German soldier, chief of staff 1891–1905, drew up Schlieffen Plan for possible invasion of France.

Schliemann, Heinrich (1822–90), German archaeological pioneer, discovered site of Troy and Mycenae.

Schmidt telescope, devised 1930 by the Estonian optical instrument-maker Bernhard Voldemar Schmidt (1879–1955).

Schnabel, Artur (1882–1951), Austrian-born pianist, major interpreter of German and Austrian Romantics.

Schnitger, Arp (1648–1718), German organ-builder, first of a distinguished family.

Schnitzer, Eduard. See **Emin Pasha.**

Schnitzler, Arthur (1862–1931), Austrian writer, best known for his short stories and plays about Viennese society.

Scholes, Percy (1877–1958), English musicologist, edited *Oxford Companion to Music.*

Schomberg, Frederick, Duke of (1615–1690), German-born commander of William III's forces in Ireland; killed at Battle of the Boyne.

Schomburgk, Robert (1804–65), and Richard (1811–90), German-born British botanists, explored British Guiana.

Schönberg, Arnold (1874–1951), Austrian composer, pioneered 12-note system; wrote opera *Moses and Aaron.*

Schongauer, Martin (*c.* 1445–1491), German engraver and painter, whose work includes the *Madonna of the Rose Garden.*

Schopenhauer, Arthur (1788–1860), German philosopher of deeply pessimistic views, wrote *The World as Will and Idea* (1818).

Schreiner, Olive (1855–1922), South African writer of *Story of an African Farm* (1883).

Schrödinger, Erwin (1887–1961), Austrian physicist, worked on wave mechanics; Nobel prizewinner 1933.

Schrödinger Wave Equation, quantum mechanics, derived and published 1926 by Erwin Schrödinger.

Schubert, Franz (1797–1828), major Austrian composer and leading Romanticist, best known for his symphonies, song cycles and string quartets.

Schumacher, Kurt Ernst (1895–1952), German Social Democrat politician, imprisoned for his opposition to the Nazis.

Schuman, Robert (1886–1963), French statesman, laid the foundations for the European Economic Community.

Schumann, Clara (1819–96), German pianist, wife of Robert Schumann.

Schumann, Elizabeth (1891–1952), German-born opera singer, worked in U.S.A. from 1938; interpreter of Richard Strauss.

Schumann, Robert (1810–56), major German Romantic composer, notably of piano works, songs and orchestral music.

Schuschnigg, Kurt von (b. 1897), Austrian statesman, chancellor of Austria 1934–38; imprisoned by the Nazis.

Schütz, Heinrich (1585–1672), German composer, best known for his church music.

Schuyler, Philip John (1733–1804), American Revolutionary soldier, led attack on Canada.

Schwann, Theodor (1810–82), German physiologist, discovered pepsin.

Schwarzenburg, Felix (1800–52), Austrian statesman, chief minister 1848–52, restored imperial authority after 1848 revolution.

Schweitzer, Albert (1875–1965), French medical missionary, theologian and musician, winner of 1952 Nobel Peace Prize.

Science Museum, London, formerly part of South Kensington Museum, founded 1857; made a separate institution 1909.

Science Research Council, established 1965 by royal charter.

Scientific and Industrial Research, Department of, London, established 1916; closed 1964.

scientist, term introduced 1840 by William Whewell, master of Trinity College, Cambridge University.

Scientology, movement originated early 1950s in U.S.A. by Ron Hubbard.

Scinde Dawk, first Indian postage stamp, issued 1 July 1852.

Scipio Africanus, Publius Cornelius (237–183 B.C.), Roman soldier, invaded Carthage, defeated Hannibal at Zama 202 B.C.

Scipio Aemilianus Africanus, Publius Cornelius (185–129 B.C.), Roman soldier, responsible for final destruction of Carthage; also victorious in Spain.

Scopas (4th cent. B.C.), Greek sculptor, whose work shows development of post-Classical emotionalism.

Scopes Trial, Dayton, Tennessee 1925; John Thomas Scopes (1900–70) tried for teaching theory of evolution in school.

Scoresby, William (1789–1857), English Arctic explorer, surveyed Greenland coast.

Scot, Michael (c. 1175–c. 1234), Scottish scholar, translator from Arabic at the emperor Frederick II's court; in legend a great magician.

Scotland, Picts and Scots under one king c. 843; whole kingdom unified by 1034; Scottish crown united with England's 1603; kingdoms united 1707.

Scott, Charles Prestwich (1846–1932), English journalist, editor of *Manchester Guardian* 1872–1929.

Scott, Cyril (1879–1970), English composer of piano music and symphonies.

Scott, Sir George Gilbert (1811–88), English architect, was a leading figure in the Gothic revival.

Scott, Robert Falcon (1868–1912), English Antarctic explorer, beaten to South Pole by Amundsen; died on return journey.

Scott, Sir Walter (1771–1832), Scottish novelist, wrote *Waverley* (1814) and other historical novels.

Scottish Labour Party, founded 1888 by Keir Hardie (q.v.).

Scotus, Duns. See **Duns Scotus.**

screw propeller, invented 1836 by the Englishman Sir Francis Pettit Smith (1808–74) and, independently, by the Swedish engineer John Ericsson (1803–1889).

screw threads, standardized 1841 by Sir Joseph Whitworth (q.v.).

Scriabin, Alexander (1872–1915), Russian composer, mainly for piano; also wrote mystically inspired works, e.g. *The Divine Poem* (1905).

Scribe, Eugène (1791–1861), French playwright, enjoyed great popularity on the Parisian stage.

Scribner, Charles (1821–71), American publisher, founder of well-known firm, 1846.

Scripps, Edward Wyllis (1854–1926), American publisher, built up newspaper empire.

Scroggs, Sir William (c. 1623–1683), English lawyer, lord chief justice 1678–81; presided at Popish Plot trials.

Scrope, Richard le (c. 1350–1405), English prelate, archbishop of York 1398–1405; joined northern rebellion; executed.

Scudéry, Madeleine de (1608–1701), French writer of long romances, e.g. *Clélie* (1654–60).

scurvy, prevention by means of lime juice suggested in 1750s by the Scottish physician James Lind (1716–94) but not effected until 1795.

scuttling, notably German Grand Fleet 21 June 1919; *Graf Spee* 17 Dec. 1939; French fleet at Toulon 27 Nov. 1942.

Sea Devil. See **Luckner,** Felix von.

seaplane, first flown by Fabre in France 1910; first practical seaplane designed 1911 by Glenn Curtiss (q.v.).

searchlights, first operational lights, using carbon arcs, developed in 1870s.

Sears Tower, Chicago, over 250 m (820 ft) high, completed 1974.

Sea Scouts, movement started in Britain 1908; adopted present name 1912.

S.E.A.T.O. See **South East Asia Treaty Organization.**

Seaton, Edward Cator (1815–80), English physician, secured adoption of compulsory vaccination.

Sebastian (1554–78), king of Portugal 1557–78, killed fighting in Morocco.

Sebastiano del Piombo (c. 1485–1547), Italian painter in Mannerist style.

second, originally defined in terms of mean solar day; redefined 1956 in terms of tropical year 1900; formally defined 1967 in terms of atomic time (using caesium-133 atom).

secondary education, first national scheme for Britain 1902; free since 1944.

secularism, as term for non-religious ethics, coined *c.* 1850 by George Jacob Holyoake (*q.v.*).

Sedan, Battle of, Prussian victory over French 1 Sept. 1870; German army's breakthrough at, May 1940.

Sedbergh School, Cumbria, English public school founded 1525 by the provost of Eton, Dr Roger Lupton (d. 1540).

Sedgemoor, Battle of, victory of forces of King James II over the rebels under the Duke of Monmouth, 6 July 1685.

Sedgwick, Adam (1785–1873), English geologist in the West Country, introduced terms 'Devonian' and 'Cambrian'.

Sedgwick, Robert (d. 1656), English colonist in America, captured Acadia from French 1654.

Sedley, Sir Charles (*c.* 1639–1701), English Restoration playwright, author of *Bellamira* (1687).

Seebeck effect, in an electric circuit, discovered 1821 by the Russian-born German physicist Thomas Johann Seebeck (1770–1831).

seed drill, invented 1701 by Jethro Tull (*q.v.*).

Seeley, Sir John (1834–95), English writer, encouraged imperialist sentiment in *The Expansion of England* (1883).

Seferiades, George (1900–71), Greek poet, author of *The Turning Point* (1931).

Segovia, Andrés (b. 1893), Spanish guitar virtuoso; many concert works were specially written for him.

Segrè, Emilio (b. 1905), Italian-born American physicist, Nobel prizewinner 1959.

Seguier, William (1771–1843), English artist and first Keeper of the National Gallery, London.

Seiber, Mátyás (1905–60), Hungarian composer, in Britain 1935–60; was also an important teacher.

Seignobos, Charles (1854–1942), French historian, author of *Political History of Contemporary Europe* (1897).

seismograph, invented *c.* A.D. 132 by a Chinese scholar Chang Heng (A.D. 78–139); horizontal pendulum device developed 1880 by the English geologist John Milne (1850–1913).

seismic methods, for discovering petroleum, first used 1922 in Mexico, reflection methods introduced 1932 in Texas, both by the Royal Dutch Shell Group.

Sejanus, Lucius Aelius (d. A.D. 31), Roman commander of Praetorian Guard, plotted for supreme power; executed.

Selborne, Roundell, Earl of (1812–95), English lawyer, lord chancellor 1872–74 and 1880–85.

Selden, John (1584–1654), English lawyer; his conversation was posthumously published as *Table-Talk* (1689).

selenium, chemical element, discovered 1817 by Baron Berzelius (*q.v.*).

Seleucid dynasty, ruled Near East 312–64 B.C.

Seleucus I (*c.* 358–280 B.C.), Macedonian soldier, founded Seleucid dynasty, ruled Seleucid Empire 306–280 B.C.

Seleucus II (d. 227 B.C.), ruler of Seleucid Empire 246–227 B.C., lost Asia Minor and Parthia.

self-raising flour, first patented by Henry Jones of Bristol, 1845.

Selfridge's, London, Oxford Street department store, opened 15 March 1909; founded by the American-born merchant Gordon Selfridge (1857–1947).

self-starter, for vehicles, invented 1911 by the American Charles Franklin Kettering (1876–1958).

Selim I (1467–1520), sultan of Turkey 1512–20, greatly enlarged empire.

Selim II (1524–74), sultan of Turkey 1566–74, defeated at Lepanto, 1571.

Selim III (1761–1808), sultan of Turkey 1789–1807, attempted reforms but deposed.

Selkirk, Alexander (1676–1721), Scottish sailor, original of Robinson Crusoe, alone on small island 1704–09.

Selwyn, George (1809–78), English prelate, first bishop of New Zealand 1841–68.

Selwyn College, Cambridge University, founded in memory of George Selwyn, 1882.

semaphore signalling, pioneered 1666 by Lord Worcester; developed 1792 by the French engineer Claude Chappe (1763–1805) and his brother Ignace; further developed 1795 by the Rev. Lord George Murray (1761–1803); perfected 1803 by Admiral Sir Home Riggs Popham (1762–1820).

Semonov, Nikolai (b. 1896), Russian chemist, carried out important researches into chemical chain reactions.

semiconductors, rectifying properties discovered 1874 by the German physicist Karl Ferdinand Braun (1850–1918); used in crystal-set radios until replaced 1906 by the triode valve (*q.v.*); widely used in electronics industry since 1948 in transistors (*q.v.*) and other devices.

Semmelweiss, Ignaz (1818–65), Hungarian physician, pioneer of antisepsis.

Semmering Pass, the Alps, railway constructed 1848–54.

Sempill, Robert (*c.* 1595–*c.* 1665), Scottish poet, author of *Habbie Simson* (1640).

Senancourt, Etienne de (1770–1846), French Romantic writer, notably of *Obermann* (1804).

Seneca, Annaeus (*c.* 54 B.C.–A.D. 39), Roman lawyer born in Spain, wrote valuable description of cases and legal techniques.

Seneca, Lucius Annaeus (c. 4 B.C.–A.D. 65), Roman Stoic philosopher and writer of tragedies; tutor, and later victim, of Nero.

Senefelder, Alois (1771–1834), German inventor of lithography, 1798.

Senegal, West Africa, reached by Portuguese in 15th century; French factories established in 17th century; French governor appointed 1854; made a French overseas territory 1946; became an independent republic 1960.

Senior, Nassau (1790–1864), English economist, wrote *An Outline of the Science of Political Economy* (1836).

Senlac, hill near Hastings, Sussex, where Battle of Hastings (*q.v.*) took place.

Sennacherib (d. 681 B.C.), king of Assyria 705–681 B.C., conquered Babylon and Syria–Palestine.

sensory and motor nerves, distinguished 1807 by the Scottish anatomist Sir Charles Bell (1774–1842).

Septuagint, earliest Greek version of the Old Testament, said to have been made by 72 Jewish elders for Ptolemy II c. 270 B.C.; parts are in fact later.

Sequoyah (c. 1770–1843), American Indian, developed written Cherokee language.

Serapeum, temple of Apis (Serapis), Egypt; ruins discovered 1850 by the French Egyptologist Auguste Mariette (*q.v.*).

Serbia, Balkan kingdom 12th–14th centuries; ruled by Turks 1459–1829; under Austrian occupation 1915–18; part of Yugoslavia since 1918.

serfdom, died out in England in late Middle Ages; abolished in Prussia 1807, in Russia 1861.

Sergius I, Saint (d. 701), Pope 687–701, encouraged missionary efforts in northern Europe.

Sergius II (d. 847), Pope 844–847; Rome was sacked by Saracens during his pontificate.

Serra, Junípero (1713–84), Spanish missionary in California, established many missions, forming a nucleus of settlements.

Sertorius, Quintus (d. 72 B.C.), Roman administrator in Spain, supported Marius against Sulla.

Servetus, Michael (1511–53), Spanish theologian, burnt at stake at Geneva for anti-Trinitarian views.

Service, Robert William (1874–1958), English-born ballad writer in Canada, e.g. *Dan McGrew,* suggested by Klondyke experiences.

Servile Wars, caused by revolts of Roman slaves, in Sicily 135–132 B.C. and 103–101 B.C.; in Italy 73–71 B.C.

Sesostris I (d. 1935 B.C.), king of Egypt c. 1980–1935 B.C., conquered Nubia.

Sesostris II (d. 1887 B.C.), king of Egypt 1906–1887 B.C., built pyramid near Faiyum.

Sesostris III (d. 1849 B.C.), king of Egypt 1887–1849 B.C., greatly extended Egyptian power.

Sesshu (1421–1507), Japanese landscape painter and Zen Buddhist priest.

Sessions, Roger (b. 1896), American composer, wrote the opera *The Trial of Lucullus* (1947).

Seth, Andrew (1856–1931), Scottish philosopher, wrote *Man's Place in the Cosmos* (1897).

Seti I (d. 1292 B.C.), king of Egypt 1313–1292, waged wars in Libya and Syria; built Abydos sanctuary.

Seton, Ernest Thompson (1860–1946), English-born writer-artist, wrote about American wild life.

set theory, mathematics, first developed 1874–97 by Georg Cantor (*q.v.*).

Settle, Elkanah (1648–1724), English poet and playwright, author of *The Empress of Morocco* (1671).

Settlement, Act of, securing Hanoverian succession to the English throne, passed 1701.

Seurat, Georges (1859–91), French painter, developed theory and practice of pointillisme.

Seven Days' Battles, near Richmond, Virginia, in American Civil War 25 June to 1 July 1862.

Seven Sleepers of Ephesus, persecuted Christians who allegedly slept in a cave c. A.D. 250–447.

Seven Weeks' War, between Prussia and Austria (and her allies), 1866.

Seven Years' War, between Prussia and Britain and France, Austria and Russia 1756–63.

Sevenoaks School, Kent, English public school, founded 1418 by the lord mayor of London Sir William Sevenoke (c. 1378–c. 1433).

Sévérac, Déodat de (1873–1921), French composer, introduced Provençal themes into his works.

Severn, Joseph (1793–1879), English painter, notable for association with the poet Keats.

Severn Bridge, carrying M4 motorway, opened 1966.

Severn Tunnel, constructed 1873–86.

Severus, Lucius Septimus (A.D. 146–211), Roman emperor A.D. 193–211, restored civil order, defeated Parthians; died at York.

Sévigné, Marquise de (1626–96), French noblewoman, wrote famous letters to her daughter.

Seward, Anna (1747–1809), English poet, called 'the swan of Lichfield'.

Sewell, Anna (1820–78), English novelist, wrote *Black Beauty* (1877).

sewers, London. See **drainage system.**

sewing machine, early ones developed 1755 and 1790; machine produced in France 1841 by Barthélemy Thimonnier; practical device invented 1846 (patented 1854) by the American Elias Howe (1819–1867); Howe's needle used 1851 in the machine of the American Isaac Merrit Singer (1811–75).

sextant, developed 1757 from the quadrant (*q.v.*) of John Hadley following a suggestion of Captain John Campbell (*c.* 1720–1790).

Seychelles, Indian Ocean, probably discovered by Portuguese *c.* 1500; French possession 1744–84; ceded to Britain 1814 and administered from Mauritius; made a separate colony 1903; became an independent republic 1976.

Seymour, Edward. See **Somerset,** Duke of.

Seymour, Thomas (*c.* 1508–49), English noble, brother of Duke of Somerset and lord high admiral; intrigued with Princess Elizabeth; executed.

Seyss-Inquart, Artur von (1892–1946), Austrian Nazi official, executed for war crimes.

Sforza, Francesco (1401–66), duke of Milan 1447–66, former mercenary soldier; overthrew the republic.

Shackleton, Sir Ernest (1874–1922), English explorer, made three expeditions to Antarctica.

Shadwell, Thomas (*c.* 1642–92), English writer, enemy and rival of Dryden, poet laureate 1688–92.

Shafi'i, al- (767–820), Arab scholar, founder of one of the four schools of Islamic law.

Shaftesbury, Anthony Ashley Cooper, 1st Earl of (1621–83), English politician, noted for his opposition to Charles II's policies.

Shaftesbury, Anthony Ashley Cooper, 3rd Earl of (1671–1713), English politician and philosopher, exponent of Neo-Platonian.

Shaftesbury, Anthony Ashley Cooper, 7th Earl of (1801–85), English philanthropist and social reformer, responsible for first Factory Acts.

Shah Jahan (1592–1666), Mogul emperor of India 1627–58, founded Delhi and built Taj Mahal.

Shakers, Society of, religious movement, seceded from Quakers 1747 under James and Jane Wardley; first settlement in America 1776 founded by Ann Lee (*q.v.*).

Shakespeare, William (1564–1616), English playwright and poet, whose works have earned him recognition as the greatest dramatic genius of all time.

Shakespeare Memorial Theatre. See **Royal Shakespeare Theatre.**

Shang dynasty, semi-legendary dynasty, ruled China, 1766–1122 B.C.

Shannon, Charles (1863–1937), English lithographer and painter, with Charles Ricketts produced *The Dial* (1889–97).

Shapley, Harlow (1885–1972), American astronomer, noted for his researches into the Milky Way.

Shapur I (3rd cent. A.D.), Sassanid king of Persia 241–272, defeated and captured Roman emperor Valerian.

Shapur II (3rd cent. A.D.), Sassanid king of Persia 310–379, tried to enforce the Zoroastrian religion.

Sharp, Cecil (1859–1924), English folksong collector, revived general interest in subject.

Sharp, Granville (1735–1813), English philanthropist, established that a slave became free once in England.

Sharp, William (*c.* 1855–1905), Scottish novelist writing as 'Fiona Macleod', author of *The Immortal Hour* (1900).

Shashtri, Lal Bahadur (1904–66), Indian statesman, prime minister of India 1964–1966.

Shaw, George Bernard (1856–1950), Irish playwright of comic genius, preface-writer, Fabian propagandist, and music and drama critic.

Shaw, Martin (1875–1958), English composer in nationalist idiom, wrote *Mr Pepys* (1926).

Shaw, Norman (1831–1912), Scottish architect, known for his design of private houses, often in Queen Anne style.

Shays, Daniel (*c.* 1747–1825), American soldier, led rebellion in Massachusetts against U.S. government 1786–87.

Shchedrin, Nikolai. See **Saltykov,** Mikhail.

Shee, Sir Martin Archer (1769–1850), Irish painter, best known as a portraitist.

Shee, Sir William (1804–68), English lawyer, first Roman Catholic judge since 1689 Revolution.

Sheffield University, South Yorkshire, formed by amalgamation of three colleges; university college 1897; acquired university status 1905.

Sheldonian Theatre, Oxford, built 1669 by Christopher Wren for Gilbert Sheldon, archbishop of Canterbury (1598–1677).

Shelley, Mary Wollstonecraft (1797–1851), English writer of *Frankenstein* (1818), wife of Percy Bysshe Shelley.

Shelley, Percy Bysshe (1792–1822), English Romantic poet of radical views, author of *Adonais*, etc.; drowned.

Shenstone, William (1714–63), English poet, wrote *The Schoolmistress* (1742).

Sheppard, Jack (1702–24), English highwayman, famous for prison escapes; hanged.

Sheraton, Thomas (1751–1806), English

cabinet maker, wrote influential *Cabinet-Maker and Upholsterer's Drawing Book* (1791).

Sherborne School, English public school, probably originated in 8th century; refounded by Edward VI 1550.

Sheridan, Richard Brinsley (1751–1816), Irish playwright, wrote classic comedy *The School for Scandal* (1777); was also a notable politician.

Sherman, William Tecumseh (1820–91), American Unionist general in Civil War; made famous march through Georgia to sea 1864.

Sherriff, Robert Cedric (1896–1975), English playwright, wrote *Journey's End* (1928) about life in the trenches in World War I.

Sherrington, Sir Charles (1857–1952), English physiologist, studied the neuron; Nobel prizewinner 1932.

Sherwood, Robert (1896–1955), American playwright, wrote *The Petrified Forest* (1935).

Shi'a, Islamic sect, founded *c.* 658, dominant in Persia, opposed to Sunni majority.

Shih Huang Ti (259–210 B.C.), first Chinese emperor 221–210 B.C., built the Great Wall of China.

Shiloh, Tennessee, American Civil War, victory of Unionist forces under Grant over the Confederates, 6–7 April 1862.

ship, first gas-turbine propelled (H.M.S. *Grey Goose*) fitted out 1955.

ship, first nuclear-powered (*Lenin*), commissioned 1959 as an icebreaker.

ship, first ocean-going iron (*The Great Britain*) built 1843 by Isambard Kingdom Brunel (*q.v.*).

ship, first steam-propelled (*Savannah*), crossed the Atlantic 1819.

ship, first turbine-propelled (*Turbinia*) demonstrated 1897 by Sir Charles Parsons.

ship money, first levied in England 1007; revived, without parliamentary consent, by Charles I 1634–36.

Shipton, Mother (16th cent.), alleged English witch and prophetess, probably never existed.

Shirley, Sir Anthony (1565–*c.* 1635), English adventurer, self-appointed ambassador to Persia, later in Russia, Morocco, etc.

Shirley, James (1596–1666), English playwright, author of *The Maid's Revenge* (1626).

Shivaji (1627–80), Mahratta leader, founder of Mahratta power in India.

Shockley, William (b. 1910), American physicist, noted for his work in developing the transistor.

Sholem Aleichem. See **Aleichem, Sholem.**

Sholes, Christopher (1819–90), American inventor, developed the first successful typewriter.

Sholokhov, Mikhail (b. 1905), Russian novelist, author of *And Quiet Flows the Don* (1934).

Shore, Jane (d. *c.* 1527), English goldsmith's wife, mistress of Edward IV, 1470–83.

shorthand, first with signs invented 1588 by the Englishman Timothy Bright (1551–1615); modern systems developed 1837 by the Englishman Sir Isaac Pitman (1813–1897) and 1888 by the Irish-born John Robert Gregg (1867–1948).

Shorthouse, Joseph Henry (1834–1903), English novelist, wrote *John Inglesant* (1880).

Shostakovich, Dmitri (1906–75), major Soviet composer of operas and symphonies of epic scale and quality.

Shovell, Sir Cloudesley (1650–1707), English admiral, after a distinguished career drowned when his flagship sank.

Shrewsbury, Treaty of, recognizing Llewelyn II's overlordship of Wales, 1265.

Shrewsbury School, English public school, founded by Edward VI 1552; augmented by Queen Elizabeth 1571.

Shrove Tuesday, day before Lent; day of preparation for Ash Wednesday.

Shute, Nevil (1899–1960), English novelist, author of *A Town Like Alice* (1949); was also an aeroplane engineer.

Siam. See **Thailand.**

Sibelius, Jean (1865–1957), Finnish composer, inspired by native land, lakes and folk-legends, best known for his symphonic work.

Siberia, conquered by Cossacks from Tatars 1581; maritime region ceded by China to Russia 1860; opened up by Trans-Siberian Railway built 1891–1905; incorporated in U.S.S.R. 1922.

Sicilian Vespers, massacre of French in Sicily, 31 March 1282.

Sicily, colonized by Greeks 8th century B.C.; conquered by Rome 3rd century B.C.; taken by Byzantines A.D. 535; conquered by Arabs 9th century and Normans in 11th century; ruled by Spanish dynasties 1302–1713 and by Bourbons 1735–1860; joined kingdom of Italy 1860.

Sickert, Walter (1860–1942), German-born English painter in Impressionist style but sombre tones, e.g. music-hall interiors.

Siddons, Sarah (1755–1831), English tragic actress, outstanding in Shakespeare; sister of John Philip Kemble.

Sidgwick, Henry (1838–1900), English philosopher, wrote chiefly on ethics.

Sidgwick, Nevil Vincent (1873–1952), English chemist, noted for his work on molecular structure.

Sidmouth, Viscount. See **Addington, Henry.**

Sidney, Algernon (1622–83), English

republican, opposed both Cromwell and Charles II; executed.

Sidney, Sir Philip (1554–86), English soldier-poet (*Astrophel and Stella*); renowned for his chivalrous death in Dutch war.

Sidney Sussex College, Cambridge University, founded under will of Lady Frances Sidney, Dowager Countess of Sussex, 1596.

Siebold, Philipp von (1796–1866), German ethnographer and naturalist, wrote much about Japan.

Siegen, Ludwig von (*c.* 1609–*c.* 1675), Dutch-born engraver, invented mezzotint process 1642.

Siemens, Werner von (1816–92), German electrical engineer and inventor, founded great business concern 1847.

Siemens, Sir William (1823–83), German-born British pioneer of electrical engineering, brother of Werner von Siemens.

Siemens-Martin Process. See **open-hearth process.**

Siena University, Italy, founded 1240.

Sienkiewicz, Henryk (1846–1916), Polish novelist, wrote *Quo Vadis?* (1896).

Sierra Leone, West Africa, earliest English settlement 1787; crown colony 1808–1960; became independent as a member of the Commonwealth of Nations 1961.

Sièyes, Abbé Emmanuel Joseph (1748–1836), French politician, prominent early in the French Revolution.

Sigebert (d. 575), king of Austrasian Franks, spurred by wife Brunhilde to engage in civil wars.

Sigismund (1368–1437), Holy Roman emperor 1411–37, defeated by Turks at Nicopolis, 1396.

Sigismund I (1467–1548), king of Poland 1506–48, involved in wars with neighbouring powers.

Sigismund II (1520–72), king of Poland 1548–72, incorporated Lithuania into Poland 1569.

Sigismund III (1566–1632), king of Poland 1587–1632, and of Sweden 1592–1604, but ousted by Charles IX (*q.v.*).

Signac, Paul (1863–1935), French pointtilliste painter, worked closely with Seurat.

sign language, for deaf and dumb, developed 1765 by Charles Michel (1712–89).

Signorelli, Luca (*c.* 1442–1523), Italian painter, created cycle of powerful frescoes in Orvieto Cathedral.

Sigurdsson, Jón (1811–79), Icelandic scholar, published early sagas; led struggle against Danes for a constitution.

Sikh religion, founded by the Indian religious leader Nanak (*q.v.*) in late 15th century.

Sikh Wars, between British and Sikhs 1845–46 and 1848–49.

Sikkim, colonized by Tibet in 16th–17th centuries; British influence began early 19th century; made a British protectorate 1895; became an Indian protectorate 1947; incorporated in India 1975.

Sikorsky, Igor (1889–1972), Russian-born American pioneer of the helicopter.

Sikorski, Władyslaw (1881–1943), Polish soldier and statesman, prime minister of his country's government in exile during World War II.

Silcoates School, Wakefield, English public school, founded 1920.

Silesia, under Polish control from late 10th century; part of Bohemia 1335–1469; ruled by Hungary 1469–90; part of Hapsburg Empire 1526–1740; ruled by Prussia 1740–1871 and by Germany 1871–1945; Polish since 1945.

Silesian Wars, between Prussia and Austria 1740–42, 1744–45 and 1756–63.

silicon, chemical element first isolated 1824 by Baron Berzelius (*q.v.*).

silk, traditionally invented in China 2640 B.C.; silkworms brought to Constantinople *c.* A.D. 550.

Silurian Period, Earth history, from *c.* 430 to *c.* 395 million years ago.

Silurist, The. Name often applied to Henry Vaughan (*q.v.*).

silver, known since ancient times; artefacts found in tombs dating back to 4000 B.C.

Silverius, Saint (d. *c.* 538), Pope 536–*c.* 538, twice exiled under Justinian.

Silvester I, Saint (d. 335), Pope 314–335, supposed (wrongly) to have baptized Constantine.

Silvester II (*c.* 940–1003), Pope 999–1003, was a noted scientific and mathematical scholar.

Simenon, Georges (b. 1903), Belgian novelist, best known for his detective stories.

Simeon I (d. 927), tsar of Bulgaria 893–927, defeated Byzantines and Magyars.

Simeon Stylites, Saint (*c.* 389–459), Syrian Christian ascetic, spent thirty years on top of a pillar.

Simhath Torah (Rejoicing of the Law), Jewish holiday 23rd day of Tishri.

Simnel, Lambert (*c.* 1477–*c.* 1534), English pretender to throne as Earl of Warwick; confessed his imposture and became a royal servant.

Simon, Sir John (1816–1904), English public health pioneer, first medical health officer for London, 1848.

Simon, John, Viscount (1873–1954), English lawyer and politician, cabinet minister 1930–40; lord chancellor 1940–45.

Simon de Montfort. See **Montfort, Simon de.**

Simonides of Ceos (556–468 B.C.), Greek lyric poet, author of odes, elegies and hymns to the gods.

Simplon Pass, Switzerland, built 1800–07 by Napoleon.

Simplon Tunnel, Italy to Switzerland, deepest and longest rail tunnel, undertaken by the German engineer Alfred Brandt (1846–99); divided into two sections, first one constructed 1898–1906, second one 1918–22.

Simpson, Maxwell (1815–1902), Irish chemist, obtained synthetically di- and tri-basic acids.

Simson, William (1800–47), Scottish painter of portraits and historical set-pieces.

Sinclair, Upton (1878–1968), American novelist, whose *The Jungle* (1906) exposed the exploitation of labour.

Sinding, Christian (1856–1941), Norwegian composer, remembered for the popular *Rustle of Spring*.

Sind War, India, between British and Baluchis, March 1843.

Singapore, founded 1819 by Sir Stamford Raffles (*q.v.*); part of Straits Settlements (*q.v.*) crown colony 1867; occupied by Japanese 1942–45; made a separate crown colony 1946; part of Federation of Malaysia 1963–65; independent republic within the Commonwealth 1965.

Sinigaglia, Leone (1868–1944), Italian composer, best known for folk-based Piedmontese dances.

Sinn Fein, Irish political party founded 1905 by Arthur Griffith (*q.v.*).

siphon, principle discovered 1577 by the Scottish mathematician William Welwood (d. after 1622).

Sirius, binary star reported as such 1844 by Friedrich Wilhelm Bessel (1784–1846); companion star detected 1862 by the American astronomer Alvan G. Clark and identified 1915 as a white dwarf (*q.v.*).

Sisley, Alfred (1839–99), French painter, was a pioneer Impressionist.

Sismondi, Jean de (1773–1842), Swiss economist and historian of the medieval Italian republics.

Sitting Bull (*c.* 1831–1890), American Indian chief, defeated and killed George Armstrong Custer (*q.v.*) at Little Big Horn, 1874.

Sitwell, Dame Edith (1887–1964), English poet, used sound-association to convey meaning.

Sitwell, Sir Osbert (1892–1969), English writer, now remembered mainly for memoirs (*Left Hand, Right Hand!* etc.).

Sitwell, Sacheverell (b. 1897), English writer of travel description and art appreciation; brother of Edith and Osbert Sitwell.

SI Units (Système International d'Unités), system of internationally agreed scientific units defined and named 1954–60.

Six-Day War, between Israel and Egypt, Jordan, Syria and Iraq 5–10 June 1967.

Siward the Strong (d. 1055), Danish Earl of Northumberland, overthrew Macbeth of Scotland in favour of Malcolm III.

Sixtus II (d. 258), Pope 257–258, martyred in reign of emperor Valentinian.

Sixtus IV (1414–84), Pope 1471–84, built Sistine Chapel.

Sixtus V (1521–90), Pope 1585–90, was a builder and patron of arts.

Skanderbeg (*c.* 1403–1468), Albanian leader in independence struggle against Turks; defeated.

Skeat, Walter (1835–1912), English philologist and notable editor of Chaucer.

Skelton, John (*c.* 1460–1529), English poet wrote effective doggerel-like satirical verse, e.g. *Philip Sparrow*.

Skinners' Company, London livery company founded 12th century; first charter granted by Edward III, 1327.

Skylab, first, American manned space laboratory (*q.v.*), launched into Earth orbit 1973.

skyscraper, first, erected 1868–70 in New York City; first with internal metal frame, erected 1884–85 in Chicago, designed by the American architect William Le Baron Jenney (1832–1907).

slavery, declared illegal on British soil 1772; abolished in British Empire 1834; abolished throughout U.S.A. by 1865.

slaves, first Negro slaves in an English colony landed at Virginia 1619.

slave trade, British, abolished 1807; American, abolished 1808.

sleeping cars. See **Pullman sleeping car.**

slide projector, invented 1640s as the magic lantern and developed 1656 by Christiaan Huygens (*q.v.*); models for projecting photographic slides used in 1840s by the American brothers W. and F. Langenheim.

slide rule, invented 1622 by the English mathematician William Oughtred (1575–1660).

slimming, by elimination of fats and starch, first undergone 1862 and popularized by an English undertaker William Banting (1797–1878).

Sloane, Sir Hans (1660–1753), Irish royal physician and naturalist; his collections formed nucleus of British Museum.

Slocum, Henry Warner (1827–94), American soldier, fought at Gettysburg and on Sherman's march through Georgia.

Slocum, Joshua (1844–1909), American sailor, first man to sail round the world alone.

Sluter, Claus (*c.* 1350–*c.* 1405), Dutch sculptor, e.g. *Well of Moses*.

smallpox, vaccine developed 1796–98 by Edward Jenner (*q.v.*).

Smart, Christopher (1722–71), English

religious poet, wrote *A Song to David* while confined in lunatic asylum.

Smeaton, John (1724–92), English engineer constructed Eddystone Lighthouse, 1759.

Smedley, Frank (1818–64), English novelist, author of *Frank Farleigh* (1850).

Smetana, Bedřich (1824–84), Bohemian composer in national idiom, notably the opera *Bartered Bride* and the symphonic poem *Má Vlast.*

Smibert, John (1688–1751), Scottish portrait painter, first professionally trained artist in America 1728–51.

Smiles, Samuel (1812–1904), Scottish writer of improving biographies, apostle of 'self-help'.

Smirke, Sir Robert (1781–1867), English architect, designed the British Museum, London.

Smith, Adam (1723–90), Scottish economist, whose *Wealth of Nations* (1776) became basis of all 'classical' economics.

Smith, Alfred Emanuel (1873–1944), U.S. politician, Democratic party nominee for the presidency and governor of New York State.

Smith, Bernard (*c.* 1630–1708), German-born organ-builder for Westminster Abbey, Sheldonian, Oxford, etc.

Smith, Bessie (*c.* 1898–1937), American Negro singer, notable exponent of blues.

Smith, Sir Francis (1808–74), English inventor of the screw propeller for steamships.

Smith, George (1840–76), English Assyriologist, noted for his decipherment of cuneiform script.

Smith, Ian Douglas (b. 1919), Rhodesian politician, was prime minister when his country declared unilateral independence in 1965.

Smith, John (1580–1631), English colonist, took a leading part in the colonization of Virginia.

Smith, Joseph (1805–44), American founder of the Mormon Church; lynched.

Smith, Sir Matthew (1879–1959), English painter, noted for his landscapes and nudes.

Smith, Stephenson Percy (1840–1922), English-born New Zealand authority on the Maoris.

Smith, Sydney (1771–1845), English clergyman, famous wit, writer and co-founder of *Edinburgh Review.*

Smith, William (1769–1839), English pioneer of geological maps.

Smith, William Henry (1825–91), English newsagent, founded the chain of bookshops which bear his name.

Smithsonian Institution, Washington, D.C., established 1846 by the bequest of the French-born English scientist James Smithson (1765–1829).

Smolensk, Battle of, French victory over the Russians 17–18 Aug. 1812.

Smollett, Tobias (1721–71), Scottish novelist, picaresque and bawdy, wrote *Roderick Random* (1748).

Smuts, Jan Christiaan (1870–1950), South African statesman, prime minister 1919–1924 and 1939–48, strove to achieve Anglo-Afrikaner unity.

Smyth, Dame Ethel (1858–1944), English composer, wrote opera *The Wreckers* (1906).

Smyth, James Carmichael (1741–1821), Scottish royal physician and pioneer in fever prevention.

Smyth, Sir James Carmichael (1779–1838), British soldier, fought at Waterloo; governor of British Guiana 1833–38; son of James Smyth.

Snorri Sturluson (1178–1241), Icelandic poet and chronicler, author of the *Prose Edda.*

Snow, Charles Percy, Baron (b. 1905), English scientist and novelist, author of *The Masters* (1951).

Snow, John (1813–58), English physician, introduced ether as an anaesthetic.

Snowden, Philip (1864–1937), English statesman, chancellor of the exchequer in Labour and National governments 1924 and 1929–31.

Snowy Mountains Hydroelectric Scheme, Australia, started 1949; completed 1974.

Snyders, Frans (1579–1657), Flemish painter of still-life and animals.

Soane, Sir John (1753–1837), English architect, built Bank of England, London; bequeathed his own house as a museum.

soap tax, imposed in England 1712; abolished 1853.

Sobieski, John (1624–96), Polish soldier, became king as John III 1674–96; drove Turks from Vienna.

Social Democratic Federation, British socialist organization, founded 1881 as the Democratic Federation by H. M. Hyndman (*q.v.*).

Socialist League, British socialist organization, founded 1884 by seceders from Social Democratic Federation and led by William Morris (*q.v.*).

Socialist Parties, foundation dates: Germany 1869; France (several) 1870s and 1880s; Switzerland 1870; Denmark 1871; Portugal 1875; U.S.A. 1877; Spain 1879; Belgium 1885; Norway 1887; Netherlands 1888; Sweden 1880s; Italy 1892; Russia 1898; Finland 1899. In Britain, Labour Representation Committee 1900 became Labour Party 1906; Socialist Labour Party 1903 became Socialist Party of Great Britain 1904. See also **Independent Labour Party; Social Democratic Federation; Socialist League.**

Social Security, Ministry of, formed 1966 by merging Ministry of Pensions and National Insurance with the National Assistance Board; became Ministry of Health and Social Security 1968.

Society for the Prevention of Cruelty to Children, U.S.A., founded 1875 by Elbridge Thomas Gerry (*q.v.*).

Society for Promoting Christian Knowledge, founded 1698 in England by Dr Thomas Bray (*q.v.*).

Society for Propagating the Gospel in Foreign Parts, London, founded 1701 by Dr Thomas Bray.

Society for Psychical Research, London, founded 1882.

Society of Antiquarians of London, founded 1717; granted royal charter 1751.

Society of Antiquaries of Scotland, founded 1780.

Society of Friends. See **Friends,** Society of.

Society of Indexers, London, founded 1957 by G. Norman Knight.

Society Islands, Polynesia, discovered 1607 by the Portuguese explorer Pedro Fernandez de Queirós (*c.* 1560–1614); French protectorate since 1843.

Socotra, Indian Ocean, British-protected 1886–1967; part of Yemen People's Democratic Republic since 1967.

Socrates (*c.* 470–399 B.C.), outstanding Athenian philosopher, sought knowledge by question and answer method.

Soddy, Frederick (1877–1956), English chemist, close associate of Lord Rutherford; Nobel prizewinner 1922.

sodium, long known in compound form, isolated as the pure element 1807 by Sir Humphry Davy.

Sodoma, Giovanni (1477–1549), Italian painter in early Mannerist style, worked mainly in Siena.

solar compass, invented 1836 by the American William Burt (1792–1858).

Solari, Cristoforo (d. *c.* 1525), Italian sculptor of Beatrice d'Este's tomb.

solar parallax, used in determining Earth–Sun distance, first measured 1672; greater accuracy obtained by the English astronomers Sir David Gill 1877 and Sir Harold Spencer Jones 1930–31.

sol-fa, tonic, system of musical notation devised by Sarah Ann Glover (*q.v.*); systemized in 1840s by John Curwen (1816–80).

Solferino, Battle of, in which the French and Piedmontese defeated the Austrians, 24 June 1859.

Solihull School, Warwickshire, English public school, origins uncertain; first recorded mention 1560.

Solís, Juan Diaz de (*c.* 1470–1516), Spanish navigator, explored the Atlantic coast of South America.

Sologub, Fyodor (1863–1927), Russian writer combining beautiful style with grotesque matter, e.g. *The Little Demon* (1907).

Solomon (*c.* 973–*c.* 933 B.C.), king of Israel, under whose rule his country reached the peak of its greatness.

Solomon Islands, Pacific, discovered 1568 by the Spanish navigator Álvaro de Mendaña; made a British protectorate 1893; became independent 1977.

Solomos, Dionysios (1798–1857), Greek poet, author of *Hymn to Liberty* (1823).

Solon (*c.* 640–*c.* 558 B.C.), Greek legislator, gave Athens a new constitution.

solstice, summer, longest day, June 21 or 22 (northern hemisphere).

solstice, winter, shortest day, Dec. 21 or 22 (northern hemisphere).

Solvay process, for producing sodium carbonate, invented 1863 by the Belgian industrial chemist Ernest Solvay (1838–1922).

Solzhenitsyn, Alexander (b. 1918), Russian novelist, author of *Cancer Ward* (1968) and *August 1914* (1971); Nobel prizewinner 1970.

Somali Democratic Republic, East Africa, established 1960 by merger of British Somaliland and Somalia.

Somalia, made Italian protectorate 1889; incorporated in Italian East Africa 1936; under British military administration 1941–49; U.N. trusteeship territory 1950–1960; independent 1960 as part of Somali Democratic Republic (*q.v.*).

Somaliland, British, protectorate established 1884; merged with Somalia as Somali Democratic Republic 1960.

Somaliland, French. See **Afars and Issas,** French Territory of the.

Somers, Sir George (1554–1610), English discoverer of the Bermuda Islands 1609.

Somerset, Edward Seymour, Duke of (*c.* 1506–1552), English Protector in reign of Edward VI until overthrown by Northumberland; beheaded.

Somerset, Robert Carr, Earl of (*c.* 1590–1645), Scottish favourite of James I, ruined by Overbury (*q.v.*) scandal.

Somerville, Mary (1780–1872), Scottish writer of popular scientific texts.

Somerville, William (1675–1742), English poet, author of *The Chase* (1735).

Somerville College, Oxford University, founded for women students 1879.

Somme, Battles of the, World War I, 1 July–13 Nov. 1916.

Sonar, echo detection of underwater objects, developed 1918 by the French physicist Paul Langevin (1872–1946) and British and American scientists.

Sophia (1630–1714), electress of Hanover; her son became George I of Great Britain.

Sophia Alexeievna (1657–1704), regent

of Russia 1682–89 for her half-brothers Ivan and Peter; ousted by Peter.

Sophia Charlotte (1668–1705), queen of Frederick I of Prussia 1701–05; sister of George I of Great Britain.

Sophia Dorothea (1666–1726), electress of Hanover, wife of George I; accused of adultery, imprisoned 1694–1726.

Sophocles (c. 496–406 B.C.), Greek playwright, author of *Oedipus Tyrannus*, *Antigone*, etc.

Sophonisba (d. c. 204 B.C.), queen of Numidia, whose tragic history inspired Corneille and other writers.

Sopwith, Thomas (b. 1888), English pioneer aviator, founded famous aircraft company.

Sorabji, Cornelia (c. 1866–1954), Indian lawyer, wrote popular books about India, e.g. *India Calling* (1934).

Sorbonne, Paris University, founded 1257 by the French priest Robert de Sorbon (1201–74).

Sordello (c. 1200–c. 1270), Italian troubadour, wrote in Provençal, notably *Lament for Blacas*.

Sorel, Agnes (c. 1422–1450), mistress of Charles VII of France 1444–50.

Sorel, Georges (1847–1922), French political thinker of extreme views, best known for *Reflections on Violence* (1908).

Sorge, Richard (1895–1944), German living in Japan, who spied for the Soviet Union.

Sorolla y Bastida, Joaquín (1863–1923), Spanish painter in Impressionist style.

SOS, international distress call signal, first used 1909; adopted by International Radiotelegraph Conference 1912.

Sotatsu (1576–1643), Japanese painter, achieved elegant effects with gold dust.

Sotheby's, London auction rooms, founded 1744 by Samuel Baker.

Soufflot, Jacques (1709–80), French architect, designed the Panthéon, Paris.

Soulé, Pierre (1801–70), French-born American politician, as minister to Spain intrigued to acquire Cuba.

Soult, Nicolas (1769–1851), French soldier, served Napoleon; minister of war under Louis Philippe.

sound recording, first made 1877 on the tin-foil cylinders of Edison's phonograph (q.v.); first flat gramophone records made 1887 by the German-born American Émile Berliner (1851–1929).

Sousa, John Philip (1854–1932), American composer of famous marches, e.g. *Stars and Stripes for Ever*.

Sousa, Martin Affonso de (c. 1500–64), Portuguese admiral, founded first Portuguese settlements in Brazil.

South, Sir James (1785–1867), English astronomer, worked with Herschel and Laplace.

South, Robert (1634–1716), English Anglican clergyman, became famous for his sermons.

South Africa, Republic of, formed 1961, replacing Union of South Africa established 1910.

Southampton, Henry Wriothesley, Earl of (1573–1624), English noble, patron of Shakespeare; involved in Essex rebellion but pardoned.

Southampton, Thomas Wriothesley, Earl of (1505–50), English diplomat and lord chancellor, influential under Henry VIII and Edward VI.

Southampton University, founded 1902; achieved university status 1952.

South Australia, formed into a province 1834; became a state in the Commonwealth of Australia 1901.

South Carolina, U.S.A., first settled permanently by English 1670; entered the Union 1788; seceded 1860; readmitted 1868.

Southcott, Joanna (1750–1814), English religious zealot of eccentric beliefs, gained many followers.

South Dakota, U.S.A., first reached 1743 by the French brothers Verendrye; first settlement established 1817; admitted to Union 1889.

South-East Asia Collective Defence Treaty, signed at Manila Sept. 1954.

South-East Asia Treaty Organization (S.E.A.T.O.), the group of nations that signed the Collective Defence Treaty.

Southerne, Thomas (1660–1746), Irish playwright, wrote *Oroonoko* (1696).

Southern Rhodesia. See Rhodesia.

Southey, Robert (1774–1843), English poet, poet laureate 1813–43, now remembered for *Life of Nelson* (1813).

South Kensington Museum, London, forerunner of Victoria and Albert Museum, founded 1857.

South Pole, first reached 14 Dec. 1911 by Roald Amundsen (q.v.); reached 18 Jan. 1912 by Robert Falcon Scott (q.v.).

South Sea Bubble, South Sea Company incorporated 1711; boom and financial collapse 1720.

Southwark Bridge, London, constructed 1913–21 by the English architect Sir Ernest George (1839–1922).

Southwell, Robert (c. 1561–95), English poet, Jesuit missionary to England; hanged.

South-West Africa. See Namibia.

Southwood, Julius Elias, Viscount (1873–1946), British newspaper proprietor, publisher of *John Bull*, *People*, *Daily Herald*, etc.

Soyer, Alexis (1809–58), French chef, worked at Reform Club, London; wrote about food and cooking.

spacecraft, first one, launched Oct. 1957,

was the Soviet satellite Sputnik I; first manned craft, launched April 1961, was the Soviet Vostok I carrying Yuri Gagarin (*q.v.*) into Earth orbit.

space laboratory, first one, the Soviet Salyut, launched 1971 and manned from the Soyuz spacecraft. See also **Skylab.**

space–time concept, first mooted 1904 by Hendrik Antoon Lorentz (*q.v.*); formalized 1907 by the Russian-born mathematician Hermann Minkowski (1864–1909); developed in the general theory of relativity (*q.v.*).

Spain, Greek settlements from 7th century B.C.; Carthaginians dominant from 5th century B.C.; Roman predominance from *c.* 200 B.C. to Vandal invasion A.D. 409; Muslim invasion 711; last Muslims defeated 1492; ruled by Hapsburgs 1516–1700; ruled by Bourbons 1700–1808 and 1814–70; republic 1873–74; ruled by Bourbons 1874–1931 (dictatorship, 1923–1930); republic 1931–39; dictatorship 1939–75; constitutional monarchy since 1975.

Spallanzani, Lazzaro (1729–99), Italian biologist, disproved the theory of spontaneous generation.

Spangenberg, August Gottlieb (1704–92), German founder of the Moravian Church in America.

Spanish–American War, April–July 1898.

Spanish Civil War, began July 1936; ended March 1939.

Spanish Guinea. See **Equatorial Guinea.**

Spanish Sahara. See **Sahara,** Western.

Spanish Succession, War of the, began 1701; ended 1713.

Spartacus (d. 71 B.C.), Thracian slave and gladiator in Rome, led slave revolt 73–71 B.C.

Speaker, House of Commons, office instituted in early 14th century; term first used 1377.

spectacles, known in Europe in 13th century; use common by 15th century.

Spectator, British periodical 1711–12 edited by Joseph Addison and Sir Richard Steele (*qq.v.*); present *Spectator* founded 1828 by Robert Rintoul (1787–1858).

spectroheliograph, for photographing the Sun, invented 1889 by the American astronomer George Ellery Hale (1868–1938).

spectroscope, first built 1859 by the German physicists Gustav Kirchhoff (1824–1887) and Robert Bunsen (1811–99).

spectrum, of sunlight, investigated 1666 by Sir Isaac Newton.

Spee, Maximilian, Graf von (1861–1914), German naval commander, victorious at Coronel; killed at Falkland Islands.

Speed, John (*c.* 1552–1629), English map-maker, published series covering England and Wales 1608–10.

speedwriting, developed *c.* 1924 by the American Emma Dearborn.

Speke, John Hanning (1827–64), English explorer, discovered source of the Nile 1862.

Spellman, Francis, Cardinal (1889–1967), American ecclesiastic, Roman Catholic archbishop of New York 1939–67.

Spencer, Herbert (1820–1903), English philosopher and social scientist, often called founder of sociology.

Spencer, Sir Stanley (1891–1959), English painter of religious subjects and portraits, often set in his native Cookham.

Spender, Stephen (b. 1909), English poet, associated with Auden and Isherwood in 1930s.

Spengler, Oswald (1880–1936), German historical philosopher, wrote *The Decline of the West* (1918–23).

Spenser, Edmund (1552–99), English poet, whose major work is *The Faerie Queen* (1590–96).

Sperry, Elmer Ambrose (1860–1930), American electrical engineer, made many inventions including gyroscopic compasses.

spin, of the electron, postulated 1925 by the Dutch-born American physicists George E. Uhlenbeck (b. 1900) and Samuel A. Goudsmit (b. 1902).

Spinello, Aretino (d. *c.* 1410), Italian painter of the Florentine school, also worked in Pisa and Siena.

spinning frame, invented 1768 by Sir Richard Arkwright (*q.v.*).

spinning jenny, invented *c.* 1764 by the English weaver James Hargreaves (d. 1778).

Spinoza, Benedict (1632–77), Dutch philosopher, broke with Jewish Church, created rationalist–pantheistic system.

spiral galaxies, first detected 1845 by the Earl of Rosse (1800–67).

Spiritualism, modern, began with the Fox sisters at Hydesville, U.S.A., 1848.

Spithead, British fleet mutiny at, 15 April 1797.

Spode, Josiah (1754–1827), English potter, created standard bone china.

Spohr, Louis (1784–1859), German Romantic composer and virtuoso violinist, influential as a teacher.

spoonerisms, originated by the English don, the Rev. William Archibald Spooner (1844–1930).

Spotsylvania Courthouse, Battle of, American Civil War 8–21 May 1864.

Spottiswoode, John (1565–1639), Scottish archbishop of St Andrews 1615–39; deposed.

spring, *c.* 21 March to *c.* 21 June in northern hemisphere.

Spurgeon, Charles Haddon (1834–92), English Baptist preacher, drew large audiences at Metropolitan Tabernacle, London.

Spurs, Battle of the, English victory over the French, 16 Aug. 1513.

Sputnik. See **satellite.**

Spyri, Johanna (1827–1901), Swiss writer of the children's classic *Heidi* (1881).

Squarcione, Francesco (1394–1474), Italian painter, famous as teacher of Mantegna, etc.

Squire, Sir John (1884–1958), English poet, general essayist, journalist and anthologist.

Sri Lanka, Buddhist civilization established 3rd century B.C.; settled by Portuguese from 1505; annexed by Dutch 1658; ceded to Britain 1802; became a crown colony 1833; achieved independence within the Commonwealth 1948.

S.S.A.F.A. (Soldiers', Sailors' and Airmen's Families Association), London, founded 1885.

Ssu-ma Ch'ien (145–*c.* 87 B.C.), Chinese scholar, wrote the first history of China.

Staël, Madame de (1766–1817), French writer, novelist (*Delphine*, 1802) and influential Romantic critic.

Staël, Nicolas de (1914–55), Russian-born French painter, an exponent of abstract expressionism.

Stafford, Edward, 3rd Duke of Buckingham (1478–1521), English nobleman, executed by order of Henry VIII for alleged treason.

Stafford, Henry, 2nd Duke of Buckingham, (*c.* 1454–1483), English noble, supported, then revolted against, Richard III; executed.

Stahl, Georg Ernst (1660–1734), German chemist, proposed existence of gas 'phlogiston' to explain combustion.

Stainer, Sir John (1840–1901), English composer and editor-critic of medieval music.

stainless steel, first made 1913 in England and 1914 in Germany.

Stair, John Dalrymple, Earl of (1673–1747), Scottish soldier, gave distinguished service under Marlborough; ambassador to France 1715–20.

Stalin, Joseph (1879–1953), leader of the Soviet Communist Party and dictator of the U.S.S.R., forced through massive industrialization and collectivization programme in the 1930s.

Stambuliski, Alexander (1879–1923), Bulgarian statesman, leader of Peasants' Party, prime minister 1920–23; assassinated.

Stambulov, Stefan (1854–95), Bulgarian statesman, prime minister 1887–94; assassinated.

Stamford School, Lincolnshire, English public school, founded by William Radcliffe of Stamford, 1532.

Stamp Act, British tax on American colonies passed 1764; repealed 1766.

stamp booklets, first used in Britain 1904.

stamp duty, regularly imposed in England since 1694.

stamped envelopes, first British issued 1840; designed by Irish artist William Mulready (1786–1863).

Standard, Battle of the, English victory over the Scots 22 Aug. 1138.

Standard Oil Company, of Ohio, founded 1870 by John D. Rockefeller.

Standish, Myles (*c.* 1584–1656), English colonist in America, travelled on *Mayflower*; leader of New Plymouth colony.

Stanford, Sir Charles (1852–1924), Irish composer, often on national subjects, e.g. *Irish Rhapsodies.*

Stanford University, California, founded 1891 through an endowment from the American railway builder Leland Stanford (1824–93).

Stanhope, Lady Hester (1776–1839), English traveller, lived in eccentric 'native' style in Palestine–Lebanon 1810–39.

Stanhope, Philip. See **Chesterfield,** Earl of.

Stanislaus I (1677–1766), king of Poland 1704–09 and 1733–35, as Swedish, and later French, candidate.

Stanislaus II (1732–98), last king of Poland 1764–95, unable to resist partitions of country by neighbours.

Stanislavski, Konstantin (1863–1938), Russian actor and director, founded Moscow Art Theatre; wrote *My Life in Art* (1924).

Stanley, Sir Henry Morton (1841–1904), Welsh explorer in Africa, opened up the Congo; famous meeting with Livingstone 1871.

Stanley, John (1713–86), blind English organist and composer, wrote *Zimri* (1760).

Stanley, Wendell (1904–71), American biochemist, noted for his work in crystallizing viruses.

Stanley, William (1858–1916), American electrical engineer, produced the first practical transformer.

Stannary Parliament, Cornish assembly, last held at Truro 1752.

Stanton, Elizabeth (1815–1902), American agitator for women's rights, launched female suffrage movement 1848.

Star, British evening newspaper, founded 1888; absorbed by *Evening News* 1960.

Star Chamber, English prerogative court inaugurated in 14th century; unpopular use by Charles I caused abolition by Long Parliament 1641.

Stark, James (1794–1859), English landscape painter of the Norwich school.

Stark effect, splitting of spectral lines, discovered 1913 by the German physicist Johannes Stark (1874–1957).

Starling, Ernest (1866–1927), English physiologist, introduced the word hormone to describe the secretions of the ductless glands.

Stationers' Company, London, livery company incorporated 1557; charter confirmed by Queen Elizabeth 1559; monopoly ended 1842.

Statius (d. A.D. 96), Roman poet, wrote the collection *Silvae.*

Statue of Liberty, New York harbour, designed 1876 by French sculptor Frédéric Auguste Bartholdi (1834–1904); unveiled 28 Oct. 1886.

Stauffenberg, Claus Schenk von (1907–1944), German army officer, executed after leading abortive plot against Hitler.

Staunton, Howard (1810–74), English chess player, supreme *c.* 1843–52; was also a Shakespearian scholar.

Stavisky, Alexandre (*c.* 1886–1934), French swindler; discovery of his huge bond fraud caused the fall of two governments; committed suicide.

STD, subscriber trunk dialling, introduced in Britain Dec. 1958.

Stead, William Thomas (1849–1912), English journalist, exposed English 'white slave trade'; drowned in *Titanic.*

steady-state theory, of the universe, proposed 1948 by the astronomers Thomas Gold (b. 1920), Hermann Bondi (b. 1919) and Fred Hoyle (b. 1915).

steamboat, prototype built from 1787 by the American John Fitch (1743–98); first working design, *Charlotte Dundas* built by William Symington (*q.v.*), launched 1802; first commercially successful vessel (*Clermont*), built by Robert Fulton (*q.v.*), launched 1807.

steam engine, first practical one invented 1698 by Thomas Savery (*q.v.*); developed 1705 by Thomas Newcomen (*q.v.*); improved version built 1769 by James Watt.

steam hammer, invented 1839 by the Scottish engineer James Nasmyth (1808–1890).

steam locomotive, first working engine, the *New Castle*, built 1803 by Richard Trevithick (*q.v.*); improved by others including George Stephenson (*q.v.*) with, first, the *Blücher* (1814), and later the *Rocket* (1829), etc.

steam turbine, invented 1884 by the British engineer Sir Charles Parsons (1854–1931).

stearic acids. See fatty acids.

steel, cast by the crucible process, developed *c.* 1740; alloy steels first commercially produced 1861.

Steele, Sir Richard (1672–1729), Irish writer, alternated with Addison (*q.v.*) in writing essays for *The Spectator.*

Steen, Jan (1626–79), Dutch painter of tavern and similar scenes.

Steer, Wilson (1860–1942), English painter, was a distinguished landscape artist in oils and watercolours.

Stein, Sir Aurel (1862–1943), Hungarian-born British archaeologist, worked extensively in Asia.

Stein, Gertrude (1874–1946), American writer in Paris, noted for her experimental style, author of *Three Lives* (1909).

Stein, Karl (1757–1831), Prussian statesman, made sweeping reforms, including abolition of serfdom.

Steinach, Eugen (1861–1944), Austrian biologist, attempted human rejuvenation by grafting animal glands.

Steinbeck, John (1902–68), American novelist, author of *The Grapes of Wrath* (1939).

Steiner, Rudolf (1861–1925), Austrian philosopher, founder of anthroposophy.

Steinitz, Wilhelm (1836–1900), Austrian-born world chess champion 1866–94, lived in Britain and U.S.A.

Steinmetz, Charles Proteus (1865–1923), German-born American electrical engineer, made many important discoveries.

Steinway, piano manufacturers, firm established Brunswick *c.* 1825; New York 1853; London 1875; Hamburg 1880.

stellar parallax, first measured 1838 for the star 61 Cygni by Friedrich Wilhelm Bessel (1784–1846).

Stendhal (pseud. of Henri Marie Beyle; 1783–1842), French writer, novelist (*Scarlet and Black*, 1831), diarist, autobiographer and writer on art.

Steno, Nicolaus (1638–86), Danish anatomist, discovered duct of parotid gland.

Stephen, Saint. See **Stephen I,** of Hungary.

Stephen II (d. 757), Pope 752–757, crowned Pepin the Short, began close papal–Frankish relationship.

Stephen (*c.* 1097–1154), king of England 1135–54, almost continually at war with rival claimant Matilda.

Stephen I, Saint (*c.* 975–1038), king of Hungary 997–1038, enforced Christianity; patron saint of Hungary.

Stephen V (1239–72), king of Hungary 1270–72, defeated Bohemians.

Stephen Bathory (1533–86), king of Poland 1575–86, made his country a leading European power.

Stephen Dushan (*c.* 1308–1355), king of Serbia 1335–55, conquered Bosnia, Macedonia and Albania from the Byzantines.

Stephen, Sir James (1829–94), English lawyer, influential writer and high court judge.

Stephen, Sir Leslie (1832–1904), English writer, editor of *Dictionary of National Biography.*

Stephen Harding, Saint. See **Harding, Saint Stephen.**

Stephens, Alexander (1812–83), American statesman, vice-president of the Confederacy 1861–65.

Stephens, George (1813–95), English archaeologist and philologist, pioneered study of runic monuments.

Stephens, James (1882–1950), Irish writer, notably of novel *The Crock of Gold* (1912).

Stephens, John (1805–52), American archaeologist and traveller, wrote about the ancient civilizations of the Americas.

Stephenson, George (1781–1848), English locomotive engineer, constructed first railway (Stockton–Darlington) 1825, and the *Rocket* 1829.

Stephenson, Robert (1803–59), English engineer, son of George Stephenson, was a notable builder of railway bridges.

Stephen the Great (c. 1431–1504), prince of Moldavia, defeated Turks at Racova 1475.

Stepniak, Sergei (1852–95), Russian Nihilist, assassinated General Mezentsev 1878; lived in England 1884–95.

stereochemistry, study initiated 1874 by the Dutch scientist Jacobus Henricus van't Hoff (1852–1911).

stereophonic reproduction, demonstrated early 1930s; stereophonic records became available 1958.

stereoscope, invented c. 1838 by Sir Charles Wheatstone (*q.v.*).

stereotype process, invented 1725 by the Scot William Ged (1690–1749); not commercially used until 1790s.

sterling, taken off British gold standard Sept. 1931.

Sterling, John (1806–44), Irish-born writer and friend of the famous; biography written by Carlyle (*q.v.*).

Sternberg, Konstantin (1852–1924), Russian-born American pianist, founded well-known school at Philadelphia.

Sterne, Laurence (1713–68), Irish-born clergyman in Yorkshire, wrote the eccentric, whimsical novel *Tristram Shandy* (1759–67).

stethoscope, invented 1816 by the French physician René Théophile Laënnec (1781–1826).

Steuben, Frederick, Baron von (1730–94), German-born soldier, served Frederick the Great; trained Washington's Continental Army.

Stevens, Alfred (1818–75), English sculptor, notably of the Wellington Monument, Saint Paul's Cathedral.

Stevens, Henry (1819–86), American book dealer in London, expert on Bible bibliography.

Stevens, John (1749–1838), American pioneer of patent legislation; steamboat builder.

Stevens, Wallace (1879–1955), American poet, author of *Collected Poems* (1954).

Stevenson, Adlai (1900–65), American political leader, a liberal Democrat he ran unsuccessfully for president against Eisenhower 1952 and 1956.

Stevenson, David (1815–86), Scottish civil engineer, built lighthouses, etc.; son of Robert Stevenson.

Stevenson, Robert (1772–1850), Scottish engineer, built lighthouses and devised their system of flashing lights.

Stevenson, Robert Louis (1850–94), Scottish novelist, wrote *Treasure Island* (1883), *Kidnapped* (1886); lived in Samoa 1889–1894.

Stevenson, Thomas (1818–87), Scottish engineer, devised screen for thermometers; father of Robert Louis Stevenson.

Stewart, Balfour (1828–87), Scottish physicist, director of Kew Observatory, and meteorologist, studied terrestrial magnetism.

Stewart, Dugald (1753–1828), Scottish philosopher, wrote *Philosophy of the Active and Moral Powers* (1828).

Stewart, Robert, Duke of Albany (c. 1340–1420), governor and regent of Scotland, dominated reign of Robert III.

Stiegel, Henry William (1729–85), German-born American glass manufacturer, founded and established factory at Mannheim, Pennsylvania.

Stieler, Adolf (1775–1836), German cartographer, produced widely used atlases.

Stifter, Adalbert (1805–68), Austrian novelist of everyday life, author of *Witiko* (1865–67).

Stigand (d. 1072), English prelate, archbishop of Canterbury 1052–66; deposed and imprisoned as usurper.

Stilicho, Flavius (d. A.D. 408), Roman general, effectively chief minister to Honorius; repelled Barbarians; executed.

Still, Andrew Taylor (1828–1917), American founder of osteopathy.

Stillingfleet, Edward (1635–99), English prelate, bishop of Worcester 1689–99, was a pugnacious Anglican controversialist.

Stirling, James (1692–1770), Scottish mathematician, also discovered Venetian technique of glass-making.

Stirling, James Hutchison (1820–1909), Scottish Idealist philosopher, introduced Hegel in Britain; attacked Huxley and Darwin.

Stirner, Max (1806–56), German philosopher, whose *Ego and his Own* advocates an almost solipsistic egoism.

Stockhausen, Karlheinz (b. 1928), German composer, an exponent of electronic music.

Stockmar, Christian Friedrich, Baron von (1787–1863), German-born adviser to Queen Victoria and Prince Albert.

Stockport Grammar School, English public school, founded by the lord mayor of London, Sir Edmund Shaa, 1487.

Stockton, Francis Richard (1834–1902), American writer, remembered for his short story *The Lady or the Tiger?* (1882).

Stockton and Darlington Railway, first to use steam-powered locomotive traction for freight and later for passengers; built and equipped by George Stephenson; opened 1825.

Stoicism, philosophical system, founded by Zeno of Citium 4th–3rd centuries B.C.

Stoker, Bram (1847–1912), Irish business manager of Sir Henry Irving (*q.v.*), wrote *Dracula* (1897).

Stokes, Sir George (1819–1903), Irish physicist, pioneer of spectrum analysis.

Stokes, Margaret M'Nair (1832–1900), Irish archaeologist, wrote *The High Crosses of Ireland*.

Stokes, William (1804–78), Irish physician, noted for his work on diseases of the heart and lungs.

Stokowski, Leopold (1887–1977), English-born American conductor of Philadelphia Symphony Orchestra 1912–36.

Stolberg, Friedrich, Graf (1750–1819), German poet, e.g. *Timoleon* (1784); often collaborated with brother Christian (1748–1821).

Stolypin, Piotr (1863–1911), Russian statesman, prime minister 1906–11, attempted some reforms; assassinated.

Stone, Lucy (1818–93), American agitator against slavery and for women's rights.

Stone, Nicolas (1586–1647), English sculptor and architect, best known for his tombs, including John Donne's.

Stone Age, Old. See **Palaeolithic.**

Stone Age, New. See **Neolithic.**

Stonehenge, Wiltshire, built at various periods between 1800 and 1400 B.C.

Stonyhurst College, English public school, founded originally at St Omers 1593; re-opened in England 1794.

Stopes, Marie (1880–1958), English pioneer of birth control.

Storm, Theodor (1817–88), German poet and novelist, e.g. *Der Schimmelreiter* (1888).

Storting, Norwegian parliament, founded 1814.

Stoss, Veit (*c.* 1438–1533), German sculptor in elaborate, dynamic Gothic style, worked at Cracow and Nuremberg.

Stothard, Thomas (1755–1834), English painter, e.g. *The Canterbury Pilgrims.*

Stow, John (*c.* 1525–1605), English antiquary, whose *Survey of London* (1598) documents the Elizabethan city.

Stowe, Harriet Beecher (1811–96), American novelist whose *Uncle Tom's Cabin* (1852) intensified anti-slavery sentiment.

Stowe Collection of Manuscripts, British Museum, London; collected by the English antiquary Thomas Astle (1735–1803).

Stowe School, English public school, founded 1923.

Strabo (*c.* 64 B.C.–*c.* A.D. 22), Greek geographer and traveller, wrote *Geography* describing the known world.

Strachan, John (1778–1867), Scottish bishop of Toronto 1839–67, struggled to secure Anglican control over university education.

Strachey, John St Loe (1860–1927), English journalist, editor of *The Spectator* 1896–1925.

Strachey, John St Loe (1901–63), English labour politician and writer, author of *Contemporary Capitalism* (1956); son of John St Loe Strachey.

Strachey, Lytton (1880–1932), English writer, member of the Bloomsbury Group, noted for his critical biography *Eminent Victorians* (1918).

Strodella, Alessandro (*c.* 1645–1681), Italian composer, notably of operas and oratorios; murdered.

Stradivari, Antonio (1644–1737), Italian violin-maker, whose superb craftsmanship brought him world-wide fame.

Strafford, Thomas Wentworth, Earl of (1593–1641), English administrator, effectively chief minister of Charles I; impeached and executed.

Straits Settlements, former British colony comprising Malacca, Penang and Singapore, formed 1867; dissolved 1946.

Strang, William (1859–1921), Scottish artist, noted as a portraitist and etcher.

Strange, Sir Robert (1721–92), Scottish engraver, often of Van Dyke's paintings.

Straparola, Giovanni (*c.* 1480–*c.* 1557), Italian short-story writer, author of *Piacevoli Notti.*

Strasbourg, France, imperial free city from *c.* 1486; ceded to France under the Treaty of Ryswyck 1697; ruled by Germany 1871–1918 and 1940–44.

Stratford, John de (d. 1348), English prelate, archbishop of Canterbury 1333–1348, chancellor and chief adviser to Edward III.

Strathallan School, Scottish public school, founded at Bridge of Allan by first headmaster, H. Riley, 1912; moved to present site 1920.

Straus, Oscar (1870–1954), Austrian musical-comedy composer, notably of *The Chocolate Soldier* (1908).

Strauss, Johann, the Elder (1804–49), Austrian composer, notably of Viennese waltzes.

Strauss, Johann, the Younger (1825–99), Austrian composer of light music, including the *Blue Danube* and the operetta *Die Fledermaus* (1874).

Strauss, Richard (1864–1949), German composer, best known for his orchestral work and operas, including *Der Rosenkavalier* (1911).

Stravinsky, Igor (1882–1971), Russian-born composer, in France and U.S.A., profoundly influenced the development of 20th-century music, notably with *Rite of Spring* (1913).

Street, George Edmund (1824–81), English Neo-Gothic architect, designed Royal Courts of Justice, London.

street lighting, in Britain, first oil 1681; gas *c.* 1812; electricity *c.* 1880.

Streicher, Julius (1885–1946), German Nazi journalist and politician, violently anti-Jewish; executed as a war criminal.

streptomycin, first isolated 1943 by the Russian-born American scientist Selman Abraham Waksman (1888–1973); first medical use 1945.

Stresemann, Gustav (1878–1929), German statesman, foreign minister 1923–29; Nobel Peace prizewinner 1926.

stretcher-bearers, introduced *c.* 1792 by Baron Pierre François Percy (1754–1825).

Stribling, Thomas Sigismund (1881–1965), American novelist, wrote *The Store* (1932).

Strickland, Agnes (1796–1874), English writer, author of *Lives of the Queens of England* (1840–48).

Strijdom, Johannes (1893–1958), South African statesman, prime minister 1954–1958; enforced apartheid.

strike, right to, legalized in Britain 1824.

Strindberg, August (1849–1912), Swedish playwright and novelist; profoundly influenced the development of modern drama, author of *The Father* (1887).

strip cartoons, originated by the German artist Wilhelm Busch (1832–1908).

Stroheim, Erich von (1885–1957), Austrian-born film director and actor, best remembered for *Greed* (1923).

Strongbow (nickname of Richard, Earl of Warwick; d. 1176), English nobleman, conquered much of Ireland.

strontium, first isolated 1808 by Sir Humphry Davy.

Strozzi, Bernardo (1581–1644), Italian painter, worked in Venice 1630–44.

Struensee, Johann Friedrich (1737–72), German-born chief minister of Denmark; overthrown and beheaded.

Strutt, Joseph (1742–1802), English antiquary, wrote studies of English costume and sports and pastimes.

Struve, Friedrich (1793–1864), German astronomer, investigated double stars.

strychnine, discovered 1818 by the French chemists Pierre Joseph Pelletier (1788–1842) and Joseph Bienaimé Caventou (1795–1877).

Stuart, Arabella (1575–1615), cousin of James I of England and next in succession to the throne; died insane in Tower of London.

Stuart, Charles Edward, the Young Pretender (1720–88), English prince, grandson of James II, leader of the 1745 Jacobite rebellion.

Stuart, James Edward, the Old Pretender (1688–1766), English prince, son of James II, made unsuccessful attempts to claim British throne.

Sturgeon, William (1783–1850), English physicist, constructed the first electromagnet.

Strype, John (1643–1737), English historian, wrote biographies and edited documents of the Tudor period.

Stuart, Frances, Duchess of Richmond and Lennox (1647–1702), English beauty, known as 'La Belle Stuart', was the original of Britannia on coinage.

Stuart, John, Earl of Bute. See **Bute,** Earl of.

Stuart, John McDouall (1815–66), Scottish explorer, first to reach centre of Australia, 1860.

Stubbs, George (1724–1806), English painter, above all of horses.

Stubbs, Henry (1632–76), English physician, classical scholar and mathematician, wrote *Oceana* (1660).

Stukeley, William (1687–1765), English antiquary, investigated Stonehenge.

Sturdee, Sir Doveton (1859–1925), English admiral, present at Battle of the Falkland Islands 1914 and of Jutland 1916.

Sture, Sten (*c.* 1440–1503), regent of Sweden, founder of Uppsala University.

Sturge, Joseph (1793–1859), English Quaker reformer, abolitionist, Chartist and pacifist.

Sturluson, Snorri. See **Snorri Sturluson.**

Sturt, Charles (1795–1869), English explorer of Australian interior.

Stuyvesant, Peter (1592–1682), Dutch governor of New Amsterdam (New York); surrendered to English 1664.

Stylites, Saint Simeon. See **Simeon Stylites,** Saint.

Suarez, Francisco (1548–1617), Spanish Jesuit theologian, follower of Saint Thomas Aquinas.

submarine, first navigable, invented 1620 by the Dutch scientist Cornelis Drebbel (1572–1633).

submarine, first nuclear-powered, the American *Nautilus,* launched 1954.

submarine telephone system, first long-distance, laid across Atlantic 1956.

submarine warfare, World War I, submarine blockade declared by Germany 4 Feb. 1915; unrestricted submarine warfare declared 1 Feb. 1917.

Suckling, Sir John (1609–42), English

Cavalier poet, wrote *Why so pale and wan, fond lover?*

Sucre, Antonio de (1793–1830), Venezuelan liberator of Bolivia and Colombia from Spain; assassinated.

Sudan, ruled by Egypt from 1820; Mahdist rebellion 1883–98; Anglo-Egyptian condominium 1899–1956; independent republic since 1956.

Sudermann, Hermann (1857–1928), German playwright, author of *Fritzchen* (1896).

Sue, Eugène (1804–57), French novelist, whose melodramatic works, e.g. *The Wandering Jew* (1844–45), enjoyed great popularity.

Suetonius (A.D. 70–160), Roman historian, wrote the colourful and scandalous *Lives of the Caesars.*

Suez Canal, constructed 1859–69 under the direction of Ferdinand de Lesseps (*q.v.*); opened Nov. 1869; nationalized by Egyptian government 1956; British and French invasion of Canal Zone Nov.–Dec. 1956; closed 1967 following Arab-Israeli War; cleared and reopened 1975.

sugar. See **glucose.**

Suger (*c.* 1081–1151), French abbot of St Denis, built first Gothic church; wrote life of Louis VI.

Suggia, Guilhermina (1888–1950), Portuguese cellist, achieved an international reputation.

suicides, in Britain, buried at crossroads transfixed by a stake until 1834.

Suidas (10th cent. A.D.), Greek lexicographer, worked at Constantinople.

Sui dynasty, China, reigned A.D. 581–618.

Sukarno, Ahmed (*c.* 1901–1970), Indonesian statesman, first president of independent Indonesia.

Sukkoth (Feast of Tabernacles), Jewish holiday, 15th day of Tishri.

Suleiman I, the Magnificent (*c.* 1494–1566), sultan of Turkey 1520–66, conqueror in Balkans, Asia and North Africa.

Suleiman II (1641–91), sultan of Turkey 1687–91, a period marked by reforms under the vizier Kuprili.

Sulla, Lucius Cornelius (138–78 B.C.), Roman soldier, headed conservative party against Marius (*q.v.*); as dictator 82–79 B.C. reorganized the state.

Sullivan, Sir Arthur (1842–1900), English composer of many light operas with W. S. Gilbert, e.g. *Patience* (1881).

Sullivan, Barry (1821–91), Irish actor, popular in provinces and Ireland, toured widely.

Sullivan, John (1740–95), American soldier, prominent in the Revolutionary War; later became a judge.

Sullivan, John Lawrence (1858–1918), American boxer, world heavyweight champion 1882–92.

Sullivan, Louis Henri (1856–1924), American architect, regarded as the founder of modernism in architecture.

Sully, Maximilien, Duc de (1560–1641), French statesman, adviser to Henry IV, improved economy and royal finances.

Sully-Prudhomme, René (1839–1907), French poet, wrote brief, reflective lyrics; Nobel prizewinner 1901.

sulphanilamide, first synthesized 1908 by the German scientist P. Gelmo.

sulphonamide drugs, first produced 1935 (Prontosil; *q.v.*) and 1938 (M & B).

sulphur, first classified as a chemical element 1777 by Antoine Lavoisier (*q.v.*); commercially produced from 1900 by the Frasch process developed by Herman Frasch (1851–1914).

sulphuric acid, most abundantly produced chemical, first prepared and described 1300; first commercially produced mid-18th century.

Sumatra, settled *c.* 1510 by Portuguese; taken over by Dutch from *c.* 1596; part of Indonesia from 1949.

summer, *c.* 21 June to *c.* 21 Sept. in the northern hemisphere.

summer time (daylight saving), in Britain, introduced May 1916; made permanent 1925.

Sumner, John Bird (1780–1862), English prelate, archbishop of Canterbury 1848–1862.

Sumter, Fort, South Carolina, bombardment 12–13 April 1861 began American Civil War.

Sun, distance from Earth, first reliably measured 1672 by the determination of the solar parallax (*q.v.*).

Sun, rotation of, first observed 1610 by Galileo.

Sunday Schools, pioneered in Gloucester 1780, chiefly by Robert Raikes (*q.v.*).

Sunday Times, British newspaper, founded 1822; issued first British colour supplement magazine 1962.

Sung dynasty, China, reigned 960–1279.

sunspots, first telescopically observed 1610–11, independently by Galileo, Johannes Fabricus, Thomas Harriot and Christoph Scheiner; cyclic variation (over about 11 years) first announced 1843 by Samuel Heinrich Schwabe (1789–1875).

Sun Yat-Sen (1866–1925), Chinese statesman, played a prominent part in the 1911 revolution.

superconductivity, discovered 1911 by the Dutch scientist Heike Kamerlingh Onnes (1853–1926).

superheterodyne receiver, radio receiver, designed *c.* 1917 by the American electrical engineer Edwin H. Armstrong (1890–1954).

supermarkets, first appeared in U.S.A. in 1930s and in Europe in 1950s.

supernovas, exploding stars, observed 1054 (Crab Nebula), 1572 (Tycho's Nova), 1604 (Kepler's Nova); studied from 1930s by astronomers including Fritz Zwicky (1898–1974), and Walter Baade (1893–1960).

Suppé, Franz von (1819–95), Austrian composer, wrote overture *Poet and Peasant*.

Supply, Ministry of, Britain, existed 1939–1959.

Supremacy, Acts of, making monarch instead of pope the head of the English Church, passed in reign of Henry VIII, 1534, and of Queen Elizabeth, 1559.

surgeon, first British woman (Miss Eleanor Davies-Colley), admitted to the Royal College of Surgeons 1911.

Surgeons, Company of, London, founded 1746.

surgical instruments, steam sterilization of introduced 1886 by the German surgeon Ernst von Bergmann (1836–1907).

Surinam, South America, first settled by English 1630; ceded to Netherlands 1667; became independent 1975.

Surrey, Henry Howard, Earl of (c. 1517–1547), English poet, first to use blank verse; with Sir Thomas Wyatt (*q.v.*) introduced sonnet; executed for treason.

Surtees, Robert Smith (1803–64), English writer, notably of such hunting stories as *Jorrocks's Jaunts and Jollities* (1838).

Suso, Heinrich (c. 1295–1366), German Dominican mystic and ascetic, wrote popular *Büchlein der Ewigen Weisheit*.

Sussex, Thomas Radclyffe, Earl of (c. 1526–1583), English lord deputy of Ireland 1556–64, established his authority over much of the country.

Sutherland, Graham (b. 1903), English painter, noted for his landscapes, religious pictures and portraits.

Sutherland, Joan (b. 1926), Australian operatic soprano, well known for her roles in Italian opera.

Suttee (Sati), compulsory or voluntary sacrifice of Hindu widows, made illegal in India 1829.

Sutter, John Augustus (1803–80), German-born pioneer in California, founded Sacramento.

Sutton, Thomas (1532–1611), English mine owner, founder of Charterhouse School 1611.

Sutton Hoo, Suffolk, Anglo-Saxon ship-burial treasure discovered 1939.

Sutton Valence School, Kent, English public school, founded 1576 by the English merchant William Lambe (1495–1580).

Suvorov, Alexander (1729–1800), Russian soldier, commanded army against Turks 1787–92 and in Italy against French 1799.

Svalbard Archipelago, Arctic, Norwegian sovereignty recognized 1920; officially incorporated in Norway 1925.

Svendsen, Johan (1840–1911), Norwegian composer and violinist, e.g. *Norwegian Rhapsodies*.

Sverdrup, Otto (1855–1930), Norwegian explorer, made several Arctic expeditions.

Sverre (d. 1202), king of Norway 1177–1202, rose from obscurity to build a strong monarchy.

Svevo, Italo (pseud. of Ettore Schmitz; 1864–1928), Italian novelist, wrote *Confessions of Zeno* (1923).

Swabian Leagues, first, formed 1331; second, formed 1376; third ('The Great'), formed by the emperor Frederick III 1488; disintegrated 1534.

Swammerdam, Jan (1637–80), Dutch biologist, first man to describe red corpuscles and values of lymph glands.

Swan, Sir Joseph (1828–1914), English pioneer in electric lighting and photographic printing.

Swan of Lichfield, The. See **Seward,** Anna.

Swarthmore College, Pennsylvania, founded by the Society of Friends 1864.

Swarthout, Gladys (1904–69), American mezzo-soprano opera singer, performed at Chicago and New York Metropolitan opera houses.

Swaziland, protected by the South African Republic 1894–99; administered by the governor of the Transvaal 1903–07; administered by a British high commissioner 1907–68; achieved independence as a kingdom within the Commonwealth 1967.

Sweden, Christian since c. 1000; united with Denmark and Norway 1397; ruled by house of Vasa 1521–1810; ruled by Bernadotte dynasty since 1810 (also ruled Norway 1814–1905).

Swedenborg, Emanuel (1688–1722), Swedish scientist, philosopher, theologian and mystic.

Swedenborgian Church, or New Church, based on writings of Emanuel Swedenborg, organized in London 1788 by Robert Hindmarsh (1759–1835).

Swedish Nightingale, The. See **Lind,** Jenny.

Sweelinck, Jan (1562–1621), Dutch organist and composer, influenced Bach.

Sweet, Henry (1845–1912), English philologist and pioneer of phonetics, model for Henry Higgins in Shaw's *Pygmalion*.

Swete, Henry Barclay (1835–1917), English theologian, was a notable Biblical scholar.

Sweyn I (d. 1014), king of Denmark c. 914–1014, led frequent raids on England.

Sweyn II (d. 1075), king of Denmark 1047–1075, founder of the Estrith dynasty.

Swift, Jonathan (1667–1745), Irish writer and master of satire, dean of St Patrick's, Dublin, author of *Gulliver's Travels* (1726).

Swinburne, Algernon (1837–1909), English poet of great musical and technical skill, e.g. *Atalanta in Calydon* (1865).

Swinton, Sir Ernest (1868–1951), British soldier, one of the originators of the tank.

Swithin, Saint (d. 862), Anglo-Saxon bishop of Winchester *c.* 852–862; wrongly associated with rain-forecasting.

Swithin's Day, Saint. See **Saint Swithin's Day.**

Switzerland, identifiable as separate area from 1291; effectively independent 15th century; French-controlled Helvetic Republic set up 1798; present area and neutrality established 1815; federation formed 1848.

Sydenham, Thomas (1624–89), English physician, the 'English Hippocrates', pioneered clinical observation.

Sydney, New South Wales, founded 1788.

Sydney Harbour Bridge, officially opened 19 March 1932.

Sylva, Carmen. See **Carmen Sylva.**

Sylvester, Pope(s). See **Silvester.**

Sylvester, James (1814–97), English mathematician, noted for his work on the theory of numbers.

Sylvester, Joshua (1563–1618), English translator of Guillaume du Bartas and other French writers.

Sylvestrines, monastic order founded 1231 by Saint Sylvester (d. 1267).

Symbolism, artistic and literary movement originating in France in the 1880s.

Symington, William (1763–1831), Scottish steam engineer, developed first practical steamboat.

Symmachus, Saint (d. 514), Pope 498–514, drove Manichaeans from Rome.

Symonds, John Addington (1840–93), English historian of the Italian Renaissance.

Symons, George James (1838–1900), English meteorologist, collected rainfall data and investigated the Krakatoa eruption.

synchrocyclotron, particle accelerator, design suggested 1945 by the American physicist Edwin M. McMillan (b. 1907) and, independently, by the Soviet physicist Vladimir Veksler (1907–66).

synchrotron. See **proton synchrotron.**

Syndicalism, founded in France at end of the 19th century; first international conference, London 1913; British version called Guild Socialism (*q.v.*).

Synge, John Millington (1871–1909), Irish playwright, prominent in his country's literary revival, author of *Playboy of the Western World* (1907).

Synod of the Clergy, first held in England at Hertford 673.

syphilis, bacillus discovered 1905 by the German scientists Fritz Schaudinn (1871–1906) and Erich Hoffmann; treatment with salvarsan (*q.v.*) introduced 1909.

Syracuse University, New York State, founded 1870.

Syria, formed part of Egyptian, Persian and Roman Empires; conquered by Arabs 7th century A.D.; ruled by Ottoman Turks 1516–1917; largely French-controlled 1923–46; achieved complete independence as a republic 1946; linked with Egypt in United Arab Republic 1958–61.

Széchenyi, Count István (1791–1860), Hungarian soldier, distinguished in Napoleonic Wars; worked to improve Danube navigation.

Szymanowski, Karol (1883–1937), Polish composer, wrote opera *King Roger* (1926).

T

Tabari, Abu Ja'far (*c.* 839–*c.* 923), Arab historian, wrote a universal history, the *Annals*.

Tabernacles, Feast of. See **Sukkoth.**

table turning, in spiritualist seances, began in U.S.A. 1948; reached Europe 1852.

Tabriz, capital of East Azerbaijan province, Iran, reputed to have been founded by Zobeidah, wife of Harun-al-Rashid, in the 8th century.

Tacca, Pietro (1577–1640), Italian sculptor to the grand dukes of Tuscany.

Tacitus, Publius Cornelius (*c.* A.D. 55–*c.* 116), Roman historian, renowned for his terse, condensed style; author of the *Annals*.

Tacitus, Marcus Claudius (d. A.D. 276), Roman emperor 275–276, made reforms; killed in army mutiny.

Tacoma Narrows, suspension bridge, Washington, collapsed after construction 1940; rebuilt 1950.

Taddeo di Bartolo (*c.* 1362–*c.* 1422), Italian painter of the Sienese school.

Tadema, Alma-. See **Alma-Tadema.**

Tadzhikistan, Soviet Socialist Republic, admitted to the U.S.S.R. 1929.

taffeta, type of woven silk, in earliest form introduced into England *c.* 14th century.

Taft, William Howard (1857–1930), American statesman, 27th president of the United States 1909–13; chief justice of the Supreme Court 1921–30.

Taganrog, port, Sea of Azov, founded 1769 on the site of a fortress erected by Peter the Great, 1698.

Taglioni, Marie (1804–84), Italian ballerina, created leading role in *La Sylphide* (1832).

Tagore, Rabindranath (1861–1941), Indian poet, philosopher and mystic, awarded Nobel Prize for Literature 1913.

Tahirites, or Tahirids, ruling dynasty in Khorassan, Persia, 813–872.

Tahiti, largest of Society Islands, French

Polynesia, discovered 1767 by the English naval captain Samuel Wallis (1728–95); made a French colony 1880.

Taillefer (d. 1066), Norman bard, said to have struck first blow at Battle of Hastings.

Taine, Hippolyte (1828–93), French historian, wrote *Origins of Contemporary France* (1876–94).

T'ai-P'ing Rebellion, China, lasted from 1851 to 1865.

Tait, Archibald (1811–82), Scottish prelate, archbishop of Canterbury 1869–82.

T'ai Tsung (597–649), emperor of China 627–649; his reign marked the zenith of the T'ang dynasty.

Taiwan, visited by Portuguese 1590; settled by Dutch early 17th century; Dutch expelled by Chinese 1661; ceded by China to Japan 1895; returned to China 1945; seat of Chinese Nationalist government since 1949; lost seat at United Nations 1971.

Taj Mahal, Agra, India, mausoleum built 1632–43 by the emperor Shah Jahan (*q.v.*) for his favourite wife Mumtaz Mahal; complex completed 1654.

Takahashi, Korekiyo (1854–1936), Japanese financier and statesman, prime minister 1921–22; assassinated.

Talana Hill, near Dundee, Natal, scene of early Boer War battle 20 Oct. 1899.

Talavera, Battle of, Peninsular War, victory of British over French 27–28 July 1809.

Talbot, William Henry Fox (1800–77), English photographic pioneer, produced 'calotype', first practical negative process.

Taliesin (6th cent.), Welsh poet, possibly legendary; credited with writing *Book of Taliesin*.

talkies, sound films, first shown in commercial cinemas 1928.

tallage, special tax on English towns, first levied by Henry I; ceased with 1332 levy; formally abolished 1340.

Tallahasee, capital of Florida, reputedly founded by Spanish in 17th century.

Talleyrand, Charles de (1754–1838), French statesman and diplomat, foreign minister 1797–1807 and 1814–15.

Tallien, Jean Lambert (1769–1820), French Revolutionary leader, overthrew Robespierre.

Tallinn, Estonia, U.S.S.R., effectively founded by Waldemar II of Denmark 1219; capital of independent Estonia 1919–40.

Tallis, Thomas (*c.* 1505–1585), English composer and organist at the Chapel Royal; wrote much church music.

Talmud, collection of Rabbinical exegesis and commentary, completed 4th–5th century; first complete edition published 1520–23 in Venice by Dutch printer Daniel Bomberg (d. 1549).

Tamar Bridge, rail bridge connecting Devon and Cornwall completed 1859, built by Isambard Brunel; road bridge completed 1961.

Tamerlaine (*c.* 1336–1405), Tatar warrior, whose armies conquered Persia and Central Asia, and severely defeated the Russians and Turks.

Tamil Nadu, Indian state, invaded by Muslims in 14th century; visited by Portuguese 1498; first British settlement 1611; larger part brought under British rule 1801; part of independent India since 1947; name changed from Madras to Tamil Nadu 1968.

Tammany Hall, New York political organization of Democratic Party, founded 1789; centre of great scandals in 1870s.

Tancred (*c.* 1078–1112), Norman soldier, joined 1st Crusade; ruler of Palestine.

Taney, Roger Brooke (1777–1864), American jurist, as chief justice defended states' rights against the federal government.

Tanganyika, German colony 1884–1914; conquered by British 1914–16; British League of Nations mandate 1920–46; United Nations trusteeship 1946–62; independent member of the Commonwealth 1962; united with Zanzibar 1964 to form Tanzania (*q.v.*).

Tanganyika, Lake, discovered 1858 by Sir Richard Burton (*q.v.*) and John Hanning Speke (*q.v.*).

T'ang dynasty, China, reigned 618–906.

Tangier, Morocco, ruled by Portugal 1471–1662, by England 1662–84, by Morocco 1684–1904; international zone 1923; integrated with Morocco 1956.

tank, first practical one tested in Britain Sept. 1915; first used by the British army on the Somme 15 Sept. 1916.

Tank Corps, British army, formation authorized 28 July 1917.

Tannenberg, Battle of, victory of Poles over Teutonic Knights 1410; of Germans over Russians 26–31 Aug. 1914.

Tanner, Thomas (1674–1735), English antiquary, bishop of St Asaph 1732–35, wrote *Notitia Monastica*.

Tannhäuser, (13th cent.), German poet and minnesinger, subject of many legends.

tantalum, metallic element, discovered 1802 by the Swedish chemist Anders Gustaf Ekeberg (1767–1813).

Tanzania, republic created 1964 by union of Tanganyika and Zanzibar (*qq.v.*).

Taoism, Chinese religion, reputedly founded by the sage Lao-tzu *c.* 6th century B.C.

tape recording. See magnetic recording.

Tarbela Dam, on the Indus River, Pakistan, completed 1975.

Tardieu, André (1876–1945), French statesman, prime minister 1929–30 and 1932.

Tariq ibn-Ziyad (d. *c.* 720), Berber chieftain, led the first Muslim invasion of Spain, 711.

Tarkington, Booth (1869–1946), American novelist, wrote *The Magnificent Ambersons* (1918).

Tarleton, Sir Banastre (1754–1833), English soldier in the American Revolutionary War; conducted several successful operations.

Tarlton, Richard (d. 1588), English actor and royal jester; perhaps 'Yorick' of Shakespeare's *Hamlet*.

Tarquin (Lucius Tarquinius Priscus; 7th–6th cent. B.C.), semi-legendary king of Rome *c.* 616–*c.* 578 B.C., successful in war against the Latins and Sabines.

Tarquin (Lucius Tarquinius Superbus; 6th cent. B.C.), semi-legendary last king of Rome *c.* 534–*c.* 510 B.C.; exiled despite help of Lars Porsena.

tartaric acid, isolated 1769 by Carl Wilhelm Scheele (*q.v.*).

Tartini, Giuseppe (1692–1770), Italian violinist and composer, teacher of Paganini.

Tasman, Abel Janszoon (1603–*c.* 1659), Dutch navigator, discovered Tasmania, New Zealand and the Fiji Islands.

Tasmania, discovered 1642 by Abel Tasman; first British settlement 1804; made a colony 1825; named Tasmania and given responsible government 1856; became a state of the Commonwealth of Australia 1901.

Tasso, Torquato (1544–95), Italian poet, wrote epic *Jerusalem Delivered* (1575).

Tata, Jamsetji Nasarwanji (1839–1904), Indian industrialist, founded great iron and steel company.

Tate, Sir Henry (1819–99), English sugar refiner, made a great fortune used in philanthropic works.

Tate, Nahum (1652–1715), Irish-born poet laureate 1692–1715, wrote second part to Dryden's *Absalom and Achitophel*.

Tate Gallery, London, founded by Sir Henry Tate (*q.v.*); opened 1897.

Tatham, Charles Heathcote (1772–1842), English architect, designed decorations for Drury Lane Theatre, London.

Tatler, English periodical edited by Sir Richard Steele (*q.v.*) 1709–11.

Tattersall's, London horse auction and sporting centre, founded by the English horse-auctioneer Richard Tattersall (1724–95).

Tauber, Richard (1892–1948), Austrian opera and musical comedy tenor, created several roles in works by Franz Lehár.

Tauchnitz, Karl (1761–1836), German publisher of the classics at Leipzig; his nephew Christian Tauchnitz (1816–95) set up his own firm, and published English and American authors.

Taeuber-Arp, Sophie (1889–1943), Swiss painter, wife of Hans Arp, pioneer of abstract work.

Tauler, Johann (*c.* 1300–1361), German Dominican monk, well known as a mystic and preacher.

Taunton School, English public school, founded 1847.

Taussig, Frank (1859–1940), American economist, wrote *Tariff History of the United States* (1888).

Taverner, Jean Baptiste (1605–89), French traveller in Asia, reached the East Indies.

Taverner, John (*c.* 1495–1545), English composer, almost exclusively of church music.

Tawney, Richard (1880–1962), English economic historian, author of *Religion and the Rise of Capitalism* (1926).

taxi-cabs, first official recognition of their existence in draft of proposed cab regulations for London issued by Home Secretary 1907.

Tay Bridge, Dundee, rail bridge built 1878, collapsed 1879, rebuilt 1887; road bridge built 1966.

Taylor, Alfred Swaine (1806–80), English medical jurist, wrote standard text, 1865.

Taylor, Jeremy (1613–67), English theologian, notable prose stylist in *Holy Living* (1650), etc.

Taylor, John (1580–1653), English writer, 'the Water Poet', was a Thames waterman.

Taylor, Zachary (1784–1850), American statesman, 12th president of the United States 1849–50, had a distinguished military career in the Mexican War 1845–47.

Tchaikovsky, Peter Ilych (1840–93), major Russian composer, strongly romantic in tone, noted for his concertos, and symphonic and ballet music.

tea, drink traditionally invented 2737 B.C. by the Chinese emperor Shen Nung; reached Holland 1610; first public sale in Britain 1657; Indian tea reached Britain 1839.

Teach, Edward (d. 1718), English pirate, known as 'Blackbeard', operated off the coast of Carolina and Virginia.

Teasdale, Sarah (1884–1935), American poet, wrote *Love Songs* (1917).

technetium, first artificially produced element, discovered 1937 by Emilio Segrè and the Italian mineralogist C. Perrier.

Tecumseh (*c.* 1768–1813), American Indian, Shawnee chief, fought on British side in 1812 war; killed in battle.

Tedder, Arthur, Baron (1890–1967), British air force commander in North Africa and Mediterranean 1940–43; Allied deputy supreme commander 1943–45.

Te Deum, Latin hymn, probably composed in the 5th century.

Tegner, Esaias (1782–1846), Swedish poet, author of *Frithiof's Saga* (1825).

Teheran Conference, World War II, between Roosevelt, Churchill and Stalin from 28 Nov. to 1 Dec. 1943.

Teilhard de Chardin, Pierre (1881–1955), French palaeontologist, Jesuit and philosopher, author of *The Phenomenon of Man* (1959).

Teisserenc de Bort, Léon (1855–1913), French meteorologist, discoverer of the stratosphere.

Teixeira, Pedro (d. 1640), Portuguese explorer in Brazil, ascended the Amazon to the Andes.

Tel-Aviv, Israel, founded 1909; capital 1948–50.

telegraph, deflecting needle type, first practical system patented and publicly demonstrated 1837 by Sir Charles Wheatstone (*q.v.*) and Sir William Fothergill Cooke (1806–79); used on railways by 1839; monopoly granted to Post Office 1869.

telegraph, electric, invented 1832, patented 1837, by Samuel Morse (*q.v.*); first public demonstration 1844, using Morse Code and a telegraph line from Baltimore to Washington.

telegraph, optical, invented *c.* 1791 by the Frenchmen Claude Chappe (1763–1805) and his brother.

telegraph cable, first laid across English Channel 1850; first laid across Atlantic 1857.

Telemann, Georg Philipp (1681–1767), German composer, stylistically between Bach and Haydn, worked at Leipzig and Hamburg.

telepathy, first so-named 1882 by the English writer F. W. H. Myers (1843–1901).

telephone, crude design made 1861 by a German schoolteacher Philipp Reis; practical one patented 1876 by Alexander Graham Bell (*q.v.*).

telephone cable, first multi-channel, laid across the Atlantic 1956.

telephone exchange, world's first automatic, at La Porte, Indiana, 1892; first automatic exchange in Britain, Epsom, 1912.

telephone exchange, world's first all-electronic opened in London 1962. See also **STD.**

telephone kiosks, in Britain, first erected 1908; standardized design introduced 1921 by the G.P.O.

telephone speaking clock, TIM, in Britain, introduced by the G.P.O. 1936.

telephone system, British, taken over by G.P.O. 1913.

telephone weather forecasting service, began in Britain 1956.

telescope, invented 1608 traditionally by Hans Lippershey (*q.v.*) using lenses (refracting telescope); first astronomical studies 1609 by Galileo (*q.v.*). See also **radio telescopes; reflecting telescope.**

telescopes, largest optical: reflecting, 600 cm, at the Soviet Academy of Sciences Astrophysical Observatory, Caucasus, in operation since 1976; refracting, 40 inch (102 cm), at Yerkes Observatory, Wisconsin, in operation since 1897.

television, first demonstrated 1926 by the Scottish inventor John Logie Baird (*q.v.*).

television, colour, first regular commercial transmissions began in New York 1951; first British colour television service inaugurated 1967.

television, commercial, began in Britain 1955.

television broadcast, first experimental 1929; first B.B.C. experimental programme transmissions 1932; world's first regular service of high-definition television launched by B.B.C. 1936.

television via satellite, first, Telstar relays, 1962.

Telford, Thomas (1757–1834), Scottish engineer, constructed many roads, canals and bridges, including the Menai suspension bridge.

Tell, William (13th cent.), Swiss patriot, said to have defied Austrian overlords.

Teller, Edward (b. 1908), Hungarian-born American physicist, prominent in the development of the hydrogen bomb.

Tellier, Charles (1828–1913), French inventor of the refrigerator, 1867.

tellurium, chemical element, discovered 1782 by the Austrian mineralogist Franz Joseph Müller von Reichenstein (1740–1825).

Telstar. See **satellite,** communications.

Tempest, Marie (1864–1942), English musical comedy star, later an internationally known comedienne.

Templars, Knights (Order of the Poor Soldiers of Christ of the Temple), founded *c.* 1119; abolished 1314.

Temple, Jerusalem, destroyed by Nebuchadnezzar 586 B.C.; rebuilt 516 B.C.; destroyed by the emperor Titus A.D. 70.

Temple, Sir William (1628–99), English diplomat, architect of the Triple Alliance 1668; also an essayist.

Temple Bar, Fleet Street, London, built 1672 by Sir Christopher Wren; re-erected at Theobalds Park, Herts 1878.

Teniers, David, the Elder (1582–1649), Flemish painter, pupil of Rubens.

Teniers, David, the Younger (1610–90), Flemish painter of peasant and tavern scenes.

Tenison, Thomas (1636–1715), English prelate, archbishop of Canterbury 1694–1715, established first London public library.

Tennant, Smithson (1761–1815), English chemist, discovered iridium 1804.

Tennessee, U.S.A.; first settled 1757; admitted to the Union 1796; seceded 1861; readmitted 1866.

Tennessee University, U.S.A.; founded at Knoxville 1794.

Tennessee Valley Authority, U.S.A., established 1933.

Tenniel, Sir John (1820–1914), English artist, *Punch* cartoonist and illustrator of *Alice's Adventures in Wonderland*.

tennis, lawn, origins in real tennis (*q.v.*); modern form introduced as 'sphairistike' by Major Walter Wingfield 1874; Lawn Tennis Association formed 1888.

tennis, real, played in France in 11th century; known in England from 14th century.

Tennis Court Oath, French Revolution, 20 June 1789.

Tennyson, Alfred, 1st Baron (1809–92), English poet, poet laureate 1850–92 and a master of technique, enjoyed great popularity in Victorian England; author of *In Memoriam* (1850).

Tenzing, Norgay (b. 1914), Nepalese mountaineer, was, with Sir Edmund Hillary, the first to climb Mount Everest.

terbium, metallic element, discovered 1843 by the Swedish chemist Karl Gustav Mosander (1797–1858).

Ter Borch, Gerard (1617–81), Dutch painter of distinctive domestic scenes, e.g. *The Singing Lesson*.

Terbrugghen, Hendrick (1588–1629), Dutch painter, whose work shows the influence of Caravaggio.

Terence (*c.* 185–*c.* 159 B.C.), Roman playwright, best known as a writer of comedy.

Teresa of Ávila, Saint (1515–82), Spanish mystic, wrote autobiography; was a noted reformer of the Carmelite order.

Terman, Lewis (1877–1956), American psychologist, noted for his work on intelligence tests.

Terpander (7th cent. B.C.), Greek poet and musician, called the father of Greek music.

Territorial Army, Britain, established 1907; disbanded 1967 and replaced by Territorial and Army Volunteer Reserve.

Terry, Ellen (1847–1928), English actress, for many years partnered Sir Henry Irving (*q.v.*) at the Lyceum Theatre.

Terry, Sir Richard (1865–1938), English composer of church music.

Tertiary Period, Earth history, from *c.* 65 to *c.* 2·5 million years ago.

Tertis, Lionel (1876–1975), English virtuoso on the viola, which he made an acceptable solo instrument.

Tertullian (*c.* A.D. 160–*c.* 230), Carthaginian Christian writer, one of the fathers of the church despite his Montanist views.

Teschen, Peace of, averting war between Austria and Prussia, signed 13 May 1779.

Tesla, Nikola (1857–1943), Croatian-born American inventor of electrical devices.

Test Act, British measure designed to prevent Catholics and Dissenters from holding office, passed 1673; repealed 1828–29.

testicles, human, structure described 1668 by the Dutch anatomist Regnier de Graaf (1641–73).

Tetrazzini, Luisa (1871–1940), Italian operatic soprano, appeared mainly in U.S.A. and Italy.

Tetzel, Johann (*c.* 1465–1519), German Dominican monk whose methods of selling indulgences provoked Martin Luther.

Teutoburg Forest, Battle of the, victory of Germanic tribes over the Romans A.D. 9.

Teutonic Order, Knights of the, German religious order founded ·*c.* 1190; suppressed by Napoleon 1809.

Tewfik Pasha (1852–92), khedive of Egypt 1879–92, effectively subordinate to the British.

Texas, U.S.A., discovered by Spanish early 16th century; French settlement late 17th century; under effective Spanish control until 1821; ruled by Mexico 1821–1836; proclaimed independent republic 1836; admitted to Union 1845; seceded 1861; readmitted 1870.

Texas Rangers, first formed 1820s; reformed 1840; merged with state highway patrol 1935.

Texas University, Austin, founded 1881.

Textile Institute, Manchester, founded 1910.

Teyte, Dame Maggie (1888–1976), English opera singer, worked much in France.

Thackeray, William Makepeace (1811–1863), major English novelist, author of *Vanity Fair* and *Henry Esmond*.

Thailand, separate kingdom formed 1350; remained absolute monarchy until 1932; constitutional monarchy 1932–51; new constitution 1959; permanent constitution promulgated 1968; abolished 1971.

Thales, (*c.* 636–546 B.C.), Greek philosopher, held that water was basic element; also a geometer and astronomer.

thalidomide, drug causing foetal malformations, prescribed as a sedative from *c.* 1959 to 1962 in Britain, West Germany and elsewhere.

thallium, metallic element discovered spectroscopically 1861 by Sir William Crookes (*q.v.*); isolated 1862, independently, by Crookes and Claude-Auguste Lamy.

Thames, first steamboat service 1905.

Thames Conservancy, founded as the Conservators of the River Thames, 1857.

Thames Rowing Club, founded as the City of London Rowing Club 1860; assumed present name 1862.

Thames Tunnel, constructed 1825–43 by Sir Marc Isambard Brunel (*q.v.*).

Thanksgiving Day, U.S.A., originated in celebration of 1621 harvest; first national Thanksgiving Day 26 Nov. 1789; now 4th Thursday in November.

Thant, U (1909–74), Burmese diplomat, secretary-general of the United Nations 1961–71.

theatre, first permanent English, opened in London 1576.

theatre footlights, first known reference to in Britain 1672.

theatre lighting, first gas 1817 (Drury Lane, London); first electric 1846 (Paris Opera); first for entire theatre 1881 (Savoy, London).

theatres, English, closed by Puritans 1642; reopened 1660.

Thelwall, John (1764–1834), English radical reformer, associate of Horne Tooke (*q.v.*).

Themistocles (*c.* 523–*c.* 458 B.C.), Athenian statesman and general, architect of naval victory over Persia at Salamis.

Theobald (d. 1161), Norman prelate, archbishop of Canterbury 1138–61, resolute defender of ecclesiastical rights.

Theocritus (*c.* 310–*c.* 250 B.C.), Greek poet, lived at Alexandria, created pastoral mode of poetry.

Theodora (*c.* 508–548), Byzantine empress, a former courtesan who married Justinian (*q.v.*); politically influential.

Theodore I (d. 649), Pope 642–649, condemned Monothelites.

Theodore I, Lascaris (d. 1222), first Nicaean emperor 1208–22, founded new empire after fall of Constantinople.

Theodore of Mopsuestia (*c.* 350–*c.* 428), Syrian theologian, teacher of Nestorius (*q.v.*); writings condemned by Justinian.

Theodore of Tarsus (602–690), Syrian monk, archbishop of Canterbury 668–690; established Church supremacy in England.

Theodoret (*c.* 393–*c.* 458), Syrian theologian, defended Nestorius (*q.v.*).

Theodoric the Great (*c.* 454–526), king of the Ostrogoths 474–526, conquered Italy 489.

Theodosius I (*c.* 346–395), Roman emperor 379–395, ruling mainly in the East.

Theodosius II (401–450), Byzantine emperor 408–450, maintained integrity of empire; published Theodosian code.

Theognis (mid-6th cent. B.C.), Greek poet of Megara, wrote elegies.

Theophrastus (*c.* 372–*c.* 286 B.C.), Greek philosopher, wrote *Characters*, illustrating moral types.

Theosophical Society, founded in the U.S.A. by Helena Blavatsky (*q.v.*); led in Britain by Annie Besant (*q.v.*).

Thérèse of Lisieux, Saint (1873–97), French Carmelite nun, known as the 'little flower of Jesus'.

Thermidor, French Revolutionary calendar month, 19th or 20th July to 17th or 18th August.

thermionic emission, first observed 1883 by Thomas Alva Edison.

thermionic valve, diode developed 1904 by Sir John Fleming; triode 1906 by Lee de Forest; tetrode 1915 by Walter Hans Schottky.

thermionics, study developed by the English physicist Sir Owen Williams Richardson (1879–1959).

thermochemistry, study developed from 1840 by the Swiss-born Russian chemist Germain Henri Hess (1802–50).

thermocouples, developed since 1821 following the discovery of the Seebeck effect.

thermodynamics, founded in 1820s by Nicolas Sadi Carnot (1796–1832); first two laws published 1850 by Rudolf Julius Clausius (1822–88); third law 1906 by Walther Nernst (*q.v.*).

Thermopylae, Battle of, between the Spartans and the Persians 480 B.C.

thermos flask. See vacuum flask.

Thibaut IV (1201–53), king of Navarre 1234–53, was a noted troubadour.

Thicknesse, Philip (1719–92), English adventurer in America, governor of Landguard Fort 1766.

Thierry, Augustin (1795–1856), French historian, wrote *Norman Conquest of England* (1825).

Thiers, Adolphe (1799–1877), French statesman and historian, prime minister under the July monarchy; crushed Commune of 1871; president of Third Republic 1871–73.

Thimonnier, Barthélemy (1793–1859), French tailor, invented a form of sewing machine, 1830.

Third Republic, France 1871–1940.

Thirty-nine Articles, of the Church of England, agreed by Convocation 1563; enforced by Parliament 1571; revised 1604.

Thirty Years' War, religious wars in Germany 1618–48.

Thistle, Order of the, founded by James III of Scotland *c.* 1480; revived in 1687 and 1703.

Thistlewood, Arthur (1770–1820), English radical, planned to assassinate cabinet ministers; betrayed and executed.

Thomas, Ambroise (1811–96), French composer, wrote *Hamlet* (1868) and other operas.

Thomas, Brandon (1857–1914), English actor and dramatist, author of *Charley's Aunt* (1892).

Thomas, Dylan (1914–50), Welsh poet, of bardic verbal exuberance, also writer for radio (*Under Milk Wood*).

Thomas, Philip Edward (1878–1917), English poet, noted for his verse about nature and the countryside.

Thomas Aquinas, Saint (c. 1225–74), Italian philosopher whose *Summa Theologiae* became received philosophy of the medieval Church.

Thomas (à) Becket. See **Becket,** Thomas.

Thomas à Kempis (1380–1471), Dutch Augustinian monk, wrote *The Imitation of Christ*.

Thomas Cook's. See **Cook,** Thomas.

Thomas of Erceldoune (13th cent.), Scottish seer, said to have foretold various events.

Thomason, George (d. 1666), English bookseller, collector of contemporary pamphlets.

Thompson, Benjamin, Count Rumford (1753–1814), American-born inventor, founded Royal Institution, London.

Thompson, David (1770–1857), English trader-explorer and map-maker in Canada; negotiated U.S.–Canadian boundary.

Thompson, Edward (1860–1935), American archaeologist, noted for his excavations of the Maya civilization.

Thompson, Francis (1859–1907), English poet, wrote *The Hound of Heaven* (1893).

Thompson, John Taliaferro (1860–1940), American inventor of the Thompson submachine gun, 1920.

Thomson, Elihu (1853–1937), English-born American co-founder of General Electric; prolific inventor of electrical equipment.

Thomson, James (1700–48), Scottish poet, wrote *The Seasons* (1726–30), foreshadowing romantic treatment of nature.

Thomson, John Turnbull (1821–84), Scottish pioneer surveyor in New Zealand.

Thomson, Sir Joseph John (1856–1940), English physicist, discovered electrons, awarded Nobel Prize for Physics 1906.

Thomson, Robert William (1822–73), Scottish engineer and inventor of pneumatic tyres 1845.

Thomson, Roy, 1st Baron (1894–1970), Canadian newspaper proprietor, controlled one of the world's largest publishing concerns.

Thomson, Virgil (b. 1896), American composer, wrote *Four Saints in Three Acts* (1934).

Thoreau, Henry David (1817–62), American poet and philosopher, author of *Walden* (1854), classic of 'natural' living.

Thoresby, John (d. 1373), English prelate, archbishop of York 1351–73, was a trusted royal administrator and diplomat.

Thoresby, Ralph (1658–1725), English antiquary, wrote *Ducatus Leodiensis* (1715).

thorium, radioactive element discovered 1828 by Baron Berzelius (*q.v.*).

Thorndike, Dame Sybil (1882–1976), English actress, had a long and distinguished career; created Shaw's *St Joan* (1924).

Thornton, William (1759–1828), American architect, helped to design National Capitol, Washington, D.C.

Thorvaldsen, Bertel (1770–1844), Danish sculptor, noted for his frigid neoclassical style.

Thou, Jacques Auguste de (1553–1617), French historian, royal political adviser, wrote in Latin *History of His Own Time*.

Thrale, Hester Lynch (1741–1821), English friend of Dr Johnson, of whom she wrote *Anecdotes* (1786).

Thrasybulus (d. c. 388 B.C.), Athenian restored democratic system of government 403 B.C.; fought Spartans.

Three Choirs Festival, annual West Country music festival, founded 1724.

threshing machine, first practical design patented 1788 by the Scottish millwright Andrew Meikle (1719–1811).

Throckmorton, Sir Nicholas (1515–71), English diplomat, imprisoned because of support for Mary Queen of Scots.

Thucydides (c. 460–c. 400 B.C.), Greek historian of the Peloponnesian War.

thulium, metallic element, discovered 1879 by the Swedish chemist Per Tesdor Cleve (1840–1905).

Thurber, James (1894–1961), American humorous writer and cartoonist for the *New Yorker*, author of *Fables for Our Time* (1940).

Thuret, Gustave Adolphe (1817–75), French botanist, investigated marine plant life.

Thurloe, John (1616–68), English secretary of state under Oliver Cromwell, constructed intelligence network of unparalleled efficiency.

Thurlow, Edward, Baron (1731–1806), English lawyer, lord chancellor 1778–83, and 1784–92; noted for his reactionary views.

Thurstan (d. 1140), Norman prelate, archbishop of York 1114–40, was also an administrator and diplomat.

Thutmose I (16th–15th cent. B.C.), king of Egypt c. 1540–1501 B.C. and c. 1496–1493 B.C., was a noted builder; involved in struggle with Thutmose III.

Thutmose II (16th–15th cent. B.C.), king of Egypt c. 1496–c. 1493 B.C., jointly with his father Thutmose I.

Thutmose III (16th–15th cent. B.C.), king of Egypt c. 1501–1496 B.C. and c. 1493–1481 B.C. jointly with wife Hatshepsut; reigned alone c. 1481–1447 B.C.; his conquests greatly expanded the Egyptian empire.

Thutmose IV (16th–15th cent. B.C.), king of Egypt c. 1420–1411 B.C., waged war in Nubia and Phoenicia.

Tiberius (42 B.C.–A.D. 37), Roman emperor A.D. 14–37, son of Livia, efficient soldier and administrator, later notorious for vices.

Tibet, independent kingdom 7th century A.D.; under Mongol influence from 13th century; Chinese suzerainty established 1720; British expedition 1904; Chinese expelled 1912; Chinese Communist occupation 1950; Tibetan rebellion 1959; made autonomous region of China 1965.

Tibullus (c. 54–c. 18 B.C.), Roman poet, noted for his elegies.

Tichborne, Chidiock (c. 1558–1586), English conspirator, joined Babington Plot 1586; executed.

Tichborne Claimant, The. See **Orton,** Arthur.

Tickell, Thomas (1686–1740), English poet, wrote ballad *Colin and Lucy*.

ticker-tape machine, invented 1867; developed by Thomas Alva Edison (q.v.) and Franklin L. Pope (1840–95).

Ticknor, William Davis (1810–64), American publisher, one of the first to pay foreign authors for publishing rights.

Tieck, Ludwig (1773–1853), German poet, playwright and short-story writer; also revised August von Schlegel's translation of Shakespeare.

Tiepolo, Giovanni Battista (c. 1696–1770), Italian painter, creator of brilliantly coloured large-scale decorations.

Tiffany, Charles Lewis (1812–1902), American jeweller, built great business with London and Paris branches.

Tigranes (140–55 B.C.), king of Armenia c. 94–55 B.C., extended kingdom until defeated by Romans.

Tillett, Ben (1860–1943), English labour leader, notably in 1889 dock strike.

Tillotson, John (1630–94), English prelate, archbishop of Canterbury 1691–94.

Tilly, Johann, Count (1559–1632), Flemish soldier, led Catholic Imperial troops in Thirty Years' War.

Tilsit, Treaty of, between Napoleon and Alexander I of Russia, 1807.

Timaeus (5th–4th cent. B.C.), Greek philosopher of Locri, Italy; Plato gave his name to a dialogue.

Timaeus (c. 345–c. 250 B.C.), Greek historian in Sicily, wrote a history of Italy.

Time and Tide, British periodical founded by Lady Rhondda (q.v.), published 1920–1953 and from 1959.

Times, The, founded 1785 by the English merchant John Walter (1739–1812); acquired present name 1788.

Timoleon (c. 410–c. 337 B.C.), Greek statesman and soldier, defended Sicilian Greeks against Carthage.

Timor, disputed between Dutch and Portuguese from 17th century; boundary finally ratified 1914; Dutch part transferred to Indonesia 1949; Portuguese part occupied by Indonesia 1975.

tin, used in bronze (tin–copper alloy) in Mesopotamia c. 3500 B.C.

Tindal, Matthew (1653–1733), English deist, asserted rights of state over church, and a non-miraculous religious ethic.

Tintoretto (1518–94), Italian painter, master of rich colour and intense drama.

Tippecanoe, Battle of, victory of the Americans over the Indians under Tecumseh 7 Nov. 1811.

Tipperary, (*It's a long way to Tipperary*), popular World War I song, composed 1912 by the English song-writer Jack Judge (1878–1938).

Tippett, Sir Michael (b. 1905), English composer, e.g. of *The Midsummer Marriage*.

Tippoo Sahib (1749–99), sultan of Mysore 1782–99, inveterate enemy of British; killed at storming of Seringapatam.

Tiptoft, John, Earl of Worcester (c. 1427–1470), English Yorkist, chief adviser to Edward IV; executed by Lancastrians.

Tiros. See **satellite,** weather.

Tirpitz, German warship, destroyed by Royal Navy in World War II, 12 Nov. 1944.

Tirpitz, Alfred von (1849–1930), German admiral, noted for his advocacy of unrestricted submarine warfare.

Tirso de Molina (c. 1571–1648), Spanish playwright, creator of Don Juan in *El Burlador de Sevilla* (1630).

Tisserand, François (1845–96), French astronomer, made observations in Japan and Santo Domingo.

tissue culture, successfully demonstrated 1907 by the American biologist Ross G. Harrison (1870–1959).

Tisza, Kalmán (1830–1902), Hungarian statesman, prime minister 1875–90.

Titan. See **Saturn.**

Titanic, British Atlantic passenger liner, sank on her maiden voyage, 15 April 1912.

titanium, discovered 1791 by the English chemist William Gregor (1761–1817); independently discovered and named 1795 by the German chemist Martin Kloproth; pure form isolated 1910 by Matthew A. Hunter.

Tit-Bits, British periodical founded 1881 by George Newnes (q.v.).

Titian (c. 1486–1576), Italian painter, outstanding artist of the Venetian Renaissance, noted for his portraits and mythological scenes.

Tito (properly Josip Broz; b. 1892), Yugoslav statesman, led partisans in resistance to Nazis, effective ruler of Yugoslavia since 1945.

Titus (A.D. 40–81), Roman emperor A.D. 79–81, captured Jerusalem A.D. 70.

TNT, trinitrotoluene, discovered 1863 by J. Wilbrand.

tobacco, brought from America to Europe in 16th century; introduced 1560 into France by Jean Nicot (*q.v.*).

Tobago, West Indies, discovered by Columbus 1498; first Dutch settlement in 1630s; occupied by various countries in 17th and 18th centuries; finally ceded to Britain 1814; united with Trinidad (*q.v.*) 1899 to form colony of Trinidad and Tobago.

Tobruk, Libya, in World War II taken by British 22 Jan. 1941; by Germans 21 June 1942; recaptured by British 13 Nov. 1942.

Tocqueville, Alexis de (1805–59), French political analyst, author of *Democracy in America*.

Togliatti, Palmiro (1893–1964), Italian politician, for many years leader of the Communist party in Italy.

Togo, West Africa, became a German protectorate 1885; captured by Anglo-French forces 1914; western part mandated to Britain and eastern part to France 1922; western part (Togoland) became a British trust territory 1946; incorporated in Ghana 1957; eastern part (French Togo) became a French trust territory 1946; achieved independence as the Republic of Togo 1960.

Togo, Heihachiro (1847–1934), Japanese admiral, destroyed Russian fleet at Tsushima 1905.

Togoland. See **Togo.**

Tojo, Hideki (1885–1948), Japanese soldier and politician, prime minister 1941–44; executed for war crimes.

Tokaido Line. See **New Tokaido Line.**

Toledo, Francisço de (c. 1515–1584), Spanish viceroy of Peru 1569–81, executed the last Inca chieftain Tupac Amaru.

Toleration, landmarks include: Peace of Augsburg (toleration of German rulers' religion) 1555; Edict of Nantes 1598 in France; in Britain, Act of Toleration 1689 and repeal of Test Acts 1828–29.

Tolkien, John Ronald (1892–1973), English novelist, author of *The Lord of the Rings* (1954–55).

Toller, Ernst (1893–1939), German playwright, of revolutionary socialist views, author of *Mass Man* (1921).

Tolpuddle Martyrs, Dorset farmhands, pioneer trade unionists, sentenced to transportation 1834; pardoned 1836.

Tolstoy, Count Leo (1828–1910), major Russian novelist, wrote *War and Peace* (1869), *Anna Karenina* (1877), etc.

tomato, brought from South America to Europe in 16th century.

Tombaugh, Clyde William (b. 1906), American astronomer, discovered the planet Pluto 1930.

Tom Thumb, General (pseud. of Charles Stratton; 1838–83), American dwarf, was exhibited by Barnum.

'Tom Thumb, The', first railway engine built in U.S.A., 1830; constructed by the American manufacturer Peter Cooper (1791–1883).

Tomkins, Thomas (1743–1816), English calligrapher, author of *The Beauties of Writing* (1777).

Tommasini, Vincenzo (1878–1950), Italian composer, e.g. of opera *Medea*; also music critic.

Tommy Gun, invented 1920 by J. T. Thompson (*q.v.*) and John N. Blish.

Tompion, Thomas (1639–1713), English clockmaker of outstanding skill.

Tonbridge School, English public school, founded by Sir Andrew Judd 1553; chartered by Edward VI 1553.

Tone, Wolfe (1763–98), Irish nationalist, inspired French attempt to invade Ireland 1796; committed suicide in prison.

Tonga, Pacific, discovered by Dutch 1616 and visited by Abel Tasman 1643; British protectorate proclaimed 1900; became an independent kingdom within the Commonwealth 1970.

tonic sol-fa system. See **sol-fa.**

Tonson, Jacob (c. 1656–1736), English publisher of almost all the great writers of his period.

Tonti, Henry de (c. 1650–1704), Italian-born explorer in Illinois, Louisiana, etc.

tontine, annuity system introduced c. 1653 by the Italian banker Lorenzo Tonti.

Tooke, Horne (1736–1812), English radical clergyman and philologist, supporter of parliamentary reform and the American colonists.

Topelius, Zachris (1818–98), Finnish writer, notably of historical novels with Finnish and Swedish settings.

Töpffer, Rodolphe (1799–1846), Swiss writer, also noted for his humorous drawings.

Topham, Thomas (1710–49), English strong man, performed feats in England and Ireland.

Toplady, Augustus (1740–78), English divine and hymn-writer, especially *Rock of Ages* (1775).

Tories, English political group, first so named 1679.

Toronto University, Canada, founded 1827.

torpedo, motor, invented by the American engineer Herschel Clifford Parker (1867–1944).

torpedo, submarine, invented 1866 by the English engineer Robert Whitehead (1823–1905).

Torquemada, Tomás de (1420–98), Spanish Dominican monk, led Inquisition in Spain, notoriously relentless and cruel.

Torrens, Sir Robert (1814–84), Irish-born settler in South Australia, of which he was the first premier.

Torricelli, Evangelista (1608–47), Italian inventor of the barometer.

Torrigiano, Pietro (1472–1522), Italian Renaissance sculptor in England, carved Henry VII's tomb in Westminster Abbey.

Toscanini, Arturo (1867–1957), Italian conductor, best known for his brilliant interpretation of Beethoven and Verdi.

Tosti, Sir Francesco (1846–1916), Italian-born composer of songs in England, was singing teacher to royal family.

Tostig, Earl of Northumbria (d. 1066), English thane, revolted against his brother King Harold; slain at Stamford Bridge.

Tottel, Richard (c. 1525–1594), English publisher of first collection of English poetry.

Toulon, scene of the sabotaging of the French fleet in World War II, 27 Nov. 1942.

Toulouse-Lautrec, Henri de (1864–1901), French painter, who excelled at the portrayal of Parisian café society and night life.

Tourneur, Cyril (c. 1575–1626), English playwright, wrote *The Atheist's Tragedy* (1611).

tourniquet, first used in Thirty Years' War by the German surgeon Fabriz von Hilden (1560–1634); screw tourniquet first used by the French surgeon Jean Louis Petit (1674–1750).

Tours, Battle of, victory of Charles Martel and the Franks over the Saracens 732.

Toussaint l'Ouverture, François (1743–1803), Haitian Negro liberator, defeated by Napoleonic army; died in French prison.

Tovey, Sir Donald (1875–1940), English musicologist and composer, wrote many books about music.

Tower Bridge, London, completed 1894.

Tower of London, begun 1067 as an earthwork; central keep (White Tower) built 1078–97; remainder mainly 12th and 13th centuries; alterations late 17th century.

Townes, Charles (b. 1915), American physicist, joint winner of 1964 Nobel Prize for Physics, investigated quantum electronics and invented the maser.

Townshend, Charles, Viscount (1674–1738), English politician, as chancellor of the exchequer heavily taxed the American colonies; later pioneer of improved agriculture.

Toynbee, Arnold (1889–1975), English historian, wrote comparative survey of civilizations *Study of History* (1934–60).

Toynbee Hall, London, social settlement founded 1884 as a memorial to the English reformer Arnold Toynbee (1852–1883).

trachoma, main cause of blindness; virus first isolated 1957 by the Chinese scientist F. F. T'ang.

Tracts for the Times, Oxford Movement (q.v.) tracts issued 1833–41.

trade marks, first given statutory recognition as assignable and transmissible property 1875; Trade Mark Registry, London, established 1876.

Trades Union Congress, Britain, formed 1868.

Trafalgar, Battle of, victory of British navy under Lord Nelson over French and Spanish fleets 21 Oct. 1805.

traffic lights, first set (with gas lanterns) operated 1868 in London; first electric lights introduced 1914 in Cleveland, Ohio, and 1926 in London; first automated, in Britain 1927.

Traherne, Thomas (c. 1637–74), English mystic and poet, had a proto-romantic conception of childhood innocence.

Trajan, (c. A.D. 53–117), Roman emperor 98–117, period of successful wars and internal improvements.

tramway, first, opened in New York 26 Nov. 1832; first introduced into England by G. F. Train 1860; first English electrified overhead tramway Leeds 1891; last London tram ran 6 July 1952.

Trans-Andean railway tunnel, between Chile and Argentina, opened 1910.

transatlantic cable, first laid 1857–58.

transatlantic flight, first non-stop, made by John William Alcock and Arthur Whitten Brown (qq.v.) June 1919; first solo flight made 20–21 May 1927 by the American aviator Charles Lindbergh (q.v.); first woman transatlantic flier Amelia Earhart (q.v.) June 1928.

transatlantic telephone cables, between the United Kingdom, Canada and the U.S.A., inaugurated 1956.

Transcendental Club, American literary-philosophical society, formed 1836.

transfinite numbers, theory propounded 1895–97 by Georg Cantor (q.v.).

transistor, invented 1948 at Bell Telephone Laboratories by the American physicists John Bardeen (b. 1908), William B. Shockley (b. 1910), and Walter H. Brattain (b. 1902).

Trans-Siberian Railway, constructed 1891–1916.

transuranic elements, unstable chemical elements with atomic numbers greater than uranium, first one, neptunium (q.v.), synthesized 1940.

Transvaal, first Boer settlements 1838; independence recognized by Britain 1852; annexed by Britain 1877; independence restored 1880; finally re-annexed 1900 during South African War; granted self-government 1906; joined Union of South Africa 1910.

Transvaal gold-bearing lode, discovered 1885.

Transylvania, ruled by Austria 1698–

1867; by Hungary 1867–1920 (as part of Austria–Hungary 1867–1918) and 1940–1945; by Romania 1920–40 and since 1945.

Trappist Order, monastic order, founded 1664 by Armand de Rancé (1626–1700).

Trasimeno, Battle of Lake, victory of Carthaginians led by Hannibal over the Romans 217 B.C.

Travers, Ben (b. 1886), English dramatist, best known for his farces including *Rookery Nook* (1926).

Trebizond, Asia Minor, capital of empire of Comneni 1204–61; captured by Turks 1461 and renamed Trabzon.

Tree, Sir Herbert Beerbohm (1853–1917), English actor-manager, a spectacular rather than faithful Shakespearian interpreter.

Treitschke, Heinrich von (1834–96), German historian of the rise of Prussia.

Trelawny, Edward John (1792–1881), English adventurer, friend of Shelley and Byron, of whom he wrote *Recollections* (1858).

Trelawny, Sir Jonathan (1650–1721), English prelate, one of the 'Seven Bishops' tried for sedition by James II 1688.

Trent, Council of, Catholic ecumenical council, met 1545–63.

Trent College, Long Eaton, Nottinghamshire, English public school, founded 1886.

Trevelyan, George Macaulay (1876–1962), English historian, author of *English Social History* (1942).

Trevisa, John of (1326–1412), English translator of Latin chronicles.

Trevithick, Richard (1771–1833), English engineer, built first steam carriage and first rail-locomotive.

Trianon, Treaty of, between Hungary and World War I Allies, signed 4 June 1920.

Triassic Period, Earth history, from *c.* 225 to *c.* 190 million years ago.

Trieste, Mediterranean port and surrounding area ruled by Austria 1382–1918; by Italy 1918–45; free territory 1947–54; partitioned between Italy and Yugoslavia 1954.

trigonometry, founded by Hipparchus (*q.v.*) in 2nd century B.C.

Trinidad and Tobago, West Indies, member of West Indies Federation 1958–1962; independent member of the Commonwealth of Nations since 1962.

Trinidad, West Indies, discovered by Columbus 1498; settled by Spanish late 16th century; ceded to Britain 1802; linked with Tobago to form colony of Trinidad and Tobago (*q.v.*) 1899.

Trinity College, Cambridge University, founded by King Henry VIII 1546.

Trinity College, Dublin, founded 1591.

Trinity College, Glenalmond, Scottish

public school, founded 1841; opened 1847.

Trinity College, Oxford University, founded 1555 by Sir Thomas Pope (d. 1559).

Trinity Hall, Cambridge University, founded by William Bateman, bishop of Norwich, 1350.

Trinity House, London, origins in the medieval Guild of Mariners, developing into the Corporation of Trinity House of Deptford Strond, granted its first charter by Henry VIII, 1514.

Trinity School, Croydon, English public school, founded 1596 by John Whitgift, archbishop of Canterbury.

triode valve, invented 1906 by the American scientist Lee de Forest (1873–1961).

Triple Alliance, between Germany, Austria and Italy, formed 1882.

Triple Entente, between Britain, France and Russia, 1904–17.

Tripura, Indian state, formed 1972.

Tristan da Cunha, Atlantic Island, discovered 1506 by the Portuguese navigator Tristão da Cunha (*c.* 1460–*c.* 1540); annexed and garrisoned by Britain 1816; settlement developed in 19th century; made dependency of Saint Helena 1938.

tritium, radioactive hydrogen isotope, discovered 1934 by the Australian physicist Marcus Oliphant (b. 1901).

trolley-bus, first used in Britain 1909; began replacing trams in London 1938.

Trollope, Anthony (1815–82), English novelist, wrote novels of clerical life, e.g. *Barchester Towers* (1857) and also on political themes, e.g. *Phineas Finn* (1869).

Tromp, Maarten (1597–1653), Dutch admiral, helped to establish the Netherlands as a great sea power.

Trotsky, Leon (1879–1940), Russian revolutionary and Marxist theoretician, creator of the Red Army, exiled by Stalin 1929; assassinated.

Troy, ancient city said to have been destroyed by Greeks *c.* 1200 B.C.; site at Hissarlik, Asia Minor, discovered 1801 by the English archaeologist Sir William Gell (1778–1836); excavation begun by Heinrich Schliemann (*q.v.*) 1870.

troy ounce. See **ounce,** troy.

Truck Act, prohibiting payment of wages in kind, passed by British Parliament 1831.

Truman, Harry S. (1884–1972), American statesman, 33rd president of the United States 1945–53, committed his country to postwar anti-Communist role.

Trucial States, Persian Gulf, seven sheikhdoms in treaty relations with Great Britain since 1820.

Trumbull, John (1756–1843), American painter of scenes from the Revolutionary War, e.g. *Declaration of Independence.*

Truro School, English public school, founded 1879.

Trusteeship System, U.N. See **Mandate.**

Truth, British periodical, founded 1877 by its first editor, the English scholar Henry Labouchère (1831–1912); ceased publication 1957.

Tshombe, Moise (1919–69), Congolese political leader, president of Katanga 1960 and prime minister of Zaïre 1964–65.

tsi dynasty, China, A.D. 479–502.

Tsin dynasty, China, A.D. 165–419.

Tsushima, Battle of, victory of Japanese over Russian fleet 27 May 1905.

tuberculosis, bacillus discovered 1882 by Robert Koch (*q.v.*).

Tubman, William (1895–1971), Liberian lawyer and statesman, president 1944–71.

Tucker, Benjamin (1854–1939), American anarchist, wrote *State Socialism and Anarchism* (1899).

Tucuman, Congress of, declared independence of Argentina 9 July 1816.

Tu Fu (712–770), Chinese poet, noted for the beauty of his lyric verse.

Tuke, Sir Brian (d. 1545), English administrator, secretary to Henry VIII.

Tulane University, New Orleans, U.S.A., founded 1834.

Tull, Jethro (1674–1741), English agricultural pioneer, invented seed drill 1701.

tungsten, or wolfram, isolated 1783 by the Spanish chemists Juan José and Fausto Elhuyar, following discovery 1781 of tungstic acid by Carl Wilhelm Scheele (*q.v.*).

tuning fork, traditionally invented 1711 by the English trumpeter and lutenist John Shore (1662–1752).

Tunisia, region under Carthage from 6th century B.C.; Roman province 2nd century B.C.; conquered by Vandals 5th century A.D. and by Muslims 7th century; ruled by Hafsid dynasty 1228–1574; annexed by Ottomans 1574; became French protectorate 1881; scene of fighting in World War II; achieved independence 1956.

Tunney, Gene (b. 1898), American boxer, world heavyweight champion 1926–28.

Tunstall, Cuthbert (1474–1559), English prelate, scholar and diplomat, bishop of Durham 1530–59, accepted Henrician Reformation but opposed Protestantism.

Tupac Amaru (*c.* 1544–1571), last Inca chieftain, executed by Spanish.

turbine, gas, first patent issued 1791 to the Englishman John Barber; greatly developed in early 20th century.

turbine, steam, invented 1884 by Sir Charles Parsons (*q.v.*).

turbine, water, first practical one built 1837 by the French engineer Benoît Fourneyron (1802–67).

turbojet aircraft, first, the de Havilland Comet 1, entered scheduled service May 1952. See also **jet engine.**

turboprop aircraft, first, the Bristol Britannia, entered scheduled service Feb. 1957.

turbo-prop engine, first (Rolls-Royce Trent), 1945.

Turenne, Henri de (1611–75), French soldier, marshal of France, served with distinction in the Thirty Years' War and the Dutch wars of Louis XIV.

Turgenev, Ivan (1818–83), outstanding Russian novelist and playwright, author of *On the Eve* (1860).

Turgot (d. 1115), Anglo-Saxon prelate, bishop of St Andrews 1109–15.

Turgot, Anne Robert (1727–81), French economist, as minister of finance 1774–76 attempted unsuccessfully to reform his country's economy.

Turina, Joaquín (1882–1949), Spanish composer in nationalist idiom, also a polemical critic.

Turkey, Turkic peoples known from the 6th century A.D.; Seljuk Turks defeated Byzantines at Manzikert 1071; defeated by Mongols 1243; Ottoman Empire founded 1288; Ottoman Turks crossed Dardanelles 1345; defeated Serbs at Kossovo 1389; defeated by Timur 1402; captured Constantinople 1453; Ottoman Empire expanded 13th–18th centuries; collapsed 1922; Turkish Republic proclaimed 1923.

Turks and Caicos Islands, West Indies, discovered early 16th century; settled late 18th century; dependency of Jamaica 1873–1962; British crown colony since 1962.

Turner, Joseph Mallord (1775–1851), English painter, particularly for his use of light and colour in landscapes and sea pictures.

Turner, Thomas (1749–1809), English potter, introduced the 'Chinese' willow pattern.

Turpin, Dick (1705–39), English highwayman, hanged at York; in legend made a famous London to York ride.

Tussaud, Marie (1761–1850), French-born founder of Madame Tussaud's exhibition of waxworks.

Tutankhamen (*c.* 1371–*c.* 1352 B.C.), king of Egypt *c.* 1361–*c.* 1352 B.C., whose magnificent tomb was discovered 1922.

Tutuola, Amos (b. 1920), Nigerian novelist, author of *The Palm-Wine Drinkard* (1952).

Tuvalu. See **Gilbert and Ellice Islands.**

Twain, Mark (pseud. of Samuel Clemens; 1835–1910), American novelist, creator of Tom Sawyer and Huckleberry Finn.

Twelfth Night (Old Christmas Day or the Feast of the Three Kings), celebrated on night of 5 Jan.

Twentieth Century, English periodical, founded 1877 as *The Nineteenth Century* by the English architect Sir James Knowles (1831–1908).

Two Thousand Guineas, Newmarket, first run 1809.

Tycho Brahe. See **Brahe,** Tycho.

Tyler, John (1790–1862), American statesman, 10th president of the United States 1841–45.

Tyler, Wat (d. 1381), English leader of Peasants' Revolt; murdered at Smithfield meeting with Richard II.

Tylor, Sir Edward (1832–1917), English anthropologist, author of *Primitive Culture* (1917).

Tyndale, William (c. 1494–1536), English translator of the New Testament (1526), the first printed; burnt as heretic.

Tyndall, John (1820–93), Irish-born scientist, noted for his investigations into radiant heat.

typewriter, first commercially produced, the Remington, built 1873 by the American Christopher Latham Scholes; shift key added 1878.

typhoid fever, bacillus described by C. J. Eberth 1880.

typhus, bacillus described 1908–09 by the American pathologist Howard T. Ricketts (1871–1910).

tyre, pneumatic. See **pneumatic tyre.**

Tyrrell, Anthony (1552–c. 1610), English Roman Catholic priest, imprisoned; became a government spy.

Tyrrell, George (1861–1909), Irish Roman Catholic priest and theologian, prominent in the controversy over modernism.

Tyuchev, Fedor (1803–73), Russian poet, remembered for his lyric verse.

Tzetzes, John (c. 1120–c. 1183), Byzantine scholar, wrote literary-historical *Chiliades*; was also a poet.

Tz'u Hsi (1834–1908), empress of China, effective ruler of her country for many years.

U

Ubaldini Petruccio (c. 1524–c. 1588), Italian scholar, published first Italian-language book in England, a life of Charlemagne (1581).

Überweg, Friedrich (1826–71), German philosopher in Hegelian tradition.

Uccello, Paolo (c. 1397–1475), Italian painter, pioneer of perspective but strongly decorative, e.g. *Rout of San Romano.*

Udall, Nicholas (1504–56), English writer of earliest comedy, *Ralph Roister Doister*; also headmaster of Eton.

U.D.I. (Unilateral Declaration of Independence), made by Rhodesia (q.v.) 11 Nov. 1965.

UFO. See **unidentified flying objects.**

Uganda, East Africa, made a British protectorate 1894; became an independent member of the Commonwealth of Nations 1962.

Ugolino di Nerio (early 14th cent.), Italian painter of Sienese school, only fragments of whose work survive.

Uhde, Fritz von (1848–1911), German painter, especially of Biblical scenes.

Uhland, Johann Ludwig (1787–1862), German Romantic poet, well known for his ballads.

Ukraine, settled in 6th century A.D.; acquired by Lithuania 14th century; incorporated in Poland 1569; divided between Poland and Russia 1667; under Russian rule from 1793; People's Republic established 1917; joined U.S.S.R. 1923.

Ulanova, Galina (b. 1910), Russian ballet dancer, for many years prima ballerina of the Bolshoi ballet.

Ulbricht, Walter (1893–1973), German Communist leader, chief minister of East Germany 1960–71.

Ulfilas (c. 311–383), bishop to the Goths, translated Bible into Gothic and invented Gothic alphabet.

Ulloa, Francisco de (d. c. 1540), Spanish navigator, explored Gulf of California.

Ulpian (c. A.D. 170–c. 228), Roman lawyer, adviser to several emperors.

ultraviolet radiation, discovered 1801 by the German physicist Johann Wilhelm Ritter (1776–1810).

Umberto I (1844–1900), king of Italy 1878–1900; assassinated by anarchist.

Umberto II (b. 1904), king of Italy 1946, abdicated after unfavourable referendum.

Unamuno, Miguel de (1864–1936), Spanish scholar and writer, author of *Tragic Sense of Life* (1913).

uncertainty principle, atomic physics, proposed 1927 by Werner Heisenberg (q.v.).

underground railroad, system by which Negro slaves in Southern U.S. states were aided in crossing north to Canada, in operation from c. 1825.

Underground Railway, London, first opened 1863 (Metropolitan Railway); first electric line 1890 (City and South London Railway).

Undset, Sigrid (1882–1949), Norwegian historical novelist, wrote *Kristin Lavransdatter* (1920–22).

UNESCO (United Nations Educational, Scientific and Cultural Organization), established 1945.

UNICEF (United Nations International Children's Emergency Fund), established 1946.

unidentified flying objects, first reported June 1947 by an American pilot, Kenneth Arnold.

Uniformity, Acts of, regulating public worship in England 1549, 1552, 1559 and 1662.

Union, Act of, between England and Scotland 1707; between Britain and Ireland 1801.

Union of Soviet Socialist Republics — Uttar Pradesh

Union of Soviet Socialist Republics, name officially adopted 1922.

Union Pacific Railway, U.S.A., first transcontinental service, finished 1869.

Unitarianism, originated in Hungary and Poland in mid-16th century; spread to England in 17th century; General Assembly of Unitarian and Free Christian Churches formed 1928.

Unitas Fratrum. See **Moravian Brethren.**

United Arab Emirates, Arabian Peninsula, in treaty relationship with Britain from 1820; became an independent federation 1971.

United Arab Republic, union of Egypt and Syria, formed 1958; effectively ended following withdrawal of Syria 1961.

United Church of Christ, U.S.A., formed 1958 by union of Congregational with Evangelical and Reformed Church.

United Kingdom, of Great Britain and Ireland, formed 1801 by union of Britain and Ireland; title officially changed to United Kingdom of Great Britain and Northern Ireland 1927. See also **England**; **Great Britain.**

United Nations, officially established 1945.

United States of America, declared independence 1776; constitution established 1787; peace with Britain 1783; Anglo-American War 1812–14; acquired new territory by Louisiana Purchase 1803 and Mexican War 1846–48; Civil War 1861–1865; Spanish–American War 1898; took part in World War I 1917–18 and World War II 1941–45; leading industrial power from beginning of 20th century.

Universal Postal Union, regularizing international mail, founded at Berne 1875.

universe, background radiation, discovered 1965 by American physicists Arno A. Penzias and Robert W. Wilson and identified by Robert Dicke.

universe, estimated age c. 10,000 million years.

universe, expanding, theory proposed c. 1916 by the Dutch astronomer Willem de Sitter (1872–1934); established 1929 by the American astronomer Edwin Powell Hubble (1889–1953).

universe, origin of. See **big-bang theory**; **steady-state theory.**

University College, London University, opened 1828.

University College, Oxford University, founded by William of Durham 1249.

University College School, London, English public school, founded 1830; moved to present site 1907.

U Nu (b. 1897), Burmese statesman, first prime minister of independent Burma 1948–62.

Upper Volta, West Africa, French protectorate established by 1897; made a separate colony 1919; partitioned among other French colonies 1932; reconstituted as a French overseas territory 1947; independent republic since 1960.

Uppingham School, Leicester and Rutland, English public school, founded by Archdeacon Johnson 1584.

uranium, radioactive element, discovered 1789 by the German chemist Martin Heinrich Klaproth (1743–1817); metal isolated 1841 by Eugene-Melchior Peligot; radioactivity of uranium discovered 1896 by Henri Becquerel (q.v.).

Uranus, discovered 1781 by Sir William Herschel (q.v.); first two satellites discovered 1787 by Herschel.

urea, first organic compound to be formed from an inorganic one (ammonium cyanate), experiment performed 1828 by the German chemist Friedrich Wöhler (1800–1882).

Urey, Harold Clayton (b. 1893), American chemist, discovered heavy hydrogen 1932.

Urfé, Honoré d' (1568–1625), French writer, author of the pastoral romance L'Astrée (1610–27).

Urfey, Thomas d' (c. 1653–1723), English playwright, wrote a Don Quixote.

Urquhart, Sir Thomas (1611–60), Scottish writer, translated Rabelais.

Urquiza, Justo José de (1800–70), Argentinian statesman, president 1854–60; assassinated.

Ursinus, Zacharias (1534–83), German Protestant theologian, one of the composers of the Heidelberg Catechism 1563.

Ursuline Order, of nuns, founded 1535 by Saint Angela Merici.

Uruguay, area explored by Spanish 1516; Portuguese settlement established 1680; under Spanish control by 1776; rebelled against Spain 1811; part of Brazil 1821–25 and of Argentina 1825–28; gained complete independence 1828.

Ussher, James (1581–1656), Irish prelate, archbishop of Armagh 1625–56, devised popular Biblical chronology.

Utah, U.S.A., settled by Mormons 1847; organized as a territory 1850; admitted to Union 1896.

Utah State University, chartered 1888.

Utah, University of, founded 1850 as Deseret University; reopened under present name 1867.

Utamaro, Kitagawa (1753–1806), Japanese master of colour prints.

Utrillo, Maurice (1833–1955), French painter, noted for his portrayal of Parisian street scenes; son of Suzanne Valadon (q.v.).

Uttar Pradesh, Indian state, formed part of Mauryan, Kushan and Gupta empires; annexed to Delhi Sultanate at end of 12th century; parts annexed to Britain in 19th

century; United Provinces of Agra and
Oudh formed 1902; acquired present
name 1950.

V

V-1 missile, German pilotless ramjet aircraft, launched against Britain, mainly
London, June 1944 to March 1945.

V-2 rocket, developed in Germany from
1936; first fired against Paris, then London, Sept. 1944.

vaccination. See **inoculation.**

vaccine. See **smallpox.**

vacuum cleaner, power operated, devised
1901 by the British engineer Hubert Cecil
Booth.

vacuum flask, or thermos flask, invented
in 1890s by the Scottish scientist Sir James
Dewar (1842–1923).

Vaihinger, Hans (1852–1933), German
philosopher, formulated 'As if' approach
to philosophy.

Valadon, Suzanne (1869–1938), French
painter, best known for her portraits and
nude studies.

Valdemar I (1131–82), king of Denmark
1157–82, strengthened the power of the
monarchy.

Valdemar II (1170–1241), king of Denmark 1202–41, made his country the most
powerful in northern Europe.

Valdemar IV (c. 1320–1375), king of Denmark 1340–75, engaged in long struggle to
maintain national unity.

Valdes, Juan de (1498–1541), Spanish
theologian, noted as a religious reformer.

Valdivia, Pedro de (c. 1498–1554), Spanish conquistador, accompanied Pizarro;
went on to conquer Chile.

valency, theory devised 1852 by the English chemist Sir Edward Frankland (1825–
1899); electron theory developed by
Richard Abegg (1900s), Gilbert Lewis
(1916) and Nevil Sidgwick (1920s).

Valens (d. 378), Roman emperor in the
East 364–378, defeated and slain by Visigoths at Adrianople.

Valentine, Saint (3rd cent.), Christian
martyr, unconnected with Valentine card.

Valentine's Day, Saint. See **Saint Valentine's Day.**

Valentinian I (A.D. 321–375), Roman
emperor 364–375, brother of Valens, to
whom he gave the Eastern Empire.

Valentinian II (A.D. 371–392), Roman
emperor 375–392, expelled from Italy and
murdered.

Valentinian III (A.D. 419–455), Roman
emperor 425–455, effectively controlled
by his mother, Galla Placidia.

Valentino, Rudolph (1895–1926), Italian-
born American film actor, idol of millions
in such films as *The Sheik.*

Valentinus (2nd cent. A.D.), Egyptian-
born philosopher, exponent of Gnosticism.

Valerian (d. c. A.D. 260), Roman emperor
253–260, defeated by Persians and kept
prisoner until his death.

Valéry, Paul (1871–1945), French poet and
essayist, associated with Symbolist movement, author of *La Jeaune Parque* (1917).

Valle-Inclan, Ramón del (1859–1936),
Spanish novelist, playwright and poet,
author of *Sonatas* (1902–05).

Vallejo, César (1892–1938), Peruvian poet,
author of *Poemas Humanos.*

Valois dynasty, ruled France 1328–1589.

Valotton, Félix (1865–1925), Swiss painter
and woodcut artist, worked in Paris.

Valparaiso, Chile, founded 1536.

value added tax. See **V.A.T.**

valve, electronic. See **thermionic valve.**

vanadium, metallic element, discovered
1801 by the Spanish scientist Andrés
Manuel del Río (1764–1849); rediscovered
1830 by the Swedish chemist Nils Gabriel
Sefström (1787–1845).

Van Allen radiation belts, discovered
1958 by the American physicist James A.
Van Allen (b. 1914) from data collected by
the American satellite Explorer I.

Vanbrugh, Sir John (1664–1726), English
architect of Blenheim Palace, and playwright in Restoration manner.

Van Buren, Martin (1782–1862), American statesman, 8th president of the United
States 1837–41.

Vancouver, George (c. 1757–1798), English navigator, explored northwest coast of
Canada.

Vandals, Barbarian people, crossed Rhine
406; entered Spain 409; crossed to Africa
429; sacked Rome 455; defeated and
destroyed by Byzantine general Belisarius
533.

Van de Graaff generator, first conceived
c. 1929, built 1931, by the American physicist Robert J. Van de Graaff (1901–67).

Vanderbilt, Cornelius (1794–1877),
American financier, made huge shipping
and railroad fortune; first of an influential
family.

Vanderbilt University, Tennessee,
U.S.A., founded 1872.

Van Doren, Carl (1885–1950), American
writer, critic and literary journalist on *The
Nation.*

Van Dyck, Sir Anthony (1599–1641),
Flemish painter, in England 1631–41,
produced portraits of wonderful refine-
ment.

Vane, Sir Henry (1613–62), English statesman, prominent supporter of Parliament
in the Civil War; executed for treason.

Van Gogh, Vincent. See **Gogh,** Vincent
van.

Van Loon, Hendrick (1882–1944), American writer, notably of *Story of Mankind.*

Van Rensselaer, Killiaen (1595–1644), Dutch merchant, bought much of (now) New York state from Indians.

Van't Hoff, Jacobus (1852–1911), Dutch chemist, best known for his work on chemical dynamics; awarded Nobel Prize 1901.

Varèse, Edgar (1885–1965), French-born composer in U.S.A., leading exponent of progressive abstract music.

Vargas, Getulio Dornelles (1883–1954), Brazilian statesman, president 1930–45 and 1951–54.

Varro, Marcus Terentius (116–27 B.C.), Roman writer and scholar, most of whose prolific output is lost.

Varthema, Lodovico (16th cent.), Italian traveller and writer, visited India, China and the Malay Archipelago.

Vasari, Giorgio (1511–74), Italian painter and writer, best known for his *Lives of the Painters* (1550–68).

Vasco da Gama. See **Gama,** Vasco da.

vascular surgery, initiated by the French surgeon Alexis Carrel (1873–1944).

V.A.T. (Value Added Tax), introduced in Britain in 1973, replacing purchase tax.

Vatican, Italy, established as papal residence since 1377.

Vatican City, created 1929.

Vatican Council, Catholic general council, held 1869–70 and 1962–65.

Vattel, Emerich de (1714–67), Swiss jurist, whose *The Right of Peoples* (1758) influenced the development of international law.

Vauban, Marquis de (1633–1707), French military engineer, developed new techniques in fortifications.

Vaughan, Henry (1622–95), Welsh poet, wrote about religious experience.

Vaughan Williams, Ralph (1872–1958), major English composer, often on national themes, e.g. *Sea Symphony*.

Vauxhall Bridge, London, opened 1906.

Vauxhall Gardens, London, open from *c.* 1600 to 1859.

Vavilov, Nikolai (1887–1943), Russian geneticist, noted for his work on cultivated plants.

Vasov, Ivan (1850–1921), Bulgarian poet and novelist, author of *Under the Yoke* (1894).

Veblen, Oswald (1880–1960), American mathematician, best known for his work in differential geometry.

Veblen, Thorstein (1857–1929), American economist, author of *Theory of the Leisure Class* (1899).

Vega, Lope de (1562–1635), Spanish dramatist, wrote nearly 2,000 plays, and also novels and poetry.

Veidt, Conrad (1894–1943), German film actor, e.g. in *Dr. Caligari* (1919); later in Hollywood.

Velazquez, Diego (1599–1660), major Spanish painter, whose work ranged from domestic to court and battle scenes, e.g. *Las Meninas.*

Velde, Willem van de (1633–1707), Dutch painter, best known for his seascapes.

Venezuela, first Spanish settlement 1520; part of New Granada 1718; independence from Spain proclaimed 1811; finally secured 1830.

Venice, first settlement in 6th century A.D.; under Byzantine rule until 11th century; independent republic until 1798; ruled by Austria 1797–1805; part of Napoleonic kingdom of Italy 1805–15; restored to Austria 1815; part of Italy since 1866.

Venizelos, Eleutherios (1864–1936), Greek statesman, prime minister 1910–15, 1917–1920 and 1928–33.

Venus, temperature and other features first measured 1967 by the Soviet Venera 4 spacecraft; first surface photographs relayed 1975 by Venera 9 and 10.

Verdi, Giuseppe (1813–1901), major Italian opera composer, wrote *Rigoletto* (1851), *Otello* (1877), etc.

Verdun, Battle of, between Germans and French, World War I, Feb.–June 1916.

Vere, Edward de (1550–1604), English poet and dramatist, fought the Armada.

Vereeniging, Treaty of, between Britain and the Boers, signed May 1902.

Vérendrye, Sieur de la (1685–1749), French-Canadian explorer, travelled extensively in western Canada and the northern U.S.A.

Verga, Giovanni (1840–1922), Italian novelist and dramatist, noted for his portrayal of Sicilian life.

Verhaeren, Émile (1855–1916), Belgian poet of Flemish life and work, e.g. *Les Villes Tentaculaires* (1895).

Verlaine, Paul (1844–96), French poet, noted for his lyric verse; had disastrous association with Rimbaud (*q.v.*).

Vermeer, Jan (1632–75), Dutch painter of luminously clear interiors.

Vermont, U.S.A., first settled 1724; admitted to the Union 1791.

Verne, Jules (1828–1905), French novelist, pioneer of science fiction, author of *Journey to the Centre of the Earth* (1864).

Verner, Karl Adolph (1846–1896), Danish philologist, noted for his work in formulating sound changes in Indo-European languages.

Vernier scale, invented 1631 by the French mathematician Pierre Vernier (1580–1637).

Veronese, (1525–88), Italian painter of the Venetian school, created colourful large-scale works.

Verrazano Narrows Bridge, New York harbour, constructed 1959–64 by the Swiss-born American engineer Othmar Herman Ammann (1879–1965).

Verrochio, Andrea del (1435–88), Florentine sculptor and painter, best known for his equestrian statue of Bartolommeo Colleoni.

Versailles, Treaty of, between World War I Allies and Germany, signed 28 June 1919.

vertebrates, first seriously studied and classified in 1740s by Linnaeus (*q.v.*).

Vertue, George (1684–1756), English engraver, left informative notebooks.

Verwey, Albert (1865–1937), Dutch poet and critic, author of the collection *Persephone* (1885).

Verwoerd, Hendrik Frensch (1910–66), South African statesman, as prime minister 1958–66 was a strong advocate of apartheid; assassinated.

Vesalius, Andreas (1514–64), Belgian physician, noted particularly for his work in anatomy.

Vespasian (A.D. 9–79), Roman emperor A.D. 69–79, first of Flavian line.

Vespucci, Amerigo (1451–1512), Italian navigator, made several voyages in the New World, which was named after him.

Vestris, Elizabeth (1797–1856), English actress, first woman theatre manager.

Vesuvius, Mount, major volcanic eruption A.D. 79, burying cities of Pompeii, Herculaneum and Stabiae.

veto, abolished in Polish Diet 1791; last used by British sovereign 1707; House of Lords veto on legislation became delaying power 1911 (two years; one year in 1949); veto established in U.N. Security Council 1945.

Vianney, Jean Marie 1787–1859, 'Curé d'Ars', the patron saint of parish priests.

viceroy, title of representative of British crown in India 1858–1947.

Vichy, French town, site of French puppet government 1940–44.

Vico, Giambattista (1668–1744), Italian philosopher of history, proposed cyclical interpretation in *The New Science* (1744).

Victor Emmanuel II (1820–78), king of Sardinia 1849–61 and first king of united Italy 1861–78.

Victor Emmanuel III (1869–1947), king of Italy 1900–46; abdicated.

Victoria (1819–1901), queen of Great Britain 1837–1901, empress of India 1876–1901.

Victoria, Australian state, first settled in the 1830s; made a separate colony 1851; granted self-government 1855; became a state in the Commonwealth of Australia 1901.

Victoria, Lake, Africa, discovered by J. H. Speke (*q.v.*) 1858.

Victoria and Albert Museum, London, originated in Museum of Manufactures (later Museum of Ornamental Art) opened at Marlborough House 1852; moved to South Kensington 1857 as part of South Kensington Museum; acquired present name 1899.

Victoria College, Jersey public school, founded to commemorate visit by Queen Victoria, opened 1852.

Victoria Cross, premier British decoration for valour, founded by Queen Victoria 1856.

Victoria Falls, Zambezi River, discovered 1855 by David Livingstone (*q.v.*).

Victoria Line, London, opened Jan. 1969; completed Walthamstow Central to Brixton July 1971.

Victorian Order, Royal, founded by Queen Victoria 1896.

Vidocq, Eugène (1775–1857), French criminal-turned-detective, helped to create Parisian detective police force.

Vienna, occupied by Romans 1st century B.C.; granted city charter 1137; residence of Holy Roman emperors 1558–1806; besieged by Turks 1529 and 1683; under four-power occupation 1945–55.

Vienna, Congress of, Sept. 1814 to June 1815.

Viète, François (1540–1603), French mathematician, noted for his work on algebra.

Vietnam, Socialist Republic of, region under Chinese domination from 3rd century B.C.; became independent A.D. 939; European traders arrived 16th century; dynasty unified whole country 1802; French protectorate established 1884; occupied by Japanese 1940–45; war between French and Communist forces 1945–54; partitioned into Communist North Vietnam and anti-Communist South Vietnam 1954; intermittent war between North and South Vietnam from early 1960s ended 1975 with victory of North; while country reunited as Socialist Republic of Vietnam 1976.

Vieuxtemps, Henri (1820–81), Belgian violin virtuoso from seven years of age, also composer for violin.

Vigfusson, Guthbrandur (1827–89), Icelandic scholar in England, completed Cleasby's *Icelandic–English Dictionary* (1874).

Vignola, Giacomo da (1507–73), Italian architect, best known for his church design.

Vigny, Alfred de (1797–1863), French poet and writer, a Romantic stoic, author of *Servitude et Grandeur Militaires* (1835).

Vikings, period of raids *c.* 800 to *c.* 1050.

Viking **spacecraft.** See **Mars.**

Villa, Pancho (1877–1923), Mexican bandit and revolutionary, active in 1910 revolution; assassinated.

Villa-Lobos, Heitor (1887–1959), Brazilian composer, used fold elements in his music, e.g. *Bachianas Brasileiras.*

Villehardouin, Geoffroy de (*c.* 1150–*c.* 1213), French nobleman and writer, took part in Fourth Crusade, which he described in his *Chronicles*.

Villiers, Barbara, Countess of Castlemaine (1641–1709), English beauty, mistress of Charles II.

Villiers, George. See **Buckingham,** Duke of.

Villon, François (b. 1431, d. after 1463), French poet and criminal, condemned to death but pardoned; noted for the quality of his lyric verse.

Vincent de Paul, Saint (*c.* 1581–1660), French Roman Catholic priest, renowned for his charitable work among the poor.

Vinci, Leonardo da. See **Leonardo da Vinci.**

Vinegar Bible, so called for misprint, 'Parable of the Vinegar' (i.e. 'Vinyard'), published 1717.

Vintners Company, London livery company, first recorded reference 1321; letters patent granted 1363; first charter 1437.

violin playing, first formal teaching method published 1740 by the Italian violinist Francesco Geminiani (*c.* 1674–*c.* 1762).

Viollet-le-Duc, Eugène (1814–79), French architect, leading figure in the Gothic revival in France.

Virchow, Rudolf (1821–1902), German founder of modern pathology; also Liberal politician, opposing Bismarck.

Virgil (Publius Vergilius Maro; 70–19 B.C.), major Roman poet, author of the *Aeneid* and *Georgics*.

Virginia, U.S.A., first settled 1607; entered Union 1788; seceded 1861; re-admitted to Union 1870.

Virgin Islands, British, West Indies, discovered by Columbus 1493; acquired by Britain 1666.

Virgin Islands, U.S., West Indies, discovered by Columbus 1493; became Danish colony 1754; finally purchased by U.S.A. 1917.

viruses, differentiated from bacteria 1898 by the Dutch botanist Martinus Willem Beijerinck (1851–1931); modern studies began *c.* 1915.

Visconti, Gian Galeazzo (1351–1402), duke of Milan, extended the power of the Visconti family over much of northern Italy.

Visigoths, Western Goths, crossed Danube A.D. 376; defeated emperor Valens 378; entered Roman service as federates 382; attacked Greece 396; invaded Italy 401; sacked Rome 410; settled in southern Gaul 418 onwards; founded kingdom also including much of Spain; defeated at Vouillé 507 and lost Gaul; Spanish Visigothic kingdom destroyed by Muslims 711.

Vitalis, Ordericus. See **Ordericus Vitalis.**

Vitamin A, existence recognized 1913; chemical nature established 1931; synthesized 1947.

Vitamin B, group of 8 vitamins including: B_1, first vitamin isolated 1926, chemical nature established, synthesized 1936; B_2, existence recognized 1933, synthesized 1935; B_6, isolated 1938, synthesized 1939; B_{12}, isolated 1948–49, structure determined 1956.

Vitamin C, isolated 1927; vitamin character recognized 1932; synthesized 1933–1934.

Vitamin D, existence recognized 1918; pure form isolated 1930–31.

Vitamin E, existence recognized 1922; isolated in pure form 1936; chemical nature established 1938.

Vitruvius (1st cent. B.C.), Roman architect whose treatise *De Architectura*, discovered in 15th century, had a lasting influence.

Vivaldi, Antonio (*c.* 1676–1741), Italian composer and violinist, best known for concerto suite *The Four Seasons*.

Vives, Juan Luis (1492–1540), Spanish humanist, noted for his work on philosophy and education.

vivisection, law regulating, passed in Britain 1876.

Vladimir I (*c.* 956–1015), prince of Kiev, first Christian ruler of Russia 980–1015.

Vlaminck, Maurice (1876–1958), French painter, was a leader in the Fauvist movement.

Vogelweide, Walther von der. See **Walther von der Vogelweide.**

Volta, Alessandro (1745–1827), Italian physicist, invented voltaic pile 1800; volt (unit) named after him.

Voltaire (pseud. of François-Marie Arouet; 1694–1778), French poet, dramatist, historian, crusader against injustice and writer of witty philosophical tales, whose life and work influenced the course of European civilization.

Volunteers of America, religious organization founded by Ballington Booth and his wife Maud Ballington Booth 1896.

Vondel, Joost van den (1587–1679), Dutch poet and dramatist, author of *Jeptha* (1859).

Vörösmarty, Mihály (1800–55), Hungarian poet, noted for his lyric verse.

Vorster, Balthazar Johannes (b. 1915), South African statesman, prime minister since 1966.

Vortigern (5th cent. A.D.), British prince, said to have brought Saxons to Britain as mercenaries.

Vries, Hugo de (1848–1935), Dutch botanist, noted for his work on mutation.

Vuillard, Jean Edouard (1868–1940), French artist, best known as a painter of domestic interiors, still life and flowers.

vulcanization. See **rubber.**

vulcanized rubber. See **ebonite.**

Vulgate, Latin translation of Bible, made by Saint Jerome *c.* 382–*c.* 405.

Vyshinsky, Andrei (1883–1954), Soviet lawyer and politician, prosecutor at Moscow treason trials 1936–38 and foreign minister 1949–53.

W

Waals, Johannes van der (1837–1923), Dutch physicist, investigated gas–liquid continuity; Nobel prizewinner 1910.

Wadham College, Oxford University, founded 1613 by bequest of Nicholas Wadham (1532–1609).

Wafd, Egyptian political party, active 1918–52.

Wagner, Cosima (1837–1930), daughter of Franz Liszt, left first husband for Richard Wagner; became artistic director, Bayreuth.

Wagner, Richard (1813–83), major German composer, revolutionized opera, e.g. 'Ring' cycle; founded Bayreuth festival.

Wagram, Battle of, victory of French, led by Napoleon, over Austrians 5–6 July 1809.

Wainewright, Thomas (1794–1847), English art critic, almost certainly a poisoner; transported to Tasmania for forgery.

Waitangi, Treaty of, signed by British and Maoris 5 Feb. 1840.

Wajda, Andrej (b. 1926), Polish film director, whose work includes *Kanal* (1956) and *Ashes and Diamonds* (1958).

Wake Island, Pacific, defended by Americans against Japanese 7–23 Dec. 1941.

Wakefield Grammar School, English public school, founded by royal charter 1591.

Waksman, Selman Abraham (1888–1973), Russian-born biochemist in U.S.A., discovered streptomycin 1943; Nobel prizewinner 1952.

Walburga, Saint. See **Walpurga,** Saint.

Waldenses, Christian sect, founded during 12th century by Peter Walds of Lyons; persecuted as heretics.

Waldemar. See **Valdemar.**

Waldheim, Kurt (b. 1918), Austrian diplomat, secretary-general of the United Nations since 1972.

Waldteufel, Emil (1837–1915), French composer, famous for waltzes.

Wales, inhabited by Celts from prehistoric times; conquered by Romans in 1st century A.D.; finally subdued by English 1284; united with England 1536.

Waley, Arthur David (1889–1966), English scholar, noted for his translations from Chinese and Japanese literature.

Walker, George (1618–90), English clergyman, co-governor of Derry during siege 1689; killed at Battle of the Boyne.

Wallace, Alfred Russel (1823–1913), English naturalist, discovered natural selection principle simultaneously with Charles Darwin.

Wallace, Edgar (1875–1932), English novelist and playwright, best known as a writer of detective stories.

Wallace, Lew (1827–1905), American Civil War general and novelist, wrote *Ben Hur* (1880).

Wallace, Sir William (*c.* 1274–1305), Scottish leader against English, victor at Stirling 1297, defeated at Falkirk 1298; executed.

Wallace Collection, London, art collection of Sir Richard Wallace (1818–90), bequeathed by his widow 1897; on public exhibition from 1900.

Wallasey Grammar School, English public school, first recorded mention 1595.

Wallenstein, Albrecht von (1583–1634), Austrian soldier, led the Imperial armies in Thirty Years' War; assassinated.

Waller, Edmund (1606–87), English poet, wrote in polished Augustan style.

Waller, Sir William (*c.* 1597–1668), English Parliamentarian general in Civil War; later an opponent of Cromwell.

Wall Game, Eton, held publicly on Saint Andrew's Day, 30 Nov.

Wallis, Sir Barnes Nevill (b. 1887), English aircraft designer, noted for his work on airships, special bombs and variable geometry aircraft.

Wallis, John (1616–1703), English mathematician, made important advances in *Arithmetica Infinitorum* (1655).

Wallis, Samuel (1728–95), English naval commander, discovered Tahiti 1767.

Wallis and Futuna Islands, Pacific, Wallis Island occupied by France 1842, Futuna Island 1887; together comprise a French overseas territory since 1959.

Walpole, Horace (1717–97), English writer, connoisseur and 'Gothick' novelist (*Castle of Otranto*, 1764).

Walpole, Sir Hugh (1884–1941), New Zealand-born English novelist, e.g. *Rogue Herries* (1930).

Walpole, Sir Robert, 1st Earl of Orford (1676–1745), English statesman, chief minister (virtually prime minister) 1721–1742.

Walpurga, Saint (*c.* 710–*c.* 777), English abbess of Heidenheim, reputedly helped to convert Germans to Christianity.

Walsingham, Sir Francis (*c.* 1530–1590), English statesman, secretary of state 1573–1590, tried to initiate aggressively Protestant policies.

Walsingham, Thomas (d. *c.* 1422), English chronicler of his own period.

Walter, Bruno (1876–1962), German-born conductor, worked in France and U.S.A.

Walter, John (1739–1812), English merchant, founded *The Times* 1785.

Walther von der Vogelweide (*c.* 1170–*c.* 1230), German poet, one of the greatest lyricists of the Middle Ages.

Walton, Isaak (1593–1683), English writer of *The Compleat Angler* (1653), also biographer of Donne, etc.

Walton, Sir William (b. 1902), English composer, e.g. *Facade* (1923), *Belshazzar's Feast* (1931), etc.

Wang Wei (699–759), Chinese painter, poet and musician, originator of monochrome painting.

Wankel, Felix (b. 1902), German engineer, inventor of the rotary internal-combustion engine.

Warbeck, Perkin (1474–99), Flemish Yorkist impostor, claimed to be Richard, brother of Edward V; executed.

Warburg Institute, founded by Professor Aby Warburg (1866–1929) at Hamburg; transferred to London 1933; part of London University from 1944.

Warburton, William (1698–1779), English critic, bishop of Gloucester 1759–79, editor of Alexander Pope and Shakespeare.

Ward, Artemus (1834–67), American journalist, noted for his humorous writings.

Ward, Mrs Humphrey (1851–1920), English novelist, wrote *Robert Elsmere* (1888).

Warham, William (*c.* 1450–1532), English prelate, archbishop of Canterbury 1504–1532, dominated by Henry VIII.

Warlock, Peter (pseud. of Philip Heseltine; 1894–1930), English composer, notably of songs.

Warner, Sylvia Townsend (b. 1893), English novelist, author of *Lolly Willowes* (1926).

War of 1812, between Great Britain and the United States, began June 1812; ended Dec. 1814.

Warren, Earl (1891–1974), American jurist, chief justice of the U.S. Supreme Court 1953–69.

Warren, Robert Penn (b. 1905), American novelist and poet, author of *All the King's Men* (1946).

Warsaw Treaty Organization, of Eastern European countries, established by signing of Warsaw Treaty May 1955.

Warwick, Richard Neville, Earl of (1428–1471), called 'the Kingmaker', helped Edward IV to secure the throne, but later opposed him; killed in battle.

Warwick School, English public school, probably founded *c.* 914; refounded by Henry VIII 1545.

Washington, D.C., planned 1790; occupied by federal government 1800.

Washington, Treaties of, between U.S.A. and Britain 1846, 1854 and 1871; multinational naval treaty 1922.

Washington, U.S.A., organized as territory 1853; admitted to Union as state 1889.

Washington, Booker (1859–1915), American Negro educationalist and writer, author of *Up From Slavery* (1901).

Washington, George (1732–99), American statesman and soldier, leader in Revolutionary War, first president of the United States 1789–97.

Wassermann, August von (1866–1925), German bacteriologist, devised Wassermann Test for syphilis 1906.

Wasserman, Jacob (1873–1934), German novelist, remembered chiefly for *The Maurizius Case* (1928).

watches, first appeared *c.* 1510 after the invention of the mainspring (*q.v.*); hairspring invented *c.* 1660 by Robert Hooke (*q.v.*); lever escapement invented 1765 by Thomas Mudge; wristwatches first appeared in 1790s.

water, first analysed 1783 by Antoine Lavoisier (*q.v.*).

water-closet, first, designed 1596 by the English courtier Sir John Harrington (1561–1612).

Waterhouse, Alfred (1830–1905), English architect, designed Manchester Town Hall.

Waterloo, Battle of, victory of British and Prussians led by Wellington and Blücher, over French led by Napoleon, 18 June 1815.

Waterloo Bridge, London; old bridge built 1811–17 by John Rennie (*q.v.*); new bridge by Sir Giles Gilbert Scott opened 1942 to vehicles; officially completed 1945.

watermark, in paper, first known example made in Italy *c.* 1285.

Water Poet, The. See **Taylor,** John.

waterproof clothing, invented 1823 by the Scottish chemist Charles Macintosh (1766–1843).

Watson, George Lennox (1851–1904), Scottish designer of yachts, including the royal *Britannia*.

Watson, John (1878–1958), American psychologist, noted for his work on behaviourism.

Watson, Richard (1737–1816), English chemist, bishop of Llandaff 1782–1816; also wrote Christian apologetics.

Watson-Watt, Sir Robert (1892–1973), Scottish physicist, pioneer in the development of radar.

Watt, James (1736–1819), Scottish engineer, inventor of the modern condensing steam engine.

Watteau, Antoine (1684–1721), French painter of melancholy-tinged festivities, e.g. *Embarkation for Cythera* (1717).

Watts, George Frederick (1817–1904), English painter and sculptor of large allegorical works.

Watts, Isaac (1674–1748), English hymn-writer, e.g. 'O God, our help in ages past'.

Waugh, Evelyn (1903–66), English satirical novelist, author of *Decline and Fall* (1928).

Wavell, Archibald, 1st Earl (1883–1950), British army officer, commanded Middle East forces 1939–41; viceroy of India 1943–47.

wave mechanics. See **quantum mechanics.**

wave theory, of light, first proposed 1690 by Christiaan Huygens (*q.v.*); experimentally established 1802 by Thomas Young (*q.v.*) and 1814 by the French physicist Augustin Fresnel (1788–1827).

Waynflete, William of (*c.* 1395–1486), English prelate, bishop of Winchester, founded Magdalen College, Oxford, 1458.

weather forecasting, study founded by Jean-Baptiste Lamarck (*q.v.*).

weather map, first one drawn 1820 by the German scientist Heinrich Brandes (1777–1834).

Weaver, John (1673–1760), English dancing master, introduced pantomime-ballets into England.

Webb, Beatrice (1858–1943), and Sydney (1859–1947), English Fabian socialists, wrote *History of Trade Unionism* (1894), etc.

Weber, Carl Maria von (1786–1826), German Romantic composer, notably of opera *Der Freischütz* (1820).

Weber, Max (1864–1920), German sociologist, pioneer in social science and critic of Marx's view of historical determinism.

Webern, Anton (1883–1945), Austrian composer, pupil of Schönberg and pioneer of the 12-note technique.

Webster, Daniel (1782–1852), American lawyer and statesman, famous for his oratory.

Webster, John (*c.* 1580–*c.* 1625), English playwright, created atmosphere of morbid lust and violence, e.g. *The White Devil.*

Webster, Noah (1758–1843), American lexicographer, originated *Webster's Dictionary* (1828).

Weddell, James (1787–1834), English navigator, noted for his Antarctic explorations.

wedding ring, changed from right to left hand in English Prayer Book of 1549, and in *Rituale Romanum* of 1614.

Wedekind, Frank (1864–1918), German playwright, expressionist in technique, pioneered sexual truthfulness, as in *Spring's Awakening* (1891).

Wedgwood, Josiah (1730–95), English potter, creator of jasperware, first to reach a mass market.

Wedgwood, Thomas (1771–1805), English photographic pioneer, son of Josiah Wedgwood, experimented with light-sensitive paper.

week, the seven days from midnight Saturday to midnight the following Saturday; Jewish week of seven days adopted by Romans 1st century A.D.

Weeks, Feast of (Sharuoth), Jewish festival, Sivan 6th.

Wegener, Alfred Lothar (1880–1930), German geophysicist and meteorologist, originated theory of continental drift.

Wei dynasty, China, A.D. 368 to 557.

Weierstrass, Karl Theodor (1815–1897), German mathematician, made important contribution to the theory of functions.

Weill, Kurt (1900–50), German composer, collaborated with Brecht, e.g. on *Threepenny Opera* (1928); later worked in U.S.A.

Weingartner, Felix (1863–1942), Austrian conductor, was also a writer on music.

Weishaupt, Adam (1748–1830), German philosopher, founded anti-clerical secret society, Illuminati 1776.

Weismann, August (1834–1914), German biologist, noted for his contribution to modern genetic theory.

Weizmann, Chaim (1874–1952), Russian-born Jewish chemist, Zionist and first president of Israel 1949–52.

Welch, William (1850–1934), American pathologist, discovered bacillus responsible for gas gangrene.

Welf, German noble family, originated in 11th century; combined duchies of Saxony and Bavaria in 12th century and rivalled Hohenstaufen dynasty.

Welles, Orson (b. 1915), American actor and director, whose films include *Citizen Kane* (1940).

Wellesley, Richard, Marquis (1760–1842), Irish-born administrator, highly effective governor-general of India 1797–1805; foreign secretary 1809–12.

Wellesz, Egon (1885–1974), Austrian composer, e.g. opera *Alcestis*; in England from 1938.

Wellington School, Somerset, English public school, founded 1841.

Wellington, Arthur Wellesley, 1st Duke of (1769–1852), Irish-born British soldier and statesman, victor of Waterloo; prime minister 1828–30.

Wellington College, English public school, founded by public subscription in memory of Duke of Wellington 1853.

Wells, Herbert George (1866–1946), English novelist, journalist, science fiction pioneer and popular historian, author of *The War of the Worlds* (1898).

Wells, Fargo & Co., American express company, founded 1852.

Welsbach mantle, in gas lighting, patented 1885 by the Austrian chemist Karl von Welsbach (1858–1929).

Welsh, Thomas (1781–1848), English singer in oratorio at Haymarket, London; also a successful teacher.

Welsh literature, first recorded works *c.* A.D. 550.

Welsh Nationalist Party. See **Plaid Cymru.**

Welty, Eudora (b. 1909), American novelist, author of *The Golden Apples* (1949).

Welwyn Garden City, Hertfordshire, established 1920.

Wembley Exhibition, British Empire Exhibition, Wembley, April–Nov. 1924.

Wenceslaus, Saint (*c.* 905–930), duke of Bohemia, introduced Christianity into his country; murdered by brother.

Wentworth, William Charles (1793–1872), Australian politician, leader of movement for self-government.

Werfel, Franz (1890–1945), Austrian expressionist writer, best known for *Song of Bernadette* (1941).

Wergeland, Henrik (1808–45), Norwegian poet and dramatist, author of *The English Pilot* (1844).

Werner, Alfred (1866–1919), Swiss chemist, awarded Nobel Prize for Chemistry 1913 for his work on the co-ordination theory of valency.

Wesker, Arnold (b. 1932), English playwright, author of *Chicken Soup with Barley.*

Wesley, Charles (1707–88), English hymnwriter, brother of John Wesley.

Wesley, John (1703–91), English evangelist, founded movement that became the Methodist Church.

West, Benjamin (1738–1820), American painter of historical scenes, e.g. *Death of Wolfe*; settled in London.

West, Mae (b. 1892), American actress, made her reputation in films like *I'm No Angel* (1933).

West, Nathaniel (1903–40), American novelist, author of *Miss Lonelyhearts* (1933).

West, Rebecca (pseud. of Cicely Fairfield; b. 1892), English writer, author of *The Meaning of Treason* (1949).

West Bengal, Indian state, established 1947. See also **Bengal.**

Western Australia, originally settled 1829; granted responsible government 1890; became a state 1900.

Western European Union, inaugurated at Strasbourg 1955.

Western Pacific High Commission, created 1877.

Western Samoa, first visited by Dutch 1722; German colony 1900–14; administered by New Zealand 1920–62; independent since 1962.

Westminster, Statute of, recognizing independence of dominions within the Commonwealth, passed 1931.

Westinghouse, George (1846–1914), American inventor, patented the air brake and automatic signalling on railways.

Westminster Abbey, London, building of present edifice began 1245.

Westminster Assembly, Puritan religious body, sat 1643–49.

Westminster Bridge, London, constructed 1854–62 by the English civil engineer Thomas Page (1803–77); replaced bridge built 1750.

Westminster Cathedral, London, built 1895–1903; opened 1903; consecrated 1910.

Westminster Gazette, British newspaper, founded 1893; absorbed into *Daily News* 1928.

Westminster School, English public school, first recorded reference 1339; re-established by Queen Elizabeth 1560.

Weston, Agnes (1840–1918), English founder of the Royal Sailors' Rests.

Westphalia, kingdom 1807–14; Prussian province from 1815.

Westphalia, Peace of, ended Thirty Years' War, 1648.

West Virginia, U.S.A., separated from Virginia 1861; admitted to Union as a state 1863.

Wetterhorn, peak ·near Grindelwald, Switzerland, first climbed by the Swiss guides Bannholzen and Jaun 1844.

Weyden, Rogier van der (*c.* 1400–64), Flemish religious painter, of brilliant, intense clarity, e.g. *Descent from the Cross*.

Weyprecht, Karl (1838–81), German explorer, discovered Franz Joseph Land 1873.

Whaling Commission, International, set up 1946.

Wharton, Edith (1862–1937), American novelist, author of *The Age of Innocence* (1920).

Wharton, Henry (1664–95), English scholar-clergyman, wrote *Anglia Sacra* (1691).

Wheatstone, Sir Charles (1802–75), English physicist, invented, 1842, the Wheatstone Bridge and a form of stereoscope.

Wheeler, Sir Mortimer (1800–1976), English archaeologist, noted for his work on the Indus Valley civilizations.

Whigs, British political grouping; word first used in this sense 1679.

Whipsnade Zoo, Bedfordshire, opened to the public 1931.

Whistler, James McNeill (1834–1903), American painter, e.g. portrait of mother; lived in London and Paris.

Whiston, Joseph (1711–80), English bookseller in Fleet Street, London, whose shop became a writers' meeting place.

Whitaker's Almanack, founded 1868 by the English publisher Joseph Whitaker (1820–95).

Whitby, Synod of, whereby the English Church adopted the Roman rite, 664.

White, Gilbert (1720–93), English naturalist and clergyman, wrote *Natural History and Antiquities of Selborne* (1789).

White, William Hale. See **Rutherford,** Mark.

white corpuscles, of the blood, existence and function discovered 1880s by the Russian scientist Elie Metchnikov (*q.v.*).

White Dwarf, first one, companion of the binary star Sirius (*q.v.*), discovered 1915 by the American astronomer Walter Sydney Adams (1876–1956).

Whitehead, Alfred North (1861–1947), English philosopher, wrote *Principia Mathematica* (1910) with Bertrand Russell.

Whitefield, George (1714–70), English evangelist, associated with Wesley, preacher of great emotional impact.

Whitehead, Robert (1823–1905), English inventor of self-projecting torpedo.

Whiteman, Paul (1890–1967), American musician, enjoyed great popularity as a jazz band conductor.

White Russia, under Polish sovereignty until 1650; ceded to Russia 1793; occupied by Poland 1919; became part of U.S.S.R. 1922.

Whitfield, Henry (1597–c. 1660), English clergyman, founder of Guildford, Connecticut, as base for mission to Indians.

Whitgift School, Croydon, founded 1596 by the Archbishop of Canterbury John Whitgift (c. 1530–1604).

Whitley Councils, on British labour problems, largely founded 1917 by John Henry Whitley (1866–1935), speaker of the House of Commons.

Whitman, Walt (1819–92), American poet, democratic, libertarian, consciously national and rhetorical, author of *Leaves of Grass.*

Whitney, Eli (1765–1825), American manufacturer, inventor of the cotton gin.

Whittier, John (1807–92), American poet and abolitionist, author of *Voices of Freedom* (1846).

Whittingham, Charles (1767–1840), English printer, first to issue india-paper editions.

Whittington, Dick (c. 1358–1423), English merchant, lord mayor of London 1397–98, 1406–07 and 1419–20; subject of many legends.

Whittle, Sir Frank (b. 1907), English aviator and inventor, pioneer of jet propulsion.

Whitworth, Sir Joseph (1803–87), English mechanical engineer, standardized screw threads, improved manufacturing techniques, etc.

Whymper, Edward (1840–1911), English mountaineer, climbed Matterhorn 1865 and Chimborazo 1880.

Whyte-Melville, George (1821–78), Scottish novelist, e.g. *The Gladiators* (1863).

Wickham, Sir Henry (1846–1928), English pioneer of rubber plantations, bringing seeds from Brazil to the East.

Widor, Charles (1844–1937), French organ virtuoso of great influence; was also a composer.

Wieland, Christoph Martin (1733–1813), German novelist and poet, author of *Oberon* (1780).

Wien, Wilhelm (1864–1928), German physicist, investigated black-body energy radiation; Nobel prizewinner 1911.

Wieniawski, Henri (1835–80), Polish violinist and composer, lived in Brussels and toured widely.

Wilberforce, Samuel (1805–73), English prelate, son of William Wilberforce, bishop of Winchester 1869–73.

Wilberforce, William (1759–1833), English philanthropist, played a prominent part in the abolition of the slave trade.

Wild, Jonathan (c. 1682–1725), English receiver of stolen goods and informer on confederates; hanged.

Wilde, Oscar (1856–1900), Irish poet, dramatist and wit, author of *The Importance of Being Ernest* (1895).

Wilder, Thornton (1897–1975), American novelist and dramatist, author of *The Bridge of San Luis Rey* (1927).

Wilfrid, Saint (634–710), English prelate, defeated Celtic Christians at Whitby 664; archbishop of York.

Wilhelm, Karl Friedrich (1815–73), German composer of the patriotic *Wacht am Rheine* (1854).

Wilhelmina (1880–1962), queen of the Netherlands 1890–1948, abdicated in favour of daughter Juliana (*q.v.*).

Wilhelmshaven, first German military port, opened officially 1869.

Wilkes, John (1727–97), English politician, opponent of George III and champion of freedom of the press.

Wilkins, Sir Herbert (1888–1958), Australian explorer and aviator, took part in numerous polar expeditions.

Wilkinson, Ellen (1891–1947), English Labour politician, associated with Jarrow March, first woman minister of education 1945–47.

William I, the Conqueror (1027–87), duke of Normandy 1035–87 and king of England 1066–87, created powerful monarchy.

William II, Rufus (c. 1056–1100), king of England 1087–1100; killed mysteriously in New Forest.

William III, of Orange (1650–1702), Dutch stadtholder 1672–1702, joint English monarch (with wife Mary) 1689–94; reigned alone 1694–1702.

William IV (1765–1837), king of Great Britain and Ireland 1830–37; succeeded by his niece Victoria.

William I (1797–1888), king of Prussia

1861–88, emperor of Germany 1871–88.

William II (1859–1941), emperor of Germany 1888–1918, abdicated at end of World War I; lived in Netherlands.

William and Mary, College of, Williamsburg, Virginia, founded 1693 by the English colonist William Randolph (c. 1651–1711).

William Hulme's Grammar School, Manchester, English public school, founded by the Hulme Trust 1887.

William of Malmesbury (c. 1095–c. 1143), English chronicler, wrote *Gesta Regum Anglorum*.

William of Ockham. See **Ockham,** William of.

William of Wykeham. See **Wykeham,** William of.

Williams, Roger (c. 1603–1683), English clergyman, founded the colony of Rhode Island, 1636.

Williams, Sir George (1821–1905), English founder of the Y.M.C.A. 1844.

Williams, Ralph Vaughan. See **Vaughan Williams,** Ralph.

Williams, Tennessee (b. 1914), American playwright, wrote *Streetcar Named Desire* (1947).

Williams, William Carlos (1883–1963), American poet, author of *Paterson* (1946–1951).

Williams's Library, London, founded by the Nonconformist leader Daniel Williams (c. 1643–1716).

Williamson, Alexander (1824–1904), English chemist, investigated ether.

William the Lion (1143–1214), king of Scotland 1165–1214, bought his country's independence from Richard I.

William the Silent (1533–84), prince of Orange, led Dutch revolt against Spain; first stadtholder 1579–84; assassinated.

Willibrord, Saint (c. 658–c. 739), English missionary, apostle to the Frisians.

willow pattern, on porcelain, introduced c. 1780 by the English potter Thomas Turner (1749–1809).

Willstätter, Richard (1872–1942), German chemist, noted for his researches into pigmentation in plants.

Wilna, Elijah (1720–97), Jewish scholar, author of commentaries on rabbinical literature.

Wilson, Alexander (1714–86), Scottish astronomer, was the first to discover the nature of sunspots.

Wilson, Angus (b. 1913), South African-born English novelist, author of *Hemlock and After* (1952).

Wilson, Charles (1869–1959), Scottish physicist, inventor of the cloud chamber for studying electrically charged particles.

Wilson, Sir Harold (b. 1916), British statesman, prime minister 1964–70 and 1974–76.

Wilson, John (1595–1674), English lutenist and composer, musician to Charles I and Charles II.

Wilson, John. See **North,** Christopher.

Wilson, Woodrow (1856–1924), American statesman, 28th president of the United States 1913–21; brought his country into World War I; helped found League of Nations.

Winchester Cathedral, built from c. 1079; rebuilt from c. 1394 by William of Wynford.

Winchester College, English public school, founded 1382 by William of Wykeham (q.v.).

Winckelmann, Johann (1717–68), German archaeologist and art critic, began the systematic study of ancient art.

Winckler, Hugo (1863–1913), German archaeologist, investigated Hittite civilization.

windmill, first mentioned in Persia c. 650, in England c. 1190.

window tax, imposed in England 1696; repealed 1851.

Windsor, adopted as name of British royal family July 1917.

Wine and Food Society, London, held first meeting at Café Royal 14 Nov. 1933.

Wingate, Orde (1903–44), British soldier, trained guerrillas who fought behind Japanese lines in Burma in World War II.

Winslow, Edward (1595–1655), English Pilgrim Father, several times governor of Plymouth Colony.

Winstanley, Gerrard (1609–52), English religious radical, led Diggers, claiming inalienable right to land.

Winterhalter, Franz (1806–73), German painter, fashionable portraitist of royalty.

Winthrop, John (1558–1649), English colonist, first governor of Massachusetts.

Winthrop, John (1606–1706), English colonist, son of John Winthrop, governor of Connecticut, 1636.

Wisconsin, U.S.A., first settled 1670; created a territory 1836; admitted to the Union 1848.

Wiseman, Nicholas, Cardinal (1802–65), English Roman Catholic prelate, first archbishop of Westminster 1849–65.

Wiseman, Richard (c. 1622–76), English surgeon, made his profession respected.

witches, last tried in England (Jane Wenham) 1712; statutes against witchcraft repealed 1736.

Witte, Count Sergei (1849–1915), Russian statesman, as minister of finance began a large-scale programme of industrialization.

Wittgenstein, Ludwig (1889–1951), Austrian-born philosopher in England, pioneered linguistic philosophy in *Tractatus Logic-Philosophicus* (1921).

Wodehouse, Sir Pelham Grenville (1881–

1975), English novelist, famous for his humorous stories featuring Bertie Wooster.

Woffington, Peg (c. 1714–1760), Irish actress, mistress of David Garrick; outstanding in comedy.

Wöhler, Friedrich (1800–92), German chemist, was the first to synthesize an organic compound.

Wolcot, John. See **Pindar,** Peter.

Wolf, Hugo (1860–1903), Austrian composer of songs, deeply influenced by Schumann.

Wolf Cubs, junior Boy Scout movement, organized in Britain 1916.

Wolfe, James (1727–1759), English soldier, commanded victorious British army at Quebec; killed in battle.

Wolfe, Thomas (1900–38), American novelist, author of *Look Homeward, Angel* (1929).

Wolf-Ferrari, Ermanno (1876–1948), Italian composer, notably of comic operas, e.g. *School for Fathers.*

wolfram. See **tungsten.**

Wolfram von Eschenbach (early 13th cent.), German poet, author of *Parzifal.*

Wollaston, William Hyde (1766–1828), English chemist, discovered rhodium 1805.

Wollstonecraft, Mary (1759–97), English reformer, wrote *Vindication of the Rights of Woman* (1792).

Wolseley, Garnet (1833–1913), Irish-born soldier, introduced important British army reforms; served in India and Canada.

Wolsey, Thomas, Cardinal (c. 1475–1530), English prelate, archbishop of York 1514–1530, chief minister until he failed to secure divorce for Henry VIII.

Wolverhampton Grammar School, English public school, founded by Sir Stephen Jenyns 1512; moved to present site 1875.

woman minister, first, was Nina Bang, Danish minister of education 1924–26; in Britain, Margaret Bondfield, minister of labour 1929–31.

woman prime minister, first, was Mrs Sirimavo Bandaranaike, Sri Lanka 1960.

Women's Legion, voluntary British wartime organization of drivers founded 1915 by the Marchioness of Londonderry (1879–1959).

Women's Royal Voluntary Service, founded by Lady Reading 1938.

women's suffrage, New Zealand 1893; Australia 1902; Norway 1906; Britain 1918–28; U.S.A. 1920; France and Italy 1946; Belgium 1948; Switzerland 1971.

Wood, Anthony à (1632–95), English antiquary, wrote history of Oxford antiquities 1674.

Wood, Mrs Henry (1814–87), English novelist whose *East Lynne* (1861) was enormously popular as melodrama.

Wood, Sir Henry (1869–1944), English conductor, founded Promenade Concerts 1895.

Wood, John (1704–54), English architect, designed many of the well-known areas of Bath.

Woodhouse Grove School, English public school, founded 1812.

Wood's Halfpence, British patent 1722 granting to ironmaster William Wood (1671–1730) exclusive right to coin halfpence and farthings in Ireland; withdrawn 1724.

Woodville, Anthony, 2nd Earl Rivers (c. 1442–1483), English noble, trusted adviser to Edward IV; executed by Richard III.

Woodville, Richard, 1st Earl Rivers (d. 1469), English soldier, father of Anthony Woodville; executed after Edward IV's defeat.

Woodward, Robert Burns (b. 1917), American chemist, best known for his work on organic synthesis.

Woolf, Virginia (1882–1941), major English novelist and critic, made an important contribution to the development of the novel, author of *To the Lighthouse* (1927).

Woolley, Sir Leonard (1880–1960), English archaeologist, best known for his excavations at Ur.

Woolner, Thomas (1825–92), English sculptor associated with Pre-Raphaelites; also a successful portraitist.

Woolworth, Frank Winfield (1852–1919), American businessman, founder, 1879, of the great chain of stores which bear his name.

Worcester, Battle of, victory of Parliamentary over Royalist forces, 3 Sept. 1651.

Worcester Cathedral, built 1084–89; burnt 1202; restored 1218.

Worcester porcelain, manufactured since 1751.

Worcester Royal Grammar School, earliest recorded reference 1290; granted charter by Queen Elizabeth 1561.

Worde, Wynkyn de (d. c. 1534), German-born printer in England, at first as assistant to Caxton; issued many works.

Wordsworth, Dorothy (1771–1855), English writer, sister of William Wordsworth; her *Journals* often provided his source material.

Wordsworth, William (1770–1850), major English Romantic poet, e.g. *The Prelude* (1805); poet laureate 1843–50.

Work, Henry Clay (1832–84), American song-writer, notably of *Marching Through Georgia.*

worker-priest movement, in France, began 1943; banned by Vatican 1959; ban lifted 1965.

Workshop College, English public school, founded by the Duke of Newcastle 1895.

World Association of Girl Guides and

Girl Scouts, formed in London 1928.

World Bank (International Bank for Reconstruction and Development), Washington, established Dec. 1945.

World Council of Churches, constituted 1948.

World Health Organization, constitution drawn up 1946; confirmed as specialized U.N. agency April 1948.

World Trade Center, New York City, twin towers completed 1973.

World War I, began 28 July 1914; Britain entered war 4 Aug. 1914, Japan 23 Aug., Turkey 1 Nov., Italy 23 May 1915, U.S.A. 6 April 1917; Russia left the war Dec. 1917; armistice signed 11 Nov. 1918; peace treaties 1919–20.

World War II, began 1 Sept. 1939; German invasion of Poland 1 Sept. 1939, of Norway 9 April 1940, of Low Countries 10 May 1940; French surrender 22 June 1940; German attack on Russia 22 June 1941; Japanese attack on Pearl Harbor 7 Dec. 1941; Italian surrender 3 Sept. 1943; D-Day 6 June 1944; German surrender 8 May 1945; Japanese surrender 14 Aug. 1945; Peace Conference, Paris, 29 July to 15 Oct. 1946.

Worms, Diet of, German assembly called to judge Martin Luther (*q.v.*) 1521.

Worth, Charles (1825–95), English dress designer, became leading figure in the creation of Parisian fashions.

Wotton, Sir Henry (1568–1639), English diplomat, ambassador to Venice 1604–24; also a poet.

Wren, Sir Christopher (1632–1723), English architect, designed many London churches, above all Saint Paul's Cathedral.

Wright, Frank Lloyd (1869–1959), major American architect, original and individual in style, e.g. Guggenheim Museum, New York.

Wright, Orville (1871–1948), American aviator, brother of Wilbur Wright.

Wright, Richard (1908–60), American Negro novelist, author of *Native Son* (1940).

Wright, Wilbur (1867–1912), American aviator, with brother Orville Wright made first powered flight at Kitty Hawk, 1903.

Wroclaw, Poland, founded 10th century; under Bohemian rule from 1335; ruled by Prussia from 1741; included in Poland since 1945.

Wui Tai. See **Five Dynasties.**

Wulfstan, Saint (*c.* 1012–1095), Anglo-Saxon prelate, bishop of Worcester 1062–1095; accepted Norman Conquest.

Wulfstan, (d. 1023), Anglo-Saxon prelate, archbishop of York 1003–23.

Wu Tao-tzu (*c.* 700–760), Chinese artist, noted for the realism of his figures and landscapes.

Wu Ti (157–87 B.C.), Chinese emperor, who brought Korea and Tonkin under Chinese rule.

Wyatt, Sir Francis (*c.* 1575–1644), English colonist, first governor of Virginia 1624–1626.

Wyatt, Sir Thomas (1503–42), English poet, introduced sonnet form from Italian; wrote fine love lyrics.

Wyatt, Sir Thomas (*c.* 1521–54), English soldier, son of Sir Thomas Wyatt, led rebellion against Queen Mary's Spanish marriage; executed.

Wycherley, William (*c.* 1640–1716), English Restoration playwright, wrote the bawdy *Country Wife* (1673).

Wyclif, John (*c.* 1320–84), English religious reformer, translated parts of Bible, forerunner of the Protestant Reformation.

Wykeham, William of (1324–1404), English prelate, bishop of Winchester, lord chancellor, founded New College, Oxford University, 1379.

Wynkyn de Worde. See **Worde,** Wynkyn de.

Wyoming, U.S.A., first settled 1834; created a territory 1868; admitted to Union as a state 1890.

X

xenon, gaseous element, discovered 1898 by Sir William Ramsay (*q.v.*) and Morris W. Travers.

Xenophon (*c.* 430–355 B.C.), Greek leader of 'the march to the sea', described in his *Anabasis.*

Xerxes I (*c.* 519–465 B.C.), king of Persia 486–465 B.C., led an abortive invasion of Greece.

X-rays, discovered 1895 by Wilhelm von Röntgen (*q.v.*).

XYZ Correspondence, Franco–American negotiations 1798.

Y

Yale, Elihu (1648–1721), American-born English administrator in India, patron of Collegiate School, later Yale University.

yale locks, designed from *c.* 1840 by the American Linus Yale (1821–68).

Yale University, Connecticut, founded as a school 1701; first called Yale College 1718; chartered 1745; made a university 1887.

Yalta, U.S.S.R., meeting-place of World War II Allied leaders Feb. 1945.

Yamagata, Aritomo (1838–1922), Japanese soldier and statesman, helped make his country a great military power.

Yamamoto, Gonnohyoe (1852–1933), Japanese statesman, prime minister 1913–1914 and 1923–24.

Yamamoto, Isoroku (1884–1943), Japanese admiral, planned the attack on Pearl Harbor.

Yamashita, Tomoyuki (1885–1946), Japanese soldier, commanded the forces which conquered Malaya, Singapore and the Philippines in World War II.

yard, imperial standard length established in Britain 1844; defined by Weights and Measures Act 1878.

Yaroslav (d. 1054), prince of Kiev, extended his rule over much of Russia.

Yarrow, Sir Albert (1842–1932), English shipbuilder, notably of military vessels.

year, solar year: 365 days 5 hrs 48 min. 46 sec.; sidereal year: 365 days 6 hrs 9 min. 10 sec.

Yeardley, Sir George (c. 1580–1627), English governor of Virginia 1619–21 and 1626–27, summoned first American representative assembly.

Year of Confusion, first year of Julian calendar, including 80 extra days, 46 B.C.

Yeats, William Butler (1865–1939), Irish poet, leader of Irish literary renaissance, founded Abbey Theatre; Nobel prizewinner 1932.

Yellow Book, quarterly English journal notable for 'decadent' writings and illustrations, published 1894–97.

yellow fever, cause, mosquito-borne virus discovered 1901 by Walter Reed (*q.v.*).

Yellowstone National Park, first American national park to be designated, 1872.

Yemen, People's Democratic Republic of, Arabian Peninsula, states in treaty relationship with Britain from c. 1840, subsequently forming the Aden Protectorate; some states established Federation of South Arabia 1959; later joined by others; became an independent republic 1967.

Yemen Arab Republic, Arabian Peninsula, ancient Minaean kingdom 2nd millennium B.C.; under Egyptian, Roman and Ethiopian rule; converted to Islam A.D. 628; under Ottoman Turkish rule 1538–1630; reoccupied by Turks in 19th century; independent monarchy established after World War I; became a republic 1962.

Yiddish language, dates from at least 10th century; manuscript literature developed 12th–13th centuries.

Yin dynasty. See **Shang dynasty.**

Yokohama, Japanese port, opened to foreign trade 1859.

Yom Kippur, holiest day in the Jewish year, falls on the 10th day of Tishri (during last two weeks of September and first two weeks of October).

Yom Kippur War. See **October War.**

Yonge, Charlotte (1823–1901), English writer, author of *Heir of Redclyffe* (1853).

Yoritomo (1147–99), Japanese ruler, founder of the Kamakura shogunate.

York Minster, erected 13th–15th centuries.

Yorktown, Virginia, scene of siege at which British commander Cornwallis surrendered to Washington, 1781.

Yosemite National Park, California, designated 1890.

Yoshida, Shigeru (1878–1967), Japanese statesman, as prime minister 1946–54 founded his country's postwar prosperity.

Youmans, Vincent (1898–1946), American musical-comedy composer, wrote *No, No, Nanette* (1924).

Young, Sir Allen (1827–1915), English naval commander, made several expeditions to the Arctic.

Young, Andrew (1807–89), Scottish hymn-writer, e.g. *There is a Happy Land.*

Young, Arthur (1741–1820), English agricultural writer, publicized new methods; his *Travels in France* (1792) is a valuable record.

Young, Brigham (1801–77), American Mormon leader, succeeded Joseph Smith (*q.v.*); founded Salt Lake City 1847.

Young, Edward (1683–1765), English poet, popular for the romantic gloom of his *Night Thoughts* (1742).

Young, James (1811–83), Scottish chemist, founded paraffin industry.

Young, Thomas (1773–1829), English physician, physicist and Egyptologist of varied achievement; described astigmatism and deciphered hieroglyphics.

Young England, romantic conservative group, active c. 1842–c. 1848.

Younghusband, Sir Francis (1863–1942), English explorer, led expeditions to Central Asia and opened up Tibet to Europeans.

Young Ireland, Irish nationalist group, active c. 1842–c. 1848.

Young Italy, Italian nationalist group, founded 1832 by Giuseppe Mazzini (*q.v.*).

Young Men's Christian Association, Y.M.C.A., founded in London 1844 by Sir George Williams (1821–1905).

Young Women's Christian Association, founded in London 1855 by Lady Kinnaird (1816–88).

Youth Hostels Association, British, founded 1930.

Ypres, Battles of, World War I; first, Oct.–Nov. 1914; second, April–May 1915; third, July–Nov. 1917.

Yriarte, Tomás de (1750–91), Spanish poet and composer, wrote *Fábulas Literarias* (1782).

Ysaÿe, Eugène (1858–1931), Belgian violin virtuoso, also a noted teacher and composer.

ytterbium, metallic element discovered 1878 by the French scientist Jean-Charles de Marignac (1817–94).

yttrium, metallic element, discovered 1794

by the Finnish chemist Johan Gadolin (1760–1852).

Yuan dynasty, China, 1280–1368.

Yüan Shi-k'ai (1859–1916), Chinese statesman, first president of the Chinese Republic.

Yugoslavia, proclaimed a kingdom Dec. 1918; absolute monarchy 1929–34; Communist republic since 1945; adopted new constitution 1963.

Yukawa, Hideki (b. 1907), Japanese physicist, first man to postulate the existence of the meson.

Yule, Sir Henry (1820–89), Scottish administrator in India, compiled *Hobson-Jobson* (1886), an Anglo-Indian glossary.

Yung Lo (1359–1424), emperor of China 1403–24, whose reign marked the peak of Ming power.

Z

Zachary, Saint (d. 752), Pope 741–752, cemented papal-Carolingian alliance by confirming crowning of Pepin the Short (*q.v.*).

Zaehnsdorff, Joseph (1816–86), Hungarian-born London bookbinder, whose work was much admired.

Zagreb University, Yugoslavia, founded 1874.

Zaharoff, Sir Basil (1849–1936), Turkish-born arms manufacturer of European-wide influence.

Zaïre, Africa, originated with establishment of Congo Free State 1885; annexed to Belgium 1908; achieved independence 1960.

Zambia, administered by British South Africa Company 1889–1924; British protectorate 1924; part of Federation of Rhodesia and Nyasaland 1953–63; became an independent member of the Commonwealth of Nations 1963.

Zamenhof, Ludovic (1859–1917), Polish linguist, invented Esperanto 1887.

Zandonai, Riccardo (1883–1944), Italian composer, wrote *Francesca da Rimini* (1914).

Zangwill, Israel (1864–1926), English novelist, often on Jewish subjects, e.g. *Children of the Ghetto* (1892).

Zanzibar, under Portuguese domination during 16th–17th centuries; united with island of Pemba 1822; became a British protectorate 1890; independent 1963; sultanate overthrown 1964, and republic proclaimed which united with Tanganyika to form Tanzania (*q.v.*).

Zapata, Emiliano (*c.* 1879–1919), Mexican revolutionary and radical agrarian reformer; assassinated.

zebra crossing. See **pedestrian crossing.**

Zeebrugge Raid, World War I, 22–23 April 1918.

Zeeman, Pieter (1865–1943), Dutch physicist, discovered the Zeeman Spectral Effect 1896; Nobel prizewinner 1902.

Zeiss, Carl (1816–88), German maker of optical instruments, founded well-known firm.

Zeller, Eduard (1814–1908), German philosopher, wrote studies of the subject.

Zemstvos, Russian provincial assemblies, formed 1864.

Zen, school of Buddhism, originated in China *c.* A.D. 520.

Zeno (426–491), Eastern Roman emperor 474–491, diverted Theodoric from Byzantium to conquest of Italy.

Zeno of Citium (*c.* 340–*c.* 270 B.C.), Greek philosopher, founded Stoic school.

Zeno of Elea (5th cent. B.C.), Greek philosopher, disciple of Parmenides and famous dialectician.

Zenobia (d. *c.* A.D. 273), queen of Palmyra 267–272, defeated by the Roman emperor Aurelian.

Zephyrinus, Saint (d. 217), Pope 198–217, involved in doctrinal disputes.

Zeppelin, rigid airship, designed by the German inventor Count Ferdinand von Zeppelin (1838–1917) and first flown 1900; first used in attack on London June 1915.

zero. See **absolute zero.**

Zeromski, Stefan (1864–1925), Polish novelist, author of *The Homeless* (1900).

Zetkin, Clara (1857–1933), German politician, Communist from 1919, member of Presidium of Third International.

Zeuss, Johann Kaspar (1806–56), German pioneer in Celtic philology.

Zevi, Sabbatai (1626–76), Jewish self-proclaimed Messiah, won huge following; recanted when threatened with death.

Zhdanov, Andrei (1896–1948), Soviet politician and soldier, defended Leningrad; enforced Socialist Realism on writers.

Zhukov, Georgi (1896–1974), Soviet military leader, outstanding general in World War II.

Zhukovski, Vassily (1783–1852), Russian poet, whose translations introduced European Romanticism to Russia.

Ziegfeld, Florenz (1869–1932), American theatre producer of lavish 'Ziegfeld Follies' shows.

Zimbabwe, Rhodesian ruins of disputed origin, dating from 11th century onwards. See also **Rhodesia.**

Zimisces, John (925–976), Byzantine emperor 969–976, recovered Bulgaria and Syria.

zinc, used in alloy form (brass) since prehistoric times; element isolated *c.* 13th century in India; rediscovered in Europe by Paracelsus (*q.v.*).

Zingarelli, Nicola (1752–1837), Italian opera composer, teacher of Bellini.

Zinoviev Letter, forged instructions for Communist rising in Britain, published Oct. 1924, purportedly written by the head of the Comintern Grigori Evseivich Zinoviev (1888–1936).

Zinzendorf, Nikolaus (1700–60), German noble, rescued the persecuted Moravian Brethren and settled them in America.

Zionist Congress, first world, held at Basel 1897.

Zionist movement, founded 1897 by Theodor Herzl (*q.v.*).

zip, invented and exhibited 1893 by the American Whitcomb L. Judson; improved versions appeared 1902 and 1913.

zirconium, metallic element, isolated 1824 by Baron Berzelius (*q.v.*).

Žižka, John (*c.* 1360–1424), Bohemian Hussite leader of the Taborites, defeated imperial armies.

Zoffany, John (*c.* 1734–1810), German-born English painter of portraits and theatrical scenes.

Zog (1895–1961), king of Albania 1928–39, driven out by Italians; deposed 1946.

Zola, Émile (1840–1902), French novelist, pioneered documentary naturalism in Rougon-Macquart series, e.g. *Germinal* (1885).

Zöllner, Johann Karl (1834–82), German astrophysicist, constructed astrophotometer.

Zollverein, German customs union, formed 1834.

Zomba, capital of Malawi, established *c.* 1880.

Zoological Society, London, founded 1826 by Sir Stamford Raffles (*q.v.*).

Zorn, Anders (1860–1920), Swedish Impressionist painter, worked in Europe and U.S.A.

Zoroaster (*c.* 6th cent. B.C.), Persian religious leader, founder of Zoroastrian religion; martyred.

Zorilla, José (1817–93), Spanish poet and playwright, author of *Don Juan Tenorio* (1844).

Zoshchenko, Mikhail (1895–1958), Soviet satirical writer, author of *The Merry Life* (1924).

Zosimus (5th cent. A.D.), Byzantine historian, wrote history of the imperial period.

Zosimus, Saint (d. 418), Pope 417–418, condemned Pelagian beliefs.

Zsigmondy, Richard (1865–1929), Austrian pioneer in development of colloidal chemistry; was awarded the Nobel Prize for Chemistry in 1925.

Zuccarelli, Francesco (1702–88), Italian painter of landscape scenes.

Zuccaro, Federigo (1543–1609), Italian painter of the Mannerist school, worked in England and Spain.

Zuccaro, Taddeo (1529–66), Italian painter, brother of Federigo Zuccaro, painted large decorative works.

Zucchi, Antonio (1726–95), Italian painter, worked in England; husband of Angelica Kauffmann (*q.v.*).

Zuckerman, Sir Solly (b. 1904), South African-born British zoologist, chief government scientific adviser 1964–71.

Zuckmayer, Carl (1896–1977), German playwright, author of *The Captain from Kopenick* (1931).

Zuider Zee, Netherlands, drainage scheme completed 1932.

Zukor, Adolph (1873–1977), Hungarian-born film producer in U.S.A., chairman of Paramount Pictures.

Zuloaga, Ignacio (1870–1945), Spanish painter of national subjects.

Zululand, Anglo–Zulu war 1879; annexed by British 1887; incorporated in Natal 1897.

Zumalacarregui, Tomás (1788–1835), Spanish soldier in Napoleonic and Carlist Wars.

Zurbarán, Francisco de (1598–*c.* 1665), Spanish painter of austerely pious works for religious houses in Spain and Spanish America.

Zutphen, Netherlands, Siege of, Sept. 1586.

Zweig, Arnold (1887–1968), German novelist, wrote *The Case of Sergeant Guischa* (1927); lived in Palestine 1933–48 and East Germany 1948–68.

Zweig, Stefan (1881–1942), Austrian writer, of poetry, novels and biographical studies.

Zwingli, Huldreich (1484–1531), Swiss Protestant reformer in Zurich; killed in battle.

zymose, yeast-cell fermenting agent discovered 1903 by Eduard Buchner (*q.v.*).

ANNIVERSARIES
PEOPLE AND EVENTS

1st JANUARY
New Year's Day. Julian Calendar began in 45 B.C. The Festival of the Circumcision.

Needle and Thread Ceremony
On this day the Bursar of Queen's College, Oxford, presents to each guest at the 'gaudy' a needle and thread – 'aiguille' and 'fil', a pun on the name of Robert de Eglesfield, founder of the College (1340) – with the words 'Take this and be thrifty'.

People
1449	Lorenzo de' Medici born.
1515	Louis XII, King of France, died.
1559	Christian III, King of Denmark and Norway, died.
1651	Charles II crowned King of Scots at Scone.
1697	Joseph Dupleix, Governor-General of India under the French, born.
1766	James Stuart, the Old Pretender, died.
1767	Maria Edgeworth, novelist, born.
1800	Francis Egerton, Earl of Ellesmere, statesman and poet, born.
1854	Francis Place, radical reformer, died.
1863	Baron Pierre de Coubertin, reviver of the Olympic Games, born.
1894	Heinrich Hertz, physicist, died.
1944	Sir Edwin Lutyens, architect, died.

Events
1801	Act of Union between Great Britain and Ireland came into force.
1804	Haiti declared its independence.
1887	Queen Victoria proclaimed Empress of India at Delhi.
1901	The Commonwealth of Australia formed.
1909	Old-age pensions became payable to people aged 70 and over in Britain.
1910	Labour Exchanges Act came into operation in Britain.
1923	Union of Soviet Socialist Republics proclaimed.
1926	Nationalist government established in China.
1948	Nationalization of all British railways came into effect.
1956	Sudan achieved independence.
1958	The European Economic Community came into existence.
1960	Cameroon achieved independence.
1962	Western Samoa achieved independence.
1973	Britain became a member of the European Economic Community.
1974	Coalition government formed in Northern Ireland.

2nd JANUARY
Berchtold's Day (Switzerland).

People
1322	Philip V, King of France, died.
1647	Nathaniel Bacon, American pioneer, born.
1727	James Wolfe, soldier, born.
1861	Frederick William IV, King of Prussia, died.
1891	A. W. Kinglake, writer and traveller, died.
1892	Sir George Airy, astronomer, died.
1898	Sir Edward Bond, antiquarian, died.
1905	Sir Michael Tippett, composer, born.

Events
1492	Spanish army took Granada from the Moors.
1896	The Jameson Raid ended.
1905	Port Arthur, Manchuria, captured by the Japanese.
1933	Anarchist rising in Barcelona.
1946	King Zog of Albania deposed *in absentia*.
1959	Luna I, first rocket to pass near the Moon, launched.

3rd JANUARY
Feast of St Geneviève, patron saint of Paris.

People

106 B.C.	Marcus Tullius Cicero, Roman statesman and writer, born.
1497	Beatrice d'Este, patron of the arts and diplomat, died.
1641	Jeremiah Horrocks, astronomer, died.
1670	George Monck, Duke of Albemarle, died.
1795	Josiah Wedgwood, English potter, died.
1840	Father Damien, missionary, born.
1858	Rachel, actress, died.
1883	Clement Attlee, statesman, born.
1883	Herbert Morrison, statesman, born.
1894	Elizabeth Palmer Peabody, kindergarten pioneer, died.
1915	James Elroy Flecker, poet, died.
1931	Joseph Joffre, soldier, died.

Events

1521	Martin Luther excommunicated.
1777	Battle of Princeton.
1959	Alaska achieved statehood.

4th JANUARY

People

1581	Archbishop Ussher, scholar, born.
1785	Jakob Grimm, philologist and folklorist, born.
1809	Louis Braille, benefactor of the blind, born.
1813	Sir Isaac Pitman, shorthand pioneer, born.
1879	Augustus John, artist, born.
1941	Henri Bergson, philosopher, died.
1958	Ralph Vaughan Williams, composer, died.
1960	Albert Camus, novelist, died.
1965	T. S. Eliot, poet, died.

Events

1642	King Charles I attempted the arrest of five members of Parliament.
1896	Utah achieved statehood.
1948	Burma became independent.

5th JANUARY
Wassail Eve (Britain).

People

1066	Edward the Confessor, King of England, died.
1589	Catherine de' Medici, Queen of France, died.
1762	The Empress Elizabeth of Russia died.
1779	Stephen Decatur, American naval commander, born.
1816	Sir George Prevost, soldier and statesman, died.
1855	King Gillette, inventor, born.
1858	Joseph Radetzky, soldier, died.
1876	Konrad Adenauer, statesman, born.
1922	Sir Ernest Shackleton, explorer, died.
1941	Amy Johnson, aviator, died.
1943	George Washington Carver, American Negro scientist, died.

Events

1477	Battle of Nancy.
1919	National Socialist (German Workers') Party founded.

6th JANUARY
Epiphany.   Twelfth Night.   Old Christmas Day.   Feast of the Three Kings.

People
- 1367   Richard II, King of England, born.
- c. 1412   Joan of Arc born.
- 1831   Rodolphe Kreutzer, violinist, died.
- 1838   Max Bruch, composer, born.
- 1840   Fanny Burney (Madame d'Arblay), novelist, died.
- 1872   Alexander Scriabin, composer, born.
- 1878   Carl Sandburg, poet, born.
- 1919   Theodore Roosevelt, statesman, died.

Events
- 871   Battle of Ashdown.
- 1579   Union of Arras.
- 1912   New Mexico achieved statehood.

7th JANUARY
Christmas Day (Orthodox Churches).

People
- 1502   Pope Gregory XIII born.
- 1536   Catherine of Aragon, Queen of England, died.
- 1655   Pope Innocent X died.
- 1715   François Fénelon, writer, died.
- 1758   Allan Ramsay, poet, died.
- 1768   Joseph Bonaparte, King of Naples, born.
- 1794   Eilhard Mitscherlich, chemist, born.
- 1800   Millard Fillmore, statesman, born.
- 1830   Sir Thomas Lawrence, painter, died.
- 1873   Adolph Zukor, film industry pioneer, born.
- 1899   Francis Poulenc, composer, born.
- 1912   Sophia Jex-Blake, champion of women's rights, died.

Events
- 1558   Calais, last English possession in France, regained by the French.
- 1789   First American national election.

8th JANUARY

People
- 1198   Pope Celestine III died.
- 1337   Giotto, artist, died.
- 1642   Galileo Galilei, astronomer, died.
- 1825   Eli Whitney, inventor, died.
- 1871   Viscount Craigavon, statesman, born.
- 1896   Paul Verlaine, poet, died.
- 1896   Jaromir Weinberger, composer, born.
- 1941   Robert Baden-Powell, founder of Boy Scouts, died.
- 1976   Chou En-lai, revolutionary and statesman, died.

Events
- 1815   Battle of New Orleans.
- 1916   Allied operations in Gallipoli ended.
- 1918   President Wilson's 'Fourteen Points' announced.
- 1926   Ibn Saud proclaimed King of the Hejaz.

9th JANUARY

People

1554   Pope Gregory XV born.
1735   Earl St Vincent, admiral, born.
1757   Bernard de Fontenelle, writer, died.
1859   Carrie Chapman Catt, suffragette, born
1873   Napoleon III, Emperor of France, died.
1890   Karel Čapek, playwright, born.
1913   Richard Nixon, statesman, born.
1923   Katherine Mansfield, novelist, died.

Events

1792   Peace of Jassy between Russia and Turkey.
1957   Anthony Eden resigned as British prime minister.

10th JANUARY

People

1276   Pope Gregory X died.
1645   Archbishop Laud executed.
1738   Ethan Allen, American patriot, born.
1778   Carl Linnaeus, naturalist, died.
1855   Mary Russell Mitford, writer, died.
1834   Lord Acton, historian, born.

Events

1308   The Templars suppressed in England
1840   Penny post came into operation in Britain.
1863   London's Underground Railway inaugurated.
1890   Cleopatra's tomb discovered.
1946   First United Nations General Assembly held in London.

11th JANUARY   Hilary Law Sittings begin.

People

1494   Ghirlandaio, artist, died.
1753   Sir Hans Sloane, physician, died.
1757   Alexander Hamilton, statesman, born.
1762   L. F. Roubillac, sculptor, died.
1829   Friedrich von Schlegel, poet, died.
1842   William James, philosopher, born.
1843   Francis Scott Key, lawyer and poet, died.
1857   Fred Archer, jockey, born.
1864   Harry Gordon Selfridge, merchant, born.
1882   Theodor Schwann, physiologist, died.
1928   Thomas Hardy, novelist, died.

Events

1861   Benito Juarez returned to Mexico City.
1946   Albania declared a republic.

12th JANUARY

People

1519   The Holy Roman Emperor Maximilian I died.
1588   John Winthrop, statesman, born.
1628   Charles Perrault, writer, born.

1729   Edmund Burke, statesman, born.
1746   J. H. Pestalozzi, educationalist, born.
1852   Joseph Joffre, soldier, born.
1860   Sir Charles Oman, historian, born.
1878   Ferenc Molnár, playwright, born.
1893   Hermann Goering, Nazi leader, born.
1960   Neville Shute, novelist, died.
1976   Dame Agatha Christie, novelist, died.

Events

1906   Landslide Liberal victory in British general election.
1964   Zanzibar proclaimed a republic.
1970   End of Nigerian civil war.

13th JANUARY

Canute's Day (Sweden).

People

86B.C. Gaius Marius, Roman soldier and statesman, died.
1691   George Fox, Quaker, died.
1864   Wilhelm Wien, physicist, born.
1864   Stephen Foster, song writer, died.
1941   James Joyce, writer, died.

Events

1864   The Zemstvos, or provincial assemblies, formed in Russia.
1874   Conscription introduced in Russia.

14th JANUARY

Mallard Day (All Souls: Oxford).

People

1575   Barbara Uttman, lace-maker, died.
1640   Lord Coventry, statesman, died.
1742   Edmund Halley, astronomer, died.
1806   Matthew Maury, oceanographer, born.
1847   The Rev. Wilson Carlile, founder of the Church Army, born.
1850   Pierre Loti, writer, born.
1867   Jean Ingres, artist, died.
1875   Albert Schweitzer, medical missionary, born.
1890   Lord Napier of Magdala, soldier, died.
1892   Cardinal Manning died.
1898   Lewis Carroll (Charles Dodgson), writer and mathematician, died.
1977   Sir Anthony Eden (Earl of Avon), statesman, died.

Events

1604   The Hampton Court Conference began.
1814   Norway ceded to the King of Sweden by the King of Denmark.
1858   Orsini's (unsuccessful) attempt on Napoleon III's life.
1935   Oil pipeline (Kirkuk to Haifa) inaugurated.
1943   Casablanca Conference began.

15th JANUARY

People

69   The Roman Emperor Galba assassinated.
1342   Philip the Bold, Duke of Burgundy, born.
1622   Molière, playwright, baptized.

15th January

1791   Franz Grillparzer, poet, born.
1815   Emma, Lady Hamilton, mistress of Lord Nelson, died.
1893   Fanny Kemble, actress, died.
1896   Matthew Brady, photographer, died.
1912   Henry Labouchère, editor, died.
1929   Martin Luther King, civil rights leader, born.

Events

1535   The Act of Supremacy in England.
1759   The British Museum opened.
1790   Lettres de cachet abolished in France.
1922   The Irish Free State came into being.

16th JANUARY

People

1599   Edmund Spenser, poet, died.
1794   Edward Gibbon, historian, died.
1809   Sir John Moore, soldier, died.
1891   Léo Delibes, composer, died.

Events

1547   The first Russian Tsar (Ivan the Terrible) crowned.
1556   The Emperor Charles V abdicated.
1809   Battle of Corunna (La Coruña).
1839   Aden annexed to British India.
1906   The Conference of Algeciras began.
1909   The Shackleton Expedition reached the Magnetic South Pole.
1920   Prohibition came into force in the United States.
1929   *The Listener* began publication.

17th JANUARY
St Anthony's Day.

People

395   The Emperor Theodosius I died.
1504   Pope Pius V born.
1600   Pedro Calderón de la Barca, playwright, born.
1706   Benjamin Franklin, statesman, scientist and writer, born.
1863   David Lloyd George, statesman, born.
1871   David, Earl Beatty, admiral, born.
1873   Compton Mackenzie, writer, born.
1903   Quintin Hogg, Polytechnic founder, died.

Events

1377   The Papal See was transferred from Avignon back to Rome.
1746   Battle of Falkirk.
1852   The Sand River Convention signed.

18th JANUARY

People

1779   Peter Mark Roget, thesaurus-writer, born.
1782   Daniel Webster, statesman, born.
1840   Austin Dobson, poet, born.
1841   Emmanuel Chabrier, composer, born.
1856   Joseph Haydn, compiler of the *Dictionary of Dates*, died.

1863   Konstantin Stanislavski, actor-manager, born.
1873   Lord Lytton, writer, died.
1936   Rudyard Kipling, poet and novelist, died.
1963   Hugh Gaitskell, statesman, died.

Events

1562   The Council of Trent reconvened after a suspension of 10 years.
1778   Hawaii discovered by Captain Cook.
1871   The German Empire proclaimed.
1912   Captain Scott reached the South Pole.
1943   The siege of Leningrad raised.

19th JANUARY

People

1544   Francis II, King of France, born.
1736   James Watt, inventor, born.
1737   Bernardin de Saint Pierre, writer, born.
1798   Auguste Comte, philosopher, born.
1807   Robert E. Lee, Confederate soldier, born.
1809   Edgar Allan Poe, writer, born.
1813   Sir Henry Bessemer, engineer, born.
1839   Paul Cézanne, artist, born.
1881   Auguste Mariette, Egyptologist, died.

Events

1563   The Heidelberg Catechism published.
1840   Captain Wilkes discovered Antarctic coast.
1899   Condominium of Britain and Egypt over the Sudan established.
1966   Indira Gandhi became prime minister of India.

20th JANUARY
St Agnes' Eve.   Inauguration Day (U.S.A.).

People

1612   The Holy Roman Emperor Rudolf II died.
1779   David Garrick, actor, died.
1790   John Howard, prison reformer, died.
1875   J. F. Millet, painter, died.
1900   John Ruskin, art critic, died.
1926   Charles Doughty, traveller and poet, died.
1936   George V, King of Great Britain, died.

Events

1841   Hong Kong ceded to Britain by China.
1961   Inauguration of John F. Kennedy as U.S. President.

21st JANUARY
Feast of St Agnes.

People

1118   Pope Paschal II died.
1547   The Earl of Surrey, poet and soldier, executed.
1609   Joseph Scaliger, scholar and critic, died.
1766   James Quin, actor, died.

1793   Louis XVI, King of France, guillotined.
1813   John Charles Frémont, explorer, born.
1814   Bernardin de Saint Pierre, writer, died.
1824   'Stonewall' Jackson, Confederate soldier, born.
1829   Oscar II, King of Sweden and Norway, born.
1840   Sophia Jex-Blake, champion of women's rights, born.
1855   Ernest Chausson, composer, born.
1872   Franz Grillparzer, poet, died.
1901   Elisha Gray, inventor, died.,
1924   Lenin, revolutionary and statesman, died.
1950   George Orwell, writer, died.

Events

1769   The letters of Junius began publication.
1772   The letters of Junius last appeared.
1907   Britain first officially recognized the existence of taxi-cabs.
1936   Edward VIII proclaimed King of Great Britain.
1954   The U.S. *Nautilus*, first nuclear-powered submarine, launched.

22nd JANUARY
St Vincent's Day.

People

1561   Francis Bacon, statesman and writer, born.
1729   Gotthold Lessing, writer, born.
1775   André Ampère, physicist, born.
1788   Lord Byron, poet, born.
1799   Horace Bénédict de Saussure, physicist, died.
1849   August Strindberg, playwright, born.
1858   Beatrice Webb, social reformer, born.
1875   D. W. Griffith, pioneer film director, born.
1887   Sir Joseph Whitworth, mechanical engineer, died.
1901   Queen Victoria died.
1906   George Jacob Holyoake, reformer and secularist, died.
1942   Richard Sickert, painter, died.
1973   Lyndon B. Johnson, statesman, died.

Events

1905   'Bloody Sunday' in St Petersburg.
1924   First Labour prime minister took office in Britain.
1944   Anzio landings in Italy began.
1976   Cease-fire agreement in Lebanon.

23rd JANUARY

People

1002   The Holy Roman Emperor Otto III died.
1783   Stendhal, novelist, born.
1806   William Pitt, statesman, died
1832   Edouard Manet, artist, born.
1837   John Field, composer, died.
1841   Benoît-Constant Coquelin, actor, born.
1875   Charles Kingsley, poet and novelist, died.
1878   Rutland Boughton, composer, born.
1931   Anna Pavlova, ballerina, died.
1936   Dame Clara Butt, singer, died.
1956   Sir Alexander Korda, film producer, died.
1976   Paul Robeson, singer, died.

Events

1571 Royal Exchange, London, opened.
1579 Treaty of Utrecht.
1719 The Principality of Liechtenstein constituted.
1943 Tripoli captured by the British.

24th JANUARY

People

1712 Frederick the Great, King of Prussia, born.
1732 Pierre de Beaumarchais, playwright, born.
1746 Gustavus III, King of Sweden, born.
1749 Charles James Fox, statesman, born.
1818 John Mason Neale, hymn-writer, born.
1862 Edith Wharton, novelist, born.
1883 Friedrich Flotow, composer, died.
1944 Edward Munch, painter, died.
1965 Sir Winston Churchill, statesman, died.

Events

1616 Cape Horn first rounded by Willem Schouten (24–31 Jan.).
1848 Gold first discovered in California.
1908 First Boy Scout troop formed in England.
1915 Naval Battle of the Dogger Bank.
1943 Casablanca Conference ended.

25th JANUARY
Feast of the Conversion of St Paul.

People

1540 Edmund Campion, Jesuit martyr, born.
1627 Robert Boyle, physicist, born.
1640 Robert Burton, writer, died.
1736 Joseph Louis Lagrange, mathematician, born.
1746 Comtesse de Genlis, writer, born.
1759 Robert Burns, poet, born.
1786 Benjamin Haydon, painter, born.
1841 Lord Fisher, naval strategist, born.
1857 Lord Lonsdale, sportsman, born.
1874 W. Somerset Maugham, writer, born.
1886 Wilhelm Furtwängler, conductor, born.
1960 Rutland Boughton, composer, died.

Events

1787 Abortive attempt to seize the U.S. Arsenal at Springfield, Mass.
1934 John Dillinger, bank robber, captured in Tucson, Arizona.
1952 Vincent Massey appointed first Canadian-born Governor-General of Canada.
1971 Milton Obote, President of Uganda, deposed by General Idi Amin.

26th JANUARY
Australia Day (Wattle Day).

People

1763 Charles XIV, King of Sweden, born.
1778 Ugo Foscolo, poet, born.

26th January

1823   Edward Jenner, pioneer in vaccination, died.
1880   Douglas MacArthur, soldier, born.
1885   General Gordon killed at Khartoum.
1939   W. B. Yeats, poet, died.

Events

1564   The decrees or definitions of the Council of Trent confirmed by Pope Pius IV.
1837   Michigan achieved statehood.
1871   The Rugby Union founded in Britain.
1885   Khartoum fell to the Mahdi's troops.
1939   Barcelona fell to the Spanish Nationalists.
1949   The first test photograph made at Mt Palomar Observatory.
1950   India proclaimed a Republic within the Commonwealth.

27th JANUARY

Feast of St John Chrysostom.

People

1720   Samuel Foote, actor and playwright, born.
1756   Wolfgang Amadeus Mozart, composer, born.
1775   Friedrich Wilhelm Joseph von Schelling, philosopher, born.
1814   Eugène Viollet-le-Duc, architect, born.
1823   Edouard Lalo, composer, born.
1832   Lewis Carroll (Charles Dodgson), writer and mathematician, born.
1851   John James Audubon, ornithologist, died.
1859   Kaiser Wilhelm II of Germany born.
1873   Adam Sedgwick, geologist, died.
1885   Jerome Kern, composer, born.
1901   Giuseppe Verdi, composer, died.
1951   Carl Mannerheim, soldier and statesman, died.

Events

1926   John Logie Baird gave first public demonstration of television in Britain.
1973   Cease-fire agreement between North Vietnam and the United States.

28th JANUARY

People

814   Charlemagne died.
1457   Henry VII, King of England, born.
1547   Henry VIII, King of England, died.
1595   Sir Francis Drake, navigator, died.
1613   Sir Thomas Bodley, book-collector, died.
1621   Pope Paul V died.
1706   John Baskerville, printer, born.
1725   Peter the Great, Tsar of Russia, died.
1791   L. J. Hérold, composer, born.
1833   General Gordon born.
1841   Sir Henry Stanley, explorer, born.
1861   Henri Murger, writer, died.
1939   W. B. Yeats, writer, died.
1947   Reynaldo Hahn, composer, died.

Events

1521   The Diet of Worms began.
1846   Battle of Aliwal, first Sikh War.
1871   Paris surrendered to the German army.

29th JANUARY

People

1119   Pope Gelasius II died.
1688   Emanuel Swedenborg, theologian, born.
1696   Ivan V, Tsar of Russia, died.
1737   Thomas Paine, reformer, born.
1782   Daniel Auber, composer, born.
1820   George III, King of Great Britain and Ireland, died.
1843   William McKinley, statesman, born.
1860   Anton Chekhov, playwright, born.
1862   Frederick Delius, composer, born.
1866   Romain Rolland, novelist, born.
1872   Sir William Rothenstein, artist, born.
1917   The Earl of Cromer, diplomat, died.
1928   Earl Haig, soldier, died.
1942   Bion Joseph Arnold, electrical engineer and inventor, died.
1963   Robert Frost, poet, died.

Events

1635   Académie Française formally established.
1728   John Gay's *The Beggar's Opera* first performed.
1820   George IV proclaimed King of Great Britain and Ireland.
1856   The Victoria Cross instituted.
1861   Kansas achieved statehood.
1935   The London County Council approved the Green Belt scheme.

30th JANUARY

Anniversary of King Charles the Martyr.   Feast of St Basil.

People

1730   Peter II, Tsar of Russia, died.
1775   Walter Savage Landor, writer, born.
1882   Franklin Delano Roosevelt, statesman, born.
1888   Edward Lear, artist and writer, died.
1889   Crown Prince Rudolf of Austria and Marie Vetsera committed suicide (the Mayerling tragedy).
1891   Charles Bradlaugh, reformer, died.
1948   Orville Wright, aviator, died.
1948   Mahatma Gandhi, Indian national leader, assassinated.
1963   Francis Poulenc, composer, died.

Events

1649   King Charles I executed.
1840   The Emperor of China forbade all trade with Britain.
1858   The Hallé Orchestra gave its first regular public concert.
1933   Adolf Hitler appointed Chancellor of Germany.
1959   First British drive-in bank opened.
1965   State funeral of Sir Winston Churchill.
1972   British troops shot 13 civilians during illegal march in Londonderry.

31st JANUARY

People

1606   Guy Fawkes, conspirator, executed.
1797   Franz Schubert, composer, born.
1885   Anna Pavlova, ballerina, born.

31st January

1892 C. H. Spurgeon, Baptist pastor, died.
1903 Tallulah Bankhead, actress, born.
1933 John Galsworthy, novelist and playwright, died.
1938 Princess Beatrix of the Netherlands born.

Events

1858 The *Great Eastern* launched.
1929 Leon Trotsky exiled from Russia.
1943 The Germans capitulated at Stalingrad.
1968 Nauru became independent.

1st FEBRUARY
Feast of St Bridget.

People

1552 Sir Edward Coke, legal expert, born.
1859 Victor Herbert, composer, born.
1873 Dame Clara Butt, singer, born.
1903 Sir George Stokes, mathematician and physicist, died.
1908 Carlos I, King of Portugal, assassinated.

Events

1790 U.S. Supreme Court held first meeting.
1811 Bell Rock Lighthouse started operating.
1910 First British state labour exchanges opened.
1917 Germany began unrestricted submarine warfare.
1939 The White Paper on Civil Defence in Britain published.
1941 The British Air Training Corps founded.
1957 First turbo-prop airliner entered into scheduled service in Britain.
1958 Egypt merged with Syria in the United Arab Republic.

2nd FEBRUARY
Candlemas.   Festival of the Purification of the Virgin.   Scottish Quarter Day.

People

1594 Giovanni da Palestrina, composer, died.
1875 Fritz Kreisler, violinist and composer, born.
1882 James Joyce, writer, born.
1901 Jascha Heifetz, violinist, born.

Events

1534 The Great Swabian League dissolved.
1808 Rome occupied by French forces.
1972 Mob burnt down British embassy in Dublin.

3rd FEBRUARY
St Blaise's Day.

People

1399 John of Gaunt died.
1809 Felix Mendelssohn-Bartholdy, composer, born.
1811 Horace Greeley, editor of the *New York Tribune*, born.
1821 Dr Elizabeth Blackwell, first English woman doctor, born.
1826 Walter Bagehot, economist and political writer, born.

1874   Gertrude Stein, writer, born.
1924   Woodrow Wilson, statesman, died.

Events
1830   Greece declared a kingdom by the Protocol of London.
1945   The Yalta Conference began.
1966   First soft landing on the Moon by Soviet spacecraft Luna 9.

4th FEBRUARY

People
211   The Roman Emperor Severus died at York.
999   Pope Gregory V died.
1617   Louis Elzevier, printer, died.
1805   Harrison Ainsworth, novelist, born.
1881   Thomas Carlyle, historian, died.
1902   Charles Lindbergh, aviator, born.
1950   Lord Norman, banker, died.

Events
1874   Battle of Kumasi ended the Ashanti War.
1915   Submarine warfare declared by Germany.
1938   Adolf Hitler took command of the German Army.
1948   Sri Lanka became independent.
1952   The United Nations Disarmament Commission first met.
1976   More than 23,000 dead in Guatemala earthquake.

5th FEBRUARY

People
1788   Sir Robert Peel, statesman, born.
1799   John Lindley, botanist, born.
1840   Sir Hiram Stevens Maxim, inventor, born.
1840   John Boyd Dunlop, inventor, born.
1848   J. K. Huysmans, writer, born.
1900   Adlai Stevenson, statesman, born.

Events
1811   Prince of Wales declared Prince Regent.
1818   Charles XIV proclaimed King of Sweden.
1920   The Royal Air Force College, Cranwell, founded.

6th FEBRUARY

People
1140   Thurstan, Archbishop of York, died.
1515   Aldus Manutius, printer, died.
1564   Christopher Marlowe, playwright, born.
1626   Mme de Sévigné, writer, born.
1665   Anne, Queen of Great Britain, born.
1685   Charles II, King of England and Scotland, died.
1804   Joseph Priestley, scientist, died.
1838   Sir Henry Irving, actor, born.
1952   George VI, King of Great Britain and Northern Ireland, died.

6th February

Events

1840   The Treaty of Waitangi.
1922   The Limitation of Armaments Conference, Washington, ended.
1934   The Stavisky riots in Paris (6–7 Feb.).
1952   Queen Elizabeth II succeeded to the British throne.
1959   National Day of New Zealand first changed to 6th February.

7th FEBRUARY

People

1478   Sir Thomas More, statesman, born.
1812   Charles Dickens, novelist, born.
1823   Mrs Radcliffe, novelist, died.
1837   Gustavus IV, King of Sweden, died.
1878   Pope Pius IX died.
1885   Sinclair Lewis, novelist, born.
1894   'Babe' Ruth, baseball player, born.
1937   Elihu Root, statesman, died.

Events

1831   The Belgian constitution published.
1941   Benghazi captured by the British.
1974   Grenada became independent.

8th FEBRUARY

People

1587   Mary, Queen of Scots, executed.
1819   John Ruskin, art critic, born.
1820   William Tecumseh Sherman, soldier, born.
1828   Jules Verne, novelist, born.
1888   Dame Edith Evans, actress, born.
1967   Sir Victor Gollancz, publisher, died.

Events

1861   The Confederate States of America formed.
1904   The outbreak of the Russo-Japanese War.
1910   The Boy Scouts of America formally incorporated.

9th FEBRUARY
St Apollonia's Day.

People

1567   Lord Darnley, husband of Mary Queen of Scots, murdered.
1670   Frederick III, King of Denmark, died.
1773   William Henry Harrison, statesman, born.
1854   Sir Edward Carson, lawyer and politician, born.
1860   John St Loe Strachey, editor, born.
1863   Anthony Hope, novelist, born.
1865   Mrs Patrick Campbell, actress, born.
1874   Jules Michelet, historian, died.
1881   Fyodor Dostoyevsky, novelist, died.
1885   Alban Berg, composer, born.
1894   Adolphe Sax, musical-instrument maker, died.
1923   Brendan Behan, playwright, born.
1960   Alexandre Benois, theatre designer, died.

Events

1830   Charles Sturt, the explorer, discovered the termination of the Murray River.
1849   The Republic of Rome proclaimed.
1870   The United States weather service established.
1934   The Balkan Entente signed at Athens.
1943   The Japanese evacuated Guadalcanal Island.

10th FEBRUARY

People

1306   John Comyn, claimant to the Scottish throne, killed.
1482   Luca della Robbia, sculptor, died.
1624   Heorge Heriot, jeweller and royal banker, died.
1775   Charles Lamb, essayist, born.
1824   Samuel Plimsoll, mercantile marine benefactor, born.
1829   Pope Leo XII died.
1837   Alexander Pushkin, writer, died.
1890   Boris Pasternak, writer, born.
1894   Harold Macmillan, statesman, born.
1912   Lord Lister, surgeon, died.
1939   Pope Pius XI died.

Events

1696   The Assassination Plot against William of Orange exposed.
1763   The Peace of Paris ceded Canada to Britain.
1840   Queen Victoria and Prince Albert married.
1840   Upper and Lower Canada united.
1931   New Delhi officially inaugurated.
1947   The U.S.S.R. signed a peace treaty with Finland.

11th FEBRUARY

People

731   Pope Gregory II died.
1435   Joanna II, Queen of Naples, died.
1535   Pope Gregory XIV, born.
1650   René Descartes, philosopher, died.
1657   Bernard de Fontenelle, writer, born.
1800   William Fox Talbot, pioneer photographer, born.
1821   Auguste Mariette, Egyptologist, born.
1847   Thomas Alva Edison, inventor, born.
1920   Farouk, King of Egypt, born.
1940   John Buchan, statesman and writer, died.
1960   Ernst von Dohnanyi, composer, died.

Events

1798   French troops captured Rome.
1858   First miracles of Lourdes.
1929   The Vatican City created an independent sovereign state.
1945   The Yalta Conference ended.
1971   Britain adopted decimal currency.

12th FEBRUARY

People

1554   Lady Jane Grey and Lord Guildford Dudley executed.
1637   Jan Swammerdam, naturalist, born.

12th February

1663	Cotton Mather, writer on witchcraft, born.
1690	Charles Le Brun, painter, died.
1746	Tadeusz Kosciusko, Polish patriot, born.
1768	Francis II, last Holy Roman Emperor, born.
1804	Immanuel Kant, philosopher, died.
1809	Charles Darwin, scientist, born.
1809	Abraham Lincoln, statesman, born.
1828	George Meredith, poet and novelist, born.
1870	Marie Lloyd, music hall comedian, born.

Events

1709	Alexander Selkirk (prototype of Robinson Crusoe) taken off Juan Fernandez Island.
1950	The European Broadcasting Union formed.

13th FEBRUARY

People

990	Ethelgar, Archbishop of Canterbury, died.
1615	Pope Innocent XII born.
1718	Lord Rodney, admiral, born.
1728	John Hunter, anatomist and surgeon, born.
1754	Prince Talleyrand, statesman, born.
1779	Captain James Cook, explorer, murdered.
1849	Lord Randolph Churchill, statesman, born.
1873	Fyodor Chaliapin, operatic singer, born.
1883	Richard Wagner, composer, died.
1908	James Knowles, editor and architect, died.
1950	Rafael Sabatini, novelist, died.
1958	Dame Christabel Pankhurst, suffragette, died.

Events

1689	William III and Mary proclaimed King and Queen of England.
1692	The massacre of Glencoe.
1859	The Corps of Commissionaires founded in Britain.
1866	The James-Younger gang robbed the bank at Liberty, Missouri (their first bank robbery).
1943	The Nuffield Foundation established.
1974	Alexander Solzhenitsyn, writer, expelled from Soviet Union.

14th FEBRUARY
St Valentine's Day.   Old Candlemas.

People

1130	Pope Honorius II died.
1400	Richard II probably murdered.
1845	Quintin Hogg, founder of the Polytechnic, born.
1945	Sir William Rothenstein, painter, died.
1975	Sir Julian Huxley, scientist, died.
1975	P. G. Wodehouse, novelist, died.

Events

1488	The Great Swabian League formed.
1797	Battle of Cape St Vincent.
1859	Oregon achieved statehood.
1912	Arizona achieved statehood.
1939	The *Bismarck* launched.
1958	The Arab Federation of Iraq and Jordan proclaimed.

15th FEBRUARY

People
1368 The Emperor Sigismund born.
1564 Galileo Galilei, scientist, born.
1680 Jan Swammerdam, naturalist, died.
1781 Gotthold Lessing, writer, died.
1809 Cyrus Hall McCormick, inventor, born.
1845 Elihu Root, statesman, born.
1857 M. I. Glinka, composer, died.
1861 A. N. Whitehead, philosopher, born.
1874 Sir Ernest Shackleton, explorer, born.
1928 The Earl of Oxford and Asquith, statesman, died.

Events
1898 The *Maine* blown up in Havana Harbour.
1922 First session of Permanent Court of International Justice.
1937 The Balkan Entente Conference held at Athens.
1942 The Japanese captured Singapore.
1945 British troops reached the Rhine.

16th FEBRUARY

People
1497 Philip Melanchthon, Church reformer, born.
1519 Gaspard de Coligny, soldier, born.
1620 Frederick William, the Great Elector, born.
1740 Giambattista Bodoni, printer, born.
1754 Richard Mead, royal physician, died.
1834 Ernst Haeckel, naturalist, born.
1838 Henry Adams, historian, born.
1848 Hugo de Vries, botanist, born.
1876 G. M. Trevelyan, historian, born.

Events
1824 The Athenaeum Club, London, founded.
1871 The capitulation of the fortress of Belfort to the German Army.
1945 Bataan, Philippines, taken by the Americans.
1959 Fidel Castro became prime minister of Cuba.

17th FEBRUARY

People
1673 Molière, playwright, died.
1688 James Renwick, Scottish Covenanter, executed.
1740 Horace de Saussure, physicist and Alpinist, born.
1766 Thomas Malthus, economist, born.
1856 Heinrich Heine, poet, died.
1862 Sir Edward German, composer, born.
1902 Marian Anderson, singer, born.
1934 Albert I, King of the Belgians, died.
1948 The Imam Yahya, King of the Yemen, murdered.

Events
1871 The Pact of Bordeaux signed.
1944 The White Paper concerning the British National Health Service published.
1965 Gambia became independent.

18th FEBRUARY

People

1478   The Duke of Clarence put to death in the Tower of London.
1516   Mary I, Queen of England, born.
1546   Martin Luther, Church reformer, died.
1564   Michelangelo Buonarroti, artist, died.
1745   Count Alessandro Volta, physicist, born.
1790   Marshall Hall, physician, born.
1795   George Peabody, philanthropist, born.
1855   Jean Jusserand, diplomat and historian, born.

Events

1678   *Pilgrim's Progress* published.
1725   The Order of the Bath revived.
1861   The Italian Parliament opened.
1915   The German submarine blockade of Britain began.
1951   The King of Nepal proclaimed a constitutional monarchy.
1965   Gambia became independent.

19th FEBRUARY

People

1473   Nicolaus Copernicus, astronomer, born.
1622   Sir Henry Savile, classical scholar and philanthropist, died.
1717   David Garrick, actor, born.
1843   Adelina Patti, operatic singer, born.
1859   Svante Arrhenius, physicist, born.
1865   Sven Hedin, traveller, born.
1941   Sir Hamilton Harty, conductor, died.
1951   André Gide, writer, died.

Events

1674   The Peace of Westminster.
1797   The Peace of Tolentino.
1940   Battle of the *Altmark*.

20th FEBRUARY

People

1431   Pope Martin V died.
1437   James I, King of Scotland, assassinated.
1500   The Holy Roman Emperor Charles V born.
1677   Baruch Spinoza, philosopher, died.
1790   The Holy Roman Emperor Joseph II died.
1810   Andreas Hofer, Tirolese patriot, executed.
1820   Henri Vieuxtemps, violinist, born.
1861   Eugène Scribe, playwright, died.
1887   Vincent Massey, statesman, born.
1920   Robert Peary, explorer, died.
1960   Sir Leonard Woolley, archaeologist, died.

Events

1909   First Manifesto of Futurism (art movement) issued.
1915   The Panama-Pacific International Exposition opened at San Francisco.
1917   The U.S.A. bought the Dutch West Indies.
1938   Anthony Eden resigned as British Foreign Secretary.

21st FEBRUARY
International Youth Day of Struggle against Colonialism (U.S.S.R. and countries of Eastern Europe).

People
1513 Pope Julius II died.
1595 Robert Southwell, poet and Jesuit martyr, hanged.
1728 Peter III, Tsar of Russia, born.
1741 Jethro Tull, agricultural writer, died.
1779 Friedrich Karl von Savigny, jurist, born.
1801 Cardinal Newman born.
1836 Léo Delibes, composer, born.
1859 George Lansbury, Labour leader, born.
1907 W. H. Auden, poet, born.
1941 Sir Frederick Banting, scientist, killed in an air-crash.

Events
1916 Battle of Verdun began.
1946 Indian naval mutiny at Bombay.
1952 Identity cards abolished in Britain.

22nd FEBRUARY

People
1440 Ladislaus V, King of Hungary, born.
1732 George Washington, soldier and statesman, born.
1788 Arthur Schopenhauer, philosopher, born.
1810 Frédéric Chopin, composer, born.
1819 James Russell Lowell, poet, born.
1827 Charles Willson Peale, painter, died.
1845 Sydney Smith, reformer, died.
1857 Lord Baden-Powell, founder of the Boy Scout movement, born.
1857 Heinrich Hertz, physicist, born.
1872 Eric Gill, artist, born.
1875 Jean Corot, painter, died.
1875 Sir Charles Lyell, geologist, died.
1890 Benno Moiseiwitsch, pianist, born.
1892 Edna St Vincent Millay, poet, born.

Events
1649 The Westminster Assembly ended.
1797 The last invasion of Britain: the French at Fishguard.
1819 Spain ceded Florida to the U.S.A.
1972 I.R.A. bomb attack at Aldershot killed seven.

23rd FEBRUARY

People
1447 Pope Eugene IV died.
1468 Johannes Gutenberg, printer, died.
1516 Ferdinand V, King of Castile and Leon, died.
1633 Samuel Pepys, diarist and administrator, born.
1685 George Frederick Handel, composer, born.
1792 Sir Joshua Reynolds, painter, died.
1817 Sir George Watts, painter, born.
1821 John Keats, poet, died.
1889 Erich Kästner, writer, born.

23rd February

1929   Sir Edward Marshall Hall, lawyer, died.
1931   Dame Nellie Melba, singer, died.
1934   Sir Edward Elgar, composer, died.
1955   Paul Claudel, writer and diplomat, died.
1976   L. S. Lowry, painter, died.

Events

1820   The Cato Street Conspiracy.
1836   The Siege of the Alamo, San Antonio, Texas, began.
1901   The United States Steel Corporation founded.
1920   First regular broadcasting service in Britain started from Chelmsford.
1942   Lease-Lend made reciprocal between the U.S.A. and Britain.

24th FEBRUARY   St Matthias' Day.

People

1547   Don John of Austria, soldier, born.
1693   James Quin, actor, born.
1786   Wilhelm Grimm, writer, born.
1810   Henry Cavendish, scientist, died.
1815   Robert Fulton, inventor, died.
1822   Thomas Coutts, banker, died.
1825   Thomas Bowdler, editor, died.
1852   George Moore, writer, born.
1856   Nicholas Lobachevsky, mathematician, died.

Events

1525   The Battle of Pavia.
1829   Cadiz made a free port.
1848   Louis Philippe, King of France, abdicated.
1966   President Kwame Nkrumah of Ghana deposed.

25th FEBRUARY

People

1601   Robert, Earl of Essex, favourite of Queen Elizabeth, executed.
1713   Frederick I, King of Prussia, died.
1723   Christopher Wren, architect, died.
1778   José de San Martin, South American patriot, born.
1841   Pierre Auguste Renoir, painter, born.
1852   Thomas Moore, poet, died.
1866   Benedetto Croce, philosopher, born.
1873   Enrico Caruso, operatic singer, born.
1890   Dame Myra Hess, pianist, born.
1914   Sir John Tenniel, artist and illustrator, died.

Events

1570   Pope Pius V excommunicated Queen Elizabeth I and declared her a usurper.
1862   'Greenbacks' first issued by Abraham Lincoln.
1913   First federal income tax became law in the U.S.A.
1938   Lord Halifax became British Foreign Secretary.

26th FEBRUARY

People

1154   Roger II, King of Sicily, died.
1266   Manfred, King of Sicily, killed in battle.
1723   Sir Christopher Wren, architect, died.

1802   Victor Hugo, writer, born.
1846   'Buffalo Bill' (William F. Cody) born.
1879   Frank Bridge, composer, born.

Events

493   The capitulation of Ravenna to Theodoric, King of the Ostrogoths.
1266   The Battle of Benevento.
1848   The Second French Republic proclaimed.

27th FEBRUARY

People

1706   John Evelyn, diarist, died.
1795   Francis Marion, American patriot and soldier, died.
1807   Henry Wadsworth Longfellow, poet, born.
1823   Ernest Renan, philosopher and theologian, born.
1848   Dame Ellen Terry, actress, born.
1848   Sir Hubert Parry, composer, born.
1850   Henry Huntington, railway promoter, born.
1854   Félicité de Lamennais, Church reformer, died.
1887   Alexander Borodin, composer, born.
1902   John Steinbeck, novelist, born.

Events

1558   Russia's first trade mission to England reached London.
1933   The burning of the Reichstag.

28th FEBRUARY

People

468   Saint Hilary, Pope, died.
1468   Pope Paul III, born.
1513   Robert Fabyan, historian, died.
1533   Michel de Montaigne, essayist, born.
1648   Christian IV, King of Denmark, died.
1683   René de Réaumur, scientist, born.
1820   Sir John Tenniel, artist and illustrator, born.
1821   Rachel, actress, born.
1865   Sir Wilfred Grenfell, medical missionary, born.
1869   Alphonse de Lamartine, poet, died.
1890   Vaslav Nijinsky, dancer, born.
1909   Stephen Spender, poet, born.
1916   Henry James, writer, died.
1941   Alfonso XIII, ex-King of Spain, died.

Events

1900   Ladysmith relieved (Boer War).
1922   The British Protectorate over Egypt ended.

29th FEBRUARY
Leap Year.

People

992   Saint Oswald, Archbishop of York, died.
1528   Patrick Hamilton, Scottish martyr, burnt at the stake.

29th February

1604	John Whitgift, Archbishop of Canterbury, died.
1712	Louis Joseph, Marquis de Montcalm, soldier, born.
1736	Ann Lee, founder of the Society of Shakers, born.
1792	Gioacchino Rossini, composer, born.

Events

1880	The junction of the galleries under the St Gothard Pass effected.
1892	The Behring Sea Arbitration Treaty signed.
1912	Military revolt in Peking.

1st MARCH
St David's Day.

People

1510	Francisco de Almeida, first Portuguese Viceroy of India, died.
1643	Girolamo Frescobaldi, organist and composer, died.
1757	Sir Samuel Romilly, lawyer, born.
1792	The Holy Roman Emperor Leopold II died.
1880	Lytton Strachey, author, born.
1883	Prince Gorchakov, statesman, died.
1886	Oskar Kokoschka, painter, born.
1938	Gabriele d'Annunzio, writer, died.

Events

1498	Mozambique discovered by Vasco da Gama's fleet.
1562	The massacre of the Huguenots at Wassy.
1711	The first number of *The Spectator* published.
1781	The articles of Confederation and Perpetual Union ratified by all states of the United States.
1803	Ohio achieved statehood.
1867	Nebraska achieved statehood.
1935	The Saar was returned to Germany.
1950	Chiang Kai-shek resumed the presidency of Nationalist China (Taiwan).
1974	Seven American officials indicted in connection with Watergate burglary.

2nd MARCH

People

986	Lothair, King of the West Franks, died.
1545	Sir Thomas Bodley, book-collector, born.
1578	George Sandys, poet and translator, born.
1791	John Wesley, Methodist, died.
1793	Sam Houston, statesman, born.
1797	Horace Walpole, Earl of Orford, writer, died.
1810	Pope Leo XIII born.
1824	Bedřich Smetana, composer, born.
1835	Francis II, last Holy Roman Emperor, died.
1855	Nicholas I, Tsar of Russia, died.
1876	Pope Pius XII born.
1916	Carmen Silva, Queen Elizabeth of Romania, died.

Events

1836	A group of 59 citizens of Mexico founded the Republic of Texas.
1924	The Turkish National Assembly abolished the Caliphate.
1943	Battle of the Bismarck Sea began.
1956	Independence restored to Morocco.
1969	Concorde aircraft made its first test flight.

3rd MARCH
Feast of Dolls (Japan).

People
1583 Lord Herbert of Cherbury, poet, born.
1606 Sir William D'Avenant, poet and dramatist, baptised.
1606 Edmund Waller, poet, born.
1633 George Herbert, poet, buried.
1652 Thomas Otway, playwright, born.
1703 Robert Hooke, scientist, died.
1756 William Godwin, political writer, born.
1792 Robert Adam, architect, died.
1803 The Duke of Bridgewater, canal pioneer, died.
1847 Alexander Graham Bell, inventor, born.
1869 Sir Henry Wood, conductor and composer, born.
1926 Sir Sidney Lee, editor, died.
1932 Ernest Griffiths, physicist, died.

Events
1845 Florida achieved statehood.
1848 Louis-Philippe of France arrived in England after his abdication.
1861 Serfdom abolished in Russia.
1918 The Treaty of Brest-Litovsk signed.
1931 The *Star-Spangled Banner* adopted by Congress as U.S. National Anthem.

4th MARCH

People
 561 Pope Pelagius I died.
1193 Saladin, Sultan of Egypt, died.
1394 Prince Henry the Navigator born.
1748 Count Casimir Pulaski, soldier, born.
1756 Sir Henry Raeburn, artist, born.
1805 J. B. Greuze, painter, died.
1852 Nicolai Gogol, writer, died.
1953 Sergei Prokofiev, composer, died.

Events
1681 King Charles II granted William Penn a patent for territory in North America.
1789 The Constitution of the United States of America came into force.
1791 Vermont achieved statehood.
1824 The Royal National Lifeboat Institution was founded.
1890 The Forth Bridge was officially opened.
1919 The Comintern was formed.
1943 The Battle of the Bismarck Sea ended.

5th MARCH

People
1512 Gerard Mercator, mapmaker, born.
1534 Antonio da Correggio, painter, died.
1625 James I, King of England and Scotland, died.
1778 Thomas Arne, composer, died.
1790 Flora Macdonald, patriot, died.
1815 Franz Anton Mesmer, physician, died.
1817 Sir Austen Henry Layard, archaeologist, born.
1827 Pierre Laplace, astronomer, died.

5th March

1827	Count Alessandro Volta, physicist, died.
1852	Lady Gregory, dramatist, born.
1853	Howard Pyle, artist, born.
1879	Lord Beveridge, economist, born.
1887	Heitor Villa-Lobos, composer, born.
1893	Hippolyte Taine, historian, died.
1953	Joseph Stalin, statesman, died.

Events

1770	The Boston 'Massacre'.
1946	(Sir) Winston Churchill's 'Iron Curtain' speech at Fulton, Missouri.
1956	The Telephone Weather Forecasting Service began in Britain.

6th MARCH

People

1475	Michelangelo Buonarroti, artist, born.
1616	Francis Beaumont, playwright, died.
1806	Elizabeth Barrett Browning, poet, born.
1834	George Du Maurier, artist and novelist, born.
1885	Ring Lardner, humorous writer, born.
1888	Louisa M. Alcott, novelist, died.
1918	John Redmond, nationalist leader, died.
1932	John Philip Sousa, composer, died.
1935	Oliver Wendell Holmes, U.S. Supreme Court judge, died.
1965	Herbert Morrison, statesman, died.
1967	Zoltan Kodaly, composer, died.

Events

1836	The Siege of the Alamo, San Antonio, Texas, ended.
1957	Ghana achieved independence.

7th MARCH
Feast of St Thomas Aquinas.

People

1724	Pope Innocent XIII died.
1785	Alessandro Manzoni, writer, died.
1792	Sir John Herschel, astronomer, born.
1802	Sir Edwin Landseer, painter, born.
1839	Ludwig Mond, chemist, born.
1842	Henry Hyndman, socialist, born.
1849	Luther Burbank, botanist, born.
1850	Thomas Masaryk, statesman, born.
1875	Maurice Ravel, composer, born.
1881	Ernest Bevin, trade unionist and statesman, born.
1911	Antonio Fogazzaro, novelist, died.
1932	Aristide Briand, statesman, died.

Events

1876	Alexander Graham Bell patented his first telephone.
1936	The Rhineland reoccupied by Germany.

8th MARCH

People

1702	William III, King of England, died.
1714	C. P. E. Bach, composer, born.

1717 Abraham Darby, sen., ironmaster, died.
1841 Oliver Wendell Holmes, U.S. Supreme Court judge, born.
1844 Charles XIV, King of Sweden, died.
1858 Ruggiero Leoncavallo, composer, born.
1869 Hector Berlioz, composer, died.
1879 Otto Hahn, nuclear physicist, born.
1889 John Ericsson, inventor, died.
1930 William Howard Taft, statesman, died.
1961 Sir Thomas Beecham, conductor, died.

Events

1801 The British Army captured Aboukir.
1865 Construction began of the Amsterdam – North Sea Canal.
1912 Foundation stone of the London County Hall laid.
1917 Russian Revolution began at Petrograd.
1949 Independence of Vietnam within the French Union proclaimed.

9th MARCH

People

1451 Amerigo Vespucci, navigator, born.
1661 Cardinal Mazarin, statesman, died.
1749 The Comte de Mirabeau, politician and writer, born.
1763 William Cobbett, writer, born.
1847 Mary Anning, fossil-collector, died.
1890 V. M. Molotov, Soviet statesman and diplomat, born.

Events

1862 The battle between the *Monitor* and the *Merrimac*.
1958 Yemen combined with the United Arab Republic to form the United Arab States.

10th MARCH

People

 483 Pope Simplicius died.
1772 Friedrich Schlegel, poet, born.
1787 William Etty, painter, born.
1810 Henry Cavendish, scientist, died.
1844 Pablo Sarasate, violinist, born.
1858 Henry Fowler, expert on English usage, born.
1864 Maximilian II, King of Bavaria, died.
1872 Giuseppe Mazzini, Italian nationalist leader, died.
1885 Tamara Karsavina, ballerina, born.
1892 Arthur Honegger, composer, born.
1934 F. Anstey, writer, died.
1943 Laurence Binyon, poet, died.
1948 Jan Masaryk, statesman, died.

Events

1848 The U.S. Senate ratified the Treaty of Guadalupe Hidalgo.
1880 The Salvation Army sent a pioneer party to the United States.
1906 The Bakerloo Line of the London Underground was opened.
1915 The Battle of Neuve-Chapelle began.

11th MARCH

People

1514 Donato Bramante, architect, died.
1544 Torquato Tasso, poet, born.

1770 William Huskisson, statesman, born.
1801 Paul I, Tsar of Russia, murdered.
1819 Sir Henry Tate, manufacturer and philanthropist, born.
1820 Benjamin West, painter, died.
1820 Sir Alexander Mackenzie, explorer, died.
1847 Johnny Appleseed, American pioneer, died.
1885 Sir Malcolm Campbell, motor racing champion, born.
1916 Sir Harold Wilson, statesman, born.
1936 Admiral Earl Beatty died.
1955 Sir Alexander Fleming, bacteriologist, died.
1957 Richard Byrd, polar aviator, died.

Events

1702 The *Daily Courant*, London's first daily newspaper, first issued.
1888 The Great Blizzard started in the U.S.A.
1917 Baghdad captured by the British.
1941 'Lease-Lend' for Britain (from the U.S.A.) became law.

12th MARCH

Feast of St Gregory the Great.

People

417 Pope Innocent I died.
604 Pope Gregory the Great died.
1613 André le Nôtre, landscape architect, born.
1685 Bishop Berkeley, philosopher, born.
1710 Thomas Arne, composer, born.
1711 Abraham Darby, jun., ironmaster, born.
1790 John Daniell, chemist, born.
1838 Sir William Perkin, scientist, born.
1863 Gabriele d'Annunzio, writer, born.
1881 Kemal Atatürk, statesman, born.
1925 Sun Yat-sen, Chinese leader, died.
1942 Sir William Bragg, scientist, died.

Events

1789 The United States Post Office established.
1912 The Girl Scouts movement started in the U.S.A.
1938 German troops entered Austria.
1968 Mauritius became independent.

13th MARCH

People

1615 Pope Innocent XII born.
1619 Richard Burbage, actor, died.
1733 Joseph Priestley, scientist, born.
1741 The Holy Roman Emperor, Joseph II, born.
1770 Daniel Lambert, fat man, born.
1855 Percival Lowell, astronomer, born.
1858 The assassin Felice Orsini executed.
1860 Hugo Wolf, composer, born.
1884 Sir Hugh Walpole, novelist, born.
1901 Benjamin Harrison, statesman, died.

Events

1758 Halley's comet came to its perihelion – as Halley had predicted in 1682.
1781 The planet Uranus discovered by Sir William Herschel.

1884 Standard time established in the U.S.A.
1930 Discovery of the planet Pluto announced.
1938 Union of Austria with Germany.

14th MARCH

People
1682 Jakob van Ruisdael, painter, died.
1757 Admiral Byng executed at Portsmouth.
1803 Friedrich Klopstock, poet, died.
1804 Johann Strauss, the elder, composer, born.
1820 Victor Emmanuel, King of Italy, born.
1835 Giovanni Schiaparelli, astronomer, born.
1854 Paul Ehrlich, bacteriologist, born.
1868 Maxim Gorki, novelist, born.
1879 Albert Einstein, scientist, born.
1884 Karl Marx, political philosopher, died.
1915 Walter Crane, painter and illustrator, died.
1932 George Eastman, photographic pioneer, died.
1975 Aristotle Onassis, shipping magnate, died.

Events
1915 The German cruiser *Dresden* sunk.
1917 Provisional government established in Russia.
1917 The German retreat to the Hindenburg Line began.
1925 The first transatlantic broadcast made.

15th MARCH

People
44B.C. Julius Caesar assassinated.
493   Odoacer slain by Theodoric, King of the Ostrogoths.
1767 Andrew Jackson, statesman, born.
1779 Viscount Melbourne, statesman, born.
1842 Luigi Cherubini, composer, died.
1891 Sir Joseph William Bazalgette, engineer, died.

Events
1079 The Jalalian (or Seljuk) Era began.
1820 Maine achieved statehood.
1848 Hungarian revolution began in Budapest.
1909 Selfridge's, London department store, opened.
1917 The Tsar of Russia abdicated.
1919 The American Legion founded.
1939 German troops invaded Bohemia and Moravia.

16th MARCH

People
1751 James Madison, statesman, born.
1787 Georg Ohm, physicist, born.
1792 Gustavus III, King of Sweden, shot (died 29 March).
1822 Rosa Bonheur, painter, born.
1878 Emil Cammaerts, writer, born.
1878 William Banting, undertaker and pioneer in slimming, died.

16th March

1892   Edward Freeman, historian, died.
1898   Aubrey Beardsley, artist, died.
1937   Sir Austen Chamberlain, statesman, died.
1940   Selma Lagerlöf, writer, died.

Events

1517   The Fifth Lateran Council ended.
1660   The Long Parliament was finally dissolved.
1802   The United States Military Academy established at West Point.
1815   William of Orange proclaimed William I, King of the Netherlands.
1909   The first meeting of the Port of London Authority.

17th MARCH
St Patrick's Day.

People

1040   Harold Harefoot, King of England, died.
1473   James IV, King of Scotland, born.
1715   Bishop Burnet, historian, died.
1787   Edmund Kean, actor, born.
1817   Pasquale Mancini, statesman, born.
1846   Kate Greenaway, artist, born.
1958   Sir Hubert Wilkins, explorer, died.

Events

1766   The Stamp Act repealed by Parliament.
1776   British troops withdrew from Boston.
1948   The Brussels Treaty signed.

18th MARCH

People

1227   Pope Honorius III died.
1455   Fra Angelico, painter, died.
1584   Ivan the Terrible, Tsar of Russia, died.
1609   Frederick III, King of Denmark, born.
1745   Sir Robert Walpole, statesman, died.
1768   Laurence Sterne, writer, died.
1781   A. R. J. Turgot, statesman, died.
1782   John Calhoun, statesman, born.
1812   John Tooke, statesman, died.
1830   Fustel de Coulanges, historian, born.
1837   Stephen Grover Cleveland, statesman, born.
1842   Stéphane Mallarmé, poet, born.
1844   Nikolai Rimsky-Korsakov, composer, born.
1858   Rudolf Diesel, inventor, born.
1869   Neville Chamberlain, statesman, born.
1913   George I, King of Greece, assassinated.
1936   Eleutherios Venizelos, statesman, died.
1965   Farouk, former King of Egypt, died.

Events

1123   The First Lateran Council began.
1314   Grand Master of the Templars, Jacques de Molay, executed.
1848   Revolution broke out in Milan.
1890   Prince Bismarck resigned the German chancellorship.
1891   The London–Paris telephone system opened.
1967   *Torrey Canyon* oil tanker disaster.

19th MARCH

Feast of St Joseph.

People

1687	Robert Cavelier, Sieur de la Salle, murdered in Texas.
1813	David Livingstone, explorer, born.
1821	Sir Richard Burton, traveller and writer, born.
1872	Sergei Diaghilev, ballet master, born.

Events

1834	The Tolpuddle Martyrs sentenced.
1859	Gounod's *Faust* first performed in Paris.
1932	Sydney Harbour Bridge officially opened.

20th MARCH

People

43B.C.	Ovid, poet, born.
1413	Henry IV, King of England, died.
1546	Sir Thomas Elyot, diplomat and writer, died.
1549	Thomas Seymour, Lord High Admiral of England, executed.
1656	Archbishop Ussher, theologian and scholar, died.
1717	Abraham Darby, sen., ironmaster, died.
1727	Sir Isaac Newton, scientist, died.
1741	Jean Houdon, sculptor, born.
1828	Henrik Ibsen, playwright, born.
1890	Beniamino Gigli, singer, born.
1894	Louis Kossuth, statesman, died.
1925	Lord Curzon, statesman, died.
1929	Ferdinand Foch, soldier, died.
1964	Brendan Behan, playwright, died.

Events

1602	The Dutch East India Company founded.
1806	The foundation stone of Dartmoor Prison laid.
1815	Napoleon arrived at Fontainebleau (beginning of 'The Hundred Days').
1819	The Burlington Arcade, London, opened.
1848	Ludwig I, King of Bavaria, abdicated.
1935	The British Council established.
1956	France recognized the independence of Tunisia.

21st MARCH

Feast of St Benedict.

People

1556	Archbishop Cranmer burnt at the stake.
1685	Johann Sebastian Bach, composer, born.
1729	John Law, financier, died.
1763	Jean Paul Richter, writer, born.
1804	The Duc d'Enghien executed.
1806	Benito Juárez, statesman, born.
1831	Dorothea Beale, educationalist, born.
1839	Modest Mussorgsky, composer, born.
1843	Robert Southey, poet, died.
1936	Alexander Glazounov, composer, died.
1942	P. Wilson Steer, painter, died.

Events

1801	The Battle of Alexandria.
1829	Duel between the Duke of Wellington and the Earl of Winchelsea.
1859	The Scottish National Gallery, Edinburgh, opened.
1871	The first Reichstag officially opened.
1918	Beginning of last German offensive on the Western front.
1960	Demonstrators shot at Sharpeville, South Africa.

22nd MARCH

People

1459	The Holy Roman Emperor Maximilian I born.
1599	Sir Anthony Van Dyck, painter, born.
1687	Jean Baptiste Lully, composer, died.
1785	Adam Sedgwick, geologist, born.
1797	Wilhelm I, Emperor of Germany, born.
1832	Johann Wolfgang von Goethe, poet and philosopher, died.
1842	Carl Rosa, impresario, born.
1868	Robert Millikan, physicist, born.
1903	Frederic William Farrar, clergyman and writer, died.

Events

1312	The Pope abolished the Order of the Templars.
1939	Memel annexed by Germany.
1945	The Arab League founded at Cairo.
1946	Jordan became independent.

23rd MARCH

People

1369	Pedro the Cruel, King of Castile and Leon, killed.
1430	Margaret of Anjou, Queen of England, born.
1555	Pope Julius III died.
1769	William Smith, geologist, born.
1819	August von Kotzebue, playwright, murdered.
1842	Stendhal, novelist, died.
1854	Alfred, Lord Milner, statesman, born.
1921	E. W. Hornung, novelist, died.
1953	Raoul Dufy, painter, died.

Events

1848	First officially organised band of settlers landed at Dunedin, New Zealand.
1933	Adolf Hitler granted dictorial powers.

24th MARCH

People

1455	Pope Nicholas V died.
1490	Georg Agricola, mineralogist, born.
1603	Elizabeth I, Queen of England, died.
1773	Lord Chesterfield, literary patron and writer, died.
1834	William Morris, writer, artist and reformer, born.
1844	Bertel Thorvaldsen, sculptor, died.
1855	Andrew William Mellon, financier, born.

1877 Walter Bagehot, political economist, died.
1882 Henry Wadsworth Longfellow, poet, died.
1884 François Mignet, historian, died.
1901 Charlotte M. Yonge, writer, died.
1916 Enrique Granados, composer, died.
1920 Mrs Humphrey Ward, novelist, died.
1950 Harold Laski, politician and economist, died.
1953 Queen Mary, consort of George V, died.
1976 Field-Marshal Earl Montgomery of Alamein died.

Events

1267 Saint Louis of France called his knights to Paris in preparation for his second crusade.
1603 Accession of King James I.
1933 Concentration camps created in Germany.
1942 The national loaf introduced in Britain.

25th MARCH

Feast of the Annunciation of the Virgin.   Lady Day.   Greek Independence Day. Maryland Day.

People

1133 Henry II, King of England, born.
1347 Saint Catherine of Siena born.
1767 Joachim Murat, King of Naples, born.
1801 'Novalis' (Friedrich von Hardenberg), poet, died.
1820 Anne Brontë, novelist, born.
1842 Antonio Fogazzaro, novelist, died.
1867 Arturo Toscanini, conductor, born.
1881 Bela Bartok, composer, born.
1913 Garnet Wolseley, soldier and army reformer, died.
1914 Frédéric Mistral, poet, died.
1918 Claude Debussy, composer, died.
1937 John Drinkwater, writer, died.

Events

1409 The Council of Pisa assembled.
1924 Greece proclaimed a Republic.
1957 The European Community established by treaty signed at Rome.

26th MARCH

People

1516 Konrad von Gesner, naturalist, born.
1726 Sir John Vanbrugh, architect and playwright, died.
1826 John VI, King of Portugal, died.
1827 Ludwig van Beethoven, composer, died.
1859 A. E. Housman, poet, born.
1868 Fuad I, King of Egypt, born.
1874 Robert Frost, poet, born.
1892 Walt Whitman, poet, died.
1902 Cecil Rhodes, statesman, died.
1911 Tennessee Williams, playwright, born.
1923 Sarah Bernhardt, actress, died.
1931 Timothy Healy, statesman, died.
1945 David Lloyd George, statesman, died.
1957 Edouard Herriot, statesman, died.
1973 Noël Coward, playwright, died.

26th March

Events

1639   First patent signed for the Drury Lane Theatre.
1674   Second Drury Lane Theatre opened.
1917   First Battle of Gaza.

27th MARCH

People

1378   Pope Gregory XI died.
1615   Marguerite de Valois, Queen of Navarre, died.
1625   James I, King of England and Scotland, died.
1676   Franz Rakoczy, patriot, born.
1785   Louis XVII, King of France, born.
1797   Alfred de Vigny, poet, born.
1822   Henri Murger, novelist, born.
1845   Wilhelm von Röntgen, physicist, born.
1851   Vincent d'Indy, composer, born.
1889   John Bright, statesman, died.
1923   Sir James Dewar, physicist, died.
1931   Arnold Bennett, novelist, died.

Events

1794   The United States Navy created.
1802   Treaty of Amiens concluded between Britain and France.

28th MARCH

People

193   The Roman Emperor Pertinax assassinated.
1592   Johann Comenius, educational reformer, born.
1660   George I, King of Great Britain, born.
1749   The Marquis de Laplace, mathematician, born.
1760   Peg Woffington, actress, died.
1819   Sir Joseph William Bazalgette, engineer, born.
1840   Emin Pasha, traveller, born.
1862   Aristide Briand, statesman, born.
1871   Willem Mengelberg, conductor, born.
1881   Modest Mussorgsky, composer, died.
1937   Karol Szymanowski, composer, died.
1941   Virginia Woolf, writer, died.
1943   Sergei Rachmaninoff, composer, died.
1944   Stephen Leacock, humorous writer, died.
1969   Dwight D. Eisenhower, soldier and statesman, died.

Events

1854   Britain declared war on Russia.
1941   The Battle of Cape Matapan.

29th MARCH

People

1058   Pope Stephen X died.
1751   Thomas Coram, philanthropist, died.
1769   Nicolas Soult, soldier, born.

1772 Emanuel Swedenborg, scientist and theologian, died.
1790 John Tyler, statesman, born.
1792 Gustavus III, King of Sweden, died.
1815 Sir Bartle Frere, statesman, born.
1837 Mrs Fitzherbert, mistress of King George IV, died.
1847 Prince Jules de Polignac, diplomat and statesman, died.
1853 Elihu Thomson, inventor, born.
1866 John Keble, divine and poet, died.
1869 Sir Edwin Lutyens, architect, born.
1891 Georges Seurat, painter, died.
1902 Sir William Walton, composer, born.
1957 Joyce Carey, novelist, died.

Events

1461 The Battle of Towton.
1871 The Royal Albert Hall, London, officially opened.
1939 The Spanish Civil War ended.
1961 End of South African Treason Trial.

30th MARCH

People

1707 Sebastien de Vauban, military engineer, died.
1746 Francisco de Goya, painter, born.
1783 William Hunter, anatomist, died.
1840 Beau Brummel, leader of fashion, died.
1844 Paul Verlaine, poet, born.
1853 Vincent Van Gogh, painter, born.
1880 Sean O'Casey, dramatist, born.
1883 Jo Davidson, sculptor, born.
1950 Léon Blum, statesman, died.

Events

1867 Alaska purchased from Russia by the U.S.A.
1912 The Treaty of Fez made Morocco a French protectorate.
1972 Northern Ireland henceforth ruled directly from London.

31th MARCH

People

1499 Pope Pius IV born.
1547 Francis I, King of France, died.
1596 René Descartes, philosopher, born.
1621 Philip III, King of Spain, died.
1631 John Donne, poet and divine, died.
1732 Franz Josef Haydn, composer, born.
1763 Abraham Darby, jun., ironmaster, died.
1809 Nikolai Gogol, writer, born.
1809 Edward FitzGerald, poet, born.
1811 Robert Bunsen, scientist, born.
1837 John Constable, painter, died.
1850 John Calhoun, statesman, died.
1855 Charlotte Brontë, novelist, died.
1913 J. Pierpont Morgan, financier, died.

Events

1282 The Sicilian Vespers (massacre of the French in Sicily).
1814 The surrender of Paris to the Allies.

1st APRIL
April Fools' Day

People
1548 Sigismund I, King of Poland, died.
1578 William Harvey, physician, born.
1815 Prince Bismarck, statesman, born.
1852 Edwin Abbey, painter, born.
1868 Edmond Rostand, playwright, born.

Events
1918 The Royal Air Force formed.
1935 The Green Belt Scheme for the environs of London came into force.
1945 The Battle of Okinawa began.
1954 The U.S. Air Force Academy created.

2nd APRIL

People
742 Charlemagne born.
1305 Jeanne, Queen of Navarre, died.
1416 Ferdinand I, King of Aragon, died.
1791 The Comte de Mirabeau, politician and writer, died.
1805 Hans Christian Andersen, writer, born.
1827 Holman Hunt, painter, born.
1838 Léon Gambetta, statesman, born.
1840 Emile Zola, novelist, born.
1865 Richard Cobden, political reformer, died.
1873 Sergei Rachmaninoff, composer, born.
1914 Sir Alec Guinness, actor, born.
1974 Georges Pompidou, statesman, died.

Events
1559 The Peace of Cateau-Cambrésis.
1792 The United States Mint established.
1801 The Naval Battle of Copenhagen.
1927 The Oxford and Cambridge Boat Race first broadcast.
1939 The official end of the Spanish Civil War.
1946 The Royal Military Academy, combining Sandhurst and Woolwich, established at Sandhurst.
1951 NATO Allied Command, Europe, came into being.

3rd APRIL

People
1245 Philip III, King of France, born.
1287 Pope Honorius IV died.
1367 Henry IV, King of England, born.
1593 George Herbert, poet, born.
1783 Washington Irving, writer and diplomat, born.
1822 Edward Everett Hale, writer, born.
1826 Bishop Reginald Heber, hymn-writer, died.
1866 J. B. Hertzog, statesman, born.
1897 Johannes Brahms, composer, died.
1901 Richard D'Oyly Carte, impresario, died.
1925 Jean de Reszke, singer, died.
1958 Lord Percy of Newcastle, pioneer in education, died.

Events

1367   The Battle of Navarrete.
1860   First Pony Express set out across the United States.
1930   Hailé Selassié proclaimed Emperor of Ethiopia.
1941   Benghazi captured by German forces.
1949   Arab armistice with Israel.

4th APRIL

People

1490   Matthias Corvinus, King of Hungary, died.
1588   Frederick II, King of Denmark, died.
1617   John Napier, inventor and mathematician, died.
1648   Grinling Gibbons, artist, born.
1752   Nicola Zingarelli, composer, born.
1758   John Hoppner, painter, born.
1774   Oliver Goldsmith, writer, died.
1807   Joseph Lalande, astronomer, died.
1817   André Masséna, soldier, died.
1823   Sir William Siemens, inventor, born.
1832   José Echegaray, writer and scientist, born.
1843   Hans Richter, conductor, born.
1932   Wilhelm Ostwald, scientist, died.
1939   Ghazi, King of Iraq, died.
1968   Martin Luther King, civil rights leader, murdered.

Events

1460   The University of Basle opened.
1939   Faisal II acceded to the throne of Iraq.
1949   The North Atlantic Treaty signed at Washington.

5th APRIL

People

1588   Thomas Hobbes, philosopher, born.
1648   Elihu Yale, merchant and administrator, born.
1732   Jean Fragonard, painter, born.
1765   Edward Young, poet, died.
1784   Ludwig Spohr, composer, born.
1794   Georges Danton, statesman, guillotined.
1795   Sir Henry Havelock, soldier, born.
1811   Robert Raikes, Sunday School founder, died.
1827   Lord Lister, surgeon, born.
1837   Algernon Swinburne, poet, born.
1869   Albert Roussel, composer, born.
1964   Douglas MacArthur, soldier, died.
1975   Chiang Kai-shek, soldier and statesman, died.

Events

1614   The Addled Parliament began sitting.
1955   Sir Winston Churchill resigned as British prime minister.
1976   Sir Harold Wilson resigned as British prime minister.

6th APRIL

People

1199   Richard I, King of England, killed in battle.
1520   Raphael, painter, died.

1528	Albrecht Dürer, artist, died.
1605	John Stow, historian, died.
1773	James Mill, philosopher and historian, born.
1826	Gustave Moreau, painter, born.
1869	Louis Raemaekers, artist, born.
1870	Oscar Straus, composer, born.
1874	Harry Houdini, professional magician, born.
1890	Anthony Fokker, aeroplane designer, born.
1971	Igor Stravinsky, composer, died.

Events

1712	Slave revolt in New York.
1851	Cardinal Manning converted to Catholicism.
1862	The Battle of Shiloh began.
1909	Commander Peary reached the North Pole.
1917	The U.S.A. declared war on Germany.
1939	Britain and the U.S.A. agreed on 50-year joint control of the Phoenix Islands.
1941	German ultimatum to Greece and Yugoslavia.
1944	P.A.Y.E. introduced in Britain.
1955	Sir Anthony Eden became prime minister.

7th APRIL

People

1506	Saint Francis Xavier born.
1614	El Greco, painter, died.
1668	Sir William D'Avenant, poet and playwright, died.
1770	William Wordsworth, poet, born.
1772	François Fourier, social reformer, born.
1780	William Channing, Unitarian, born.
1836	William Godwin, writer, died.
1858	Anton Diabelli, music publisher and composer, died.
1891	P. T. Barnum, showman, died.
1891	Sir David Low, cartoonist, born.
1947	Henry Ford, pioneer motor manufacturer, died.

Events

560	Cuckoo has traditionally first sung in Wales at St Brynach since this date.
1862	The Battle of Shiloh ended.
1906	The Conference of Algeciras ended.
1936	President Zamora of Spain deposed.
1948	The World Health Organization confirmed as a specialized U.N. agency.
1956	Spain relinquished its protectorate in Morocco.

8th APRIL

People

1143	John II, Byzantine emperor, killed accidentally.
1492	Lorenzo de' Medici, statesman, died.
1605	Philip IV, King of Spain, born.
1848	Gaetano Donizetti, composer, born.
1860	Count Stephen Széchenyi, statesman, died.
1875	Albert I, King of the Belgians, born.
1892	Mary Pickford, film actress, born.
1937	Sir Henry Hadow, musicologist, died.
1941	Marcel Prévost, novelist, died.
1950	Vaslav Nijinsky, ballet-dancer, died.
1973	Pablo Picasso, painter, died.

Events

1213 The Assembly of Soissons.
1898 Battle of Atbara.
1904 The Entente Cordiale: signature of the Anglo-French agreement.

9th APRIL

People

1483 Edward IV, King of England, died.
1553 François Rabelais, writer, died.
1626 Francis Bacon, statesman and writer, died.
1761 William Law, theologian, died.
1802 Elias Lönnrot, Finnish folklorist, born.
1804 Jacques Necker, statesman, died.
1806 Isambard Brunel, engineer, born.
1807 John Opie, painter, died.
1821 Charles Baudelaire, poet, born.
1835 Leopold II, King of the Belgians, born.
1865 Erich von Ludendorff, soldier, born.
1865 Charles Steinmetz, electrical engineer, born.
1870 Lenin, revolutionary and statesman, born.
1872 Léon Blum, statesman, born.
1882 Dante Gabriel Rossetti, painter and poet, died.
1889 Efrem Zimbalist, violinist, born.
1898 Paul Robeson, singer, born.
1904 Isabella II, Queen of Spain, died.
1906 Hugh Gaitskell, statesman, born.
1940 Mrs Patrick Campbell, actress, died.

Events

1770 James Cook discovered Botany Bay.
1865 General Robert E. Lee surrendered to General Ulysses S. Grant at Appomattox.
1917 The Canadians stormed Vimy Ridge (capturing it 10 April).
1942 Bataan surrendered to the Japanese.

10th APRIL

People

1512 James V, King of Scotland, born.
1583 Hugo Grotius, jurist, born.
1585 Pope Gregory XIII died.
1778 William Hazlitt, essayist and critic, born.
1794 Commodore Perry of the U.S. Navy born.
1813 Joseph Lagrange, mathematician, died.
1829 William Booth, Salvation Army founder, born.
1847 Joseph Pulitzer, journalist, born.
1867 George Russell ('A.E.'), writer, born.
1954 Auguste Lumière, pioneer in cinematography, died.
1966 Evelyn Waugh, novelist, died.

Events

1790 The United States patent system established.
1814 Battle of Toulouse.
1841 The *New York (Herald) Tribune* first published.
1848 The Chartists presented their Petition to Parliament.
1858 Big Ben cast.
1864 Maximilian made Emperor of Mexico.
1945 U.S. troops captured Hanover.

11th APRIL

People

1492   Marguerite d'Angoulême, Queen of Navarre, born.
1767   Jean Baptiste Isabey, painter, born.
1770   George Canning, statesman, born.
1772   Manuel Quintana, writer, born.
1794   Edward Everett, statesman, born.
1825   Ferdinand Lassalle, socialist, born.
1934   Sir Gerald Du Maurier, actor-manager, died.

Events

1713   The Treaty of Utrecht signed.
1814   The Treaty of Fontainebleau signed.
1814   Napoleon abdicated.
1814   Louis XVIII acceded to the throne of France.
1935   The Stresa Conference began.

12th APRIL

People

1684   Niccolò Amati, violin-maker, died.
1704   Jacques Bossuet, orator and historian, died.
1726   Charles Burney, music historian, born.
1748   William Kent, architect, died.
1777   Henry Clay, statesman, born.
1792   The Earl of Durham, statesman, born.
1814   Charles Burney, music historian, died.
1868   J. L. Garvin, editor, born.
1938   Fyodor Chaliapin, operatic singer, died.
1945   Franklin Delano Roosevelt, statesman, died.

Events

1709   *The Tatler* first published.
1782   Admiral Rodney defeated the French fleet in the West Indies.
1861   The American Civil War began.
1861   The Battle of Fort Sumter began.
1961   First man into space (Yuri Gagarin) – Cosmonaut's Day (U.S.S.R.).
1971   Bangladesh government claimed sovereignty over East Pakistan.

13th APRIL

People

1593   Thomas Wentworth, Earl of Strafford, statesman, born.
1695   Jean de La Fontaine, writer, died.
1743   Thomas Jefferson, statesman, born.
1748   Joseph Bramah, inventor, born.
1771   Richard Trevithick, engineer, born.
1817   George Holyoake, reformer and secularist, born.
1852   Frank Winfield Woolworth, merchant, born.
1944   Lord Lonsdale, sportsman, died.

Events

1598   The Edict of Nantes issued.
1772   Warren Hastings appointed governor of Bengal.
1829   The Catholic Emancipation Act became law in Britain.
1868   Magdala, Abyssinia, finally taken by the British.
1975   Outbreak of fighting between Christians and Muslims in Beirut.

14th APRIL
Pan American Day (throughout the Americas).

People
911 Pope Sergius III died.
1053 Godwin, Earl of Wessex, died.
1471 Warwick the Kingmaker killed at Battle of Barnet.
1578 Philip III, King of Spain, born.
1629 Christian Huygens, physicist, born.
1759 George Frederick Handel, composer, died.
1865 Abraham Lincoln, statesman, shot by assassin (died 15th).
1889 Arnold Toynbee, historian, born.
1900 Osman Pasha, soldier, died.
1904 Sir John Gielgud, actor, born.
1951 Ernest Bevin, statesman and trade unionist, died.

Events
1828 Noah Webster's *Dictionary* first published.
1861 Battle of Fort Sumter ended.
1890 The Pan American Union established at the first International Conference of American States.
1912 S.S. *Titanic* sank (night of 14/15) on maiden voyage.
1931 Alfonso XIII, King of Spain, abdicated.
1935 The Stresa Conference ended.

15th APRIL

People
69 The Roman Emperor Otho committed suicide.
1741 Charles Peale, painter, born.
1764 Madame de Pompadour, mistress of Louis XV of France, died.
1814 John Motley, historian, born.
1817 Benjamin Jowett, classical scholar and theologian, born.
1843 Henry James, writer, born.
1874 Johannes Stark, physicist, born.
1888 Matthew Arnold, educationalist and poet, died.
1925 J. S. Sargent, painter, died.

Events
1797 Naval mutiny at Spithead.
1920 The murders were committed for which Sacco and Vanzetti were later executed.
1942 Malta awarded the George Cross by King George VI.

16th APRIL

People
1446 Filippo Brunelleschi, architect, died.
1660 Sir Hans Sloane, physician and collector, born.
1682 John Hadley, mathematician, born.
1786 Sir John Franklin, explorer, born.
1828 Francisco de Goya, painter, died.
1838 Ernest Solvay, industrial chemist, born.
1844 Anatole France, novelist, born.
1850 Madame Tussaud, waxworks founder, died.
1859 Alexis de Tocqueville, writer, died.
1871 John Millington Synge, poet and playwright, born.
1881 Lord Halifax, statesman, born.
1889 Sir Charles Chaplin, actor, born.

16th April

1904   Samuel Smiles, writer, died.
1940   Margrethe, Queen of Denmark, born.
1968   Edna Ferber, writer, died.

Events

1521   Martin Luther arrived at the Diet of Worms.
1746   Battle of Culloden.
1797   The mutiny of the fleet at Spithead.
1855   The Declaration of Paris signed.
1912   The *Daily Herald* began publication in London.
1912   The Channel first flown by a woman, Harriet Quimby.
1948   The Organization for European Economic Co-operation set up.

17th APRIL

People

1586   John Ford, playwright, born.
1711   The Holy Roman Emperor Joseph I died.
1790   Benjamin Franklin, statesman, died.
1837   John Pierpont Morgan, the elder, financier, born.
1876   Ian Hay, writer, born.
1954   Theodore Komisarjevsky, theatre director, died.

Events

1521   Martin Luther excommunicated by the Diet of Worms.
1559   The Act of Supremacy partly re-enacted in England.
1839   The Republic of Guatemala established.
1897   Turkey declared war on Greece.
1969   Alexander Dubček replaced as first secretary of Czech Communist Party.
1975   End of civil war in Cambodia.

18th APRIL

People

1552   John Leland, antiquary, died.
1587   John Foxe, martyrologist, died.
1689   Judge Jeffreys died in the Tower of London.
1797   Louis Adolphe Thiers, statesman, born.
1802   Erasmus Darwin, physician and writer, died.
1819   Franz von Suppé, composer, born.
1867   Sir Robert Smirke, architect, died.
1887   Leopold Stokowski, conductor, born.
1940   H. A. L. Fisher, historian, died.
1955   Albert Einstein, scientist, died.

Events

1775   Paul Revere's ride from Charleston to Lexington.
1906   The San Francisco earthquake and fire began.
1949   The Republic of Ireland Act, 1948, came into operation.
1951   The European Steel and Coal Community set up.
1955   The First Bandung Conference began.

19th APRIL
Primrose Day.

People

1054   Pope Leo IX died.
1560   Philip Melanchthon, Church reformer, died.

1588	Paolo Veronese, artist, died.
1645	Anton van Diemen, explorer, died.
1689	Queen Christina of Sweden died.
1757	Admiral Lord Exmouth born.
1772	David Ricardo, economist, born.
1813	Benjamin Rush, physician and abolitionist, died.
1824	Lord Byron, poet, died.
1874	Owen Jones, architect, died.
1881	Benjamin Disraeli, statesman, died.
1882	Charles Darwin, biologist, died.
1893	John Addington Symonds, critic and poet, died.
1938	Sir Henry Newbolt, writer, died.
1967	Konrad Adenauer, statesman, died.

Events

1775	Battle of Lexington.
1839	The Treaty of London signed.
1906	The San Francisco earthquake ended.
1956	Prince Rainier of Monaco married Grace Kelly (civil ceremony 18 April).

20th APRIL

People

1820	Arthur Young, agricultural pioneer, died.
1889	Adolf Hitler born.
1893	Joan Miró, painter, born.
1947	Christian X, King of Denmark, died.

Events

1653	The Long Parliament dissolved (temporarily) by Cromwell.
1770	The discovery of New South Wales by Captain James Cook.
1896	The Bimetallist Conference met at Brussels.
1945	Russian forces reached Berlin.

21st APRIL

People

1073	Pope Alexander II died.
1109	Archbishop Anselm died.
1142	Peter Abelard, philosopher and theologian, died.
1509	Henry VII, King of England, died.
1671	John Law, financier, born.
1699	Jean Racine, playwright, died.
1736	Prince Eugene of Savoy, soldier, died.
1782	Friedrich Froebel, education pioneer, born.
1816	Charlotte Brontë, novelist, born.
1828	Hippolyte Taine, historian, born.
1896	Léon Say, statesman, died.
1926	Elizabeth II, Queen of Great Britain and Northern Ireland, born.
1946	Lord Keynes, economist, died.
1958	Margery Fry, social reformer, died.

Events

753B.C.	Traditional date of the foundation of Rome.
1836	Battle of San Jacinto.
1869	The Metaphysical Society founded by James Knowles.
1906	The San Francisco fire ended.
1967	Greek military junta took over the government of the country.

22nd APRIL

People

1451   Isabella, Queen of Castile and Leon, born.
1707   Henry Fielding, novelist, born.
1724   Immanuel Kant, philosopher, born.
1766   Madame de Staël, writer, born.
1892   Edouard Lalo, composer, died.
1912   Kathleen Ferrier, singer, born.
1916   Yehudi Menuhin, violinist, born.

Events

1500   Brazil discovered by Pedro Alvarez Cabral.
1823   The Baltic Exchange formally established as the Baltic Club, London.
1834   Saint Helena became a Crown Colony.
1915   Poison gas first used by the Germans on the Western Front.
1918   Battle of Zeebrugge began.
1944   Allies landed troops in New Guinea.

23rd APRIL
St George's Day.

People

1564   William Shakespeare born (traditional date).
1616   William Shakespeare died.
1616   Miguel de Cervantes, novelist, died.
1697   Lord Anson, explorer, born.
1728   Samuel Wallis, navigator, born.
1775   J. M. W. Turner, painter, born.
1791   James Buchanan, statesman, born.
1818   J. A. Froude, historian, born.
1850   William Wordsworth, poet, died.
1858   Max Planck, physicist, born.
1858   Dame Ethel Smyth, composer, born.
1861   Lord Allenby, soldier, born.
1891   Sergei Prokofiev, composer, born.
1899   Vladimir Nabokov, writer, born.
1952   Elizabeth Schumann, singer, died.

Events

1795   Warren Hastings acquitted of high treason.
1826   The Turks captured Missolonghi.
1860   The explorer John Stuart reached the centre of Australia.
1918   The Battle of Zeebrugge ended.
1924   The British Empire Exhibition, Wembley, opened.
1932   The new Shakespeare Memorial Theatre opened at Stratford-on-Avon.
1945   Allied forces reached River Po.
1952   The oil pipe-line, Kirkuk to Banias, completed.
1959   Britain's first Heliport opened on the Thames.

24th APRIL

People

1533   William the Silent, Prince of Orange, born.
1743   Edmund Cartwright, inventor, born.
1815   Anthony Trollope, novelist, born.
1856   Philippe Pétain, soldier and statesman, born.
1889   Sir Stafford Cripps, statesman, born.

Events

1792	The *Marseillaise* composed by Rouget de Lisle (night of 24/25).
1800	The Library of Congress, Washington, established.
1955	First Bandung Conference ended.

25th APRIL

Feast of Saint Mark the Evangelist.   Anzac Day.

People

1214	Saint Louis, King of France, born.
1284	Edward II, King of England, born.
1599	Oliver Cromwell, soldier and statesman, born.
1710	James Ferguson, astronomer, born.
1769	Sir Marc Isambard Brunel, engineer, born.
1792	John Keble, divine and poet, born.
1800	William Cowper, poet, died.
1862	Edward (Viscount) Grey, statesman, born.
1874	Guglielmo Marconi, radio pioneer, born.
1882	J. K. F. Zöllner, scientist, died.

Events

1792	The guillotine first erected in Paris at the Place de Grève.
1859	Work began on the construction of the Suez Canal.
1915	Allied operations in Gallipoli began.
1916	Anzac Day first celebrated in London.

26th APRIL

People

121	Marcus Aurelius, Roman Emperor, born.
1573	Marie de' Medici, Queen of France, born.
1731	Daniel Defoe, writer, died.
1765	Emma, Lady Hamilton, mistress of Lord Nelson, born.
1785	John James Audubon, ornithologist, born.
1798	Eugène Delacroix, painter, born.
1812	Friedrich Flotow, composer, born.
1834	Artemus Ward, humorist, born.
1868	H. S. Harmsworth, Lord Rothermere, newspaper publisher, born.
1880	Michel Fokine, choreographer, born.
1910	Björnstjerne Björnson, writer, died.

Events

1478	The Pazzi Conspiracy in Florence.
1915	The (Secret) Pact of London between the Allies and Italy.
1923	The marriage of the future King George VI and Queen Elizabeth.
1925	The election of President Hindenburg in Germany.
1928	Madame Tussaud's new building opened in London.
1937	Guernica, Spain, destroyed by German aircraft.
1962	Ariel, first Anglo-American satellite, launched.
1964	Union of Tanganyika and Zanzibar to form Tanzania.

27th APRIL

People

1404	Philip the Bold, Duke of Burgundy, died.
1521	Ferdinand Magellan, navigator, died.
1682	Theodore III, Tsar of Russia, died.

1737   Edward Gibbon, historian, born.
1791   Samuel Morse, inventor, born.
1820   Herbert Spencer, philosopher, born.
1822   Ulysses S. Grant, soldier and statesman, born.
1840   Edward Whymper, mountaineer, born.
1873   William Macready, actor, died.
1882   Ralph Waldo Emerson, writer, died.

Events

1296   Battle of Dunbar.
1910   (27–28 April) Louis Paulhan won the *Daily Mail* London–Manchester flight.
1960   Togo achieved independence.

28th APRIL

People

32   The Roman Emperor Otto born.
1442   Edward IV, King of England, born.
1710   Thomas Betterton, actor, died.
1758   James Monroe, statesman, born.
1772   Count von Struensee, statesman, executed.
1801   Lord Shaftesbury, social reformer, born.
1813   Mikhail Kutuzov, soldier and diplomat, died.
1831   John Abernethy, surgeon, died.
1889   Antonio de Oliveira Salazar, statesman, born.
1936   Fuad I, King of Egypt, died.
1940   Luisa Tetrazzini, operatic soprano, died.
1945   Benito Mussolini executed.

Events

1789   The mutiny on the *Bounty*.
1919   The League of Nations founded.
1936   Farouk became King of Egypt.
1939   The Anglo-French Naval Agreement denounced by Hitler.
1952   Japan regained its sovereignty.
1969   Charles de Gaulle resigned as president of France.

29th APRIL

People

1380   Saint Catherine of Siena died (feast day 30 April).
1676   Michel de Ruyter, naval officer, died.
1769   The Duke of Wellington, soldier and statesman, born.
1818   Alexander II, Tsar of Russia, born.
1879   Sir Thomas Beecham, conductor, born.
1895   Sir Malcolm Sargent, conductor, born.
1901   Hirohito, Emperor of Japan, born.

Events

1507   Louis XII, King of France, led his troops into Genoa.
1770   Botany Bay discovered by Captain Cook.
1945   The German Army in Italy surrendered unconditionally to the Allies.
1986   Halley's Comet will return to its perihelion.

30th APRIL   Feast of Saint Catherine of Siena.

People

1524   The Chevalier de Bayard, French soldier, killed.
1602   William Lilly, astrologer, born.

1632 Jan, Count of Tilly, soldier, died.
1777 J. K. F. Gauss, mathematician and astronomer, born.
1870 Franz Lehár, composer, born.
1889 Carl Rosa, impresario, died.
1909 Juliana, Queen of the Netherlands, born.
1912 Wilbur Wright, aviator, died.
1936 A. E. Housman, poet, died.
1945 Adolf Hitler committed suicide.

Events
1789 General Washington inaugurated as first president of the U.S.A.
1803 The U.S.A. purchased Louisiana from France.
1812 Louisiana achieved statehood.
1926 General strike began in Britain.
1948 Organization of American States founded.

1st MAY
May Day. Labour Day. Feast of SS Philip and James.

People
1218 Rudolf I, King of Germany, born.
1572 Pope Pius V died.
1672 Joseph Addison, writer, born.
1700 John Dryden, poet and playwright, died.
1769 Arthur Wellesley, Duke of Wellington, born.
1873 David Livingstone, explorer, died.
1904 Antonin Dvořák, composer, died.

Events
1851 The Great Exhibition opened at Hyde Park, London.
1865 Argentina, Brazil and Uruguay formed an alliance against Paraguay.
1876 Queen Victoria proclaimed Empress of India.
1898 Battle of Manila Bay.
1919 The reclamation of the Zuider Zee began.
1945 Berlin captured by the Russians.

2nd MAY

People
1519 Leonardo da Vinci, artist, died.
1551 William Camden, historian, born.
1729 Catherine the Great, Empress of Russia, born.
1772 'Novalis', poet, born.
1779 John Galt, novelist, born.
1821 Mrs Thrale (Mrs Hester Piozzi), writer, died.
1844 William Beckford, writer, died.
1857 Alfred de Musset, playwright, died.
1859 Jerome Klapka Jerome, writer, born.
1860 Theodor Herzl, founder of Zionism, born.
1864 Giacomo Meyerbeer, composer, died.
1892 Baron Manfred von Richthofen, aviator, born.
1905 Alan Rawsthorne, composer, born.
1935 Faisal II, King of Iraq, born.
1957 Senator Joe McCarthy, politician, died.
1964 Nancy, Viscountess Astor, first woman M.P. to sit in House of Commons, died.

Events
1668 Treaty of Aix-la-Chapelle.
1670 The Hudson's Bay Company chartered.

2nd May

1813 Battle of Lutzen.
1955 Public VHF broadcasting introduced in Britain.
1968 Student riots in Paris.

3rd MAY

People

1469 Niccolò Machiavelli, diplomat and writer, born.
1761 August von Kotzebue, playwright, born.
1763 George Psalmanazar, adventurer, died.
1844 Richard D'Oyly Carte, impresario, born.
1845 Thomas Hood, poet, died.
1849 Bernhard von Bülow, statesman, born.
1860 John Scott Haldane, physiologist, born.

Events

1512 The Fifth Lateran Council began.
1791 The Polish Constitution reformed.
1951 The Festival of Britain opened.

4th MAY

People

1769 Sir Thomas Lawrence, painter, born.
1776 J. F. Herbart, philosopher, born.
1796 William Prescott, historian, born.
1825 Thomas Huxley, scientist, born.
1889 Cardinal Francis J. Spellman, Archbishop of New York, born.

Events

1471 Battle of Tewkesbury.
1780 The Derby first run.
1839 The Cunard Company founded.
1886 The Colonial and Indian Exhibition officially opened at South Kensington.
1970 Four students killed at Kent State University, U.S.A., during anti-war
      demonstration.

5th MAY
Feast of Flags (Japan).

People

1352 Rupert, King of Germany, born.
1705 The Holy Roman Emperor Leopold I died.
1747 The Holy Roman Emperor Leopold II born.
1813 Søren Kierkegaard, philosopher, born.
1818 Karl Marx, political philosopher, born.
1821 Napoleon died at Saint Helena.
1826 The Empress Eugénie of France born.
1837 Nicola Antonio Zingarelli, composer, died.
1882 Sir Douglas Mawson, explorer, born.
1883 Lord Wavell, soldier, born.
1887 Sir Charles R. Fairey, aeroplane designer, born.
1902 Bret Harte, writer, died.

Events

1659 Saint Helena occupied by Captain John Dutton of the East India Company.
1789 The States-General assembled at Versailles.

1811 The Battle of Fuentes de Onoro.
1865 First train robbery in the U.S.A. carried out near North Bend, Ohio.
1936 Italian troops captured Addis Ababa.
1942 British troops invaded Madagascar.
1949 Statute establishing the Council of Europe signed in London.
1955 The Federal Republic of Germany became a sovereign independent state.

6th MAY

People

1574 Pope Innocent X born.
1638 Cornelis Jansen, theologian, died.
1758 André Masséna, soldier, born.
1758 Maximilien Robespierre, revolutionary leader, born.
1856 Sigmund Freud, psychoanalyst, born.
1856 Robert Peary, explorer, born.
1859 Alexander von Humboldt, naturalist and explorer, died.
1861 Rabindranath Tagore, philosopher and writer, born.
1862 H. D. Thoreau, writer, died.
1880 Lord Ironside, soldier, born.
1910 Edward VII, King of Great Britain and Ireland, died.
1949 Maurice Maeterlinck, writer, died.
1952 Maria Montessori, educationalist, died.

Events

1092 Lincoln Cathedral consecrated.
1536 The Bible ordered to be placed in every English church by King Henry VIII.
1626 Manhattan bought from the Indians for a few trinkets by Peter Minuit.
1840 The first postage stamp issued.
1882 Epping Forest dedicated for the perpetual use of the people by Queen Victoria.
1882 The Phoenix Park murders, Dublin.
1910 George V acceded to the British throne.
1942 Corregidor surrendered to the Japanese.

7th MAY

People

973 The Holy Roman Emperor, Otto I, died.
1711 David Hume, philosopher, born.
1763 Prince Joseph Poniatowski, soldier, born.
1812 Robert Browning, poet, born.
1833 Johannes Brahms, composer, born.
1840 Peter Ilyich Tchaikovsky, composer, born.
1847 Lord Rosebery, statesman, born.
1868 Lord Brougham, statesman, died.
1880 Gustave Flaubert, novelist, died.
1892 Archibald MacLeish, poet, born.
1940 George Lansbury, Labour Party leader, died.
1941 Sir James Frazer, social anthropologist, died.
1942 Felix Weingartner, conductor, died.

Events

1663 The first Drury Lane Theatre opened.
1832 Greece proclaimed an independent kingdom.
1915 The *Lusitania* torpedoed.
1942 The Battle of the Coral Sea began.
1943 Allied forces captured Tunis.
1955 Inaugural meeting of the Western European Union Council.

8th MAY
Saint Michael's Day.   Furry Day (Helston, Cornwall).

People
1794   Antoine Lavoisier, chemist, guillotined.
1796   François Mignet, historian, born.
1828   Jean Henri Dunant, Red Cross founder, born.
1873   John Stuart Mill, philosopher, died.
1880   Gustave Flaubert, novelist, died.
1884   Midhat Pasha, statesman, died.
1884   Harry S. Truman, statesman, born.
1944   Dame Ethel Smyth, composer, died.
1947   Harry Gordon Selfridge, department store pioneer, died.

Events
1559   The Act of Uniformity signed by Queen Elizabeth I.
1864   The Battle of Spotsylvania Courthouse began.
1942   The Battle of the Coral Sea ended.
1945   The unconditional surrender of the German armed forces.
1945   VE Day in Britain.

9th MAY

People
1688   Frederick William, the Great Elector, died.
1773   Jean de Sismondi, economist, born.
1800   John Brown, abolitionist, born.
1805   Friedrich von Schiller, poet and playwright, died.
1850   Joseph Gay-Lussac, scientist, died.
1860   Sir James Barrie, writer, born.
1874   Lilian Baylis, theatre manager, born.
1946   Victor Emmanuel III, King of Italy, abdicated.
1949   Louis II, Prince of Monaco, died.

Events
1671   Colonel Thomas Blood attempted to steal the Crown Jewels.
1926   The North Pole first flown over by Richard E. Byrd and Floyd Bennett.
1932   Piccadilly Circus first lit by electricity.
1936   The King of Italy proclaimed Emperor of Abyssinia.
1945   Official end of war in Europe (World War II).

10th MAY

People
1696   Jean de La Bruyère, essayist, died.
1727   A. R. J. Turgot, statesman, born.
1774   Louis XV, King of France, died.
1795   Augustin Thierry, historian, born.
1838   James, Viscount Bryce, statesman, born.
1850   Sir Thomas Lipton, merchant and sportsman, born.
1863   'Stonewall' Jackson, Confederate general, died.
1904   Sir Henry Morton Stanley, explorer, died.

Events
1774   Louis XVI acceded to the French throne.
1775   Fort Ticonderoga captured by Ethan Allen.
1787   Edmund Burke impeached Warren Hastings.

1857 Indian Mutiny began.
1869 The Central Pacific and Union Pacific Railways linked up west of Ogden, thus completing the first transcontinental U.S. railway.
1871 Peace of Frankfurt-am-Main.
1893 Imperial Institute, London, officially opened.
1940 Neville Chamberlain resigned the Premiership.
1940 (Sir) Winston Churchill appointed Prime Minister.

11th MAY

People

1778 William Pitt, Earl of Chatham, statesman, died.
1812 Spencer Perceval, Prime Minister, assassinated.
1828 Alfred Stevens, painter, born.
1849 Madame Récamier, society leader, died.
1854 Ottmar Mergenthaler, inventor, born.
1871 Sir John Herschel, astronomer, died.
1888 Irving Berlin, composer, born.
1889 Paul Nash, painter, born.
1916 Max Reger, composer, died.

Events

1745 Battle of Fontenoy.
1858 Minnesota achieved statehood.
1920 Oxford University passed statute admitting women to degrees.

12th MAY

People

1003 Pope Silvester II died.
1496 Gustavus Vasa, King of Sweden, born.
1641 The Earl of Strafford, statesman, executed.
1784 James Knowles, playwright, born.
1803 Justus von Liebig, chemist, born.
1812 Edward Lear, artist and writer, born.
1820 Florence Nightingale, nursing pioneer, born.
1828 Dante Gabriel Rossetti, poet and painter, born.
1842 Jules Massenet, composer, born.
1845 August Schlegel, poet and critic, died.
1845 Gabriel Fauré, composer, born.
1880 Lincoln Ellsworth, aviator, born.
1884 Bedrich Smetana, composer, died.
1935 Jozef Pilsudski, statesman, died.
1967 John Masefield, poet, died.

Events

1588 The 'Day of the Barricades' in France.
1906 Horatio Bottomley began the publication of *John Bull*.
1926 General strike ended in Britain.
1937 The coronation of King George VI.
1949 The Berlin Blockade lifted.

13th MAY

People

1619 Jan van Oldenbarneveldt, statesman, executed.
1655 Pope Innocent XIII born.
1717 Maria Theresa, Empress of Austria, born.

13th May

1769	John VI, King of Portugal, born.
1792	Pope Pius IX born.
1828	Josephine Butler, social reformer, born.
1840	Alphonse Daudet, novelist, born.
1842	Sir Arthur Sullivan, composer, born.
1857	Sir Ronald Ross, scientist, born.
1867	Sir Frank Brangwyn, artist, born.
1883	James Young, chemist, died.
1884	Cyrus Hall McCormick, inventor, died.
1925	Lord Milner, statesman, died.
1930	Fridtjof Nansen, explorer, died.

Events

1607	First permanent English settlement made at Jamestown, Virginia.
1830	The Presidency of Quito became the Republic of Ecuador.

14th MAY

Feast of St John Nepomuk.

People

1316	The Holy Roman Emperor Charles IV born.
1553	Marguerite de Valois, Queen of Navarre, born.
1610	Henry IV, King of France, assassinated.
1643	Louis XIII, King of France, died.
1686	Gabriel Fahrenheit, physicist, born.
1771	Robert Owen, social reformer, born.
1841	Sir Squire Bancroft, actor-manager, born.
1853	Sir Hall Caine, novelist, born.
1885	Otto Klemperer, conductor, born.
1936	Lord Allenby, soldier, died.

Events

1264	The Battle of Lewes.
1796	Edward Jenner made his first successful experiment in vaccination.
1811	The independence of Paraguay proclaimed.
1842	The *Illustrated London News* first published.
1940	The Local Defence Volunteers (later Home Guard) formed in Britain.
1948	Israel proclaimed an independent state.

15th MAY

People

1773	Prince Metternich, statesman, born.
1833	Edmund Kean, actor, died.
1847	Daniel O'Connell, Irish patriot, died.
1858	Robert Hare, chemist, died.
1859	Pierre Curie, scientist, born.
1932	Premier Tsuyoshi Inukai assassinated in Tokyo.

Events

1525	The Battle of Frankenhausen.
1602	The first white man (Captain Bartholomew Gosnold) set foot in New England.
1858	The (third) Royal Opera House opened at Covent Garden.
1862	U.S. Department of Agriculture created.
1918	U.S.A. inaugurated world's first regular air mail service.
1935	The first broadcast quiz programme made in Canada.
1943	The Third International dissolved.
1960	Sputnik IV, the first space ship, launched.

16th MAY

People

1611   Pope Innocent XI born.
1703   Charles Perrault, story-teller, died.
1777   Button Gwinnett, American patriot, died after being wounded in a duel.
1804   Elizabeth Peabody, kindergarten pioneer, born.
1830   J. B. J. Fourier, mathematician, died.
1835   Felicia Hemans, hymn-writer, died.
1928   Sir Edmund Gosse, writer, died.
1929   Lilli Lehmann, singer, died.

Events

1633   Charles I crowned King of Scotland at Edinburgh.
1811   Battle of Albuera.
1875   The Kentucky Derby first run.

17th MAY

People

1510   Sandro Botticeili, artist, died.
1575   Matthew Parker, Archbishop of Canterbury, died.
1749   Edward Jenner, physician, born.
1799   Pierre de Beaumarchais, playwright, died.
1838   Prince Talleyrand, statesman, died.
1855   Timothy Healy, statesman, born.
1935   Paul Dukas, composer, died.

Events

1630   The belts of the planet Jupiter first recognized.
1814   The independence of Norway proclaimed.
1900   Mafeking relieved by the British.
1916   The Summer Time Act came into force in Britain.

18th MAY

People

1410   Rupert, King of Germany, died.
1812   John Bellingham, assassin (of the Prime Minister, Spencer Perceval), hanged.
1836   Wilhelm Steinitz, chess champion, born.
1868   Nicholas II, Tsar of Russia, born.
1872   Bertrand Russell, philosopher, born.
1883   Walter Gropius, architect, born.
1909   George Meredith, writer, died.
1909   Isaac Albeniz, composer, died.
1917   John Maskelyne, professional magician, died.

Events

1756   Britain declared war on France.
1804   Napoleon proclaimed Emperor of France.
1843   The Free Church of Scotland founded.
1845   Don Carlos relinquished his rights to the Spanish crown in favour of his son.
1900   Mafeking Night in Britain.
1900   Tonga proclaimed a British protectorate.
1943   U.N.R.R.A. founded.
1943   The Hot Springs Conference began.
1954   European Convention on Human Rights came into force.

19th MAY

People

1218	The Holy Roman Emperor Otto IV died.
1536	Anne Boleyn beheaded.
1762	J. G. Fichte, philosopher, born.
1767	Sir George Prevost, soldier and statesman, born.
1795	James Boswell, biographer of Dr Johnson, died.
1861	Dame Nellie Melba, singer, born.
1864	Nathaniel Hawthorne, writer, died.
1898	W. E. Gladstone, statesman, died.
1935	T. E. Lawrence, explorer and writer, killed in a road accident.

Events

1579	Treaty of the Malcontents with the Prince of Parma signed.
1643	Battle of Rocroi.
1692	The British destroyed a French fleet off Cap de la Hogue.
1802	The order of the Légion d'Honneur created.
1906	The Simplon Tunnel officially opened.

20th MAY

People

1506	Christopher Columbus, explorer, died.
1799	Honoré de Balzac, novelist, born.
1806	John Stuart Mill, philosopher, born.
1834	The Marquis de Lafayette, statesman, died.
1864	John Clare, poet, died.
1882	Sigrid Undset, novelist, born.
1896	Clara Schumann, pianist, died.
1956	Sir Max Beerbohm, writer, died.

Events

1775	The Mecklenburg declaration of independence adopted at Charlotte, North Carolina.
1867	The foundation stone of the Royal Albert Hall, South Kensington, officially laid.
1927	The Treaty of Jedda signed.
1927	Charles Lindbergh began first non-stop solo transatlantic flight.
1956	The first American hydrogen bomb dropped over Bikini atoll.

21st MAY

The Feasts of Saint Helen and Saint Constantine (Greek calendar).

People

1471	Henry VI, King of England, murdered.
1471	Albrecht Dürer, artist, born.
1527	Philip II, King of Spain, born.
1542	Hernando de Soto, soldier and explorer, died.
1688	Alexander Pope, poet, born.
1736	The Duke of Bridgewater, canal pioneer, born.
1771	Christopher Smart, poet, died.
1780	Elizabeth Fry, prison reformer, born.
1786	Carl Scheele, chemist, died.
1855	Emile Verhaeren, poet, born.
1878	Glenn Curtiss, aviation pioneer, born.
1884	Sir Claude Auchinleck, soldier, born.
1895	Franz von Suppé, composer, died.

Events

1502   João de Nova discovered the island of Saint Helena.
1553   Lady Jane Grey forced to marry Lord Guildford Dudley.
1864   The Battle of Spotsylvania Courthouse ended.
1871   The Treaty of Frankfurt ratified.
1894   The Manchester Ship Canal officially opened.
1927   Charles Lindbergh reached Paris at the end of his transatlantic flight.

22nd MAY

People

1813   Richard Wagner, composer, born.
1856   Augustin Thierry, historian, died.
1859   Sir Arthur Conan Doyle, writer, born.
1868   Julius Plücker, scientist, died.
1885   Victor Hugo, poet, novelist and playwright, died.
1907   Lord Olivier, actor, born.
1925   Sir John French, soldier, died.
1932   Lady Gregory, playwright, died.

Events

1216   Louis VIII of France invaded England, landing at Stonor.
1931   Whipsnade Zoo opened to the public.
1939   The Italo-German alliance signed in Berlin.

23rd MAY

People

1498   Girolamo Savonarola, reformer, strangled and burnt at the stake.
1701   Captain William Kidd, pirate, hanged.
1707   Carl Linnaeus, botanist, born.
1734   Franz Anton Mesmer, physician, born.
1799   Thomas Hood, poet, born.
1906   Henrik Ibsen, playwright, died.

Events

1618   The Defenestration of Prague.
1660   King Charles II sailed from Scheveningen for England on his return from exile.
1706   Battle of Ramillies.
1797   The Mutiny at the Nore.

24th MAY
Commonwealth Day.

People

1089   Lanfranc, Archbishop of Canterbury, died.
1543   Nicolaus Copernicus, astronomer, died.
1743   Jean Paul Marat, revolutionary leader, born.
1819   Victoria, Queen of Great Britain and Ireland, born.
1855   Sir Arthur Pinero, playwright, born.
1870   Jan Christian Smuts, soldier and statesman, born.
1879   William Lloyd Garrison, abolitionist, died.

24th May

1912 Joan Hammond, operatic singer, born.
1959 John Foster Dulles, statesman, died.
1974 'Duke' Ellington, musician, died.

Events

1658 Battle of the Dunes.
1809 Dartmoor Prison opened.
1815 The Lachlan River (Australia) discovered by the explorer George Evans.
1822 The Battle of Pinchincha.
1844 Samuel Morse sent the first public message over his electric telegraph between Washington and Baltimore.
1902 Empire Day first celebrated in Britain.
1909 Bristol University granted a Royal Charter.
1941 The battleship *Hood* sunk.
1959 Empire Day renamed Commonwealth Day.

25th MAY

Independence Day (Argentina).

People

1085 Pope Gregory VII died.
1681 Pedro Calderón, playwright, died.
1803 Ralph Waldo Emerson, writer, born.
1803 Lord Lytton, novelist, born.
1805 William Paley, philosopher, died.
1818 Jacob Burckhardt, historian, died.
1826 Tom Sayers, pugilist, born.
1828 John Oxley, explorer of Australia, died.
1865 P. Zeeman, physicist, born.
1879 Lord Beaverbrook, newspaper publisher, born.
1892 Josip Broz Tito, statesman, born.
1899 Rosa Bonheur, artist, died.
1934 Gustav Holst, composer, died.

Events

1734 The Battle of Bitonto.
1921 The first British woman barrister qualified.
1923 Transjordan (now Jordan) achieved independence.
1953 The world's first atomic shell fired in Nevada.
1955 A British expedition climbed Kanchenjunga.

26th MAY

Feast of Saint Augustine of Canterbury.

People

1391 Charles, Duc d'Orléans, poet, born.
1613 Sir Harry Vane, statesman, born.
1623 Sir William Petty, economist, born.
1703 Samuel Pepys, diarist and administrator, died.
1799 Alexander Pushkin, writer, born.
1822 Edmond de Goncourt, writer, born.
1844 Jacques Laffitte, banker and politician, died.
1867 Queen Mary, wife of King George V, born.
1893 Eugene Goossens, composer, born.
1922 Ernest Solvay, industrial chemist, died.
1939 Charles Mayo, surgeon, died.

Events

1637 Pequod Fort, Connecticut, destroyed.
1660 King Charles II landed at Dover.

1805	Napoleon crowned King of Italy.

1805 Napoleon crowned King of Italy.
1828 Kaspar Hauser, the wild boy, found in the Nuremberg market-place.
1865 American Civil War ended with surrender of last Confederate army.
1871 Ismailia annexed to Egypt.
1906 Vauxhall Bridge, London, officially opened.
1913 The first British woman magistrate, Emily Duncan, appointed.
1966 Guyana became independent.

27th MAY

People

1564 John Calvin, Church reformer, died.
1661 The 8th Earl of Argyll, soldier, beheaded.
1756 Maximilian I, King of Bavaria, born.
1799 Jacques Halévy, composer, born.
1867 Arnold Bennett, novelist, born.
1878 Isadora Duncan, dancer, born.
1964 Jawaharlal Nehru, statesman, died.

Events

1679 The Habeas Corpus Act became law.
1905 The Naval Battle of Tsushima.
1937 The Golden Gate Bridge, San Francisco, opened.
1941 The battleship *Bismarck* sunk.
1952 The European Defence Community set up.
1958 State of emergency in Ceylon (Sri Lanka).

28th MAY

People

1738 Dr Joseph Guillotin, adviser on capital punishment, born.
1759 William Pitt the Younger, statesman, born.
1779 Thomas Moore, poet, born.
1807 Jean Agassiz, naturalist, born.
1849 Anne Brontë, novelist, died.
1878 Lord John (Earl) Russell, statesman, died.
1884 Eduard Beneš, statesman, born.
1972 The Duke of Windsor died.

Events

1812 The Treaty of Bucharest signed.
1932 The closing of the 20-mile dyke connecting North Holland with Friesland, reduced the Zuider Zee to an inland lake.
1937 Neville Chamberlain appointed British Prime Minister.
1940 The Belgian Army surrendered to the Germans.

29th MAY
Oak Apple Day.

People

1439 Pope Pius III died.
1500 Bartolomeu Diaz, explorer, lost at sea.
1630 Charles II, King of England and Scotland, born.
1660 Sarah, Duchess of Marlborough, born.
1736 Patrick Henry, orator and statesman, born.

29th May

1829   Sir Humphry Davy, scientist, died.
1846   Sir Henry Wickham, pioneer rubber planter, born.
1860   Isaac Albeniz, composer, born.
1874   G. K. Chesterton, writer, born.
1911   Sir William Gilbert, playwright, died.
1917   John F. Kennedy, statesman, born.

Events

1453   Constantinople fell to the Turks.
1660   King Charles II entered London.
1848   Wisconsin achieved statehood.
1940   The evacuation of Dunkirk began.
1953   Sir Edmund Hillary and the Sherpa Tensing climbed Mount Everest.
1959   Charles de Gaulle formed government of national safety in France.

30th MAY

Feast of Saint Joan of Arc.   Memorial Day (U.S.A.).

People

1431   Saint Joan of Arc burnt at the stake.
1593   Christopher Marlowe, playwright, killed.
1640   Peter Paul Rubens, artist, died.
1672   Peter the Great, Tsar of Russia, born.
1744   Alexander Pope, poet, died.
1770   François Boucher, painter, died.
1778   Voltaire, writer, died.

Events

1656   The Grenadier Guards formed.
1814   The first Treaty of Paris signed.
1869   Memorial Day (Decoration Day) first observed in the U.S.A.
1913   The Treaty of London signed.

31st MAY

People

1809   Franz Josef Haydn, composer, died.
1819   Walt Whitman, poet, born.
1837   Joseph Grimaldi, clown, died.
1857   Pope Pius XI born.
1860   Walter Sickert, painter, born.
1863   Sir Francis Younghusband, explorer, born.
1923   Rainier III, Prince of Monaco, born.

Events

1669   Samuel Pepys ended his Diary.
1902   The Peace of Vereeniging.
1910   The Union of South Africa formed.
1916   The Naval Battle of Jutland.
1952   The Volga-Don Canal opened.

1st JUNE

People

1793   Henry Francis Lyte, hymn-writer, born.
1801   Brigham Young, Mormon, born.
1804   Mikhail Glinka, composer, born.

1815 James Gillray, caricaturist, died.
1815 Otto I, King of Greece, born.
1878 John Masefield, poet, born.
1879 Eugène, Prince Imperial of France, killed in the Zulu campaign.
1882 John Drinkwater, writer, born.
1941 Hugh Walpole, novelist, died.
1968 Helen Keller, blind and deaf scholar, died.

Events

1792 Kentucky achieved statehood.
1794 The Battle of the Glorious First of June.
1796 Tennessee achieved statehood.
1835 Otto I assumed the government of Greece.
1841 Mehemet Ali became hereditary Viceroy of Egypt.
1939 The submarine *Thetis* lost.
1941 The Hot Springs Conference ended.
1946 A combined television and sound broadcasting receiving licence introduced in Britain.

2nd JUNE

People

959 Odo, Archbishop of Canterbury, died.
1453 Alvaro de Luna, courtier and poet, executed.
1624 John Sobieski, King of Poland, born.
1701 Madeleine de Scudéry, novelist, died.
1776 Robert Foulis, printer, died.
1835 Pope Pius X born.
1840 Thomas Hardy, writer, born.
1857 Sir Edward Elgar, composer, born.
1863 Felix Weingartner, conductor, born.
1882 Giuseppe Garibaldi, Italian nationalist leader, died.

Events

1780 Lord George Gordon's 'No Popery' riots began.
1864 Greek troops occupied Corfu.
1895 Japan took formal possession of Formosa (Taiwan) from China.
1896 Marconi granted world's first patent for system of wireless telegraphy.
1953 The coronation of Queen Elizabeth II.

3rd JUNE

People

1657 William Harvey, physician, died.
1771 Sydney Smith, reformer and writer, born.
1804 Richard Cobden, political reformer, born.
1808 Jefferson Davis, statesman, born.
1832 Charles Lecocq, composer, born.
1853 W. F. Petrie, archaeologist, born.
1865 George V, King of Great Britain and Ireland, born.
1875 Georges Bizet, composer, died.
1899 Johann Strauss the Younger, composer, died.
1963 Pope John XXIII died.

Events

1665 The Naval Battle of Lowestoft.
1745 The Battle of Hohenfriedberg (3–4 June).
1887 The foundation stone of the opening lock of Kiel Canal laid.

3rd June

1937   The Duke of Windsor married Mrs Wallis Warfield.
1940   The evacuation of Dunkirk ended.
1942   The Battle of Midway Island began.
1956   British 3rd class railway travel abolished.

4th JUNE
Eton College Celebrations on the birthday of George III.

People

1738   George III, King of Great Britain, born.
1792   John Burgoyne, soldier and playwright, died.
1798   Casanova, adventurer and writer, died.
1833   Viscount Wolseley, army reformer, born.
1864   Nassau Senior, economist, born.
1867   Karl Mannerheim, soldier and statesman, born.
1931   Ibn Hussein, King of the Hejaz, died.
1945   Georg Kaiser, playwright, died.
1951   Serge Koussevitsky, conductor, died.

Events

1831   Leopold, Duke of Kendal, elected first King of the Belgians.
1859   The Battle of Magenta.
1944   The Allies entered Rome.
1970   Tonga became independent.

5th JUNE
Feast of Saint Boniface.

People

1316   Louis X, King of France, died.
1625   Orlando Gibbons, composer, died.
1723   Adam Smith, economist, born.
1826   Carl von Weber, composer, died.
1883   Lord Keynes, economist, born.
1900   Stephen Crane, writer, died.
1916   Lord Kitchener, soldier, perished at sea.
1968   Robert Kennedy, statesman, assassinated.

Events

1783   The hot-air balloon invented by the brothers Montgolfier.
1863   Protocol between Britain, France and Russia provided for the incorporation of the Ionian Islands into Greece.
1916   Outbreak of Arab revolt against the Turks.
1947   The Marshall Plan announced.
1967   Outbreak of war between Arab states and Israel.

6th JUNE

People

1502   John III, King of Portugal, born.
1557   John III, King of Portugal, died.
1599   Diego Velazquez, painter, born.
1606   Pierre Corneille, dramatist, born.
1756   John Trumbull, artist, born.

1762 Lord Anson, sailor and explorer, died.
1799 Alexander Pushkin, writer, born.
1826 Léon Say, statesman, born.
1832 Jeremy Bentham, philosopher, died.
1840 Sir John Stainer, composer, born.
1860 Dean Inge, theologian, born.
1862 Sir Henry Newbolt, writer, born.
1868 Robert Falcon Scott, explorer, born.
1875 Thomas Mann, novelist, born.
1881 Henri Vieuxtemps, violinist and composer, died.
1903 Aram Khachaturian, composer, born.
1935 George Grossmith, actor and writer, died.
1941 Louis Chevrolet, pioneer automobile designer, died.
1968 Robert Kennedy, statesman, assassinated.

Events
1520 Field of the Cloth of Gold.
1918 The Battle of Belleau Wood began.
1942 The Battle of Midway Island ended.
1944 D-Day landings in Normandy.
1954 The birth of Eurovision through the direct relay on the European network of the *Fête des Narcisses* at Montreux.

7th JUNE

People

1329 Robert Bruce, King of Scotland, died.
1761 John Rennie, engineer, born.
1778 Beau Brummel, leader of fashion, born.
1848 Paul Gauguin, painter, born.
1859 David Cox, artist, died.
1879 Knud Rasmussen, explorer, born.

Events

1099 The Crusaders arrived in front of Jerusalem.
1494 The Treaty of Tordesillas signed.
1614 The Addled Parliament dissolved.
1832 Parliamentary Reform Bill became law.
1905 Norway proclaimed the dissolution of the union of Norway and Sweden.
1906 The *Lusitania* launched.
1917 The Battle of Messines.
1935 Stanley Baldwin appointed British Prime Minister.
2004 The next transit of Venus over the sun.

8th JUNE

People

632 The Prophet Mohammed died.
1695 Christian Huygens, physicist, died.
1714 Sophia, Electress of Hanover, died.
1724 John Smeaton, civil engineer, born.
1772 Robert Stevenson, engineer, born.
1795 The death of Louis XVII, King of France, announced.
1809 Tom Paine, political writer and agitator, died.
1810 Robert Schumann, composer, born.
1814 Charles Reade, novelist, born.
1829 Sir John Millais, painter, born.
1831 Mrs Sarah Siddons, actress, died.

8th June

1845 Andrew Jackson, statesman, born.
1857 Douglas Jerrold, writer, died.
1865 Sir Joseph Paxton, architect and ornamental gardener, died.
1869 Frank Lloyd Wright, architect, born.
1876 George Sand, writer, died.

Events

1815 The Congress of Vienna ended.
1930 King Carol returned to the throne of Romania.

9th JUNE

People

1640 The Holy Roman Emperor Leopold I born.
1681 William Lilly, astrologer, died.
1781 George Stephenson, engineer, born.
1810 Otto Nicolai, composer, born.
1846 Pope Gregory XVI died.
1870 Charles Dickens, novelist, died.
1892 Cole Porter, composer, born.
1964 Lord Beaverbrook, newspaper publisher, died.
1976 Dame Sybil Thorndyke, actress, died.

Events

1904 First concert of the London Symphony Orchestra.
1904 First meeting of the Ladies' Automobile Club, London.

10th JUNE

People

1190 The Holy Roman Emperor, Frederick Barbarossa, died.
1580 Luis de Camões, poet, died.
1688 James Stuart, the Old Pretender, born.
1727 George I, King of Great Britain, died.
1819 Gustave Courbet, painter, born.
1836 André Ampère, physicist, died.
1899 Ernest Chausson, composer, died.
1921 Prince Philip, Duke of Edinburgh, born.
1934 Frederick Delius, composer, died.
1974 The Duke of Gloucester died.

Events

1809 Napoleon excommunicated.
1826 The final revolt of the Janissaries in Turkey began.
1829 First Oxford and Cambridge University Boat Race.
1854 Crystal Palace officially opened.
1918 Battle of Belleau Wood ended.
1940 Italy declared war on Great Britain and France.
1946 Italy became a republic.

11th JUNE
Feast of Saint Barnabas.

People

1488 James III, King of Scotland, assassinated.
1665 Sir Kenelm Digby, writer, died.
1727 George II proclaimed King of Great Britain.
1776 John Constable, painter, born.

1847 Dame Millicent Fawcett, reformer, born.
1847 Sir John Franklin, explorer, died.
1851 Mrs Humphrey Ward, novelist, born.
1859 Prince Metternich, statesman, died.
1864 Richard Strauss, composer, born.

Events

1509 King Henry VIII married Catherine of Aragon.
1903 King Alexander of Serbia and Queen Draga assassinated in Belgrade.
1975 First oil pumped ashore from Britain's North Sea oilfields.

12th JUNE

People

1759 William Collins, poet, died.
1802 Harriet Martineau, writer, born.
1806 John Roebling, engineer, born.
1819 Charles Kingsley, poet and novelist, born.
1842 Thomas Arnold, headmaster of Rugby, died.
1842 Rikard Nordraak, composer and folksong collector, born.
1897 Sir Anthony Eden (Earl of Avon), statesman, born.

Events

1458 Magdalen College, Oxford, founded.
1908 The Rotherhithe-Stepney Tunnel, London, opened.

13th JUNE

People

1231 Saint Anthony of Padua died.
1396 Philip the Good, Duke of Burgundy, born.
1752 Fanny Burney (Mme D'Arblay), novelist, born.
1795 Thomas Arnold, headmaster of Rugby, born.
1831 James Clerk Maxwell, physicist, born.
1865 William Butler Yeats, poet, born.
1886 Ludwig II, King of Bavaria, drowned.
1888 Elizabeth Schumann, singer, born.
1958 Pierre Flandin, statesman, died.

Events

1700 Peter the Great concluded peace with Turkey.
1900 The Boxer Rising in China.
1944 First Flying Bombs (13–14 June) fell on London.
1956 Last British troops left the Suez base.

14th JUNE
Flag Day (U.S.A.).

People

1594 Orlando di Lasso, composer, died.
1662 Sir Harry Vane, statesman, executed.
1811 Harriet Beecher Stowe, writer, born.
1848 Bernard Bosanquet, philosopher, born.
1883 Edward FitzGerald, poet, died.

14th June

1884 Count John McCormack, singer, born.
1927 Jerome K. Jerome, writer, died.
1936 G. K. Chesterton, writer, died.
1946 J. L. Baird, television pioneer, died.

Events

1381 King Richard II persuaded the Essex rebels to return home.
1645 The Battle of Naseby.
1777 The Stars and Stripes adopted by the Continental Congress.
1800 The Battle of Marengo.
1900 The Hawaiian Islands constituted as United States territory.
1940 The Germans entered Paris.
1958 The withdrawal of French forces from Morocco announced.

15th JUNE
Feast of Saint Vitus.

People

 923 Robert I, King of France, killed in battle.
1330 Edward, the Black Prince, born.
1381 Wat Tyler killed at Smithfield.
1467 Philip the Good, Duke of Burgundy, died.
1563 George Heriot jeweller and royal banker, born.
1815 'Phiz' (Hablot K. Browne), artist, born.
1843 Edvard Grieg, composer, born.
1844 Thomas Campbell, poet, died.
1858 Ary Scheffer, painter, died.
1865 Paul Gilson, composer, born.
1888 Frederick III, Emperor of Germany, died.
1893 Franz Erkel, composer, died.

Events

1215 Magna Carta signed.
1752 Benjamin Franklin demonstrated electricity by means of a kite.
1836 Arkansas achieved statehood.
1858 The massacre of the Christians at Jedda.
1919 Alcock and Brown completed first non-stop transatlantic flight.

16th JUNE

People

1514 Sir John Cheke, classical scholar, born.
1722 The Duke of Marlborough, soldier, died.
1779 Siege of Gibraltar began.
1801 Julius Plücker, scientist, born.
1858 Gustav V, King of Sweden, born.
1930 Elmer Ambrose Sperry, inventor, died.

Events

1487 The Battle of Stoke.
1815 The Battle of Quatre Bras.
1826 The insurrection of the Janissaries at Constantinople ended.
1880 The Berlin Conference.
1930 Mixed bathing in the Serpentine, Hyde Park, first permitted.
1940 The Soviet Union sent an ultimatum to Estonia.
1972 Burglars arrested in the Democratic Party headquarters, Watergate Building, Washington.

17th JUNE

People

1239	Edward I, King of England, born.
1682	Charles XII, King of Sweden, born.
1696	John III, King of Poland, died.
1703	John Wesley born.
1719	Joseph Addison, writer, died.
1762	P. J. de Crébillon, poet, died.
1800	The Earl of Rosse, astronomer, born.
1810	Ferdinand Freiligrath, poet, born.
1818	Charles Gounod, composer, born.
1845	Richard Barham, poet, died.
1882	Igor Stravinsky, composer, born.
1958	Imre Nagy, statesman, executed.

Events

1745	The French surrendered Louisburg, Cape Breton Island, to the British.
1775	The Battle of Bunker Hill.
1789	The Third Estate constituted themselves the French National Assembly.
1860	*Great Eastern* left the Needles on her first transatlantic voyage.
1869	Wilhelmshaven, Germany's first military port, officially inaugurated.
1873	The Roumelian Railway opened.
1905	The River Steamboat Service on the Thames began.
1940	Latvia occupied by the Russians.
1940	The evacuation of the British Expeditionary Force from France completed.
1944	Iceland proclaimed an independent republic.
1967	China claimed to have exploded a hydrogen bomb.

18th JUNE

People

1769	Viscount Castlereagh, statesman, born.
1835	William Cobbett, writer and politician, died.
1868	Miklós Horthy, statesman, born.
1871	George Grote, historian, died.
1880	John Sutter, pioneer in the U.S.A., died.
1902	Samuel Butler, writer, died.
1936	Maxim Gorki, writer, died.

Events

1429	The Battle of Patay.
1812	War between Britain and the U.S.A. began.
1815	The Battle of Waterloo.
1928	The Atlantic first flown by a woman aviator (Amelia Earhart).
1953	Egypt proclaimed a republic.

19th JUNE

People

1566	James I, King of England and Scotland, born.
1623	Blaise Pascal, philosopher and mathematician, born.
1782	Félicité de Lamennais, church reformer, born.
1820	Sir Joseph Banks, naturalist, died.
1834	Charles Spurgeon, Baptist leader, born.
1861	Earl Haig, soldier, born.
1867	The Emperor Maximilian of Mexico executed.
1889	John Percy, metallurgist, died.
1937	Sir James Barrie, writer, died.

19th June

Events

1829   Act passed founding Metropolitan Police.
1850   The Earl of Rosse publicly announced his discovery of the Spiral Nebulae.
1895   The Kiel Canal opened.
1910   The first Zeppelin airliner (*Deutschland*) launched.
1961   Kuwait became independent.

20th JUNE

People

1819   Jacques Offenbach, composer, born.
1836   Emmanuel Sieyès, statesman, died.
1837   William IV, King of Great Britain and Ireland, died.
1870   Jules de Goncourt, writer, died.
1965   Bernard Baruch, financier, died.

Events

1756   The Black Hole of Calcutta.
1789   The oath of the Tennis Court (French Revolution).
1791   Louis XVI's attempted flight to Varennes.
1792   The mob invaded the Tuileries.
1837   Queen Victoria ascended the throne.
1863   West Virginia achieved statehood.
1927   Greyhound racing began at White City, London.

21st JUNE

The Summer Solstice (except in Leap Years).

People

1002   Pope Leo IX born.
1377   Edward III, King of England, died.
1529   John Skelton, poet, died.
1631   John Smith, colonizer of Virginia, died.
1639   Increase Mather, President of Harvard College, born.
1652   Inigo Jones, architect, died.
1852   Friedrich Froebel, educationalist, died.
1882   Rockwell Kent, artist, born.
1908   Nikolai Rimsky-Korsakov, composer, died.
1935   Françoise Sagan, novelist, born.
1940   John Thompson, soldier and inventor, died.

Events

1619   Dulwich College, London, founded.
1788   The American Constitution came into force.
1813   The Battle of Vitoria.
1843   The Royal College of Surgeons, London, founded.
1919   The German Fleet scuttled at Scapa Flow.
1942   Tobruk fell to German forces.

22nd JUNE

The Summer Solstice in Leap Years.

People

1101   Roger I, King of Sicily, died.
1276   Pope Innocent V died.
1527   Niccolò Machiavelli, diplomat and writer, died.

1535   Bishop John Fisher executed.
1748   Thomas Day, writer, born.
1805   Giuseppe Mazzini, nationalist leader, born.
1830   Theodore Leschetizky, pianist, born.
1846   Benjamin Robert Haydon, painter, committed suicide.
1856   Sir H. Rider Haggard, novelist, born.
1887   Sir Julian Huxley, biologist, born.

Events

1476   The Battle of Morat.
1559   Queen Elizabeth's Prayer Book issued.
1679   The Battle of Bothwell Bridge.
1774   The Quebec Act received the Royal Assent.
1817   Windham Sadler crossed the St George's Channel by balloon.
1900   The Wallace Collection, London, opened.
1907   The Northern Underground Line, London, opened.
1933   The Social Democrat Party suppressed in Germany.
1941   Germany invaded Russia.
1945   The Battle of Okinawa ended.

23rd JUNE

Midsummer Eve.

People

1703   Marie Leszczynska, Queen of France, born.
1763   The Empress Josephine, wife of Napoleon, born.
1836   James Mill, philosopher and historian, died.
1839   Lady Hester Stanhope, traveller, died.
1894   The Duke of Windsor born.
1924   Cecil Sharp, folk-music collector, died.

Events

1585   The Star Chamber suppressed all provincial printing offices.
1611   The navigator Henry Hudson cast adrift to perish.
1683   William Penn signed a treaty of peace and friendship with the Indians.
1757   The Battle of Plassey.
1793   The beginning of the Reign of Terror in France.
1848   The 'June Days' (23–24) in France.
1956   Gamal Nasser elected President of the Republic of Egypt.

24th JUNE

The Feast of Saint John the Baptist.   Midsummer Day.

People

1065   Ferdinand I, King of Castile and Leon, died.
1340   John of Gaunt, Duke of Lancaster, born.
1519   Lucrezia Borgia, Duchess of Ferrara, died.
1542   Saint John of the Cross born.
1643   John Hampden, statesman, died.
1650   The Duke of Marlborough, soldier, born.
1768   Marie Leszcynska, Queen of France, died.
1768   Lazare Hoche, soldier, born.
1771   Eleuthère du Pont, American powder manufacturer, born.
1813   Henry Ward Beecher, divine, born.
1850   Lord Kitchener, soldier, born.
1870   Adam Lindsay Gordon, poet, committed suicide.

Events

1314   The Battle of Bannockburn.
1497   John Cabot reached the North American shore.

24th June

1717 The Mother Grand Lodge of Freemasonry inaugurated in London.
1812 Napoleon invaded Russia.
1859 The Battle of Solferino.
1860 The training of nurses in Britain started in St Thomas's Hospital, London.
1948 The Russian blockade of Berlin began.

25th JUNE

People

1483 Earl Rivers, statesman, executed.
1634 John Marston, dramatist, died.
1736 John Horne Tooke, politician and philologist, born.
1876 George Armstrong Custer, soldier, died.
1900 Earl Mountbatten of Burma, soldier and administrator, born.
1908 Grover Cleveland, statesman, died.
1912 Sir Lawrence Alma-Tadema, artist, died.
1913 Esteban Eitler, composer, born.

Events

841   The Battle of Fontenoy.
1530 The Confession of Augsburg read to the Diet.
1862 The Seven Days' Battles began.
1876 The Battle of Little Big Horn (Custer's Last Stand).
1950 The Korean War began.
1975 Mozambique became independent.

26th JUNE

People

363   Julian the Apostate, Roman Emperor, died of wounds.
1541 Francisco Pizarro, conquistador, assassinated.
1666 Sir Richard Fanshawe, diplomat and translator, died.
1763 George Morland, painter, born.
1793 Gilbert White, writer on natural history, died.
1824 Lord Kelvin, scientist, born.
1827 Samuel Crompton, inventor, died.
1830 George IV, King of Great Britain and Ireland, died.
1836 C. J. Rouget de Lisle, composer of the *Marseillaise*, died.
1892 Pearl S. Buck, writer, born.
1938 E. V. Lucas, essayist, died.

Events

1830 William IV ascended the British throne.
1846 The Corn Laws repealed.
1853 The Russians issue a manifesto against Turkey.
1857 Massacre at Cawnpore.
1857 Queen Victoria distributed Victoria Crosses at Hyde Park.
1909 The present buildings of the Victoria and Albert Museum opened officially.
1912 The first Queen Alexandra Day held.
1917 The American Expeditionary Force reached France.
1945 The United Nations Charter signed at San Francisco.

27th JUNE

People

1682 Charles XII, King of Sweden, born.
1829 James Smithson, scientist, died.
1846 Charles Stewart Parnell, Irish nationalist leader, born.

1872 Paul Lawrence Dunbar, poet, born.
1880 Helen Keller, blind and deaf scholar, born.
1888 Guilhermina Suggia, 'cellist, born.

Events

1743 The Battle of Dettingen.
1900 The Central London Electric Railway opened.
1944 Cherbourg taken by the Allies.

28th JUNE

People

767 Pope Paul I died.
1476 Pope Paul IV born.
1491 Henry VIII, King of England, born.
1712 Jean Jacques Rousseau, writer and philosopher, born.
1805 Giuseppe Mazzini, Italian nationalist leader, born.
1815 Robert Franz, composer, born.
1831 Joseph Joachim, violinist, born.
1855 Lord Raglan, soldier, died.
1867 Luigi Pirandello, playwright, born.
1871 Luisa Tetrazzini, operatic singer, born.
1873 Alexis Carrel, scientist, born.
1914 The Archduke Ferdinand and his wife assassinated at Sarajevo.
1915 Victor Trumper, cricketer, died.

Events

1776 The British repulsed at Charleston.
1778 The Battle of Monmouth, New Jersey.
1910 The first Zeppelin airliner (*Deutschland*) crashed.
1910 Westminster Cathedral consecrated.
1919 The Treaty of Versailles signed.
1948 The Anglo-U.S. airlift to Berlin began.

29th JUNE   The Feasts of Saint Peter and Saint Paul.

People

1577 Peter Paul Rubens, painter, born.
1798 Giacomo Leopardi, poet, born.
1810 Robert Schumann, composer, born.
1841 Sir Henry Morton Stanley, explorer, born (traditional date).
1858 George Washington Goethals, Panama Canal builder, born.
1861 William Mayo, surgeon, born.
1868 George Hale, astronomer, born.
1895 T. H. Huxley, scientist, died.
1911 Prince Bernhard of the Netherlands born.
1941 Ignaz Jan Paderewski, pianist and statesman, died.

Events

1734 The Battle of Parma.
1871 Trade unions legalized by Act of Parliament.
1943 U.S. forces landed in New Guinea.

30th JUNE

People

1803 Thomas Beddoes, writer, born.
1843 Sir Herbert Stewart, soldier, born.
1861 Elizabeth Barrett Browning, poet, died.

Events

1688	William of Orange invited to England.
1708	Battle of Oudenarde began.
1860	The British Association's first annual meeting held at Oxford.
1855	The Newspaper Stamp Tax abolished in Britain.
1893	Harold Laski, economist and politician, born.
1924	The first International Power Conference held at Wembley.
1934	The 'Night of the Long Knives' in Germany.
1960	Zaïre became independent.
1970	Negotiations began for British membership of the European Economic Community.

1st JULY

Dominion Day (Canada).

People

1534	Frederick II, King of Denmark, born.
1574	Bishop Joseph Hall, writer, born.
1589	Christopher Plantin, printer, died.
1646	Gottfried Leibniz, philosopher and mathematician, born.
1725	Comte de Rochambeau, soldier, born.
1804	George Sand, writer, born.
1839	Mahmud II, Sultan of Turkey, died.
1860	Charles Goodyear, inventor, died.
1872	Louis Blériot, pioneer aviator, born.
1896	Harriet Beecher Stowe, writer, died.
1904	George Frederick Watts, painter, died.
1925	Eric Satie, composer, died.
1964	Pierre Monteux, musician, died.
1974	Juan Perón, political leader, died.

Events

1643	The Westminster Assembly began.
1690	The Battle of the Boyne.
1858	The Darwinian theory of evolution by natural selection first communicated to the Linnean Society.
1863	Slavery ceased in the Dutch West Indies.
1863	The Battle of Gettysburg began.
1867	The German federal constitution came into force.
1867	The Provinces of Canada united under the British North America Act.
1873	Prince Edward Island admitted to the Canadian Confederation.
1885	The sovereignty of King Leopold I of Belgium over the Congo proclaimed.
1912	First Variety 'Command Performance' in Britain.
1916	Battle of the Somme began.
1920	The British civil administration of Palestine began.
1944	The Bretton Woods Conference began.
1946	The first of the atom bomb tests over Bikini atoll.
1960	The Somali Republic formed.
1962	Burundi and Rwanda became independent.
1969	Prince Charles invested as Prince of Wales.

2nd JULY

People

936	Henry the Fowler, King of Germany, died.
1489	Thomas Cranmer, Archbishop of Canterbury, born.
1566	Nostradamus, astrologer, died.
1714	Christoph Gluck, composer, born.
1724	Friedrich Klopstock, poet, born.
1778	Jean-Jacques Rousseau, philosopher and writer, died.
1850	Sir Robert Peel, statesman, died.

1862	Sir William Bragg, scientist, born.
1881	James Garfield, statesman, shot (died 19th Sept.).
1903	Sir Alec Douglas-Home, statesman, born.
1903	Olav V, King of Norway, born.
1914	Joseph Chamberlain, statesman, died.
1917	Sir Herbert Beerbohm Tree, actor-manager, died.
1932	Manuel II, ex-King of Portugal, died.

Events

1644	The Battle of Marston Moor.
1862	The Seven Days' Battles ended.
1940	The Vichy Government set up in France.

3rd JULY

People

1423	Louis XI, King of France, born.
1642	Marie de Médicis, Queen of France, died.
1728	Robert Adam, architect, born.
1738	John Copley, painter, born.
1746	Henry Grattan, statesman, born.
1816	Dorothy Jordan, actress and royal mistress, died (generally accepted date).
1908	Joel Harris, humorous writer, died.

Events

323	The Battle of Adrianople.
1608	The settlement of Quebec began.
1620	The Treaty of Ulm signed.
1778	The Massacre at Wyoming, Pennsylvania.
1815	King Louis XVIII entered Paris (end of the 'Hundred Days').
1863	The Battle of Gettysburg ended.
1890	Idaho achieved statehood.
1898	The Naval Battle of Santiago.
1953	Nanga Parbat climbed by an Austro-German expedition.
1962	Algeria became independent.

4th JULY

Independence Day in the United States of America.

People

1623	William Byrd, composer, died.
1761	Samuel Richardson, novelist, died.
1804	Nathaniel Hawthorne, novelist, born.
1807	Giuseppe Garibaldi, Italian patriot and soldier, born.
1826	Stephen Foster, song-writer, born.
1826	John Adams, statesman, died.
1826	Thomas Jefferson, statesman, died.
1831	James Monroe, statesman, died.
1848	François de Chateaubriand, writer, died.
1857	Joseph Pennell, etcher, born.
1872	Calvin Coolidge, statesman, born.
1910	Giovanni Schiaparelli, astronomer, died.
1934	Marie Curie, scientist, died.
1942	Prince Michael of Kent born.

Events

1187	The Battle of the Horns of Hattin.
1399	Henry of Lancaster (Henry IV) landed at Ravenspur, Yorkshire.
1636	Providence, Rhode Island, founded.

1653	Barebones Parliament began sitting.
1776	The American Declaration of Independence.
1817	Work on the Erie Canal began.
1828	Don Miguel assumed the title of King of Portugal.
1829	The first London bus ran from Marylebone Road to the Bank.
1863	The surrender of Vicksburg.
1904	The construction of the Panama Canal began.
1946	The Republic of the Philippines established.

5th JULY

People

1755	Mrs Sarah Siddons, actress, born.
1764	Ivan VI, Tsar of Russia, murdered.
1781	Sir Stamford Raffles, administrator, born.
1801	David Farragut, naval officer, born.
1803	George Borrow, writer, born.
1810	Phineas Barnum, showman, born.
1822	Ernst Hoffmann, writer and composer, died.
1826	Sir Stamford Raffles, administrator, died.
1843	Bishop Mandell Creighton, historian, born.
1849	W. T. Stead, social reformer, born.
1853	Cecil Rhodes, statesman, born.
1877	Wanda Landowska, musician, born.
1880	Jan Kubelik, violinist, born.
1889	Jean Cocteau, writer, born.
1894	Sir Austen Layard, archaeologist, died.

Events

1841	Thomas Cook's, travel agents, founded, with running of world's first excursion train.
1933	The German Catholic Party dissolved.
1948	The British National Health Service came into operation.
1955	The first Assembly of the Western European Union opened at Strasbourg.
1975	Cape Verde Islands became independent.

6th JULY
Feast of Saint Thomas More.

People

1189	Henry II, King of England, died.
1415	Jan Huss, religious reformer, burnt at the stake.
1535	Sir Thomas More, scholar and statesman, executed.
1553	Edward VI, King of England, died.
1572	Sigismund II, King of Poland, died.
1747	John Paul Jones, naval officer, born.
1755	John Flaxman, sculptor, born.
1796	Nicholas I, Tsar of Russia, born.
1832	The Emperor Maximilian of Mexico born.
1847	Lord Runciman, shipowner, born.
1893	Guy de Maupassant, writer, died.
1968	Sarah Millin, writer, died.
1971	Louis Armstrong, musician, died.

Events

1096	Grand Council of Nimes opened.
1560	The Treaty of Edinburgh signed.
1685	The Battle of Sedgemoor.

1809	The Battle of Wagram.
1859	Queensland, Australia, formed into a separate colony.
1907	Brooklands Motor Racecourse opened.
1923	The U.S.S.R. formally constituted.
1950	The Oder-Neisse Line declared the permanent frontier between Germany and Poland (by the German Democratic Republic and Poland).
1952	The last London tram ran.
1964	Malawi became independent.
1967	Outbreak of civil war in Nigeria.

7th JULY

Feasts of Saint Cyril and Saint Methodius.

People

1307	Edward I, King of England, died.
1752	Joseph Jacquard, inventor, born.
1816	Richard Brinsley Sheridan, playwright, died.
1860	Gustav Mahler, composer, born.
1884	Lion Feuchtwanger, novelist, born.
1930	Sir Arthur Conan Doyle, writer, died.

Events

| 1807 | The Treaty of Tilsit signed. |
| 1898 | Hawaii annexed by the United States. |

8th JULY

People

1621	Jean de La Fontaine, writer, born.
1623	Pope Gregory XV died.
1822	Percy Bysshe Shelley, poet, died.
1823	Sir Henry Raeburn, painter, died.
1836	Joseph Chamberlain, statesman, born.
1838	Count Zeppelin, inventor, born.
1839	John D. Rockefeller, sen., industrialist, born.
1851	Sir Arthur Evans, archaeologist, born.
1882	Percy Grainger, composer, born.
1939	Havelock Ellis, physician and writer, died.

Events

1709	The Battle of Poltava.
1833	The Treaty of Unkiar Skelessi signed.
1924	Adolf Hitler resumed leadership of the National Socialist Party in Germany.

9th JULY

People

1228	Stephen Langton, Archbishop of Canterbury, died.
1440	Jan van Eyck, painter, died.
1746	Philip V, King of Spain, died.
1764	Ann Radcliffe, novelist, born.
1777	Henry Hallam, historian, born.
1797	Edmund Burke, orator and writer, died.

9th July

1819   Elias Howe, inventor, born.
1856   Nikola Tesla, inventor, born.
1863   Baron von Stockmar, statesman, died.
1909   The Marquess of Ripon, statesman, died.
1916   Edward Heath, statesman, born.
1932   King Gillette, manufacturer, died.

Events

1386   The Battle of Sempach.
1755   General Braddock's troops attacked by the French and Indians near Fort Duquesne.
1810   Holland united to France.
1816   The Congress of Tucumán.
1816   Argentina declared its independence from Spain.
1857   Madeleine Smith acquitted at Edinburgh of the murder of her lover.
1860   Massacre of the Christians in Damascus began.
1944   Caen captured by the Allies.

10th JULY

People

1290   Ladislaus IV, King of Hungary, murdered.
1509   John Calvin, Church reformer, born.
1559   Henry II, King of France, killed.
1605   Theodore II, Tsar of Russia, murdered.
1723   Sir William Blackstone, jurist, born.
1792   Frederick Marryat, writer, born.
1834   James McNeill Whistler, painter, born.
1835   Henri Wieniawski, composer, born.
1871   Marcel Proust, writer, born.
1886   Lord Gort, soldier, born.
1888   Toyohiko Kagawa, reformer and writer, born.
1920   Lord Fisher, naval reformer, died.
1923   Albert Chevalier, music-hall singer, died.

Events

1553   Lady Jane Grey proclaimed Queen of England.
1762   Peter III, Tsar of Russia, dethroned.
1890   Wyoming achieved statehood.
1921   Mongolia proclaimed an independent state.
1938   Reims Cathedral reopened.
1962   Telstar, communications satellite, launched.
1968   First purges in Chinese Cultural Revolution announced.

11th JULY

People

1274   Robert Bruce, King of Scotland, born.
1657   Frederick I, King of Prussia, born.
1732   Joseph Lalande, astronomer, born.
1754   Thomas Bowdler, literary editor, born.
1767   John Quincy Adams, statesman, born.
1797   Charles Macklin, actor, died.
1903   William Henley, poet, died.
1926   Gertrude Bell, traveller, died.
1937   George Gershwin, composer, died.
1941   Sir Arthur Evans, archaeologist, died.
1946   Paul Nash, artist, died.
1957   The Aga Khan III died.

Events

1302   The Battle of the Spurs (Battle of Courtrai).
1637   The number of typefounders in England restricted to four by Star Chamber decree.
1708   The Battle of Oudenarde ended.
1804   Alexander Hamilton fatally wounded in a duel with Aaron Burr.
1859   The Treaty of Villafranca signed.
1860   Massacre of the Christians at Damascus ended.
1960   Province of Katanga, Zaïre, proclaimed independent.

12th JULY

Orangeman's Day (Northern Ireland).

People

100B.C.Julius Caesar born.
1536   Desiderius Erasmus, scholar, died.
1584   William the Silent, Prince of Orange, assassinated.
1705   Titus Oates, conspirator, died.
1730   Josiah Wedgwood, potter, born.
1803   Thomas Guthrie, promoter of Ragged Schools, born.
1817   Henry Thoreau, writer, born.
1849   Sir William Osler, physician, born.
1854   George Eastman, photographic pioneer, born.
1859   Robert Stephenson, engineer, died.
1872   F. E. Smith, Lord Birkenhead, statesman, born.
1895   Kirsten Flagstad, operatic singer, born.
1910   The Hon. C. S. Rolls, pioneer aviator and motor motor car manufacturer, killed.
1935   Alfred Dreyfus, army officer, died.

Events

1691   The Battle of Aughrim.
1806   The formation of the Confederation of the Rhine.
1878   The British took possession of Cyprus.
1906   Alfred Dreyfus vindicated and rehabilitated.
1941   Anglo-Russian agreement signed in Moscow.
1967   Race riots in Newark, New Jersey.
1975   São Tomé and Principe became independent.

13th JULY

People

1380   Bertrand du Guesclin, Constable of France, died.
1755   Edward Braddock, soldier, died.
1793   John Clare, poet, born.
1793   Jean Paul Marat, statesman, assassinated.
1816   Gustav Freytag, writer, born.
1859   Sidney Webb, Lord Passfield, economist and Fabian, born.
1886   Clifford Bax, playwright, born.
1890   John Frémont, explorer, died.
1951   Arnold Schönberg, composer, died.

BROMLEY LIBRARIES

Events

1191   Acre taken by the Crusaders.
1798   Wordsworth wrote his 'Lines' composed a few miles above Tintern Abbey.
1868   The Scottish Reform Act passed.
1878   The Treaty of Berlin signed.
1878   Romania proclaimed independent.
1919   The airship *R34* landed in England after its flight from the U.S.A.

14th JULY   Bastile Day (France).

People

1223   Philip Augustus, King of France, died.
1602   Cardinal Mazarin, statesman, born.
1816   Francisco Miranda, nationalist leader, died.
1816   The Comte de Gobineau, traveller and writer, born.
1817   Madame de Staël, writer, died.
1858   Emmeline Pankhurst, champion of women's rights, born.
1868   Gertrude Bell, explorer, born.
1887   Alfred Krupp, industrialist, died.
1904   Stephanus Kruger, Boer leader, died.
1958   Faisal II, King of Iraq, assassinated.
1965   Adlai Stevenson, statesman, died.

Events

1096   Grand Council of Nîmes ended.
1789   The storming of the Bastille began the French Revolution.
1833   The Oxford Movement launched.

15th JULY   Saint Swithin's Day.

People

1291   Rudolf I, King of Germany, died.
1573   Inigo Jones, architect, born.
1606   Rembrandt van Rijn, painter, born.
1685   The Duke of Monmouth beheaded.
1704   Bishop August Spangenberg, founder of the Moravian Church of America, born.
1864   Marie Tempest, actress, born.
1865   Lord Northcliffe, newspaper proprietor, born.
1948   John Pershing, soldier, died.
1958   Nuri-es-Said, soldier and statesman, assassinated.

Events

1099   Jerusalem captured by the Crusaders.
1662   The Royal Society received a royal charter.
1840   The Treaty of London signed.
1912   Social insurance came into effect in Britain.
1974   Makarios government in Cyprus temporarily overthrown.

16th JULY

People

1216   Pope Innocent III died.
1723   Sir Joshua Reynolds, painter, born.
1796   Jean Baptiste Corot, painter, born.
1821   Mrs Mary Baker Eddy, religious leader, born.
1827   Josiah Spode, potter, died.
1828   Jean Antoine Houdon, sculptor, died.
1857   Pierre de Béranger, writer, died.
1872   Roald Amundsen, explorer, born.
1896   Edmond de Goncourt, writer, died.
1896   Trygve Lie, statesman, born.
1918   Nicolas II, Tsar of Russia, murdered.
1953   Hilaire Belloc, writer, died.

Events

622   Muslim Era began.
1790   The District of Columbia established.

1945   The first atomic bomb explosion carried out in New Mexico.
1951   Leopold III, King of the Belgians, abdicated.

17th JULY

People

1674   Isaac Watts, hymn-writer, born.
1762   Peter III, Tsar of Russia, murdered.
1763   John Jacob Astor, merchant and financier, born.
1790   Adam Smith, economist, died.
1793   Charlotte Corday, assassin, executed.
1810   Martin Tupper, writer, born.
1832   A. J. Sodermann, composer, born.
1845   2nd Earl Grey, statesman, died.
1875   Sir Donald Tovey, musicologist, born.
1903   James McNeill Whistler, painter, died.

Events

1791   The Champs de Mars massacre.
1821   Florida formally ceded to the U.S.A. by Spain.
1841   *Punch* first issued.
1917   The British Royal Family adopted the name Windsor.
1936   The Spanish Civil War began.
1940   The Baghdad Railway was completed.
1945   The Potsdam Conference began.
1975   Soviet–U.S. linkup in spacecraft (17th–19th).

18th JULY

People

1100   Godfrey of Bouillon, first crusader King of Jerusalem, died.
1552   The Holy Roman Emperor Rudolf II born.
1721   Antoine Watteau, painter, died.
1792   John Paul Jones, naval officer, died.
1811   William Makepeace Thackeray, writer, born.
1817   Jane Austen, writer, died.
1848   W. G. Grace, cricketer, born.
1853   H. A. Lorentz, physicist, born.
1864   Lord Snowden, statesman, born.
1865   Laurence Housman, writer, born.
1872   Benito Juárez, statesman, died.
1892   Thomas Cook, travel agent, died.
1894   Leconte de Lisle, poet, died.
1938   Marie, Queen of Romania, died.

Events

1870   The infallibility of the Pope and the universality of his episcopate proclaimed by the Vatican Council.
1918   The Second Battle of the Marne.
1925   The first part of Hitler's *Mein Kampf* published.
1934   The Mersey Tunnel formally opened.

19th JULY   Feast of Saint Vincent de Paul.

People

1814   Matthew Flinders, explorer, died.
1814   Samuel Colt, inventor, born.
1819   Gottfried Keller, novelist, born.

1834	Edgar Degas, painter, born.
1839	Maurice de Guérin, poet, died.
1865	Charles Mayo, surgeon, born.
1896	A. J. Cronin, novelist, born.

Events

1333	The Battle of Halidon Hill.
1870	The Franco-Prussian War began.
1904	The building of Liverpool Cathedral began.
1919	Peace celebrations at the end of World War I.
1924	Liverpool Cathedral consecrated.
1930	The King's Prize at Bisley first won by a woman.
1949	Laos became independent.

20th JULY

People

1031	Robert II, King of France, died.
1304	Petrarch, poet, born.
1838	Augustin Daly, theatre manager, born.
1860	Margaret McMillan, nursery school pioneer, born.
1873	J. M. D. de Sévérac, composer, born.
1873	Alberto Santos-Dumont, aviator, born.
1903	Pope Leo XIII, died.
1937	Guglielmo Marconi, inventor, died.

Events

1845	The first white man (Charles Sturt) entered Simpson's Desert in Central Australia.
1877	The First Battle of Plevna.
1932	Franz von Papen's *coup d'état* in Prussia.
1944	Attempt on Adolf Hitler's life.
1946	The Paris Peace Conference began.
1974	Turkish invasion of Cyprus.

21st JULY

Belgian Independence Day.

People

1664	Matthew Prior, poet, born.
1796	Robert Burns, poet, died.
1809	Daniel Lambert, fat man, died.
1898	Ernest Hemingway, writer, born.
1928	Ellen Terry, actress, died.

Events

1588	The beginning of the assembly of the Spanish Armada.
1595	Alvaro Mendaña discovered the Marquesas Islands.
1773	The Pope dissolved the Society of Jesus.
1798	The Battle of the Pyramids.
1831	Leopold I proclaimed King of the Belgians.
1861	The first Battle of Bull Run.
1873	The James-Younger gang carried out a train robbery near Adair, Iowa (the first in the American West).
1897	The Tate Gallery, London, officially opened.
1944	The Americans occupied Guam.
1953	The first meeting of the Press Council in London.
1969	Neil Armstrong, astronaut, was the first man to land on the Moon.
1976	British ambassador to Ireland killed by landmine.

22nd JULY
Feast of Saint Mary Magdalen.

People
1478 Philip III, King of Spain, born.
1812 The Comte d'Antraigues and his wife murdered by their servant.
1822 Gregor Mendel, botanist, born.
1844 The Rev. William Spooner, originator of spoonerisms, born.
1852 William Poel, theatrical producer, born.
1909 Detlev von Liliencron, writer, died.
1922 Michael Collins, Irish nationalist leader, killed.
1950 Mackenzie King, statesman, died.
1967 Carl Sandburg, poet, died.
1976 Sir Mortimer Wheeler, archaeologist, died.

Events
1298 The Battle of Falkirk.
1812 The Battle of Salamanca.
1847 The Mormons entered Salt Lake City.
1932 The Imperial Economic Conference began at Ottawa.
1944 The Bretton Woods Conference ended.
1953 Construction of Calder Hall atomic power station began.

23rd JULY

People
1403 Hotspur (Sir Henry Percy) killed in battle.
1883 Lord Alanbrooke, soldier, born.
1885 Ulysses S. Grant, soldier and statesman, died.
1886 Salvador de Madariaga, writer and diplomat, born.
1892 Hailé Selassié, Emperor of Ethiopia, born.
1930 Glenn Curtiss, aviator, died.
1951 Philippe Pétain, soldier and statesman, died.
1955 Cordell Hull, statesman, died.

Events
1403 The Battle of Shrewsbury.
1858 The Jewish Disabilities Removal Act passed by Parliament.
1870 The Emperor Napoleon III appointed the Empress Eugénie Regent of France.
1974 Greek military junta resigned.

24th JULY

People
1345 Jacob van Artevelde, statesman, murdered.
1783 Simón Bolivar, soldier and statesman, born.
1802 Alexandre Dumas, père, writer, born.
1842 John Cotman, painter, died.
1864 Franz Wedekind, dramatist, born.
1880 Ernest Bloch, composer, born.
1883 Captain Matthew Webb, swimmer, died.
1898 Amelia Earheart, aviator, born.

Events
1704 Admiral Sir George Rooke took Gibraltar from the Spaniards.
1882 A Holy War in Egypt declared by Arabi Pasha.
1923 The Treaty of Lausanne signed.
1927 The Menin Gate unveiled.
1956 The first guided-missile ship commissioned.

25th JULY

The Feasts of Saint James the Great and Saint Christopher.

People

1492   Pope Innocent VIII died.
1834   Samuel Taylor Coleridge, poet, died.
1842   Jean de Sismondi, historian, died.
1843   Charles Macintosh, inventor, died.
1848   The Earl of Balfour, statesman, born.
1876   Elizabeth, Queen of the Belgians, born.
1934   Engelbert Dollfuss, statesman, murdered.

Events

1139   The Moors defeated by Alfonso I of Portugal.
1581   The Netherlands proclaimed their independence from Spain.
1799   Napoleon defeated the Turks near Aboukir.
1859   The last performance at Vauxhall Gardens, London.
1909   Louis Blériot flew the Channel.
1943   Fall of Mussolini.
1948   The Brussels Treaty concerning Western Union came into force.
1952   The European Steel and Coal Community came into being.

26th JULY

Feast of Saint Anne.

People

1471   Pope Paul II died.
1678   The Holy Roman Emperor Joseph I born.
1782   John Field, composer, born.
1856   George Bernard Shaw, writer, born.
1867   Otto I, King of Greece, died.
1874   Serge Koussevitsky, conductor, born.
1875   Carl Gustav Jung, psychoanalyst, born.
1881   George Borrow, writer, died.
1885   André Maurois, writer, born.
1894   Aldous Huxley, writer, born.

Events

1847   The independence of Liberia proclaimed.
1869   The Royal Assent given to the Irish Church Bill.
1956   The Suez Canal Company nationalized.

27th JULY

People

1689   John Graham of Claverhouse, soldier, killed.
1844   John Dalton, scientist, died.
1877   Ernst von Dohnányi, composer, born.
1942   Sir Flinders Petrie, Egyptologist, died.
1965   The Maldive Islands became independent.

Events

1689   The Battle of Killiecrankie.
1809   The Battle of Talavera began.
1830   Revolution broke out in Paris.
1866   The Atlantic telegraph cable completed.
1953   The Korean armistice signed.
1955   Austria regained its sovereignty.

28th JULY

People

1750	Johann Sebastian Bach, composer, died.
1794	Maximilien Robespierre, revolutionary leader, guillotined.
1794	Louis de St Just, revolutionary leader, guillotined.
1811	Giulia Grisi, operatic singer, born.
1939	William James Mayo, surgeon, died.

Events

388	Theodosius I, Byzantine emperor, defeated Roman emperor Maximus near Aquileia.
1656	The Battle of Warsaw began.
1790	Forth and Clyde Canal opened.
1809	The Walcheren Expedition set out.
1809	The Battle of Talavera ended.
1821	Peru declared its independence from Spain.
1914	Austria-Hungary declared war on Serbia.
1943	Italian Fascist Party dissolved.
1976	Major earthquake in China.

29th JULY

Feasts of Saint Olaf and Saint Theodor.

People

1108	Philip I, King of France, died.
1805	Alexis de Tocqueville, writer, born.
1833	William Wilberforce, philanthropist, died.
1846	John Owens, merchant and philanthropist, died.
1856	Robert Schumann, composer, died.
1867	Enrique Granados, composer, born.
1869	Booth Tarkington, writer, born.
1883	Benito Mussolini, Fascist dictator, born.
1887	Sigmund Romberg, composer, born.
1946	Gertrude Stein, writer, died.

Events

1588	The Spanish Armada defeated.
1899	The Permanent Court of Arbitration established at The Hague.
1930	(29 July–1 Aug.) The dirigible *R100* crossed the Atlantic.
1945	The BBC Light Programme began broadcasting.
1945	The Treaty of Moscow signed.
1975	Military coup in Nigeria.

30th JULY

People

1511	Giorgio Vasari, art critic and historian, born.
1718	William Penn, Quaker, writer and founder of Pennsylvania, died.
1771	Thomas Gray, poet, died.
1784	Denis Diderot, encyclopaedist, died.
1857	Thorstein Veblen, economist, born.
1863	Henry Ford, motor-car manufacturer, born.
1894	Walter Pater, writer, died.
1898	Otto von Bismarck, statesman, died.
1898	Henry Moore, sculptor, born.

Events

1656	The Battle of Warsaw ended.
1877	The Second Battle of Plevna.

30th July

1930   The airship *R101* flew the Atlantic.
1934   Kurt von Schuschnigg appointed Chancellor of Austria.
1948   The world's first port radar station opened at Liverpool.

31st JULY
Feast of Saint Ignatius Loyola.

People

1527   The Holy Roman Emperor Maximilian II born.
1556   Ignatius Loyola, founder of the Jesuits, died.
1803   John Ericsson, inventor, born.
1849   Alexander Petöfi, poet, died.
1886   Franz Liszt, composer, died.
1950   Guilhermina Suggia, 'cellist, died.

Events

1917   The Third Battle of Ypres began.
1934   The murderers of Dollfuss executed.
1954   The mountain K2 (Godwin-Austen) climbed by an Italian expedition.

1st AUGUST
Lammas Day.   Swiss Independence Day.

People

527   The Byzantine Emperor Justin I died.
1137   Louis VI, King of France, died.
1589   Henry III, King of France, murdered.
1714   Anne, Queen of Great Britain, died.
1743   Richard Savage, poet, died.
1744   The Chevalier de Lamarck, naturalist, born.
1770   William Clark, explorer, born.
1815   Richard Dana, writer, born.
1819   Herman Melville, writer, born.
1936   Louis Blériot, pioneer aviator, died.

Events

1714   George I proclaimed King of Great Britain.
1715   Doggett's Coat and Badge Race first rowed on the Thames.
1798   The Battle of the Nile.
1831   New London Bridge opened.
1834   Slavery abolished in all British possessions.
1876   Colorado achieved statehood.
1883   Inland parcel post began in Britain.
1914   The Central Powers declared war on Russia.
1960   Dahomey became independent.
1966   Military coup in Nigeria.

2nd AUGUST

People

1100   William Rufus, King of England, killed.
1788   Thomas Gainsborough, painter, died.
1802   Nicolas Wiseman, first Archbishop of Westminster, born.
1820   John Tyndall, physicist, born.

1823   Edward Freeman, historian, born.
1835   Elisha Gray, inventor, born.
1849   Mehemet Ali, Pasha of Egypt, died.
1891   Sir Arthur Bliss, composer, born.
1921   Enrico Caruso, operatic singer, died.
1934   Paul von Hindenburg, soldier and statesman, died.
1976   Fritz Lang, film director, died.

Events

1718   The Quadruple Alliance concluded in London.
1858   The government of India transferred from the East India Company to the British government.
1858   British Columbia constituted a crown colony.
1945   The Potsdam Conference ended.

3rd AUGUST

People

1422   Henry V, King of England, died.
1460   James II, King of Scotland, killed.
1721   Grinling Gibbons, artist, died.
1792   Sir Richard Arkwright, inventor, died.
1801   Sir Joseph Paxton, designer, born.
1819   Sir George Stokes, mathematician and physicist, born.
1857   Eugène Sue, novelist, died.
1867   Stanley Baldwin, statesman, born.
1872   Haakon VII, King of Norway, born.
1887   Rupert Brooke, poet, born.
1896   Sir William Robert Grove, lawyer and scientist, died.
1907   Augustus St Gaudens, sculptor, died.
1916   Sir Roger Casement executed for treason.
1924   Joseph Conrad, novelist, died.

Events

1610   Henry Hudson discovered Hudson Bay.
1759   Eugene Aram, murderer, tried at York.
1830   The July Revolution in France ended.
1858   The source of the Nile discovered by John Speke.
1882   Suez occupied by British marines.
1914   Germany declared war on France.
1940   Latvia admitted to the Soviet Union.
1949   The Council of Europe came into being.
1960   Niger became independent.

4th AUGUST

Feast of Saint Dominic.

People

1060   Henry I, King of France, died.
1265   Simon de Montfort, Earl of Leicester, killed in battle.
1578   Sebastian, King of Portugal, killed in battle.
1598   Lord Burghley, statesman, died.
1792   Percy Bysshe Shelley, poet, born.
1792   Edward Irving, founder of the Irvingites, born.
1810   Maurice de Guérin, poet, born.
1839   Walter Pater, writer, born.
1859   Knut Hamsun, writer, born.
1870   Sir Harry Lauder, comedian, born.

4th August

1900 Queen Elizabeth, the Queen Mother, born.
1976 Lord Thomson of Fleet, newspaper publisher, died.

Events

1265 The Battle of Evesham.
1511 Affonso de Albuquerque captured Malacca.
1578 The Battle of Al Kasr al Kebir.
1789 Feudal system abolished in France.
1853 Newspaper advertisements duty abolished in Britain.
1914 Germany invaded Belgium.
1914 Britain declared war on Germany.

5th AUGUST

People

882   Louis III, King of France, died.
1799 Lord Howe, naval officer, died.
1809 A. W. Kinglake, traveller and writer, born.
1811 Ambroise Thomas, composer, born.
1850 Guy de Maupassant, writer, born.
1858 Alexis Soyer, chef, died.
1895 Friedrich Engels, political philosopher, died.

Events

1864 The Battle of Mobile Bay.
1890 A French protectorate declared over Madagascar.
1939 British transatlantic airmail service inaugurated.
1955 The European Monetary Agreement signed.
1955 The French Southern and Antarctic Territories created.
1960 Upper Volta became independent.
1972 Expulsion of Asians from Uganda announced.

6th AUGUST
Feast of the Transfiguration.

People

258   Pope Sixtus II martyred.
1272 Stephen V, King of Hungary, died.
1458 Pope Callistus III died.
1504 Archbishop Parker, theologian, born.
1623 Anne Hathaway, wife of William Shakespeare, died.
1637 Ben Jonson, dramatist, died.
1651 François Fénélon, dramatist, born.
1660 Diego Velazquez, painter, died.
1759 Eugene Aram, murderer, hanged.
1775 Daniel O'Connell, Irish patriot, born.
1789 Friedrich List, economist, born.
1809 Alfred, Lord Tennyson, poet, born.
1866 John Neale, hymn-writer, died.
1881 Sir Alexander Fleming, scientist, born.
1900 Wilhelm Liebknecht, socialist leader, died.

Events

1806 Francis II renounced the crown of the Holy Roman Empire.
1825 Bolivia declared its independence from Peru.
1915 The Allied landings at Suvla in the Dardanelles began.
1945 The first atomic bomb dropped on Hiroshima.
1962 Jamaica became independent.

7th AUGUST

People

1831   Dean Frederick Farrar, theologian, born.
1834   Joseph Jacquard, inventor, died.
1868   Sir Granville Bantock, composer, born.
1941   Rabindranath Tagore, writer, died.

Events

1409   The Council of Pisa dissolved.
1479   The Battle of Guinegatte.
1485   Henry Tudor (Henry VII) landed at Milford Haven.
1790   Alexander McGillivray, chief of the Muskogian Indians, signed a treaty of peace and friendship with President Washington.
1830   Louis Philippe accepted the crown of France.
1858   Ottawa selected as capital of Canada.
1925   Summer Time Act made permanent in Britain.
1960   The Ivory Coast became independent.

8th AUGUST

People

869   Lothair, King of Lotharingia, died.
1646   Sir Godfrey Kneller, painter, born.
1827   George Canning, statesman, died.
1856   Madame Vestris, actress, died.
1901   Ernest Lawrence, physicist, born.

Events

870   The Treaty of Mersen signed.
1288   Pope Nicholas IV proclaimed a crusade against Ladislaus IV of Hungary.
1588   Queen Elizabeth reviewed her troops at Tilbury.
1902   The British Academy, London, was granted a Royal Charter.
1918   The Battle of Amiens began.
1919   The Treaty of Rawalpindi was signed.
1940   The Battle of Britain began.

9th AUGUST

People

1593   Izaak Walton, writer, born.
1631   John Dryden, poet and playwright, born.
1757   Thomas Telford, engineer, born.
1848   Frederick Marryat, writer, died.
1875   Reynaldo Hahn, composer, born.
1896   Léonide Massine, choreographer, born.
1919   Ruggiero Leoncavallo, composer, died.
1919   Ernst Haeckel, naturalist, died.

Events

378   The Battle of Adrianople.
1690   The Siege of Limerick began.
1842   The Canada-U.S.A. frontier defined.
1858   The first Atlantic cable completed.
1890   Heligoland formally transferred to Germany.
1945   An atomic bomb dropped on Nagasaki.
1946   The Arts Council of Great Britain incorporated.

9th August

1965   Singapore became independent.
1971   Detention without trial introduced in Northern Ireland.
1974   Richard Nixon resigned as U.S. President.

10th AUGUST   Saint Lawrence's Day.

People

1740   Samuel Arnold, hymn-writer, born.
1759   Ferdinand VI, King of Spain, died.
1782   Sir Charles Napier, naval reformer, born.
1810   The Count di Cavour, statesman, born.
1821   Jay Cooke, banker, born.
1845   Karl Wilhelm Naundorff, pretender to the throne of France, died.
1853   The Comte de Richemont, pretender to the throne of France, died.
1865   Alexander Glazunov, composer, born.
1874   Herbert Hoover, statesman, born.

Events

1388   The Battle of Otterburn.
1557   The Battle of St Quentin.
1675   Greenwich Observatory founded.
1792   Imprisonment of the French royal family.
1809   Ecuador finally revolted against Spanish domination.
1815   Napoleon banished to Saint Helena.
1846   The Smithsonian Institution established in Washington.
1910   Airmail service first organized in Britain.
1920   The Treaty of Sèvres.
1952   The High Authority (Luxembourg) of the European Steel and Coal Community inaugurated.
1954   The Saint Lawrence Seaway Project officially launched.

11th AUGUST

People

1433   John I, King of Portugal, died.
1456   János Hunyadi, Hungarian patriot, died.
1656   Prince Octavio Piccolomini, military commander, died.
1737   Joseph Nollekens, sculptor, born.
1823   Charlotte M. Yonge, novelist, born.
1857   Marshall Hall, physiologist, died.
1890   Cardinal Newman died.
1919   Andrew Carnegie, industrialist and philanthropist, died.

Events

1711   The first Ascot race meeting held.
1909   Wireless distress call 'SOS' first used.
1936   Joachim von Ribbentrop appointed German ambassador to London.
1939   The Axis Conference at Salzburg began.
1942   The new Waterloo Bridge, London, opened to traffic.
1943   The Quebec Conference opened.
1952   King Talal deposed by the Parliament of Jordan and succeeded by King Hussein.
1960   Chad became independent.

12th AUGUST   Grouse shooting begins.

People

1350   Philip VI, King of France, died.
1484   Pope Sixtus IV, died.

1676   King Philip, American Indian Chief, killed.
1689   Pope Innocent XI died.
1715   Nahum Tate, playwright, died.
1753   Thomas Bewick, engraver, born.
1762   George IV, King of Great Britain and Ireland, born.
1774   Robert Southey, poet, born.
1774   Stephen Rigaud, mathematician and astronomer, born.
1822   Lord Castlereagh, statesman, committed suicide.
1827   William Blake, painter and poet, died.
1832   Dr Hely Hutchinson Almond, educationalist, born.
1848   George Stephenson, engineer, died.
1866   Jacinto Benavente, playwright, born.
1884   Frank Swinnerton, writer, born.
1891   James Lowell, writer, died.
1955   Thomas Mann, writer, died.

Events
1676   The Indian War in New England ended.
1678   Titus Oates' Popish Plot made known to King Charles II.
1898   The U.S.A. formally annexed Hawaii.
1944   The 'Pluto' pipeline came into action.

13th AUGUST
Old Lammas Day.

People
1667   Jeremy Taylor, theologian, died.
1765   Francis I, Holy Roman Emperor, died.
1863   Eugène Delacroix, painter, died.
1879   John Ireland, composer, born.
1888   John Logie Baird, television pioneer, born.
1896   Sir John Millais, painter, died.
1910   Florence Nightingale, nursing pioneer, died.
1912   Jules Massenet, composer, died.
1937   Lord Runciman, shipowner, died.
1946   H. G. Wells, writer, died.

Events
1704   The Battle of Blenheim.
1960   The Central African Republic became independent.

14th AUGUST

People
1040   Duncan I, King of Scotland, murdered (traditional date).
1464   Pope Pius II died.
1740   Pope Pius VII born.
1778   Augustus Toplady, hymn-writer, died.
1840   Richard Krafft-Ebing, physician, born.
1861   Bion Joseph Arnold, electrical engineer and inventor, born.
1867   John Galsworthy, writer, born.
1870   David Farragut, naval officer, died.
1887   Richard Jefferies, writer, died.
1951   William Randolph Hearst, newspaper proprietor, died.
1956   Bertold Brecht, playwright, died.

Events
1385   The Battle of Aljubarrota.
1920   The Little Entente formed.

14th August

1941   The Atlantic Charter made public.
1945   Japan surrendered, ending World War II.
1969   British troops moved into Londonderry to separate rioting Catholics and Protestants.

15th AUGUST
Feast of the Assumption of the Blessed Virgin Mary.

People

778   Roland, French hero, died in battle (according to tradition).
1057   Macbeth, King of Scotland, slain in battle.
1769   Napoleon born.
1771   Sir Walter Scott, writer, born.
1785   Thomas De Quincey, writer, born.
1845   Walter Crane, painter, born.
1856   Keir Hardie, socialist leader, born.
1875   Samuel Coleridge-Taylor, composer, born.
1879   Ethel Barrymore, actress, born.
1883   Ivan Meštrovič, sculptor, born.
1888   T. E. Lawrence, explorer, soldier and writer, born.
1890   Jacques Ibert, composer, born.
1907   Joseph Joachim, violinist, died.
1935   Wiley Post, aviator, died.
1935   Will Rogers, humorist, died.
1950   Princess Anne born.

Events

1237   Berlin founded.
1799   The Battle of Novi.
1914   The Panama Canal officially opened.
1915   The Allied landings at Suvla in the Dardanelles completed.
1947   India became independent.
1947   Pakistan separated from India and became independent.
1948   The Republic of Korea (South Korea) proclaimed.
1960   The (French) Congo became independent.
1971   Bahrain became independent.

16th AUGUST

People

1678   Andrew Marvell, poet, died.
1854   Duncan Phyfe, cabinet-maker, died.

Events

1513   The Battle of the Spurs.
1777   The Battle of Bennington, Vermont.
1780   The Battle of Camden, South Carolina.
1812   The Battle of Smolensk began.
1819   The Peterloo Massacre.
1825   The Republic of Bolivia proclaimed.
1870   The Battle of Vionville.
1960   Cyprus became independent.

17th AUGUST

People

1657   Robert Blake, naval officer, died.
1786   Frederick the Great, King of Prussia, died.
1786   David Crockett, American pioneer, born.

1834 Pierre Benoît, composer, born.
1840 Wilfrid Scawen Blunt, poet, born.
1850 Homoré de Balzac, novelist, died.
1955 Fernand Léger, painter, died.
1945 Indonesia proclaimed an independent republic.

Events

1812 The Battle of Smolensk ended.

18th AUGUST

People

1559 Pope Paul IV died.
1587 Virginia Dare first white child of English parentage to be born in America.
1765 Francis I, Holy Roman Emperor, died.
1774 Meriwether Lewis, explorer, born.
1792 Earl Russell, statesman, born.
1803 James Beattie, poet, born.
1809 Matthew Boulton, engineer, died.
1834 Marshall Field, merchant, born.
1874 Sir William Fairbairn, engineer and inventor, died.
1922 William Hudson, naturalist and writer, died.

Events

1870 The Battle of Gravelotte.
1917 The Verdun offensive began.

19th AUGUST

People

1560 James ('The Admirable') Crichton, scholar, born.
1646 John Flamstead, first astronomer royal, born.
1662 Blaise Pascal, theologian and mathematician, died.
1819 James Watt, engineer, died.
1823 Robert Bloomfield, poet, died.
1843 Charles M. Doughty, traveller and poet, born.
1871 Orville Wright, pioneer aviator, born.
1881 Georges Enesco, composer and violinist, born.
1928 Viscount Haldane, statesman and reformer, died.
1929 Serge Diaghilev, ballet master, died.
1934 Sir Nigel Playfair, actor-manager, died.
1944 Sir Henry Wood, conductor and composer, died.
1959 Sir Jacob Epstein, sculptor, died.

Events

1561 Mary Queen of Scots returned from France.
1792 The French Revolutionary Tribunal set up.
1861 The passport system introduced in the U.S.A.

20th AUGUST

Feast of Saint Bernard of Clairvaux.

People

1153 Saint Bernard of Clairvaux died.
1592 The Duke of Buckingham, courtier and royal favourite, born.
1648 Lord Herbert of Cherbury, poet, died.

20th August

1672 Jan de Witt, statesman, died.
1701 Sir Charles Sedley, playwright, died.
1778 Bernardo O'Higgins, Chilean patriot, born.
1779 Baron Berzelius, chemist, born.
1818 Emily Brontë, writer, born.
1823 Pope Pius VII died.
1833 Benjamin Harrison, statesman, born.
1854 Friedrich von Schelling, philosopher, died.
1860 Raymond Poincaré, statesman, born.
1902 Christian Bérard, painter, born.
1912 William Booth, Salvation Army leader, died.
1915 Paul Ehrlich, scientist, died.

Events

1914 The Germans entered Brussels.
1932 The Imperial Economic Conference at Ottawa ended.
1960 Senegal became independent.
1968 Soviet troops invaded Czechoslovakia.

21st AUGUST

People

1165 Philip Augustus, King of France, born.
1567 Saint Francis de Sales born.
1754 William Murdock, engineer and inventor, born.
1762 Lady Mary Wortley Montagu, traveller, died.
1765 William IV, King of Great Britain and Ireland, born.
1798 Jules Michelet, historian, born.
1930 Princess Margaret born.
1940 Leon Trotsky assassinated in Mexico.
1951 Constant Lambert, composer, died.

Events

1808 The Battle of Vimiero.
1810 Marshal Bernadotte chosen Crown Prince of Sweden.
1863 The Quantrill Raid on Lawrence, Kansas.
1918 The Battle of Bapaume-Peronne began.
1944 The Dumbarton Oaks Conference began.
1954 Hawaii became the 50th state of the U.S.A.

22nd AUGUST

People

1241 Pope Gregory IX died.
1485 Richard III, King of England, killed in battle.
1741 Jean la Pérouse, sailor and explorer, born.
1760 Pope Leo XII born.
1806 Jean Fragonard, painter, died.
1818 Warren Hastings, administrator, died.
1862 Claude Debussy, composer, born.
1889 John Sanger, circus manager, died.
1940 Sir Oliver Lodge, scientist and writer, died.

Events

1138 The Battle of the Standard.
1485 The Battle of Bosworth Field.
1642 Civil War in England began.

1798 French forces landed in Ireland.
1864 The International Red Cross founded.
1910 Korea formally annexed by Japan.
1932 The first regular BBC television service began.

23rd AUGUST

People

  408 Flavius Stilicho, soldier, assassinated.
1305 William Wallace, Scottish patriot, executed.
1540 Guillaume Budé, classical scholar, died.
1628 The Duke of Buckingham, courtier and royal favourite, assassinated.
1754 Louis XVI, King of France, born.
1802 John Randall, shipbuilder, died.
1849 William Ernest Henley, poet, born.
1864 Eleutherios Venizelos, statesman, born.
1905 Constant Lambert, composer, born.
1927 Sacco and Vanzetti executed at Charleston, Massachusetts.
1937 Albert Roussel, composer, died.
1942 Michel Fokine, choreographer, died.

Events

1328 The Battle of Cassel.
1914 Japan declared war on Germany.
1914 Namur captured by the Germans.
1914 The Battle of Mons.
1939 The Soviet–German Non-Aggression Pact signed.
1948 The World Council of Churches formed.
1967 Race riots in Detroit.

24th AUGUST
Feast of Saint Bartholomew.

People

1540 Francesco Parmigianino, artist, died.
1572 Gaspard de Coligny, Huguenot leader, killed.
1680 Colonel Thomas Blood, adventurer, died.
1759 William Wilberforce, statesman, born.
1770 Thomas Chatterton, poet, committed suicide.
1831 August von Gneisenau, soldier, died.
1841 Theodore Hook, writer, died.
1846 Adam Krusenstern, circumnavigator of the world, died.
1872 Sir Max Beerbohm, writer, born.
1906 Alfred Stevens, painter, died.
1958 J. G. Strijdom, statesman, died.

Events

1572 The Massacre of Saint Bartholomew.
1814 British troops captured Washington, D.C.
1943 The Quebec Conference ended.

25th AUGUST
Feast of Saint Louis.

People

  79 Pliny the Elder, naturalist, died.
1270 Saint Louis, King of France, died.

25th August

1482   Margaret of Anjou, Queen of England, died.
1530   Ivan IV, 'the Terrible', Tsar of Russia, born.
1649   Richard Crashaw, poet, died.
1744   J. G. von Herder, writer, born.
1767   Louis de St Just, revolutionary leader, born.
1770   Thomas Chatterton, poet, died.
1776   David Hume, philosopher, died.
1786   Ludwig I, King of Bavaria, born.
1822   Sir William Herschel, astronomer, died.
1839   Bret Harte, writer, born.
1845   Ludwig II, King of Bavaria, born.
1867   Michael Faraday, scientist, died.
1908   Henri Becquerel, physicist, died.

Events

1768   James Cook set sail on first voyage of discovery.
1825   The independence of Uruguay proclaimed.
1830   Revolution against the Netherlands broke out in Brussels.
1914   The Germans sacked Louvain.
1919   Daily service by air between London and Paris began.
1921   The Treaty of Berlin signed.
1944   The Allies liberated Paris.

26th AUGUST

People

1278   Ottocar II, King of Bohemia, killed in battle.
1676   Sir Robert Walpole, statesman, born.
1743   Antoine Lavoisier, chemist, born.
1819   Albert, Prince Consort, born.
1833   Henry Fawcett, economist, born.
1833   Stephen Perry, astronomer, born.
1850   Louis Philippe, King of the French, died.
1875   John Buchan, statesman and writer, born.
1900   Friedrich Nietzsche, philosopher, died.
1910   William James, psychologist, died.
1974   Charles Lindbergh, aviation pioneer, died.

Events

55B.C.   Julius Caesar's first invasion of Britain.
1346   The Battle of Crecy.
1914   Louvain destroyed by the Germans.
1914   The Battle of Tannenberg began.
1920   Women's suffrage came into force in the U.S.A.
1936   The Anglo-Egyptian Alliance signed.

27th AUGUST

People

551B.C.   Confucius, philosopher, born.
1576   Titian, painter, died.
1590   Pope Sixtus V died.
1635   Lope de Vega, poet, died.
1770   George Friedrich Hegel, philosopher, born.
1879   Sir Rowland Hill, pioneer in postal services, died.
1886   Eric Coates, composer, born.

1908 Sir Donald Bradman, cricketer, born.
1919 Louis Botha, soldier and statesman, died.
1965 'Le Corbusier', architect, died.
1975 Hailé Selassié, deposed Emperor of Ethiopia, died.

Events

1776 The Battle of Long Island.
1789 French National Assembly issued the Declaration of the Rights of Man.
1859 The first oil well drilled in West Pennsylvania.
1928 The Kellogg Pact signed.
1950 BBC transmitted its first television programme from the Continent.

28th AUGUST
The Feast of Saint Augustine, Bishop of Hippo.

People

1749 Wolfgang von Goethe, writer and scientist, born.
1828 Count Leo Tolstoy, writer, born.
1833 Sir Edward Burne-Jones, painter, born.
1840 Ira Sankey, revivalist, born.
1859 Leigh Hunt, writer, died.
1863 Eilhardt Mitscherlich, chemist, died.
1943 Boris III, Tsar of Bulgaria, died.
1958 Ernest Lawrence, physicist, died.

Events

1839 (28th–29th) The Eglinton Tournament.
1914 The Battle of Heligoland Bight.

29th AUGUST

People

1619 Jean Baptiste Colbert, statesman, born.
1632 John Locke, philosopher, born.
1645 Hugo Grotius, statesman, died.
1780 Jean Ingres, painter, born.
1799 Pope Pius VI died.
1809 Oliver Wendell Holmes, writer, born.
1817 John Leech, artist, born.
1853 Sir Charles Napier, statesman, died.
1862 Maurice Maeterlinck, writer, born.
1877 Brigham Young, Mormon leader, died.
1890 Richard Casey, statesman, born.
1930 The Rev. William Spooner, originator of Spoonerisms, died.
1975 Eamon de Valera, statesman, died.

Events

1782 The loss of the *Royal George* off Spithead.
1835 Melbourne, Australia, founded.
1842 The Treaty of Nanking, ending the Opium War, signed.
1882 'The Ashes' instituted in cricket.
1929 The airship *Graf Zeppelin* completed the circumnavigation of the world.

30th AUGUST

People

1334 Pedro the Cruel, King of Castile and Leon, born.
1483 Louis XI, King of France, died.

1797   Mary Shelley, writer, born.
1871   Lord Rutherford, scientist, born.
1928   Wilhelm Wien, physicist, died.
1940   Professor Sir J. J. Thomson, scientist, died.

Events

1721   The conclusion of the Peace of Nystad.
1860   First British tramway inaugurated at Birkenhead.

31st AUGUST

People

1688   John Bunyan, religious writer, died.
1811   Théophile Gautier, writer, born.
1821   Hermann von Helmholtz, physicist, born.
1864   Ferdinand Lassalle, socialist, killed in a duel.
1867   Charles Baudelaire, poet, died.
1880   Wilhelmina, Queen of the Netherlands, born.
1887   Friedrich Paneth, scientist, born.
1931   Sir Hall Caine, writer, died.

Events

1709   Battle of Malplaquet began.
1914   The Battle of Tannenberg ended.
1957   Malaya achieved independence.
1962   Trinidad achieved independence.

1st SEPTEMBER

People

1159   Pope Adrian IV (the Englishman Nicholas Breakspear) died.
1566   Edward Alleyn, philanthropist, born.
1715   Louis XIV, King of France, died.
1729   Richard Steele, writer, died.
1804   Zerah Colburn, calculating prodigy, born.
1854   Engelbert Humperdinck, composer, born.
1874   Edwin Evans, musicologist, born.
1877   Francis Aston, physicist, born.
1912   Samuel Coleridge-Taylor, composer, died.
1943   W. W. Jacobs, humorous writer, died.
1967   Siegfried Sassoon, writer, died.

Events

1853   The first triangular Cape of Good Hope stamps issued.
1860   Foundation stone of the Parliament Buildings, Ottawa, laid.
1870   Siege of Metz began.
1870   The Battle of Sedan ended.
1894   The use of postcards with adhesive stamps first permitted in Britain.
1939   The German Army invaded Poland.
1939   The BBC Home Service began.
1971   Qatar became independent.

2nd SEPTEMBER

People

1685   Lady Alice Lisle, supporter of religious dissent, beheaded.
1726   John Howard, prison reformer, born.
1851   William Nicol, physicist, died.

1853   Wilhelm Ostwald, scientist, born.
1877   Frederick Soddy, scientist, born.
1937   Baron Pierre de Coubertin, reviver of the Olympic Games, died.

Events

31 B.C.   The Battle of Actium.
1666   The Great Fire of London began.
1898   Omdurman captured by Lord Kitchener.
1945   The formal surrender of the Japanese armed forces to the Allies signed on the U.S. battleship *Missouri*.
1958   China opened its first television station at Peking.

3rd SEPTEMBER

People

1592   Robert Greene, dramatist, died.
1658   Oliver Cromwell, soldier and statesman, died.
1728   Matthias Boulton, engineer, born.
1739   George Lillo, dramatist, died.
1847   James Hannington, first Bishop of Eastern Equatorial Africa, born.
1877   Louis Adolphe Thiers, statesman, died.
1948   Eduard Beneš, statesman, died.

Events

590   Gregory the Great consecrated Pope.
1650   The Battle of Dunbar.
1651   The Battle of Worcester.
1783   The Treaty of Paris signed.
1916   The first Zeppelin destroyed in England.
1925   U.S. dirigible *Shenandoah* broke apart at Caldwell, Ohio.
1939   Britain and France declared war on Germany.
1939   Excess Profits Tax came into force in Britain.

4th SEPTEMBER

People

1768   François de Chateaubriand, writer, born.
1824   Anton Bruckner, composer, born.
1892   Darius Milhaud, composer, born.
1907   Edvard Grieg, composer, died.
1965   Albert Schweitzer, medical missionary, died.

Events

1260   The Battle of Monte Aperto.
1870   The Third Republic proclaimed in France.
1909   The first Boy Scout Rally held at Crystal Palace.

5th SEPTEMBER

People

1187   Louis VIII, King of France, born.
1548   Catherine Parr, Queen-Dowager of England, died.
1638   Louis XIV, King of France, born.
1781   Anton Diabelli, music publisher and composer, born.

5th September

1791   Giacomo Meyerbeer, composer, born.
1808   John Home, playwright, died.
1831   Victorien Sardou, playwright, born.

Events
1774   The first Continental Congress assembled at Philadelphia.
1905   The Treaty of Portsmouth, New Hampshire, signed.
1972   Black September massacre at Munich.

6th SEPTEMBER

People
1757   The Marquis de Lafayette, statesman, born.
1766   John Dalton, scientist, born.
1858   Ando Hiroshige, artist, died.
1869   Sir Walford Davies, composer, born.
1871   Montague Norman, banker, born.
1923   King Peter of Yugoslavia born.
1939   Arthur Rackham, artist, died.

Events
1620   The *Mayflower* set sail from Plymouth.
1651   The future King Charles II hid in an oak tree after the Battle of Worcester.
1666   The Great Fire of London ended.
1901   President McKinley shot by an anarchist.
1914   The Battle of the Marne began.
1954   The Manila Conference began.
1968   Swaziland became independent.

7th SEPTEMBER

People
1312   Ferdinand IV, King of Castile and Leon, died.
1496   Ferdinand II, King of Naples, died.
1533   Elizabeth I, Queen of England, born.
1707   The Comte de Buffon, naturalist, born.
1735   Thomas Coutts, banker, born.
1833   Hannah More, religious writer, died.
1836   Sir Henry Campbell-Bannerman, statesman, born.
1859   Isambard Kingdom Brunel, engineer, died.
1910   Holman Hunt, painter, died.
1930   Baudouin, King of the Belgians, born.

Events
1822   Brazil proclaimed its independence from Portugal.

8th SEPTEMBER

People
1157   Richard I, King of England, born.
1474   Ludovico Ariosto, poet, born.
1560   Amy Robsart, wife of the Earl of Leicester, died.
1644   Francis Quarles, poet, died.
1767   August von Schlegel, poet, born.
1804   Eduard Mörike, poet, born.

1830 Frédéric Mistral, poet, born.
1841 Antonin Dvořák, composer, born.
1886 Siegfried Sassoon, writer, born.
1894 Hermann von Helmholtz, physicist, died.
1933 Faisal I, King of Iraq, died.
1949 Richard Strauss, composer, died.

Events

1565 The raising of the Great Siege of Malta.
1664 The Dutch surrendered New Amsterdam (now New York) to the English.
1760 Montreal capitulated to British forces.
1944 The first V2 landed in England.
1951 San Francisco Treaty of Peace with Japan signed.
1954 The Manila Conference ended.

9th SEPTEMBER

People

1087 William the Conqueror, King of England, died.
1513 James IV, King of Scotland, killed in battle.
1583 Sir Humphrey Gilbert, explorer, drowned at sea.
1585 Cardinal Richelieu, statesman, born.
1737 Luigi Galvani, scientist, born.
1855 Houston Chamberlain, writer, born.
1954 André Derain, painter, died.
1976 Mao Tse-tung, revolutionary and statesman, died.

Events

1513 The Battle of Flodden Field.
1850 California achieved statehood.
1914 The Battle of the Marne ended.
1943 The Allies landed at Salerno.
1948 North Korea established as an independent country.

10th SEPTEMBER

People

954 Louis IV, King of France, died.
1487 Pope Julius III born.
1624 Thomas Sydenham, physician, born.
1753 John Soane, architect, born.
1771 Mungo Park, explorer, born.
1797 Mary Wollstonecraft, champion of women's rights, died.
1890 Franz Werfel, writer, born.

Events

1547 The Battle of Pinkie.
1813 The Battle of Lake Erie.
1919 The Treaty of Saint Germain signed.
1974 Guinea-Bissau became independent.

11th SEPTEMBER

People

1524 Pierre de Ronsard, poet, born.
1611 Henri de Turenne, soldier, born.
1618 Thomas Ross, libeller, beheaded.

11th September

1700 James Thomson, poet, born.
1823 David Ricardo, economist, died.
1860 Ben Tillett, Labour leader, born.
1862 O. Henry, writer, born.
1877 Sir James Jeans, scientist, born.
1885 D. H. Lawrence, writer, born.
1950 J. C. Smuts, soldier and statesman, died.

Events

1709 The Battle of Malplaquet ended.
1855 Allies entered Sebastopol after the Russian capitulation.
1877 The Third Battle of Plevna.
1909 Halley's Comet first observed at Heidelberg.
1922 The British mandate proclaimed in Palestine.
1973 Military coup in Chile ousted left-wing government.

12th SEPTEMBER

People

1362 Pope Innocent VI died.
1494 Francis I, King of France, born.
1733 François Couperin, composer, died.
1764 Jean-Philippe Rameau, composer, died.
1818 Richard Gatling, inventor, born.
1819 Gebhard von Blücher, soldier, died.
1852 The Earl of Oxford and Asquith, statesman, born.
1874 François Guizot, historian and statesman, died.
1948 Rupert D'Oyly Carte, impresario, died.

Events

1609 The Hudson River discovered by Henry Hudson.
1649 Sack of Drogheda.
1683 Vienna besieged by the Turks.
1814 The defence of Baltimore against the British.
1914 Battle of the Marne ended.
1932 The dissolution of the Reichstag in Germany.
1940 Five boys discovered the painted caves at Lascaux.
1943 Mussolini rescued from prison by the Germans.
1970 Arab commandos blew up hijacked airliners in Jordan.

13th SEPTEMBER

People

1520 Lord Burghley, statesman, born.
1557 Sir John Cheke, classical scholar, died.
1592 Michel de Montaigne, essayist, died.
1598 Philip II, King of Spain, died.
1759 James Wolfe, soldier, died.
1759 The Marquis de Montcalm, soldier, mortally wounded (died 14th).
1806 Charles James Fox, statesman, died.
1810 Clara Schumann, pianist, born.
1851 Walter Reed, bacteriologist, born.
1860 John Pershing, soldier, born.
1874 Arnold Schönberg, composer, born.
1894 Emmanuel Chabrier, composer, died.
1944 W. Heath Robinson, artist, died.

Events

1515 The Battle of Marignano began.
1759 The Battle of Quebec began.

1791   Louis XVI took his oath as constitutional monarch of France.
1814   Francis Scott Key wrote the words of 'The Star-Spangled Banner'.
1918   The Battle of Saint Mihiel.
1943   General Chiang Kai-shek elected President of the Chinese Republic.

14th SEPTEMBER

People

258   Saint Cyprian martyred.
407   Saint John Chrysostom died.
1321   Dante Alighieri, poet, died.
1646   The Earl of Essex, Parliamentary soldier, died.
1735   Robert Raikes, Sunday School pioneer, born.
1759   The Marquis de Montcalm died.
1760   Luigi Cherubini, composer, born.
1769   Alexander von Humboldt, naturalist and explorer, born.
1817   Theodor Storm, poet and novelist, born.
1852   The Duke of Wellington, soldier and statesman, died.
1852   Augustus Pugin, architect, died.
1901   William McKinley, statesman, died of wounds.
1916   José Echegaray, writer and scientist, died.
1937   Thomas Masaryk, statesman, died.

Events

1515   The Battle of Marignano ended.
1752   The Gregorian calendar adopted in Britain.
1812   Napoleon entered Moscow.
1829   The Treaty of Adrianople signed.
1854   British and French forces landed in the Crimea.
1860   Niagara Falls illuminated for the first time.
1917   Russia proclaimed a republic.

15th SEPTEMBER
Battle of Britain Day.

People

1583   Albrecht von Wallenstein, soldier and statesman, born.
1613   François de La Rochefoucauld, writer, born.
1666   Sophia Dorothea, Electress of Hanover, born.
1712   The Earl of Godolphin, statesman, died.
1789   James Fenimore Cooper, novelist, born.
1830   William Huskisson, statesman, killed.
1834   Heinrich von Treitschke, historian, born.
1857   William Howard Taft, statesman, born.
1851   James Fenimore Cooper, writer, died.
1859   Isambard Kingdom Brunel, engineer, died.
1876   Bruno Walter, conductor, born.

Events

1821   The Central American republics proclaimed their independence from Spain.
1830   The Manchester–Liverpool Railway opened.
1916   Tanks first used in World War I.
1938   Hitler and Chamberlain met at Berchtesgaden.
1940   Heavy German air-raid on London.
1946   The Bulgarian People's Republic proclaimed.
1949   Konrad Adenauer elected Chancellor of West Germany.
1952   Britain handed over the sovereignty of Eritrea to Ethiopia.

16th SEPTEMBER

People

655 Pope Martin I died.
1498 Tomás de Torquemada, Inquisitor-General, died.
1519 John Colet, theologian, died.
1736 Daniel Fahrenheit, physicist, died.
1745 Mikhail Kutuzov, soldier and diplomat, born.
1797 Sir Anthony Panizzi, librarian, born.
1823 Francis Parkman, historian, born.
1824 Louis XVIII, King of France, died.
1858 Andrew Bonar Law, statesman, born.
1858 Sir Edward Marshall-Hall, lawyer, born.
1893 Sir Alexander Korda, film producer, born.
1911 Edward Whymper, mountaineer, died.
1932 Sir Ronald Ross, physician, died.
1945 Count John McCormack, singer, died.
1946 Sir James Jeans, scientist, died.

Events

1639 Maarten Tromp defeated the Spanish fleet.
1810 The Mexican revolt against Spain began.
1812 Moscow almost entirely destroyed by fire.
1859 Lake Nyasa discovered by David Livingstone.
1861 Post Office Savings Banks introduced in Britain.
1862 The Battle of Antietam began.
1941 Reza Khan Pahlavi, Shah of Iran, abdicated.
1963 Malaysia became an independent state.

17th SEPTEMBER
Constitution Day in the United States.

People

1552 Pope Paul V born.
1665 Philip IV, King of Spain, died.
1701 James II, former King of England, died.
1730 Baron von Steuben, army reformer, born.
1743 Marquis de Condorcet, philosopher, born.
1771 Tobias Smollett, novelist, died.
1863 Alfred de Vigny, poet, died.
1864 Walter Savage Landor, writer, died.
1958 Friedrich Paneth, scientist, died.

Events

1745 Edinburgh occupied by Jacobite forces.
1759 The Battle of Quebec ended.
1787 The U.S. Constitution signed.
1862 The Battle of Antietam ended.
1871 The Mont Cenis Tunnel opened.
1949 The first meeting of the North Atlantic Treaty Council held.

18th SEPTEMBER

People

1180 Louis VII, King of France, died.
1709 Dr Samuel Johnson, writer and lexicographer, born.
1721 Matthew Prior, poet, died.

1765   Pope Gregory XVI born.
1775   Andrew Foulis, printer, died.
1783   Leonhard Euler, mathematician, died.
1792   Bishop August Spangenberg, founder of the Moravian Church in America, died.
1797   Lazare Hoche, soldier, died.
1819   Jean Foucault, scientist, born.
1830   William Hazlitt, writer and critic, died.
1860   Joseph Locke, civil engineer, died.
1905   Greta Garbo, actress, born.
1964   Sean O'Casey, playwright, died.

Events

1810   The independence of Chile from Spain proclaimed.
1838   Anti-Corn Law League established by Richard Cobden.
1851   The *New York Times* began publication.
1918   The Battle of Megiddo began.

19th SEPTEMBER

People

1551   Henry III, King of France, born.
1802   Lajos Kossuth, statesman, born.
1839   George Cadbury, manufacturer, born.
1867   Arthur Rackham, artist, born.
1881   James Abram Garfield, statesman, died.

Events

1356   The Battle of Poitiers.
1734   The Battle of Luzzara.
1870   The Siege of Paris (by the Germans) began.
1950   The European Payments Union established.

20th SEPTEMBER

People

1803   Sir Titus Salt, manufacturer and philanthropist, born.
1803   Robert Emmet, Irish patriot, executed.
1863   Jakob Grimm, writer and philologist, died.
1876   Sir Titus Salt, manufacturer and philanthropist, died.
1878   Upton Sinclair, novelist, born.
1898   Theodor Fontane, poet and novelist, died.
1908   Pablo de Sarasate, violinist, died.
1933   Annie Besant, theosophist, died.
1957   Jean Sibelius, composer, died.

Events

1258   Salisbury Cathedral consecrated.
1562   The Treaty of Hampton Court signed.
1697   The Treaty of Ryswick signed.
1792   The Battle of Valmy.
1854   The Battle of Alma.
1857   Delhi recaptured by the British.
1861   The Battle of Lexington.
1906   The *Mauretania* launched.
1909   The South Africa Act received the Royal Assent.
1931   Sterling taken off the Gold Standard.
1932   The Methodist Church of Great Britain and Ireland came into being.
1959   Last fly-past of Hurricanes over London commemorating the Battle of Britain.

21st SEPTEMBER
The Feast of Saint Matthew.

People
1327   Edward II, King of England, murdered.
1452   Girolamo Savonarola, Church reformer, born.
1549   Marguerite d'Angoulême, Queen of Navarre, died.
1645   Louis Joliet, explorer, born.
1722   John Home, playwright, born.
1756   John McAdam, engineer, born.
1832   Sir Walter Scott, novelist, died.
1860   Arthur Schopenhauer, philosopher, died.
1866   H. G. Wells, writer, born.
1874   Gustav Holst, composer, born.
1883   Karol Szymanowski, composer, born.
1953   Roger Quilter, composer, died.
1957   Haakon VII, King of Norway, died.

Events
1745   The Battle of Prestonpans.
1792   Beginning (midnight) of the era of the French Republic and the French Revolutionary Calendar.
1809   Duel between Lord Castlereagh and George Canning.
1917   Latvia proclaimed its independence.
1933   The Reichstag Fire Trial opened at Leipzig.
1949   The Federal Republic of Germany formally came into existence.
1964   Malta became independent.

22nd SEPTEMBER

People
1241   Snorri Sturlason, historian, killed.
1694   Lord Chesterfield, literary patron and writer, born.
1776   Nathan Hale, American patriot, hanged.
1788   Theodore Hook, humorous writer, born.
1791   Michael Faraday, scientist, born.
1880   Dame Christabel Pankhurst, suffragette, born.
1914   Alain-Fournier, writer, killed in action.

Events
1586   The Battle of Zutphen.
1862   Abraham Lincoln's emancipation proclamation.
1955   Commercial television began in Britain.
1955   Juan Perón, statesman, deposed.
1960   Mali became independent.

23rd SEPTEMBER
Autumnal Equinox.

People
63B.C.   Augustus Caesar, Roman emperor, born.
1625   Jan de Witt, statesman, born.
1713   Ferdinand VI, King of Spain, born.
1764   Robert Dodsley, bookseller, died.
1854   Dr Cornelis Lely, statesman and engineer, born.
1880   Lord Boyd Orr, biologist, born.
1889   Wilkie Collins, novelist, died.

1923 Lord Morley, statesman, died.
1939 Sigmund Freud, psychoanalyst, died.

Events

1779 The naval battle between the *Bonhomme Richard* and the *Serapis* off Flamborough Head.
1803 The Battle of Assaye.
1846 The planet Neptune discovered by Johann Galle.
1862 Bismarck appointed Prime Minister of Prussia.
1940 The George Cross and the George Medal instituted.
1955 Pakistan joined the Baghdad Pact.

24th SEPTEMBER

People

768   Pepin III, King of the Franks, died.
1143 Pope Innocent II died.
1717 Horace Walpole, writer, born.
1795 Antoine Barye, sculptor, born.
1813 André Grétry, composer, died.
1860 Samuel Crockett, novelist, born.
1890 Sir Alan Herbert, writer, born.
1892 Patrick Gilmore, bandmaster and composer, died.

Events

1841 (Sir) James Brooke appointed raja of Sarawak.
1916 The second Zeppelin destroyed in England.
1916 Krupps Works at Essen bombed by the French.

25th SEPTEMBER

People

1066 Harald Haardraade, King of Norway, killed in battle.
1506 Philip the Handsome, King of Spain, died.
1680 Samuel Butler, satirist, died.
1683 Jean-Philippe Rameau, composer, born.
1849 Johann Strauss, the elder, composer, died.

Events

1066 The Battle of Stamford Bridge.
1513 Vasco Balboa discovered the Pacific Ocean.
1857 The relief of Lucknow began.
1882 The reconstituted Polytechnic, Regent St., London, opened.
1915 The Battle of Loos began.
1956 Transatlantic telephone cables operational between Britain and North America.

26th SEPTEMBER
Dominion Day in New Zealand.

People

1626 Bishop Lancelot Andrews, theologian, died.
1750 Lord Collingwood, naval officer, born.
1790 Nassau William Senior, economist, born.
1897 Pope Paul VI born.

1898   George Gershwin, composer, born.
1917   Edgar Degas, painter, died.
1942   The Rev. Wilson Carlile, founder of the Church Army, died.
1945   Bela Bartok, composer, died.

Events

1815   Holy Alliance made between the Emperors of Russia and Austria and the King of Prussia.
1907   New Zealand declared a Dominion.
1918   The Battle of the Meuse-Argonne began.
1934   The *Queen Mary* launched.

27th SEPTEMBER

People

1404   William of Wykeham, Bishop of Winchester, died.
1627   Jacques Bossuet, orator and historian, born.
1660   Saint Vincent de Paul, founder of charities, died.
1696   Saint Alfonso Maria dei Liguori, theologian, born.
1700   Pope Innocent XII died.
1722   Samuel Adams, patriot, born.
1792   George Cruikshank, artist, born.
1817   Paul Féval, novelist, born.
1840   Alfred Mahan, naval historian, born.
1862   Louis Botha, soldier and statesman, born.
1879   Cyril Scott, composer, born.
1919   Adelina Patti, singer, died.
1921   Engelbert Humperdinck, composer, died.
1928   Sir Henry Wickham, pioneer rubber planter, died.
1944   Aimee Semple McPherson, evangelist, died.

Events

1829   Mount Ararat first climbed.
1938   The *Queen Elizabeth* launched.
1938   League of Nations denounced Japanese aggression in China.

28th SEPTEMBER
Feast of Saint Wenceslaus.

People

1197   The Holy Roman Emperor Henry VI died.
1789   Thomas Day, writer, died.
1803   Prosper Mérimée, novelist, born.
1824   Francis Palgrave, anthologist, born.
1841   Georges Clemenceau, statesman, born.
1851   Henry Jones, dramatist, born.
1873   Emile Gaboriau, writer, died.
1895   Louis Pasteur, chemist, died.
1970   Gamal Abdul Nasser, statesman, died.

Events

1862   Bismarck made his 'Blood and Iron' speech.
1864   The First International founded.
1900   The 'Khaki' Election began in Britain.
1923   The *Radio Times* first published.
1940   German troops reached Warsaw.
1944   Canadian forces entered Calais.
1958   Referendum on the constitution of the Fifth French Republic held.

29th SEPTEMBER
Feast of Saint Michael and All Angels.   Michaelmas.

People
1518   Tintoretto, painter, born.
1560   Gustavus Vasa, King of Sweden, died.
1725   Robert Clive, Indian Empire pioneer, born.
1758   Lord Nelson born.
1810   Mrs Gaskell, novelist, born.
1833   Ferdinand VII, King of Spain, died.
1867   Walter Rathenau, statesman, born.
1902   Emile Zola, novelist, died.
1931   Sir William Orpen, painter, died.

Events
1613   The New River water supply for London opened.
1818   The Congress of Aix-la-Chapelle began.
1918   The Hindenburg Line broken by the Allies.
1923   British Mandate in Palestine proclaimed.
1930   The Pilgrim Trust established.
1938   The Munich Conference began.
1946   The BBC Third Programme began.

30th SEPTEMBER

People
420   Saint Jerome, Doctor of the Church, died.
1628   Sir Fulke Greville, poet, murdered.
1732   Jacques Necker, financier, born.
1770   George Whitfield, religious leader, died.
1772   James Brindley, engineer, died.
1832   Lord Roberts, soldier, born.
1852   Sir Charles Stanford, composer, born.
1857   Hermann Sudermann, playwright, born.
1913   Rudolf Diesel, engineer, died.
1930   Lord Birkenhead, lawyer and statesman, died.

Events
1399   The coronation of Henry IV, King of England.
1810   The University of Berlin opened.
1929   The first BBC experimental television broadcast took place.
1938   The Munich Agreement signed.
1939   Identity cards first issued in Britain.
1951   The Festival of Britain ended.
1966   Botswana became independent.

1st OCTOBER
National Holiday in China commemorating the formation of the Central People's
Government 1949.

People
1207   Henry III, King of England, born.
1578   Don John of Austria, soldier, died.
1684   Pierre Corneille, playwright, died.
1754   Paul I, Tsar of Russia, born.
1865   Paul Dukas, composer, born.
1873   Sir Edwin Landseer, painter, died.

1893 Benjamin Jowett, classical scholar, died.
1904 Vladimir Horowitz, pianist, born.

Events

1529 The Colloquy of Marburg began.
1795 Belgium incorporated in the French Republic.
1802 The Peace of Amiens: preliminary articles signed.
1843 The *News of the World* began publication.
1870 Halfpenny postage introduced in Britain.
1870 Stamped postcards first issued in Britain.
1918 T. E. Lawrence and the Arabs occupied Damascus.
1938 German troops entered Sudetenland.
1949 The People's Republic of China proclaimed.
1960 Nigeria became independent.
1974 Watergate trial began in the United States.

2nd OCTOBER

People

1452 Richard III, King of England, born.
1780 John André, army officer, executed for spying.
1847 Paul von Hindenburg, statesman and soldier, born.
1851 Ferdinand Foch, soldier, born.
1869 Mahatma Gandhi, nationalist leader, born.
1871 Cordell Hull, statesman, born.
1904 Graham Greene, novelist, born.
1920 Max Bruch, composer, died.
1931 Sir Thomas Lipton, sportsman, died.

Events

1187 Saladin entered Jerusalem.
1799 The Duke of York captured Alkmaar in the Netherlands.
1901 The first British submarine launched at Barrow.
1909 The first rugby football match played at Twickenham.
1940 A Royal Charter of incorporation granted to the British Council.
1958 Guinea proclaimed an independent republic.

3rd OCTOBER
Feast of Saint Thérèse of Lisieux.

People

1226 Saint Francis of Assisi died.
1658 Myles Standish, leader of the Pilgrim Fathers, died.
1859 Eleonora Duse, actress, born.
1867 Elias Howe, inventor, died.
1886 Alain-Fournier, writer, born.
1896 William Morris, artist and writer, died.
1929 Gustav Stresemann, statesman, died.
1953 Sir Arnold Bax, composer, died.
1967 Sir Malcolm Sargent, conductor, died.

Events

1574 The relief of Leyden.
1691 The surrender of Limerick.
1918 Tsar Ferdinand of Bulgaria abdicated.
1929 Yugoslavia first so named.
1952 First test of British atomic bomb, at the Monte Bello Islands.

4th OCTOBER
Feast of Saint Francis of Assisi.

People

1289	Louis X, King of France, born.
1669	Rembrandt van Rijn, painter, died.
1720	Giovanni Piranesi, architect, born.
1741	Edmond Malone, Shakespearian scholar, born.
1743	Henry Carey, poet and musician, died.
1787	François Guizot, historian and statesman, born.
1814	Jean François Millet, painter, born.
1821	John Rennie, engineer, died.
1832	William Griggs, inventor, born.
1861	Frederick Remington, artist, born.
1872	Sir Roger Keyes, naval officer, born.

Events

1535	Printing of the first English-language Bible completed.
1830	The independence of Belgium proclaimed.
1883	The Boys' Brigade founded at Glasgow.
1957	The first Soviet earth-satellite launched (Sputnik I).
1966	Lesotho became independent.

5th OCTOBER

People

1285	Philip III, King of France, died.
1713	Denis Diderot, encyclopaedist, born.
1789	William Scoresby, Arctic explorer, born.
1805	Charles, Marquess Cornwallis, statesman, died.
1830	Chester Arthur, statesman, born.
1880	Jacques Offenbach, composer, died.

Events

1930	The airship *R101* crashed at Beauvais.
1938	President Beneš of Czechoslovakia resigned.
1947	The Cominform formed at Belgrade.
1958	The constitution of the Fifth Republic of France came into force.

6th OCTOBER

People

1536	William Tyndale, theologian, burnt at the stake.
1773	Louis Philippe, King of the French, born.
1820	Jenny Lind, singer, born.
1846	George Westinghouse, inventor, born.
1891	Charles Stewart Parnell, Irish political leader, died.
1892	Alfred, Lord Tennyson, poet, died.
1893	Ford Madox Brown, painter, died.

Events

1238	Peterborough Cathedral consecrated.
1600	Henry IV of France married Marie de' Medici.
1895	The Promenade Concerts, London, founded by Sir Henry Wood.
1903	Manchester University formally opened,
1949	The Berlin airlift ended.
1973	Outbreak of war between Israel and Arab states.

7th OCTOBER

People

1468   Sigismondo Malatesta, tyrant and soldier, died.
1573   William Laud, Archbishop of Canterbury, born.
1577   George Gascoigne, poet and playwright, died.
1734   Sir Ralph Abercromby, soldier, born.
1780   Patrick Ferguson, soldier and inventor, killed in action.
1849   Edgar Allan Poe, writer, died.
1849   James Riley, poet, born.
1894   Oliver Wendell Holmes, writer, died.
1918   Sir Hubert Parry, composer, died.
1922   Marie Lloyd, music hall singer, died.

Events

1391   Saint Bridget of Sweden canonized.
1571   The Battle of Lepanto.
1906   The Persian Assembly opened by the Shah.
1944   The Dumbarton Oaks Conference ended.
1949   The constitution of the German Democratic Republic enacted.
1959   Lunik III took first photographs of the far side of the Moon.

8th OCTOBER

People

1354   Cola di Rienzi, reformer, murdered.
1469   Fra Filippo Lippi, painter, died.
1754   Henry Fielding, novelist, died.
1803   Vittorio Alfieri, poet, died.
1837   François Fourier, social reformer, died.
1838   Lord Rowton, philanthropist, born.
1878   Sir Alfred Munnings, painter, born.
1953   Kathleen Ferrier, singer, died.
1967   Clement Attlee, statesman, died.

Events

1871   The outbreak of the Great Fire of Chicago.
1912   War broke out in the Balkans against Turkey (First Balkan War).
1918   Beirut taken by the British.

9th OCTOBER
Feast of Saint Denis.   Leif Ericson Day (Norway).

People

1253   Robert Grosseteste, theologian, died.
1757   Charles X, King of France, born.
1835   Camille Saint-Saëns, composer, born.
1859   Alfred Dreyfus, army officer, born.
1890   Aimee Semple McPherson, evangelist, born.
1934   Alexander, King of Yugoslavia, assassinated.
1935   The Duke of Kent born.
1958   Pope Pius XII died.
1967   André Maurois, writer, died.

Events

1514   Louis XII, King of France, married Mary Tudor.
1561   The Colloquy of Poissy broke up.

1875   The Universal Postal Union founded at Berne.
1914   First Battle of Ypres began.
1962   Uganda became independent.

10th OCTOBER

People

1685   Antoine Watteau, painter, born.
1731   Henry Cavendish, scientist, born.
1738   Benjamin West, painter, born.
1813   Giuseppe Verdi, composer, born.
1825   Paul Kruger, statesman, born.
1827   Ugo Foscolo, poet, died.
1830   Isabella II, Queen of Spain, born.
1861   Fridtjof Nansen, explorer, born.
1877   Lord Nuffield, motor manufacturer and philanthropist, born.
1894   Dr William Moon, inventor of an alphabet of the blind, died.
1940   Sir Wilfred Grenfell, medical missionary, died.

Events

43B.C. Lyons founded by Lucius Plancus.
1774   The Battle of Point Pleasant.
1911   The outbreak of the Chinese Revolution.

11th OCTOBER

People

1531   Huldreich Zwingli, reformer, killed.
1542   Sir Thomas Wyatt, poet, died.
1821   Sir George Williams, founder of the Y.M.C.A., born.
1837   Samuel Wesley, composer, died.
1884   Eleanor Roosevelt, lecturer and writer, born.
1889   James Prescott Joule, physicist, died.
1896   Anton Bruckner, composer, died.
1963   Jean Cocteau, writer, died.

Events

1216   King John's baggage lost in The Wash.
1797   The Battle of Camperdown.
1871   The great Chicago fire ended.

12th OCTOBER

Columbus Day in the United States.

People

1537   Edward VI, King of England, born.
1576   The Holy Roman Emperor Maximilian II died.
1654   Carel Fabritius, painter, killed.
1844   Helen Modjeska, actress, born.
1845   Elizabeth Fry, prison reformer, died.
1859   Robert Stephenson, engineer, died.
1860   Elmer Sperry, inventor, born.
1866   J. Ramsay Macdonald, statesman, born.
1870   Robert E. Lee, soldier, died.

12th October

1872   Ralph Vaughan Williams, composer, born.
1892   Ernest Renan, philosopher, died.
1915   Nurse Edith Cavell executed by the Germans.
1924   Anatole France, writer, died.

Events

1654   The great explosion at Delft.
1950   The College of Europe, Bruges, opened.
1968   Equatorial Guinea became independent.

13th OCTOBER

People

1815   Joachim Murat, King of the Two Sicilies, executed.
1821   Rudolf Virchow, pathologist, born.
1822   Antonio Canova, sculptor, born.
1825   Maximilian I, King of Bavaria, died.
1831   Sir James Knowles, editor and architect, born.
1862   Mary Kingsley, traveller and writer, born.
1905   Sir Henry Irving, actor, died.

Events

1307   The arrest of the Templars in Paris.
1812   Battle of Queenston Heights.

14th OCTOBER

People

1066   Harold, King of the English, slain in battle.
1630   Sophia, Electress of Hanover, born.
1633   James II, King of England and Scotland, born.
1644   William Penn, founder of Pennsylvania, born.
1784   Ferdinand VII, King of Spain, born.
1882   Eamon de Valera, statesman, born.
1890   Dwight D. Eisenhower, soldier and statesman, born.
1942   Dame Marie Tempest, actress, died.
1976   Dame Edith Evans, actress, died.

Events

1066   The Battle of Hastings.
1806   The Battle of Jena.
1809   The Peace of Vienna.
1929   The first trials of the airship *R101*.
1939   The *Royal Oak* torpedoed in Scapa Flow.
1958   The Malagasy Republic (Madagascar) became independent.
1974   United Nations recognized Palestine Liberation Organization.

15th OCTOBER

People

70B.C.   Virgil, poet, born.
1553   Lucas Cranach, painter, died.
1686   Allan Ramsay, poet, born.
1762   Samuel Holyoke, hymn-writer, born.
1817   Tadeusz Kosciuszko, patriot, died.
1836   James Tissot, painter, born.
1844   Friedrich Nietzsche, philosopher, born.
1881   P. G. Wodehouse, novelist, born.

1905   Lord Snow (C. P. Snow), scientist and novelist, born.
1934   Raymond Poincaré, statesman, died.

Events

1582   The Gregorian Calendar introduced into Roman Catholic countries.
1846   Ether first publicly demonstrated as an anaesthetic.
1851   The Great Exhibition closed.
1928   The airship *Graf Zeppelin* completed its first transatlantic flight.
1946   The Paris Peace Conference ended.
1957   The naval base of Trincomalee handed over to Sri Lanka by Britain.
1971   Legislation passed curbing immigration into the United Kingdom.

16th OCTOBER

People

1430   James II, King of Scotland, born.
1555   Hugh Latimer, religious reformer, burnt at the stake.
1555   Nicholas Ridley, religious reformer, burnt at the stake.
1591   Pope Gregory XIV died.
1621   Jan Sweelinck, organist, died.
1758   Noah Webster, lexicographer, born.
1793   Marie Antoinette, Queen of France, guillotined.
1793   John Hunter, surgeon, died.
1803   Robert Stephenson, engineer, born.
1854   Oscar Wilde, writer, born.
1886   David Ben-Gurion, statesman, born.
1888   Eugene O'Neill, playwright, born.
1946   Sir Granville Bantock, composer, died.

Events

1759   Official opening of Smeaton's Eddystone Lighthouse.
1859   John Brown raided Harper's Ferry.
1869   Girton College, Cambridge University, opened.
1900   The 'Khaki' Election ended.
1964   China exploded a nuclear weapon.

17th OCTOBER

People

1586   Sir Philip Sidney, soldier and writer, died.
1727   John Wilkes, political agitator, born.
1757   R. A. de Réaumur, scientist, died.
1813   Georg Büchner, playwright, born.
1849   Frédéric Chopin, composer, died.
1921   Ludwig III, King of Bavaria, died.

Events

1346   The Battle of Neville's Cross.
1662   Charles II sold Dunkirk to the French (Treaty of Dunkirk).
1777   General Burgoyne surrendered at Saratoga.
1956   The Calder Hall Atomic Power Station opened.

18th OCTOBER

Feast of Saint Luke.

People

1405   Pope Pius II born.
1417   Pope Gregory XII died.

1503 Pope Pius III died.
1541 Margaret, Queen of Scotland, died.
1663 Prince Eugene of Savoy, soldier, born.
1674 Beau Nash, master of ceremonies, born.
1715 Peter II, Tsar of Russia, born.
1777 Heinrich von Kleist, poet and dramatist, born.
1785 Thomas Love Peacock, writer, born.
1831 Frederick III, Emperor of Germany, born.
1859 Henri Bergson, philosopher, born.
1865 Lord Palmerston, statesman, died.
1893 Charles-François Gounod, composer, died.
1931 Thomas Alva Edison, inventor, died.

Events

1685 King Louis XIV revoked the Edict of Nantes.
1775 Falmouth (now Portland, Maine) bombarded by the British.
1826 The last state lottery drawn in Britain.
1905 Aldwych, London, opened.
1905 Kingsway, London, opened.
1937 Rheims Cathedral reconsecrated.

19th OCTOBER

People

1605 Sir Thomas Browne, writer, born.
1745 Jonathan Swift, satirist, died.
1784 Leigh Hunt, writer, born.
1862 Auguste Lumière, pioneer in photography, born.
1875 Sir Charles Wheatstone, physicist, died.
1909 Cesare Lombroso, criminologist, died.
1937 Lord Rutherford, scientist, died.

Events

1781 Lord Cornwallis surrendered at Yorktown.
1807 Sir Humphry Davy publicly announced his discovery of sodium.
1812 Napoleon's army began the retreat from Moscow.
1864 Battle of Cedar Creek.
1954 Anglo-Egyptian agreement concerning the Suez Canal base signed.

20th OCTOBER

People

1524 Thomas Linacre, physician, died.
1632 Sir Christopher Wren, architect, born.
1784 Lord Palmerston, statesman, born.
1822 Thomas Hughes, writer, born.
1842 Grace Darling, heroine, died.
1858 John Burns, statesman, born.
1859 John Dewey, philosopher, born.
1867 Sarah Ann Glover, inventor of the Tonic Sol-fa system, died.
1890 Sir Richard Burton, traveller and writer, died.
1894 J. A. Froude, historian, died.
1922 Mussolini seized power in Italy after march on Rome.
1964 Herbert Hoover, statesman, died.

Events

480B.C. The Battle of Salamis.
1805 The Battle of Ulm.

1818 Anglo-American convention defined border between Canada and the United States.
1827 The Battle of Navarino.
1944 The Allies captured Aachen.
1962 Chinese troops attacked Indian border positions.

21st OCTOBER

People

1558 Julius Scaliger, philosopher and scientist, died.
1687 Edmund Waller, poet, died.
1760 Hokusai, painter, born.
1772 Samuel Taylor Coleridge, poet, born.
1777 Samuel Foote, actor and playwright, died.
1790 Alphonse de Lamartine, poet and statesman, born.
1805 Lord Nelson died.
1833 Alfred Nobel, manufacturer and philanthropist, born.

Events

1097 The Crusaders first arrived in front of Antioch.
1803 The Louisiana Purchase ratified.
1805 The Battle of Trafalgar.
1909 Halley's comet sighted from Cambridge Observatory.
1929 The BBC began regional broadcasting services.
1940 Purchase tax introduced in Britain.
1966 Aberfan slag heap disaster.

22nd OCTOBER

People

1383 Ferdinand I, King of Portugal, died.
1565 Jean Grolier, statesman, died.
1689 John V, King of Portugal, born.
1806 Thomas Sheraton, cabinet-maker, died.
1811 Franz Liszt, composer, born.
1843 Stephen Babcock, scientist, born.
1845 Sarah Bernhardt, actress, born.
1859 Ludwig Spohr, composer, died.
1933 Sir John Fortescue, historian, died.
1935 Sir Edward (Lord) Carson, lawyer and politician, died.
1973 Pablo Casals, cellist, died.
1976 Arnold Toynbee, historian, died.

Events

1883 The Metropolitan Opera House in New York opened.
1910 Dr Hawley Crippen convicted of murdering his wife.
1975 Juan Carlos proclaimed King of Spain.

23rd OCTOBER

People

42B.C. Marcus Brutus committed suicide.
1658 Thomas Pride, Parliamentary soldier, died.
1805 Adalbert Stifter, writer, born.
1844 Robert Bridges, poet, born.

23rd October

1845 George Saintsbury, literary historian and critic, born.
1906 Paul Cézanne, painter, died.
1915 W. G. Grace, cricketer, died.

Events

42B.C. The Second Battle of Philippi.
1642 The Battle of Edgehill.
1917 The Battle of Caporetto began.
1942 The Battle of El Alamein began.
1956 The Hungarian Revolution broke out.

24th OCTOBER
Feast of Saint Raphael the Archangel.

People

1601 Tycho Brahe, astronomer, died.
1632 Anthony van Leeuwenhoek, naturalist, born.
1645 Sir William Rollo, Royalist soldier, executed.
1767 Jacques Laffitte, banker and politician, born.
1897 Francis Palgrave, anthologist, died.
1918 Charles Lecocq, composer, died.
1948 Franz Lehar, composer, died.

Events

1648 The Treaty of Westphalia signed.
1861 The transcontinental telegraph line across the U.S.A. completed.
1945 The United Nations formally came into existence.
1964 Zambia became independent.

25th OCTOBER
Feast of Saint Crispin.

People

1400 Geoffrey Chaucer, poet, died.
1510 Giorgione, painter, died.
1735 James Beattie, poet, born.
1760 George II, King of Great Britain and Ireland, died.
1764 William Hogarth, painter, died.
1800 Lord Macaulay, historian, born.
1825 Johann Strauss, the younger, composer, born.
1838 Georges Bizet, composer, born.
1888 Richard Byrd, aviator and explorer, born.
1920 Terence MacSwiney, Irish patriot, died of starvation.

Events

1415 The Battle of Agincourt.
1760 George III proclaimed King of Great Britain.
1854 The Charge of the Light Brigade at Balaklava.
1924 The Zinoviev Letter published in Britain.
1971 Chinese People's Republic admitted to the United Nations.

26th OCTOBER

People

1440 Gilles de Rais, Marshal of France, hanged.
1759 Georges Danton, statesman, born.
1764 William Hogarth, painter, died.

1800   Helmuth, Graf von Moltke, soldier, born.
1919   Mohammad Reza Pahlavi, Shah of Iran, born.

Events

1825   The Erie Canal opened to traffic.
1905   Sweden agreed to the repeal of the union of Sweden and Norway.
1907   The Territorial Army inaugurated in Britain.
1956   The United Nations approved the establishment of the International Atomic Energy Agency.

27th OCTOBER

People

1553   Michael Servetus, theologian, burnt at the stake.
1670   Vavasour Powell, itinerant preacher, died in prison.
1760   August von Gneisenau, soldier, born.
1782   Nicolò Paganini, violinist, born.
1854   Sir William Smith, founder of the Boys' Brigade, born.
1858   Theodore Roosevelt, statesman, born.

Events

1775   The Continental Congress established the United States Navy.
1806   Berlin captured by the French.
1918   President Wilson's Fourteen Points accepted by Germany.
1930   The Courtauld Institute of Art established in London.
1930   The London Naval Treaty ratified.

28th OCTOBER

Feast of Saints Simon and Jude.

People

901   Alfred the Great, King of England, died.
1412   Margaret, Queen of Denmark, Norway and Sweden, died.
1585   Cornelis Jansen, theologian, born.
1696   Maurice de Saxe, soldier, born.
1704   John Locke, philosopher, died.
1728   James Cook, navigator and explorer, born.
1792   John Smeaton, civil engineer, died.
1899   Ottmar Mergenthaler, inventor, died.
1914   Jonas Salk, scientist, born.

Events

1636   Harvard College founded.
1870   Capitulation of Metz to the German army.
1886   The Statue of Liberty dedicated.
1918   Independence of Czechoslovakia proclaimed.

29th OCTOBER

People

1618   Sir Walter Raleigh, navigator and writer, executed.
1656   Edmund Halley, astronomer, born.
1740   James Boswell, Dr Johnson's biographer, born.
1783   Jean d'Alembert, mathematician and philosopher, died.
1864   John Leech, artist, died.

29th October

1879 Franz von Papen, statesman, born.
1885 James Hannington, first Bishop of Eastern Equatorial Africa, murdered.
1897 Joseph Goebbels, Nazi leader, born.
1911 Joseph Pulitzer, newspaper publisher, died.
1950 Gustaf V, King of Sweden, died.

Events

1888 The Convention of Constantinople declared the Suez Canal open to the vessels of all nations and free from blockade.
1945 The Atomic Energy Research Establishment set up at Harwell.
1956 Israeli forces invaded the Sinai Peninsula.

30th OCTOBER

People

1741 Angelica Kauffmann, painter, born.
1751 Richard Brinsley Sheridan, playwright, born.
1823 Edmund Cartwright, inventor, died.
1894 Peter Warlock, composer, born.
1895 Gerhard Domagk, pathologist, born.
1910 Henri Dunant, founder of the International Red Cross, died.
1923 Andrew Bonar Law, statesman, died.
1958 Dame Rose Macaulay, novelist, died.

Events

1841 Fire at the Tower of London.

31st OCTOBER
Hallowe'en.

People

1620 John Evelyn, diarist, born.
1632 Jan Vermeer, painter, born.
1638 Meindert Hobbema, painter, born.
1867 The Earl of Rosse, astronomer, died.
1887 Chiang Kai-shek, soldier and statesman, born.

Events

1517 Luther nailed his theses on indulgences to the church door at Wittenberg.
1795 John Keats, poet, born.
1864 Nevada achieved statehood.
1902 The Pacific cable completed at Suva.
1909 The National University of Ireland, Dublin, came into being.
1909 Queen's University, Belfast, came into being.
1925 The Persian Majles deposed the Shah, Sultan Ahmad.

1st NOVEMBER
All Saints' Day.

People

846 Louis II, King of France, born.
1500 Benvenuto Cellini, sculptor, born.
1636 Nicolas Boileau, poet, born.
1714 John Radcliffe, physician, died.

1770   Alexander Cruden, concordancer, died.
1778   Gustavus IV, King of Sweden, born.
1793   Lord George Gordon, political agitator, died.
1865   John Lindley, botanist, died.
1871   Stephen Crane, writer, born.
1894   Alexander III, Tsar of Russia, died.
1896   Edmund Blunden, poet, born.
1903   Theodor Mommsen, historian and archaeologist, died.
1972   Ezra Pound, poet, died.

Events

1755   The great earthquake at Lisbon.
1814   The Congress of Vienna opened.
1914   The Battle of Coronel.
1922   Radio receiving licences introduced in Britain.
1924   The British Empire Exhibition, Wembley, closed.
1943   U.S. forces landed in the Solomon Islands.
1956   The States Reorganization Act came into force in India.

2nd NOVEMBER

All Souls' Day.

People

1148   Saint Malachy, Church reformer, died.
1470   Edward V, King of England, born.
1483   The Duke of Buckingham, courtier, executed.
1600   Richard Hooker, theologian, died.
1734   Daniel Boone, American pioneer, born.
1755   Marie Antoinette, Queen of France, born.
1795   James Polk, statesman, born.
1818   Sir Samuel Romilly, lawyer, committed suicide.
1865   Warren Harding, statesman, born.
1887   Jenny Lind, singer, died.
1950   George Bernard Shaw, dramatist, died.

Events

1308   Castellat, last of the Templars' stronghold, fell.
1889   North and South Dakota achieved statehood.
1917   The Balfour Declaration about a national home for the Jews in Palestine.
1920   KDKA Pittsburgh, world's first regular broadcasting station, went on the air.
1930   Hailé Selassié crowned Emperor of Ethiopia.
1959   M1 motorway officially opened.
1976   James Earl Carter elected U.S. President.

3rd NOVEMBER

People

1801   Karl Baedeker, guidebook publisher, born.
1901   Leopold III, King of the Belgians, born.
1954   Henri Matisse, painter, died.

Events

1640   The Long Parliament assembled.
1706   Abruzzi destroyed by an earthquake.
1840   Acre taken by British forces.
1903   The independence of Panama proclaimed.
1918   German fleet mutinied at Kiel.
1957   First animal-carrying satellite launched.

4th NOVEMBER

People

1702 John Benbow, naval officer, died.
1740 Augustus Toplady, hymn-writer, born.
1787 Edmund Kean, actor, born.
1840 Auguste Rodin, sculptor, born.
1847 Felix Mendelssohn-Bartholdy, composer, died.
1856 Paul Delaroche, painter, died.
1859 Joseph Rowntree, Quaker educationalist, died.
1862 Eden Phillpotts, writer, born.
1879 Will Rogers, humorist, born.
1924 Gabriel Fauré, composer, died.

Events

1814 Norway granted separate constitution and joined in personal union with Swedish monarchy.
1942 The Battle of El Alamein ended.
1948 The Indian constitution formally introduced in the Constituent Assembly.
1957 The second Soviet earth-satellite launched.

5th NOVEMBER
Guy Fawkes' Day.

People

1494 Hans Sachs, poet and dramatist, born.
1800 Jesse Ramsden, instrument maker, died.
1807 Angelica Kauffman, painter, died.
1895 Walter Gieseking, pianist, born.
1955 Maurice Utrillo, painter, died.

Events

1605 Guy Fawkes' attempt on the Houses of Parliament.
1688 William of Orange landed at Torbay.
1854 The Battle of Inkerman.

6th NOVEMBER

People

1406 Pope Innocent VII died.
1612 Henry Frederick, Prince of Wales, died.
1656 John IV, King of Portugal, died.
1671 Colley Cibber, writer, born.
1771 Alois Senefelder, inventor of lithography, born.
1793 John Murray, publisher, died.
1814 Adolphe Sax, musical instrument maker, born.
1833 Jonas Lie, novelist, born.
1854 John Philip Sousa, composer, born.
1860 Sir Charles Napier, naval officer, died.
1870 Viscount Samuel, statesman, born.
1884 Henry Fawcett, economist, died.
1892 Sir John Alcock, pioneer aviator, born.
1893 Peter Tchaikovsky, composer, died.

Events

1860 Abraham Lincoln elected President of the United States.
1956 Cease-fire agreed at Suez.
1956 Work began on the Kariba High Dam.

7th NOVEMBER

People
1723   Sir Godfrey Kneller, painter, died.
1810   Franz Erkel, composer, born.
1862   Bahadur Shah II, last titular Mogul Emperor of India, died.
1867   Marie Curie, scientist, born.
1912   Richard Shaw, architect, died.

Events
1619   Elizabeth, daughter of James I, crowned Queen of Bohemia.
1631   Transit of Mercury (first observation of the transit of a planet) observed by Pierre Gassendi.
1811   The Battle of Tippecanoe.
1917   The October Revolution began in Russia.

8th NOVEMBER

People
1226   Louis VIII, King of France, died.
1308   Duns Scotus, philosopher, died.
1674   John Milton, poet, died.
1828   Thomas Bewick, engraver, died.
1834   J. K. F. Zöllner, scientist, born.
1865   Tom Sayers, pugilist, died.
1883   Sir Arnold Bax, composer, born.
1886   Fred Archer, jockey, committed suicide.
1890   César Franck, composer, died.
1908   Victorien Sardou, playwright, died.
1933   Mohammed Nadir Shah, King of Afghanistan, assassinated.

Events
1861   The Unionist warship *San Jacinto* removed Confederate commissioners from the British mailship *Trent*.
1889   Montana achieved statehood.
1923   Adolf Hitler's attempted putsch in Munich.
1942   British and American forces landed in North Africa.

9th NOVEMBER

People
1623   William Camden, antiquary, died.
1677   Gilbert Sheldon, Archbishop of Canterbury, died.
1818   Ivan Turgenev, writer, born.
1841   Edward VII, King of Great Britain and Ireland, born.
1880   Sir Giles Scott, architect, born.
1937   J. Ramsay MacDonald, statesman, died.
1940   Neville Chamberlain, statesman, died.
1951   Sigmund Romberg, composer, died.
1953   Ibn Saud, King of Saudi Arabia, died.
1953   Dylan Thomas, poet, died.
1970   Charles de Gaulle, soldier and statesman, died.

Events
1858   The first concert of the New York Symphony Orchestra.
1908   Britain's first woman mayor, Mrs Garrett Anderson, elected at Aldeburgh.
1917   Georges Glemenceau elected Premier of France.
1918   William II of Germany abdicated.
1918   The German Republic proclaimed.

9th November

1943 The U.N.R.R.A. agreement signed.
1944 The beginning of the Moscow Conference.
1953 Cambodia became independent.

10th NOVEMBER

People

461   Pope Leo the Great died.
1444 Ladislas III, King of Poland, died.
1483 Martin Luther, Church reformer, born.
1549 Pope Paul III died.
1556 Richard Chancellor, navigator, lost at sea.
1668 François Couperin, composer, born.
1683 George II, King of Great Britain and Ireland, born.
1697 William Hogarth, painter, born.
1728 Oliver Goldsmith, writer, born.
1759 Friedrich Schiller, playwright, born.
1796 Catherine II, Empress of Russia, died.
1852 Gideon Mantell, geologist, died.
1880 Jacob Epstein, sculptor, born.
1887 Arnold Zweig, novelist, born.
1924 Sir Archibald Geikie, geologist, died.
1938 Kemal Atatürk, statesman, died.

Events

1559 Queen Elizabeth I confirmed the Charter of the Stationers' Company.
1775 The United States Marine Corps formed.
1798 Alois Senefelder invented the lithographic process.
1915 The Gilbert and Ellice Islands annexed by Britain.

11th NOVEMBER
Martinmas.

People

1599 Prince Octavio Piccolomini, military commander, born.
1729 L. A. de Bougainville, explorer, born.
1821 Fyodor Dostoyevsky, novelist, born.
1855 Søren Kierkegaard, philosopher, died.
1858 Hugh Pattinson, metallurgical chemist, died.
1882 Gustaf VI Adolf, King of Sweden, born.
1936 Sir Edward German, composer, died.
1945 Jerome Kern, composer, died.

Events

1889 Washington achieved statehood.
1918 The Battle of the Meuse-Argonne ended.
1918 Armistice Day: World War I.
1920 The Cenotaph in Whitehall, London, unveiled.
1940 British attack on Italian fleet at Taranto.
1973 Cease-fire between Israel and Egypt.
1975 Angola became independent.

12th NOVEMBER

People

1035 Canute II, King of England and Denmark, died.
1555 Bishop Gardiner, theologian, died.
1595 Sir John Hawkins, navigator, died.

1615   Richard Baxter, divine, born.
1671   Thomas Fairfax, Parliamentary soldier, died.
1684   Edward Vernon, naval officer, born.
1755   Gerhard von Scharnhorst, soldier, born.
1769   Amelia Opie, novelist, born.
1841   Lord Rayleigh, physicist, born.
1854   Charles Kemble, actor, died.
1865   Mrs Gaskell, novelist, died.

Events

1630   The Day of Dupes (in France).
1893   The Durand Agreement, defining the frontier between Afghanistan and India, signed.
1921   The Limitation of Armaments Conference began at Washington.
1933   The first elections under the Nazi régime held in Germany.
1944   The German battleship *Tirpitz* sunk.

13th NOVEMBER

People

 867   Pope Nicholas I died.
1093   Malcolm III, King of the Scots, killed.
1312   Edward III, King of England, born.
1460   Prince Henry the Navigator died.
1736   George Sale, orientalist, died.
1792   E. J. Trelawny, traveller and writer, born.
1804   Captain Samuel Wallis, navigator, died.
1825   Charles Worth, dress designer, born.
1831   James Clerk-Maxwell, physicist, born.
1833   Edwin Booth, actor, born.
1849   William Etty, painter, died.
1850   Robert Louis Stevenson, writer, born.
1907   Francis Thompson, poet, died.
1916   Percival Lowell, astronomer, died.

Events

1564   The Tridentine Creed promulgated.
1916   Battle of the Somme ended.
1929   The Bank for International Settlements founded.

14th NOVEMBER

People

 565   The Byzantine Emperor Justinian I died.
1635   'Old Parr' (born about 1483), died.
1716   Gottfried Leibniz, philosopher, died.
1765   Robert Fulton, inventor, born.
1797   Sir Charles Lyell, geologist, born.
1831   G. W. F. Hegel, philosopher, died.
1840   Claude Monet, painter, born.
1863   Leo Baekeland, inventor, born.
1889   Jawaharlal Nehru, statesman, born.
1891   Sir Frederick Banting, scientist, born.
1909   Joseph McCarthy, politician, born.
1914   Lord Roberts, soldier, died.
1916   Henryk Sienkiewicz, novelist, died.
1935   Hussein, King of Jordan, born.
1946   Manuel de Falla, composer, died.
1948   The Prince of Wales born.
1955   Robert E. Sherwood, writer, died.

14th November

Events

1770   James Bruce discovered the source of the Blue Nile.
1918   Thomas Masaryk elected president of the Republic of Czechoslovakia.
1922   The British Broadcasting Company began its first daily broadcasting service.

15th NOVEMBER

People

1397   Pope Nicholas V born.
1607   Madeleine de Scudéry, writer, born.
1630   Johannes Kepler, astronomer, died.
1638   Catharine of Braganza, wife of Charles II of England, born.
1708   William Pitt, Earl of Chatham, statesman, born.
1738   Sir William Herschel, astronomer, born.
1741   J. K. Lavater, poet and mystic, born.
1776   Per Ling, pioneer in gymnastic training, born.
1787   Christoph Gluck, composer, died.
1802   George Romney, painter, died.
1862   Gerhardt Hauptmann, dramatist, born.
1863   Frederik VII, King of Denmark, died.
1882   Felix Frankfurter, Supreme Court judge, born.
1889   Manuel II, King of Portugal, born.

Events

1831   The Treaty of London.
1837   Isaac Pitman first published his stenographic phonography.
1889   Brazil became a republic.

16th NOVEMBER

People

42B.C.   Tiberius, Roman emperor, born.
1272   Henry III, King of England, died.
1632   Gustavus Adolphus, King of Sweden, killed in battle.
1724   Jack Sheppard, highwayman, hanged.
1766   Rodolphe Kreutzer, violinist, born.
1776   James Ferguson, astronomer, died.
1811   John Bright, statesman, born.
1839   William de Morgan, novelist, born.
1889   George S. Kaufman, playwright, born.
1895   Paul Hindemith, composer, born.

Events

1632   The Battle of Lützen.
1776   British forces captured Fort Washington.
1824   The Murray River discovered by the Australian explorer, Hamilton Hume.
1846   Austria annexed Cracow.
1869   The formal opening of the Suez Canal at Port Said.
1907   Oklahoma achieved statehood.
1918   Hungary proclaimed an independent republic.

17th NOVEMBER

People

1093   Saint Margaret, Queen of Scotland, died.
1558   Mary I, Queen of England, died.
1665   John Earle, writer, died.

1747 A. R. Le Sage, novelist and dramatist, died.
1755 Louis XVIII, King of France, born.
1794 George Grote, historian, born.
1858 Robert Owen, social reformer, died.
1917 Auguste Rodin, sculptor, died.
1959 Heitor Villa-Lobos, composer, died.

Events

1869 Procession of ships made the first passage through the Suez Canal.
1921 Polish constitution established.
1956 Kashmir voted to become part of India.

18th NOVEMBER

People

1785 Sir David Wilkie, painter, born.
1789 Louis Daguerre, pioneer in photography, born.
1830 Adam Weishaupt, philosopher, died.
1831 Karl von Clausewitz, military strategist, died.
1836 Sir W. S. Gilbert, playwright, born.
1860 Ignaz Jan Paderewski, pianist, composer and statesman, born.
1889 Amelita Galli-Curci, singer, born.
1899 Eugène Ormandy, conductor, born.
1922 Marcel Proust, novelist, died.

Events

1883 Standard time introduced in the U.S.A.
1903 The U.S.A. and Panama signed a treaty concerning the construction, government and use of the Panama Canal and the Canal Zone.
1905 Prince Carl of Denmark formally elected as King Haakon VII of Norway.
1918 Latvia proclaimed an independent republic.

19th NOVEMBER

People

1600 Charles I, King of England and Scotland, born.
1665 Nicolas Poussin, painter, died.
1692 Thomas Shadwell, poet and dramatist, died.
1770 Bertel Thorvaldsen, sculptor, born.
1805 Ferdinand de Lesseps, engineer, born.
1828 Franz Schubert, composer, died.
1831 James Garfield, statesman, born.
1883 Sir William Siemens, inventor, died.

Events

1942 German army at Stalingrad surrounded.
1946 The first General Conference of U.N.E.S.C.O. held in Paris.
1951 The world's first atomic central heating plant started operating at Harwell.

20th NOVEMBER

People

1591 Sir Christopher Hatton, statesman, died.
1752 Thomas Chatterton, poet, born.

1761   Pope Pius VIII born.
1841   Sir Wilfrid Laurier, statesman, born.
1847   Henry Francis Lyte, hymn-writer, died.
1855   Josiah Royce, philosopher, born.
1858   Selma Lagerlöf, writer, born.
1894   Anton Rubinstein, composer, died.
1910   Count Leo Tolstoy, writer, died.
1925   Queen Alexandra, wife of King Edward VII, died.
1925   Robert Kennedy, statesman, born.
1935   Lord Jellicoe, naval officer, died.
1938   Maud, Queen of Norway, died.
1945   Francis Aston, experimental physicist, died.

Events

1759   The Battle of Quiberon Bay.
1917   The Battle of Cambrai.
1945   The Nuremberg War Crimes Tribunal began.
1947   The wedding of Princess Elizabeth (Queen Elizabeth II).

21st NOVEMBER

People

1579   Sir Thomas Gresham, founder of the Royal Exchange, died.
1682   Claude Lorrain, painter, died.
1694   Voltaire, writer, born (reputed date).
1695   Henry Purcell, composer, died.
1811   Heinrich von Kleist, poet and dramatist, committed suicide.
1835   James Hogg, poet, died.
1863   Sir Arthur Quiller-Couch, writer, born.
1877   Siegfried Karg-Elert, composer, born.
1895   William Gerhardi, writer, born.
1916   Franz Josef, Emperor of Austria, died.
1942   J. B. M. Hertzog, soldier and statesman, died.

Events

1818   The Congress of Aix-la-Chapelle ended.
1843   The vulcanization of rubber patented.
1890   The Lincoln Judgment (concerning the jurisdiction of the Archbishop of
       Canterbury) delivered.
1918   The surrender of the German battle fleet to the Allies.
1944   The Moscow Conference ended.
1955   The inaugural meeting of the Permanent Council of the Baghdad Pact (later
       C.E.N.T.O.) at Baghdad.
1958   The construction of the Forth Road Bridge begun.
1974   I.R.A. bombs in Birmingham killed 19 people.

22nd NOVEMBER

People

1594   Sir Martin Frobisher, explorer, died.
1643   The Sieur de la Salle, explorer, born.
1767   Andreas Hofer, Tirolese patriot, born.
1774   Robert Clive, Indian Empire pioneer, died.
1808   Thomas Cook, travel agent, born.
1819   George Eliot, novelist, born.
1859   Cecil Sharp, folk-music collector, born.
1869   André Gide, writer, born.
1873   L. S. Amery, statesman, born.
1890   Charles de Gaulle, soldier and statesman, born.
1896   George Ferris, engineer, died. ʼ

1900 Sir Arthur Sullivan, composer, died.
1913 Benjamin Britten, composer, born.
1944 Sir Arthur Eddington, scientist, died.
1963 Aldous Huxley, writer, died.
1963 John F. Kennedy, statesman, assassinated.
1963 C. S. Lewis, scholar and writer, died.

Events

1497 Vasco da Gama rounded the Cape of Good Hope.
1921 The Anglo-Afghan Treaty concluded in Kabul.
1956 The Olympic Games opened at Melbourne.

23rd NOVEMBER

People

912 The Holy Roman Emperor Otto the Great born.
1457 Ladislas V, King of Hungary, died.
1499 Perkin Warbeck, pretender, executed.
1585 Thomas Tallis, composer, died.
1616 Richard Hakluyt, geographer, died.
1726 Sophia Dorothea, Electress of Hanover, died in captivity.
1804 Franklin Pierce, statesman, born.
1837 J. van der Waals, physicist, born.
1860 Marie Bashkirtseff, painter, born.
1876 Manuel de Falla, composer, born.
1910 Dr Hawley Crippen executed at Pentonville.
1934 Sir Arthur Pinero, playwright, died.

Events

1858 The General Medical Council held its first meeting in London.
1914 Royal Navy bombarded Zeebrugge.

24th NOVEMBER

People

1504 Isabella, Queen of Castile and Leon, died.
1572 John Knox, Church reformer, died.
1632 Baruch Spinoza, philosopher, born.
1713 Laurence Sterne, writer, born.
1784 Zachary Taylor, statesman, born.
1815 Grace Darling, heroine, born.
1848 Lord Melbourne, statesman, died.
1848 Lilli Lehmann, operatic singer, born.
1857 Sir Henry Havelock, soldier, died.
1929 Georges Clemenceau, statesman, died.
1937 Lilian Bayliss, theatre manager, died.
1940 Lord Craigavon, statesman, died.

Events

1639 The transit of Venus first observed by Jeremiah Horrocks.
1642 Abel Tasman discovered Van Diemen's Land.
1793 The republican calendar adopted in France.

25th NOVEMBER

People

1562 Lope de Vega, poet and playwright, born.
1626 Edward Alleyn, actor, died.

25th November

1686 Nicolaus Steno, scientist, died.
1748 Isaac Watts, hymn-writer, died.
1775 Charles Kemble, actor, born.
1835 Andrew Carnegie, financier and philanthropist, born.
1841 Sir Francis Chantrey, sculptor, died.
1877 Harley Granville Barker, actor and critic, born.
1878 Georg Kaiser, playwright, born.
1881 Pope John XXIII born.
1974 U Thant, statesman, died.

Events

1542 The Battle of Solway Moss.
1783 British troops evacuated New York.
1859 The London Irish Volunteer Rifles formed.
1892 Pierre de Coubertin proposed the revival of the Olympic Games.
1918 French troops entered Strasbourg.

26th NOVEMBER

People

1607 John Harvard, philanthropist, born.
1731 William Cowper, poet, born.
1810 Lord Armstrong, inventor and engineer, born.
1836 John McAdam, engineer, died.
1851 Nicolas Soult, soldier, died.
1869 Maud, Queen of Norway, born.
1896 Coventry Patmore, poet, died.
1917 Sir Leander Jameson, statesman, died.
1930 Otto Sverdrup, explorer, died.
1968 Arnold Zweig, novelist, died.

Events

1703 (night of 26–27) The Great Storm of London.
1764 Suppression of the Jesuits in France.
1789 First national Thanksgiving Day (celebrating the harvest of 1623) in the United States.
1812 Battle of the Berezina.
1955 State of emergency in Cyprus.

27th NOVEMBER

People

1635 Madame de Maintenon, wife of Louis XIV of France, born.
1680 Athanasius Kircher, scientist and inventor, died.
1701 Anders Celsius, inventor, died.
1758 Perdita (Mary Robinson), actress, born.
1809 Fanny Kemble, actress, born.
1811 Andrew Meikle, millwright and inventor, died.
1953 Eugene O'Neill, playwright, died.
1955 Arthur Honegger, composer, died.

Events

1095 Pope Urban II began to preach the First Crusade at Clermont.
1518 Daniel Bomberg completed the Rabbinical Bible.
1912 Spain established a protectorate in Morocco.
1919 The Treaty of Neuilly signed.
1942 The French fleet sabotaged at Toulon.

28th NOVEMBER

People

1757 William Blake, poet and painter, born.
1811 Maximilian II, King of Bavaria, born.
1829 Anton Rubinstein, composer, born.
1855 Adam Mickiewicz, poet, died.
1859 Washington Irving, writer and diplomat, died.
1911 'Lord' George Sanger, circus pioneer, murdered.
1954 Enrico Fermi, atomic scientist, died.

Events

1660 The Royal Society formally founded.
1885 The British entered Mandalay.
1905 The Sinn Fein Party organized.
1912 The independence of Albania proclaimed.
1960 Mauritania became independent.

29th NOVEMBER

People

1314 Philip IV, King of France, died.
1378 The Holy Roman Emperor Charles IV died.
1489 Margaret, Queen of Scotland, born.
1516 Giovanni Bellini, painter, born.
1530 Cardinal Wolsey, statesman, died.
1632 Jean Baptiste Lully, composer, born.
1682 Prince Rupert, soldier, died.
1695 Anthony à Wood, antiquary, died.
1780 Maria Theresa, Empress of Austria, died.
1832 Louisa May Alcott, writer, born.
1856 Theobald von Bethmann-Hollweg, statesman, born.
1869 Giulia Grisi, operatic singer, died.
1872 Horace Greeley, editor of the *New York Tribune*, died.
1898 C. S. Lewis, scholar and writer, born.
1924 Giacomo Puccini, composer, died.

Events

1945 Yugoslavia proclaimed a Federal People's Republic.
1962 Franco-British agreement to develop 'Concorde' supersonic airliner.

30th NOVEMBER
Eton College Wall Game.   Saint Andrew's Day.

People

1554 Sir Philip Sidney, poet and statesman, born.
1628 John Bunyan, religious leader and writer, baptized.
1654 John Selden, jurist and antiquary, died.
1667 Jonathan Swift, writer, born.
1750 Maurice de Saxe, soldier, died.
1807 William Farr, statistician, born.
1809 Mark Lemon, editor of *Punch*, born.
1817 Theodor Mommsen, historian, born.
1835 Mark Twain, writer, born.
1856 Viscount Haldane, statesman and reformer, born.
1858 Sir Jagadis Chandra Bose, scientist, born.
1862 James Sheridan Knowles, playwright, died.

30th November

1874   Sir Winston Churchill, statesman, born.
1900   Oscar Wilde, writer, died.
1901   Edward Eyre, explorer and statesman, died.
1954   Wilhelm Furtwängler, conductor, died.
1957   Beniamino Gigli, singer, died.

Events

1924   Radio photographs first transmitted from Britain to the U.S.A.
1936   The Crystal Palace destroyed by fire.
1940   U.S.S.R. invaded Finland.
1966   Barbados became independent.
1967   People's Democratic Republic of Yemen became independent.

1st DECEMBER

People

1135   Henry I, King of England, died.
1455   Lorenzo Ghiberti, sculptor, died.
1521   Pope Leo X died.
1525   Blanche of Castile, wife of Louis VIII of France, died.
1795   Leopold von Ranke, historian, born.
1825   Alexander I, Tsar of Russia, died.
1830   Pope Pius VIII died.
1844   Queen Alexandra, wife of King Edward VII, born.
1849   Ebenezer Elliott, Corn Law poet, died.
1964   J. B. S. Haldane, scientist, died.
1973   David Ben-Gurion, statesman, died.

Events

1918   The British Second Army entered Germany.
1919   The first British woman M.P. (Lady Astor) took her seat in the House of Commons.
1925   A pact of mutual agreement between Belgium and Britain signed in London.
1932   The Tate Gallery reassumed its original name.
1941   'Points' rationing began in Britain.
1942   The Beveridge Report on social security in Britain issued.

2nd DECEMBER

People

1547   Hernando Cortes, conquistador, died.
1825   Pedro II, Emperor of Brazil, born.
1853   Amelia Opie, novelist, died.
1859   John Brown, abolitionist, hanged.
1859   Georges Seurat, painter, born.
1899   Sir John Barbirolli, conductor, born.
1931   Vincent d'Indy, composer, died.
1967   Francis, Cardinal Spellman, Archbishop of New York, died.

Events

1254   The Battle of Foggia.
1804   Napoleon crowned by the Pope.
1805   The Battle of Austerlitz.
1823   Birkbeck College (University of London) founded.
1823   The Monroe Doctrine proclaimed.
1852   The proclamation of the Second French Empire.
1942   The first atomic pile began operating in Chicago.
1971   The United Arab Emirates became independent.

3rd DECEMBER
Feast of Saint Francis Xavier.

People
1596 Nicolo Amati, violin-maker, born.
1753 Samuel Crompton, inventor, born.
1795 Sir Rowland Hill, postal pioneer, born.
1826 John Flaxman, sculptor, died.
1857 Joseph Conrad, novelist, born.
1894 Robert Louis Stevenson, writer, died.
1910 Mrs Mary Baker Eddy, religious leader, died.
1919 Pierre Auguste Renoir, painter, died.

Events
1800 The Battle of Hohenlinden.
1808 Madrid surrendered to Napoleon.
1810 The British captured Mauritius from the French.
1818 Illinois achieved statehood.
1917 The Battle of Cambrai ended.

4th DECEMBER

People
1334 Pope John XXII died.
1637 Nicholas Ferrar, religious leader, died.
1642 Cardinal Richelieu, statesman, died.
1649 William Drummond of Hawthornden, writer, died.
1679 Thomas Hobbes, philosopher, died.
1732 John Gay, poet and playwright, died.
1777 Madame Récamier, society leader, born.
1795 Thomas Carlyle, historian and writer, born.
1798 Luigi Galvani, scientist, died.
1865 Edith Cavell, nurse and patriot, born.
1879 Sir Hamilton Harty, conductor, born.

Events
1563 The Council of Trent dissolved.
1896 Brighton Chain Pier completely destroyed during gales.
1966 Harold Wilson met Ian Smith aboard H.M.S. *Tiger*.

5th DECEMBER

People
1560 Francis II, King of France, died.
1594 Gerhard Mercator, geographer, died.
1782 Martin Van Buren, statesman, born.
1791 Wolfgang Amadeus Mozart, composer, died.
1830 Christina Rossetti, poet, born.
1859 Earl Jellicoe, naval officer, born.
1867 Marshal Pilsudski, statesman, born.
1870 Alexandre Dumas, père, writer, died.
1891 Pedro II, Emperor of Brazil, died.
1899 Sir Henry Tate, manufacturer and philanthropist, died.
1901 Walt Disney, animated cartoon film producer, born.
1926 Claude Monet, painter, died.
1940 Jan Kubelik, violinist, died.

5th December

Events

1492 Columbus discovered the island of Santo Domingo.
1757 The Battle of Leuthen.
1925 Medina capitulated to Ibn Saud.
1933 Prohibition in the U.S.A. repealed.
1941 Britain declared war on Finland, Hungary and Romania.
1956 The union of British Togoland with Ghana approved.
1958 The Preston Bypass, Britain's first section of motorway, officially opened.

6th DECEMBER

Feast of Saint Nicholas.

People

1421 Henry VI, King of England, born.
1608 George Monk, soldier and statesman, born.
1721 Chrétien Malesherbes, statesman, born.
1732 Warren Hastings, statesman, born.
1778 Joseph Gay-Lussac, scientist, born.
1788 Richard Harris Barham ('Thomas Ingoldsby'), writer, born.
1857 Joseph Conrad, writer, born.
1882 Anthony Trollope, novelist, died.
1889 Jefferson Davis, statesman, died.
1892 Ernst von Siemens, inventor, died.
1892 Sir Osbert Sitwell, writer, born.

Events

1492 Columbus discovered Haïti.
1648 Pride's Purge of Parliament.
1857 The Battle of Cawnpore (Kanpur).
1897 The Treaty of Constantinople signed.
1917 The independence of Finland proclaimed.
1921 Establishment of Irish Free State.
1925 The Libyan frontier agreement between Italy and Egypt signed.
1971 War broke out between India and Pakistan.

7th DECEMBER

Feast of Saint Ambrose.

People

983 The Holy Roman Emperor Otto II died.
1254 Pope Innocent IV died.
1542 Mary Queen of Scots born.
1549 Robert Kett, rebel leader, hanged.
1598 Giovanni Bernini, architect, born.
1709 Meindert Hobbema, painter, died.
1793 Madame du Barry, mistress of Louis XV of France, guillotined.
1810 Theodor Schwann, physiologist, born.
1815 Michel Ney, soldier, executed.
1826 John Flaxman, sculptor, died.
1834 Edward Irving, founder of the Irvingites, died.
1863 Pietro Mascagni, composer, born.
1876 Willa Cather, novelist, born.
1879 Rudolf Friml, composer, born.

Events

1917 United States declared war on Austria-Hungary.
1941 The Japanese attack on Pearl Harbor.

8th DECEMBER

People

65B.C. Horace, writer, born.
1626   Queen Christina of Sweden born.
1708   Francis I, Holy Roman Emperor, born.
1832   Björnstjerne Björnson, dramatist, born.
1859   Thomas De Quincey, writer, died.
1865   Jean Sibelius, composer, born.
1903   Herbert Spencer, philosopher, died.

Events

1660   The first (unnamed) actress appeared on the English stage.
1914   The Battle of the Falkland Islands.
1941   Britain and the United States declared war on Japan.

9th DECEMBER

People

1165   Malcolm IV, King of Scotland, died.
1437   The Holy Roman Emperor Sigismund died.
1565   Pope Pius IV died.
1594   Gustavus Adolphus, King of Sweden, born.
1608   John Milton, poet, born.
1641   Sir Anthony Van Dyck, painter, died.
1814   Joseph Bramah, inventor, died.
1848   Joel Chandler Harris, writer, born.
1921   Sir Arthur Pearson, publisher and philanthropist, died.
1964   Dame Edith Sitwell, writer, died.

Events

1813   The Macquarie River (Australia) discovered by the explorer George Evans.
1824   The Battle of Ayacucho.
1905   Law promulgating the separation of the Church from the State in France.
1917   Jerusalem surrendered to the British.

10th DECEMBER

People

1495   Hans Memling, artist, died.
1626   Edmund Gunter, mathematician, died.
1805   William Lloyd Garrison, abolitionist, born.
1822   César Franck, composer, born.
1830   Emily Dickinson, poet, born.
1851   Melvil Dewey, pioneer in book classification, born.
1865   Leopold I, King of the Belgians, died.
1891   Lord Alexander, soldier, born.
1896   Alfred Nobel, chemist and philanthropist, died.

Events

1508   The Treaty of Cambrai signed.
1599   The Assembly of the Convention of States at Edinburgh.
1710   The Battle of Villaviciosa.
1768   The Royal Academy, London, founded.
1817   Mississippi achieved statehood.
1845   Robert Thomson patented the first pneumatic tyres.

10th December

1898	Cuba became an independent state.
1902	The ceremonial opening of the Aswan Dam.
1908	The National Farmers' Union, London, founded.
1928	The new underground station in Piccadilly Circus, London, opened.
1941	Battleships *Prince of Wales* and *Repulse* sunk by Japanese aircraft.
1945	Waterloo Bridge formally opened.
1948	The Declaration of Human Rights issued by the U.N. General Assembly.

11th DECEMBER

People

1475	Pope Leo X born.
1718	Charles XII, King of Sweden, killed.
1757	Charles Wesley, composer, born.
1803	Hector Berlioz, composer, born.
1810	Alfred de Musset, poet, born.
1843	Casimir Delavigne, writer, died.
1843	Robert Koch, scientist, born.
1909	Ludwig Mond, chemist, died.
1913	Menelek II, Emperor of Ethiopia, died.

Events

1816	Indiana achieved statehood.
1848	Louis Napoleon elected president of the French Republic.
1899	The Battle of Magersfontein.
1931	The Statute of Westminster became law.
1936	Edward VIII, King of Great Britain and Ireland, abdicated.
1936	George VI acceded to the throne.

12th DECEMBER

People

1574	Selim II, Sultan of Turkey, died.
1582	The Duke of Alva, statesman and soldier, died.
1724	Viscount Hood, naval officer, born.
1731	Erasmus Darwin, physician and writer, born.
1745	John Jay, statesman, born.
1751	Lord Bolingbroke, statesman, died.
1821	Gustave Flaubert, writer, born.
1837	John Green, historian, born.
1849	Sir Mark Isambard Brunel, engineer, died.
1889	Robert Browning, poet, died.
1929	John Osborne, playwright and actor, born.
1939	Douglas Fairbanks, sen., film actor, died.
1968	Tallulah Bankhead, actress, died.

Events

1688	Judge Jeffreys took refuge in the Tower of London from the mob.
1901	Marconi transmitted the first transatlantic radio signal.
1963	Kenya became independent.

13th DECEMBER

People

1466	Donatello, sculptor, died.
1521	Pope Sixtus V born.

1521   Manuel I, King of Portugal, died.
1565   Konrad von Gesner, naturalist, died.
1585   William Drummond of Hawthornden, writer, born.
1675   Jan Vermeer, painter, died.
1784   Dr Samuel Johnson, writer and lexicographer, died.
1797   Heinrich Heine, poet, born.
1816   Ernst von Siemens, inventor, born.
1903   John Piper, painter, born.

Events

1545   The Council of Trent began.
1577   Sir Francis Drake began his voyage round the world from Plymouth.
1653   The Barebones Parliament ended.
1862   The Battle of Fredericksburg.
1916   The Germans sent a peace note to the Allies.

14th DECEMBER

People

1417   Sir John Oldcastle (prototype of Shakespeare's Falstaff) hanged.
1503   Nostradamus, astrologer, born.
1542   James V, King of Scotland, died.
1546   Tycho Brahe, astronomer, born.
1553   Henry IV, King of France, born.
1799   George Washington, soldier and statesman, died.
1824   Puvis de Chavannes, artist, born.
1861   Albert, Prince Consort, died.
1873   Jean Agassiz, naturalist, died.
1895   George VI, King of Great Britain and Northern Ireland, born.
1901   Paul I, King of Greece, born.
1947   Earl Baldwin, statesman, died.
1974   Walter Lippmann, news commentator, died.

Events

1911   Roald Amundsen reached the South Pole.
1911   The first woman surgeon was admitted to the Royal College of Surgeons.
1918   Women first voted in a British General Election.
1939   The Battle of the River Plate.

15th DECEMBER

People

1263   Haakon IV, King of Norway, died.
1675   Jan Vermeer, painter, died.
1683   Isaak Walton, writer (particularly on angling), died.
1788   K.P.E. Bach, composer, died.
1832   Gustav Eiffel, engineer, born.
1852   Henri Antoine Becquerel, physicist, born.
1859   Dr Lazarus Zamenhof, inventor of Esperanto, born.
1890   Sitting Bull, American Indian chief, killed.
1916   Gregory Rasputin, monk and Tsarist court favourite, murdered.

Events

1791   The United States Bill of Rights ratified by the states.
1899   The Battle of Colenso.
1906   The Piccadilly Tube opened.
1916   The Battle of Verdun ended.
1970   Food riots in Poland.

16th DECEMBER

Dingaan's Day, Republic of South Africa.

People

714 Pepin II, ruler of the Franks, died.
1714 George Whitefield, evangelist, born.
1742 Gebhard Blücher, soldier, born.
1770 Ludwig van Beethoven, composer, born.
1775 Jane Austen, novelist, born.
1787 Mary Russell Mitford, writer, born.
1790 Leopold I, King of the Belgians, born.
1859 Wilhelm Grimm, philologist and writer, died.
1882 Zoltán Kodály, composer, born.
1899 Noël Coward, playwright, born.
1921 Camille Saint-Saëns, composer, died.

Events

1653 Oliver Cromwell became Lord Protector of England.
1773 The Boston Tea Party.
1838 The Boers defeated the Zulus under Dingaan.
1879 The Transvaal Republic founded.
1925 The construction of the Mersey Tunnel began.
1944 The Battle of the Bulge began.
1955 The new terminal buildings at London Airport opened.

17th DECEMBER

People

1187 Pope Gregory VIII died.
1493 Paracelsus, scientist, born.
1619 Prince Rupert, soldier, born.
1724 Thomas Guy, philanthropist, died.
1778 Sir Humphry Davy, scientist, born.
1830 Simón Bolivar, revolutionary and statesman, died.
1830 Jules de Goncourt, writer, born.
1833 Kaspar Hauser, the wild boy, died.
1907 Lord Kelvin, scientist, died.
1909 Leopold II, King of the Belgians, died.

Events

1807 The Milan Decree issued.
1858 The Geologists' Association, London, founded.
1903 The Wright brothers flew their first plane at Kitty Hawk, North Carolina.
1938 The Franco-Italian Agreement of 1935 denounced by Italy.
1939 The battleship *Graf Spee* scuttled.
1940 President Roosevelt proposed 'Lease-Lend' for Britain.

18th DECEMBER

People

1737 Antonio Stradivarius, violin-maker, died.
1779 Joseph Grimaldi, clown, born.
1786 Carl Maria von Weber, composer, born.
1803 Johann Herder, writer, died.
1818 Dr William Moon, inventor of an alphabet for the blind, born.
1829 The Chevalier de Lamarck, naturalist, died.
1856 Sir J. J. Thomson, scientist, born.

1859   Francis Thompson, poet, born.
1861   Edward MacDowell, composer, born.
1907   Christopher Fry, playwright, born.
1913   Willy Brandt, statesman, born.

Events
1745   The Battle of Clifton Moor.
1792   Thomas Paine tried *in absentia* for publishing *The Rights of Man*.
1865   Slavery finally abolished in the United States.
1912   The discovery of the Piltdown Man announced.
1917   The United States Congress submitted prohibition legislation to the states.
1923   The International Zone of Tangier set up.

19th DECEMBER

People
1498   Andreas Osiander, religious reformer, born.
1683   Philip V, King of Spain, born.
1741   Vitus Bering, explorer, died.
1742   Carl Wilhelm von Scheele, chemist, born.
1790   Sir William Edward Parry, explorer, born.
1848   Emily Brontë, novelist, died.
1851   Joseph Turner, painter, died.
1852   Albert Michelson, scientist, born.
1884   Sir Stanley Unwin, publisher, born.
1953   Robert Millikan, physicist, died.

Events
1562   The Battle of Dreux.
1941   The British evacuated Penang.
1957   Air service between London and Moscow inaugurated.

20th DECEMBER

People
1894   Sir Robert Menzies, statesman, born.
1937   Erich Ludendorff, soldier, died.
1954   James Hilton, novelist, died.

Events
1699   Peter the Great's reform of the Russian calendar.
1860   South Carolina seceded from the Union (first state to do so).
1888   The Battle of Suakin.
1959   The first atomic ice-breaker (the *Lenin*) started operations.

21st DECEMBER
Winter Solstice on an average of two years in every four. Feast of Saint Thomas. Forefathers' Day (U.S.A.).

People
1375   Giovanni Boccaccio, writer, died.
1803   Sir Joseph Whitworth, mechanical engineer, born.
1823   Jean Henri Fabre, naturalist and writer, born.
1879   Joseph Stalin, statesman, born.

21st December

Events

1620	The landing of the Pilgrim Fathers on Plymouth Rock.
1845	The Battle of Ferozeshah began.
1846	Anaesthetics first used in surgery in Britain.
1908	The Port of London Authority constituted.
1958	General Charles de Gaulle elected President of the Fifth French Republic.

22nd DECEMBER

Winter Solstice on an average of two years in every four.

People

1552	Saint Francis Xavier died.
1590	Ambroise Paré, surgeon, died.
1639	Jean Racine, dramatist, christened.
1804	Benjamin Disraeli, statesman, born.
1839	John Maskelyne, professional magician, born.
1858	Giacomo Puccini, composer, born (now accepted as the correct date by most authorities).
1880	George Eliot, novelist, died.

Events

1845	The Battle of Ferozeshah ended.
1935	Anthony Eden appointed British Foreign Secretary.
1956	The withdrawal of Anglo-French forces from Port Said completed.

23rd DECEMBER

People

1568	Roger Ascham, writer, died.
1588	Henri de Lorraine, Duc de Guise, assassinated.
1732	Sir Richard Arkwright, inventor, born.
1761	Alastair Macdonnell, 'Pickle the spy', died.
1804	Charles Sainte-Beuve, writer, born.
1812	Samuel Smiles, writer, born.
1908	Yousuf Karsh, photographer, born.
1959	The Earl of Halifax, statesman, died.

Events

1834	Hansom cabs patented by Joseph Hansom.
1861	Britain presented a Note on the Trent Affair to the U.S. Government.
1913	The Federal Reserve Bank in the United States founded.
1933	The sentences announced at the Reichstag Fire Trial.

24th DECEMBER

Christmas Eve. The Festival of Nine Lessons and Nine Carols (King's College, Cambridge).

People

1167	John, King of England, born.
1317	Jean de Joinville, crusader and historian, died.
1491	Saint Ignatius Loyola, religious reformer, born.
1524	Vasco da Gama, navigator, died.
1754	George Crabbe, poet, born.
1791	Eugène Scribe, playwright, born.

1798 Adam Mickiewicz, poet, born.
1809 Kit Carson, soldier, born.
1818 James Joule, physicist, born.
1822 Matthew Arnold, poet, born.
1845 George I, King of Greece, born.
1863 William Makepeace Thackeray, novelist, died.
1894 Frances Buss, pioneer of high schools for girls, died.
1935 Alban Berg, composer, died.
1942 Admiral Darlan assassinated in Algiers.

Events

1814 The Treaty of Ghent signed.
1933 The Codex Sinaiticus arrived in London.
1941 British forces gained control of Cyrenaica.
1951 Libya achieved independence.
1951 King Idriss I acceded to the throne of Libya.

25th DECEMBER
Christmas Day.

People

1642 Sir Isaac Newton, scientist, born.
1721 William Collins, poet, born.
1759 Richard Porson, classical scholar, born.
1796 Hugh Pattinson, metallurgical chemist, born.
1808 Richard Porson, classical scholar, died.
1810 Alexandres Rhankaves, scholar, poet and statesman, born.
1885 Paul Manship, sculptor, born.
1938 Karel Čapek, writer, died.

Events

 800 Charlemagne crowned first Holy Roman Emperor by Pope Leo III.
1497 Natal discovered by Vasco da Gama.
1926 The Emperor Hirohito acceded to the throne of Japan.
1941 Hong Kong surrendered to the Japanese.
1974 Darwin, Australia, devastated by cyclone.

26th DECEMBER
Feast of Saint Stephen. Boxing Day.

People

1716 Thomas Gray, poet, born.
1734 George Romney, painter, born.
1797 John Wilkes, political agitator, died.
1829 Patrick Gilmore, bandmaster and composer, born.
1888 Pasquale Mancini, statesman, died.
1931 Melvil Dewey, pioneer in book classification, died.
1950 James Stephens, writer, died.
1972 Harry S. Truman, statesman, died.

Events

1776 The Battle of Trenton.
1805 The Treaty of Pressburg signed.
1825 Decembrist army revolt in Russia crushed.
1898 Radium discovered by Pierre and Marie Curie.
1941 British commando raid on Norway.
1943 The battleship *Scharnhorst* sunk off North Cape.

27th DECEMBER
Feast of Saint John the Evangelist.

People

1571 Johannes Kepler, astronomer, born.
1585 Pierre de Ronsard, poet, died (27th/28th).
1717 Pope Pius VI born.
1814 Joanna Southcott, prophet, died.
1822 Louis Pasteur, chemist, born.
1834 Charles Lamb, essayist, died.
1859 Sir Henry Hadow, musicologist, born.
1889 Stephen Perry, astronomer, died.

Events

1703 The Methuen Treaty signed.
1927 Trotsky expelled from Soviet Communist Party.
1956 Clearance of Suez Canal began.

28th DECEMBER
Childermas (Holy Innocents' Day).

People

1622 Saint Francis de Sales, nobleman and ecclesiastic, died.
1835 Sir Archibald Geikie, geologist, born.
1856 Woodrow Wilson, statesman, born.
1859 Lord Macaulay, historian, died.
1937 Maurice Ravel, composer, died.
1947 Victor Emanuel III, former King of Italy, died.
1963 Paul Hindemith, composer, died.

Events

1846 Iowa achieved statehood.
1908 The Messina earthquake.

29th DECEMBER

People

1170 Saint Thomas Becket, Archbishop of Canterbury, murdered.
1766 Charles Macintosh, inventor, born.
1800 Charles Goodyear, inventor, born.
1808 Andrew Johnson, statesman, born.
1809 William Ewart Gladstone, statesman, born.
1813 Alexander Parkes, chemist, born.
1843 Carmen Silva, Queen Elizabeth of Romania, born.
1890 Octave Feuillet, novelist, died.
1894 Christina Rossetti, poet, died.
1926 Rainer Maria Rilke, poet, died.

Events

1775 Sarah Siddons made her début on the London stage.
1798 Formation of Second Coalition against France.
1843 The Battle of Maharajpur.
1845 Texas achieved statehood.
1860 H.M.S. *Warrior*, Britain's first seagoing ironclad, launched.
1895 The Jameson Raid began.
1931 The scientist H. C. Urey publicly announced the discovery of heavy water.
1959 Durgapur Steel Works, West Bengal, officially opened.

30th DECEMBER

People

1591 Pope Innocent IX died.
1853 André Messager, composer, born.
1865 Rudyard Kipling, writer, born.
1867 Simon Guggenheim, philanthropist, born.
1869 Stephen Leacock, humorous writer, born.
1894 Amelia Jenks Bloomer, champion of women's rights, died.
1899 Sir James Paget, surgeon, died.
1904 Dmitri Kabalevsky, composer, born.
1956 Ruth Draper, actress, died.
1967 Vincent Massey, statesman, died.
1968 Trygve Lie, statesman, died.

Events

1460 The Battle of Wakefield.
1897 Zululand annexed to Natal.
1922 The Treaty of Union adopted by the first Soviet Congress of the U.S.S.R.
1947 King Michael of Romania abdicated.

31st DECEMBER

New Year's Eve. Saint Sylvester's Eve. Hogmanay.

People

1384 John Wyclif, reformer, died.
1491 Jacques Cartier, explorer, born.
1705 Catherine of Braganza, wife of King Charles II, died.
1719 John Flamsteed, first Astronomer Royal, died.
1720 Charles Edward Stuart, the Young Pretender, born.
1738 Marquess Cornwallis, statesman and soldier, born.
1815 Sir Edward Bond, antiquarian, born.
1830 Comtesse de Genlis, writer, died.

Events

1775 Failure of American attack on Quebec.
1805 Napoleon abandoned the use of the Revolutionary Calendar.
1923 The chimes of Big Ben first broadcast.
1927 The use of the lance in the British Army abandoned, except for ceremonial use.
1940 Firewatching became compulsory in Britain.

12" SINGLE
£3·29